In Defense of My People
Alonso S. Perales and the Development of Mexican-American Public Intellectuals

Edited by Michael A. Olivas

Arte Público Press
Houston, Texas

This volume is made possible through grants from the City of Houston through the Houston Arts Alliance; Humanities Texas; and the University of Houston's Center for Mexican American Studies, College of Liberal Arts and Social Sciences, Law Center and M. D. Anderson Library.

Recovering the past, creating the future

Arte Público Press
University of Houston
4902 Gulf Fwy, Rm 100
Houston, Texas 77204-2004

Cotton Picker document, located in University of Texas-Permian Basin, Dungan Library, Archives / Special Collections, in personal library of John Bell Shepperd. Reprinted with permission.

Cover design by Adelaida Mendoza
Cover photo courtesy of Alonso S. Perales Collection,
Recovering the US Hispanic Literary Heritage

Perales, Alonso S.
    In defense of my people : Alonso S. Perales and the development of Mexican-American public intellectuals / Michael A. Olivas, editor.
    p. cm.
    ISBN 978-1-55885-760-5 (alk. paper)
    1. Perales, Alonso S., 1898-1960. 2. Perales, Alonso S., 1898-1960—Influence. 3. Mexican Americans—Civil rights—Texas—History—20th century. 4. Mexican Americans—Civil rights—History—20th century. 5. Mexican Americans—Intellectual life—20th century. 6. League of United Latin American Citizens—History. 7. Mexican Americans—Texas—Biography. I. Olivas, Michael A., author, editor of compilation.
    F391.P4I6 2013
    973'.046872—dc23
    [B]
                                                            2012046350
                                                            CIP

∞ The paper used in this publication meets the requirements of the American National Standard for Information Sciences—Permanence of Paper for Printed Library Materials, ANSI Z39.48-1984.

12 13 14 15 16 17 18   10 9 8 7 6 5 4 3 2 1

December 21, 2011

To: Alonso S. Perales Conference Organizers
(Perales.confer12@gmail.com)

From: Vilma S. Martinez

Congratulations and thanks to the University of Houston for organizing a conference on January 13, 2012 to honor the many accomplishments of Alonso S. Perales.

Mr. Perales practiced law in San Antonio, Texas at the International Building. When I was 15 years old, I volunteered to help out at his firm in order to learn what lawyers actually do! (I was presumptuous enough to think I might be able to do that someday.)

What I learned was that lawyers, through their education and training, are able to help people in times of need. Mr. Perales assured that a couple who wanted to adopt a child had this fond wish fulfilled. I saw him comfort and guide through the legal process a young widow from a foreign country who needed to repatriate herself and her husband's body to their homeland.

What I did not know was what a spectacular and singular role he had played in the early days of the Mexican-American civil rights movement. The conference will go a long way towards educating this new generation of leaders concerning his important contributions.

I regret that I cannot be there in person to share these few memories (and learn more about this man who encouraged me to pursue my dream of becoming a lawyer); but I send my very best wishes to the University and Mr. Perales' loving family for a most successful conference.

Sincerely,

Vilma S. Martinez

TABLE OF CONTENTS

Preface and Acknowledgements

Michael A. Olivas

If ever there were an enterprise that is a team effort involving the whole village, it is a scholarly conference and a book project as a result. The logistics of each are daunting, and in different ways, but when they work out they are very satisfying, especially when the whole is greater than the sum of its various parts. Each of the dozen scholars who worked together on this book had known of Alonso Perales, some quite well, but none knew him like we know him now. The papers and materials in the wonderful Perales Collection now housed at the M.D. Anderson Library at the University of Houston will allow many scholars to come to know him in all his manifestations. The Collection will soon become an acknowledged source of information about early Mexican and Mexican American organizations in the United States, political issues in the Southwestern U.S. and especially Texas during the period of 1925-1960.Evident in the papers is the role of various social influences that both served as accommodationist and restrictionist mediators for the rise of the Mexican-American community during this period, including the courts and legislatures, state and local governments, the Catholic Church, inter-American and diplomatic venues, newspapers and other media, and the many other discursive vehicles that Alonso Perales employed to improve the lot of his Raza.

My list of acknowledgements is as long as the list of Perales' correspondents. I thank Brown Foundation Professor Nicolás Kanellos, who drew me into this project as a follow-up to our successful collaboration that led to the 2006 Arte Público Press volume, *"Colored Men" and "Hombres Aquí": Hernandez v. Texas and the Emergence of Mexican-American Lawyering*, itself a wonderful resource with a different cohort of colleagues. He also provided substantive feedback on my pieces in this project, as did Texas A&M historian Carlos K. Blanton.

The Arte Público Press staff included Marina Tristán, Rebeca Reyes, Carmen Peña Abrego, Ashley Hess, Matthew Hall, and Nellie González, all of whom helped in one way or the other for the January, 2012 conference. Brown Foundation Director of Research for Recovering the US Hispanic Heritage program, Dr. Carolina Villarroel, guided us at every turn from start to finish of the project. Arte Público Press executive editor, Professor Gabriela Baeza Ventura, worked carefully and conscientiously with me and with the authors to edit the large and complex project. From the UH M.D. Anderson Library, Head of Special Collections Pat Bozeman and her many staff members collaborated on this project, and it was their exceptional archival and media skills that made the Collection and this book possible. They include: Valerie

Prilop, Nelda Cervantes, Chinh Doan, Rachel Vacek, J. Fisher, Nam-Anh Vu, Michele Reilly, Nicole Westbrook, Dan Johnson, Justin Elbert, Katie Buehner, and Carolyn Meanley. All those who follow in this Collection will follow the archival and digitized paths they carved from the materials.

UH resources were made available by Provost John Antel, Library Dean Dana Rooks, CLASS Dean John W. Roberts, UHLC Dean Raymond T. Nimmer, and IHELG program director Deborah Y. Jones. Carrie A. Criado and John Kling assisted with the media and publicity for the conference. UH History Professors Raúl Ramos and Mónica Perales were active participants in the conference, helping coordinate the participation of the more than one hundred persons who attended.

In a class apart are the talented and generous authors who contributed original and creative work for this book. While I approached some of the obvious and usual suspects who had written about Alonso Perales earlier, based on other documentation and second-hand materials, and was delighted when each of them took me up on this offer, we also held a national call for papers that resulted in other scholars, including exceptionally-talented graduate students, applying to be part of this book project. The array of interests and approaches to the material and the man are wide-ranging and fresh, but all of us know we are only starting our work in this Collection, with more certain to come in the future. It will be fascinating to see how this Collection fills out our early knowledge of the events touched and shaped by Attorney Perales. We also hope that valuable materials will come forward from others, now that the Collection is established.

Finally, we all acknowledge the generosity of the Perales family, as represented by his two children, Martha Perales Carrizales and Raymond A. Perales, who made the resources available. By my imperfect count, there were more than two dozen of his immediate family and extended family in attendance at the conference, willing and able to add nuance and to share their memories. These were materials that simply had to make their way into the sunlight to inform and instruct us. It has been more than fifty years that he passed, but his lessons and efforts seem fresh and necessary to us today. One of the many canards applied to Mexican-Americans by those who do not know better, is that we have passively accepted our fate and did not work to resist the many depredations visited upon the community. If there is any single figure whose entire life did not conform to this stereotype, it was Alonso S. Perales, who worked tirelessly and effectively in defense of his *Raza*. This Collection reveals the many ways and the many places that this work was undertaken, and they reveal a remarkable if not perfect man, who himself was greater than the sum of his parts. Indeed, he should become a model for all of us, products of our times as he clearly was, but also willing to render extraordinary service, so that others might prosper.

Michael A. Olivas
Christmas, 2012, Santa Fe, NM

Introduction

Alonso S. Perales, The Rule of Law and the Development of Mexican-American Public Intellectuals

Michael A. Olivas

In 2011, the University of Houston, Arte Público Press, through the Recovering the U.S. Hispanic Literary Heritage Program, the Special Collections Department of the M.D. Anderson Library, and the UH Law Center announced that the papers of early Tejano lawyer Alonso S. Perales had been acquired from his family and were available for scholarly examination. Alonso S. Perales (1898-1960) was among the most important organizational figures and public intellectuals of his time, and was instrumental in early and mid-twentieth-century Mexican-American political development in Texas. Perales graduated from George Washington University School of Law in 1925, making him one of the earliest Mexican-American attorneys to practice law in Texas. Over time, he not only had a successful law practice, but helped found the League of United Latin American Citizens (LULAC), served his country in several diplomatic capacities and was a prolific writer and public figure, one who employed all the discursive avenues available to him.

The University of Houston and Arte Público Press, through the Recovering the U.S. Hispanic Literary Heritage Program, acquired his papers and archives in 2009, and this treasure trove, which had not been widely cited in significant scholarship, was the source of a scholarly conference held at the University of Houston in January 12-13, 2012, by means of solicitations and a call for papers derived from this collection that have resulted in this book project. This conference was held in conjunction with an M.D. Anderson Library-curated exhibit of the papers, correspondence, and other materials from the Perales Collection. Conference sponsors invited proposals from historians, legal scholars, political scientists, sociologists, literary scholars and others from the humanities and social sciences with an interest in early twentieth-century Texas political development concerning Mexicans, Mexican Americans and other groups in the state and region, drawn from the collection and other available materials. We invited doctoral students, scholars of all ranks and independent researchers with interests in this important period, particularly those with interests in the early Mexican-American social and political organizations, especially LULAC, Order Sons of America (OSA) and 100 Loyal Citizens. Work derived from access to these papers had suggested that Mexican-American political organizing and social consciousness arose much earlier than has been generally credited in the work of most historians, political scientists and other scholars. Whereas many scholars had placed these origins in the late 1920s, especially with the events leading up to the 1929 founding of LULAC, in Corpus Christi, Texas, the Perales papers and materials reveal roots to predecessor groups and to events from the end of the dictatorship of Porfirio Díaz, the Mexican Revolution, and the early 1920s. These family-held papers, now available in the original and on microfilm at UH Special Collections, promise to fill out the record on the structured role of Mexican-American men and women in these mutual aid societies and civic organizations, as well as the behind-the-scenes role of lawyers—in this instance, not primarily as litigators, but as civic leaders and elected officials. Perales also carried on an extraordinary correspondence with many Latino and Latina and other political figures, revealing wide and deep contacts and affiliations. (Examples include Adela Sloss-Vento, George I. Sánchez, Archbishop Robert Lucey and Anastasio Somoza.) In addition, he carried on a remarkable correspondence with ordinary Mexican-American citizens and *Mejicanos de afuera* (Mexican nationals residing in the United States), on a variety of cultural and religious topics, ranging from marital counseling, Catholic pieties and other affirmations of the race, designed to share his views and expertise widely and deeply. There is virtually no other parallel to the significant and fascinating materials now archived and ripe for examination.

As every section of this book project reveals, Alonso S. Perales was a fascinating and complex man, one best-identified by his unstinting efforts on behalf of Mexican-origin people in the United States, especially in Texas, and his unceasing search for the best public or private venue in which to advance these interests. He was without equal either in his community or that of the larger community, finding extensive public involvement in his law practice, organizational involvement and leadership, the Catholic Church, efforts to gain elected office, diplomatic and international participation, lobbying and advocacy before governmental entities, private correspondence, writing op-eds and media venues, publishing books and recording public and private instances of discrimination and engagement in a number of other discourses that allowed him to seek equality and to improve the lot in life of his community, what he termed his *raza*. Unusual as it was for his time, approximately 1925 until his death in 1960, such a wide-ranging polity is rarely seen in his contemporaries or even in the present day. The cache of papers and materials has unlocked many unknown aspects of his long and distinguished career, and also fleshed out the more quotidian and personal aspects of his character.

The organization of this book

In his useful chapter where he explains the editorial approach and choices of which resources to utilize, the accomplished senior historian F. Arturo Rosales sets out in "Writing a Biography of Alonso Sandoval Perales" the decisions he is using to organize and write the full-length biography that will result from these archives. He notes the several options available to him, including chronological and thematic means, and he helpfully sets out his choices, weaving both published commentary already available on Perales and the letters and other materials he has selected to highlight. He writes:

This essay outlines the challenges which I will face in producing a biography of Alonso Sandoval Perales. Although he is one of the most important figures in Mexican-American civil rights history, his trajectory is relatively unknown, primarily because until recently his papers were unavailable . . . I agreed to produce the biography before reviewing the compilation of data, imagining the content would provide thematic avenues. But after a preliminary but thorough assessment of the papers, the task became more daunting because the repository supports almost infinite pathways to understanding Perales. I have also examined other primary sources, not in the collection, but related to Perales, in Mexico City, at the National Archives in Maryland, at the Benson Collection at the University of Texas and in other repositories. I then decided that the biography should explain political and ideological trends which influenced and motivated this San Antonio attorney in the 1930s, 1940s and 1950s.

Besides appreciating and understanding the civil rights efforts Perales and his cohorts mustered, the biography should further demonstrate how important it is for academicians to transcend post-1960s points of reference which have guided much of our assessment of this generation. Activists of the Chicano Movement accused civil rights advocates of Perales' generation of denying their "Mexicanness" and instead claimed whiteness. This era also influenced a foundation for more serious scholarly appraisals which to lesser degree also viewed the generation negatively. (Rosales, p. 267)

My aim in writing the Introduction to this edited conference volume is more modest and less-comprehensive than was Rosales' task: I am attempting to sort the chapters that resulted from the UH conference into a framework, introduce the contributions, comment upon the themes that have emerged from this inter-disciplinary collection, add my own observations upon his legal practice (a topic that has not been examined before this project) and note the many promising avenues that can now be pursued, due to the availability of these materials in a collection far-too-rich for any one undertaking. The chapters fell into several thematic niches, ones that also roughly track the chronology of Perales' life. Accordingly, I have situated them into five large domains: Organizing, Creating LULAC and Texas Politics; The Mexican-American Generation, Revisited; Religion and Race; Letters, Piety and Politics; Diplomacy, Law and Biography.

Organizing, Creating LULAC and Texas Politics

Having grown up in Alice, and then Corpus Christi, Texas, Alonso S. Perales was orphaned when he was just twelve years old. He left Texas then went East to join the military, and to attend college and law school, which he completed in 1925 by graduating from the law school that later became George Washington University (GWU, 2012). He returned to Texas as the third Mexican-American lawyer, following the first two, J.T. Canales and M.C. Gonzales. Canales graduated from the Uni-

versity of Michigan Law School in 1899 and likewise returned to Texas, where he
practiced law and entered politics; Manuel C. Gonzales attended law school at St.
Louis University and graduated from the University of Texas Law School in 1924.
Not surprisingly, both interacted with the young Perales over the years. There was a
small number of Mexican-American lawyers—even as late as the 1950s, there were
only a few dozen in Texas, educated both out-of-state and at the premier public law
school in the State, the University of Texas at Austin. As one history of the early half-
century of the UT Law School, the site of *Sweatt v. Painter*, the 1950 SCOTUS case
that struck down the makeshift parallel law school for Negroes, has noted, "The University of Texas School of Law has long lived under a shadow of racial discrimination. For a period of over sixty years, the Law School had no African American law
students and less than twenty Mexican-American law school graduates" (Barrera,
1998, p. 108). That most of the Mexican-American lawyers went on to distinguished
legal careers is evidence of how few they were and what remarkable careers they
carved out, against all odds.

As a sidebar, this history of early Texas Mexican-American lawyers and other
Latino and Latina lawyers is very sketchy and incomplete, and calls out for more historical work. (That I have personally met several of these pioneers since my 1982
arrival in Texas is left-handed acknowledgement of how small and recent the number
was.) For some time, I had believed and written that the first Latinos to argue a case
before the U.S. Supreme Court were the lawyers of the *Hernandez v. Texas* case, who
did so in early 1954 (close to the time that the *Brown v. Board* lawyers re-argued their
case). I have also recently written that the 2006 Voting Rights Act case *Perry v. Texas*
was the first SCOTUS case where Latinos and Latinas were on both sides of the case
(Nina Perales, Puerto Rican, on the MALDEF side, and Teodoro Cruz, Cuban, arguing on the side of the State). It turns out that I have been wrong in both instances. I
am happy to correct this record, even at the risk of still getting it wrong.

There are likely some Puerto Rican lawyers who argued Puerto Rico cases that
came to the U.S. Supreme court before 1950, and someone needs to examine these
records. I have not done so, and will consult others about this. One Puerto Rican
attorney who signed a number of the briefs on behalf of the Department of the Interior in cases involving Native American Tribes before the U.S. Supreme Court was
Pedro Capó-Rodríguez. He was born on the Island, studied law in the States, and
became a member of the Vermont bar. It is unclear whether he actually tried the
cases. He published articles on the cases in the *American Journal of International
Law* in the 1910s, a fairly unusual level of access to this publication for someone not
an academic. There may be other Latinos/as who served as government lawyers during these years, and the identification of Latino ethnicity is, as always, problematic.
This type of identification is an art, not a science. (Ramirez, 2011; Chavez, 2011;
Olivas, 2006; 2012)

In 1951, Manuel Ruiz, Jr. (1905-1986), a Mexican-American lawyer and civil
rights activist in the Los Angeles area, argued *Buck v. California*, 353 U.S. 99
(1952), before the Supreme Court. Of course, this predates the *Hernandez* arguments
and decision in 1954. I have looked at the Manuel Ruiz, Jr. files, which are archived
in the Stanford Special Collections—where the MALDEF collection is also housed,

which I have used for several years to trace the *Plyler* case. (Olivas, 2005) The finding tool for the Manuel Ruiz, Jr. collection is online at: http://www-sul.stanford.edu/depts/spc/xml/m0295.xml.

Interestingly, however, neither the Stanford collection headings nor the extensive introductory biography include mention of his having argued *Buck*, a case involving taxi licenses. (His clients lost the case, in a 5-4 decision.) While his civic involvement is well-known, and has been examined by several leading Latino scholars of the period (such as George J. Sánchez, 1993, p. 250; and Richard Griswold del Castillo, 2008, pp. 148-158, among others), his status as apparently the first Mexican American to argue before the SCOTUS is not mentioned. As a very minor footnote, he also appears in 1963 public records as the family law attorney to socialite Joan Tyler in a paternity suit involving actor George Jessel, suggesting that he was a well-connected and successful lawyer across several fields, certainly transcending civil rights and ethnic litigation. I spoke about the *Hernandez* case quite extensively with one of the four Mexican-American lawyers involved in the case, Judge James DeAnda, and he was of the impression that no Latino or Latina attorney had argued before SCOTUS prior to his case (Olivas, 2006). My recent discovery now leads me to believe he was mistaken, and it likely reflects the lack of a national Latino bar at the time, the non-civil rights nature of his practice, and the poor state of professional communications then, in contrast to the present day, where we are all so well-connected with thriving personal and professional networks and Google@ access to so many data sources. In contrast, I was recently involved in a complex conference call with nearly twenty participants—virtually all lawyers of color—plotting strategy to submit *amicus* briefs to the California State Supreme Court on behalf of an undocumented law graduate being certified to practice law (DeBenedictis, 2012; Sloan, 2012).

Harold R. Medina Sr., later federal Judge Medina, argued several SCOTUS cases, beginning with a 1922 case early in his long career: *New York, N.H. & H.R. Co. v. Fruchter*. Medina's father, Joaquin Adolfo Medina, was born in Merida, Mexico (Medina, 1959, p. v) but the son never self-identified—and was not widely identified—as being Latino. Interestingly, Harold Sr.'s son, Harold Jr., also argued a case before SCOTUS, with Richard M. Nixon as opposing counsel (*Time Inc. v. Hill*, 1967). Some of this is, of course, very much an idiosyncratic matter of ethnic and racial self-identification, ascription, opportunity, politics at the time, etc.

With the caveat that I have not been able to review all the SCOTUS cases argued on Puerto Rican issues, the first-known Latina to argue before the U.S. Supreme Court appears to have been Miriam Naveira de Rodon, then the Solicitor General of Puerto Rico, who argued *Examining Board v. Flores de Otero*, 426 U.S. 572 (1976) in 1975. Naveira de Rodon argued against Max Ramirez de Arellano, and both parties were on the brief. I now believe this to be the first time two Latinos appeared on both sides of a Supreme Court matter. This revises my earlier assertion that *Perry v. Texas* was the first such case. *Flores de Otero* is an interesting immigration case, well-known to immigration teachers. To an extent, Puerto Rican lawyers arguing Puerto Rican cases in the U.S. Supreme Court are a special jurisdictional category, but are no less important to the history of Latino/Latina lawyering. Following Naveira de Rodon's argument, Vilma S. Martinez, the first known Mexican-American woman to appear before the Supreme Court, argued *East Texas Motor Freight Sys., v. Rodriguez*, 431 U.S. 395 (1977). At the time, she was the President and General Counsel of MALDEF; at present, she is President Barack Obama's Ambassador to Argentina. Recent research on Latinas to argue before the nation's high court, from 1950 to 2009, reveals that only fifteen known Latinas have argued before the Supreme Court of the United States (Mendoza, 2011).

In sum, the total number of Latino and Latina lawyers at the peak of Supreme Court practice has been very small, even though several have had considerable professional success. Teodoro Cruz and Miguel Estrada have become members of the elite club who have argued several SCOTUS cases and also gained attention for their conservative politics (Goldstein, 2006; Batheja, 2012). I will also note, however, that the confusion also reflects the poor state of Mexican-American archives in this dimension, and the resulting gap in Chicano historiography concerning the important role of Latino and Latina lawyers, not all of them Mexican American. Similarly, we do not know the history of Anglo lawyers taking up cases for Mexican-American clients in important civil rights litigation (Carpio, 2012). Until recently, I had not put two and two together to connect the appearances of A.L. Wirin, who served as co-counsel in both the 1947 *Mendez* and the 1948 *Delgado* cases; for that matter, I had not known he had been involved in litigation following the earlier Sleepy Lagoon violence against Mexican Americans, or that afterward, he had gone on to do the Lord's work in Arizona, or that he had later argued before the U.S. Supreme Court (Valencia, 2006, pp. 53-55 also missed this connection in his discussion of *Gonzales v. Sheely*, the 1951 Maricopa County, Arizona desegregation case). Through its journey to the Ninth Circuit, *Mendez* drew upon white, Jewish, Asian and African American lawyers, but not a single Latino or Mexican-American attorney.

In his smaller universe, Alonso S. Perales set out early in his career not only to establish his legal practice in San Antonio, and later elsewhere in the State, but to become active in community work and organization-building, most notably in his efforts to consolidate several fledgling Tejano mutual aid and advocacy organizations into LULAC, the League of United Latin American Citizens, in 1929; he served as the organization's National President in 1930-31. As examined by historian Cynthia E. Orozco in "Alonso S. Perales and His Struggle for the Civil Rights of *La Raza* through the League of United Latin American Citizens (LULAC) in Texas in the 1930s: *Incansable Soldado del Civismo Pro-Raza*" and political scientist Benjamin Márquez, in "In Defense of My People: Alonso S. Perales and the Moral Construction of Citizenship," this central role in LULAC dominated the early career of Perales, and accounts for most of the available scholarly commentary on him. Marquez is among the leading scholars who have systematically looked at LULAC over the years (Márquez, 1993, 2003), while Orozco's 1992 PhD dissertation and 2009 book on the history of LULAC both drew from the Perales records. As she explains in the chapter, she had virtually unprecedented access to the family files, even before they were acquired and processed by the University of Houston. (This access also shows how prodigious talent and being in the right place at the right time can shape a scholar's career.)

Orozco supplements our knowledge of the young Perales, who in 1933, joined the San Antonio law firm of Still, Wright, Davis, and Perales and also undertook work for the Bexar County Attorney's office in 1934. She carefully documents his organizational work in steering the many competing groups that merged to form LULAC in 1929, and she notes his selflessness in assisting others to cultivate their leadership skills. The record makes it clear he could have been the symbolically significant first National President, but he encouraged Ben Garza to assume this position. The chapter contains new and fresh detailed information about the tenuousness of the first years of the group, especially its fragile finances, intermittent leadership and internecine politics. A reader also comes away with a sense of the incredible manner in which he threw himself into the development of the organization, traveling the state, exhorting its members, flogging its early activities and engaging in the politicking required for any nascent organization. After his presidential year ended in 1931, he remained a Board member until 1937, when he essentially withdrew from active membership and the politics over a second San Antonio council. Nonetheless, his vision took root, and LULAC remains a significant Latino organization to the present day.

Although she makes many original contributions in this chapter, especially as she re-assesses his work in light of all the materials now available to her, perhaps her most useful contribution will be the way she maps how these papers will require other senior historians who have written about Perales without the access she had to revise and reconsider their earlier work. I urge all the persons (named by her but omitted here) to take into account her generous questions and recommendations. She summarizes, citing chapter and verse, literally: This paper based on the Perales archives suggests several needed Chicano history revisions:

First, LULAC's work (and that of Perales) was primarily motivated by collective interests not individual interests.

Second, LULAC did not abandon Mexican immigrants. LULAC was silent about deportations in the 1930s, but otherwise fought for immigrant rights, especially their rights to attend schools and LULAC promoted their efforts to obtain U.S. citizenship.

Third, Perales should be honored for helping to found the School Improvement League for which Eleuterio Escobar has received most of the attention but which came out of Council 16, which Perales founded. Perales, not Escobar, initiated the call for major school improvements.

Fourth, LULAC waged a multi-faceted activist agenda not just legal desegregation work in the 1930s, Extending the traditional Chicano movement bias against LULAC framework, [one historian] wrote that the Liga Defensa was "more confrontational" than LULAC and that "Escobar challenged the San Antonio School Board directly." He suggested "LULAC primarily addressed segregation through the courts." But LULAC 16 initiated that struggle, Escobar was a member of Council 16 and it is Perales who must truly be credited for that effort.

Fifth, LULAC addressed national policy/legislation in the 1930s not just local or state issues.

Sixth, Perales (and thus LULAC) was not a super-assimilationist organization demanding English-only. Perales should not be used as an example of internalized racism . . . Perales did not blame La Raza for its own oppression, but he did realize La Raza needed to take advantage of any educational opportunities available and needed to empower themselves.

Seven, scholars must also consider gender when writing about the League and La Raza's empowerment. Perales (and other LULACers) missed opportunities to empower women of Mexican descent. LULAC was gendered and Perales' mentoring of future leaders was too. This paper confirms activist Sloss-Vento's account of Perales. Sloss-Vento's portrayal is not simply a laudatory, biased tribute by a friend. She did not exaggerate his achievements or simply pay homage to a local man.

Eight, this paper confirms research by [an historian] who accurately portrayed Perales' ideology. [He] was unable to document Perales' actions in the 1930s because the Perales papers were not available. (Citations omitted, Orozco, pp. 24-25)

Benjamin Márquez, whose scholarship on the establishment of LULAC did not have access to these archives as Orozco had, has taken an opportunity to revisit his earlier work, and to resituate Perales as a complex transitional figure, particularly in his many efforts to thread the needle in a highly structured and racialized social hierarchy that was Jaime Crow Texas—the peculiar mix of social exclusion and *de facto* segregation that occurred in post-World War I Texas, the only jurisdiction in the South with substantial numbers of African Americans and Mexican Americans. He notes:

As a founding member of LULAC and a political activist with a career that spanned almost fifty years, Perales' was a pivotal figure in these debates. He fought for equality before the law, equal employment opportunity, school desegregation and increased political representation. Perales argued Mexican Americans were Caucasian and rejected the option of a political alliance with African Americans. At first glance, these ideas place him solidly within the LULAC tradition of biculturalism and faith that Mexican Americans would soon be incorporated into American society. However, it will be demonstrated that he departed from his organization's ideological foundation in significant respects, enough to warrant a reexamination of the relationships early activists had with one another and where they agreed or disagreed on these questions. Given the central role he played in the creation of LULAC, it is surprising how pessimistic he was about the prospects for social change. He doubted Anglo Americans could be trusted or were willing to apply the ideals of equality and justice to Mexican Americans. Perales endorsed the idea of individual responsibility for one's social mobility in the abstract, but placed much of the blame for Mexican-American subordination on the Anglo Saxon. He accused them of using their numbers and political power to maintain a rigid racial hierarchy.

Indeed, race so profoundly determined one's life chances that Perales often argued group identity and individual interests were virtually the same thing. (Márquez, p. 30)

He carefully uses the new letters to extend our understanding of the extraordinary range of civic and political matters in which Perales was engaged, especially after he matter-of-factly exited from regular LULAC involvement. He cites dozens of letters, proceedings, opinion pieces, articles, *testimonios*, books, and other materials that constitute the Perales correspondence. He admiringly documents the many intersections Perales carved out, and the unusual public intellectual aspects of his mission. Even when the record reveals warts and all, especially Perales' growing conservatism, anti-union animus and anti-Communism fervor, he generously notes: "Scholars must take great care in generalizing about the political work of an individual, and in assessing the influence of an individual activist—particularly one who lived many years before" (Márquez, p. 44). Thus, he deftly escapes the mistake of presentism so prevalent in a wide swath of Chicano history, where it is tempting to use present day pieties and paradigms to assess complex historical records, accomplishments and events that seem so obvious in hindsight. With the light of day and this extraordinary record to reevaluate, Márquez leaves his subject with an admiring view, but he is by no means unaware of the manner in which Perales' attachment to these strong principles likely blinded him to other glaring inequalities and obscured his vision. He allows, "Another issue that merits further study is the way civil liberties and constitutional protections were understood by early Mexican-American civil rights activists. Given the severity of racial exclusion Perales experienced and witnessed, it is paradoxical that he was so intolerant of groups and ideas he disliked" (p. 47).

It is a remarkable event to note that these two scholars, whose important work has largely determined the scholarly trajectory concerning LULAC and how to understand that important time, are both absorbing the new materials and reconsidering their earlier work, in the service of all observers developing a more thorough and nuanced appreciation of this important organization. This process of reconsideration is likely to increase, given just how much material is now available, and how many talented scholars, more senior and more junior, are engaged in the reevaluation of Perales and his times.

The Mexican-American Generation, Revisited

These chapters, authored by two senior law professors and two history graduate students, all cover the terrain earlier labeled as "The Mexican-American Generation" by another author, historian Mario T. García. The term "Mexican-American Generation" is not just any generic reference, but a nuanced and significant trope by historians, particularly Mexican-American historians, who have mined its meaning for over two decades, since García named the period in his masterful 1989 work, *Mexican Americans: Leadership, Ideology, and Identity, 1930-1960*. In this important analytic book, García identified the salience of this period, before and after World War II:

Possessing a complex and heterogeneous history, Mexican Americans have evolved through several historical stages. This study concerns one of these—what I call the Mexican-American Era . . . Recruited and exploited as a cheap labor force, and indispensable to the important economic growth of the Southwest during the late nineteenth and early twentieth centuries, Mexican Americans remained rooted in the working class, although their intraclass positions shifted by the 1930s and 1940s to more urban industrial and service occupations. With urbanization came education. A rising although limited U.S.-born middle class likewise arose . . . The convulsions of the Great Depression combined with new economic and political opportunities during World War II and with the historic discrimination in the Southwest against Mexicans and rising expectations among Mexican Americans to give birth to a new leadership, cognizant of its rights as U.S. citizens and determined to address them. (M.T. Garcia, 1989, p. 2)

Perales, whose professional life spanned the mid-1920s through his death in 1960 traced this arc of "rising expectations," has historically been situated as among the most important and recognizable leaders of the Mexican-American Era. Now that the extensive archival materials can be employed to elaborate upon the existing record, it is likely that he will become even more identified with this period and his range of public obligations even better understood. Doctoral student Joseph Orbock Medina, in "The trials of Unity: Rethinking the Mexican-American Generation in Texas, 1948-1960," perceptively notes:

Scholars have rightly acknowledged Alonso S. Perales as a leading crusader in the fight to defend the essential dignity of the "Latin Race," particularly with his treatise *En Defensa de mi Raza*. Like many of his fellow activists of the "Mexican-American Generation," he had a diverse set of ideas on how to best achieve the specific business of reform. Perales also had political commitments, loyalties, and grudges that tempered the character of his involvement with other activists and organizations.

Rather than view Alonso S. Perales and his legacy as part of a triumphal teleology of mid-twentieth-century Mexican-American social and political progress, [I place] him within the volatile partisan politics and grand ideological battles of the post-war era. With such a relatively small cadre of movement insiders, personal relationships, and individual philosophies held great sway in the paternalistic organizations of the Mexican-American Generation. Pointed internal divisions among these leaders mirrored and reinforced broader (pan-) American debates on labor, social class, and identity. Compromise and contestation from within would define the Movement. (Orbock Medina, p. 53)

With the deep resources now evident in these archives, scholars will be able to track and better analyze the details of his "personal relationships and individual philosophies" that "held great sway," as have virtually all the authors in this preliminary project. Accordingly, law professor Lupe S. Salinas, who wrote earlier on the career and contributions of lawyer Gustavo (Gus) García, (Salinas, 2003, pp. 159-

160) can locate many traces of Perales' life as an ambitious young man in a hurry, and in "Legally White, Socially Brown: Alonso S. Perales and His Crusade for Justice for *La Raza*," he details the remarkable rise of this young lawyer who, within a few years of his membership in the Texas bar, had literally transformed the political and organizational landscape for Mexican Americans:

> Fueled by his observations and experiences in Texas, Perales sought to create a strong organization to protect "the best interests and welfare of our Race" and to strive "for their progress." However, due to his youth and lack of training, several years passed until the idea went beyond the discussion stage. Once he received his honorable discharge from the U.S. Army in January 1920, he proceeded to Washington, D.C. in order to pursue his studies and his training to be "equipped to help solve the problems of our people in Texas." Perales and his two friends discussed the idea for a time and then communicated by mail to further the dream of establishing an organization that would become "a bulwark for the protection of all our Racial brethren." (p. 78)

By tracing these activities, Professor Salinas helps clarify the many influences that later manifested themselves in Perales' complex professional biography, most notably his high aspirations for group solidarity, organizational development and communication skills (Salinas, p. 78).

Aarón E. Sánchez, in *"Mendigos de nacionalidad*: Mexican-Americanism and Ideologies of Belonging in a New Era of Citizenship, Texas 1910-1967," has effectively used the archives to show how Perales and other colleagues were mythologizing Mexican Americans to inculcate their stories, including stories with their origins in Mexico, into the American narrative, such as J.T. Canales' retelling of the Juan Cortina story (*Juan N. Cortina: Bandit or Patriot?*), stripping it of its *bandido* folk roots and the efforts of Ruben Rendon Lozano, a San Antonio lawyer and LULACer who published *Viva Tejas: The Story of the Mexican-born Patriots of the Republic of Texas.* These projects of literary reconstitution by Mexican-American lawyers attempted to reframe the story of the Republic of Texas to one more consonant with the mythic role of Tejanos as patriots and citizen soldiers, prepared to go to war for their country. Of course, after World War II, when it became clear that the American polity and Texas decision-makers had not traded unusual and fervent patriotism in exchange for improved civil rights in benefits, accommodations, and public acceptance, the Faustian bargain was cruelly revealed. Lawyer Perales then began his self-financed large-scale project of *testimonios* and notarized statements to document the gap between the rhetoric and the actual conditions, where even Tejano genuine soldier heroes with Congressional Medals of Honor could be excluded from restaurants, theaters, and other private spaces and public accommodations, such as veterans' housing and the like. The nationally publicized dustup with the refusal to honor Private Felix Longoria in the U.S. Cemetery in Three Rivers, Texas, and the incident with Sgt. Macario García and the Oasis Café in the rural Houston area gave impetus to the American G.I. Forum, founded by Corpus Christi Dr. Hector P. García to channel attention to *veteranos* (Ramos 1998; Olivas, 2008; I. García, 2003, 2008).

In a fresh and compelling way, one that will likely draw the attention of Latino and Latina literary scholars, historians, and linguists, doctoral student Sánchez recounts the new way that these early Mexican-American lawyers used the tricks of the trade, even with skill sets not often found in lawyers: literary criticism and folklore. Their attempt to employ this discourse was one of the many organized efforts to employ available discursive folkways to reconstitute Mexican Americans away from foreign "others" to full and active and patriotic U.S. Citizens:

The intellectual project of reconceptualizing U.S.-Mexican belonging as an American ethnic was a departure from previous modes of imagining in U.S.-Mexican thought. This change required a reformulation of the position of U.S.-Mexicans in the region, nation, and world. Calling themselves Mexican American came with a direct intent and entailed an ideological shift. They were responding to the global change in citizenship and the evolving homeland politics in the Southwest in the years after the Mexican Revolution. Many U.S.-Mexicans found themselves outside of the mainstream American social imaginary and excluded from the imagined community of *México de afuera*. This forced many people on a search for belonging. For a group of U.S.-Mexicans, they were Americans—including the exclusive racial, class, and linguistic connotations the word carried with it. They emphasized whiteness and promoted a specific modernist worldview that underwrote racial and social hierarchies. Leaders like Alonso S. Perales and Andres de Luna, as well as organizations like the Order Sons of America and LULAC cooperated in ideas that, while not necessarily hegemonic, were definitely homogenizing.

It would be impossible, and nearly foolhardy, to argue that citizenship did not provide U.S.-Mexicans with political and material benefits. Being recognized as citizens gave them power to access a legal system that offered avenues of protection and redress. By being citizens, U.S.-Mexicans could claim inclusion into an important imagined community. However, the change towards the emphasis on citizenship did indeed limit the intellectual and ideological possibilities of other human connections between people of the world. It is difficult to criticize Mexican Americans for the social distance they kept from African Americans during the period, but the ideology of Mexican-Americanism did not co-opt the racial regime of the twentieth century; it cooperated in its reproduction. For that reason and many others, Mexican-Americanism was a limited and, at time, limiting ideology. (Sánchez, p. 114)

Legal scholar George A. Martínez, whose most significant earlier work has been to examine closely the long and hidden history of Mexican-American litigation, especially in twentieth-century desegregation, public accommodations, and other areas where *de facto* discrimination was deeply imbedded, takes a different approach in "Alonso S. Perales and the Effort to Establish the Civil Rights of Mexican Americans as Seen through the Lens of Contemporary Critical Legal Theory: Post-racialism, Reality Construction, Interest Convergence, and Other Critical Themes."

Here, he employs various postmodernist and critical theory frameworks to understand the complex web of exclusion, discrimination, and informal racism that permeated the Mexican-American existence in the Southwestern United States. He paints a convincing picture of Perales' efforts to frame the issues and to engage in the discourse. His most convincing analysis is the dramatic explanation of why Perales, a lawyer and former court stenographer, used legal terminology and notarized formats in the 1948 *Good Neighbors*, an unusual volume for its sheer level of repeated detail of the lived and observed stories by WWII *veteranos*, which he then turns into testimony for governmental hearings and legislative purposes. Martínez deftly suggests that this rhetorical device anticipated the qualitative and normative framing devices of the twenty-first century, or at the least, critical theory of the late twentieth-century: "Looking to the bottom—adopting the perspective of those who have seen and felt the falsity of the liberal promise—can assist critical scholars in the task of fathoming the phenomenology of law and defining the elements of justice." He specifies:

[W]e can observe that Perales has sought to invalidate and deconstruct the socially constructed reality of post-racialism—a worldview which holds that racism does not play a significant role in the lives of Mexican Americans. In its place, he substitutes a new more accurate reality based on the actual experiences of Mexican Americans in which they describe an alternative reality that is permeated with racism against Mexican Americans.

It is worth noting that Perales' task of reality construction is a large one. In Perales' day, most people were operating well within a black/white paradigm regarding civil rights—*i.e.*, "the conception that race in America consists, either exclusively or primarily, of only two constituent groups, the Black and the White." Accordingly, civil rights discourse focused primarily on black/white relations. Mexican Americans fell outside of this black/white paradigm. This point is highly significant. As philosopher of science Thomas Kuhn has explained, phenomena that do not fit within the prevailing paradigm or "normal science" of the day "are often not seen at all." Accordingly, the phenomena regarding Mexican Americans that Perales was seeking to publicize would generally be invisible or not seen because of the prevailing black/white paradigm. (Martínez, p. 127)

This is exhilarating work, seeing the spores of later critical theory in these earlier writings. Other new evidence on the origins of this 1948 Perales publishing project may have been the epistolary nature of a WWI diary published by Perales' friend and collaborator José de la Luz Saenz, with who he had traveled the Rio Grande Valley early in his career. Saenz had published his diary in 1933 with the San Antonio Spanish-language publisher Artes Gráficas. This authentic work collected letters, editorials, souvenirs and wartime letters-from-the-front that appeared in *La Prensa* and elsewhere (Zamora, 2002, 2012). Inasmuch as many Chicano historians have, with some justification in the earlier and incomplete record, contested the Mexican-American generation as conservative and regressive—especially those who have projected more modern expectations upon older events—this may and likely will spur a complete reconsideration of the teleology and political economy of this important cohort.

Religion and Race

If there is any constant theme that permeates every corner of Alonso S. Perales' life, even more than the advancement of his *raza*, it is the advancement of his *raza*'s religion, more specifically, Roman Catholicism. Not only was he a devout and practicing Catholic, but his entire ethos of *raza* advancement embraced a strict and conservative Catholicism that he urged as a feature of political action, personal behavior, organizational development and community spirituality. In his book *Católicos: Resistance and Affirmation in Chicano Catholic History* and in the co-edited *Mexican-American Religions: Spirituality, Activism, and Culture* (with Gastón Espinosa), historian Mario T. García has drawn the close connections between Mexican-American civic and political leaders (such as Perales' close friend and compatriot Cleofas Calleros) and their spiritual and religious moorings. In his important analysis of Catholic social doctrine, García noted that the tenets of the doctrine "recognize[d] the human dimension of people— the incarnational—and, as such, further recognize[d] the social and political in human beings" (García, 2008, p. 55).

Even by these historical standards, the integration of Perales' personal piety and his general theory of Mexican-American advancement were notable. In "Alonso S. Perales and the Catholic Imaginary: Religion and the Mexican-American Mind," García notes that this religious-politic doctrinal blend stressed "human dignity, truth, justice, charity, freedom, and civil and political as well as social and economic human rights. In their many writings in both Spanish- and English-language newspaper columns, in their correspondence, and in their praxis as civil rights leaders, Perales and Calleros identified with the principles of Catholic social doctrine. . . . [Y]ou cannot fully understand Perales without understanding the central role that his faith, Catholicism, played in his personal, social, and political formation and mindset. It is his Catholic imaginary—his imagining his world and the new world he sought for Mexican Americans through his Catholic faith—that envelops his life and career" (p. 52). After reviewing the dozens of letters, advice columns, and essays by Perales, he summarizes:

But if Catholic social doctrine represented the more public face of Perales' Catholicism, his foreign policy if you will, there is another and more personal side to his Catholicism that represents his "domestic policy" aimed not at an outside non-Mexican-American audience but at Mexican Americans themselves. That is, Perales employed Catholic social doctrine as a way of influencing Anglos, especially policy-makers about the civil rights concerns of Mexican Americans in a way that gave his views more credibility because they coincided with those of the Catholic Church itself. At the same time, he employed his more personal Catholicism and faith to socialize or attempt to socialize Mexican Americans in Texas or his part of Texas to observe, respect, and practice their Catholic faith not only for their own redemption, but to show the outside world that Mexican Americans represented a strong and observant religious American people who as such should be fully accepted and integrated by other God-fearing Americans. In order for Perales to convincingly argue for integration and equal opportunities for Mexican Americans, he needed to also display that Mexican Americans were worthy of such inclusion by showing that they constituted a strong Christian community based, as with other Americans, on solid Christian family values. This domestic side of Perales' Catholicism is especially observed in his many personal advice columns and other writing in the San Antonio Spanish-language Catholic newspaper *La Voz* during the 1950s. (García, pp. 152-153)

While his religious advice and public piety may strain credulity in today's more secular discourse, it is a noteworthy aspect of Perales' constant search for dialogic space: to be good citizens and community members, Mexican Americans must be chaste, pious, (Roman Catholic) God-fearing and on best behavior, to be accepted as good and Christian participants in the polity and in community advancement. Virtually no secular political figure occupied this niche, in either English or in Spanish; thus, Perales played all four corners of the court, as almost no Mexican-American leader before or since. As García notes, UFW leader and iconic political figure César Chávez came closest in his blend of activism and invocation of religious values, even though they were not as strident or as singularly Catholic as those of Perales.

Even allowing for the value of hindsight, it is clear that Perales lay down with dogs and woke up with fleas. This disturbing corner of Perales' life, where his virulent anti-Communism and conservative Catholicism led him to make political alliances with a wide range of troubling and contested figures, whose intersection with him was all the more ironic and remarkable for their own conservatism and lack of solidarity on the overarching feature of Perales' entire life, the advancement of Mexican Americans, has not been widely known or analyzed. In a remarkable study, "Faithful Dissident: Alonso S. Perales, Discrimination, and the Catholic Church," Virginia Marie Raymond has carefully filled out these interstices, drawing upon the newly available archival materials. He carried on correspondence and became politically involved with Latin American dictator Anastacio Somoza, segregationist Texas Governor Allan Shivers, and others whose own work clearly impeded the progress of Mexican Americans. She notes:

Perales was an outsider both in the secular and religious worlds in which he circulated. Both as a Mexican American and layperson, he found himself at the margins of the Catholic Church. He was also outside some secular political circles as a Mexican American, a Catholic, or a social conservative.

From one point of view, Perales' religious and political commitments might seem complicated: sometimes overlapping or identical and at other times tense. Even to assign "religion" and "politics" to separate categories, however, might betray and mislead us. This paper will focus on the dual political aspects of Mr. Perales' Catholicism. I mean "political" in the broadest sense, that is, having to do with power relations between and among people . . .

Our protagonist was a sometime ally of the both the highest-ranking secular executive and the highest-ranking member of the Catholic hierarchy in
Texas. To be a Mexican-American civil rights advocate politically positioned
uncomfortably between Governor Allan Shivers and Archbishop Robert E.
Lucey is the essence of the Perales paradox. The trajectories of Perales' anti-
communism, and the relationship of his anti-communism to his Catholicism,
warrant close attention. (Raymond, pp. 171-172)

Raymond's "close attention" brings sunlight to the many progressive struggles
waged by Perales; in this instance, against the segregation of Catholic parish creation
and ethnic siting for congregations, against segregated Catholic schooling and
against the exclusion of pious Mexican Americans from the Church's lay leadership.
Some of these examples are staggering, such as the clear racial separation among the
races by Catholic policy and practice, especially in Texas, where she shows embarrassing details about the history of the Church, especially affecting the predominantly Catholic Mexican-American population. As an observer of the longstanding
segregatory practices in Texas schooling, I was reminded more than once of that sad
history in her reading of Catholic education and parish-formation.

But as tragic as that rendering is (San Miguel, 2000; Valencia, 2008), I confess
that I was squirming as I read in her chapter of Perales' cozying up to Texas Governor Allan Shivers, who was characterized in *Yellow Dogs And Republicans: Allan
Shivers And Texas Two-party Politics* (Dobbs, 2005) as being the significant transitional figure who transformed Texas in the 1940s and 1950s from essentially a one-
party conservative Dixiecrat state to one that has become thoroughly Republican
since. By 2012, not a single Democrat had held statewide office at any level for a
decade (Dunham and Wilkins, 2012). Shivers accomplished the beginnings of this
transformation in a variety of racialized ways, from inveighing against *Brown v.
Board* to supporting segregation efforts in schooling, in voting districts, and in dis-
pensing political favors. Surely, dealing with the various secular and political leaders in Texas meant that anyone such as Perales would have had to deal regularly with
unsavory persons, but he used this proximity and influence to bait in a way reminis-
cent of Sen. Joseph McCarthy at the national and international level, as when he
wrote a private letter to Shivers in 1954, several months after the *Hernandez* and
Brown cases: "Shivers also accused his challenger, former Judge Ralph Yarborough,
of both being a Communist and an integrationist. Perales agreed, writing to Governor Shivers that in his opinion, both Yarborough and state representative Maury
Maverick, Jr., were 'soft' on communism. Maverick, Jr., had opposed Shivers'
attempt to make membership in the Community Party a capital offense" (p. 201).
She cites a fawning letter that Perales wrote to Shivers:

. . . [Y]ou jumped the fence and declared yourself unequivocally against communism, and that is exactly what we Americans must insist that each and every
candidate do in determining whether [sic] or not we are going to support him;
and that any candidate who refuses to do that is not deserving of our consideration at the polls. . . . Here are the names of some persons who campaigned

against Your Excellency [sic] recently: Gus C. Garcia, Dr. George I. Sanchez, D,. [sic] Hector Garcia, J.J. Herrera, Ed Idar, Jr., Virgilio C. Rosel, Tomas M. Rodriguez. (references omitted, Raymond, p. 201)

It is sad duty to see the obsequious style ("Your Excellency") and perfidious identification of extraordinary fellow Mexican-American legal and political leaders as if they were enemies for real or imagined transgressions against Perales. She is even-handed beyond warrant when she notes these strange bedfellows: "It might have been possible for Alonso S. Perales to have worked—in harmony with other Mexican-American advocates—simultaneously for civil rights, against what he saw as the evils of communism, and within the Catholic Church until his death. His new political alliances as well as his denunciation of other Mexican-American civil rights lawyers, complicated that possibility" (p. 203). To see it in the service of a political figure who actively opposed progress for Perales' *raza* is jarring and noteworthy, even if likely a corollary to his fierce conservatism and anti-Communism. To contrast this letter-writing indictment is all the more perplexing when the archives reveal a number of earlier letters written to create a discourse and purposive medium of exchange—endorsements of officials running for elected office to encourage their hiring named Mexican-American constituents in affirmative action and the appointments process (Márquez, pp. 29-48).

Letters, Piety, and Politics

When I began to read through the thousands of letters and the widespread materials in the extraordinary Perales archives, I realized I had not read so many letters since a graduate seminar in the epistolary novel, taken in my early 1970s stint as an English graduate student, when I had occasion to read letters in collections of Nathaniel Hawthorne and James Thurber. I had forgotten how complex it was to reconstruct a world through letters, especially if they are incomplete (one does not always know the denominator of the full correspondence), asymmetrical (not all the correspondents are collected, making the discourse lopsided), or bilingual (not all authors are equally fluent in two languages, introducing subtle issues of translation and nuance). Some of these problems exist in this archive, but given how organized Perales was and how complete his materials are, both sides are remarkably well-archived. Moreover, they are real letters, not fictitious ones in a narrative discourse. It has been since the early 1970s that I read literary theory (earning foreign language credits as well, given my unfamiliarity with the postmodernist scholarship on the rise then), but in preparation for this section and overall access to this collection, I drank deeply from several scholarly books and articles on the genre. (I confess that these too often reminded me of the jibe, "Q: What do you get when you cross a mafioso with a postmodernist? A: An answer you cannot understand.") But I started with the obligatory Derrida, and worked my way through until I understood parts:

As Jacques Derrida observes, texts, particularly novels, usually contain unmistakable marks indicating their genre. These marks may refer to particular books or to a mode of discourse, such as Valmont's gleanings from "romans." Their function in the text, however, extends beyond mere allusion: they constitute intertextual extensions of the narrative by investing the text with a second, already determined, narrative matrix, creating a palimpsestic relationship of narrated events. Thus references to earlier epistolary novels establish an analogous textualization (lettering) of the events, and similar occurrences at the level of event are in some degree overdetermined by the anterior text; moreover, the reader's response is in some degree overdetermined. References to the "novel" or "romance" raise more complex epistemological questions, since a fictional discourse is being used to measure truth within another fiction. These generic references are often meta-textually significant both in constructing and in deconstructing the illusion of reality necessary for a sympathetic response to the textual society, just as the existence of real literary works in a fictional universe both gives that universe credibility and opens to question the fiction's representation of life. A third means of genre marking involves the use of specific formal conventions, and epistolary novels are especially adept in applying such transmission conventions as reflexivity, enclosure, intermediary transmission, and the confidant. (Bernard Duyfhuizen, 1985, "Epistolary Narratives of Transmission and Transgression")

What I took was that the letters formed a "relationship of narrated events," not Tristram Shandy writing to his family about life and sex or Bram Stoker's 1897 *Dracula*, but the Alonso S. Perales letters and materials were significant, "both in constructing and in deconstructing the illusion of reality necessary for a sympathetic response to the textual society," or Texas in Perales' times. On the completeness aspect of the Perales letters, the Samuel Richardson scholar Alan D. McKillop has usefully written, "The writing of the letters is only the beginning; they are copied, sent, received, shown about, discussed, answered, even perhaps hidden, intercepted, stolen, altered, or forged. The relation of the earlier letters in an epistolary novel to the later may thus be quite different from the relation of the earlier chapters of a novel to the later" ("Epistolary Technique in Richardson's Novels," in *Samuel Richardson: A Collection of Critical Essays*, ed. John J. Carroll, 1969, p. 139). This is a useful organizing principle for such a sprawling narrative as these archives.

Independent scholar Norma Adelfa Mouton, in "Changing Voices: Approaching Modernity from Mexican to Mexican American to Chicano in the Epistolary Archives of Alonso S. Perales," reviews many of the *testimonios* and notarized letters from Mexican Americans to Perales gathered in *Are We Good Neighbors?*, having to do with the post-WW II treatment of these adults, particularly the *veteranos* who had returned from foreign fields of battle to encounter increased Anglo hostility as they began to claim their new found status as full American citizens and military patriots:

The letters in the collection, when taken together chronologically, whether written by men or by women, present an increasingly bolder voice. The letters written before 1941 and making no reference to the military service rendered by Mexican Americans during World War II tend to acknowledge a total separation or isolation from the dominant Anglo-Saxon culture. . . . Letters written during and after 1941, or those earlier letters mentioning military service during the war, tend to make clearer reference to ways in which individuals are expected to suppress or eliminate their Mexican culture in order to be accepted by the Anglo Saxons around them.

The cases of discrimination also change after World War II and after laws began to be enacted that change the political status of the Mexican American by law if not by practice. Prior to 1946 most of the letters relate incidents of discrimination that tend to attempt to eliminate the Mexican American from establishments reserved for "whites" or Anglo Saxons. During World War II, Mexican Americans begin to voice their displeasure at having to send their boys to war while being discriminated against at home. When those same servicemen and women return home either after the war or while on leave, they too complain, and more vehemently, at the discrimination they must endure at home while fighting in the same trenches with Anglo Saxons at the battlefront. After World War II and especially after the 1960s, when the few laws that have been passed to protect against discrimination gain wider recognition, the nature of the discrimination begins to change. No longer can Mexican Americans be eliminated from participating in public forums and patronizing public establishments, so Anglo Saxons begin to point out the cultural differences that separate the two ethnic groups and belittle those values dear to the Mexican-American traditions. In all cases a "modernity of subtraction" applies. In the earlier letters it is a complete subtraction of the individual subaltern from the dominant culture, while in the later letters it is the subtraction of specific cultural traits of the subaltern that do not fit into the framework of the dominant culture. Just as the nature of the discrimination changes from subtraction of the person to subtraction of cultural characteristics, so the voice of the Mexican-American protest changes from acquiescent and accepting to questioning and finally militant. Letters written after 1950 also begin to reflect a tendency to defend unknown victims . . . This change has taken the focus from defense of the individual to defense of the community. (Mouton, pp. 235-236)

The letters became the backdrop for legislative hearings and governmental records. As unusual as letters were for such civil rights law enactment, so too was the discursive format of the op-eds and published letters to and from entreaties by Mexican-American Catholic women, as well as local men. Mouton has carefully tracked many of the letters and materials not only to keep evident the discursive synchronicity, but to situate them as a belated return to private life for so many Mexican Americans.

Literary theorist Donna M. Kabalen de Bichara, in "Self-Writing and Collective Representation: The Literary Enuciation of Historical Reality and Cultural Values," situates Perales in a broad narrative and discursive tradition of autobiography, even as it is clear that Perales is in a complex multilateral project, not in a narrow, singular act of autobiography:

As I argue in this chapter, *En Defensa de mi Raza / In Defense of My People*, provides the reader with information that serves as a starting point for coming to a more clear understanding of various aspects of Alonso S. Perales' life project which involves deconstructing systems of thought that attempt to radically limit the rights of Mexican Americans as citizens of the United States. This project takes on larger dimensions over time as it includes the support of those Mexicans residing in the United States as well. So as to broaden this initial focus, the corpus of my study also focuses on letters exchanged between Alonso S. Perales and Adela Sloss Vento, those exchanged between Marta Perales and Adela Sloss Vento, as well as those letters written by Marta Perales. I suggest that these letters can be seen as literary artifacts embedded within a specific historical reality. My intention in this direction is a critical reading of a select number of letters so as to highlight the type of discourse production evident within these texts. Although literary theorists have tended to marginalize letters as a sub-genre of autobiography, I propose that they clearly involve a type of self-writing that reveals elements that contribute to a cultural understanding of the writer and his life project. My major goal, therefore, is to demonstrate that the content of these letters presents self-writing that emanates from a cultural community; that is, these letters reflect the concerns of a collectivity of men and women of Mexican descent living in the United States. . . .

It is through the letters written by Alonso S. Perales, then, that we find a type of life writing which, as noted by Genaro Padilla, "transforms life history into textual permanence" in the form of "diaries, family histories, personal poetry and collections of self-disclosing correspondence" (Padilla, p. 4). It is precisely through various types of "self-disclosing correspondence" that the reader encounters information that focuses on specific dates and types of information that functions as a historical inscription of facts that represent "a major articulation of resistance to American social and cultural hegemony." (pp. 242-243)

This section's two nuanced, insightful chapters reveal the extent to which the Perales materials, particularly the voluminous correspondence and epistolary dialogues, have an organic and synoptic meaning, indicating the extent to which they are in a long-standing dialogic tradition, one often rooted in fictional narrative, but also showing the connectedness between his over-arching worldview in advancing his people's cause and the many real historical events swirling around him in these important times. These are important and thoughtful contributions to our understanding of Perales the letter writer. Reading these chapters, however, also makes one realize that the full understanding of the archives is beyond the ken or reach of any one scholar, inasmuch as it is such a large collection covering so many years and subjects. His role as a public intellectual is yet to be fully measured or appreciated.

Diplomacy, Law, and Biography: Assessing Alonso S. Perales

In the final chapters, we return to Perales' biographer F. Arturo Rosales—noted earlier—and historian Emilio Zamora ("Connecting Causes: Alonso S. Perales,

Hemispheric Unity, and Mexican Rights in the United States"). I have gained the admiration usually reserved for extraordinary athletes and artists, considering just how shapeshifting and malleable Alonso S. Perales appears, now that we have the intellectual DNA that made up his nearly thirty years of public discursive life.

In what is perhaps the most novel treatment of the Perales papers, Zamora extracts the details of the final stage of his career, that of diplomat and international lawyer, playing on a large post-WWII stage. He notes:

The United Nations conference held at San Francisco's Veteran's War Memorial Building began winding down as delegations from fifty countries prepared to take part in the signing ceremony of the new organization's charter. When it came time for Nicaragua to sign, on June 23, 1945, Dr. Mariano Arguello Vargas, Minister of Foreign Affairs, walked to the austere stage of the Herbst Theatre and seated himself at a large round table. The rest of the Nicaraguan delegation, made up of government and military officials, stood between him and a raised display of national flags as the official photographers recorded yet another nation committing to international cooperation for global peace, democracy, and justice.

Although the event looked like all the other forty-nine signing ceremonies, Nicaraguan officials had dispensed with tradition and assigned one of the coveted positions in their delegation to a person who had been born and raised in the United States. Alonso S. Perales, a co-founder of the League of United Latin American Citizens (LULAC) and one of the most prominent U.S. civil rights leaders of the twentieth century, held the post of lead counselor to the delegation. His selection and assignment may have seemed odd to a casual observer, but not to someone who had followed Perales' extensive and distinguished diplomatic career for Nicaragua and the United States, or knew of his close relationship with the Anastasio Somoza regime. By the time the first UN meeting took place, Perales had served as the Nicaraguan Consul General in San Antonio, Texas for eleven years; he also had participated in at least thirteen U.S. diplomatic missions in Latin America since the 1920s. . . .

With some exceptions, historians have overlooked the relationship between the heightened wartime attention to prejudice, racial thinking, and discrimination and the treatment of Mexicans in the United States, and they have failed to examine this community as a point where local and hemispheric issues began to correspond and connect. Building on my prior work on Mexicans in the United States, here I underscore the importance of Perales as an insightful, prescient, and determined civil rights figure. Through his role in hemispheric diplomacy, Perales brought international attention to the discriminatory treatment of Mexicans in the American Southwest. (Zamora, pp. 288-289, citations omitted)

In sum, Perales used the nuanced and elegant offices of the U.S. and pan-American diplomatic world as his final discursive project, seizing these developing opportunities to gain traction for his lifelong dream, identifying anti-Mexican and anti-Mexican-American political strains and building support for the international human rights and civil rights antidiscrimination projects that he had envisioned all his life, building LULAC and other organizations, gathering *testimonios*, engaging in litigation and legislative efforts to improve their lives, and above all, urging his people to meet their side of the bargain with the larger community: if we do our part and be good neighbors, they will accept us or at least not actively oppose our civil rights. Of course, in an ironic sense, this strategy required the racializing of the struggle. As Zamora notes,

> I suggest that just as government and non-government representatives elevated racial thinking to prominence in the diplomatic arena, civil rights activists in Mexican communities from Texas also made the connection with a grounded civil rights cause as their principal point of departure. The story of race as a wartime issue, in other words, can be best appreciated by examining diplomatic relations, the Mexican civil rights cause in Texas, and their connection in the political biography of Perales. (Zamora, p. 289)

I characterize this as "ironic," or perhaps better, "double-edged," given the uneven relationship Perales and his contemporaries had with legal whiteness, their being a "class apart," and their inconsistent attempts to advance their *raza* without being racialized. As legal historian Ariela Gross has perceptively noted (also using the term "ironically"): "The notion of mestizaje, or racial mixture, also created a sense of the fluidity among groups and reinforced the importance of culture in defining identity: Mexican Americans often saw themselves and their culture as stronger because they were a mixed-race, or mestizo, people. Ironically, at the very moment that some Mexican-American advocates on the U.S. side of the border were claiming whiteness strategically, the newly independent government of Mexico was propagating the national mythos of la raza—the Mexican race uniquely strengthened by its combination of Spanish and Indian" (Gross, 2007, p. 345).

But for the first time in his life, diplomat Perales interacted routinely with educated and powerful Latin Americans, particularly Mexicans, in a clear attempt to elevate the quotidian racial violence and political oppression faced by *Mexicanos de afuera* to this bigger and more visible stage. That he failed to live long enough to harvest his efforts in the successful civil rights antidiscrimination legislation of the 1960s is no fair critique. Perhaps without equal among Mexican Americans and among most Anglos, his discursive behavior, civil rights efforts, and longstanding leadership marked the transition from the Mexican-American Generation, largely centered around post-WWII to the period where civil rights were the center of the polity, fueled largely by fellow Texan President Lyndon Johnson, whose own time as a schoolteacher in a Mexican school seared him with anger and a desire for fairness (Pycior, 1997). Perales is not Woody Allen's *Zelig*, but he is the closest analog in the Mexican-American community, and perhaps the U.S. biography of the time, certainly for a person who never held formal appointive or elected offices or a held full of diplomatic portfolio. He is also the person who combined being of Mexican origin and being Mexican American in a fluid and transformative fashion—born a U.S. citizen, he had all the relative advantages that flowed to his community, but his interaction with and advocacy for Mexicans in exile transformed him into an advocate who never accepted his lot in life.

Each of these chapters reveals more of lawyer Alonso S. Perales than we knew, as if the half century his letters were hidden now enable us to see his good and bad sides, his generous importunings, selflessly advanced on behalf of his people, and his weak religious pieties directed at advice-seekers, steeped in his conservative cultural Catholicism. He could privately and publicly cultivate and serve as a mentor to others, even as he outed political enemies to Governor Shivers, in what can only be fairly described as a creepy and mean-spirited fashion. But we come away with a certain sense of service and dedication to egalitarian principles, and insight into a man who used every strategy possibly available to him to serve his *raza*. He even participates in the quintessential discursive act for a person politically inclined: he runs for office himself, unsuccessfully, for the San Antonio school board, a disappointment that paves the way for Gus Garcia's subsequent victory to that body. The papers should lead to a fundamental reconsideration of this important transitional figure, and we are grateful to his family, these accomplished authors and the many others who have made these insights possible.

One regret is that the many legal documents that he must have accumulated through his years of practice are not well-represented in the archives. There are, to be sure, any number of such materials, but we do not come away with the fuller sense of Perales as a lawyer, dealing with poor clients, arguing cases in various tribunals and legal venues, collecting fees and dealing with the business side of a small practice. Perhaps more such documents, which were likely removed for confidentiality purposes upon his death, will appear in archival format or in the various places where they could be sequestered: old law office files held by his collaborators or libraries where they have not yet surfaced. Or a garage.

Even with this scant legal record—scant surely in contrast to his more fulsome and comprehensive packrattish private record—it is possible to evaluate the extent to which his legal career added value to his organizing and political efforts, and I have examined all the cases he tried for which there are published opinions. Given the extent to which the early Mexican-American lawyers dominated the polity, his legal career is an exemplar of understanding the crucial role of *Tejano* lawyers in this history, and as Emilio Zamora and others have noted, his international legal practice was substantial and successful.

In "The Legal Career of Alonso S. Perales," I look at the record he built up as an attorney in practice from approximately 1925 through 1960. While there are scattered files that shed light on his long legal career, regrettably, the complete files and papers of his practice have not survived, so observers of this interesting period of his career do not have a full or clear record of his thirty-plus years of practice. However, he built a substantial practice that allowed him and his family to enjoy a solid middle class life, one that was characteristically modest and that involved adopting children. He tried a number of cases that establish a record of both his general commercial practice, representing Mexican-American clients and his civil rights practice, trying to strike down punitive practices and discriminatory policies that harmed community members, such as racially restrictive covenants and excessive police force. These particular cases were tried in a twenty year stretch from 1939 until months before his 1960 death, although the record reveals involvement other cases where he was not the trial attorney of record, such as 1930s *Salvatierra v. Del Rio ISD*. I am hopeful that this preliminary work will lead to more research on the early *Tejano* and other Mexican-American lawyers and other professionals in other states (Muñoz, 2001; Valencia, 2008; García, Yosso, and Barajas, 2012). These leaders who figure in this record show the centrality of lawyers in the Mexican-American struggle, and reading their stories fills any reader with a sense of outrage and admiration in equal parts.

References and Cases Cited

Arellano, G. (May 6, 2010). Mi casa es mi casa: How Fullerton resident Alex Bernal's 1943 battle against housing discrimination helped change the course of American civil rights. *Orange County Weekly*. (n.p.)

Bender, S. (2010). *Tierra y libertad: Land, liberty, and Latino housing*. New York, N.Y: New York University Press.

Blanton, C. K. (2006). George I. Sanchez, ideology, and whiteness in the making of the Mexican American civil rights movement, 1930-1960. *The Journal of Southern History, 72*(3), 569-604.

Blanton, C. K. (2012). A legacy of neglect: George I. Sanchez, Mexican American education, and the ideal of integration, 1940-1970. *Teachers College Record, 114*(6), 1-34.

Carpio, G. (2012). Unexpected allies: David C. Marcus and his impact on the advancement of civil rights in the Mexican-American legal landscape of southern California (Sanchez, G. J., Ed.), in *Beyond alliances: The Jewish role in reshaping the racial landscape of southern California* (pp. 1-32). West Lafayette: Purdue University Press.

Carrigan, W. D., & Webb, C. (2003). The lynching of persons of Mexican origin or descent in the United States, 1848 to 1928. *Journal of Social History, 37*(2), 411-438.

Chávez, M. (2011). *Everyday injustice: Latino professionals and racism*. Lanham, Md: Rowman & Littlefield Publishers.

Chin, G. J., Hartley, R. E., & University of Arizona. (2006). Still on the books: Jim Crow and segregation laws fifty years after Brown v. Board of Education, a report on laws remaining in the codes of Georgia, Louisiana, Mississippi, Missouri, South Carolina, Virginia and West Virginia. East Lansing, Mich.: *Michigan State Law Review*, 447-476.

Chin, G. J. (2010). Sweatt v. Painter and undocumented college students in Texas. *Thurgood Marshall Law Review 36*, 39-61.

Christian, C. E. (1989). Joining the American mainstream: Texas's Mexican Americans during World War I. *The Southwestern Historical Quarterly, 92*(4), 559-595.

Cruz, J. L., & Molina, M. S. (2010). Hispanic National Bar Association national study on the status of Latinas in the legal profession; few and far between: The reality of Latina lawyers. *Pepperdine Law Review, 37*(3), 971-1038.

De León, A. (1982). *The Tejano community, 1836-1900*. Albuquerque: University of New Mexico Press.

De León, A. (1983). *They called them greasers*. Austin: University of Texas Press.

Dobbs, R. F. (2005). *Yellow dogs and Republicans: Allan Shivers and Texas two-party politics*. College Station: Texas A&M University Press.

Dudziak, M. L. (2000). *Cold War civil rights: race and the image of American democracy*. Princeton: Princeton University Press.

Gándara, P. C., & Contreras, F. (2010). *The Latino education crisis: The consequences of failed social policies*. Cambridge, Mass: Harvard University Press.

García, D. G., Yosso, T. J., & Barajas, F. P. (2012). 'A few of the brightest, cleanest Mexican children': School segregation as a form of mundane racism in Oxnard, California, 1900-1940. *Harvard Educational Review, 82*(1), 1-25.

García, I. M. (2000). *Viva Kennedy: Mexican Americans in search of Camelot*. College Station, Texas: Texas A & M University Press.

García, I. M. (2003). *Hector P. Garcia: In relentless pursuit of justice*. Houston, Texas: Arte Publico Press.

García, I. M. (2009). *White but not equal: Mexican Americans, jury discrimination, and the Supreme Court*. Tucson: University of Arizona Press.

García, M. T. (1989). *Mexican Americans: Leadership, ideology & identity, 1930-1960*. New Haven: Yale University Press.

Garcia, R. A. (1991). *Rise of the Mexican American middle class: San Antonio, 1929-1941*. College Station: Texas A & M University Press.

Gómez, L. E. (2007). *Manifest destinies: The making of the Mexican American race*. New York: New York University Press.

Gonzales, P. B. (2006). Whither the Nuevomexicanos: The career of a southwestern intellectual discourse, 1907-2004. *The Social Science Journal (43)*2, 273-286.

Gonzales, P. B. & Massmann A. (2006). Loyalty questioned: Nuevomexicanos in the Great War. *Pacific Historical Review, 75*(4), 629-666.

Griswold del Castillo, R. (2008). *World War II and Mexican American civil rights*. Austin: University of Texas Press.

Gross, A. J. (2003). Texas Mexicans and the politics of whiteness. *Law and History Review, 21*, 195-206.

Gross, A. J. (2007). "The Caucasian cloak": Mexican Americans and the politics of whiteness in the twentieth-century southwest. *The Georgetown Law Journal, 95*(2) 337-392.

Guglielmo, T. (2006). Fighting for Caucasian rights: Mexicans, Mexican Americans, and the transnational struggle for Civil Rights in World War II Texas. *Journal of American History, 92*, 1212-1237.

History of GWU Law School. (n.d.). *George Washington University*, from http://www.law.gwu.edu/School/Pages/History.aspx/.

Jones-Correa, M. (2001). The origins and diffusion of racial restrictive covenants. *Political Science Quarterly, 115* 541-568.

Kohout, M. D. (n.d.). Cadena, Carlos Cristian. *Handbook of Texas Online*. Retrieved August 2, 2012, from http://www.tshaonline.org/handbook/online/articles/fcaas.

Lopez, I. H. & Olivas M. A. (2008). Hernandez v. Texas: Jim Crow, Mexican Americans, and the Anti-Subordination Constitution (Moran R.l & Carbado D., Eds.). In *Race Law Stories* (pp. 269-306). New York: Foundation Press.

Kanellos, N. (2007). Recovering and reconstructing early twentieth-century Hispanic immigrant print culture in the U.S., *Hispanic Literary History 21*, 438-455.

Kanellos, N., & Martell, H. (2000). *Hispanic periodicals in the United States, origins to 1960: A brief history and comprehensive bibliography*. Houston, Texas: Arte Público Press.

Márquez, B. (1993). *LULAC: The evolution of a Mexican American political organization*. Austin: University of Texas Press.

Martinez, G. A. (1994). Legal indeterminacy, judicial discretion and the Mexican American litigation experience: 1930-1980. *U.C. Davis Law Review 27*, 555-618.

Mazon, M. (1998). *The zoot-suit riots: the psychology of symbolic annihilation*. Austin: University of Texas Press.

Mendoza, M. G. (n.d.). Very few Latino attorneys argue before the Supreme Court. In *National Law Journal*. Retrieved February 8, 2012 from http://www.law.com/jsp/nlj/PubArticleNLJ.jsp?id=1202541721954

Molina, M. S. (2011). Role models: theory, practice, and effectiveness among Latina lawyers, *Journal of Civil Rights & Economic Development 25*, 125-139.

Montejano, D. (1987). *Anglos and Mexicans in the making of Texas, 1836-1986*. Austin: University of Texas Press.

Munoz, L. K. (2001) Separate but equal? A case study of Romo v. Laird and Mexican American schooling. *OAH Magazine of History 15*, 28-35.

Olivas, M. A. (Ed.). (2006). 'Colored men' and 'hombres aquí': Hernandez v. Texas and the emergence of Mexican-American lawyering. Houston: Arte Público Press.

Olivas, M. A. (2008). The 'trial of the century' that never was: Staff Sgt. Macario Garcia, the Congressional Medal of Honor, and the Oasis Café. *Indiana Law Journal 83*, 1391-1403.

Olivas, M. A. (2010). Review essay — The arc of triumph and the agony of defeat: Mexican Americans and the law, *Journal of Legal Education 60*, 354-367.

Orozco, C. E. (2009). *No Mexicans, women, or dogs allowed: The rise of the Mexican American civil rights movement*. Austin: University of Texas Press.

Orozco, C. E. (2012a). Lozano, Alicia Guadalupe Elizondo de. *Handbook of Texas Online* Retrieved July 31, 2012 from http://www.tshaonline.org/handbook/online/articles/flo69.

Orozco, C. E. (2012b). Clínica De La Beneficencia Mexicana. *Handbook of Texas Online* Retrieved July 31, 2012 from http://www.tshaonline.org/handbook/online/articles/pqcpu).

Leininger Pycior, J. (1997). *LBJ and Mexican Americans: The paradox of power*. Austin: University of Texas Press.

Ramirez, J. A. (2009). *To the line of fire: Mexican Texans and WWI*. College Station: Texas A&M University Press.

Ramos, C. (2001). Educational legacy of racially restrictive covenants: their long term impact on Mexican Americans. *The Scholar: St. Mary's Law Review on Minority Issues 4*, 149–84.

Ramos, R. A. (2008) *Beyond the Alamo: Forging Mexican ethnicity in San Antonio, 1821-1861*. Chapel Hill: University of North Carolina Press.

Rangel, J. C. & Alcala C. M. (1972) Project report: De jure segregation of Chicanos in Texas schools. *Harvard Civil Rights-Civil Liberties Law Review 7*, 307-391.

Rivas-Rodriguez, M. (Ed.). (2005). *Mexican Americans and World War II*. Austin: University of Texas Press.

Rivera, J. M. (2006). *The emergence of Mexican America: Recovering stories of Mexican peoplehood in U.S. culture*. New York: NYU Press.

Romero II, T. I. (2004). Our Selma is here: The political and legal struggle for education equality in Denver, Colorado, and multiracial conundrums in American jurisprudence. *Seattle Journal for Social Justice 3*, 73-142.

Romero II, T. I. (2007). Bound between & beyond the borderlands: Region, race, scale and a subnational legal history. *Oregon Review of International Law 9*, 301-336.

Rosales, A. F. (1985). Shifting self-perceptions and ethnic consciousness among Mexicans in Houston 1908–1946, *Aztlán: A Journal of Chicano Studies 16*, 71-94.

Ross, D. L. (1998). Examining the liability factors of sudden wrongful deaths in police custody. *Police Quarterly 1*, 65-91.

Portes, A. & Rumbaut, R. G. (2006). *Immigrant America: A portrait*. Berkeley: University of California.

Salinas, G. (1971). Mexican-Americans and the desegregation of schools in the southwest. *Houston Law Review 8*, 939-951.

Salinas, L. S. (2003) Gus Garcia and Thurgood Marshall: Two legal giants fighting for justice. *Thurgood Marshall Law Review 28*, 145-175.

Salinas, L. S. (2005). Latinos and criminal justice in Texas: has the new millennium brought progress. *Thurgood Marshall Law Review 30*, 289-346.

Sanchez, G. J. (1993) *Becoming Mexican American: Ethnicity, culture and identity in Chicano Los Angeles, 1900-1945*. Oxford: Oxford University Press.

San Miguel Jr., G. (1987). *'Let all of them take heed': Mexican Americans and the campaign for educational equality in Texas, 1910-1981*. Austin: University of Texas Press.

San Miguel Jr., G. (2005). *Brown, not white: School integration and the Chicano movement in Houston*. College Station: Texas A&M University Press.

Saucedo, L. M. (2012). Mexicans, immigrants, cultural narratives, and national origin. *Arizona State Law Journal 44*, 305-341.

Shabazz, A. (2004). *Advancing democracy: African Americans and the struggle for access and equity in higher education in Texas*. Chapel Hill: University of North Carolina Press.

Sheridan, C. (2003). 'Another white race': Mexican Americans and the paradox of whiteness in jury selection. *Law and History Review 21*, 109-144.

Steele, R. (2008). Violence in Los Angeles: Sleepy lagoon, the zoot suit riots, and the liberal response. In del Castillo, R. G. (Ed.) *World War II and Mexican American civil rights*. Austin: University of Texas Press.

Strum, P. (2010). *Mendez v. Westminster: School desegregation and Mexican-American rights*. Lawrence: University Press of Kansas.

Tushnet, M. V. (1987). *The NAACP's legal strategy against segregated education, 1925-1950*. Chapel Hill: University of North Carolina Press.

Valencia, R. R. (2008). *Chicano students and the courts: The Mexican American legal struggle for educational equality*. New York: NYU Press.

Valenzuela, A. (1999). *Subtractive schooling: U.S.-Mexican youth and the politics of caring*. Albany: SUNY Press.

Ware, L. B. (1989). Invisible walls: An examination of the legal strategy of the restrictive covenant cases. *Washington University Law Quarterly 67*, 737-772.

Ware, L. B. (1993). New weapons for an old battle: The enforcement provisions of the 1988 Amendments to the Fair Housing Act. *Admininstrative Law Journal 7*, 59-119.

Ware, L. B. (2002). Race and urban space: Hypersegregated housing patterns and the failure of school desegregation. *Widener Law Symposium Journal 9*, 55-71

Wilson, S. H. (2003) 'Brown' over 'other white': Mexican Americans' legal arguments and litigation strategy in school desegregation. *Law and History Review 21*, 145-194

Zamora, E. (2002). Fighting on two fronts: José de la Luz Saenz and the language of the Mexican American civil rights movement. In *Recovering the U.S. Hispanic Literary Heritage Volume IV*, Aranda, Jr. J. F. & Torres-Saillant, S. (Eds). Houston: Arte Público Press.

Zamora, E. (2005). Mexico's wartime intervention on behalf of Mexicans in the United States. In *Mexican Americans and World War II*, Rivas-Rodriguez, M. (Ed.). Austin: University of Texas Press.

Zamora, E. (2009). *Claiming rights and righting wrongs in Texas, Mexican workers and job politics during World War II*. College Station: Texas A&M University Press.

Zamora, E. (Forthcoming). José de la Luz Saenz: Experiences and autobiographical consciousness. In *Mexican American civil rights pioneers*, Quiroz, A. (Ed.). Champaign, Illinois: University of Illinois Press.

Cases tried to decision by Alonso S. Perales:

Spanish Book & Stationery Co. v. U.S., United States Customs Court July 06, 1939, Not Reported in F.Supp, 3 Cust. Ct. 512, 1939 WL 7271

Lozano v. De Martinez, Court of Civil Appeals of Texas, San Antonio. July 22, 1942 164 S.W.2d 196

Clifton v. Puente, 218 S.W.2d 272 (Tex. Civ. App.—San Antonio 1948, writ ref'd n.r.e

Alaniz v. State, Court of Criminal Appeals of Texas. May 04, 1949 153 Tex.Crim. 374

Mendoza v. Mendoza, Court of Civil Appeals of Texas, San Antonio. February 04, 1953 255 S.W.2d 251

Powe v. Powe, Court of Civil Appeals of Texas, San Antonio. April 28, 1954 268 S.W. 2d 558

Barrera v. Barrera, Court of Civil Appeals of Texas, San Antonio (October 24, 1956) 294 S. W. 2d 865

Ydrogo v. Haltom, Court of Civil Appeals of Texas, Eastland. May 10, 1957, 302 S.W. 2d 670

Villarreal v. U.S., 254 F. 2d 595 (5th Cir. 1958)
Valdez v. Amaya, Court of Civil Appeals of Texas, San Antonio. September 9, 1959
327 S.W. 2d 708
Also: Counsel on "Statement as to Jurisdiction on Appeal," Indep. Sch. Dist. v. Sal-
vatierra, 33 S.W.2d 790 (Tex. Civ. App.—San Antonio 1930, writ dism'd w.o.j.);
[Statement as to Jurisdiction on Appeal, Salvatierra v. Indep. School Dist., 1931
WL 32417 (U.S. 1931) (No. 195)]; cert. den., 284 U.S. 580 (1931)

Other cases cited:

Romo v. Laird, et al., No. 21617, Maricopa County Superior Court (1925) [unpub-
lished, reprinted in Laura K. Muñoz, Separate But Equal? A Case Study of Romo
v. Laird]
Doss v. Bernal [Superior Court of the State of California, Orange County, No.
41466, 1943]
Mendez v. Westminster, 161 F.2d 774 (9th Cir. 1947)
Delgado v. Bastrop, Civ. No. 388 (W.D. Tex. June 15, 1948) (unpublished opinion)
Shelley v. Kramer, 334 U.S. 1 (1948)
Gonzales v. Sheely, 96 F. Supp. 1004 (D. Ariz. 1951)
Hernandez v. Texas, 347 U.S. 475 (1954)
Brown v. Board (Brown I), 347 U.S. 483 (1954)
Brown v. Board (Brown II), 349 U. S. 294, 301 (1955)
Herminio Hernandez et al. v. Driscoll Consolidated Independent School District;
Civil Action (Civ.A.) 1384, U.S. District Court for the Southern District of Texas
(S.D.Tex., 1957), Corpus Christi Division [published opinion at 2 Race Relations
Law Reporter 329 (S. D. Tex., 1957)]
Trinidad Villareal et al. v. Mathis Independent School District of San Patricio City et
al., Civ. A. 1385 (S. D. Tex., Corpus Christi Division, 2 May 1957)
Lopez v. Texas, 378 U.S. 567 (1964)
Chapa v. Odem Independent School District (S.D.Tex., 1967) [Corpus Christi Divi-
sion, Civ. No. 66-C-72]
Cisneros v. Corpus Christi ISD, 324 F. Supp. 599 (S. D. Tex., 1970), 404 U.S. 1211
(1971) ("The stay will be reinstated pending action on the merits in the Fifth Circuit or action by the full Court") 459 F.2d 13 (5th Cir. 1972), cert den. 413 U.S.
920 (1973)

Organizing, Creating
LULAC, and Texas Politics

Alonso S. Perales and His Struggle for the Civil Rights of *La Raza* through the League of United Latin American Citizens (LULAC) in Texas in the 1930s: *Incansable Soldado del Civismo Pro-Raza*

Cynthia E. Orozco

Remembering Perales

The year is 2012 and we still know little about Alonso S. Perales: activist, civil rights leader, lawyer, U.S. diplomat, author, columnist, orator, teacher, publisher and translator. Historians and political scientists have overlooked, minimized and misunderstood him despite the fact that he was one of the most important Mexican American activists/public intellectuals in the United States in the twentieth century.

I learned about Perales in 1978 when I was a sophomore and was given the charge to write a twenty page research paper for a Chicano history class. My topic was the origins of the League of United Latin American Citizens (LULAC), the most important Latino civil rights organization in the twentieth century. Several sources like *LULAC News* had profiled him as a past president and the University of Texas Austin libraries owned his two published books *En Defensa de mi Raza* (1937) and *Are We Good Neighbors?* (1948). I was fortunate to be a work/study student at the Center for Mexican American Studies at UT Austin where Dr. Arnoldo Vento learned of my work. He informed me of his mother's book *Alonso S. Perales: His Struggle for the Rights of Mexican Americans* published in 1978. (Adela Sloss-Vento, *Alonso S. Perales: His Struggle for the Rights of Mexican Americans* (San Antonio: Artes Gráficas, 1977). Adela Sloss-Vento, a colleague and activist with Perales, wrote the book when she was in her 70s, realizing there were too few historians interested in the history of *la raza* despite the existence of Chicano Studies since 1968. Indeed, this book is four decades late.

Even in the 1930s Sloss-Vento recognized Perales' significance. She penned "The League of United Latin Americans by Its Founder, Attorney Alonso S. Perales" for *La Prensa*, the only statewide Spanish-language newspaper in Texas, and a similar essay for *LULAC News*. (Sloss, 1932, p. 15). She began her activism in 1927 when she graduated from Pharr-San Juan High and did not marry until 1935. (*Latinas in the United States,* 2006, pp. 686-687). Ben Garza, the first national president of LULAC, died in 1937 and as a result the League began to reflect on its history and founders. Perales himself sought to tell his version of the founding and document his contributions to the League; he did so in *En Defensa de mi Raza* in 1937.

Despite this documentation, Garza would be referred to as the "Father of LULAC," even being referred to as such by LULAC co-founder M.C. Gonzales, one of eleven key founders in an address delivered by M.C. Gonzales at the Latin Quarter on the occasion of a banquet given by LULAC Council #2 in his honor (San Antonio, Texas, November 9, 1944, Alonso S. Perales Papers [hereafter AP], M.D. Anderson Library, University of Houston, Box 3, Folder 47). It is not clear if he gave Garza this title to spite Perales or to honor Garza because he was deceased.

Perales was active beginning in the late 1910s until he died in 1961, before the emergence of Chicano Studies, and has hardly been remembered. National LULAC recognized Perales through its parade of brief presidential biographies appearing in *LULAC News*, a tradition that started around 1939 ("The Parade of Past Presidents General, Alonso S. Perales," *LULAC News*, June 1947: 25, 29, AP, Box 4, Folder 7). Perales' books might have kept his memory alive but they were self-printed with limited funds in limited editions. Still, San Antonio LULAC, and especially Luis Alvarado (a son-in-law of Perales' co-activist J. Luz Saenz) of Council 2, honored Perales throughout the years (Resolution by Luis Alvarado, Feb. 12, 1960, LULAC Hall of Fame, AP, Box 3, Folder 40). In 1969 Alice, Texas resident Rafael Trevino and twenty others tried to get Alice High named after the hometown boy ("Alice's New High School to be Named After City," *Corpus Christi Caller*, September 10, 1969, AP, Box 14 (oversize), Folder: Newspaper Articles Saved: Perales' life and work). In 1974, Sloss-Vento sought to bring Perales' name to the attention of national LULAC but without success (Letter from Adela Sloss-Vento to Joe Benitez, 1974, National LULAC President, AP, Box 4, Folder 34). IMAGE honored Perales that year in San Antonio and Arno Press reissued *Are We Good Neighbors?* (Golden Years Appreciation Banquet Program, a Banquet Honoring Distinguished Mexican-Americans, September 16, 1974, San Antonio, Author's files). In 1975, San Antonio Chicano activists discovered Perales' legacy; *Chicano Times* published a biography based on talks with Marta Perez Perales, his wife. ("An Interview with Mrs. Perales," *Chicano Times*, Feb. 14 thru Feb. 28, 1975, AP, Box 14). And around 1977 the Alonso S. Perales School was named in San Antonio.

Even so, when national LULAC celebrated its 50th anniversary in Houston in 1979, much more was made of first president Ben Garza than Perales, the second president. But he was the second president only because he orchestrated Garza's presidency (Orozco, 2009, chapter 6). The 1980s passed with little memory of him.

Finally, in 1990, Mrs. Perales sought and received recognition for her husband at the national LULAC convention in Albuquerque. Historian Richard García revived his memory when he published the insightful *The Rise of the Mexican-American Middle Class* in 1991; this book was the first to place Perales in historical context. Garcia did an excellent job without use of Perales' papers. Professional historians, especially Chicano historians, had known of Perales for decades. In 1994 Erasmo Figueroa of San Antonio tried to create a LULAC Scholarship Foundation in his honor ("Name of Scholarship Leads to Controversy," *San Antonio Express News*, September 17, 1994, Author's files). In 1999, he was honored during LULAC Week in Alice (Guy H. Lawrence, "LULAC co-founder Alonso Perales honored," *Corpus Christi Caller*, February 16, 1999, Author's files). In 2000, Araceli Perez Davis, Perales' wife's relative, resurrected him in *El Mesteño*, a popular South Texas history and culture magazine (Araceli Perez Davis, "Marta Perez de Perales," *El Mesteño* 4: 37 (October 2000): 16). In 2003, Josh Gottheimer included him in *Ripples of Hope: Great American Civil Right Speeches,* but the same year the *San Antonio News* reported "Unsung Hero of Civil Rights 'Father of LULAC' a Fading Memory" (Gottheimer, 2003; "Unsung Hero of Civil Rights 'Father of LULAC' a Fading Memory" *San Antonio Express*, September 14, 2003). All these tributes were written without access to Perales' papers.

History of My Work on Perales and LULAC

My work to remember Perales began in 1978. Sloss-Vento urged me to visit Sra. Perales hoping that I would help give Perales, J. Luz Saenz and J.T. Canales their due as LULAC founders. She wrote a letter of introduction for me and Sra. Perales accepted my request to visit her and her husband's archive. Sra. Perales was friendly and gracious, and gave me access to the papers in the house. (There was also a garage full of boxes.) The papers were not available to scholars after my visit. In 1980 I wrote a senior honors thesis using Perales' papers, especially 1920s documents (Orozco, 1980). Later as a UCLA graduate student writing my dissertation and Research Associate for the *New Handbook of Texas*, a Texas history encyclopedia, I wrote a short bio about Perales for the *Handbook* that was published in 1996 (*New Handbook of Texas,* 1996, p. 148-149). My book on the origins of LULAC and Perales' significant role in the founding of LULAC was published in 2009.

In 2002, national LULAC held its annual convention in San Antonio where I happened to run into Perales' daughter, Marta Perales Carrizales. She visited the LULAC history booth organized by Benny Martinez of Goliad. I introduced myself, noting that I had visited her mother and the archives in the late 70s. She gasped, "La niña, la niña. Eres la niña." (Author's translation: The girl. The girl. You are that girl.) (Indeed, I was a young woman scholar in the making). She suggested I visit with her and brother Raymond at the family home. I advised the family of the importance of archives, as had numerous librarians and archivists over the years. I suggested they request immediate archival processing and a public conference. I am happy they chose the U.S. Hispanic Recovery Project at the University of Houston. Now with the Perales papers available to scholars we can learn much more. My review of the papers allows me to discuss his ideology, activism, and character in the 1930s, particularly as they relate to LULAC.

This chapter will 1) assess the community's memory of Perales (see above); 2) address his activism in LULAC in San Antonio in the 1930s; 3) assess his national presidency of LULAC from 1930 to 1931; 4) document his work in/with LULAC after the presidency; 5) describe his role in founding a second LULAC men's council in San Antonio; 6) explain his work in founding another organization-the League of Loyal Americans; 7) inquire into his role in mentoring gendered leadership; and 8) provide insight into his character.

Perales and San Antonio LULAC in the 1930s

Perales made San Antonio his permanent home in 1933, opening his law office in the law firm of Still, Wright, Davis, and Perales and working for the County Attorney's office in 1934 ("An Interview"). He had lived in San Antonio and Rio Grande Valley towns in the 1920s. Most of Perales' time was spent organizing, giving talks and radio addresses, writing letters, publishing articles, pamphlets and books, doing pro-bono legal work and teaching.

The Spanish founded San Antonio in 1718 and after 1836 it became a town with a subordinated Mexican community. Ninety thousand persons of Mexican descent lived there during the Depression. By 1930 *la raza* worked in railroad yards, packing plants, military bases, garment factories, service establishments, retail trade and an informal market. A small Mexican-American male lower middle class had emerged by the 1920s; historian Richard García estimated their number at 5,000 (Ramos, 2008; R. García 1991, pp. 29, 184). But most of *la raza* was working-class and undocumented.

San Antonio witnessed the arrival of numerous Mexican immigrants from 1910 to 1930 due to the Mexican Revolution. Mexican barrios expanded. Schools were racially segregated into brown, black and white. San Antonio had a political machine dependent on Mexican and Black voters, but without representation on the city council or county commission between 1930 and 1940 (Ibid, 37). Around 1940, only 9% of the city's high school graduates were of Mexican descent (Ibid, 179). Perales reported only 9 of 350 college students in the city were Spanish-surnamed in 1932, including Catholic colleges such as St. Mary's and Our Lady of the Lake (Perales, 1937, p. 16). Tuberculosis and intestinal disease were major causes of death; housing conditions were dismal (R. Garcia, 39). The Depression made this Mexican working-class existence even more difficult.

As residents of the United States, we now live in a much more prosperous time. Mind you in 1929 and for most of the 1930s there was no minimum wage, unemployment benefits, Social Security, Medicare or Medicaid, or Aid to Dependent Children. Veterans' benefits were minimal. Moreover, minimum wage laws passed in 1938 meant .25 cents an hour and did not cover domestics and farm workers. Pecan-shellers earned $1.29 a week (Leininger Pycior, 1997, p. 41). Nor were there any Pell college grants; scholarships for *la raza* did not exist.

Perales, Gonzales, Garza, Saenz, Canales and others founded LULAC in February 1929, only months before the Great Depression. Not only would LULAC address racial/class subordination, segregation, and poverty, it would attempt to fight these odds when LULACers themselves were financially challenged. The Depression affected the middle class. LULAC had no central administrative office in any city, state, or in the nation throughout the 1930s. There was no endowment, no corporate donors or white liberals funding the League in the 1930s. There were no major fundraising events. LULAC was not a business—it was a non-profit organization run by volunteers and funded by these volunteers, numerous local small business owners and a few Mexican-descent professionals.

Despite funding issues, LULAC survived, occasionally contracted and even expanded between 1929 and 1940. In 1930, 800 attended the 2nd national convention and in 1931 1,000 did so (*El Paladín*, May 7, 1931, UCLA Chicano Studies Research Center [hereafter UCLA]); *LULAC News*, May 1933, Center for American History [hereafter CAH). These were Texas conventions as no other state had LULAC in the early 1930s. In May 1932 there were twenty-four local LULAC councils and twenty-nine by December (Letter to J.T. Canales from AP, May 13, 1932; J. T. Canales, "To Whom this May Concern," May 24, 1932; J.T. Canales, "To Whom this May Concern," December 30, 1932, AP, Box 3, Folder 36). In May 1933, 23 of 45 councils were present at the state convention with 500 persons attending. By 1936 Perales referred to LULAC as a national organization ("Carta Dirigida Por Los Concilios de San Antonio Numeros 16, 12 Y 2 de La Liga De Ciudadanos Unidos Latinoamericanos a los Industriales y Hombres de Negocios y Otras Personas de San Antonio, Texas, Solicitando un Jornal Mas Alto par los Trabajadores Mexicanos," *En Defensa* 1: 66-67). LULAC was first planted in New Mexico in 1934 and by 1938 national LULAC had a New Mexican president (Orozco, 1998, pp. 459-483). By 1940 LULAC had established over 100 men's councils and over 20 "ladies" councils ("Presidents of Local Councils," n.d., AP, Box 3, Folder 37). On the eve of U.S. entrance into World War II, LULAC was a national organization with chapters firmly rooted in New Mexico and with chapters in Colorado, Arizona, California and Washington D.C. California chapters appeared in Los Angeles and Sacramento (Orozco, 1998).

The Perales papers reveal the League's financial challenges during the Depression. It was expensive to work for the LULAC cause. Membership was $20.00 annually. Other expenses including funding the *LULAC News*, the monthly magazine which began in 1931, at a suggested cost of $1.00 a month; publication totaled $25.00 monthly (Letter to AP from JT Canales, May 17, 1932, AP, Box 4, Folder 10). It was a challenge to publish *LULAC News* monthly (Letter to J.H. Contreras from AP, April 2, 1934, AP, Box 4, Folder 14; see March 20, 1934 letter, ASP, Box 4, Folder 15). A thousand copies were printed in May 1932 (Letter to Mauro Machado from AP, June 2, 1932, AP, Box 4, Folder 29). *LULAC News* was also funded by advertisements from Mexican-descent-owned businesses; typically sponsorship of the monthly magazine moved from one local council to another. In November 1934 a one-page mimeograph constituted the *LULAC News* (*LULAC News*, November 1934, AP, Box 4, Folder 6). When LULAC national president Mauro Machado's administration (1934-35) published several *LULAC News* in 1934, Perales called this one of his outstanding accomplishments (Letter to H.H. Contreras from AP, April 2, 1934, AP, Box 4, Folder 14).

There were other expenses. These included desegregation legal work; a World War I veterans' memorial; a college scholarship fund; and special, regional, state and national conventions. Perales himself told a friend he may not have the $20.00 needed to attend the 1934 national convention (Letter to AP from J. Luz Saenz, April 29, 1934, AP, Box 4, Folder 28). Moreover, travel expenses included car repairs, gas, lodging and food to spread LULAC to other towns and cities ("Editorial," *LULAC News*, August 1931, p. 3). San Antonio LULAC Council #2 acted as the "Flying Squadron," traveling LULACkers who introduced LULAC to surrounding towns on the weekends (Sandoval, 1979). Being a good LULACer also required payment of one's poll tax. In short, it cost the middle class to empower working-class *raza* and others.

Perales' papers contain scattered references to the difficulty of fundraising. Likewise, LULAC sought to fund a monument to World War I veterans of San Antonio, but could not afford to continue to raise monies. Instead, this money was transferred to funding segregation lawsuits in Mission and Del Rio (Letter to AP from JT

Canales, Aug. 7, 1931, AP, Box 4, Folder 10; "To the Various Councils of the League of United Latin-American Citizens," June 1, 1932, AP, Box 3, Folder 38). Despite the Depression each LULAC council was to raise $45.00 by October 1, 1931 for "school defense" (Tomas A. Garza, "The Kingsville Convention," *LULAC News,* August 1931, p. 4, CAH). Likewise, this money was moved again to pay for college scholarships. National President JT Canales (1932-33) asked the Hebbronville LULAC council to raise money for four or five scholarships (Letter to Fernando Ximenez from JT Canales, April 3, 1933, AP, Box 4, Folder 11).

Perales' papers also show that sometimes LULAC chapters (councils) folded because members could not afford dues. In May 1933, Perales told a LULAC council "En cuanto a la depression, pues parece que todos estamos siendo victimas de ella" (Due to the Depression it looks like we are all victims of it.) and he advised a LULAC council to tell LULAC national, "No hemos pagada nuestras cuotas porque no tenemos dinero, pero el pabellon de la LULAC continua flameando" (We haven't paid our dues because we don't have any money. Still the torch of LULAC is still lit.) (Letter to Candelario V. Barrientos from AP, May 31, 1933, AP, Box 4, Folder 9). Perales did not chastise or pity them. Likewise, Canales wrote LULAC national president M.C. Gonzales in 1932, "I doubt however whether the Penitas, La Grulla and McAllen councils can be re-organized for the reason that the people haven't got any money. . . ." (Letter to Candelario V. Barrientos from AP, May 31, 1933, AP, Box 4, Folder 9). In fact, keeping a LULAC council alive during the 1930s meant financial success. Council 2 of San Antonio, for instance, never folded but Council 16 of Crystal City did. So when Perales founded a second LULAC council in San Antonio, he used the number 16 from this defunct chapter. LULAC called these "inactive," "dormant" or "dead" councils. It cost even more to be a LULAC national president since there was no travel, phone, postal or secretarial budget.

Perales as National LULAC President, 1930-1931

Perales was the second national president of LULAC. He was a major founder of LULAC in 1929, orchestrating the rejection of the precursor organization called the Order Sons of America. The OSA was founded in 1921 in San Antonio, but also had chapters in Pearsall, Somerset, Beeville, Alice, Robstown and Corpus Christi. In 1924 Perales gave lectures in the Valley preparing for future organization. In 1927 he founded an alternative club called the Latin American Citizens League (LACL, which later merged with others to become LULAC). This expanded to La Grulla, Penitas, Mission, Pharr, Mercedes, Harlingen and Brownsville. He later forged a union among these two groups and a third called the Order Knights of America of San Antonio. He was the major voice behind unification in 1929 to found LULAC and he attended the February 1929 founding convention in Corpus Christi. He was unable to attend the May constitutional convention at which a photo was taken because he was busy conducting diplomatic work on behalf of the federal government.

Serving as the second national president from May 1930 to May 1931, Perales had a successful and productive national administration. During his tenure he: 1) gave twenty-one lectures to LULAC councils; 2) gave twenty-five other lectures to other groups; 3) helped the Mission and Del Rio School Defense Committee raise funds to fight segregation; 4) translated the constitution to Spanish; and 5) "kept in close contact with the various councils of the League and has offered many valuable suggestions and good advice" (Letter to "Mr. President" from Alonso S. Perales, May 4, 1931, AP, Box 3, Folder 40). LULAC's continued expansion into South Texas was facilitated by Perales. He "laid the foundation for new councils in Houston, Raymondville, Mercedes, Guerra, Hebbronville, San Juan, Kingsville, Rivera and Salinera" (Unsigned [J.T. Canales ?], List of "Some of the things Alonso S. Perales has done for the League of United Latin American Citizens," ca. 1931, AP, Box 3, Folder 40; Letter to "Mr. President"). Likewise, he corresponded with others in Gulf, San Angelo and Wharton, all outside of South Texas ("Letter to "Mr. President"). Perales and F.G. Garza of McAllen served as attorneys for the Mission school issue ("Documents related to segregation of Mission, Texas Mexican Students," December 30, 1930, AP, Box 3, Folder 40). Perales did all this with a minimal budget. "Of all the Councils visited Del Rio was the only one that defrayed my expenses," he wrote, "and I accepted only at the urgent insistence of the members of said Council. All the work was done by me free of charge with greatest pleasure" (Letter to Mr. President from AP, May 4, 1931, AP, Box 3, Folder 1). President Perales used pamphlets, newspapers and books to educate members and the general *raza* public. "La prensa es indispensable para la solución satisfactoria de dichos problemas, y nadie necesita tanto de la valiosa ayuda de la prensa libre come los grupos minoritarios," he argued. (The press is a necessity to solve our problems in a satisfactory manner and no one needs a brave press as do minorities.) (AP, "Un Periodico es util cuando sirve los interes de la colectividad," February 13, 1946, AP, Box 8, Folder 5). Perales' goal as president was to "keep up the spirit of the membership by sending them lectures, etc. once a week or at least twice a month" (Letter to J.T. Canales from AP, ca. 1930, AP, Box 4, Folder 10). He realized his writings served to inspire activism.

Despite the fact that English was the official language of LULAC as stated in its constitution, Perales communicated in English and Spanish and even translated the LULAC constitution into Spanish. He could thereby reach a broader audience, an audience not always literate in English. (*LULAC News*, November 1934, AP). In doing so, Perales acknowledged that many LULACers and potential LULAC members were Spanish dominant. He did not believe in English-only and did not privilege the English language. He was fully bilingual, valuing the Spanish language and worked as a translator. Likewise, he used Spanish-language radio. ("Platica sostentada por el Lic. Alonso S. Perales en la transmission de La Voz de la Raza la noche del 23 de marzo de 1932," AP, Box 8, Folder 15; see also Box 8, Folder 16). LULAC also published citizenship manuals in English and Spanish. (*LULAC News*, November 1934, AP). There is no evidence that any LULACer complained of use of the Spanish language since most LULACers were bilingual.

Perales published works he believed relevant to *la raza*'s cause. He sought to document the history of the League's founding by re-publishing political scientist Oliver Douglas Weeks' journal article about LULAC's founding as well as one by J.O. Loftin. (Weeks, 1929). Weeks had attended LULAC's constitutional convention and it is because of his published work that today's scholars know of the Order Sons of America, key activists, and the 1920s. Perales also translated into Spanish Weeks' "Mexican Americans and the Politics of South Texas" because he believed it would "stimulate interest in the "poll-tax" (Letter to Roberto Austin from AP, Jan. 8, 1932, AP, Box 4, Folder 9). He published it with his commentaries, "El Poll Tax y el Ciudadano," (The Poll Tax and the Citizen) and "Nuestra Evolucion General" (Our General Evolution); over 500 copies were printed. Activist Roberto E. Austin of Mission ordered 2,000 copies of one of Perales' writings. Perales also lauded the work of Canales in a pamphlet (Lic. Alonso S. Perales, "El Lic. Jose T. Canales Como Presidente General," (San Antonio: professionally printed by Perales?, April 30, 1932), AP, Box 4, Folder 8). In 1937, he published two volumes of *En Defensa*, the first volume costing $360.00, the second $446.25, significant amounts during the Depression. (Letter to Mrs. Ben Garza, July 30, 1937 from AP, AP, Box 4, Folder 18).

Despite all of his work, Perales noted there was indeed an "erroneous impression in the minds of some of my fellow-members that during my incumbency I did nothing for the League." Because of this impression, Perales wrote a memo documenting his activism. Likewise, a friend (likely Canales) reinforced his contributions, writing "Some of the things Alonso S. Perales has done for the League of United Latin American Citizens" (Unsigned, List of "Some of the Things"). Perhaps members' criticism or lack of faith was because Perales spent six months out of the country while president—he was still a U.S. diplomat. Between 1925 and 1933 he served on thirteen diplomatic missions ("An Interview"). In fact shortly after Perales' presidency in December 1932, Perales was in Nicaragua ("To the Members of the League of United Latin American Citizens," *LULAC News*, December 1932, p. 6 CAH). Moreover, *LULAC News* did not report all of Perales' activities, and members continued to experience racial/class subordination despite all of Perales' good deeds.

Perales as a Member of LULAC, 1931-1940

Although Perales' presidency ended in May 1931, he continued in work in national LULAC in various offices and capacities, remaining a Board of Trustee member from 1931-1937 (Garza, 1951, pp. 14-15). During the Manuel C. Gonzales administration (May 1931-May 1932), Perales was involved with the Special convention held in Nov. 1931 in San Antonio which addressed the Del Rio segregation case and scholarship guidelines. ("Arrangements for San Antonio Convention," *LULAC News*, November 1931, p. 10). During the Canales presidency (May 1932-May 1933) Perales served as "Special organizer" and had the "authority to organize new councils where no councils existed" and also re-organized inactive councils in McAllen, Penitas, Kingsville, Alice and Laredo (Letter to J.T. Canales from AP, March 18, 1933, AP, Box 4, Folder 11). In June 1932, he chaired the Educational Committee which gave five $100.00 scholarships to Latino college students (Minutes, Robstown Special Convention, June 1, 1932, AP, Box 3). He also presided over the special Del Rio convention ("To the Various Councils of the League of United Latin-American Citizens," June 1, 1932, AP, Box 3, Folder 38.) He continued to support *LULAC News;* one of his May 1932 notes read, "I will gather all the material for the May issues and we shall have it printed immediately after we confer with you" (Letter from A. Perales to J.T. Canales, May 17, 1932, AP, Box 4,

Folder 10). During the Mauro Machado presidency (1933-1934) Perales also "issued several circulars and bulletins to the Councils and had [sic] same published in the newspapers" (Ibid.) and he served as Organizer General and Inspector General. ("The Parade of Past Presidents General," *LULAC News*, June 1947: 23, 29, AP, Box 4, Folder 7). In 1935 Perales addressed the Houston national convention; reportedly 4,000 attended the Houston City Auditorium social that evening (Kreneck, 2001, pp. 67-68). Under the Frank Galvan presidency (1935-36) Perales acted as Inspector General (Letter to John W. Brown, State Health Officer from AP, November 28, 1936, AP, Box 4, Folder 9). By 1937, there was a Legislative Committee, chaired by Canales and with six others including Perales (*LULAC News*, July 1937, n.p, Benson Latin American Collection [hereafter BLAC], University of Texas at Austin). By 1937 Perales, by now a delegate of LULAC Council 16, began to address national legislation at the national conventions; these resolutions addressed support for the Black-Connery bill for minimum wage/maximum work hours and prohibited child labor. National LULAC also proposed support for the Wagner-Steagall bill for better housing for the poor ("Resumen de Resoluciones presentados por el Lic. Alonso S. Perales, Delegado del Concilio Num. 16, de San Antonio, Texas, de la Liga de Ciudadanos Unidos Latinoamericanos, en la Novena Convencion Anual de la Liga, verificado en Houston, Texas, los dias 5 y 6 de Junio de 1937," *En Defensa* 2: 74-75). And national LULAC also supported the McComrach Bill which warned against the "evils in Communism, fascism and any other 'isms' not in harmony with our form of government and our American institutions" (*En Defensa* 2, 1937, pp. 74-75). The 1937 national convention was Perales' last. Even so, in 1938 during the Ramon Longoria presidency (1937-38) Perales served as an attorney for Hondo LULAC council 37 addressing inadequate school facilities (Letter to L.A. Woods from AP, February 18, 1938, AP Box 4, Folder 36; AP to L.A. Woods, AP, Box 4, Folder 36). Perales' activist agenda was synonymous with LULAC's. When Canales' presidency ended in 1933, he issued a "Program of Activities Recommended by the retiring Pres. General to local councils." He recommended: "1) the investigation of schools; 2) health; 3) PTA noting LULAC "should encourage each Latin-American mother to be a member of said association"; 4) hospitals; 5) red-light districts; and 6) school attendance ("Program for Activities Recommended by the retiring Pres. General to Local Councils," AP, Box 3, Folder 35). Perales' priorities were the same. In 1934 Perales recommended these activities: 1) "schools/sanitation/mental retarded?/playground"; 2) health and tuberculosis; 3) PTA, encouraging "each Latin-American mother to be a member of said Association"; 4) hospital; 5) red light district; 6) school attendance; 7) Boy Scouts; and 8) Lecture: civic/hygiene/disease" (Resolution introduced by AP, May 16, 1934, AP, Box 3, Folder 42 Council 16). Perales and Canales believed that the schooling of the *raza* masses mattered most and health was key especially given the preponderance of tuberculosis. These were issues affecting the working and middle class and not elitist or petty bourgeoisie.

Perales' Role in San Antonio LULAC Council 2 & Council 16, 1929-1940

Besides his presidency and various positions at the national level, Perales was also active at the local level. When LULAC was founded in 1929, members of the

Order Sons of America (OSA) and the Order Knights of America merged to form LULAC Council 2 in San Antonio. Its key leaders included Gonzales, John Solis, and Machado. When Perales became national president there was already a history of differences/conflict with Gonzales. Perales had already been a member of the OSA in the early 20s. He and Gonzales had differing positions on the question of whether Mexican citizens should be admitted to civil rights organizations at the Harlingen convention. They also disagreed as to whether Perales and Canales should have testified before a Congressional immigration hearing in 1930 on behalf of LULAC (Letter to Manuel C. Gonzales from AP, January 30, 1931, *En Defensa* 2: 88-89).

So after a few years as a member of Council 2, Perales charged its members with inappropriate activity in electoral politics. LULAC was founded with the intention of staying independent of electoral politics and combating political bossism. Its 1929 constitution read: Aim and Principle 12: "This organization is not a political club, but as citizens we will participate in the local, state, and national contests. However, in doing so we shall ever bear in mind the general welfare of our people, and we disregard and abjure once for all any personal obligation which is not in harmony with the principles." Yet Perales believed, "We must play an independent role in politics without allegiance to a single party or faction" (Garcia, 1991, p. 287). Without Council 2 archives it is difficult to tell if its members acted on behalf of individual interests instead of *la raza*'s collective interests or if an individual saw his rise/inclusion/influence as synonymous with *la raza*'s interests.

Perales also conflicted with Gonzales and other Council 2 members on the issue of national LULAC leadership. For instance, in April 14, 1932, Gonzales and Tomas F. Garza sent a "Dear LULAC Brother" letter in support of Solis' bid for national presidency (Letter to "Dear LULAC Brother" from M.C. Gonzales and Tomas F. Garza, April 14, 1932, AP, Box 4, Folder 20). Apparently Perales did not believe Solis capable, perhaps because he had not finished high school, lacked written skills or because he was friends with Gonzales or sided with Gonzales. (Perales seemed to have been concerned with presidents' and other members' writing skills. In a letter to Canales around 1930 he suggested national president Ben Garza get a stenographer, probably because he had limited writing skills.) (Letter to J.T. Canales from AP, n.d., ca. 1930, AP, Box 4, Folder 10). Or perhaps Perales was concerned with Solis' resignation as Gonzales' secretary during Gonzales' national administration (Letter to M.C. Gonzales from Juan Solis, May 18, 1931, J.T. Canales Estate Collection [hereafter JTCEC], James C. Jernigan Library, South Texas Archives, Texas A&M University at Kingsville, Box 436, Folder 20. Solis was president of Council 2 at the time). Solis never became national president.

Another sign of conflict was when Perales referred to Gonzales, Solis, and Machado as the "San Antonio gang" in his correspondence. He noted that *LULAC News* director Felipe Valencia "admitted to me this morning that he was with the San Antonio gang" and that the bunch would instruct Valencia what to publish (Letter to J.T. Canales from AP, May 17, 1932, JTCEC, Box 4, Folder 10). Perales advised Canales not to appoint the gang to his presidential staff.

Because of this tension, Perales founded a second LULAC men's council in San Antonio. He said that LULAC councils in Edinburg and Mission had already established a precedent for a second chapter in each town. Perhaps he felt Council 2 did not welcome him, noting, "donde una puerta se cierra otra se abre" (When one door closes another opens.) (García, 1991, p. 287). Moreover, he wrote that "friendly, constructive competition" was healthy as the example of the American Legion had shown.

A major controversy emerged over the question of whether San Antonio needed or should have two councils. National President Canales asked Solis, Machado and Adolfo Garza to invite potential members to join Council 2, and Solis asked potential members not to join a rival council (A Letter to "San Antonio Council No. 2 of the LULAC" from President General J.T. Canales, n.d. AP, Box 4, Folder 3). At first Perales conceded to Canales but later wrote, "[let me] remind you that there are about 90,000 Mexicans in this city and our League should aid to serve the whole community. To do this, the number of LULACers in this city must be increased" (Letter to JT Canales from AP, May 27, 1932, AP, Box 4, Folder 10). Potential members (of a second council) "are not the type that can be herded or controlled," he argued. "See what they can do and if not, I shall insist that you authorize me to install a new council in San Antonio."

Almost a year later Canales wrote Perales, noting "Watch closely what the disturbing element of the San Antonio council, to-wit: Juan C. Solis and M.C. Gonzales are going to do" (Letter to AP from J.T. Canales, February 21, 1933, AP, Box 10, Folder 4; Letter to J.T. Canales from AP, May 27, 1932, AP, Box 4, Folder 10). This time Canales conceded to Perales and mentioned the possibility of a new council. But Canales still tried to prevent the birth of a second council remaining independent in thought and action from Perales, before and after Council 16 was ultimately created.

Perales explained this "friction" with Council 2. He believed that Council 2 was "compose[d] chiefly of young Hispanic-American lawyers employed either at the Court House or at the City Hall. . . . Interests and activities centered principally around the objective of keeping their own jobs and helping other members of Council No. 2 secure political positions. This group did little or nothing to further the real aims and purposes of the [LULAC] Organization." In contrast he said council 16 consisted of "*independent* (emphasis his) business and professional men" (Ts., Memorandum: Conditions in San Antonio, Texas, Proposed revisions/corrections by Perales, February 23, 1939, AP, Box 3, Folder 42).

This conflict between Perales and M.C. Gonzales (or Council 16 and Council 2) should not be construed as an inactive Council #2. According to Gonzales, its activities included 1) public school segregation; 2) no jury service for Mexican Americans; 3) segregated public accommodations; 4) racial covenants in real estate; and 5) voting rights (Garcia, 1991, p. 294). But perhaps Perales wanted more and better committee work tackling these problems, more independent thinkers and a more educated middle class.

Perales' Role in Founding LULAC Council 16 of San Antonio

As noted, Council 16's council number originally belonged to Crystal City and not San Antonio (Unsigned letter (AP?) to J. T. Canales, May 13, 1932, AP, Box 4, Folder 10). Perales enlightened skeptics about the prospects of a second chapter; he wrote, "This council does not propose to antagonize or obstruct the efforts of any other Council, but rather seeks to cooperate in the realization of this work," noting that 95% of its membership were new to LULAC. ("By Their Fruit Ye Shall Know Them," *LULAC News*, April 1933, p. 4).

For Perales, the purpose of a second San Antonio council was to improve the leadership/membership of Council 2; to increase League activities; to be more pro-active and more professional; and to locate men free of political bossism and obligations to city hall. Council 16 seems to have had more professionals than Council 2. Council 2 presidents in the 1930s included M.C. Gonzales, John Solis, Tomas A. Garza, Carlos A. Ramirez, Adolph A. Garza, Jake Rodriguez, and Severino Martinez.

Perales did not found the council because of egotism or a desire to control. In fact, he was not its first president. When the council was founded around March 18, 1933, the president was Pablo G. Gonzalez, a brother of folklorist Jovita Gonzalez. Nor was Perales president in 1934, 1935, or 1936. Presidents included Dr. Orlando Gerodetti (1934); Matias Trub (1935), and Charles Albidress (1936) (Ts. on founding of LULAC Council 16, March 18, 1933, ASP, Box 3, Folder 37; "Lic. P.G. Gonzales, Pres. del Nuevo Concilio," *LULAC News*, April 1933: 17, CAH; Letter to R.S. Menefee, Pres. San Antonio Board of Education from Greg Salinas, Eleuterio Escobar Jr. Papers [hereafter EEJP], BLAC, Box 1, Folder 12, April 9, 1934; Letter from Louis Wilmot to Gregory R. Salinas, August 13, 1936, Andres de Luna Sr. Papers [hereafter ADLP], BLAC, Folder 14; "List of members of LULAC Council #16," EEJP, BLAC, Box 2, Folder 2).

Council 16 had numerous committees: education, school facilities, boy scouts, judiciary auxiliary, health, housing, recreational centers, poll tax, justice, Latin-American cadets, Pro-Plaza Tipica Mexicana, and Children's Protective League, perhaps suggesting that Council 16 had more active committees than Council 2 (The Latin-American cadets referred to the fact that LULAC got Maury Maverick's help to appoint Zeferino Martinez to West Point; no title, *LULAC News*, Feb. 1937, BLAC). Perales believed the power of LULAC lay in its active/activist committees. He wrote, "The success of our labors depends largely upon how diligently, actively and enthusiastically the standing committees work" (Letter to Antonia Gomez from AP, January 11, 1933, AP, Box 4, Folder 20. She was one of a few women who wrote Perales).

The size and class composition of Council 16 made it different from Council 2. Council 2 had about 130 members while Council 16 had about 35 members ("LULAC Council No. 2 Membership Roster," (ca. 1930s); "List of Members of LULAC Council #16," EEJP). A "List of Approved Prospective Members" for Council 16 included Eleuterio Escobar Jr., Dr. Delagoa, Dr. H.N. Gonzalez, Henry Guerra, Juvencio Idar related to the Idar family of Laredo, and Carlos Cadena, a man in his 20s, who would eventually argue before the Supreme Court in the 1950s ("List of Approved Prospective Members," ca. mid-1930s, AP, Box 3, Folder 36). So both a smaller organization as well as more educated professionals could make a difference, Perales believed.

Perales not only founded Council 16 but also was an extremely active member. He chaired the education, pro-justice, and Mexican plaza tipica committees and was a member of school facilities, recreation centers and poll tax committees ("La Liga de Ciudadanos Unidos Latino Americanos," ca. mid-1930s, AP, Box 14, Folder: Newspapers articles saved: Perales' life & work). In honor of the Texas Centennial,

Council 16 sought to make a Mexican plaza on the West Side to represent the state's Spanish colonial past and foster San Antonio tourism (*En Defensa* 1: 24). Council 16 had great success in addressing inadequate/insufficient schools on the Westside and Southside. It initiated a "Survey made by the Committee on Public School Buildings and Recreational Facilities of the LULAC" ("Survey made by the Committee on Public School Buildings and Recreational Facilities of the LULAC," September 27, 1934, AP, Box 3, Folder 35). The council printed stationary reading, "The League of United Latin-American Citizens Asks for More and Better Schools for the Western Section of the City" (Stationary, AP, Box 3, Folder 42). It cooperated with Council 2 on this issue and also garnered the support of fifty *raza* organizations. (Letter to Ignacio E. Lozano from Dr. Orlando F. Gerodetti, Jan 15, 1935, AP, Box 4, Folder 20.) Later this effort took on a life and organization of its own as the Liga Defensa Pro-Escolar, headed by Escobar. ("Solicitando Facilidades Escolares Para Nuestra Ninez," *En Defensa* 2: 72.)

Council 16 also addressed racial classification by the U.S. Census. Registrars of Vital Statistics in San Antonio, Houston, Dallas and Fort Worth "had, for some time, been classifying Mexicans as colored in rendering their vital statistics reports to the Census Bureau of the U.S. Department of Commerce. Naturally, a very vigorous protest has been registered by our people through the entire State of Texas." And he said "white" included Mexicans (Letter to John W. Brown, M.D., State Health Office from AP, Nov. 28, 1936, AP, Box 4, Folder 9). A few scholars such as Steven Wilson believe that this reclassification may have been a move to better count and simply count *la raza*. Perales explicitly noted that his call for an appropriate racial classification was not about shame in being Mexican. "We are very proud of our racial extraction and we did not wish to convey the impression that we are ashamed to be called Mexicans" (Ibid.). In 1936, national president Frank J. Galvan Jr. wrote a letter to all LULAC councils noting, "There is no question in my mind but that the Census Bureau of the Department of Commerce has insulted our race in classifying us as colored in their statistics reports" (Letter from Frank J. Galvan Jr., LULAC National President, to "All LULAC Councils," Oct. 8, 1936, AP, Box 4, Folder 20). Perales did not consider whiteness superior to Mexicanness but like most members of *la raza* he believed Mexicanness superior to Blackness. The council also sought to expand LULAC's statewide expanse and worked to organize LULAC in New Braunfels, Seguin, and San Marcos in Spring 1938 (Letter to J.T. Canales from Alonso S. Perales, March 7, 1938, AP, Box 4, Folder 11).

Council 16 also addressed pending state legislation and was the only Texas council to do so. It addressed equitable funding for equal educational facilities, urging state legislators that a rider be attached to the next appropriation bill (El Que no Llora no Mama," *LULAC News*, February 1937: 4, BLAC; Letter to W. B. Carssow, Texas House of Representatives, January 14, 1937, AP, Box 4, Folder 15). At the 1937 convention Perales presented a host of resolutions, some addressing support for various bills in Congress. The LULAC body approved the resolutions but Gonzales voiced opposition ("Resumen de Resoluciones presentadas por el Lic. Alonso S. Perales," *En Defensa* 2: 74-75). It is unclear if he did so because Perales presented them, or because Gonzales may have interpreted the resolutions as an entrance into partisan politics which was contrary to the 1929 constitution. Perales saw these bills as pro-*raza*.

Conflict Between Council 2 and Council 16

Even with separate chapters conflict between Council 2 and Council 16 continued. They disagreed about future national LULAC leadership. Perales warned
Canales, "get ready for a big fight to prevent Council No. 2 from getting the President General next May" (Letter to J.T. Canales from AP, January 14, 1934, AP, Box
4, Folder 11). In a letter to Dr. Carlos Castaneda, a University of Texas history pro-
fessor and LULAC ally, Perales noted that Canales and Gonzales wanted Ermilio
Lozano as President for 1934-35 while Perales and Council 16 supported Pablo G.
Gonzalez ("Letter to Carlos Castaneda from AP," AP, April 2, 1934, Box 4, Folder
43). While noting Pablo Gonzalez' inexperience Perales told Canales he would train
Pablo and that he was trying to "safeguard the interests" of the League. That's all"
(Letter from AP to J.T. Canales, April 3, 1933, AP, Box 4, Folder 11). Perales wrote,
"I am seriously considering Mr. Pablo G. Gonzalez for the presidency . . . he can
appoint Mr. Gregorio R. Salinas, Secretary and Mr. George D. Vann, Treasurer"
(Ibid.). Perales believed he knew which leaders the League needed.

Upset with Council 16, some members of Council 2 decided to act against Perales'
council in 1937. Council 2 and Council 1 members (Corpus Christi) introduced a resolution at the national convention to force Council 2 to merge with Council 16. Resolution 8 asked the national president to order a merger when two councils existed in one
city; he was to do so within 30 days. M.C. Gonzales, Leo Duran (Council 1), and two
others who introduced the resolution said there was a "strong impression upon the
Anglo-Saxon public that a division of opinion, animosity, hatred, and social feeling
exist between the two" and that Council 16 looked down on Council 2 due to its "poor
and humble members" (Letter from Frank J. Galvan, Jr.). Perales disagreed.

Council 16 responded to this suggested merger by putting down the national president. On May 22, 1937, Council 16 sent out a form letter about National President
Ramon Longoria; it read: "cualquiera puede llega a ser Presidente General, aunque no
hay trabajado para nuestra Raza o nuestra Liga y aunque tenga unos cuantos dias de
ser socio" (Anyone can be President General even if he has not worked on behalf of
our race or our League and even if he has only been a member a few days.) (Form letter from President Charles Albidress, President Council 16, May 22, 1937, AP, Box 3,
Folder 37). By October 1937, Canales entered into the fray by penning an essay, "The
Right of LULAC Councils to Secede and Form a Rival Organization." He argued for
unity but also concluded that a council was a legal entity worthy of preservation; moreover, he added that the resolution introduced should not have been retroactive. He then
called for the special convention (JT Canales, "The Right of LULAC Councils to
Secede and Form a Rival Organization," *LULAC News*, Oct. 1937, BLAC). By February 1938, some LULAC councils, realized it had been a mistake to force Council 16
to merge and a new resolution followed. But the new resolution failed—Council 16
was not re-instated (Resolutions at National LULAC Convention, listed in *LULAC
News*, July 1937, BLAC; *LULAC News*, March 1938: 19-20, BLAC).

Despite this attempted reversal, Council 16 was permanently voted out of existence. Perales reported the events as follows: "The President General of the League
then ordered Council No. 16 to surrender its charter, which it did" ("Conditions in
San Antonio"). One letter suggests that Perales got pushed out, and noted that some

LULACers were not happy about a Perales-less LULAC. "Bear in mind that our race will be much stronger if we all belong to LULAC instead of having two Leagues for the same purpose," another said, adding, "You are a glorious leader of our race" (Letter to Perales from unknown, ca. 1937, AP, Box 4, Folder 9). By 1939, personality/ideological differences were so prominent in LULAC moving one author to write "Machine Politics and Methods in LULAC" for *LULAC News* in August 1939 ("Machine Politics and Methods in LULAC," *LULAC News*, August 1939: 21-22, AP). These "methods" included two problems Perales noted in 1937: the problem of electing friends and trading promises (Letter to AP from Adolfo de la Garza, June 18, 1937, AP, Box 4, Folder 20).

Refusing to join Council 2, Perales disappeared from the LULAC membership by the summer of 1937. He held no LULAC office between 1937 and 1938 and he was not a speaker at the June 1939 national convention (No title, 11th Annual LULAC Convention Program, June 3-4, 1939, Louis Wilmot Collection [hereafter LWC], BLAC). A man of principles, Perales refused to join Council 2.

Perales and the Founding of the League of Loyal Americans

While it may appear that Perales was booted out of LULAC, it would be more appropriate to see his actions as secession. Moreover, Perales took this political *movida* (move) and created a new opportunity. Shortly after he exited LULAC, he founded yet another civic organization—the League of Loyal Americans (LLA) which had three chapters in San Antonio by February 1939. Once again, Perales showed that he did not seek to be *the* leader or the one and only leader. He was happy with more activist groups and he would not even let LULAC stand in his way.

The Loyal Americans' purpose was "To develop within the members of the Hispanic-American Race loyal and progressive citizens of the United States of America; to uphold and defend our American form of Government and our American Institutions; to take an active interest in the civic, social and moral welfare of the community; to unite the members in the bonds of friendship, good fellowship and mutual undertakings; and for these purposes to establish subsidiary councils in different localities throughout the State of Texas" ("Conditions," 2). Its name revealed an awareness of Nazi, fascist, and Communist organizations prominent in the United States, Germany, Spain, Italy and Russia. Around 1939, Perales was its "National Director General" ("Arrangements Completed for Huge Americanism Meeting," *San Antonio Express* (?), ca. late 1930s, AP, Box 3, Folder 37). He worked as its attorney protesting the racial classification issue ("White Classification in Vital Statistics to Include Mexicans," *San Antonio News*, August 19, 1939, AP, Box 14, Folder: Newspaper Articles saved: Perales' life and work). He wrote Canales in 1942: "As I have said to you before, it makes no difference what organizations each one of [sic] belongs to or what anyone says about us. . . ." (Letter to J.T. Canales from AP, March 13, 1942, JTEC, Box 431, Folder 15). Perales did not care which organization he used; he just needed an organization because he valued his role in the context of collective action.

Perales and Mentoring Gendered Leadership

Throughout the 1930s, LULAC and the Loyal Americans rallied and mentored members of *la raza* into activism. As Canales was Perales' role model, Perales asked him for advice after law school. In 1927 Canales told him that he could be appointed as Rio Grande City attorney (Letter to AP from J.T. Canales, October 9, 1926, AP, Box 4, Folder 10). But he also let him know that his diplomatic and international law experience would be of no use. To practice civil and criminal law Perales needed experience, Canales told him (Letter to AP from J.T. Canales, Oct 9, 1926, AP, Box 4, Folder 10). The two would remain friends for decades despite occasional disagreements (Letter to AP from J.T. Canales, Oct 9, 1926, AP, Box 4, Folder 10).

Perales mentored the leadership of San Antonio's Mexican-American political elite focusing on men. This included Council 16 members like Carlos Cadena who became a lawyer, the first Latino law professor and a lawyer who argued before the Supreme Court; Gustavo Garcia, whom he helped enter high school and argued before the Supreme Court with Cadena; Henry B. Gonzalez, whom he helped find employment and who would become the first Tejano Congressperson ("Interview," 12). Perales had contact with politically active women in the 1930s including LULAC Ladies auxiliary members in San Antonio, members of Ladies LULAC in San Antonio, Mexican-descent women club members, and prominent Tejana feminists in the 1930s, but he did not mentor them. In the 1930s it would have been out of gender norms for men to mentor women.

Perales believed women and men in LULAC should work separately and he supported the idea of separate councils for women called Ladies LULAC. Perales had an opportunity to mentor Adela Sloss and Alice Dickerson Montemayor, prominent feminists working with and in LULAC. In San Antonio he might have mentored leaders Mexicanist María Hernández, communist Emma Tenayuca, benevolent maternalist Carolina Munguia and Mrs. Ruben R. Lozano, President of the Latin American Civic Club. ("Presidents of Local Councils," n.d., AP, Box 3, Folder 36. This civic club was not a LULAC chapter).

Perales collaborated with and respected Sloss from afar. Alice Dickerson Montemayor wrote him twice while he was national LULAC Inspector General, but there is no evidence he responded (Letter to AP from Mrs. F.I. Montemayor, Nov. 15, 1936, AP, Box 4, Folder 1). Hernández was one of his allies and Perales did not collaborate with Tenayuca when she was briefly connected to Ladies LULAC in her teens. Around 1939, Tenayuca lauded LULAC for its work on behalf of Mexican rights (Emma Tenayuca and Homer Brooks, "The Mexican Question in the Southwest," *The Communist* (March 1939): 257-268, CAH). In the 1980s, she told me she thought Perales was a "lunatic" perhaps because he was a staunch U.S. nationalist and anti-Communist. In the late 1930s he had written, "we neither need nor desire the advice, assistance or support of the Communists or any other un-American group" ("Arrangement Completed for Huge Americanism Meeting," nd. , ca. late 1930s., AP, Box 3, Folder 36). Perales opposed the CIO or AFL's policy of admitting Communists, Nazists or Fascists in their ranks ("Conditions in San Antonio," 2). His position on the Pecan Shellers' strike, a major conflict in the city in the late 1930s over wages, is not black or white. In 1938, Perales and LULAC supported the pecan shellers' strike on the condition that communist Tenayuca be kicked out (Richard Garcia, 271). Perales was "Presidente de la Comision Pro-Aumento de Jornales de la Liga de Ciudadanos Unidos Latinoamericanos." He said, "Para remediar la situation de nuestra gente es indispensable que se les pague lo que vale su trabajo" (To remedy our people's problems they need to be paid what their work is worth) and he suggested *la raza* speak to representatives of pecan factories, nothing that workers could only afford $5.00 rent per month ("Toma Impetu el Movimiento de los Lulacs en Pro de Aumento de Jornales Para los Mexicanos,"AP, Box 3, Folder 39).

LULAC in the 1930s was mostly gender segregated and Perales was a traditionalist in this regard. Middle-class Mexican-American women in San Antonio were mostly active in Ladies LULAC, the Spanish-speaking PTA or the Pan American Round Table. In February 1932, LULAC men installed Latin American PTAs, organizing three in February 1932 ("La Liga de Ciudadanos Latino-Americanos Logra Instalar Una Asociation Mas de Padres y Maestros," *Alma Latina:* 10, M.C. Gonzales Collection, BLAC). Likewise, Council 2 and 16 organized three boy scout troops on the West Side and gave girls less attention (M.C. Trub, "Boy Scouts and Scouters in L.U.L.A.C," *LULAC News*, Nov. 1934, Houston Metropolitan Research Center [hereafter HMRC]). LULAC men fostered male leadership. More progressive stances on gender and sexuality would have to wait decades.

By the 1950s, Perales was open to the idea of mentoring a young woman. Vilma Martinez was the daughter of a personal friend, Salvador Martinez. Martinez worked for Perales and he wrote letters on her behalf. A counselor directed her to a trade school; perhaps Perales and another teacher directed her otherwise. At minimum, Perales was a role model. She attended college at the University of Texas in Austin and law school at Columbia. She became the first women on the board of the Mexican American Legal Defense and Education Fund (MALDEF), founded in 1968 by leaders which would include LULAC. She also became its first woman president and general counsel ("Vilma Socorro Martinez," 2000, pp. 141-142). Moreover, like Perales, Martinez would go on to become a diplomat when President Barack Obama named her U.S. ambassador to Argentina in 2009 ("Vilma Socorro Martinez," 2012).

Thus into the twentieth century, Perales' mentorship of men and at least one woman would continue to bear fruit.

Perales' Character

Perales was a not a self-interested elitist or opportunistic coconut (brown on the outside and white inside). Perales believed foremost in the collective empowerment of *la raza,* the community of Mexican Americans, Mexicans in the United States and Latinos regardless of citizenship. Like all LULAC members, he realized participation in electoral politics was part of *raza* empowerment. U.S. citizens could vote, support candidates, serve on juries, run for office and serve as office holders. The 1929 constitution Aim and Principle 13 read: "With our vote and influence we shall endeavor to place in public office men who show by their deeds, respect and consideration for our people" (Orozco, 2009, p. 238).

As part of this empowerment, Perales ran for office once. He ran for the San Antonio Independent School District, lost and never ran for office again ("Interview," 12). According to Sra. Perales, M.C. Gonzales and Tafolla (Sr.? or Jr.?) campaigned against him. Perales was not disillusioned. He campaigned for those who he believed had *la raza*'s interest at heart. For example, he wrote about his political preferences for candidates such as Maury Maverick, a liberal and pro-CIO candidate for mayor, but also broke ties with Maverick when he failed to meet his political promises ("Mensaje del Lic. Alonso S. Perales a la Colonia Mexicana de San Antonio, Texas, ca. 1930s, ASP, Box 1, Folder 9; Acuña, 2011, p. 152; Alonso S. Perales, "La Verdadera Causa y Razon de la Ruptura de Relaciones Entre Maverick and Perales," ca. 1940, AP, Box 8, Folder 11).

Perales campaigned for individuals but showed less preference for a particular political party, probably since the Democrats and Republicans were both racist toward *la raza*. In the 1930s Perales and other Mexican Americans created the Association of Independent Voters, a sign that they were dissatisfied with both Democrats and Republicans. But by March 1934 it was dead (Letter to AP from J. Luz Saenz, March 22, 1934, AP, Box 4, Folder 28). In 1930, he wrote of conditions for support of candidates: 1) when the candidate or the whole ticket did not, in any way, denigrate or insult the Mexican community; 2) if the candidate or ticket advocated placing Mexican Americans on jury duty; and 3) if they advocated placing Mexican Americans in city or county government positions (R. Garcia, 1991, p. 287). He warned, "Our support of a political party or faction in Bexar County should be conditioned upon two things: 1. That no insults be cast upon our race at any time by members of said political party or faction. 2. Fair political representation for our race in the city and county government. We should have at least the following offices:

1 County Commissioner
1 Justice of the Peace
1 Assistant District Attorney
1 Assistant County Attorney
At least 35% of all District and county minor offices.
1 City commissioner
1 Assistant City Attorney
At least 25% of all city minor offices
"one seat in the state legislature." (AP?, no title, ca. 1938 AP, Box 4, Folder 3.)

He believed that "in election time they {Mexican Americans} must support men who were unquestionably friends of our race" (Ibid.). Perales was not interested in tokenism. In 1940 he resigned as board member of the San Antonio Board of Public Health. He did want to be a mere figurehead, objecting to the lack of Spanish-surnamed employees in city government ("Perales sees Discrimination," *San Antonio Light*, June 29, 1940; "Peticiones en Favor de los Mexicanos de San Antonio, Texas," *La Prensa*, June 24, 1940, AP, Box 14, Folder: Newspaper articles saved: Perales' life and work).

Perales concerned himself with working-class interests. He cared about uplifting the working class, not through unionization and wage increases, but through knowledge and education. He believed knowledge was power and sought to inform *la raza* of its rights and responsibilities. Perales wanted to uplift through adult education and night school for "Latinoamericanos." He argued that "todos los mexicanos, sin consideración de ciudadanía" should take these classes (*En Defensa* 1, p. 21). Council 16 supported night school attended by 1,400 at Sidney Lanier School on the Westside and sent a petition protesting the school's proposed closure in September 1934 (Letter to San Antonio Chamber of Commerce from Educational Committee, Council 16, ASP, Box 3, Folder 41; Letter to J. Luz Saenz from AP, March 17, 1934, AP, Box 4, Folder 28). Perales proved his caring nature when he himself taught at this night school.

Perales concerned himself with the interests of Mexican immigrants too. He did not make the lives of Mexicans in Mexico his business. He wrote "Nosotros los habitantes de origen mexicano de Texas, sin consideración a ciudadanía, tenemos problemas cívicos-sociales importantísmos que solucionar" (We Texas Mexican origin residents, irrespective of citizenship, have civic and social problems that need solving.) (Lic. Alonso S. Perales, "Visitantes Mexicanos que Mucho Nos Benefician," *En Defensa* 1, p. 69). He realized racism trumped citizenship. In a 1928 letter to Canales he noted, "the murderers did not stop to think whether or not this would-be victims were American citizens or not" (Letter to J.T. Canales from AP, January 2, 1928, AP, Box 4, Folder 10). Even after the Harlingen convention, Perales noted, "The object of the organization is to promote the general welfare of Mexican-Americans and Spanish-speaking peoples generally throughout Texas" (English typescript, news report of the Harlingen Convention, 1927, AP, Box 3, Folder 38). He along with Canales and Garza testified in 1930 to protest quotas on Mexican immigration (Leininger Pycior, 17). He helped to establish a night school open to women, people of all ages, and citizenship status ("Se Establece en San Antonio una Escuela," *La Prensa*?, ca.1933, AP, Box 8, Folder 10). His 1937 book included "Notes Toward Immigration Laws of the United States of America" since he sought to inform immigrants about how citizenship changed after 1924 (After July 1, 1924 immigrants were not eligible to become citizens if they entered without documents.) ("Apuntes Sobre Las Leyes de Inmigracion de Los Estados Unidos de America," *En Defensa* 2: 76-77). He also informed immigrants of a free citizenship manual (Alonso S. Perales, "Catecismo Civico de los Derechos y Deberes de los Ciudadanos Americanos," *En Defensa* 2, p. 75). No doubt, Perales filed many pro-bono cases for the poor, including undocumented immigrants.

Perales was not an opportunist. He did not seek to be the first LULAC national president and nor did he seek the presidency of a LULAC local council. He sought public office only once. He wrote, "I harbor no ill-feeling toward any man or group of men who seek to achieve personal fame and glory by holding themselves out as guardians and defenders of our race" . . . "I feel impelled to say vehemently that I must decline, and I do decline, to identify myself with any man or group of men who would use our downtrodden race as an instrument whereby to further selfish, individual ends" (Ms., AP, LULAC related, 2, AP, Box 3, Folder 39). Perales could have cast himself as one of the most outstanding Mexican-American leaders in the United States in the 1930s but he did not. Only a handful of men such as Senator Dennis Chavez or women like Concha Ortiz y Pino of New Mexico could have cast themselves in this manner. Despite the fact that he was the most active public Mexican-American intellectual in the 1930s, he did not seek self-aggrandizement.

Perales was not an elitist. In 1928 he either suggested or agreed to the idea that Ben Garza should be the League's first president. He wrote, "Ben is a very active young man, has money and, although he says he did not receive a very good education, I believe he would make a good President" (Ms., AP, LULAC related, 2, AP, Box 3, Folder 39). He did not assert his college education or law degree over Garza. He did not argue that only lawyers, the college-educated, or professionals were qualified to run LULAC. Perales believed in educating ordinary people about politics, so he wrote a simple question and answer essay or flyer "El 'Poll-Tax' o Impuesto Electoral" (Lic. Alonso S. Perales, "El "Poll-Tax" or Impuesto Electoral," *En Defensa* 2, pp. 62-65).

Perales did not seek whiteness. At one point he seems to have rejected use of the term "white." In a 1939 Memorandum on Conditions in San Antonio, Perales advised "Say: 'Anglo-American Women' instead of 'White Women.' The less we use the word 'white' in contradistinction to the word 'Mexican,' the better it will be." He wanted to erase the binary idea of white versus Mexican and perhaps even erase the idea that *la raza* was not also of European descent as Spanish people. In 1932 the Texas State Democratic Party changed the meaning of "white citizens" to include "Mexicans." Perales stated that "Mexicans belong to the Caucasian Race . . ." (Letter to White Man's Union Association of Wharton County from Alonso S. Perales, July 5, 1937, *En Defensa*, 2: 93-94). Later, Perales seems to have embraced a shift to the label "white" as part of political strategy for the empowerment of *la raza.* (See Mario T. Garcia, "Mexican Americans the Politics of Citizenship: The Case of El Paso, 1936," *New Mexico Historical Review* 59:2 (April 1984): 187-204; Carlos Kevin Blanton, "George I. Sanchez, Ideology, and Whiteness in the Making of the Mexican American Civil Rights Movement, 1930-1960," *Journal of Southern History* 72:3 (August 2006): 569-604; and Neil Foley, *Quest for Equality, The Failed Promise of Black-Brown Solidarity* (Cambridge: Harvard University Press, 2010).

Perales was an exceptional community leader who cared about *la raza,* LULAC, and its leadership. "The only reason I am working so hard is because I firmly believe that this League of ours is destined to become the greatest thing of its kind that we Mexican Americans have ever had in our entire history," he wrote (Letter from AP to J.T. Canales, November 2, 1927, AP, Box 4, Folder 10). And it was in the committee that was truly active that he saw the results of what LULAC could accomplish (Letter to Antonia Gomez from AP, January 11, 1933, AP, Box 4, Folder 9).

Perales cared about who led LULAC. In 1927 he wrote about the future LULAC leadership, "Our organization is destined to be the greatest thing of its kind we Mexican Americans ever had, but we must keep the reigns in good hands" (Letter to J.T. Canales from AP, AP, Box 4, Folder 10). On advocating for Pablo G. Gonzalez over Ermilio Lozano as potential LULAC president, he noted "I am trying to safeguard the interests of our League. That's all." (Letter to AP from J.T. Canales, April 3, 1933, AP, Box 4, Folder 11). He did not want LULAC to fall apart as had the Association of Independent Voters. Likewise in April 1934 he noted, "delegates, with few exceptions, do not take trouble to think." And LULACers need to "elect a man who is qualified in every respect" (Letter to H. H. Contreras from AP, April 2, 1934, AP, Box 4, Folder 14).

Leadership mattered. Criticizing weak leaders and opportunists, he stated, "I hold that the solution to our problem of unification depends largely upon intelligent, honest, and unselfish leadership." He added:

1. Our leaders must be intelligent in order that they may best guide the destiny of our race in this country.
2. They must be honest. They must really believe in and practice what they preach. They must not deceive our race by organizing it under false pretenses.
3. They must be unselfish. They must place the general welfare of all above their own. For instance, in election times they must support men who are unquestionably friends of our race." (Ts. by AP?, AP, Box 3, Folder 39).

His concept of leadership allowed many men (and not women) to lead; "Cada hombre tiene un talento, no importa cuan pequeño sea éste, y este talento deber ser desarrollado si la sociedad se ha de elevar más . . ." (Every man has a talent. It doesn't matter how small. And this talent should be developed if society is to elevate itself). (Perales, *En Defensa* 1, p. 20)

Like any leader, Perales was flawed. He thought he knew what was best for *la raza* and he believed co-activists should be loyal to him and agree with him. He said of Machado, "I used to think that he was my friend, that he was loyal, sincere, and all that. . . ." But then he learned otherwise (Letter to J.T. Canales from AP, May 27, 1932, AP, Box 4, Folder 10). Likewise, he liked to choose or influence who would be LULAC's national presidents (Letter to J.T. Canales from AP, March 18, 1933, AP, Box 4, Folder 11; Letter to JT Canales from AP, January 14, 1934; Letter to J.T. Canales from AP, April 2, 1934, AP, Box 4, Folder 11).

Perales did not blame *la raza's* oppression on *la raza* and he should not be used as an example of internalized racism. In 1927 Perales wrote, ". . . the conqueror can't assimilate conquered people. Reason: Snobbishness on the part of our fellow citizens of Nordic extraction" (Letter to JT Canales from AP, October 31, 1927, AP, Box 4, Folder 10). And in 1940 he wrote, "Ours must be a war against prejudice, ignorance, injustice, and poverty" (AP speech, "What Kind of Education Do Latin-American Citizens Want for Their Children," June 13, 1940, AP, Box 8, Folder 11).

Conclusion and Chicano History Revisions

Perales was remembered by a number of co-activists and admirers years before 2012. But there are not enough historians studying this particular history. *La raza* Perales' papers were needed for study. Perales was one of LULAC's most productive and successful national presidents. He made significant contributions to local LULAC in San Antonio, founding Council 16. Perales was ethical, leading him to form a second LULAC council in San Antonio because he saw jealousy and political opportunism (Letter to AP from J. Luz Saenz, April 16, 1934, AP, Box 4, Folder 28). Perales believed LULAC councils in the same town or city could be good neighbors; Council 2 did not prove neighborly. When he was kicked out, he seceded, and did not quit. Perales' tensions with Council 2 explain the rise of the League of Loyal Americans. His critics disagreed with a second chapter. This council was also male; Perales' activism was homosocial in the 1930s. But he changed with the times, and by the 1950s he mentored Vilma Martinez.

Ironically, LULAC men did not complain about gender division in the same town or city. Having a men's council and a ladies council in the same town or city was duplication. But this duplication in the 1930s kept women "in their place." Women's separate councils, however, were also a source of empowerment whereby women determined their own agendas. Today LULAC has multiple councils in town and cities; LULAC thrives with diversity (class, gender, age, college status, citizenship and sexuality) within geographical borders. The U in LULAC continues to be both a goal and myth.

This work based on the Perales archives suggests several needed Chicano history revisions: First, LULAC's work (and that of Perales) appears to have been primarily motivated by collective interests not individual interests. (This would revise the early work by political scientist Benjamin Marquez, *The Evolution of a Mexican American Political Organization* (Austin: University of Texas Press, 1993). Second, LULAC did not abandon Mexican immigrants as suggested by historian David Gutierrez (Gutierrez, 1995). LULAC was silent about deportations in the 1930s and the federal government's exclusion of Mexican immigrants from government jobs during the Depression. But LULAC did not advocate for deportation or repatriation. LULAC fought for immigrant rights, especially their rights to attend schools; and LULAC promoted their efforts to obtain U.S. citizenship during the Depression. Gutierrez had no access to Perales' archives.

Third, Perales should be honored for helping to found the School Improvement League for which Eleuterio Escobar has received most of the attention. Perales, not Escobar, initiated the call for major school improvements. And it was Council 16, founded by Perales, which initiated this struggle. Historian Mario T. García did not have access to the Perales papers before now (García, 1989, pp. 62-83. See the chapter "Education and the Mexican American: Eleuterio Escobar and the School Improvement League of San Antonio"). Historian Mario T. Garcia had no access to the Perales papers to know this when he conducted his study according Escobar all the credit.

Fourth, LULAC waged a multi-faceted activist agenda, not just legal desegregation work, in the 1930s (This revises Brian D. Behknen, *Fighting Their Own Battles* (Chapel Hill: University of North Carolina Press, 2011): 33-34; see Cynthia E. Orozco, "Eleuterio Escobar" *New Handbook of Texas* 2: 890-891). Extending the traditional Chicano movement bias against LULAC framework, historian Brian D. Behnken wrote that the Liga Defensa was "more confrontational" than LULAC and that "Escobar challenged the San Antonio School Board directly." He suggested "LULAC primarily addressed segregation through the courts" (Ibid.). But LULAC 16 initiated that struggle; Escobar was a member of Council 16 and it is Perales who must truly be credited for that effort.

Fifth, LULAC addressed federal policy/legislation in the 1930s not just local or state issues (Craig A. Kaplowitz *LULAC and Mexican Americans and National Policy* (College Station: Texas A&M University, 2005): 34.). Historian Kaplowitz has argued that LULAC was not working at the national level.

Sixth, Perales should not be used as an example of internalized racism. Benjamin Márquez's early writings noted that Perales blamed *la raza* for its own oppression arguing that he put the "onus of failure on the Mexican people themselves" (Márquez, 1993, p. 25). But Márquez had no access to the Perales papers at that time. Perales did not blame *la raza* for its own oppression, but he did realize *la raza* needed to take advantage of any educational opportunities available and needed to empower themselves. Perales (and thus LULAC) was not a super-assimiliationist organization demanding English-only. Recently, historian Rodolfo Acuña incorrectly suggested LULAC required its members to be "fluent in English" (Acuña, 2011, p. 11). This is false.

Seven, scholars must also consider gender when writing about the League and *la raza*'s empowerment. LULAC was gendered with Council 2 and Council 16's male membership. Perales' mentorship was too. Perales (and other LULACers) missed opportunities to empower women of Mexican descent.

Eight, this work confirms research by historian Richard Garcia and Adela Sloss-Vento. Garcia accurately portrayed Perales' ideology. He was unable to further document Perales' actions in the 1930s because the Perales papers were not yet available. My work confirms activist Sloss-Vento's positive account of Perales. Sloss-Vento's portrayal is not simply a laudatory, biased tribute by a friend. She did not amplify his character, exaggerate his achievements or simply pay homage to a man with local influence. Indeed, her book is an important tribute and documentation of Perales' life.

Perales was a selfless soldier for *la raza*. He wrote Mrs. Ben (Adelaida) Garza in July 30, 1937 noting "18 years of work done by me for my people free of charge" (Letter to Mrs. Ben Garza from AP, July 30, 1937, AP, Box 4, Folder 18). Adding decades, he could have written the same letter in 1961. In 1975, the *Chicano Times* reported that Marta Perales found her husband crying one day. He was worried about "what she was going to do with his papers after he died." Perales did not see his papers as a monument to himself; his archive is a monument to *la raza*, a monument to the history of *la raza*, a marker honoring our battles and token successes.

As we remember Perales, let us also honor the women responsible for keeping his legacy alive. Historian Sloss-Vento, acknowledged his value when no other historian had, and Mrs. Perales preserved her husband's legacy by keeping a vigilant eye on his archives. As we honor Perales, let us honor her, wife and historical preservationist, for without her stewardship we could not remember him. I too take my place as a woman who has unveiled Perales' legacy. He has earned my respect; perhaps we might now refer to him as Don Lic. Alonso S. Perales ("Don" being a title of respect and "Licenciado" referring to his education and profession as a lawyer). Perales was a man of the people for the people.

Works Cited

Archival and Primary Sources

Books, Articles, Government Documents

Perales, A. S. 1948. *Are we good neighbors?* San Antonio: Artes Gráficas.

Perales, A. S. (1931) El México Americano y la política del sur de Texas: Comentarios. San Antonio: Artes Gráficas. Translation of and commentary on Weeks, O. D. (1920) The Texas-Mexican and the politics of south Texas, *American Political Science Review 24*, 606-627. Print.

Perales, A. S. (1937). *En defensa de mi raza.* San Antonio: Artes Gráficas.

Sloss-Vento, A. (1977). Alonso S. Perales: His struggle for the rights of Mexican Americans. San Antonio: Artes Gráficas.

Tenayuca, E. & Brooks, H. (1939). The Mexican question in the southwest. *The Communist*, 257-268.

Collections

Benson Latin American Collection (hereafter BLAC), University of Texas at Austin
de Luna, Andres Sr., Papers
Dickerson Montemayor, Alice, Collection
Escobar, Eleuterio Jr., Papers
Gonzales, M.C. Collection
Wilmot, Louis Collection
Center for American History, University of Texas at Austin
LULAC News
Houston Metropolitan Research Center
LULAC News
M. D. Anderson Library, University of Houston
Alonso S. Perales Collection
Private Collections
Orozco, Cynthia E.

Secondary Sources

Articles

Blanton, C. K. (2006). George I. Sanchez, ideology, and whiteness in the making of the Mexican American civil rights movement, 1930-1960. *Journal of Southern History LXXII 3*, 569-604.

Orozco, C. E. (1997). Alice Dickerson Montemayor: Feminism and Mexican American politics in the 1930s. In Jameson, E. & Armitage, S. (Eds.), *Writing the Range: Race, Class, and Culture in the Women's West* (pp. 434-456). Norman: University of Oklahoma Press.

Orozco, C. E. (1998). Regionalism, politics, and gender in southwestern history: The League of United Latin American Citizens' (LULAC) expansion into New Mexico from Texas 1919-1945. *Western Historical Quarterly 29*(4), 459-483.

Weeks, O. D. (1929). The League of United Latin-American Citizens: A Texas-Mexican civic organization. *Southwestern Political and Social Science Quarterly 10*(3), 257-278.

Books

Acuña, R. F. (2011). *The making of Chicana/o studies*. New Brunswick: Rutgers U.

Behnken, B. D. (2011). *Fighting their own battles: Mexican Americans, African Americans, and the struggle for civil rights in Texas*. Chapel Hill: University of North Carolina Press.

Foley, N. (2010). *Quest for equality, the failed promise of black-brown solidarity*. Boston: Harvard University Press.

García, M. T. (1989). *Mexican Americans: Leadership, ideology, and identity*. New Haven, CT: Yale University Press.

García, R. A. (1991). *The rise of the Mexican American middle class*. College Station: Texas A & M University.

Gottheimer, J. (2003). *Ripples of hope: Great American civil rights speeches*. New York: Basic Civitas Books.

Gutiérrez, D. G. (1995). *Walls and mirrors: Mexican Americans, Mexican immigrants, and the politics of ethnicity.* Berkeley: University of California Press.

Kaplowitz, C. A. (2005). *LULAC: Mexican Americans and national policy.* College Station: Texas A & M University.

Kreneck, T. H. (2001). *Mexican American odyssey, Felix Tijerina, entrepreneur and civic leader, 1905-1965.* College Station: Texas A&M University Press.

Leininger Pycior, J. (1997). *LBJ & Mexican Americans, the paradox of power.* Austin: University of Texas, 1997.

Márquez, B. (1993). *LULAC: The evolution of a Mexican American political organization.* Austin: University of Texas Press.

Orozco, C. E. (2009). *No Mexicans, women or dogs allowed: The rise of the Mexican American civil rights movement.* Austin: University of Texas.

Sandoval, M. (1979). *Our legacy: The first fifty years.* Washington, DC: LULAC.

Encyclopedic Articles

Alice Dickerson Montemayor. (2006). In Ruiz, V. L. & Sánchez-Korrol, V (Eds.) *Latinas in the United States: A Historical Encyclopedia*, 3 vols. Bloomington: Indiana U Press.

Adela Sloss-Vento. (2006). In Ruiz, V. L. & Sánchez-Korrol, V (Eds.) *Latinas in the United States: A Historical Encyclopedia*, 3 vols. Bloomington: Indiana U Press Anders, E. (1996).

José Tomas Canales. (1996). In Tyler, R. C., Barnett D. E., & Barkley R. R (Eds.) *New Handbook of Texas.*, 6 vols (pp. 953-954). Austin: Texas State Historical Association.

League of United Latin-American Citizens. (2006). In Ruiz, V. L. & Sánchez-Korrol, V (Eds.) *Latinas in the United States: A Historical Encyclopedia*, 3 vols. Bloomington: Indiana U Press.

Maria Latigo Hernandez. (2006). In Ruiz, V. L. & Sánchez-Korrol, V (Eds.) *Latinas in the United States: A Historical Encyclopedia*, 3 vols. Bloomington: Indiana U Press.

Alice Dickerson Montemayor (1996). In Tyler, R. C., Barnett D. E., & Barkley R. R (Eds.) *New Handbook of Texas.*, 6 vols. Austin: Texas State Historical Association.

Alonso S. Perales. (1996). In Tyler, R. C., Barnett D. E., & Barkley R. R (Eds.) *New Handbook of Texas.*, 6 vols. Austin: Texas State Historical Association.

Bernardo F. Garza. (1996). In Tyler, R. C., Barnett D. E., & Barkley R. R (Eds.) *New Handbook of Texas.*, 6 vols. Austin: Texas State Historical Association.

Carolina Munguia. (1996). In Tyler, R. C., Barnett D. E., & Barkley R. R (Eds.) *New Handbook of Texas.*, 6 vols. Austin: Texas State Historical Association.

Del Rio v. Salvatierra. (1996). In Tyler, R. C., Barnett D. E., & Barkley R. R (Eds.) *New Handbook of Texas.*, 6 vols. Austin: Texas State Historical Association.

Eleuterio Escobar Jr. (1996). In Tyler, R. C., Barnett D. E., & Barkley R. R (Eds.) *New Handbook of Texas.*, 6 vols. Austin: Texas State Historical Association.

Gustavo Garcia. (1996). In Tyler, R. C., Barnett D. E., & Barkley R. R (Eds.) *New Handbook of Texas.*, 6 vols. Austin: Texas State Historical Association.

Harlingen Convention. (1996). In Tyler, R. C., Barnett D. E., & Barkley R. R (Eds.) *New Handbook of Texas.*, 6 vols. Austin: Texas State Historical Association.

John C. Solis. (1996). In Tyler, R. C., Barnett D. E., & Barkley R. R (Eds.) *New Handbook of Texas.*, 6 vols. Austin: Texas State Historical Association.
Ladies LULAC. (1996). In Tyler, R. C., Barnett D. E., & Barkley R. R (Eds.) *New Handbook of Texas.*, 6 vols. Austin: Texas State Historical Association.
League of United Latin American Citizens. (1996). In Tyler, R. C., Barnett D. E., & Barkley R. R (Eds.) *New Handbook of Texas.*, 6 vols. Austin: Texas State Historical Association.
Manuel C. Gonzales. (1996). In Tyler, R. C., Barnett D. E., & Barkley R. R (Eds.) *New Handbook of Texas.*, 6 vols. Austin: Texas State Historical Association.
Maria L. Hernandez. (1996). In Tyler, R. C., Barnett D. E., & Barkley R. R (Eds.) *New Handbook of Texas.*, 6 vols. Austin: Texas State Historical Association.
Mexican American Women. (1996). In Tyler, R. C., Barnett D. E., & Barkley R. R (Eds.) *New Handbook of Texas.*, 6 vols. Austin: Texas State Historical Association.
Order Knights of America. (1996). In Tyler, R. C., Barnett D. E., & Barkley R. R (Eds.) *New Handbook of Texas.*, 6 vols. Austin: Texas State Historical Association.
Orders Sons of America. (1996). In Tyler, R. C., Barnett D. E., & Barkley R. R (Eds.) *New Handbook of Texas.*, 6 vols. Austin: Texas State Historical Association.
School Improvement League. (1996). In Tyler, R. C., Barnett D. E., & Barkley R. R (Eds.) *New Handbook of Texas.*, 6 vols. Austin: Texas State Historical Association.
Spanish Speaking PTA. (1996). In Tyler, R. C., Barnett D. E., & Barkley R. R (Eds.) *New Handbook of Texas.*, 6 vols. Austin: Texas State Historical Association.
Vilma Socorro Martinez. (2000). In Meier, M.S. & Gutierrez, M. (Eds.). *Encyclopedia of the Mexican American Civil Rights Movement* (pp. 141-142). Westport, Conn.: Greenwood Press.

Newspapers and newspaper articles

El Paladín, UCLA Chicano Studies Research Center.
Orozco, C. E. (1996, February 17). New Mexico LULAC celebrates its 50th year. *Albuquerque Journal.*
Orozco, C. E. (1999, July 2). Ben and Adelaida Garza fought for equality. *Corpus Christi Times..*
Orozco, C. E. (2010, July 16). LULAC has long history in New Mexico. *Albuquerque Journal.*
Orozco, C. E. (2011, August 26). Valley's role in foundation of LULAC. *McAllen Monitor.*

Theses

Garza, E. D. (1957). *LULAC: League of United Latin-American Citizens* (Master's thesis). Southwest Texas State Teachers College.
Orozco, C. E. (1980). *Mexican and Mexican American conflict at the Harlingen convention of 1927: The genesis of LULAC* (Senior honors thesis). University of Texas at Austin.

In Defense of My People: Alonso S. Perales and the Moral Construction of Citizenship

Benjamin Márquez

Introduction

The recently available papers of Alonso S. Perales offer a unique opportunity to expand our understanding of early twentieth-century Mexican-American politics and assess the role of an important political actor. Perales was a founding member of the League of United Latin American Citizens (LULAC) and affiliated with other early civil rights organizations like the Sons of America, the League of Loyal Americans, and the Knights of America. His voluminous correspondence, newspaper articles, books, speeches, radio broadcasts and other written materials contain richly detailed descriptions of early to mid-twentieth century politics. These materials provide a vivid portrait of Mexican-American politics from the 1920s through the 1950s and the day-to-day life of an important activist grappling with the problems facing the community. Perales kept abreast of developments in the Texas courts, the state legislature and communities throughout the state, but he was especially attuned to politics in San Antonio where he lived and practiced law most of his life. His detailed commentary on the Mexican-American civil rights organizations expands our understanding of the movement's origins by virtue of his long and sustained political career. Perales worked on city and state commissions, participated in local, state and national electoral campaigns and belonged to non-ethnic organizations like the Chamber of Commerce, Optimist Club, and the Boy Scouts, in addition to religious organizations. He was also a member of the Democratic Party and, later in his life, the Republican Party.

The content of a Mexican-American ethnic identity as expressed through community leaders' positions on cultural assimilation, and attitudes toward American government and politics has long received academic scrutiny. Scholarly debates center on whether or not early leaders believed racial and economic subordination had deep-seated, systemic causes, or if inequalities between the races could be resolved through persuasion, civic engagement and lobbying. Of equal importance is the emphasis leaders like Alonso S. Perales placed on the need to celebrate and promote their culture. Cultural maintenance was a pressing issue because, in most places, Mexican Americans were outnumbered by Anglos, had little political power, and did not control the major institutions of socialization like the media or public schools.

Nevertheless, cultural preservation had political ramifications. Organizations investing a large amount of time and energy preserving one's cultural distinctiveness might
provoke a negative reaction from the majority and label the group as incapable of
social integration. However, neglecting cultural practices would accelerate the loss
of Mexican-American heritage and undermine group cohesion without any assurance of Anglo social acceptance (San Miguel, 1987; Ignacio García, 1989; Gutierrez, 1995; Márquez, 1993; Kaplowitz, 2005; Orozco, Cynthia E. 2009). Finally,
activists had to determine where Mexican Americans stood in a racialized society
defined by a black white binary (Ignatiev, 1995; Marx, 1998; Guglielmo, 2006;
Jacobson, 1999; Roediger, 2006, 2007). How they interpreted that racial status influenced their assumptions about racial reconciliation and determined, in part, their
alliances and strategic choices (Behnken, 2011).

    As a founding member of LULAC and a political activist with a career that
spanned almost fifty years, Perales' was a pivotal figure in these debates. He fought
for equality before the law, equal employment opportunity, school desegregation and
increased political representation (Perales, Alonso S. 1936–37. *En Defensa de mi
Raza Volume 2.* (San Antonio: Artes Gráficas), 16; Perales, Alonso. 1948. "Nuestro
pueblo puede ayudarse a sí mismo." Nov. 20, 1948. Reel 12; "Preparacion Para un
Hogar Feliz." *La Voz.* May 23, 1952. Reel 14; "El Matrimonio Cristiano." *La Voz.*
September 12, 1952. Reel 14). Perales argued Mexican Americans were Caucasian
and rejected the option of a political alliance with African Americans. At first glance,
these ideas place him solidly within the LULAC tradition of biculturalism and faith
that Mexican Americans would soon be incorporated into American society. However, it will be demonstrated that he departed from his organization's ideological foundation in significant respects, enough to warrant a reexamination of the relationships
early activists had with one another and where they agreed or disagreed on these
questions. Given the central role he played in the creation of LULAC, it is surprising
how pessimistic he was about the prospects for social change. He doubted Anglo
Americans could be trusted or were willing to apply the ideals of equality and justice
to Mexican Americans. Perales endorsed the idea of individual responsibility for
social mobility in the abstract, but placed much of the blame for Mexican-American
subordination on the Anglo Saxon. He accused them of using their numbers and political power to maintain a rigid racial hierarchy. Indeed, race so profoundly determined
one's life chances that Perales often argued group identity and individual interests
were virtually the same thing.

    Two other themes, a Mexican American white identity and anti-communism,
were important elements of Perales' worldview. When Perales argued Mexican
Americans were white, his immediate goal was to help them avoid the restrictions of
legal segregation in Texas, but he never assumed Mexican Americans were in fact
racially white. Nor did he argue that Mexican Americans existed on a racial contin-
uum, somewhere between Anglos and African Americans. Instead, he believed that
Mexican Americans were a distinct and self-sustaining ethnic group bound together
by a common history, racial identity, and culture (see Garcia, 1989). Racism reinforced group boundaries, but Mexican Americans possessed enduring community
ties based on their common cultural practices and social networks. Perales was a

fervent anti-communist, an important—but underexamined—aspect of the early Mexican-American civil rights movement. Perales' ideological rigidy occasionally brought him into conflict with other activists and political organizations—sometimes in inexplicable ways. If he suspected that a policy, politician or organization was in any way enabling a socialist agenda or any radical social movement, he would vigorously protest via correspondence and public forums, oftentimes to the exclusion of other issues.

Perales' archives record the work of a man deeply engaged in politics with all of its uncertainty and frustration. He wrote for a popular audience and there are many inconsistencies in his thinking about politics, but the sheer volume of his writing provides new insights into Mexican-American politics in the first half of the twentieth century. When Perales reflected on racism, poverty and cultural hegemony in the United States, his thinking always carried a clear normative message. In this way, he is part of a long tradition of identity construction in Mexican-American politics (Beltran, 2010; Barvosa, 2008). Like other activists, Alonso S. Perales carved out his own vision of an ethnic identity from its basic elements: judgments about the power of racial discrimination, economic stratification and cultural preservation (Marquez, 2003). Perales tried to solve some difficult problems but, when removed from the context of his time, the problems he encountered resonate with those Latinos face today (Fraga et al, 2010; De la Garza et al, 1992).

Race, Pride and Group Solidarity

Alonso S. Perales spent considerable time documenting incidents of racism in Texas. He uncovered numerous cases of restrictive housing covenants and police brutality (AP "Protesta en contra de una compañía de terrenos." No date. Reel 13; AP Letter to McAllen Real Estate Board. Jan. 29, 1927; AP "Carta enviada al Presidente Coolidge protestando contra los asesinatos de Raymondville." Feb. 14, 1927. Reel 13; AP "En defensa de los mexicanos" to Delta Development Co. Feb. 15, 1927. Reel 13). He found that Mexican Americans were discriminated against in hiring and paid less for the same work performed by Anglos (AP "Mr. Chairman, Ladies and Gentleman: I am indeed very happy to have . . ." RE: "What kind of education do Latin-American citizens want for their children?" no date. Reel 13). Indeed, Perales uncovered evidence of discrimination against Mexican Americans in almost every aspect of life. His files are filled with accounts of discrimination in restaurants, segregation in hospitals, segregation in theaters, racially restricted public events, discriminatory treatment by health care professionals, and segregated public parks (AP "Some places where Mexicans are discriminated against in Texas either by denying them service or by segregating them from Anglo-Americans." No date. Reel 13). Perales found cases where Mexican Americans were not allowed to attend Catholic religious services with Anglos, denied the use of public auditoriums, and overcharged for goods and services (AP "Some places where Mexicans are discriminated against in Texas either by denying them service or by segregating them from Anglo-Americans." No date. Reel 13). Mexican Americans were even segregated in jails (AP "Some places where Mexicans are discriminated against in Texas either by denying them service or by segregating them from Anglo-Americans." No date. Reel 13). Discrimination in the public schools was disturbing to Perales because education constituted the only avenue for mobility available to Mexican Americans possessed. As part of a LULAC research team, Perales published data comparing Mexican-American and Anglo schools in terms of funding, number of pupils, rooms, teachers, students per room, value of property, size of campus, operating costs, property values, revenues yielded and average cost per pupil. Systematic underfunding of Mexican-American schools resulted in "shameful" overcrowding, deteriorating infrastructure and a poor quality of instruction (AP September 27, 1934. "Statistics of All Elementary Schools of the S.A. School District." Reel 26). Perales found that Mexican Americans suffered disproportionate casualties during wartime, discrimination in war industries, unequal government pensions and segregation in New Deal programs (AP to Kilday, Paul. November 24, 1944. Reel 18; AP to Kilday, Paul. July 6, 1946. Reel 18. "Otra protesta con respeto a las pensiones." Nov. 15, 1935. Reel 13; AP "Protesta contra la segregación de nuestra juventud en los campos del gobierno." Aug. 27, 1935. Reel 13).

One form of racism Perales found especially damaging was stereotyping, and he spent much of his career railing against distorted and demeaning characterizations of Mexican Americans. Perales was alarmed by stereotypes because they were founded on an ideology of white supremacy and were employed to justify overt racist acts. The damage inflicted by stereotyping was immediate and palpable, but he was equally alarmed by its psychological harm. Perales' correspondence is filled with condemnations of the insults and humiliation Mexican Americans endured on a daily basis ("Several leading Mexican-Americans met a San Antonio . . ." Reel 13; Perales to Watson Miller, Commissioner of immigration. November 24, 1947 Reel 20; "Statement Made by Alonso S. Perales, San Antonio Attorney, with reference to the Spears Anti-Discrimination Bill." April 1945. Reel 13; Perales to Anderson. October 28, 1941. Reel 25). He was particularly infuriated by the fact that military veterans, individuals who had proven their patriotism and valor on the battlefield, found themselves subjected to degrading treatment. Upon returning to the United States, these individuals ". . . could not secure employment or that if they found it they could not receive equal wages for equal work merely because of their racial origin, or that the owner of any restaurant, barber shop, or theater could continue to humiliate them as he saw fit just because they were of Mexican descent" ("Fair Employment Practices Act. Hearings Before a Subcommittee of the Committee on Education and Labor United States Senate." Reel 28). Fighting stereotypes was a battle of ideas, one that Mexican Americans needed to win. Thus, it was important that Mexican Americans recognize their own great accomplishments, including the sophisticated civilization the Indians created long before the Spanish conquest ("La ignorancia como causa de los prejuicios raciales." Aug. 20, 1923. Reel 13). In his radio programs, he reminded community members that they were a dignified and proud people and challenged Anglos to recognize the merits and virtues of a "dignified and noble" race[1] ("Conferencias en pro del mejoramiento de los mexicanos." Aug. 2, 1924. Reel 13).

There were a number of other things that could be done in order to counter the negative impact of racial stereotyping. Perales advised Mexican Americans to work hard, educate their children, maintain their property, and tend to their personal hygiene (AP "Rambling Around." No date. Reel 13; AP "A propósito de un concurso para embellecer solares." La Prensa, April 11, 1936. Reel 13). Perales believed that Mexican Americans needed to have their contributions recognized in public and he was involved in a campaign to erect a monument memorializing Mexican-American World War I veterans. Perales hoped the costly memorial would serve as a statement, a reminder that Mexican Americans fought and died defending their country (AP "Honremos la memoria de los héroes de origen Mexicano." Managua, Nicaragua, June 30, 1928. Reel 13). Perales would not let stereotypes uttered in the public sphere stand without a rejoinder. He tirelessly criticized comments by public officials, newspaper editors, and academics that he believed wrongly characterized or cast aspersions on Mexican Americans (AP "Una presentación teatral que no hace justicia al pueblo mexicano." May 15, 1923 Published in *The Washington Post* in May of 1923. Reel 13).

He was not afraid to attack powerful politicians and organizations that maligned his people's honor. In 1936, Perales filed a complaint against the Daughters of the Republic protesting the fact that a ceremony commemorating the battle of the Alamo did not mention the names of Mexican Americans who died along with the others. He added that most of the others who died fighting the Mexican army immigrated to Texas from other states and countries (Perales and Isidoro Flores to Daughters of the Republic December March 15, 1936. Reel 15). He reminded Anglos that individuals with surnames like ". . . Seguin, Navarro, Ruiz and Menchaca and other Texas patriots of Hispanic origins [who] worked with their Anglo American brothers who created the Republic of Texas . . ." (AP "Mis estimados radiooyentes." No date. Reel 13). In 1940, Perales was outraged when San Antonio Mayor Maury Maverick called prostitution an "old Spanish custom." (AP letter to Maury Maverick. April 6, 1940. Reel 26). He immediately launched a protest and argued that no Mexican parent would ever send their daughters into prostitution: "they would rather starve to death or commit suicide than consent to their offspring going into prostitution" (AP "Comments Upon the Report Submitted Recently by Mr. S.C. Menefee, Associate Social Economist, W.P.A. Division of Social G.C.S." Reel 17). Perales went on to cite a report that found most prostitutes in San Antonio were Anglo (AP to Floyd McGown. April 20, 1940. Reel 25).

Perales wrote extensively about race, much of which centered on his argument that Mexican Americans were white. He was part of a campaign to have Mexican Americans legally classified as white, in part, to avoid the sanctions of Jim Crow legislation, especially in the public schools. The practical benefits of a white identity would help Mexican Americans realize ". . . some of the blessings of our American civilization, such as good schools, houses fit for human habitation, [and] a living wage . . ." (AP letter to Hudson, Estelle Ripley, Jan. 22, 1938. Reel 18). He helped parents lobby school boards against racial segregation, arguing that the law did not call for the segregation of Mexican-American children and that Texas, segregation statues were only intended for ". . . all persons of mixed blood descended from negro ancestry." ("Como pedir facilidades escolares para nuestra niñez." Sept. 1936. Reel 13). Mexican Americans, he argued, were "descendants of the Caucasian or white race" thereby protected by the Texas constitution, the 14th amendment to the U.S.

constitution, and the Treaty of Guadalupe Hidalgo. His fight to have Mexican Americans categorized as white eventually involved two Texas senators, the mayor of San Antonio, the Department of Commerce, the Bureau of the Census, Congressman Maury Maverick, and Senator Dennis Chavez of New Mexico (AP letter "To the Honorable Board of Trustees of the Mission Independent School District." December 30, 1930. Reel 17. See Quinn, C. K., letters Nov. 28–Dec. 2, 1936. Reel 16). He proved to be persuasive and most of the politicians and bureaucrats with whom he worked agreed that the current system was obsolete, with one going as far as to call it "humiliating and embarrassing" (William L. Austin to Maury Maverick. October 26, 1936. Reel 26; Maury Maverick to William Austin. October 19, 1936. Reel 26).

Scholars have pointed to the futility and moral hazards inherent in the claim of a white identity (Foley, 2010; Behnken, 2011). However, Perales recognized that a white identity gave Mexican Americans significant legal tools and protections.[2] For example, Mexican Americans could vote and participate in the Democratic Party because they were legally white for the purpose of voting in Texas (AP Letter to David Casas. April 14, 1941). He invoked this line of reasoning when protesting the segregation of Mexican Americans from whites in the armed forces (AP letter to Paul Kilday. August 4, 1945. Reel 19). Political advantage was not the only motive driving Perales to argue that Mexican Americans were white, he also believed black people were socially inferior. Perales thought that categorizing Mexican Americans as colored was a 'deadly insult.' In other words, he felt it was demeaning to classify his people as colored and "jumble them in as *Negroes* [sic], which they are not" and that doing so "naturally causes the most violent feelings" (AP letter to Austin, William L. October 15, 1936. Reel 18). Perales once demanded an apology after a speaker in San Antonio suggested Mexican Americans were not white. He warned that there would be serious consequences for such actions and predicted that "so long as there are people among the Anglo Saxons who unjustly classify ALL the Latin Americans as indigent, ignorant riff-raff, so long shall there be Latin Americans who will refuse to cooperate with you in civil affairs" (AP letter to Dohrn, G.F. April 13, 1948. Reel 18).

Perales once observed that black people had the same claim to equal rights as everyone else but because African Americans stood at the bottom of America's racial hierarchy, there was a clear disincitive for Mexican Americans to cast their lot with blacks. In his words, ". . . the negro is entitled to JUSTICE, but if we champion his cause, we are doomed." Hence, he invested considerable energy opposing racial misclassification schemes because they branded Mexican Americans as racial outsiders. Significantly, Perales never argued that Mexican Americans were racially identical or culturally similar to Anglos nor did he believe cultural assimilation was a desirable goal. In his more defiant moments, Perales declared that Mexican Americans were not begging for social interaction with Anglos. What his people wanted, he said, were all the rights and privileges of citizenship, and progress without Anglo interference (AP "El ideal de los México-Americanos." Oct. 1924. Reel 13).

When Perales asserted that Mexican and Anglo Americans were Caucasians, his understanding of the term was rooted in the complex construction of race in the Americas. Perales proudly referred to himself as "prieto" (dark skinned), but that did not mean he was black. Rather, he was dark-skinned Mexican American (AP "Muy estimados conciudadanos y hermanos de raza." Begins with "Me congratulo de tener la oportunidad . . ." Reel 13). His own prejudices and asumptions about race in Mexico and Latin America limited his understanding of race relations outside of the southwestern United States as well as the emerging black civil rights movement. A revealing episode came in 1944 when Carlos Castañeda, Regional Director of the President's Fair Employment Practices Committee, asked Perales to testify before a congressional committee. Congress was considering a proposal to make the FEPC permanent and Castañeda wanted Perales to talk about his decades of work against employment discrimination in the Southwest. However, he warned Perales not to raise the issue of a Caucasian identity or his aversion to the categorization of Mexican Americans as 'colored' ". . . as that would be discriminatory in itself." In the margins of the letter, Castañeda reiterated: "do not use this in any of your arguments, just *entre nous.*" (underline in text). He coached Perales to speak up for all Americans regardless of "race, creed, color, or national origin" (Carlos Castañeda letter to Perales. May 27, 1944. Reel 25). Castañeda had a more sophisticated understanding of national politics but neither man was accustomed to thinking of a racial division with whites on one side and people of color on the other. Hence, Perales believed he was reiterating a social fact of life when he said Mexican Americans were Caucasians 'who have Indian blood' (Perales to Carlos Castañeda. December 9, 1944. Reel 25).

Perales' understanding of group identity eventually brought him into conflict with the League of United Latin American Citizens and the American GI Forum over the publication of *The Wetback in the Lower Rio Grande Valley of Texas,* a book written by University of Texas professor Olen Leonard and University of New Mexico professor Lyle Saunders (Saunders and Leonard, 1951). The book was one of the first studies on undocumented labor in South Texas agriculture but Perales contended that the book was filled with damaging insults because it quoted anonymous residents, ranchers, and politicians who characterized Mexican workers as docile and disease-ridden. Perales publicized his indignation in *La Verdad* and demanded that the authors identify their anonymous respondents (AP article "Arquetectros de Nuestros Propios Destinos." *La Verdad.* Dec 14, 1951. Reel 14; AP letter to Manuel J. Raymond. December 13, 1951. Reel 20). The two professors, he said, "insulted" people of Mexican origin, something he deeply resented. He stated his intention to file a criminal libel suit because of the psychic harm inflicted on Mexican Americans and the damage it would do to their social and economic progress (AP letter to Canales, J. T. December 4, 1951. Reel 15).

LULAC and the American GI Forum were perplexed by Perales' strong reaction to quotes that reflected what civil rights activists knew were widely held attitudes about Mexican Americans. Both organizations believed that the new research brought much needed data and analysis to bear on the long-standing problem of low wage migrant labor in Texas. In order to deflect the criticisms of the book and its authors, the LULAC Supreme Council rebuked Perales by passing a resolution praising the study's method and documentation. The two sides differed over the roles respect and recognition should play in the public discourse as well as the limits of free speech and academic discourse. South Texas Attorney Manuel Raymond joined

Perales in his condemnation of the book and the failure of civil rights organizations to comprehend the damage inflicted by the Leonard and Saunders book. He was incredulous at LULAC's myopia and the implication that the book's critics ". . . are a bunch of dum-bells because the study is merely academic and a reporting job and that we fail to view it as such" (Raymond, Manuel J. Letter to Alonso Perales. December 19, 1951. Reel 20). Breaking with his colleagues in LULAC and the American GI Forum, Perales was determined to rectify what he considered a terrible injustice. Moreover, he wanted to punish the individuals who uttered the damaging words and announced his ". . . intention is to take this matter to court, if necessary, in an effort to compel them to give the names and addresses of the defamers of our people in the Lower Rio Grande Valley" (Perales to Contreras, Hermán H., December 4, 1951. Reel 18). He also wanted to sue the University of Texas and its President for group libel and seek a million dollars in damages ("danos y perjuicios") (AP letter to Luz, Saenz, J. de la. December 11, 1951. Reel 16; AP letter to Luz, Saenz, J. de la. December 4, 1951. Reel 16). Although he did not formulate a legal strategy or explain how the money would be distributed should he prevail in court, Perales believed that the book injured Mexican Americans and the authors should be held accountable.

The Politics of Group Solidarity

Perales believed that racism's greatest harm was that it condemned an entire group rather than distinguishing individuals by their own character and merit (AP "La ignorancia como causa de los prejuicios raciales." Aug. 20, 1923. Reel 13). Racism, segregation, and inequalities in wealth were a harsh reality and more Mexican Americans needed to become more involved in public affairs if these problems were to be eliminated ("La evolución de los México-Americanos" Oct. 1924. Reel 13). To that end, Perales established a night school to teach government and politics so that community members could learn and understand the mechanics of government (AP "Se establece en San Antonio una escuela de gobierno y ciudadanía." No date. Reel 13). He urged young people to pursue a legal career (AP "Jóvenes Mexico-Americanos, estudiad derecho!" no date. Reel 13). He advised his compatriots to serve on city, state, and national commissions, and to join civic organizations like Boy Scouts and the Optimists. Most importantly, he wanted everyone of voting age to pay their Poll Tax and remain vigilant during electoral campaigns in order to hold public officials to all the promises they made to the community (AP 1948. "Nuestro pueblo puede ayudarse a sí mismo." Nov. 20, 1948. Reel 12).

Perales displayed an acute understanding of the political process and how the structure of government influenced decision-making. For example, he railed against the city manager form of government because it concentrated too much power in the hands of one person. He believed that a mayor-city council form like San Antonio's was preferable because their system required individual council members to head city departments thereby rendering them more subject to political pressure (AP "Radio Talk to be made by Alonso S. Perales, local attorney, over station KABC, Friday May 2nd, at 6:45 PM."). By the mid 1930s, Perales was passing along his knowledge of law and government to parents fighting segregation and unequal funding in the public school system. He coached community members how to petition public officials and pressure them to change their policies. He wrote a fill-in-the blank form that parent groups could use when lodging a complaint. It explained to whom it should be addressed, how to present the petition, which parties had standing, and how many copies to provide and who gets those copies (school board, state board of education, superintendent of public schools, etc). The document further explained why it was illegal to segregate Mexican-American students, why they needed a response in writing, and what to do if they did not get a satisfactory resolution ("Como pedir facilidades escolares para nuestra niñez." Sept. 1936. Reel 13). Perales cited the relevant statues mandating education for children between 6 and 18, the right to attend the closest school, receive tutoring if necessary, and state policies on transfers, absences and reform school ("La educación de la niñez es obligatoria." No date. Reel 13). Finally, he kept abreast of pending legislation in the state legislature on funding inequities and lobbied for a bill that would empower the State Superintendent of Public Instruction to reduce a school district's funding when it did not provide equitable distribution of school facilities (Perales to Leonard, Homer, January 20, 1937. Reel 16).

When mobilizing the Mexican-American vote, one of his primary goals was to win a more equitable share of public resources (AP "To the Texas Pan American Round Tables, Rotary, Lions, and Kiwanis Clubs . . ." Reel 13). Specifically, he wanted affirmative action in public employment and demanded that successful candidates for public office hire a proportional number of Mexican Americans to work for their administration or face the consequences in the next election (AP letter to Anderson. April 5, 1941. Reel 18; AP "Speech to be delivered by Alonso S. Perales, local attorney, at 1:45 pm today, in behalf of the anti-Maverick ticket." Reel 13; AP "Radio talk to be delivered by Mr. Alonso S. Perales during the "Hora Anahuac" program at 1:45 pm today." Begins with, "Mis dignos conciudadanos y Hermanos de Raza." No date. Reel 13). In San Antonio, for example, Perales believed that 1/6 of the entire city workforce should be Mexican American (AP letter to P.L. Anderson. May 31, 1941. Roll 25; AP letter to Owen W. Kilday. May 11, 1940. Roll 26). His insistence on proportional hiring belied a lack of faith in the good will of Anglo politicians, a hallmark of LULAC politics, and observed that most were likely to renege on their promises to the community (AP "Mis estimados radiooyentes." No date. Reel 13). In 1950, he noted that there were no Mexican American state senators in the Texas Legislature, a fact he felt was dangerous because Anglo politicians would not represent their interests. As he asked in his weekly radio address, "do you think, mis queridos radio-oyantes, that this is just?" ("Plática sustentada por el Lic. Alonso S. Perales a través de la estación KIWW, a las 7 de la tarde, el jueves, 24 de agosto de 1950. Reel 13).

Perales practiced what he preached. He was an enthusiastic supporter of Mayor Maury Maverick when first elected as mayor of San Antonio. After Mayor Maverick failed to hire as many Mexican Americans as Perales thought appropriate, he retaliated in the next election by campaigning for Maverick's opponent and referring to the mayor as the "little dictator" (AP "Radio Talk to be made by Alonso S.

Perales, local attorney, over station KABC, Friday May 2nd, at 6:45 PM"). When candidates or tickets were non-responsive or did not act as he felt they should he vowed to "whip [them] as American citizens in the American way." In other words, he threatened offending politicians with a large Mexican-American voter turnout and defeat at the polls (AP "Speech to be delivered by Alonso S. Perales, local attorney, at 4pm today, on Station KABC (hora nacional)" no date. Reel 13).

In order to generate a credible electoral threat, he delivered lectures and wrote essays on the need for Mexican Americans to pay their poll tax and vote ("Plática sustentada por el Lic. Alonso S. Perales a través de los micrófonos de "Hora Nacional" el día 22 del actual." Jan 22, 1943. Reel 13). Perales did not think political participation was an abstract civic duty, rather, it should yield concrete results for the community. Perales believed Mexican Americans had unambiguous material interests and they should support the party or faction that offered the best deal (ventajas) to them (AP letter to Garcia, Carlos. January 7, 1932. Reel 18). Even politicians like Maury Maverick, whom Perales previously excoriated as a dictator, received his support after Maverick changed his policies (AP "Plática sustentada por el Lic. Alonso S. Perales en favor de la planilla Maverick, el 20 de mayo de 1947, a través de la estación KCOR"). However, there was nothing sacred about participating in the electoral process. If no candidate for public office met the standard of proportional representation, then it was "a thousand times better not to vote" ("El sufragio de los Mexico-Americanos." June 25, 1924. Reel 12).

If Mexican Americans organized on behalf of a successful candidate for public office that candidate incurred a debt payable upon election. In 1936, Perales wrote a letter to congratulate newly elected Governor James Allred and enclosed a list of 91 people who campaigned on Allred's behalf, a list he merely "jotted down" (AP letter to Hall, Marvin. July 28, 1936. Reel 18). In 1940, Perales reminded Owen W. Kilday, the newly elected Bexar County Sheriff, that many Mexican Americans campaigned for Kilday and the entire 'Bexar County Ticket' (Owen W. Kilday letter to Perales September 5, 1940. Reel 26; AP letter to Kilday November 28, 1940. Reel 26). In exchange, Perales gave Kilday a detailed list of individuals qualified to work as elevator operator, janitor, jail guard and doormen.[3] The following year Perales sent newly elected San Antonio Mayor C. K. Quin a long list of Mexican Americans recommended for employment, twenty-three in all, for high administrative positions as well as jobs like office clerks, staff members, stenographers, and truck drivers (May 30, 1941. Perales to C. K. Quin. Reel 27. See others Reel 27). He also sent San Antonio's Commissioner of Fire and Police another list of individuals he believed were qualified to work at every level of administration and service provision. Perales included data documenting the low numbers of Mexican-American police officers and firefighters in San Antonio. He demanded that the Commissioner of Fire and Police take immediate action to correct the disparity.[4] Equity in government hiring would correct a long-standing racial injustice and further empower Mexican Americans to leverage additional reforms. When Perales presented the Committee of One Hundred with a list of the organization's members who were employed by the City of San Antonio he celebrated the accomplishment and added that these individuals ". . . are now representing our people in the City Administration." The list included police officers, tax auditors and health inspectors, as well as luminaries like Gus Garcia who became San Antonio's First Assistant City Attorney and Carlos Cadena an attorney for the Back Tax Department ("Report Rendered by the Chairman of the Committee of One hundred, at a General Meeting of the Committee, on July 22, 1941." July 22, 1941. Reel 28).

The Dilemma of Minority Activism

A key feature of LULAC's philosophy was the belief that the United States would eventually accept and incorporate Mexican Americans as full equals. As a founding member of LULAC, Perales endorsed this ideal, but a deep pessimism ran through his thinking about American politics and he often doubted incorporation would ever occur, "I have always contended that the greatest defect of our nation as a conqueror is its inability to assimilate its conquered peoples" (AP Letter to Canales, J. T. October 31, 1927. Reel 15). In the face of relentless discrimination, Mexican Americans had little chance of being elected to public office, their only recourse was to elect Anglo politicians who were 'democratic, courageous and patriotic' (Perales to Congressman Pat Dwyer. March 15, 1941. Reel 26). However, Perales believed that few Anglos cared about racial justice, leading him to support some unlikely proposals. For example, he often argued that, in order to improve race relations, Anglos needed to embark upon an ideological campaign in the form of anti-racist talks or discussion groups (AP "A las mesas redondas panamericanas, clubes de rotarios, leones, y Kiwanis . . ." "Protesta contra unos versos ofensivos para el pueblo mexicano." May 20, 1936). Perales once argued that even the Texas Rangers could be utilized to protect Mexican Americans. He reasoned that if the Rangers were used to violate Mexican-Americans rights, they could be used to defend them (AP "La respuesta del gobernador" Feb. 17, 1944; AP "La contestacion del Lic. Perales." Feb. 25, 1944). Finally, Perales believed anti-discrimination legislation was absolutely necessary to protect Mexican Americans because only the fear of prosecution, fines, and jail time would deter racist acts. Nonetheless, he fully understood that many of the abuses suffered by Mexican Americans were committed by the same government officials (autoridades del país) he was asking for protection (Perales, Clemente Idar and J Luz Saenz. Ca1929. "una Aclaracion Al Margen de la Convención de Harligen. Reel 17; AP letter to J.T. Canales. November 2, 1927. Reel 15).

During the mid-1940s, any hope he had in the governmental process to produce just results was shattered. In 1944, when the Fourth Circuit Court of Appeals ruled that private property owners could legally discriminate against minorities in restaurants, dance halls, theaters and barbershops, Perales asked the governor to call a special session of the legislature to make racial discrimination illegal in Texas (AP "El reciente fallo de la cuarta corte de apelaciones civiles y la doctrina del buen vecino." No date. Reel 12). In the early 1940s, he lobbied for the introduction of anti-discrimination bills in the Texas legislature and kept close watch on their progress. He knew when a bill was introduced and to which committee it was assigned, and how in one case it was scrapped because of a technicality (AP Perales to Coke R. Steven-

son. August 14, 1941. Reel 26). He also knew which legislators actively opposed
anti-discrimination legislation (Perales to Franklin Delano Roosevelt. March 31,
1944. Reel 27). When an anti-discrimination bill failed in 1941, Perales asked the
governor to introduce it himself by calling the legislature into special session (Coke
Stevenson to Perales. September 2, 1941. Reel 26).

Perales witnessed the Texas Legislature's refusal to pass anti-discrimination
three times, even as acts of violence against Mexican Americans continued unabated (AP letter to Barnes, Stuart J., Oct. 7 – 9, 1945; AP "Mr. Chairman, Ladies and
Gentleman: I am indeed very happy to have . . ."; AP "What kind of education do
Latin-American citizens want for their children?" No date. Reel 13). He understood
that the Anti-Discrimination Bill did not pass in the Texas legislature because of per-
vasive discrimination against Mexican Americans. Moreover, the problem did not lie
with the beliefs of a small number of Anglos: "it is really among ninety-five percent,
if not ninety-nine, of the people in the Southwest. It may be that only 20% actually
come out and openly express their feelings, but they have the backing of the rest,
who, on the QT, say'Amen'." (AP letter to Carlos Castañeda. December 9, 1944.
Reel 25). Compounding the injury was the hypocracy that permeated the political
process. Perales observed that Anglo politicians were generally unconcerned about
the problems facing Mexican Americans except during the campaign season at
which time they exhibited ". . . a great interest in the Spanish speaking people." At
political gatherings,

> "The politicians generally select the best Spanish speakers, for those occasions
> and it is then when the florid rhetorical figures of Spanish are brought out. The
> lawyers, public men, the teachers and especially the professional politicians
> use the Spanish language freely making good use of the witty, and cutting sar-
> casms of the language in assailing their enemies." "These songs—'corridos'
> inject a great deal of enthusiasm in all the political crowds and at the end they
> holler and yell, !!Viva Davis, Viva Perales!!" (AP "Spanish Language and Pol-
> itics in the Frontier States." Reel 13)

The bitter irony of these charades was that Anglo politicians, the very people who
abused Mexican Americans, would then turn around and ask for their votes (AP letter to Carlos Castañeda. October 8, 1954. Reel 25).

Perales' frustration with the electoral process helps explain his enthusiasm for
the Good Neighbor Commission's work in Latin America and the goal of hemispheric unity through the rule of law. If the state of Texas would not pass protective
legislation, the federal government might via an international treaty. In other words,
Perales thought that a treaty among the United States, Mexico, and all Latin American countries might serve the same purpose. The United States was pressing all Latin
American countries to guard against communist expansion into the region, a strategy Perales embraced. He also believed that the treaty should contain an anti-racist
provision because of the danger that America's enemies would exploit social and
national divisions to foment discontent.[5] If realized as he envisioned, such a treaty
could serve as a short-term proxy for national anti-racism laws and leverage against

the state of Texas (AP "El reciente fallo de la cuarta corte de apelaciones civiles y la doctrina del buen vecino." No date; AP "Resolution introduced by Alonso S. Perales Delegate to the Texas Bar Association."; AP letter to Carlos Castañeda December 9, 1944. Reel 25; Perales, Alonso, ed. 1948. "Fair Employment Practices Act Hearings." in *Are We Good Neighbors?* pp. 86-91).

Perales' anti-communist fervor and hopes for civil rights protection through the Good Neighbor Commission explains why he considered racial discrimination to be a threat to national security. Racial discrimination in the United States, he predicted, would undermine the nation's credibility in Latin America, thereby making the region vulnerable to the propaganda of its enemies (AP "Speech to be delivered by Alonso S. Perales" Addressed "Mis dignos ciudadanos" and begins with "En primer lugar deseo saludar . . ." No date. Reel 13). When Perales asked the governor to call a special session of the legislature to consider anti-discrimination legislation he invoked the goals of the Good Neighbor Commission. He asserted that a racist 'fifth column' was undermining the country's security by ". . . humiliating Hispanics in public places like theaters, barber shops, restaurants, swimming pools, parks, etc." (AP "La respuesta del gobernador" Feb. 17, 1944; AP "La contestacion del Lic. Perales." Feb. 25, 1944. Reel 10; AP letter to Coke R. Stevenson. Feb. 9, 1944. Reel 10). He used the same argument when protesting incidents of discrimination and said it was ". . . intended to strengthen the ties of friendship happily existing between our two great Races of the Western Hemisphere . . ." He argued the drive for better relations would fail without the cooperation of every American citizen, particularly elected officials (AP Perales to Mayor, San Angelo, Texas, April 30, 1937. Reel 20). But in the end, even Perales doubted the utility of his tortured logic and admitted that all Mexican Americans were getting from their allies was empty promises (AP letter to Carlos Castañeda. December 9, 1944. Reel 25).

Freedom of Speech and Association

Given his extensive civil rights activism, it is surprising Alonso Perales did not have much to say about individual freedom. When he spoke about rights, he focused on group rights, equal opportunity and freedom from discrimination, not individual liberty (AP "Nuestros Deberes y Derechos Cívicos." December 31, 1941. Reel 14). However, it is clear that Perales did not believe that individual freedom constituted a license to do as one pleased, especially when it came to groups he disliked. Perales was willing to deny the right of free speech and association to anyone he suspected of involvement in radical or revolutionary activity. He condemned the American Civil Liberties Union for protecting the first amendment rights of groups espousing revolutionary politics (Perales to American Civil Liberties Union. March 1, 1938. Reel 18). He demanded that candidates for public office sign a document swearing they were not communists (AP "Será suficiente con que un candidato declare que es anti-comunista?" Sept. 19, 1954. Reel 13). He was even suspicious of attorney Gus Garcia, who argued before the U.S. Supreme Court in 1954 to end the exclusion of Mexican Americans from jury duty, because he once defended a company Perales considered 'communistic' (Perales to Carlos Castañeda. November 30, 1953. Reel).

Finally, Perales distrusted unions because they colluded with management to relegate Mexican Americans to menial jobs and a lower wage scale than that applied to Anglos (AP letter to Kilday, Paul. July 6, 1946. Reel 18). He also alleged that most unions were infiltrated by radicals who should be purged from the organization: "my honest opinion is that *all* labor unions and in fact all organizations in our country ought to deny membership to Communists, Nazists [sic] and Fascits [sic]" (AP letter to Menefee, Mr. Selden C., WPA Director of Research, Washington DC. Feb. 24, 1939. Reel 20). He supported the creation of a Senate and House Committee on Anti American Activities, advocated the deportation of foreign communists, Nazis, and fascists and, if they were naturalized, the revocation of their citizenship. He wanted to put an end to what he believed were communist-instigated strikes and make the Congress of Industrial Organizations identify its communist members. He wanted to outlaw all unions that had communist or fascist leaders as well as organizations under the control of foreign dictators, groups he alleged had seven million members in the United States (AP "Speech to be delivered by Alonso S. Perales" Addressed "Mis dignos ciudadanos" and begins with "En primer lugar deseo saludar . . ." No date. Reel 13).

Perales spared no one. He accused many politicians of receiving support from or being under the control of communists, even at one point claiming the State Department hired communists, one of whom was a close advisor to President Franklin Roosevelt (AP "Será suficiente con que un candidato declare que es anticomunista?" Sept. 19, 1954. Reel 13). Perales once charged that Congressman Maury Maverick gave aid to the communist cause through his support of the Congress of Idustrial Organizations, a union he believed sponsored 'lawless acts' like sit down strikes that blatantly violated the principle of property ownership (AP Letter to Maury Maverick. July 14, 1937. Reel 26). Perales accused Senator Lyndon B. Johnson of not having the nation's interests at heart because of his ties to the CIO and tolerance of 'subversive elements' (AP "Speech to be delivered by Alonso S. Perales, Local Attorney, Over KABC and K?SA today (June 27, 1941)" Addressed "Mis dignos conciudadanos . . ."). In 1954, he declared he was "100%" in support of Senator Joe McCarthy's anti-communist investigations, just months before the U.S. Senate censured the Wisconsin politician (AP letter to Carlos Castañeda. March 17, 1954. Reel 25).

Perales was also an advocate of a tough foreign policy. When living in Nicaragua he said ". . . the best remedy that Uncle Sam could invent for radicals and bolshevists [sic] in the United States would be to ship them to Nicaragua, all expenses paid, and keep them here for about six months. They would be cured forever and would be tickled to death to return to the good old U.S.A." (AP Letter to Canales, J. T. June 9, 1928. Reel 15). In a series of letters to President Dwight D. Eisenhower, Perales called for a more confrontational approach with the Soviet Union, especially for its growing influence in Cuba. He told the President it was time for the United States to say "those Nations who are not with us are against us." He called for a revival of the Monroe Doctrine and, more ominously, war: "I know that such action on the part of our Government would probably hasten the day when we must come to blows with Russia, but we have to meet Russia in the battlefield some day . . . so we might as well meet her right now." (AP letter to Eisenhower, Dwight D., Oct. 1, 1957–May 16, 1959. Reel 18).

Alonso Perales did not suffer dissidents gladly. He was infuriated when communist labor organizers Homer Brooks and Emma Tenayuca were invited to speak in San Antonio's municipal auditorium (Vargas, 1997). Brooks and Tenayuca were organizing Mexican-American pecan shellers in San Antonio who labored under poor working conditions and were facing a reduction in their wages. However, Perales wanted nothing to do with either of them. In a radio address he strongly condemned anyone who gave who gave aid and comfort to the two activists and those who suggested their work aided San Antonio's Mexican-American population (AP "Radio Talk to be made by Alonso S. Perales Over station KABC, Friday, May 2nd, at 6:45 PM." Addressed to "My fellow Americans." Begins with "I am very happy to have . . ." No date. [ca May 2, 1944] Reel 13).

An exchange between Perales and Congressman Maury Maverick over this incident reveals the degree to which anti-communist fanaticism clouded his thinking about American politics and civil rights. Perales accused the Congressman of supporting the communist movement by backing labor unions like the CIO. Maverick countered by asking Perales if it was lawless for workers to be shot by the police or if it was Constitutional to arrest picketers. He added that workers organized unions because of the injustices they bore, not because of communist agitation (Maury Maverick letter to Perales. July 17, 1937. Reel 26). When Perales then asked him to sign a document declaring he was not a communist, an exasperated Maverick replied, "it is absolutely false that I have ever catered to any communists—you know that yourself, and I regret very much indeed that a man of your intelligence would repeat such a thing." He reminded Perales that the United States Constitution protected minorities ". . . such as Latin-Americans who are so often persecuted by brutal and ignorant police officials." He then accused Perales of making paranoid claims about 'certain forces' at work to undermine the government and said the best way to defeat communism was to achieve economic justice, especially for ". . . your people, *who have the lowest wage scale of any group in the entire United States of America.*" (Maverick, Maury. Letter to Perales. April 4, 1938. Reel 26). Maverick told Perales to quit wasting both their time on the issue and that other things of much greater importance like housing, wages, discrimination, and ". . . staying out of Mr. Hitler's war" demanded his attention (Maury Maverick letter to Perales. September 7, 1939. Reel 26). He told Perales that a democracy could not be sustained through dictatorial tactics and it was patriotic to protect freedom of speech, ". . . and by that I mean freedom for all who care to speak." (Maury Maverick letter to Perales. April 4, 1938. Reel 26).

Perales appeared not to comprehend Maverick's argument. Nor did he appreciate the benefits that might accrue to Mexican Americans through protected speech, unionization and an expanded social welfare state. In an odd series of letters, Perales continued to hound Maverick with accusations, telling him that "the issue will not be whether a man is a good American or not for one may be a Communist, a Fascist or a Nazist [sic] and still be a good American [rather] the issue will be whether you believe in the *present form* of the US. Government . . . and whether you continue to encourage those that do not believe in them and are working to overthrow the same."

(AP Perales to Maury Maverick. March 31, 1938. Reel 26). In a follow up letter, Perales added to the confusion by asserting he supported Constitutionally guaranteed protection of free speech, but not if it were used ". . . to bring about a change in our present system of government . . ." (AP letter to Maverick. April 6, 1938. Reel 26).

Perales never clarified what kinds of change were acceptable within a constitutional framework or his understanding of the relationship between politics, race, and socio economic mobility. A defining feature of LULAC politics was the belief that, once free of racial discrimination, individual Mexican Americans would find their place in the socio-economic order according to their abilities and industriousness (Constitution and By-Laws of _____ Council League of United Latin American Citizens of _____ , 1929. [draft] Reel 17). Perales endorsed this egalitarian ethic, arguing that Mexican Americans were up to the challenge and demonstrated the ability to match or even surpass the accomplishments of any other group (AP "Conferencias en pro del mejoramiento de los mexicanos." Aug. 2, 1924. Reel 13). Nonetheless, Perales had little more to say about social change or the economics of race, even at the height of the Great Depression. He spoke out against the starvation wages pecan shellers received while farmers reaped high profits, yet failed to explore the foundation of that unequal relationship (AP "Mr. Chairman, Ladies and Gentleman: I am indeed very happy to have . . ." RE: "What kind of education do Latin-American citizens want for their children?" no date. Reel 13). In the late 1940s, Perales denounced the Bracero Program, arguing that Mexican workers would undercut native worker wages and force them into the migrant stream (AP Perales to Watson Miller, Commissioner of Immigration. November 24, 1947. Reel 20). However, beyond a vague call for wage fairness, he did not probe the causes of poverty and unemployment or identify policies that might alleviate their consequences (AP "Mexicanos: Educad a vuestros hijos." No date. Reel 13; AP letter to Menefee, Mr. Selden C., WPA Director of Research, Washington DC. Feb. 24, 1939. Reel 20).

Conclusion

Scholars must take great care in generalizing from the political work of an individual, and in assessing the influence of an individual activist—particularly one who lived many years before. Alonso Perales' importance stems from his central role in founding the League of United Latin American Citizens and a decades-long leadership role in the Mexican-American civil rights movement. One can more reliably analyze the significance of an organization and social movement by utilizing multiple data sources like articles in the popular press, internal publications, speeches by various leaders and the written materials left by activists in order to assess their significance and impact (See Torres and George Katsiaficas, eds. 1999; Vigil 1999; Warren 2001; Garcia, Ignacio 1989; Munoz, 2007). Individual activists, on the other hand, often lead messy, conflict-ridden lives that can diverge significantly from the movements in which they participate. Their lives are also complicated by the ebb and flow of politics, the details of which are found in great abundance in Perales' archival collection. For example, he did not hesitate to make his views known and could be brutally frank when it came to the political organizations of his day or his associates.[6] Perales thought the Order Knights of America, a precursor of LULAC, was ineffective, producing more talk than results (AP letter to Mauro M. Machado. February 5, 1927. Reel 16). He criticized LULAC for creating a leadership selection system that resulted in presidents he felt were incompetent or unqualified. Perales called one LULAC President a tool of the Mexican Consulate and another 'rotten and good for nothing' who was given to drinking and, when intoxicated, violent and abusive (AP "Muy estimados conciudadanos y hermanos de raza." Begins with "Me congratulo de tener la oportunidad . . ." No date. Reel 13). He criticized other activists for their poor judgment, lack of commitment, ineffectiveness and cowardice (AP letter to Contreras, Hernán H. No date. Reel 15; Perales to Luz, Saenz, J. de la. Saenz May 21, 1927. Reel 16; AP letter to Carlos Castañeda. November 30, 1953. Reel 25; AP letter to Contreras, Hernán H. April 2, 1934. Perales to Luz, Saenz, J. de la June 8, 1928. Reel 16). During election years, Perales believed he knew which candidates were best qualified for office and thought less of those who disagreed with him (Perales to Carlos Castañeda. September 13, 1954. Reel 25).

We learn Perales was frustrated by a lack of support from other Mexican Americans. He despaired at times, and once confided to a friend that they ". . . will just simply not back us up. The only time they show interest is when they are hurt. On the spur of the moment they holler 'murder' but they then go to sleep and forget all about it" (AP Letter to Castañeda, Carlos E. April 9, 1946).[7] Long an advocate of economic incorporation, Perales was disappointed to see Mexican Americans graduate from college and successfully pursue their careers without contributing time or energy to their community (AP Perales to Garza, Luis R., March 26, 1938. Reel 18).[8] He was particularly annoyed that his self-published book *Are We Good Neighbors?* sold so few copies (AP Perales to Jack Danciger. October 19, 1948. Reel 26).[9] Perales invested a substantial sum of money on the project and thought the poor sales reflected a lack of support from 'his own people' (AP Letter to Jack Danciger. August 26, 1949. Reel 26).

There are enough gaps and inconsistencies in his writing to suggest that the ideological foundation of LULAC and other groups in which Perales participated were collaborative projects. Perales was a key player in the early and formative years of LULAC, but his thinking departed from the organization's tenets in significant ways. First, he held that racial discrimination was more severe and resilient than did LULAC's official doctrine. He assumed that most Anglo politicians and the great majority of the white population held deeply racist sentiments and negotiated with Mexican Americans in bad faith. Although Perales admired the American society's constitutional government and its democratic ideals, he doubted Mexican Americans would ever be allowed meaningful participation in its system of checks and balances. Perales repeatedly said that LULAC was doing its part to produce the "best, purest citizens—true and loyal" but feared that America would not reciprocate and assimilate Mexican Americans as it had other groups. Group solidarity was necessary in order to overcome racism, but Perales doubted equality would be achieved during his lifetime. Hence, Perales' insistence on proportional representation in government and public employment was born of a deep mistrust of Anglo Americans. These negative sentiments were articulated when Perales was engaged in struggles whose outcome was not known, but it is a reminder that even the most conservative Mexican-American civil rights leaders had serious misgivings about the society they venerated.

Perales' perspective on the power of group boundaries and identity complicated his relationship with LULAC and its belief in social incorporation. He assumed that, given an equal opportunity, Mexican Americans were fully capable of economic incorporation into American society, but he was so committed to his cultural heritage it is difficult to imagine that he would endorse complete cultural assimilation. Perales believed every social group had its own unique culture and Mexican Americans were no different. He defended the community's history, cultural practices and language because it was under constant attack in Anglo dominated society, but his working assumption was that they were intrinsically valuable and needed no further justification. It is less clear how he believed Mexican Americans should contend with the cultural pressures imposed by the Anglo majority. LULAC resolved this dilemma by urging its members to become bilingual and bicultural, and to adopt the culture and mores of the majority while preserving and promoting their own heritage. Perales lived this ideal, writing and speaking English and Spanish with ease, but came close to characterizing Mexican-American culture as an inherent trait. He knew that his extraordinary abilities earned him a place in an Anglo dominated profession and a leadership position in Texas politics that few could emulate. What remains unclear is the degree to which Perales and the civil rights leadership elite believed straddling both worlds was a realistic option for others.

Perales' claim for a white identity should be understood in a similar light. The argument that Mexican Americans were Caucasian was more than a personal bias or an attempt to avoid the legal restrictions of Jim Crow laws. Perales argued vehemently that Mexican Americans were Caucasians, but he believed the racial and cultural differences between groups were profoundly important. Perales struggled for social incorporation but held fast to his cultural traditions, always relishing the opportunity to be a part of community events and celebrations. Perhaps he did not discuss the ways economic incorporation and cultural distinctiveness could exist side by side because the prospects for group mobility appeared so remote, but he did write extensively on religion—a potential bridging identity between the races. Perales was a deeply religious man who delivered religious lectures, radio broadcasts and wrote extensively for Catholic newspapers. He never politicized his religion and the first LULAC Constitution, which he helped write, stipulated that its members ". . . respect religious views and never refer to them in our institutions . . ." (Constitution and By-Laws of _____ Council League of United Latin American Citizens of _____ , 1929. Reel 17). However, there is evidence to suggest that he did not think of Catholicism as a bridge between the racial divide. At various points he referred to Mexican-American religious practices as unique cultural practices, distinct from those of the Anglo majority (AP "El Matrimonio Cristiano." September 12, 1952; AP "Preparacion Para un Hogar Feliz." May 23, 1952. Reel 14).[10]

Another issue that merits further study is the way civil liberties and constitutional protections were understood by early Mexican-American civil rights activists. Given the severity of racial exclusion Perales experienced and witnessed, it is paradoxical that he was so intolerant of groups and ideas he disliked. His aversion to any person or group with a remote or imagined link to revolutionary activity drew his ire and hobbled his thinking, even in the face of strong counter-arguments. One route would be to explore the relationship between Mexican-American civil rights organizations and labor unions. Perales' ideological rigidity made him suspicious of labor unions, even as poorly paid agricultural workers struggled to organize in Texas and other parts of the Southwest. Perales disapproved of Emma Tenayuca's organizing work among San Antonio's pecan shellers, all while being sympathetic to their plight. However, he offered no alternate to unionization and did not say how civil rights activism was different from labor organizing, or how it might help society's most vulnerable workers.

Finally, Perales was oddly silent on the political economy and economic mobility. Education was the key to a better life but he never explored the relationships between the need for greater educational opportunities, grinding poverty and the harsh discrimination Mexican Americans confronted at every turn. He had an unfailing faith in the abilities of his people to overcome adversity, but wrote little about poverty or *how* it might be overcome. Moreover, Perales declared his lasting allegiance to an unresponsive government and free market capitalism, making it difficult to discern what he believed constituted a just state of affairs. He once said that social stratification was the result of 'natural' forces in society and that real integration came over the long term with better education and interracial understanding but he never returned to the topic. ("Rambling Around." No date. Reel 13). It is possible he believed that solving the problems of voting rights, educational reform, segregation, and all the other issues that consumed his attention constituted the roadmap to a better society. If this is true, then activism was democracy in action and, given enough time, his people would eventually find their own solutions.

References

Alonso S. Perales Papers. Courtesy of Special Collections, University of Houston Libraries.

Notes

[1]He addressed listeners with phrases like "Mis distinguidos conciudadnos," "Mis dignos conciudadanos y hermanos de Raza," "Mis dignos conciudadanos," and "Mis dignos conciudadanos." See Reel 13.
[2]He published many of his letters on the subject in *En Defensa de mi Raza*, pp. 25-47.
[3]In a series of letters Perales listed his expectations. [Kilday to Perales September 9, 1940]; Deputy Sheriff [Perales to Kilday October 5, 1940]; janitor [Perales to Kilday October 128, 1940; 'jail matron' [Kilday to Perales October 22, 1940]; clerk at county jail [Perales to kilday November 1, 1940]; elevator operator [Kilday to Perales November 2, 1940]; janitor [Kilday to Perales November 2, 1940]; jail guard or doorman [Perales to Kilday November 18, 1940. Reel 26.
[4]See Committee of One Hundred Citizens and League of Loyal Citizens. Reel 25.
[5]"Ladies and Gentlemen: The Public Affairs Forum takes pleasure . . ." KONO Broadcasting Station, March 3, 1941.

[6]His own history of LULAC's formation is a narrative of these conflicts. See "El Verdadero Origin de la Liga de Ciudadanos Unidos Latinoamericanos." In Perales, Alonso S. 1937. *En Defensa de mi Raza* Vol 2. (San Antonio: Artes Gráficas), pp. 110-116.

[7]Letter to Castañeda, Carlos E. April 9, 1946.

[8]Perales to Garza, Luis R., March 26, 1938. Reel 18.

[9]Perales claimed *Are We Good Neighbors?* cost $2,475 to publish or $23,097 in 2010 dollars.

[10]"El Matrimonio Cristiano." September 12, 1952; "Preparación Para un Hogar Feliz." May 23, 1952. Reel 14.

The Mexican-American
Generation, Revisited

The Trials of Unity: Rethinking the Mexican-American Generation in Texas, 1948-1960

Joseph Orbock Medina

Introduction

When Alonso S. Perales, José Tomás Canales, Eduardo Idar Sr. and several other Mexican-American leaders founded the League of United Latin American Citizens (LULAC) in 1929, they consolidated elite and middle-class power that would dominate the organizational landscape for the next two decades. LULAC bore the vestments of officialdom for Latino U.S. citizens in their quest for equality with Anglo Americans.[1] Previous groups, such as El Primer Congreso Mexicanista, the numerous *mutualistas* (mutual aid societies), and the Order Sons of America, advocated for Latino interests and politicized the Latino population (Orozco, 2009, p. 66). However, none of these organizations captured the Mexican-American public sphere in Texas as completely as LULAC would.

With a strategy of conspicuous U.S. patriotism and innocuous middle-class assimilationism, LULACers offered a program of group progress that would be palatable in a society dominated by Anglos. Furthermore, the founders succeeded in generating enough cohesion to form a viable, if embattled, political bloc. By the end of the Great Depression, nearly every prominent, educated, Mexican-American man in Texas had joined a LULAC council.

As troops returned home from the battlefields of World War II, many Latinos became disenchanted with how little LULAC strategy was benefitting average Mexican Americans. In an effort to address the shortcomings of incremental reform, some progressive Mexican-American leaders formed alternative organizations with more aggressive tactics. George I. Sánchez's American Council of Spanish-Speaking People and Hector P. García's American G.I. Forum were two of the most significant formations of the 1940s.

Historian Mario T. García popularized the term "Mexican-American Generation" to recognize the broad cohort of movement participants from the 1930s through the 1950s. Distinct from the nostalgia of "Mexicanist" activists of the early twentieth century and the cultural nationalism of Chicanos, those in the Mexican-American Generation emphasized a claim to equal civil rights by virtue of their U.S. citizenship.

García carefully acknowledges the subgroupings of "middle class, working class, radicals, and intellectuals" in the Mexican-American Generation, but emphasizes that a political unity prevailed due to disillusionment with the "contradictions between American ideals and practices" (M. García, 1989, pp. 19-20). His seminal book, *Mexican Americans*, identified LULAC as this "generation's" organizational centerpiece (M. García, 1989, pp. 1-3). Others portray post-World War II Texas Mexican-American activists as more aggressive, yet ideologically similar versions of the pre-war ethnic leadership (D. Gutiérrez, 1995, p. 155; Rodriguez, 2007, p. 196).

Mexican-American leaders universally opposed *de facto* segregation. Aside from this accord, the supposed unity of their namesake "generation" continuously broke down in the 1950s. Pitched infighting reveals conflicts over political philosophy and legitimacy that split the most prominent Mexican-American leaders in Texas. Rather than arising strictly from social class or whiteness, these conflicts engaged competing visions of political heritage.

Historian Carlos Kevin Blanton has recognized some of the internal contentions of the postwar period, but frames his argument around the alienation of Mexican nationals from the Mexican-American civil rights movement in the early 1950s (Blanton, 2009, p. 299). Although many postwar Mexican-American leaders advocated against both legal and undocumented workers from Mexico, the Mexican-American Generation had long established a tradition of *tactically* excluding Mexicans from the civil rights movement based on citizenship. This sterling contradiction was not new in the 1950s—in 1927 Mexican citizens had been dramatically barred from the talks that led to the formation of LULAC (Orozco, 2009, p. 120). The younger, postwar Mexican-American leadership did not emphasize the broad transnational racial unity that would be constructed in the later Chicano Movement, but neither did they pioneer the exclusion of Mexican nationals from civil rights advocacy in Texas. Furthermore, this strategy did not necessarily reveal the innermost desires of Mexican-American leaders. They certainly recognized the connectedness of Mexican and U.S. Latinos. Rather, Mexican Americans in the mid-twentieth century found U.S. citizenship as their most potent weapon. Though perhaps repugnant from a post-Chicano perspective, Mexican Americans largely excluded Mexican nationals from their advocacy as a *pragmatic* measure in the high-stakes struggle against white supremacy.

While prominent Mexican-American leaders in Texas outwardly preached ethnic unity (at least among their fellow U.S. citizens,) organizational and tactical changes following World War II created tension in the broader movement. The Mexican-American movement for civil rights and equality had been nominally consolidated under LULAC in 1929, but by the early 1950s, the postwar settling of Mexican-American activism in Texas has spawned organizational challenges to LULAC's hegemony. The American Council of Spanish-Speaking People and the American G.I. Forum, among others, sapped power from LULAC, even though at times they made similar public calls for Mexican-American equality. These new groups emphasized the working-class interests of their membership in addition to broader ethnic goals, such as desegregation.

From the end of World War II through the1950s, Mexican-American Civil Rights activists in Texas struggled to redefine the Mexican-American political agenda. Conservatives, progressives and radicals, representing varied social classes, all vied for intellectual dominance over the Mexican-American public sphere. More than any one organization or generation, the collective public consciousness of Latinos across the state is best conceptualized as an arena unto itself. While historians have used LULAC, or the "Mexican-American Generation," or even the G.I. Forum as synecdoche for prevailing Mexican-American politics, these groups were themselves severely fractured. In an effort to control the *prize* of ethnic unity, various leaders waged wars of legitimacy against each other in order bring particular partisan ideologies to the fore. On the occasion of this present conference honoring the acquisition of Alonso S. Perales' personal papers by the University of Houston, it is fitting to situate him within the postwar milieu.

Scholars have rightly acknowledged Alonso S. Perales as a leading crusader in the fight to defend the essential dignity of the "Latin Race," particularly with his treatise *En Defensa de mi Raza*. Like many of his fellow activists of the "Mexican-American Generation," he had a diverse set of ideas on how to best achieve the specific business of reform. Perales also had political commitments, loyalties, and grudges that tempered the character of his involvement with other activists and organizations.

Rather than view Alonso S. Perales and his legacy as part of a triumphal teleology of mid-twentieth-century Mexican-American social and political progress, this essay places him within the volatile partisan politics and grand ideological battles of the post-war era. With such a relatively small cadre of movement insiders, personal relationships, and individual philosophies held great sway in the paternalistic organizations of the Mexican-American Generation. Pointed internal divisions among these leaders mirrored and reinforced broader American debates on labor, social class, and identity. Compromise and contestation from within would define the Movement.

The Formation of LULAC

In Texas, the early leaders of the Mexican-American Generation solidified their reputation when in the late 1920s statewide Latinos, citizens and noncitizens alike, met in Harlingen and again in Corpus Christi to discuss the problems of *la raza* and attempt the formation of a meta-organization to advocate their interests. A wide constellation of Latino organizations operated in the early twentieth century. *Mutualistas* comprised of both U.S. Latinos and Mexican nationals provided support to Latino workers on an equal basis. Organizations such as the Order of Knights of America were open to all members of the "Mexican Race." Other organizations were more restrictive. The Order of Sons of America, for example, catered to U.S. citizens. The Harlingen convention of 1927 brought together leaders from many such groups representing varied social interests and nationalities.

J. Luz Saenz, J.T. Canales, Alonso S. Perales, Clemente Idar, Ed Idar, Sr. and other prominent Mexican Americans called for an organization that would unify disparate efforts at ethnic progress. When talks began, however, issues of citizenship split the convention delegates. Presiding middle-class and elite Mexican Americans insisted that membership in any new organization be restricted to U.S. citizens. Perales, the

Idar brothers and Canales spoke against including Mexican nationals, arguing that their citizenship status would undermine civil rights efforts. After an uproar over the issue, most of the delegates left in protest before the conference resumed with a focus on U.S. citizens (Orozco, 2009, pp. 120-125).

After two more years of intense negotiations, Texas "Latin-American" leaders in Corpus Christi unified several civic organizations into the League of United Latin American Citizens in 1929. As a result of concerted efforts of unified Mexican Americans, LULAC became the foremost organization in the movement for U.S. Latino civil rights. The resulting strategy emphasized middle-class assimilation, one-hundred percent American nationalism, alliance with mainstream Anglos and a respect for Latino culture. Doctors, lawyers, printers and other professionals led the invigorated effort for Latin Americans to gain respectability and equal treatment among Anglos. David Montejano reminds us that some of the race ideas of Anglos regarding respectability, beauty and cleanliness—class aesthetics—were the cultural ground upon which these ideas became salient (Montejano, 1987, p. 232). With such a focus on elites and professionals, these Mexican-American leaders were "inclined to ignore the plight of the poor Mexican workers" (Vargas, 2005, p. 63)

New Forms of Mexican-American Organizing after World War II

Texas Latino soldiers served with distinction in World War II and held high hopes of increased equality after the war, but they found pre-war patterns of discrimination and segregation still prevalent throughout the state. Most beneficial to the self-conception of Mexican Americans, however, was the distinguished war record of these troops. Mexican Americans served throughout the world and died for their country at a higher rate than Anglo soldiers. Most pointedly, out of fourteen Texas soldiers who received the Congressional Medal of Honor, six of them were "Latin Americans."[2] Mexican Americans had undoubtedly served with distinction, and when they returned to the United States, their expectations for an improved stake in the American economy and society increased dramatically.

In South Texas, Mexican-American agricultural workers were locked in cyclical exploitation as Anglo agricultural interests secured post-war legislation allowing them to pay these workers much less than minimum wage.[3] Latinos still found themselves segregated from Anglos in schools, movie theaters and parks. Poll taxes and white primaries hindered political participation. Legal justice also eluded Mexican Americans, for they were excluded from serving on juries in many places throughout the state. Many Mexican-American veterans encountered the unfortunate return to normalcy when unsuccessfully attempting to collect G. I. benefits promised to them by the federal government (Allsup, 1982, pp. 33-35). Motivated by their wartime experience, patriotic Mexican Americans joined existing civil rights organizations and created new ones in order to challenge to the racist establishment in Texas.

In 1948 Dr. Hector P. García of Corpus Christi organized the American G.I. Forum with the initial intention of helping U.S. Latino veterans obtain their G.I. benefits from the sometimes-discriminatory government bureaucracy. Very quickly, the G.I. Forum branched out into agricultural labor reform efforts, poll tax payment drives and health initiatives aimed at bettering the conditions for average working Mexican Americans in Texas.

While the American G.I. Forum had a modest start in securing benefits for veterans and contributing to civil rights efforts initiated by others, the organization rose in power and influence during the 1948-1949 Felix Longoria Affair. The United States Army planned to return the body of Private Felix Longoria to his family in Three Rivers, Texas, after he was killed on a volunteer mission in Luzon, Philippines. When his family contacted the funeral home in Three Rivers to make arrangements, they were told the facilities were not available to "Mexicans."

Felix Longoria's sister-in-law worked with a girl's club sponsored by the G.I. Forum and knew of Dr. García through her involvement in the auxiliary. The Longoria family contacted García and asked for assistance in securing use of the forbidden chapel in Three Rivers, or for arrangements to be made in Corpus Christi. Upon confirming the refusal of service from the Three Rivers funeral home, Dr. García contacted George Groh, a reporter from the *Corpus Christi Caller-Times* who publicized the incident. The G.I. Forum mobilized their entire organization for the cause and significant publicity followed. Messages of support came to the Forum from throughout the state. Dr. García also wrote Senator Lyndon B. Johnson outlining the clear instance of discrimination. Senator Johnson responded with a sharp condemnation of discrimination and secured a tremendous public relations victory for the G.I. Forum. On January 11, 1949, the Senator wrote to Hector García with the news that he had arranged for a fully subsidized burial for Felix Longoria at Arlington National Cemetery (Allsup, 1982, pp. 41-43).

The interment of Pvt. Longoria at Arlington National Cemetery established the American G.I. Forum as a significant force in the Mexican-American civil rights movement. Although the Forum succeeded in the Longoria Affair, the tactics they employed signified a shift from the conciliatory politics of the older, more conservative LULAC founders. Certainly no Mexican-American civil rights activists opposed Longoria's burial in Washington, D.C., but the manner of resolution posed concerns for older LULAC powerbrokers.

In conducting the publicity campaign for the Longoria Affair, the American G.I. Forum and the *Corpus Christi Caller-Times* publicized the names of Anglos in Three Rivers who were connected with the incident, including the funeral home director and the mayor of the town. Despite overwhelming evidence, many Anglos in Three Rivers denied any discrimination had taken place (Allsup, 1982, p. 42). By waging a vigorous media campaign and allying with liberal politicians, the Forum took the Mexican-American movement in Texas in a new direction that achieved a major public relations victory, but increased tensions between the Anglo and Mexican-American communities. Alonso S. Perales, for example, had often forwarded instances of discrimination to the State of Texas or to Mexican officials, but did not necessarily embrace the tactic of publicly embarrassing racists.[4] Even so, Perales recognized the coup and congratulated García in a personal letter regarding the incident (I. Garcia, 2002, pp. 136-137). These two leaders continued cordial correspondence throughout 1950 as Perales sought the G.I.'s support for an anti-discrimination bill (H.P. García, letter to Perales, 20 Dec 1950, Microfilm 2309, Reel 15, Alonso S. Perales Papers).

When LULAC initially formed, the founders imagined they had achieved a substantial measure of control over the direction of Mexican-American civil rights activity, but post-war developments showed that the LULAC monopoly had been broken. Organizationally, LULAC now competed with the popular G.I. Forum, but also with many smaller organizations such as Dr. George I. Sánchez's left-leaning American Council of Spanish-Speaking People (M. García, 1989, p. 253). These more liberal and progressive organizations challenged the status quo in Mexican-American activism, but not due to lack of indoctrination of the conservative LULAC perspectives. Dr. Hector García had served as president of his local LULAC council in Corpus Christi and Dr. George I. Sánchez served as national President of LULAC from 1941-1942. The new ideas emerging from progressive Mexican-American leaders following World War II emphasized results in economic anti-discrimination struggles over the desire that Anglo leaders in the State accept them as social equals.

Texas Pro Human Relations Forum Committee

"En la union está la fuerza."[5]—J.T. Canales

Increased politicization and organizing of Latinos encouraged most Mexican American leaders, but the proliferation of new organizations and activities renewed concern to preserve unification and control of the ethnic movement as a whole. As the G.I. Forum and their allies began to look at labor reform, older LULACers sought to reconsolidate the broader movement. For older Tejano activists, the apparent fractionalization of Mexican Americans among civil rights groups reminded them of the late 1920s. Elite and middle-class LULAC founders such as Judge J.T. Canales, Alonso S. Perales, and J. Luz Saenz had endured difficult negotiations to unite Mexican-American organizations and leaders under the LULAC banner in 1929 (M. García, 1989, p. 29).

LULAC insiders under the conservative leadership of J.T. Canales appealed to all Mexican Americans statewide to come together under a new organization, the Texas Pro-Human Relations Fund Committee. This attempt at unification initially received broad support from all sectors of Mexican-American leadership, but ultimately failed over irresolvable divisions over strategies for opposing Anglo racism that more aggressive, progressive activists pursued.

As a pragmatic organization, the G.I. Forum welcomed the opportunity to collaborate with interested parties. In the summer of 1951, J.T. Canales sent out a proclamation requesting a meeting of all Texas "Latin American" leaders to discuss issues of unification and "modern progress" (Executive Committee Pamphlet, Texas Pro Human Relations Fund Committee, Box 436b, Canales Papers). After a preliminary organizational meeting in Austin, a large group of Mexican-American leaders gathered at the White Plaza Hotel in Corpus Christi on July 29, 1951 to select state officers and a name for what was to be an organization combining their various efforts at social reform. The group included Judge J.T. Canales, Professor Carlos Castañeda, Louis Wilmot, Ed Idar, Jr., Dr. Hector P. García, and many of the other prominent Mexican Americans in the state. A conspicuous absence was that of liberal professor George I. Sánchez, who was invited, but did not attend.

In calling the convention, Canales stressed putting order to the myriad directions of the Texas Mexican-American civil rights movement. He envisioned the creation of "not a new group or organization, but simply a meeting group for the already functioning groups of Latin Americans, joined for a common purpose, and dedicated to the uplifting, in every way, of Citizens of Latin American extraction of Texas" (Executive Committee Pamphlet, Texas Pro Human Relations Fund Committee, Box 436b, Canales Papers). With such a broadly stated purpose, no one could reasonably object in principle to Canales' call. Enthusiasm and a spirit of unity enveloped the conference. After debating names such as "Texas Civic Foundation, Inc." and "Latin Anglo Relations Fund Committee," the group decided upon the "Texas Pro-Human Relations Fund Committee" as the name for the new umbrella organization (Ts. "Minutes of the Latin American State Convention Held at the White Plaza Hotel, Corpus Christi, Texas, on Sunday, July 29, 1951," p. 7, Box 436b, J.T. Canales Papers).

The group selected Dr. H. N. Gonzales, J.T. Canales's nephew, as Chairman of the State Executive Committee and Dr. Hector Garcia as First Vice-Chairman. In turn, Dr. García nominated Canales as Chairman over the convention, and Canales was unanimously approved. Canales asked lawyer Gus García to give the opening address. In a few months the attorney would join James de Anda and Johnny Herrera in the defense of accused murderer Pete Hernandez. Their victory in *Hernandez v Texas* proved to be one of the most significant in the history of civil rights litigation. The eloquent speech outlined the sentiments of the Texas Pro-Human Relations Fund Committee organizers:

We, the so-called Latin-Americans, or Mexican-Americans, or Texas-Mexicans—take your choice as to terms because it really does not matter—I say we are here now because we were here first. We have nowhere else to go, and regardless of the wishes on the part of some of our fellow citizens, here we shall remain. Since the birth rate has no respect for the desires of a finicky few, you can expect us to be here in increasingly greater numbers as the years roll by . . . Specifically, the problem of Anglo-Latin relations in Texas can be reduced to its lowest denominator—if at all—on the basis of better educational and job opportunities for the minority—and of a more understanding and less unbending attitude on the part of the majority . . . Let there be no mistake about this: we are not here to form a new organization. If anything, we have too many organizations already—many of whose leaders have grown indolent and sedentary—who assume stuffy poses and bask in the glory of lofty title, while the world around their ivory towers is on fire . . . I believe that it is high time you and I assumed our full responsibility and that, working together unselfishly in a spirit of harmony and mutual respect, we raise our fellow men, and ourselves, to the position to which we are entitled in a truly democratic society. (Ts. "Minutes of the Latin American State Convention Held at the White Plaza Hotel, Corpus Christi, Texas, on Sunday, July 29, 1951," p. 11-16, Box 436b, J.T. Canales Papers).

Immediately following the convention at the White Plaza Hotel, Judge Canales and the Executive Committee of the Texas Pro-Human Relations Fund publicized their organization throughout the state. In the initial statement of the Fund to the state's "Latin-American component," the Executive Committee outlined the three purposes agreed on at the convention: 1) to promote understanding between Latin and Anglo-descended people, 2) to aid and promote any movement seeking to improve the social, economic, educational or political welfare of citizens and residents of Mexican descent, and 3) render financial aid to any organization promoting the defense and protection of American citizen's Constitutional rights (Ts. "Aims and Purposes of the Texas Pro-Human Relations Fund Committee," Microfilm 2309, Reel 22, Perales Papers). Canales urged Latinos throughout Texas to unite under the Texas Pro-Human Relations Fund and to "face the crisis" and "confusion" in the Mexican-American community and to take necessary measures to end the ill-defined "chaos."

Despite the exuberant start, the Texas Pro-Human Relations Fund began to fall apart by the end of the year. In large part, the "chaos" feared by Canales was the operation of Mexican-American civil rights activists outside the conservative rubric he helped establish with LULAC. Certainly nothing in the aims and purposes of the Texas Pro-Human Relations Fund spoke to the methodologies to be employed by the groups the Fund oversaw. Likewise, there was no official definition of the "chaos," what constituted it, nor how the group planned to alleviate it, beyond vague assurances of unity. For the Texas Pro-Human Relations Fund, the core agreements were in rhetoric and the general acknowledgement of discrimination against Latinos.

The Political Establishment in the Rio Grande Valley

More conservative Mexican-American leaders, especially those from the Valley, could enjoy a significant degree of parity with Anglos of their same class. They maintained a tenuous alliance with racial moderates in the Anglo mainstream and preferred to fight overt segregation rather than the stark systemic inequalities suffered by the Mexican-American working class. These particular leaders could find it useful to downplay Anglo racism and systemic discrimination against farm workers. Their commitments to ethnic progress relied on maintaining status within the Anglo establishment and promoting a respectable sentiment towards Latinos in the dominant society. While the Anglo establishment in the Rio Grande Valley overwhelmingly supported the interests of agribusiness, Mexican-American leaders had difficulty formulating a uniform response to labor issues.

In the 1940s, Texas, along with many states in the Southwest, began to supplement their native agricultural workforce with contracted Mexican laborers known as *braceros*. A federally run Bracero Program provided workers to fill *apparent* wartime labor shortages claimed by growers and other employers in the United States. In addition, undocumented workers from Mexico without Bracero contracts—commonly derided as "wetbacks"—found ample farm work in the Rio Grande Valley of South Texas. When either *braceros* or undocumented workers came to Texas, they diluted the labor pool and wages fell for farm workers overall. This led to an upsurge in labor advocacy from within some segments of Mexican-

American leadership. Advocates for U.S. citizen farm workers claimed that sufficient labor already existed, but was simply unable to accept the miniscule wages that prevailed due to an unregulated Mexican workforce.

A series of record cotton crops from the late 1940s to the early 1950s caused anxiety about farm workers because many local Anglos doubted the quantity and quality of domestic Latino labor.[6] As legislators reviewed annual extension of the Bracero program, many Anglos in the Valley lobbied for growers' interests. "The (Latin) American labor is far too inadequate," wrote one Anglo farmer to U.S. Senator Lyndon Johnson, "They could not do this type of labor if they would, and they would not if they could. When can we expect to lessen the stranglehold that labor has on the United States?" (E.G. Gregory, Brownsville, Texas, letter to LBJ, Washington, D.C., 11 May 1951, Senate Papers 1949-1961, Box 232, Legislative File on Alien Labor, LBJ Papers).

The failure of the 1951 citrus crop in the Rio Grande Valley due to a January freeze caused a particularly acute panic by farmers because it ruined a whole season of produce. Out of thirteen million Valley citrus trees, only five million escaped unharmed that season. The distressed Mayor of Donna, Texas, emphasized to Senator Johnson that as of July 1951, his city had been unable to collect the *ad valorem* tax due to the citrus freeze and that he expected the balances to be paid from the cotton crop (Mayor, Donna, Texas, letter to LBJ, Washington, D.C., 3 July 1951, Senate Papers 1949-1961, Box 233, LBJ Papers). Growers ripped out countless dead trees and planted cotton in their stead, hoping to recoup some of the losses. The region's cotton growers predicted that they would need 500,000 *braceros* to complete the harvest.[7] While generally less expensive than domestic farm workers, *braceros* had wage and workplace protections under an international agreement between the United States and Mexico. Undocumented farm workers did not have such protections and were thus favorable to growers looking to pay the lowest amount possible. Borrowing from the American Revolutionary discourse of freedom and liberty, growers lobbied for the cessation of all enforcement designed to regulate such "illegal" labor (W.A. Mitchell, letter to LBJ, Washington, D.C., 29 January 1952, Senate Papers 1949-1961, Box 232, LBJ Papers).

What Price Wetbacks?

Almost concurrently with the organization of the Texas Pro-Human Relations Fund, the G.I. Forum took an overt interest in the affairs of working-class agricultural laborers, overwhelmingly Latinos, in South Texas. Hector García himself had migrated to the United States and saw firsthand the low standard of living for Latino workers along the border. Following García's service as a field doctor in World War II, he treated many Mexican-American and Mexican agricultural workers in his Corpus Christi clinic. Dr. García carried his ideas on the issue to the national stage in August, 1950 when he testified before President Harry Truman's Commission on Migratory Labor. The Commission studied the effects of foreign migrant labor on the Mexican-American population and made recommendations to the U.S. Congress on extension of the Bracero Program. Speaking on the detrimental effect of inexpensive foreign labor in physically displacing domestic Mexican-American workers, García asked, "Would 30,000 Americans migrate out of this area if they did not have to? Would they expose their children to sickness and death if they did not have to? Would they leave their homes and schools to migrate to uncertainty if they could make a living at home?" (Allsup, 1992, pp. 105-106).

LULAC, in contrast, traditionally focused on creating opportunities for the middle class, especially through a strict program of cultural Americanization. A lucky few of the LULAC founders were able to access Anglo education. Many more received training from the United States military in World War I (Kaplowitz, 2005, p. 12). Despite a few of these older LULACers being able to "pass" (or at least get by) in the white world, most were not able to experience real equality. Nevertheless, LULAC embraced one-hundred percent Americanism and continued their strategic support of capitalism, democracy and Cold War notions of progress. As such, more conservative LULAC leaders had some intellectual problems with aggressively pursuing workers rights—particularly for culturally unAmericanized Mexican Americans in South Texas.

Mexican Americans picking fruit, vegetables and cotton in the Rio Grande Valley faced difficult living and working conditions in the late 1940s and early 1950s. When Texas Good Neighbor Commissioner member Pauline Kibbe issued a report on Valley Agricultural labor in 1947, she claimed that the prevailing wage laborers earned was 25 cents per hour—50 cents lower than the national minimum wage. Valley farmers replied that she was misinformed; the prevailing wage was actually 20 cents per hour.[8]

In addition to the "official" reports on Valley labor made by government officials such as Kibbe, academic researchers began to take interest in the labor crisis that had developed since World War II. Sociologists Olin Leonard from Vanderbilt University and Lyle Saunders from the University of New Mexico released a study titled "The Wetback in the lower Rio Grande Valley of Texas" in 1951. The University of Texas at Austin published the report and faculty member George I. Sánchez supervised the project. Like previous studies, the "Wetback Report" (as it was called) elaborated on the poor conditions in which Valley agricultural workers lived. The report created controversy, however, due to its criticism of Anglo discrimination in South Texas.

The lynchpin of their report hinged on the observation that "since the wetback is often identified with the Spanish-speaking citizen population, the latter suffers any stigma resulting from such behavior" (Saunders and Leonard, 1951, p. 46). Undocumented Mexican workers in the Rio Grande Valley undoubtedly affected Mexican Americans. Anglos in Texas were well aware of the differentiation between "Latin Americans" and Mexican citizens. In normal discourse and treatment, however, Anglos often classified both as "Mexican." This uncomplicated characterization carried significant prejudices that justified ethnic inequality. In an effort to present vivid evidence of their conclusions, Saunders and Leonard interviewed several prominent Anglos in the Valley to glean their ideas about Spanish-speaking people. They interviewed a Valley politician, an employee of the Texas Employment Commission, a farmer and immigration enforcement officials. These interviews, all anonymously presented, provide candid interpretations of the interplay among ethnicity, citizenship and labor.

Saunders and Leonard alleged a "definite pattern of uniformity in the attitudes of English-speaking people towards wetbacks in the Valley." They further contended that an "elaborate system of rationalizations" had evolved to explain their utilization. Anglos in the Valley claimed an acute understanding of Spanish-speaking people, both Mexican and U.S. citizens. Constructed characterizations of both Latino groups justified the status quo. According to the unnamed politician from the Valley:

The local situation is not so bad. It works out to just about the best advantage of everyone. The farmer needs labor; the wetbacks need work; and the local Spanish-speaking people have a gypsy spirit that makes them want to travel. They just can't resist going north each year, and it is fortunate that there are wetbacks around to take their place. Then, too, the local Spanish-speaking people are tending to leave agriculture. They don't like the hard work. They are beginning to want to get white-collar jobs . . . Relations between English-speaking and Spanish-speaking people are good. The people eat together and visit together. They don't intermarry much. Although there is no discrimination in the Valley, of course there is segregation in a few things, but that is for hygienic, not racial reasons. Spanish-speaking people live in their own part of town and have their own businesses. They prefer it that way. They are excluded from swimming pools and barber shops. The exclusion from pools is because it is not possible to tell the clean ones from the dirty, so we just keep them all out (Saunders and Leonard, 1951, pp. 66-67).

The authors also interviewed a farmer with sizable acreage west of Mission, Texas. He also claimed that Mexican Americans were lazy and unwilling to work in agriculture:

They lack initiative and ambition; they are content to go north and earn some money during the summer and then return here and live on it the rest of the year. They've been spoiled by too many advantages; too many welfare, education, and other services. If you give a man something for nothing, you ruin him. As soon as you begin to Americanize a Mexican he's no longer any good. He just won't work anymore . . . They've been spoiled by the unions with their talk of a forty-hour week and security for everybody. What a man needs is to get out and work and earn his own security . . . I know, because I've ruined some Mexicans by being too good to them. (Saunders and Leonard, 1951, p. 70)

Several other interviews made similar claims.

The report initiated heated debate. Saunders, Leonard, and Sánchez had created a polemic that distressed many Anglos in the State, but also divided leaders within the Mexican-American civil rights movement. Ostensibly the study advocated economic justice for Mexican-American workers, but those ends did not necessarily fit the strategic aims of all the Mexican-American leadership. Throughout the year after the report's release, influential Mexican Americans were forced to choose sides as various factions responded to the controversy and reformed the civil rights movement.

Backlash

The aggressive techniques of Sánchez, Leonard, and Saunders ignited immediate controversy. The content of the interviews certainly disturbed Latino critics of the report, but the open condemnation of the Valley Anglo population conflicted with the fundamental principles of the LULAC generation. Alonso S. Perales, always a defender of *la raza,* became incensed over the interviews. He wrote to Hector García in December 1951:

I sincerely hope that your Organization will continue to press for the names of the individuals who insulted our people on pages 65 to 88 in the pamphlet entitled: THE WETBACK IN THE LOWER RIO GRANDE VALLEY OF TEXAS. Don't give up under any circumstances. Keep up the struggle until you get the names of the offenders. I wrote to Dr. George I. Sánchez requesting the names, but he declined to give them . . . I sincerely hope also that your organization will not, under any circumstances, give anyone a clean bill or OK in connection with the preparation and publication of said pamphlet. To do so would amount to placing the stamp of approval upon the utterances of those who stated that all Mexicans have syphilis, lice, and are stupid and cowards. Sánchez never should have approved the pamphlet much less made possible its publication . . ." (A. Perales, letter to to H. P. García, 06 December 1951, Box 436a, J.T. Canales Papers)

Sánchez, who despite being invited, had never participated in a function of the Texas Pro-Human Relations Fund Committee, increasingly came under attack for his role in the "Wetback Report." Criticism of the professor increased when he openly defended both the substance and methodology of the study. Amidst the controversy, Texas State Chairman of the G.I. Forum Ed Idar, Jr., wrote to Sánchez, asking him to clarify the debate from his perspective. Sánchez responded to his detractors with a vigorous defense:

The question the critics raise about those four pages are: (1) Are the statements attributed to (the anonymous Anglos) true reproductions of interviews with those men? (2) Should those anonymous opinions be publicized . . . As to the first of these questions: emphatically "yes!" . . . These statements were in formal interviews, to two highly trained and widely experienced sociologists . . . As to the second of the questions: it is difficult to answer this question to the satisfaction of laymen; that is, to the satisfaction of those unfamiliar with what is common procedure in sociological research . . . before a malady can be cured it must be identified-whether that malady be a disease, ignorance, or prejudice . . . The facts must be faced *for our own good.* (George I. Sánchez, letter to to Ed Idar, Jr., 18 January 1952, Activities and Organizations Box 5, Folder 4, Ed Idar, Jr. Papers)

Gus García supported the academic perspective on the issue taken by the report and wrote to LULAC co-founder Alonzo Perales expressing his views:

I do not agree with you when you say that is cowardly because the authors do not give a source of quotes. If you will look into the ethics of social researchers you will learn that they, like us lawyers, have certain restrictions placed upon divulging information as to sources of material . . . (Gus García, letter to Alonso S. Perales, 06 December 1951, Box 214, Folder 15, J.T. Canales Papers)

Fault lines within the Texas Mexican-American community increasingly divided more conservative from more liberal-minded reformers. Organizations and chapters of Mexican Americans around the state faced a difficult decision when deciding to endorse or condemn the report. LULACers, prodded by conservative founders, largely rejected the study while the American G.I. Forum of Texas endorsed the entire report. When local chapters questioned or strayed from the official position of the state organizations in regards to the "Wetback Report," they were quickly castigated, as in the case of the dissident McAllen G.I. Forum in January, 1952.[9] The controversy over the tactical soundness of the report threatened the future of the Texas Pro-Human Relations Fund Committee and its mission of unity for Mexican-American activists. Both J.T. Canales and Hector García pled for a calm and measured debate that would not be divisive. Hector García initially viewed the debate as a personal dispute between George Sánchez and Alonso S. Perales, but the implications of the "Wetback Report" proved more severe (Hector García, letter to the Editor of *La Prensa,*13 December 1951, Box 214, Folder 15, H.P. García papers).

Hector García had offered support of Sánchez and the "Wetback Report" in a December 1951 letter to the editor of *La Prensa* newspaper, while J.T. Canales consistently opposed the report's methodology. Despite their difference of opinion, both leaders attempted to follow through on their obligations to the Texas Pro-Human Relations Fund Committee until an *ad hoc* convention in Mission, Texas further escalated hostilities. Some conservative Mexican Americans, including Alonso S. Perales and J. Luz Saenz met at Mission on March 9, 1952 and passed a harsh resolution that was publicized throughout the state in both Spanish and English.

. . . BE IT RESOLVED by the Mexican people of the Lower Rio Grande Valley as well as of other sections of the State, in general convention assembled in the City of Mission . . . FIRST: that (Olen Leonard, Lyle Saunders, and George I. Sánchez) as well as the University of Texas be and they are hereby publicly condemned by the Latin American citizenry of the Lower Rio Grande Valley . . . SECONDLY: That all individuals and organizations who have gone on record as approving and praising the publication of said insults to the Mexican people of the Lower Rio Grande Valley generally be and are likewise hereby condemned . . . (Ms. J. Luz Saenz and Santos De La Paz,"Draft of Resolution Adopted by Leaders of the Latin American Citizenry of the Rio Grande Valley", Box 215, Folder 4, H.P. García Papers)

J. T. Canales had preached unity and calm for months, but he played an active role in designing the harsh condemnations of other Mexican-American leaders when he showed up at Mission. Alonso S. Perales wrote to Canales, "Those guys have it coming. You gave them a good blasting at Mission and I congratulate you, Prof. Saenz, Mr. De la Paz and all others who helped. You all did a grand job indeed" (Alonso S. Perales, letter to J.T. Canales, 29 March 1952, Box 436a, J.T. Canales Papers). The desire for pan-Latino unity in Texas all but disappeared among the conservative LULAC founders. These men would not put the goal of maintaining ethnic solidarity above their political and social ideologies. LULAC co-founder J. Luz Saenz wrote to J.T. Canales in early April, 1952, "Yes, indeed, echoes and re-echoes are still resounding over there in the north, east, and west about our convention at Mission . . . why are we to invite everybody, including *bolsheviques* who do not approve our doings to our meetings when we are still in an effervescence [sic] state? I think it is our duty to consolidate our lines first and then attack or resist outside attacks" (J. Luz Saenz, letter to J.T. Canales, 02 April 1952, Box 436a, J.T. Canales Papers).

Soon after the release of the Mission resolution, it became clear several influential members of the Texas Pro-Human Relations Fund Committee were leaving the group. Gus García and Ed Idar, Jr. had worked with George Sánchez in the American Council of Spanish-Speaking People. They, Hector García, and the American G.I. Forum had been publicly attacked in the Mission resolution. J.T. Canales and other prominent Texas Pro-Human Relations Committee Fund members had orchestrated the condemnations in Mission, but claimed nothing more than a desire for unity. With no productive discussion on resolving the debates, it became clear within weeks that the Texas Pro-Human Relations Fund would dissolve. Hector García, Gus García, Ed Idar, Jr. and J.T. Canales himself had all left the Fund by the spring of 1952 (J.T. Canales, letter to H.N. Gonzales, 21 March 1952, Box 436a, J.T. Canales Papers). With no effective mechanisms for problem solving, the Texas Pro-Human Relations Fund Committee failed to achieve the aims that were set out in their opening convention at the White Plaza Hotel in Corpus Christi. Although originally intended to promote unity, the organization essentially functioned as an attempt of the older generation of Mexican Americans who founded LULAC to rein in younger activists who had advocated liberal and sometimes confrontational strategies for success.

Controversy over the "Wetback in the Lower Rio Grande Valley" ostensibly centered on the use of anonymous quotes and the "insults" printed about people of "Latin-American extraction" in South Texas. The divide among Mexican-American leaders in the early 1950s, though, ran along strict lines of social and economic class interest. Despite many recently released reports on the reprehensible conditions for Latino laborers in the Valley, J.T. Canales sympathized with Anglo farmers. In a letter to State Senator Rogers Kelley, Canales addressed Anglo concerns over the "Wetback Report:"

> It was inspired by Dr. George I. Sánchez of the University of Texas. He is a native of New Mexico and he has an extreme left psychology . . . I personally told Dr. Sánchez that his investigation and cases that he cited were misleading;

that for every case of injustice and mistreatment of our Latin Americans by Anglo Americans in the Valley, I would mention ten cases where Anglo Americans have been both kind and generous to the Latin American laborers. (J.T. Canales, letter to Rogers Kelley, 17 November 1951, 436a, J.T. Canales Papers)

The established Mexican Americans in the Valley who organized against the "Wetback Report" at the Mission convention had little to gain from supporting working-class Latinos. Indeed, they had much to lose in their goal of achieving equal social standing with their Anglo peers in the middle and upper-class ranks of mainstream American society. The desire to maintain the level of social and economic progress of some Mexican Americans in the early 1950s prohibited the formation of a unified Mexican-American movement. Clashing strategies, as well as divisive class-politics, ensured that the spirit of unity emphasized by the Texas Pro-Human Relations Fund Committee was short lived.

By 1952, the depth and permanence of the split between Mexican-American leaders was undeniable. J.T. Canales, Alonso S. Perales and their collaborators desperately struggled to hold together the old regime in the Texas Mexican-American civil rights movement. Through pleas of ethnic unity they attempted organizational solutions to the fissures over agricultural labor in the Mexican-American Civil Rights movement. Clear ideological shifts occurred, however, when a regional LULAC convention in Corpus Christi approved of the *The Wetback in the Lower Rio Grande Valley* in early 1952, much the same way that the G.I. Forum had. The actions by the LULAC regional came after the very public scuffling over the content and tone of the report.

J.T. Canales became distraught over the condition of both the organization and movement he helped create. He became further distressed when LULACers in San Antonio chose to support George Sánchez as well. He wrote to his nephew Dr. H.N. Gonzalez, a Mexican-American leader in Houston, lamenting the new developments:

If the people in San Antonio think that we have no right to criticize Dr. Sánchez when he does wrong, then there is no democracy in our organization and he is not considered a human being, but a god, and we do not entertain any such views of any human being! Dr. Sánchez never consulted us, or any of his friends, when he approved the Wetback pamphlet, unconditionally, and neither did the G.I. Forum, nor the LULAC Regional Convention. (J.T. Canales, letter to H.N. Gonzales, Houston, 19 Mar 1952, Canales Papers)

The leadership of the Mexican-American movement in Texas had effectively split in 1951 over the issues instigated by the Saunders and Leonard Report. The economic concerns of Tejano landed elites, such as J.T. Canales, differed dramatically from average Mexican Americans. As capitalist agricultural producers, these *patrones* sought to maximize profits and gain favorable political influence to secure their positions. According to Ignacio García, ". . . these *patrones* needed alliances with Anglo-American bosses, who in turn were allied with state politicians, such as the governor or even the U.S. senators" (I. García, 2002, p. 141).

The positions advocated by the G.I. Forum leaders began to prevail in the ethnic community. In 1953 Ed Idar reinforced the Forum's stance on undocumented labor and domestic worker's rights when he coauthored a report entitled "What Price Wetbacks." Largely modeled on the work by Saunders and Leonard, this report was produced with funding from both the G.I. Forum and the American Federation of Labor (Ms., Ed Idar, Jr. and Andrew C. McLennan, "What Price Wetbacks?" Box 5, Folder 6, Ed Idar, Jr. Papers).

Poll Tax Drive

Another series of incidents stoked the unrest between Texas Mexican Americans in the fall of 1955. At this time Texans were required to pay a poll tax prior to voting. This practice directly affected working-class Mexican Americans who voted in low numbers. The G.I. Forum organized a poll tax payment drive in the Rio Grande Valley for the purpose of qualifying Latino citizens to vote who had previously been disenfranchised. Unable to support such a large operation alone, the Forum again teamed up with labor unions. The newly united American Federation of Labor and the Congress of Industrial Organization (AFL-CIO) eagerly supported American workers and joined the poll tax drive.

As Executive Secretary for the American G.I. Forum of Texas, Ed Idar Jr. coordinated the major organizational programs in the state. In 1955, while completing his law degree at the University of Texas, Idar appointed his friend, Valley attorney R.P. (Beto) Sanchez to coordinate the poll tax drive. Five thousand dollars were budgeted for the drive, the cost of which would be shared by both the Forum and the AFL-CIO. The drive operated under the auspices of the Rio Grande Valley Democratic Club, specifically organized for that purpose. With great personal sacrifice, including "letting his law practice go for three months," Sanchez led a successful program that directly challenged the conservative establishment in South Texas (Idar, Jr., letter to Jerry R. Holleman, Executive Secretary Texas State Federation of Labor, AFL, 07 Nov 1955, Box 5, Folder 1, Ed Idar, Jr. Papers).

After the fiasco of the Texas Pro-Human Relations Fund Committee and the controversies over the "wetback" publications, a measured détente of sorts had settled over LULACers and G.I. Forum members. The organizations both endorsed the successful *Hernandez v Texas* case in 1954 that ensured Mexican Americans the right to serve on juries, but generally they avoided close interaction. Old rivalries would soon reignite.

In December 1955, Anglo Texas State Senator Rogers Kelley addressed a LULAC chapter in his McAllen district of the Lower Rio Grand Valley. Kelley charged the G.I. Forum with initiating "class and racial warfare" motivated by "divisive, selfish, and misguided interests, pitting "race against race" and "group against group" with the poll tax drive (H.P. García, letter to Sen. Rogers Kelley, 12 Dec 1955, Box 5, Folder 1, Ed Idar, Jr. Papers). Kelley reasserted the anticommunist sentiment permeating Anglo culture in Texas and perpetuated the popular assumptions of an emasculated and powerless Mexican-American underclass. Though LULAC and the G.I. Forum had their strategic differences, the opposition to Mexican-American voting rights opposed the basic principles of both organizations. Without condemning Senator Kelley directly, LULAC National President Oscar Laurel answered G.I. Forum protests by mentioning LULAC's history of conducting its own poll tax drives. Though varying alliances entangled LULAC and prohibited much active support, the organization was not officially opposed to the G.I. Forum's Valley initiatives in 1955 (Allsup, 1982, p. 71). Even so, LULAC preferred not to become embroiled in the growing hostility between the Forum and Valley Anglos.

The Anglo press throughout the Rio Grande Valley condemned the poll tax drive with the same rhetoric as Senator Kelley. In a letter to Jerry R. Holleman, the Executive Secretary of the Texas State Federation of Labor who represented the AFL's interest in the poll tax drive, Idar related some of the response from Valley media:

> You have probably been given reports concerning the organization of the Rio Grande Democratic Club for the purpose of conducting a poll tax drive in the three counties of the Valley and of subsequent developments thereto, including the most recent ones wherein the Valley press has launched an intensive and vicious campaign against the Forum . . . by virtue of the Forum's "political" affiliation with labor organizations in the poll tax drive. (Idar, Jr., letter to Jerry R. Holleman, 07 Nov 1955, Box 5, Folder 1, Ed Idar, Jr. Papers)

Many of the leading Anglo attorneys and powerbrokers in the Valley favored the antiunion and anticommunist policies of Texas Governor Allan Shivers. They attacked the G.I. Forum through their AFL-CIO ties as well. Writing to Ed Idar in Austin, Beto Sanchez reported on the "smear campaign" being waged by these groups as well:

> The leading Shivercrats like the Edinburg law firms of Kelly, Looney, McLean & Littleton; Rankin, Kilgore, & Cherry; Hendrickson, Bates, & Hall are already rallying their forces to open up at us with the famous CIO smear, a familiar and devastating weapon in the Valley. Carl Brazil, a strong union man, liberal democrat but practiced politician, is in tears. He thinks this will kill the Forum, the last of the liberal Democrats in the Valley, and anything else that is anti-Shivers. But I had a good talk with him yesterday here in my office and in the end he walked out feeling not near as bad as when he walked in. (R.P. Sanchez, letter to Idar, Jr., 07 Oct 1955, Box 5, Folder 1, Ed Idar, Jr. Papers)

Ed Idar and Beto Sanchez expected sharp resistance from conservatives in the Valley, including accusations of un-American sympathies. However, their members' unfailingly patriotic military service to the United States was the key element of the Forum's credibility as a civil rights organization. Idar took particular offense to a series of columns in the *Valley Morning Star* newspaper that discussed the Forum and the Valley poll tax drive of 1955. This newspaper, and many others like it called themselves "freedom newspapers," and adamantly opposed changes to the socioeconomic order in the Valley (Allsup, 1982, p. 71).

Against charges of instigating class warfare, Idar revealed his ideological underpinnings in a letter to the editor:

You print in your masthead the face that the so-called "Freedom" Newspapers believe that one truth is always consistent with another truth, and that your newspapers endeavor to be consistent with the truths expressed in such great moral guides as the Golden Rule, the Ten Commandments, and the Declaration of Independence. This sounds fine, but did your papers ever hear of the saying that you are your brother's keeper, that you should do unto others like you would have them do unto you, that participation in government was the corner-stone of the Jeffersonian philosophy in contrast to the discredited Hamiltonian philosophy that only the aristocratic classes were qualified to govern, and that every man is entitled to life, liberty, and the pursuit of happiness- including Mexicans or Latins as well as members of organized labor . . . p.s. Before you start hollerin' "outside influence," I might caution you that I was born and raised in South Texas, the third generation of my family to do so; that my roots in the Southwest go back prior to the arrival of the Anglo-Saxon colonists from the North . . . (Idar, Jr., letter to Editor of the Valley Morning Star, 1955, Box 5, Folder 1, Ed Idar, Jr. Papers)

Idar and the Forum not only felt they had a defensible position in regards to their poll tax drive, but also a strong sense of geographical and ideological entitlement in the Valley specifically.

Perhaps the most personally offensive developments of the Rio Grande Valley poll tax campaign surrounded a parade. For Veteran's Day in 1955, the American G.I. Forum had been scheduled to march alongside the American Legion, Veterans of Foreign Wars and a National Guard Unit in McAllen for the Hidalgo County Veteran's Day observance (Ramos, 1998, p. 83). First Lieutenant Doug Werner, who led the National Guard unit, withdrew his soldiers' participation in the parade due to the presence of the G.I. Forum. Werner stated that because they met with labor unions and organized a poll tax drive, the G.I. Forum was a political organization, and he did not want to "confuse a patriotic issue with a so-called political movement and that political involvement with the organizations participating with the G.I. Forum in the poll tax drive had no place with Veteran's Day Observance" (Ts., Statement by Idar Jr., 1955, Box 5, Folder 1, Ed Idar, Jr. Papers).

Despite the attempts by the Forum to strictly focus on citizen rights, highly politi-cized goals and techniques continued to influence alliances. State Representative Eli-gio (Kika) de la Garza, with whom the G.I. Forum sought (and expected) an alliance in dealing with the Veteran's Day parade incident, refused to participate in the drive or help with the controversy over the march. Many in the Forum stood by de la Garza when he ran for office, and as the only "Latin American" in the legislature, he occu-pied a significant symbolic role as well. After several attempts by Idar and the Forum to utilize their supposed ally's office for civil rights work, de la Garza wrote them a letter saying, "As to a statement from me concerning this controversy (Veteran's Day parade) which you explain in this letter, all I can say is that I was not involved in it in any form or manner and that I do not want to be involved in it now" (Eligio de la Garza, II, letter to Idar, Jr., 10 Nov 1955, Box 5, Folder 1, Ed Idar, Jr. Papers).

The strong faction of more conservative, incrementalist Mexican Americans and their leaders, like de la Garza, had been resisting the political implications of the G.I. Forum's aggressive policies for years. Regardless of their rhetoric, the Forum did aggravate class relations in Texas with advocacy of worker's rights and they did challenge the established alliances between Mexican Americans and Anglos. The Forum aggravated many older Mexican-American activists with their refusal to accept eventual or partial progress, but in the Valley poll tax drive the G.I.s began to find important friends within the ethnic community who were willing to embrace their tactics. Essentially, the G.I.'s were calling for the reform of class relations between conservative Mexican Americans and the Anglo establishment.

In December 1955, the G.I. Forum asked United States Senator Dennis Chavez of New Mexico to come to the Rio Grande Valley and support the Poll Tax drive. The only Latino in the Senate, Chavez both commanded respect as a Senator and as one of the most distinguished Mexican Americans in the country. After being informed of the political situation in the area, Chavez readily agreed to participate in the Forum's campaign:

I fully agree with the drive that you boys are making to get the American citizens of Mexican descent to express their opinion on Election Day. I would be glad to address three of your gatherings on the border during the month of January. Voting is a duty. I happen to know that in certain areas, including Australia, it is compulsory by law. Of course qualifications must be met, including that of the payment of poll taxes if necessary. Between you and me, poll taxes as such in national elections will be a thing of the past in the not too distant future. I had a short talk with our mutual friend, Lyndon Johnson, leader of the majority in the Senate and like you a fellow Texan. He thought your program was grand and that you should carry it out. He wants you boys to register and vote. How you vote is your business, but nevertheless vote. (Senator Dennis Chavez, letter to Idar, Jr., 29 Dec1955, Box 5, Folder 1, Ed Idar, Jr. Papers)

The patterns of excluding basic rights from working-class Mexican Americans were entrenched in the Valley, but average "Latin Americans" now had powerful friends invested in changing the status quo.

The Valley poll tax drive made people question what they truly believed about citizen's rights, ethnicity and class. For many Mexican Americans, particularly those of the more conservative LULAC variety, the strategies of incremental progress and Anglo accommodation conflicted with the focus on the most basic citizen's rights advocated by the Forum. As LULAC President Oscar Laurel reiterated to the Forum, LULAC had conducted many poll tax drives itself. More progressive activists often accused conservative Anglos of employing a "divide and conquer" strategy among Mexican Americans by allying with the small middle and upper classes at the expense of the large working-class of "Latin Americans." Now the G.I. Forum began to see the same success in dividing some of the traditional LULACers from tenuous conservative alliances.

The Rio Grande Valley had been a hotbed of conservative LULAC resistance to Forum efforts just a few years earlier during the controversy over the "wetback" publications. LULAC founders organized a protest convention against Forum policies at Mission in 1952 and the McAllen chapter of the G.I. Forum defected from the state organization in favor of more conservative practices in the same year. Nevertheless, the Valley poll tax drive elicited such a harsh response from conservative Anglos that many solid LULACers reevaluated their position on the G.I. Forum.

Prominent Houston Attorney John J. Herrera served the President of LULAC during the turbulent years of 1952 and 1953 where he witnessed these incidents, as well as the breakdown and collapse of the Texas Pro-Human Relations Fund that created so much animosity within the ethnic community. Herrera had been instrumental in the *Hernandez* civil rights case, among others, and he certainly advocated the full exercise of such rights by the whole Mexican-American community. In a letter to Ed Idar marked "CONFIDENTIAL!," Herrera elaborated on the growing rift within the LULAC leadership as well as his personal solidarity with the G.I.'s Valley campaign:

> I read with interest your letter to Oscar Laurel (regarding State Senator Kelley's comments) on December 12, 1955. Of course, you have always understood my difference of opinion with the Laredo Clique of Lulac and myself, in that they have always rode along with the status quo and the so-called conservative element of Lulac . . . I have always maintained along with yourself and Dr. Hector García that Shivers has never given our people the representation that they merit in considering us for state jobs such as the state highway patrol, the Texas Rangers and all of the different state boards which carry with them both honorary and remunerative jobs. . . . The recent American G.I. Forum poll tax drive in the Valley naturally was bound to arouse alarm among those politicians who have used the "divide and conquer" strategy among our people. Potentially, the Valley is a great source of political strength for our pole and if the G.I. Forum can cause a civic awakefullness in our people in the Valley it will be the greatest contribution toward the liberation of our pole in the history of Texas . . . Personally Ed, I think all of the Hullabaloo is caused by the basic fear that the Valley Farmer-Rancher-Politico has always had of the labor unions and the possibility of a strong liaison between the Latino and the basic benefits that unionism will grant them. (John J. Herrera, letter to Idar, Jr., 21 Dec. 1955, Box 5, Folder 1, Ed Idar, Jr. Papers)

Herrera, like fellow civil rights attorney Gus García, straddled both LULAC and the G.I. Forum but stood most firmly with the LULAC brand. The League was a well-established voice for Mexican Americans, even if it was weighted towards the elite. Rather than abandon LULAC or publicly crusade for the G.I. Forum exclusively, these more moderate activists sought to harden the LULAC position and bring the organizational leadership out of the conservative "clique" that had been defining the LULAC mission in terms of elite, exclusionary objectives. Furthermore, as the G.I. Forum gained more traction in their efforts, LULAC conservatives and moderates found a growing hostility among Anglos for Mexican Americans in general. In fact, LULACers and Mexican Americans had not benefitted politically in their incrementalist strategy under Governor Shivers. With a poor record of Latino political placement and persistent discrimination, the system of alliances for upper-class Mexican Americans had not proved to be productive. In one of his frequent reports on the Valley poll tax drive, Beto Sanchez outlined the tenuous position of many more conservative Mexican Americans, "One last word- The conservatives are scared, and the Mexican-American conservatives, after the treatment they got from the conservative Anglos in the last major campaign, are beginning to line up with us; the bastards have nowhere else to go . . ." (R.P. Sanchez, letter to Idar, Jr., 07 Oct 1955, Box 5, Folder 1, Ed Idar, Jr. Papers).

The G.I. Forum's role in rallying the Mexican-American vote in 1955 did not result in the immediate repeal of poll taxes or the mass-election of Mexican Americans to public office. They did, however, initiate a shift in the pattern of alliances and expectations of Mexican-American leaders in Texas. Though they had exerted considerable effort, LULAC's leaders had failed to rein in the Forum in the early 1950s. By the middle of the decade, the fiercely independent-minded G.I. Forum reformed the focus of the larger Mexican-American movement to concentrate on the impediments to basic civil rights for average, working-class Mexican Americans. The rise of liberal and moderate reformers signaled a change in the way Mexican-American leaders conducted the business of civil rights in Texas.

Conclusion

The internal conflicts and compromises presented here complicate one of the least-studied periods in Mexican-American civil rights activism. With these ideological contentions layered alongside more traditional Anglo v. Mexican divides, the evolution of activism becomes more dynamic, realistic, and pliable. This casts doubt upon a temporal stasis articulated generationally, framed by the structural changes of the meta-events of the twentieth century. The ever-present concerns of Texas Latino activists representing a variety of class interests, social changes, geographic loyalties and nationalisms have been locked in struggle among one another, as well as against the inequities they all confronted. To ignore the pro-labor, popular interests that challenged LULAC in the 1950s would be as much of an intellectual disservice as downplaying the Mexican-American challenges to the cultural nationalism of the Chicano renaissance. It is becoming increasingly clear that each generation refights the attendant battles of the many peoples carrying a Latino banner. While often sought after, proclaimed and asserted, a deep and comprehensive Latino unity remains elusive.

If Texas Mexican Americans made a "citizenship sacrifice" by strategically excluding Mexican citizens from their organizations, it originated in the early 1900s when Mexican citizens were excluded from the nascent civil rights organizations in South Texas. LULAC's citizenship limitations in the 1920s are only the most conspicuous example. While instructive, paradigms that focus squarely on citizenship tend to obscure the particular context of 1950s Latino activism in Texas. By focusing on the politics within the Mexican-American generation, it becomes clear that the battle for equality was not just against outsiders and not against all Anglos. The struggle for the movement was an ideological one.

Future battles between those "Latin Americans" and emerging Chicano activists in the 1960s reinvigorated internal arguments within the state's ethnic leadership. Chicanos would lament the G.I. Forum and other progressive reformers from the Mexican-American Generation calling them *Tío Tacos*. Though Ed Idar Jr., George Sánchez and Hector García successfully refocused ethnic activism from middle-class assimilationism to social justice for Mexican-American workers, their stance and tactics in opposing Mexican labor rendered them at odds with the Chicano racial revolution that demanded fundamental Latino unity, *la raza unida*.

The determined reformers who reframed Latino politics after World War II treaded the lonely ground between the elite driven ideology of the older Mexican-American leadership and the popular ethnic nationalism embraced by Chicanos. Scholars of both the Mexican-American Generation and the Chicano movement should reconsider the transitional role of these postwar activists. Additionally, brown skin and Latino ethnicity must not be automatically interchanged with any particular set of politics.

Criticism can surely be levied at Perales, Canales, Sánchez, García, Idar and others in the Mexican-American Generation for their various stances on party politics, gender, labor issues, citizenship, whiteness, etc. However, this broadly construed generation incubated a fundamental message of Latinos' racial dignity and social validity. In ugly tactical fights that slighted Mexican nationals, both the LULAC founders and the American G.I. Forum's 1950s leadership continued to offer a vision of Latino racial pride and legitimacy. Perales rightfully occupies a prominent place in Mexican-American history as perhaps the foremost proponent of Latino racial pride. Everyone from the Mexicanist *ricos* in his adoptive home of San Antonio to the most militant Chicano activists can appreciate his intellectual contributions to the improvement of the "Latin race" (R. García, 1991, p. 232; Acuña, 1988, p. 241). In a movement characterized by internal class dissentions, Perales' work has transcended the complications of his time, girding the soldiers of *la raza* as they continue the struggle for equality—and unity.

Bibliography

Archives

J.T. Canales Papers, South Texas Archives, James C. Jernigan Library, Texas A&M University-Kingsville
Dr. Hector P. Garcia Papers, Mary and Jeff Bell Library, Texas A&M-Corpus Christi.
Eduardo Idar, Jr. Papers, Benson Latin American Library, University of Texas at Austin.
Lyndon Baines Johnson Papers, LBJ Presidential Library, Austin, Texas.
Alonso S. Perales Papers. Courtesy of Special Collections, University of Houston Libraries.
United States Congressional Records

Newspapers

Austin American (Statesman)
Corpus Christi Caller-Times
Valley Morning Star
Wall Street Journal

Secondary Sources

Acuña, R. (1988). *Occupied America: A history of Chicanos* 3rd ed. New York: Harper Collins.
Allsup, C. (1982) .*The American G.I. forum: Origins and evolution.* Austin: Center for Mexican American Studies, The University of Texas at Austin.
Blanton, C. K. (2009). The citizenship sacrifice: Mexican Americans, the Saunders–Leonard report, and the politics of immigration, 1951-1952. *The Western Historical Quarterly 40*, 299-320.
García, I. M. (2002). *Hector P. García: In relentless pursuit of justice.* Houston: Arte Público Press.
García, M. T. (1989). *Mexican Americans.* New Haven: Yale University Press.
García, R. A. (1991). *Rise of the Mexican American middle class: San Antonio, 1929-1941.* College Station: Texas A&M University Press.
Gutiérrez, D. G. (1995). *Walls and mirrors: Mexican Americans, Mexican immigrants and the politics of ethnicity.* Berkeley: University of California Press.
Kaplowitz, C. A. (2005). *LULAC: Mexican Americans and national policy.* College Station: Texas A&M University Press.
Montejano, D. (1987). *Anglos and Mexicans in the making of Texas, 1836-1986.* Austin: University of Texas Press.
Orozco, C. E. (2009). *No Mexicans, women, or dogs allowed: The rise of the Mexican civil rights movement.* Austin: The University of Texas Press.
Ramos, H. A. J. (1998). *The American G.I. forum: In pursuit of the dream, 1948-1983.* Houston: Arte Público Press.
Rodriguez, G. (2007). *Mongrels, bastards, orphans, and vagabonds: Mexican immigration and the future of race in America.* New York: Pantheon Books.
San Miguel, Jr., G. (1987). *'Let all of them take heed:' Mexican Americans and the campaign for educational equality in Texas, 1910-1981.* Austin: University of Texas Press.
Saunders, L. & Leonard, O. E. (1951). The wetback in the lower Rio Grande Valley of Texas. *Inter-America Education Occasional Papers*, no. 7. Austin: University of Texas.
Vargas, Z. (2005). *Labor rights are civil rights: Mexican American workers in twentieth-century America.* Princeton, N.J.: Princeton University Press.

Notes

[1]Before the Chicano Movement the 1960s, many Latinos holding United States citizenship referred to themselves as "Latin Americans." This allowed them to empha-

size their U.S. citizenship without invoking the widespread nationalist discrimination against Mexico and Mexicans. "Mexican American," "Tejano," and "Latin American" are used throughout this paper to refer to U.S. citizens, while the term "Latino" is used for traditionally Spanish-speaking people regardless of nationality.

[2]U.S. Congress, Senate, Committee of Labor and Public Welfare, Subcommittee on Labor and Labor-Management Relations, 82nd Congress., 2nd sess., part 1., February-March 1952, 131.

[3]"Information Concerning Entry of Mexican Agricultural Workers to United States," Public Law 78, 82nd Congress, Approved August 1951, Senate Papers 1949-1961, Box 232, Legislative Files on Alien Labor, LBJ Presidential Library, University of Texas at Austin.; Subsequent citations for this archive will be listed parenthetically as "LBJ Papers."

[4]Alonso S. Perales to Sr. don Manuel González Martínez, Presidente del Comite Mexicano contra El Racismo, 21 July 1945, microfilm 2309, reel 22, Alonso S. Perales Papers, Courtesy of Special Collections, University of Houston; Perales to Hon. John W. Brown, M.D., Texas State Health Officer, 28 November 1936, microfilm 2309, reel 15, Perales Papers.; Special thanks are due to the Recovering the U.S. Hispanic Literary Heritage Program, University of Houston for collecting these invaluable documents. Subsequent citations for this archive will be listed parenthetically as "Perales Papers."

[5]"Our strength is in unity"—author's translation. J.T. Canales to Ed Idar, Jr., 11 March 1952, Activities and Organizations Box 5, Folder 4, Eduardo Idar, Jr. Papers, Benson Latin American Library, University of Texas at Austin; subsequent citations from this archive will be listed parenthetically as "Idar, Jr. Papers."

[6]Winston C. Fournier, "Texas Cotton: Top Producing State Expects a Record 1951 Crop, Twice '50 Output," *Wall Street Journal*, 19 June 1951, p. 1.

[7]"Ginners Say Huge Texas Cotton Crop Doomed without 500,000 Braceros," *Valley Morning Star*, 25 May 1951, p. 1.

[8]"Kibbe Answered by Claim 25 Cents not Prevailing Wage," *Austin American,* 05 September 1947.

[9]Ed Idar, Jr. to Trinidad Gonzales, 12 January 1952, Box 214, Folder 15, Dr. Hector P. García Papers, Mary and Jeff Bell Library, Texas A&M-Corpus Christi.; subsequent citations from this archive will be listed parenthetically as the "H.P. García Papers."

Legally White, Socially Brown: Alonso S. Perales and His Crusade for Justice for *La Raza*

Lupe S. Salinas

Introduction

This chapter, based on information gleaned from the Alonso S. Perales Collection,[1] addresses the Texas perspective and experience regarding the so-called *raza mexicana* or "Mexican race." Many professionals and other persons deem the term "race" a misnomer when discussing the Mexican nationality group. Nevertheless, a foundation exists for both agreement and disagreement with these two perceptions. Unquestionably, the anthropologist views the concept of race as limited to three dominant groups. However, from a sociological perspective, the manner in which distinct peoples interact speaks volumes as to how the dominant group regards the other discrete group or groups.

In this chapter, the term "white" or "Anglo" refers to Caucasians of European backgrounds other than Spaniards. The terms Mexican, Mexican American, Latino and Latin American refer to Mexican-origin members of the Caucasian race. However, this population possesses certain distinctive ethnic or racial characteristics. Since Indians populated pre-Hispanic Mexico, the arrival of Spaniards and their sexual interaction with Indian women produced the predominantly *mestizo* population of Mexico. Obviously, some Mexicans possess one hundred percent Spanish blood, some have pure Indian blood, and most possess a blend of the two.

The extensive mistreatment of Mexican-descent persons in areas of education, employment, voting and public accommodations is well-documented. This abuse at the hands of Anglos unhesitatingly leads to the conclusion that Mexican-descent persons experienced discrimination on the basis of their different "race" status. The racial tenor of the actions against Latinos by the dominant Anglo governing group clearly conveyed their motives. The comparable discrimination by this same Anglo group against African Americans further corroborated the assertion that the actions against Latinos constituted racial discrimination.

While legal construction might state that the white race includes persons of Mexican descent, the common understanding among the dominant group, comprised of Anglos, has not universally agreed with this concept (Lopez, 1996, pp. 8, 131). The majority Anglo group has historically categorized white persons of Mexican descent into a separate ethnic or racial group. Even though legally classified as white, Mexican Americans historically encountered discrimination perpetrated by the dominant Caucasian or Anglo population by virtue of a common understanding that Mexicans belong to a racial group other than white (Gómez, 2007; López, 1996, pp. 8, 131; Rodriguez, 1897, p. 353).

For example, in the legislative discussions about the imminent inclusion of Mexicans to the United States population, Senator John C. Calhoun of South Carolina voiced objections. Calhoun specifically stated: "Ours . . . is the Government of a white race. The greatest misfortunes of Spanish America are to be traced to the fatal error of placing these colored races on an equality with the white race" (Weber, ed., 1973, p. 135). In other words, the mixed blood and swarthy complexion of Mexicans provided Anglos with sufficient justification upon which to exclude Mexicans from the perceived privileges of "whiteness."

On the other hand, Mexican Americans and other Latinos have historically identified themselves as *la raza* (literally "The Race;" figuratively, "The People"). While the term *la raza* indicates, to some extent, separatist principles, the attitudes and actions of this population hardly coincide with a desire to avoid integration into American society. First, although racially restrictive covenants barred African Americans and persons of Mexican descent from purchasing land in Anglo residential areas, the historical evidence established the desire among Latinos to live in these neighborhoods (Clifton, 1948, p. 131; Matthews, 1948, p. 66).

Second, signing up for military service speaks volumes about the desire to be "American." Even though business establishments excluded Mexican Americans and school boards assigned the children to segregated Mexican Schools, Latinos volunteered to represent their country. In addition, their service proved to be outstanding. Of the Texas military delegation in World War II who received Congressional Medals of Honor, Latinos accounted for six, or forty-three percent, of the fourteen recipients. (Migratory Labor, 1952, p. 131). Remarkably, in the 1940s, Latinos accounted for only eleven percent of the Texas population (Gibson and Jung, Census, Table 58, 1940).

Furthermore, Mexican Americans engaged politically to further their dreams of a better America, one in which they would have representatives of their choice as well as Presidents and United States Senators. Unfortunately, during the Perales era, Mexican Americans did not encounter many successes. First, the racial discrimination they experienced generally alienated them from the political process. Second, election administrators, all of Anglo descent in those years, imposed voting obstacles, such as the poll tax and in some parts of Texas, the custom that the Democratic Primary was equivalent to the White Man's Primary where only "White Citizens" could vote. Specifically, the rules did not allow a "Mexican" to vote unless he was of "full Spanish blood" (Perales, 1937, p. 93).

The poll tax provided a means by which the dominant Anglo population conditioned the ability to vote on those able to pay for the right to vote. Effectively, this practice excluded poor and predominantly minority voters who viewed the payment as problematical when they had to choose between a voting permit and food for their families. Notwithstanding this reality, Perales urged his *raza* to pay the poll tax so that they could vote to remove city, county, and state officials that mistreat Mexicans

(Perales, 1937, pp. 72-75). Perales acknowledged that differences in language and the steadfast nationalistic pride to Mexico among American citizens of Mexican descent contributed to their low participation in the electoral process (AP Editorial, Box 8, Folder 8).

A few years after Perales' death, the United States Supreme Court voided the poll tax (Harper, 1966, p. 663). Surprisingly, in his writings, Perales did not aggressively question the constitutional validity of imposing a tax on the exercise of the right to vote (Perales, 1937, pp. 72-75). He appeared more interested in motivating his *raza* to get involved in the electoral process, regardless of the cost. However, when the issue involved the right not to be excluded from public accommodations, Perales emphatically presented his case and urged the Justice Department's Assistant Attorney General to ask President Roosevelt for remedial federal legislation (Letter from AP to Tom Clark, Oct. 26, 1944, Box 4, Folder 41). Congress finally enacted a law similar to that advocated by Perales (Civil Rights Act of 1964, 42 U.S.C. § 2000, Title II).

The Life and Times of Alonso S. Perales, 1898-1960

A. The Early Years—Alice, Texas, San Antonio, Texas and Washington, DC

Alonso Sandoval Perales was born in Alice, Texas on October 17, 1898 to Nicolas Perales and Susana Sandoval. By the time he was six years old, both parents had died. He attended public schools in Alice from 1905 until 1912. He then moved to San Antonio where he attended a business school (Orozco, 2009, p. 111; Application for Appointment as Army Field Clerk, Sept. 19, 1918, Box 1, Folder 8). Amazingly, the small community of Alice also counts J. Luz Saenz, a companion of Alonso Perales in the founding of LULAC, as one of its own. Saenz graduated from Alice High School in 1908 (Orozco, 2009, p. 97).

After working for a while in San Antonio, Perales gained proficiency as a stenographer. Perales then moved to the nation's capital. After working as a clerk, he received his military orders on his twentieth birthday. Perales' military career lasted slightly more than one year (Honorable Discharge Document, Jan. 6, 1920, Box 1, Folder 7). Upon his discharge, he continued his studies in Washington, D. C. at the Washington Preparatory School. He later enrolled in classes at the National University School of Economics and Government.

Before he entered law school, Perales utilized his linguistic and governmental affairs skills and joined the Diplomatic Corps as secretary to Sumner Welles. In 1922, President Harding appointed the group to serve as special representative of the United States to the Dominican Republic. Perales' bilingual skills and knowledge of Hispanic protocol served him well in other missions to Central America (Perales Biography, Dedication Ceremony of Perales Elementary School, 1974, Box 1, Folder 1).

Records indicate that he enrolled for his first year of law at Georgetown University School during 1922-23 (Box 1, Folder 13). However, another document indicates he attended the law school that became George Washington University Law School (Letter to AP, Jan. 12, 1923, Box 1, Folder 13).

Perales later served as Chief Attorney for the mission on the Tacna and Arica Arbitration under the guidance of General John J. Pershing. President Calvin

Coolidge appointed Pershing to monitor this land dispute that arose over a war several decades before between Perú and Chile. The two nations requested President Coolidge to arbitrate the dispute.

Before completing his legal studies, Perales returned to Texas, worked with a law firm, and continued his study of law under the supervision of a lawyer. After he passed the Texas state bar examination in 1925, Perales petitioned the Dean of George Washington University Law School to grant him permission to obtain his LL.B. degree (Letter from AP, Oct. 8, 1926, Box 1, Folder 13). Perales apparently later obtained his law degree from National University (Perales, 1948, p. 5). While some sources indicate that he received his law school education at George Washington, the apparent inconsistency as to where Perales earned his law degree seems to derive from the merger between George Washington and the National University in 1954, years after this correspondence (George Washington University, History).

B. LULAC and Perales' Dominant Role in Its Formation

At the age of seventeen, when most youth concern themselves with other issues, Perales began to plot the future of his *raza*. He mentioned two school friends from San Antonio as co-conspirators in this great plan for an organization which would take "our people" to a level of respect and political participation.

Fueled by his observations and experiences in Texas, Perales sought to create a strong organization to protect "the best interests and welfare of our Race" and to strive "for their progress." However, due to his youth and lack of training, several years passed until the idea went beyond the discussion stage.

Once he received his honorable discharge from the U.S. Army in January 1920, he proceeded to Washington, D. C. in order to pursue his studies and his training to be "equipped to help solve the problems of our people in Texas." Perales and his two friends discussed the idea for a time and then communicated by mail to further the dream of establishing an organization that would become "a bulwark for the protection of all our Racial brethren" (Perales, 1937, pp. 101-116 (Bilingual version); Ts., Perales, *The True Origin of the League of United Latin American Citizens (LULAC)*, July 1937, Box 3, Folder 36 (English version)).

While in Washington, he heard by way of San Antonio newspapers of the creation of groups known as the *Orden Hijos de América* (Order of the Sons of America) in 1921 and *Orden Hijos de Texas* (Order of the Sons of Texas) in 1922. In June 1923, Perales returned to San Antonio and, accompanied by J. Luz Saenz, joined the Sons of Texas to learn more about the group. Saenz, Perales and the other two friends concluded that the Sons of Texas did not fulfill the ideal of the organization they had conceived—one which worked towards the "goal of progress and welfare of our Race in Texas." They wanted an organization that would labor "unflinchingly" for the good of "our people." They did not want a group that would merely serve to impress political bosses and public officials with "the sole aim of securing this or that favor and jobs in City Hall or the red Court House" (Ts., Perales, *The True Origin of the League of United Latin American Citizens (LULAC)*, July 1937, Box 3, Folder 36).

In the summer of 1924, Perales and Saenz embarked on a tour of various Texas towns to lecture on education, unification and constitutional rights. Of course, they conducted these trips with the plans to lay the foundation for the organization they desired. In February 1927, a group which included attorney Manuel C. Gonzales founded the Order Knights of America in San Antonio. The group's track record also failed to convince Perales that this group represented his dream.

Perales then decided to move his practice to the Rio Grande Valley in South Texas, opening offices in McAllen and Rio Grande City. Before he made the move, he issued a press release that appeared in *La Prensa* in San Antonio and other Valley newspapers in which he declared his plans to open an office by July 15, 1927. In his announcement, he added that he would deliver lectures on behalf of "our Race" and to take the initial steps to establish a center, first in the Valley and then in other cities of Texas.

Perales dreamed of "working sincerely towards improving the intellectual, economic, social and political status of Mexican-Americans in particular, and the Mexican Race in General." To accomplish this, he demanded four qualities in the potential leaders: first, they must be honest, to avoid exploitation of our "unfortunate Race;" second, they should be quite active, to reach the goals more rapidly; third, they must be "brave and not fear to demand justice whenever their rights as citizens of the United States of America are violated;" and fourth, they must be intelligent so as to better direct our destinies (Ts., Perales, *The True Origin of the League of United Latin American Citizens (LULAC)*, July 1937, Box 3, Folder 36).

Perales spoke with the conviction that the organization he envisioned would develop and that "our Race may count on having a large number of leaders who possess these high qualities." Additionally, he wanted Mexican Americans to sense the confidence of an organization "crowned with complete success." On August 14, 1927, Perales met in Harlingen, Texas with Professor Saenz and attorney José T. Canales and created the League of Latin American Citizens. A few years later, Perales and his companions found others with whom to collaborate in the effort to pave the road for the merger of the three active Latino groups. (Ts., Perales, *The True Origin of the League of United Latin American Citizens (LULAC)*, July 1937, Box 3, Folder 36; Perales, 1937, pp. 101-116).

Perales' Political Philosophy

In May 1928, in one of his earliest recorded comments about the political process, Perales told Ben Garza, the future first President of LULAC, that if the precursor organization, the League of Latin American Citizens, became a political club then he would have no choice but to abandon the organization. Perales explained to Garza that he obviously wanted the members to vote, as it is their duty as good Americans, but he wanted them to vote intelligently and conscientiously for those candidates "who are true friends of our race [so] we can improve our political condition." Perales expressed concerns that voting en masse in compliance with the wishes of a politician did not "improve our condition one iota, although it might improve the condition of one or more members of our race." Another concern he had was that such unintelligent voting would make the Mexican people "a negligible factor in politics" (Ts., Perales, *The True Origin of the League of United Latin American Citizens (LULAC)*, July 1937, Box 3, Folder 36).

In his continuing discussions with Ben Garza and others about the merger of the various groups, Perales, sounding somewhat frustrated, stated the following about the refusal of James Tafolla, Sr., to agree to a merger of the organizations:

We Latin-Americans must organize. We must get out of the rut and forge ahead. Let us catch up with and keep abreast of our harddriving [sic] fellow-citizens of Anglo-Saxon extraction. To accomplish this, no man should be allowed to stand in our way. No man is big enough to block our progress. A fraction is not larger than the whole. For the sake of posterity and the good name of our race, let us get together, my friends, and begin to solve our great problems. We can only do it thru [sic] a well disciplined, solid, powerful organization.

The three groups convened in Corpus Christi, Texas on February 17, 1929, and agreed to merge under the name "United Latin American Citizens." At a later time, the organization added the word "League" to the name. As proposed by Canales, the LULAC slogan reads, "All for one, and One for all" (LULAC History, 2011). Perales proudly described his service in LULAC as Founder, President General, and Life Member (Perales, 1948, pp. 5-6).

In closing his report on the founding of LULAC and "for the information of those who are interested in knowing the truth," Perales wrote that he was the initiator of the idea and the main founder of our present-day League of United Latin American Citizens. Although this claim indicates an egotistical attitude, the documentation supports this assertion. However, in a less self-centered moment, Perales generously added that all the men who attended the Corpus Christi gathering "were and are the founders" of the group (Ts., Perales, *The True Origin of the League of United Latin American Citizens (LULAC)*, July 1937, Box 3, Folder 36). In addition, in his 1930 appearance before Congress, he more humbly identified himself as "a founder" of LULAC (Orozco, 2009, p. 112).

In his capacity as Director General of the Committee of 100 Citizens and the League of Loyal Americans, Perales declared that as Americans citizens of Texas, Mexicans should support leaders who abstain from racially discriminatory policies and who pledge to treat Mexicans with respect. He continued to urge his *raza* to pay the poll tax to remove city, county, and state officials from power if they mistreat Mexicans (AP Editorial, July 27, 1945, Box 8, Folder 3). Perales continued through the early 1950s with his support for Mexican Americans to obtain their poll tax to make a difference in the elections. In a speech entitled *Power at the Polls*, he argued that this participation was the only means by which the ethnic group could attain representation (AP Speech, April 23-25, 1952, Box 8, Folder 8).

A related voting problem centered on the low rate of citizenship applications among those of Mexican descent. In an editorial entitled *El Porvenir de los Mexico-Americanos* (The Future of Mexican Americans), Perales attributed the failure of

Mexicans to Americanize in great part to Anglo American racial prejudice. He complained about Anglos who regard persons of Mexican descent as foreigners, whether American citizens or not. Perales further observed that Anglos perceive Mexican Americans as technically American citizens only when it comes to issues that relate to the federal government and their obligations in general to the American people (AP Editorial, Box 8, Folder 8).

Participation in World War II serves as an excellent example of this observation. All Americans, regardless of ethnicity, united as one people for the purpose of defeating the common enemy. In contrast, before and after the war, when the issue concerned the purchase of real estate, voting, education, public accommodations and employment opportunity, the Anglo population denied Mexican Americans the full respect and equality they deserved.

Perales aggressively motivated his people to become involved in the political process. On one occasion, he ran for office. An unidentified document endorsed Alonso S. Perales for membership on the Board of Trustees of the San Antonio Independent School District because he is "admirably qualified for the post" (Letter of endorsement, undated, Box 1, Folder 1). Apparently, his effort did not succeed, and he never held public office.

Perales' Personality and Character

Perales' commitment to racial equality, education, ethics and leadership could not be derailed. His all-encompassing collection at the University of Houston M. D. Anderson Library reveals his persistent theme of racial equality, one from which he never deviated. His position adhered to the tenet that persons of Mexican descent are white, i.e., members of the Caucasian race. Nonetheless, he described the incongruent treatment of Latin Americans from that accorded to Anglos, the other members of the white race, as a violation of equal protection, at times referring to this disparate treatment as "racial" discrimination. To his credit, the Supreme Court of the United States later acknowledged his beliefs in *Hernandez v. Texas*, a unanimous decision which declared that Latin Americans are entitled to equal protection as a class distinct from other whites in the selection of grand and petit jurors (Hernandez, 1954, p. 478).

Perales possessed a unique courage and, from some perspectives, an obstinate tenacity when he addressed complaints to top officials. For example, in February 1927, he wrote to President Coolidge to request action from the federal government in the deaths of five men at the hands of the Sheriff of Willacy County in South Texas. The sheriff claimed unknown persons ambushed the group. In classic debate style, Perales impeached this claim by observing how the surprise attackers killed only the Mexican detainees while not one single deputy sheriff received an injury (AP Letter to the President, Feb. 14, 1927, Box 2, Folder 13).

Since Perales did not receive a response, he wrote the President again and expressed his discontent. He told the President of a lecture tour he would soon conduct in Texas, stating "much to my regret, [I] have to inform my fellow-citizens of Mexican extraction that I failed in my efforts to induce our Government to take action in the case I have alluded to, since neither Your Excellency nor the governor of Texas . . . even acknowledged receipt of the communications in which I asked you to be good enough to use your good offices to bring the slayers of defenseless citizens above mentioned before the bars of justice" (AP Letter to the President, April 30, 1927, Box 2, Folder 13).

In addition, Perales challenged Texas Governor Beauford Jester's assertion that the discrimination against persons of Mexican descent was difficult to solve due to the discrimination of social classes that exists in Mexico. As in the Willacy County Sheriff's claim, Perales questioned the official claims by pointing out that, unlike Texas, Mexican people are not treated differently in Mexico for the mere fact of being Mexican. Instead of social class discrimination, Perales referred to the treatment of Mexican-descent people in Texas as blatant racial discrimination. After all, Perales argued, if it were a social matter, Mexican consular and other top Mexican officials or University of Texas students would not be banned from certain restaurants (AP Editorial, Oct. 12, 1947, Box 9, Folder 1).

Perales and his persistence at times annoyed persons with whom he had, or once had, an apparently amiable working relationship. For instance, in 1931, he received a letter from Dr. George I. Sánchez of the University of Texas regarding the need to have educational experts in school segregation cases like Del Rio where authorities justified segregation of Latino children on the basis of "pedagogical reasons" (Letter from George I. Sánchez to AP, April 30, 1931, Box 2, Folder 19). Twelve years later, Dr. Sánchez wrote Perales about grant money at the University of Texas since he knew Perales had a "sincere interest and leadership" in educational matters (Letter from George I. Sánchez to AP, Feb. 17, 1943, Box 2, Folder 19).

A few years later, matters got somewhat heated when Perales wrote to Sánchez to complain about derogatory comments made in a pamphlet sponsored by the University of Texas in general and Dr. Sánchez in particular. Speaking on his own behalf and that of many friends from the Rio Grande Valley, Perales stated: "[W]e hereby demand that you furnish us at once the names and addresses of each and everyone [sic] of the persons noted" as informants in the pamphlet (AP Letter to George I. Sánchez, Dec. 3, 1951, Box 2, Folder 19). Sánchez quickly and sarcastically responded: "It is with a certain degree of both amazement and amusement that I read your letter of December 3 . . . I am amused . . . that you should think that you are thereby entitled to *demand* anything of me. Not even to my closest friends do I grant the privilege of making peremptory demands of me" (Letter from George I. Sánchez to AP, Dec. 5, 1951, Box 2, Folder 19, Emphasis in Original).

The Legal Career of Alonso S. Perales in San Antonio, Texas

A. The Direct and Indirect Collaboration with Civil Rights Litigation

After a brief effort at launching his private practice in the Rio Grande Valley, Perales returned to San Antonio. Aside from his legal practice, his Valley efforts met with success. While in South Texas, he founded the League of United Latin American Citizens in 1927. He then strengthened it to such a level that by 1929, it could negotiate a merger with other groups to build LULAC, a more respected and powerful union.

In his battles for justice for *la raza,* Perales encountered lonely moments during the early years of a career which began in the late 1920s. However, this loneliness did not discourage him in justice battles. Fortunately, Perales had a working relationship with a few other Mexican-American lawyers. They included, among others, Texas State Representative José Tomás "J. T." Canales, who in 1918 had filed a complaint regarding widespread brutality against Mexicans by the Texas Rangers (Salinas, 2005, p. 294). In 1931, Perales collaborated with M. C. Gonzales and J. T. Canales after they had tried the case, to request a hearing before the United States Supreme Court in the Del Rio, Texas school segregation case wherein the school district justified the segregation of Latin children for language-based pedagogical reasons, but the Court denied *certiorari* (Salvatierra, 1931; Salvatierra, 1930, p. 795).

In 1948 Perales joined forces with Carlos C. Cadena in the successful litigation to ban racially restrictive covenants that prohibited the conveyance of land to persons of "Mexican descent" (Clifton, 1948, p. 274). The United States Supreme Court previously ruled that state judicial approval of covenants that barred the sale of property to African Americans violated the Fourteenth Amendment's Equal Protection Clause (Shelley, 1948, p. 1).

B. Perales' Crusade for Justice for La Raza

In his introductory comments to his book *Are We Good Neighbors?*, Perales contended that discrimination against people of Mexican or Spanish descent would end by conducting campaigns and informing Anglos of the cultural background and virtues of the Mexican people. In this fashion, he expected governing bodies to terminate the segregation of Mexican children in public schools and to enact federal and state legislation forbidding discrimination against them "and other descendants of the Caucasian Race" (Perales, 1948, pp. 8-9). To set an example for others, Perales led his less eloquent and educated fellow Mexican Americans in the crusade for justice for *la raza.* The specific issues Perales tackled are set forth below.

1. Immigration Rights

Perales began his efforts early in life when he appeared before Congress to defend his people. In January 1930, he and J. T. Canales appeared before the Committee on Immigration and Naturalization of the United States Congress to defend "our race." Congress entertained a bill that sought to limit Mexican immigration, with one of the grounds including the claim that Mexicans were an "inferior and degenerate race" (Perales, 1937, pp. 81-86). As Perales stated, "Clearly, our League (LULAC) could not remain quiet" (News article, *La Prensa, La convención de los Lulacs en Laredo, Tex.* (The LULAC Convention in Laredo, Tex.), June 5, 1936; Gottheimer, ed., 2003, p. 157).

2. Exclusions from Public Accommodations and Commercial Establishments

Perales firmly believed that discriminatory treatment could be eliminated by legislation. As a result, in the 1940s, Perales and M. C. Gonzales requested a San

Antonio representative to introduce a bill that provided: "[A]ll persons of the Caucasian race [within] the jurisdiction of this state are entitled to the full and equal
accommodations, advantages, facilities and privileges of all public places of business or amusement." Additionally, it would be unlawful for anyone to discriminate
against Mexicans, whom the bill describes as Caucasians. The predominantly Anglo
membership in the House of Representatives met the offer of the bill with "laughs,
murmurs of disapproval and a few shouts of dissent" (News article, *"Mexican" bill
introduced,* April 15 [year not included], Box 9, Folder 30).

An avid collector of news articles, manuscripts, affidavits and letters, Perales
possessed an article from *La Prensa,* a prominent Spanish-language newspaper. The
news article addressed an incident where the Laredo Hispanic American Union of
Texas joined the Austin LULAC chapter and filed a complaint with the Austin City
Council for authorizing the creation of a segregated waiting room for whites and
another one exclusively for Blacks and Latinos in the city hospital. Dr. Castañeda and
Latino groups complained that persons of Mexican descent legally qualify as white
or Caucasian. In that regard, the segregation of Mexican descent persons apart from
other whites violated the law (News article, *La Prensa, Protesta de la Unión Hispa-
no Americana* (Hispanic American Union Protest), June 26, 1939, Box 9, Folder 32).

In other cases involving commercial establishments, Perales complained to a
general at Fort Sam Houston that two barber shops in San Antonio denied service to
a Mexican-American Army soldier while dressed in his military uniform. Perales
described the denials as "un-American" and detrimental to the country, adding that
"every citizen and every inhabitant of our land should cooperate with our Government in its national defense program instead of creating unpleasant situations" (Letter from AP to Major General James L. Collins, Dec. 24, 1940, Box 4, Folder 41).

Perales further documented the exclusion of Latinos from movie theaters. In one
incident, a manager at a theater excluded a man and his children. The man described
the emotional dilemma of having two sons at that time in military action overseas
and yet suffering this humiliation at home (Letter from Pedro Enriquez to AP, Nov.
30, 1944, Box 8, Folder 3).

In a predominantly Anglo-German community, New Braunfels, Texas, three
Mexican-American women entered a restaurant, but the manager told them to go to
the rear of the café behind a screen for food service (Letter from Lay Council for the
Spanish Speaking to "Whom it may concern," Feb. 28, 1947, Box 6, Folder 26). This
small town already had a bad reputation for discriminatory treatment of its Mexican-
American population. First, the city's school district created a "Mexican" school in
1910. Years later, the Anglo leadership built a school that effectively served the Mexican part of town. In a school desegregation civil rights action, a federal appellate
court in the 1970s found that this newer segregated school violated the equal protection rights of Mexican-American children (Zamora, 1975, p. 1084).

Additionally, Perales filed a LULAC complaint against the City of New Braunfels which criticized the existence of segregated benches at Main Plaza and the
exclusion and eviction of Mexican people from Camp Warnecke and Landa Park,
including Henry B. Gonzalez, a future Member of Congress (Aguinaldo "Nayo"
Zamora, 1998; Montejano, 2010, p. 91). The benches in the park had signs that read

"For Whites" and others marked "For Mexicans" (Perales, 1937, pp. 96-98). Perales obtained numerous notarized declarations of humiliating civil rights violations in general and exclusions from restaurants and other public accommodations in particular (Perales, 1948, pp. 139-213). He specifically documented the Texas cities which reported complaints of denials of service, which evidence indicated the existence of a statewide problem (Perales, 1948, pp. 213-223).

As mentioned earlier, Perales carried on a debate with Assistant Attorney General Tom Clark in 1944. Perales requested that the War Department inform "owners of establishments that our Federal Government will not tolerate the humiliation of American soldiers of Mexican descent simply because of their racial lineage." Perales asked Clark to inform President Roosevelt that three million Americans of Mexican descent would appreciate his requesting Congress to pass a law immediately forbidding the degradation of people of Mexican descent anywhere in the United States merely because of their ancestry (Letter from AP to Tom Clark, Oct. 26, 1944, Box 4, Folder 41).

Clark acknowledged the receipt of the report that contained locations in Texas where Mexicans experience discrimination. However, Clark noted that the Supreme Court held in the *Civil Rights Cases* that Congress did not have any authority to legislate concerning discrimination by private individuals or businesses. As a result, the Department of Justice lacked the power to provide a remedy (Letter from Tom Clark to AP, Oct. 31, 1944, Box 4, Folder 41).

Perales, living up to the ideals he personally mentioned as desirable in a LULAC leader, persisted in his demand for action. He argued that things had changed since the 1883 *Civil Rights Cases* decision. Americans of all races and ancestries had fought in two world wars and did not return to the United States "in order that some Tom, Dick or Harry may remain free to humiliate them when they return merely because of their race or national origin" (Letter from AP to Tom Clark, Nov. 6, 1944, Box 4, Folder 41).

Receiving no response, Perales persisted by writing Clark to determine what had happened regarding his questions (Letter from AP to Tom Clark, Dec. 14, 1944, Box 4, Folder 41). As to his reasoning for reversing the teachings of the *Civil Rights Cases,* Perales argued that privately owned public places can be regulated or controlled by federal law pursuant to the preamble of the Constitution which declares that the Constitution sought to "provide for the common defense [and] promote the general welfare."

Perales emphasized the need for a federal approach since the extreme level of prejudice in Texas made any state remedy practically unenforceable (Letter from AP to Tom Connally, Feb. 28, 1941, Box 4, Folder 41). In a subsequent editorial, Perales stated that the Texas Legislature, for the third time, refused to enact a law that prohibited public humiliation of Mexicans for simply being of Mexican descent. The proposed anti-discriminatory law lacked majority support from Anglo-Americans, from the Anglo-American Chamber of Commerce, and from the Anglo press (Perales Editorial, July 27, 1945, Box 8, Folder 3). The always-persistent advocate, Perales made another effort a few years later to enact an anti-discrimination law in Texas (AP Press Release, May 1, 1951, Box 8, Folder 8).

Perhaps the most notorious incident resulting in the denial of restaurant service involved a recipient of the Congressional Medal of Honor. Sgt. Macario García, recently home from World War II, went to the Oasis Café in Richmond, Texas in September 1945 (Perales, 1948, p-p. 156-57). Dressed in his military uniform, Sgt. García asked for a cup of coffee. Only one month earlier, on August 23, 1945, President Harry S. Truman awarded this Mexican immigrant the nation's most coveted military honor. Sgt. García received the hero's treatment then, taking photographs with his Commander in Chief. However, back in his Texas hometown, a business member of the Anglo community saw him as "just another Mexican" when the owner informed him they did not serve Mexicans.

3. Hate Crimes

In an editorial, Perales recounted an event where three Anglo men assaulted Francisco Ramirez, a bus passenger, because of his Mexican descent. The attack occurred after Ramirez walked out of a café. Perales contends that those who assaulted Ramirez acted out of "ignorance" and allowed "blind prejudice [to] void their sense of reasoning and humanity." He then offered a series of questions that challenged whether people should be treated as inferior simply because they have a different skin color (Editorial, Sonora, Texas, Box 8, Folder 3).

4. Employment Discrimination

As with every issue critical to the interests of the Latino community, Perales continuously promoted the need for fairness and equality of treatment. He specifically sought better employment opportunities with equal wages and responsibilities for the Mexican American. During the 1941 re-election campaign of Mayor Maury Maverick, Sr., Perales criticized the mayor for "not giving Latin-Americans recognition" (News article, *Money waste by mayor charged*, undated, Box 9, Folder 25).

Before the end of the war in 1945, Perales appeared before a subcommittee of the United States Senate headed by Senator Dennis Chávez of New Mexico and advocated for a law that would strengthen federal efforts to eliminate discrimination in employment (Perales, 1948, 114-133). Near this same time period, he collaborated with Dr. Carlos E. Castañeda of the President's Committee on Fair Employment Practices. Castañeda, who also served as a professor at the University of Texas, agreed with Perales that ninety-nine percent of the non-discriminatory law's failure resulted from opposition of "our Anglo-American fellow citizens." He informed Perales that he would send a copy of a recent Congressional bill which would create a commission with far more powers than those available under the executive order that his agency operated under (Letter from Carlos E. Castañeda to AP, Jan. 25, 1944, Box 4, Folder 13). Several months later, Perales advised Castañeda that he and others sent letters to Congressman Kilday, Senator Connally, and to the twenty members of the Committee on Labor stating that three million loyal Latin Americans in the Southwest would appreciate their support of the Anti-Mexican American discrimination bill (known as Dawson-Scanlon-LaFollette Bill) (Letter from AP to Carlos E. Castañeda, June 3, 1944, Box 4, Folder 13).

While Perales knew that ethnic discrimination kept many Latinos from gainful employment, he needed actual cases to help prove the bigotry in this field. As a result, he engaged in the practice, almost to the point of an obsession, of notarizing incidents of discrimination (Perales, 1948, pp. 139-213). One incident involved a seventeen-year-old female, a high school graduate, who applied for an office position in San Antonio, but the person who received the application candidly stated they did not have any "openings for Latin Americans" (Affidavit from Alice Martinez, May 29, 1950, Box 6, Folder 30).

5. Residential Segregation

Perales criticized real estate agents and governing bodies of residential districts in San Antonio and surrounding communities where Mexicans, regardless of their social position, encountered difficulties in the purchase of real estate (AP Editorial, Aug. 20, 1923, Box 8, Folder 12). During the 1934 race for the San Antonio area congressional district, Thurman Barrett, a homebuilder, sought the Latino vote. After failing to make it into the run-off election, Barrett then began to demean "hyphenated Americans," the very group he solicited for votes. Perales answered Barrett's insults against American citizens of Mexican descent by stating that this ethnic group represents "fullfledged [sic], genuine, loyal Americans" unlike Barrett who issued restrictive deeds in the Harlandale section of San Antonio, yet hypocritically sought the Mexican-American vote during the election (Letter from AP to Thurman Barrett, April 20, 1940, Box 4, Folder 41). Perales continued to question the motives behind the denial of the sale of property to persons of Mexican descent. If the exclusion of Mexicans was "social," then, "Why do Anglo real estate people deny honorable and wealthy Mexicans the purchase of houses in certain residential neighborhoods?" (AP Editorial, Oct. 12, 1947, Box 9, Folder 1).

Notwithstanding the principle set forth in *Shelley* and *Clifton v. Puente*, Anglo San Antonio real estate agents schemed as to how to maintain segregation of the races and the preservation of the recently rejected racial restrictive covenants. In the year following these rulings, San Antonio real estate officials, acting through the Home Owners Protective League, sought to circumvent these rulings by allowing parties to a real estate contract to enter into an agreement to observe all covenants, even those dealing with racial exclusions (San Antonio Light, Aug. 26, 1949, Box 9, Folder 25). In San Antonio, agents in 1950 continued to abide by restrictive covenants based on race. A Latino and his wife visited with an Anglo real estate agent and paid $200 as earnest money towards the purchase of a home in the Woodlawn Heights subdivision. When the buyer returned, the agent first stated that the house had already been sold, but he then conceded that Woodlawn Heights was "restricted as to Latin Americans" (Affidavit of Carlos Santos, July 31, 1950, Box 6, Folder 32).

6. School Segregation and Educational Equality

In his quest for educational equality for his people, Perales joined other lawyers in seeking a Supreme Court hearing in the *Salvatierra* language segregation case. Perales viewed the education of Mexican-descent children as perhaps his primary concern. He objected to separate schools for Mexican children. In other circumstances, Perales appeared to concede the existence of segregated schools, although he asserted that these "Mexican Schools" should be comparably adequate or equal to those provided to the Anglo kids.

He further complained that thousands of Mexican children did not attend school, others attended school for only half a day, and the school district assigned over 2,000 Mexican children to temporary wooden buildings. He observed that Anglo schools had more sinks to wash hands and more land for recreation. For instance, Jefferson High School in the Anglo North Side had thirty-three acres while Sidney Lanier High School in the Mexican West Side had only two and a half acres of recreation land (AP Editorial, Oct. 19, 1947, Box 9, Folder 1).

In another editorial shortly thereafter, Perales referred to the petition in the U.S. District court in Austin. In that case, *Delgado v. Bastrop Independent School District*, attorney Gus García complained of the official segregation of Latin American children in Texas schools. García asserted that the Texas Constitution barred the segregation of Latin Americans from other white students (AP Editorial, Nov. 23, 1947, Box 9, Folder 1). The State of Texas and the Delgado family entered into a consent decree in 1948 in which the state merely declared to school districts around the state that Texas law barred the segregation of scholastics on the basis of their Latin American extraction (Salinas, 2003, p. 166). However, it did sustain the *Salvatierra* exception of segregation of Latino children if the district could provide a linguistic or pedagogical reason (Salinas, 2003, p. 168).

The Hondo, Texas schools have continually provided problems for the Mexican-American community. The complaints discussed in this article relate to incidents that began as early as the 1930s. Perales, as the lawyer for LULAC Council No. 37 in Hondo, complained to the state superintendent of public instruction about the failure of Hondo school officials to provide Latin American children with adequate school facilities. Perales mentioned that school officials placed only eleven Latino children in the "main school" with Anglos while several Latin American children were demoted from fifth to fourth grade in order to prevent them from being eligible to go to the "main school."

Perales further complained that the Hondo School Board failed to comply with the State Superintendent's demand to give all children within the school district equal education opportunities. In addition, the board had not "erected a modern and well-equipped primary building for the Latin American children" as promised. Perales concluded that there is nothing further to do other than file suit to get relief for equality in the schools in Hondo since that district had failed to follow the State Superintendent's demand (Letter from AP to L. A. Woods, Feb. 18, 1938, Box 4, Folder 36).

Perales waged a similar battle with the Pleasanton school district. Perales complained to the Board of Education that schools should unite rather than divide citizens. If the school district persisted in the segregation of the children, then how, Perales questioned, will we "bring about a better understanding between the two peoples?" (Letter from AP to Pleasanton Board of Education, Sept. 24, 1946, Box 5, Folder 52). Since he did not receive a response to this letter, Perales again complained (Letter from AP to Pleasanton Board of Education, Oct. 10, 1946, Box 5, Folder 52). After another slight, Perales informed the State Superintendent of Public Instruction that the Pleasanton Board failed to address his request for desegregation (Letter from AP to L. A. Woods, Oct. 18, 1946, Box 5, Folder 52). The Pleasanton superintendent responded to Dr. Woods, but he did not provide Perales with a courtesy copy (Letter from W. J. Everitt to L. A. Woods, Oct. 12, 1946, Box 5, Folder 52). The State Superintendent told the Pleasanton official that Latin American children also deserve "nice school rooms, good equipment, textbooks, and an uncrowded situation as the Anglo Americans" (Letter from L. A. Woods to W. J. Everitt, Oct. 18, 1946, Box 5, Folder 52).

Legally White, Socially Brown: The Legal Foundations and the Social Realities

A. The Legal Construction of Race

The Mexican population is approximately sixty percent *mestizo* (Caucasian and Indian blood) and thirty percent Indian (Gopel, ed., 2005, p. 802). The initial racial classification of the Mexican population as predominantly Indian led to potential exclusion from citizenship by the terms of the 1836 constitution for the independent Texas republic (Gómez, 2007, p. 141). The Indian features also led to the exclusion of Manuel Domínguez, a Mexican-American citizen, from testifying in a trial in California in the 1850s. Domínguez, a signer of the California constitution and a county supervisor from Los Angeles, appeared in court to testify. Once the Anglo lawyer claimed Domínguez had Indian blood, he was declared ineligible as a witness (Pitt, 1966, p. 202).

Half a century after the conquest of Mexico by American forces and the 1848 signing of the Treaty of Guadalupe Hidalgo, the legal issue as to the citizenship eligibility and racial status of persons of Mexican descent surfaced. In the *Rodriguez* case, the applicant, a Mexican citizen by birth, applied for American citizenship. The court acknowledged that by the terms of the treaty, thousands of Mexicans were included "into our common [American] citizenship" (Rodriguez, 1897, p. 348). *Rodríguez* provided the first opportunity for a court to determine if a Mexican-descent person qualified under the law for individual naturalization. Since only white persons qualified under the statutes in effect, the government's lawyer contended that the applicant's color barred him from naturalization.

The judge in *Rodriguez* stated that a "strict scientific classification of the anthropologist" would probably not include Rodríguez under the white classification (Rodriguez, 1897, p. 349). On the color factor, the court discarded his classification as of African descent, a relevant consideration in view of the 1868 passage of the Fourteenth Amendment which provided citizenship to the freed slaves. Instead, the judge focused on the terms of the 1848 treaty as those terms related to Mexicans that remained in the territory previously belonging to Mexico. Article VIII of the treaty declared that these Mexicans may either retain the title and rights of Mexican citizens or "acquire those of citizens of the United States" (Rodriguez, 1897, p. 351). In the event that the Mexicans failed to make any affirmative decision, the treaty lan-

guage specifically declared that those Mexicans "shall be considered to have elected to become citizens of the United States" (Rodríguez, 1897, p. 351). Under these
circumstances, the judge decided that Rodríguez possessed the requisite qualifications for citizenship.

B. Hernandez v. Texas: The White-Black Two-Class Theory of Equal Protection

Notwithstanding the efforts of LULAC and other civil rights groups to promote
the "white" classification among Latinos, counsel for the litigant in *Hernandez v.
Texas* resorted to the concept that he and others similarly situated constituted a
unique ethnic group distinct from other whites (Hernandez, 1954, p. 475). The advocates had different motives for this decision. First, persons of Mexican descent had
been effectively and thus legally classified as white by means of the Treaty of
Guadalupe Hidalgo as explained in the *Rodriguez* case (Treaty of Guadalupe Hidalgo). However, for purposes of seeking equal protection of the laws from disparate
treatment by other whites, persons of Mexican descent effectively had to establish
that they were an identifiable ethnic group that had been subjected to impermissible
discrimination.

In the precedent-setting *Hernandez* court battle, the Supreme Court recognized
that "differences in race and color have defined easily identifiable groups which have
at times required the aid of the courts in securing equal treatment under the laws"
(Hernandez, 1954, p. 478). The customary practice of treating persons of Mexican
descent as non-white surfaced in the oral arguments before the Supreme Court when
the state's attorney inadvertently utilized the term "Latin American race" (García,
2009, p. 144).

C. Socially Brown: Anglo and Latino Attitudes Lead to the Same Construction

Perales' references to *la raza mexicana* (the Mexican Race) contribute to or at
least suggest the inference that Mexican Americans consider themselves as non-
white persons. Throughout his career and his efforts to obtain justice for his people,
Perales utilized the term "the Mexican race." In 1930, Perales made the following
remarks to a committee of Congress, which then had restrictive immigration legislation under consideration:

> At the outset, Mr. Chairman and members of the committee, I want to state
> that I am not here to oppose the Box bill or the Johnson bill or any other bill,
> but to promote the welfare of Texas—of the American people. Therefore I am
> not going to discuss the economic phases of this problem.
>
> However, I do wish to refer to the statements made by some sponsors of this
> quota bill, to the effect that the Mexican people is [sic] an inferior and degen-
> erate race. Being a Mexican by blood, and being just as proud of my racial
> extraction as I am of my American citizenship, I feel it my duty to deny most
> emphatically that the Mexican race is inferior to any other race. . . . (Got-
> theimer, 2003, p. 157)

The term *la raza* suggests that Mexican-descent Latinos regard themselves as a group identifiable and distinct from other whites. This identity comes from the reality of their Spanish and Indian blood mix, a characteristic which a Mexican secretary of education in the 1920s referred to as *La Raza Cósmica* (The Cosmic Race) (Vasconcelos, 1926). The term *la raza* appears even earlier when a Mexican-American newspaper editor used the term to describe Mexican Californians in the 1850s (Kanellos, 1996, p. 91).

In his comments to Congress, Perales further contributed to the view that Mexicans perceive themselves as having a separate "racial" identification. He stated:

> The charge is also made that Mexicans ought to be restricted because they do not become American citizens. I am one of the founders of what is known in Texas as the League of United Latin American Citizens. . . . The main objects of this organization are to develop within the members of our *race* the best, purest, and most perfect type of a true and loyal citizen of the United States of America; and to define with absolute and unmistakable clearness our unquestionable loyalty to the ideals, principles, and citizenship of the United States of America. (Emphasis added; Gottheimer, ed., 2003, p. 157)

Perales could have said "community" in lieu of "race," but he consistently utilized the term "race" as the correct translation for the Spanish word *raza*, a term which historically and correctly applied to this community of people primarily comprised of mixed blood persons (*mestizos*).

Did Perales' *hispano-indio* blend contribute to his constant use of the term *raza* in his writings and oral expressions? Officials described Perales in his 1925 U.S. passport as having a "dark complexion" (AP U.S. Passport, Box 1, Folder 6). Yet in public debates regarding discrimination against persons of Mexican descent, Perales asserted that Mexicans, or Latin Americans, constitute members of the white race. That view reflects the legal construction. However, the history and the discriminatory treatment of Mexican Americans reflect the social construction. Perhaps these two perspectives explain the seemingly contradictory postures taken by Perales during his advocacy in defense of his *raza*.

VI. Conclusion

One cannot fully appreciate the lifetime dedication of one person unless he or she directly benefitted from that person's sacrifice. Nonetheless, an objective examination of Perales' life establishes his contribution to the advancement of civil rights gains for Mexican Americans. The type of documentation which Perales accumulated in his books and papers, in one way or another, contributed to the enactment of legislation to prohibit discrimination on the basis, not only of race and color, but also of national origin (Perales, 1948; Civil Rights Act of 1964, 42 U.S.C. § 2000 *et seq.*).

Perales died in 1960. During the debates on the Civil Rights Act of 1964, opponents of the civil rights bill remarked that morality cannot be legislated. In other words, the minds of those inclined to treat one group as "lesser persons" could not be changed by the simple passage of a law. Perales perceptively responded to this type of comment by stating:

> To those who argue that one cannot legislate democracy or Christianity, we reply that murder and robbery run counter to the TEN COMMANDMENTS which rely for enforcement only on the appeal to man's heart and reason. Because this has proven insufficient, society has had to enact laws forbidding robbery and murder. It is true that neither medium has proved successful in abolishing crime completely. But we can well imagine what the situation would be if it were not for our schools, our churches, the press, the radio, and THE LAW. (Emphasis in original; Perales, 1948, p. 9)

Perales fought incessantly for state and federal legislation to prohibit discrimination against Mexican Americans. He complained that since the early 1920s Anglo leaders responded that cooperation and education provided the best avenue to eliminate discriminatory practices in employment and public accommodations. Perales protested that this approach had "accomplished nothing" during the twenty-five years leading up to the publication of *Are We Good Neighbors?* Perales adhered to his position that legislation with effective enforcement powers provided the only realistic solution (Perales, 1948, p. 131).

In one area of civil rights concerns, the vote, Perales seemed to deviate from the protection of his people. For example, his adamant views with regards to the payment of a poll tax appeared somewhat elitist. By taking this position and not questioning the validity of paying to vote, he disregarded the financial impositions this prerequisite for voting had on an impoverished population. He apparently never questioned why the State of Texas made this a condition for voting. His extreme patriotic beliefs apparently blinded him on this matter. After all, to Perales, the vote provided a direct means by which one could become an "American."

Undoubtedly, Perales' example, along with that of J.T. Canales and M.C. Gonzales, incited others to fight for the rights of *la raza*. As previously described, Perales worked with Carlos Cadena, one of the *Hernandez v. Texas* lawyers, in the *Clifton v. Puente* restrictive covenant case in 1948. In all fairness, the efforts of Perales and other Latino legal crusaders, such as Cadena and Gustavo C. García, who both joined Perales in the late 1930s in San Antonio, served as incentives to other new lawyers to sacrifice on behalf of *la raza*. Some of those new lawyers included Albert Peña, Pete Tijerina, Mario G. Obledo, John J. Herrera and James De Anda. In 1968, several of these outstanding lawyers collaborated in the founding of the Mexican American Legal Defense and Educational Fund.

Perales unfortunately did not gain the respect he deserved. As noted by a historian, some activists and scholars of the 1970s referred to Perales and other leaders of his era as *vendidos* (sell-outs) because of the concessions they made to the dominant Anglo political system (Orozco, 2009, p. 92). In rebuttal, at times, Perales honestly came across as somewhat assertive. Referring to his Mexican and Indian roots, and, by inference, his *raza*, Perales boldly stated that "Americans should not despise and slander, but rather welcome, even salute and respect the founders of this continent"

(AP Editorial, B8, F12). In this instance, Perales appeared to be somewhat of a militant, almost demanding equality.

Personally, this writer desires that Perales' accomplishments and good deeds will be etched into historical monuments at a future American Latino museum. While Perales did not have many impact litigation cases, he nevertheless achieved a lasting legacy. First, as one of the first Mexican-American lawyers in Texas and the nation, Perales assumed the duty of speaking for his people. Fortunately, Perales possessed this leadership characteristic even before he became a licensed attorney in 1925. His example and his impressive documentation of the history and suffering of Mexican Americans, at his own expense, will always now be remembered via the Alonso S. Perales Collection at the University of Houston.

The fact that Perales had a few shortcomings in the political and legal arena should not detract from his many accomplishments. His silence and tacit acceptance of the poll tax contradicted his fight for equal rights (Orozco, 2009, p. 214), but it also consistently represented his desire to incite Mexican Americans into civic involvement. At the same time, his unyielding anti-communist stance conflicted with his stand on the need to respect the Constitution of the United States, even when it disallowed an American citizen the opportunity to engage in free speech (Marquez, 2012, p. 24).

In closing this discussion of the Latino population's status of being legally white and yet socially brown, I wish I would be writing about a past. Instead, I have written—albeit briefly—about a history of racial superiority and advantage that endures in our country. Blame the tenacity of Latinos in wanting to adhere to cultural values, particularly the Spanish language. Blame the continuous Latino immigration. Blame the Anglo intellectuals such as Huntington and fear mongers like Lou Dobbs and Patrick Buchanan who decry the "browning" of America. (Huntington, 1996, p. 8; Lopez, 1996, p. 18). Clearly, we need more leaders like Alonso S. Perales to assist in the battle for Latino equality.

To Marta Pérez de Perales who allowed her husband to give so much to his community, to the Perales children who provided the University of Houston with his papers, and to those individuals who anonymously assisted Alonso S. Perales in his crusade for justice for his people, we can only say Mil Gracias (a thousand times "thank you"). All Latinos, not just Mexican-descent persons, owe Alonso S. Perales, this illustrious person, an incredible and immeasurable appreciation for making life a better one for Latinos in the United States.

Bibliography

Books

Garcia, I. M. (2009). *White but not equal: Mexican Americans, jury discrimination, and the Supreme Court*. Tucson: University of Arizona Press.

Gopel, E. C. (Ed.). (2005). *The world almanac and book of facts, 2005*. New York: World Almanac Books.

Gómez, L. E. (2007). *Manifest destinies: The making of the Mexican American race*. New York: New York University.

Gottheimer, J. (2003). *Ripples of hope: Great American civil rights speeches*. New York: Basic Civitas Books.

Hearings on Migratory Labor Before the Subcommittee on Labor And Labor-Management Relations of the Senate Committee on Labor and Public Welfare. 82d Cong., 2d Sess., 1, 131. (1952).

Huntington, S. P. (1996). *The clash of civilizations and the remaking of world order*. New York: Simon & Schuster.

Kanellos, N. & Martell, H. (2000). *Hispanic periodicals in the United States, origins to 1960: A brief history and comprehensive bibliography*. Houston, TX: Arte Público Press.

Haney Lopez, I. F. (1996). *White by law: The legal construction of race*. New York: New York University Press.

Montejano, D. (2010). *Quixote's soldiers: A local history of the Chicano movement, 1966-1981*. Austin: University of Texas Press.

Orozco, C. E. (2009). *No Mexicans, women, or dogs allowed: The rise of the Mexican American civil rights movement*. Austin: University of Texas Press.

Perales, A. S. (Ed). (1974). *Are we good neighbors?* New York: Arno Press.

Perales, A. S. (1937) *En defensa de mi raza, vol II*. San Antonio: Artes Gráficas.

Pitt, L. (1966). *The decline of the Californios: A social history of the Spanish-speaking Californians, 1846-1890*. Berkeley: University of California Press.

Vasconcelos, J. (1940). *La raza cosmica: Mision de la raza iberoamericana; notas de viajes a la America del Sur*. Barcelona: Agencia Mundial de Librería.

Weber, D. J. (Ed.). (1973). *Foreigners in their native land: Historical roots of the Mexican Americans*. Albuquerque: University of New Mexico Press.

Journal articles

Salinas, G. (1971). Mexican Americans and the desegregation of schools in the Southwest. *Houston Law Review 8*, 929-951.

Salinas, L. S. (2003). Gus Garcia and Thurgood Marshall: Two legal giants fighting for justice. *Thurgood Marshall Law Review 28*, 145-175.

Salinas, L. S. (2005). Latinos and criminal justice in Texas: Has the new millennium brought progress? *Thurgood Marshall Law Review 30*, 289-346.

Judicial Opinions

Brown v. Board of Education, 347 U.S. 483 (1954).

Clifton v. Puente, 218 S.W.2d 272 (Tex. Civ. App.—San Antonio 1948)

Delgado v. Bastrop Ind. School Dist., Civ. No. 388 (W.D. Tex. June 15, 1948).

Harper v. Virginia Bd. of Elections, 383 U.S. 663 (1966).

Hernandez v. Texas, 347 U.S. 475 (1954).

Independent School Dist. v. Salvatierra, 33 S.W.2d 790 (Tex Civ. App.-San Antonio 1930), *cert. denied*, 284 U.S. 580 (1931).

In re Rodriguez, 81 F. 337 (W.D. Tex. 1897).

League of United Latin American Citizens v. Perry, 548 U.S. 399 (2006).

Matthews v. Andrade, 198 P.2d 66 (Cal. App. 1948).
Salvatierra v. Independent School District (Del Rio, Texas), Statement as to Jurisdiction on Appeal, 1931 WL 32417 (U.S. No. 195, July 27, 1931).
Shelley v. Kraemer, 334 U.S. 1 (1948).
Zamora v. New Braunfels Ind. School Dist., 519 F.2d 1084 (5th Cir. 1975), *rev'g* 362 F. Supp. 552 (W.D. Tex. 1973).

Treaties and Statutes

Title II, Civil Rights Act of 1964, 42 U.S.C. § 2000 *et seq.*
Treaty of Guadalupe Hidalgo, 9 Stat. 922 (1848).

Newspapers and Online Sources

Gutiérrez, Dr. J. A. (1998, January 16). Oral history interview with Aguinaldo Zamora. *Tejano Voices*. Retrieved 2012, September 2 from http://library.uta.edu/tejanovoices/xml/CMAS_136.xml

Gibson, C. & Jung, K. (2002). Historical census statistics on population totals by race, 1790 to 1990, and by Hispanic origin, 1970 to 1990, for the United States, regions, divisions, and states, population division. *U. S. Census Bureau*. Working Paper Series No. 56. Retrieved 2012, March 15 from http://www.census.gov/population/www/documentation/twps0056/tab58.pdf.

History. (n.d.). *George Washington University*. Retrieved 2012, September 2 from http://www.law.gwu.edu/School/Pages/History.aspx.

LULAC history - All for one and one for all. (n.d.). *LULAC*. Retrieved 2011, December 4 from http://lulac.org/about/history/.

Márquez, B. (2012). In defense of my people: Alonso S. Perales and the moral construction of citizenship. *Latinoteca*. Retrieved 2012, September 2 from http://www.latinoteca.com/recovery/recovery-content/papers-perales-conference/MarquezPeralesEssaywStandardCitations.pdf.

Notes

[1] I extend my sincerest gratitude to the University of Houston and Arte Público Press in general and Dr. Nicolás Kanellos and the Recovering the U.S. Hispanic Literary Heritage Program, University of Houston, in particular for obtaining the Alonso S. Perales papers. Over forty years ago, Perales' *Are We Good Neighbors?* inspired me in writing my first law review article about the operation of Mexican Schools in Texas and the Southwest. (Salinas, 1971, 936 n. 51). Finally, I thank Texas Southern University and Thurgood Marshall School of Law for their generous summer 2011 research stipend and Danny Norris, Merari Meza, Arpita Baweja and Karine Neumann for their many hours of reviewing and editing the Perales collection with me.

Mendigos de nacionalidad: Mexican-Americanism and Ideologies of Belonging in a New Era of Citizenship, Texas 1910-1967[1]

Aarón E. Sánchez

In 1934, University of California Economist Paul S. Taylor commented on a growing group of U.S.-Mexicans who had begun to call themselves "Mexican-Americans." He explained that, "the term Mexican-American is as yet little used. I have employed it here, however, to denote a small but significant group in south Texas, which, as its members have become conscious of their American citizenship, has assumed this name" (241). He continued, "'Mexican-American' conforms more closely to the ideals which the group holds for its people, and is used consciously by them" (241). Taylor astutely observed an important ideological change occurring in the ethnic Mexican community in Texas and later across the Southwest. This group of middling and middle-class native-born Mexicans had recently begun to call themselves Mexican Americans for specific reasons.

Many historians have written about the importance of World War I and World War II in the creation of the Mexican-American Generation (García 1989, Gutiérrez 1995, Orozco 2009, Ramírez 2009, Sánchez 1993, Zamora 2009). These historians have argued that the wars and the subsequent discrimination veterans encountered were the most important influences on the mid-twentieth century U.S.-Mexicans (Monroy, 1999, p. 257-258). Indeed, many veterans returned to their hometowns to a rude awakening after fighting abroad for the American dream. However, this was not just a generational cohort but a new imaginary, a new way of seeing and understanding the world. Mexican-Americanism was not simply a reaction to the discrimination veterans received after returning from war, nor was it a simple acknowledgment of citizenship. Instead, it was a long ideological and intellectual transformation that responded to changing notions of belonging that had been occurring since the late nineteenth century in the form of citizenship and a response to evolving homeland politics in the U.S. Southwest during the first decades of the twentieth century.

Citizenship, the Nation-State and the Legitimate Means of Belonging

Mexicans living within the territory ceded by Mexico after the signing of the Treaty of Guadalupe Hidalgo in 1848 had been awarded citizenship, but citizenship in this remote region did not carry the weight that it would in later years. Citizenship began to change globally, in dramatic ways, and emerged by the 1920s as the legitimate means of belonging. Citizenship became increasingly important in an era of global migrations that occurred during the late nineteenth century. Prior to the aggressive emergence of the modern capitalist world-system, national authorities tried to keep subjects bound to the land (Torpey, 2000, p. 57). Gradually that system became unsustainable. While prior modes of production demanded immobile workers in order to reproduce themselves, capitalism needed mobile workers in flux with the local, regional, national, and international labor markets. The new found mobility of people during the nineteenth century threw off the balance of the previous system's ability to regulate membership and the right to benefits of belonging (Torpey, 2000, p. 71). Under the previous system, the experience of being rooted physically in a specific place, voluntarily or by force, for long stretches of time allowed for identities between "locals" and "outsiders" to be made quite easily. The breakdown of this system forced national authorities to redefine belonging in concrete, bureaucratic terms. "Governments became increasingly oriented to making distinctions between their own citizens/subjects and others," explains historical sociologist John Torpey (2000), and that "distinction that could be made only on the basis of documents" (p. 93). The nation-state needed its people to have a new identity, one that was categorical and defined. So it issued them one and called them citizens (Torpey, 2000, p. 108).

In addition to the disruptions caused by a growing capitalist world-system, the two World Wars that tore across Europe in the first half of the twentieth century had important consequences on how people imagined belonging. The First World War put an end to the laissez-faire sentiment regarding the movement of peoples driven by economic liberalism. The outbreak of war made the distinction between citizens who belonged and dangerous interlopers important. The passport and other authoritative documents that officially declared citizenship aided nation-states in figuring out who the state could embrace and demand services from. Many governments reintroduced stiff passport regulations: France in 1912, Britain and Italy in 1914, Germany in 1916, and the United States in 1917 (Torpey, 2000, p. 108-118). The temporary measures, mostly introduced during the War, became permanent afterwards. The demise of non nation-state configurations (such as the Austro-Hungarian and Ottoman empires) in 1918 and the large amounts of refugees after World War II elevated the importance of citizenship and its attendant documents (Torpey, 2000, p. 122). Without a state, or without citizenship, refugees could make no claim to access national territory or claim any rights. By mid-century, citizenship became a form of access to rights and nation-states began to develop the bureaucratic systems and networks necessary to issue, control, investigate and validate identity.

In the United States citizenship gained equal importance, with one critical distinction. Citizenship in the United States became racialized. This caused problems for many ethnic groups that called the U.S. home. As early as the middle of the nineteenth century U.S. authorities had struggled to assert the imperative of a state-centered identity for its citizens, within the nation and without. In 1882, Congress passed the Chinese Exclusion Act, which barred Chinese immigration for ten years and prohibited Chinese already in the nation from becoming citizens. This historic act was important because it marked a definite change in immigration policy for the nation. The United States became a "gate-keeping nation," interested in keeping citizens and citizenship free of racial contamination (Lee, 2003, p. 6). In 1888, the U.S. Supreme Court upheld exclusion as a legitimate power of the state in *Chae Chan Ping v. United States* (Salyer, 1995, p. 23). In its ruling, the court pushed past the previous legal precedent that allowed Congress to control immigration—namely, that Congress had the constitutional authority to regulate international commerce—towards a larger paradigmatic conception that emphasized that sovereignty and territoriality were one, meaning the state had an inherent right to control its borders (Torpey, 2000, pp. 99-100; Salyer, 1995, p. 23). The power of the state to control access to citizenship through documents would have lasting impacts on people who were physically present in the nation, but who were legally and politically excluded.

Exclusion clarified and narrowed the definition of American. "Aliens" were, historian Mae Ngai (2004) explains, a caste "unambiguously situated outside the boundaries of formal membership and social legitimacy" (p. 2). The connections between racialized migrants and ethnic groups in the United States created a caste of "alien citizens" (Ngai, 2004, p. 8). Ethnic minorities in the United States shared cultural and racial otherness with the legally excluded "aliens," despite being U.S. citizens by birth. These shared traits often undermined their claims of citizenship, since many saw them as non-white. Since 1790 (and until 1954), citizenship in the United States was reserved for white persons only (Haney López, 1996, p. 1; Jacobson, 1999, p. 13). The difficulty with this stipulation for many ethnic minorities was that whiteness was still in the making. For some groups, like the Italians and the Irish, whiteness, and subsequently citizenship, was more easily obtained. For others, a combination of immigration laws and court opinions were responsible for their inclusion or occlusion.

Beginning in 1878 and ending in 1952, there was a series of fifty-two prerequisite cases in which judges systematically identified who was not white, as opposed to offering a complete typology of who was (Haney López, 1996, p. 27). Using a mixture of scientific racism and "common knowledge," judges decided which groups were non-white. A very important intellectual and legal precedent was made in 1909 in *In re Najour*, when the judge developed the important connections between Caucasian, whiteness, and citizens (Haney López, 1996, p. 71). In his opinion, he reasoned that these terms were all linked. When eugenics failed to fully exclude groups like Syrians, Japanese and Asian Indians, judges used "common knowledge" or what was popularly understood to be a white person, to strip them of their whiteness and deny them citizenship. Throughout all of the prerequisite cases, the relationship between whiteness and citizenship was continuously emphasized and upheld. Interestingly, in the 1897 case *In re Rodriguez* the judge opined that Rodriguez and other Mexicans, regardless of nationality, were not white. However, Mexicans were allowed to become citizens, not because of their whiteness but because of previous treaties (Haney López, 1996, p. 61). Nonetheless, the political, legal and social ties that connected citizenship and whiteness were sufficiently established.

In 1924, Congress passed the Johnson-Reed Act, a comprehensive immigration act that established numerical limits on immigration and created a global racial hierarchy that favored certain nationalities over others (Ngai, 2004, p. 3). The Johnson-

Reed Act helped reinforce the racial boundaries of citizenship in the twentieth century. The quota system that emerged after the passing of the act considered all Europeans, regardless of nationality, as white. Because officials assigned all Europeans whiteness, they became assimilable and ready citizens (Ngai, 2004, p. 25). The conglomeration of all Europeans as white brought an end to a previous era of variegated whiteness (Jacobson, 1999, p. 52). In the post Johnson-Reed era, a "monolithic whiteness" emerged which represented and new "epistemological realm of certainty" for whiteness in which those who could claim it had access to power, citizenship, and authority (Jacobson, 1999, pp. 93-95).

Citizenship, then, in the face of the collapse of previous modes of imagining that had organized belonging, became the defining characteristic of belonging during the twentieth century. By the 1920s, the discursive authority of the nation-state predicated on complex bureaucratic structures and a specialized core of civil servants trained to manipulate them had replaced previous, spatially conceived notions of homeland and belonging that had shaped relationships between individuals and communities (Chávez, 1984; Chávez, 2009). By codifying the rights and meaning of citizenship, the nation-state changed the way that people viewed their relationship and responsibilities to other human beings. While citizenship had always been racialized, the racial epistemological foundations and legal authority had changed. It was this new form of citizenship, not a common humanity, which became the conceptual framework for defining the limits of moral, ethical and political responsibilities between people. Citizenship in the form of documents that legally identified people became the dominant mode of imagining across the globe. The state then used these documents, which had legal and international standing, to render certain groups unrecognizable and not worthy of belonging by declaring them aliens. This new emphasis on citizenship impacted U.S.-Mexican thinking in the United States.

Afuera del México de afuera

In addition to the changing importance of citizenship across the globe and its effect on belonging, U.S.-Mexicans found themselves in the middle of, what historian Emilio Zamora (1993) calls the "evolving homeland politics" of the twentieth century (p. 92). Because of the upheavals of the Mexican Revolution, millions of Mexican nationals moved into the border states, seeking refuge from the violence. These Mexican nationals not only intruded upon and disrupted already established Mexican communities, but brought with them their own sense of "Mexicanness" and belonging. While previously the communities of U.S.-Mexicans considered themselves "Mexicanos," or Mexican in language, comportment, race and culture, the newly arrived Mexican nationals scoffed at their cultural differences (Paredes, 1976, pp. 153-161; Paredes, 1958, p. xi). The Mexican nationals that fled the Revolution were in the midst of re-making their nation in the form of an exiled imagined community they called *México de afuera*. U.S.-Mexican proscription from belonging to the ideological world of *México de afuera* affected the way in which some U.S.-Mexicans thought about their own regional, national and international positioning.

Mexican nationals fled the violence of the Revolution. Most abhorred the political chaos in their country. Many of these Mexican nationals in cities like San Antonio, Brownsville, Laredo and El Paso, among many others, began to see themselves as the truest Mexicans and truest patriots. Their duty in the United States was to maintain a pristine Mexican culture in order to return and redeem their country. They saw themselves as the only hope for Mexico. In one 1916 article entitled "México Emigrado y México Esclavo," (Emigrated Mexico and Enslaved Mexico) the author explained

> We represent the nation's thought in its essence and furthermore, our urgent obligation consists in unifying ourselves and then unifying the energies and incoherent aspirations of a nation that awaits our return like salvation . . . emigrated Mexico will redeem enslaved Mexico.[1] . . . the exiled will return to reconstruct the Nation. If they do not do it they deserve . . . the curse of history for not handing down to their children the inheritance of an intact and autonomous nation that their parents received. (México Emigrado y México Esclavo)

Exiled Mexican nationals saw the cultural negotiations of U.S.-Mexicans as a form of treason because they thought the only hope for the future of Mexico lay in the hands of the Mexican nationals in the United States. In the ideological world of *México de afuera*, U.S.-Mexicans were the lowest form of traitors and renegades (Kanellos, 2001, p. 28). Mexican nationals negated U.S.-Mexicanness and started to call them insults, like *pocha* and *pocho*. In a 1919 article entitled "Las Que Tienen Novios Gringos," (The Women Who Have Gringo Boyfriends) Benjamín Padilla criticized U.S.-Mexicans for dating Anglos. He saw this as tantamount to another invasion of Mexican sovereignty and territory: "The Yankee danger, which has already invaded our mines, merchants, and industry, threatens something that should be exclusively ours, something intimate, that belongs to only those of this country, the virgin hearts of our little chicks: the ineffable love of our Mexican women." The heart, body, and soul, as well as the "ineffable love" and sexuality of Mexican women, belonged to Mexico and were the patrimony of Mexican men. Padilla believed that U.S.-Mexican women were likely to disregard traditional Mexican morality in exchange for a chance to be with an American, which in turn would lead to a soiled reputation or a pregnancy out of wedlock. Padilla finished his article with a resounding lesson for *pocha* mothers and daughters, "Oh, women, partisans of the gringos! In your sin you will carry your penance!"

Negative characterizations of U.S.-Mexicans abounded. In his 1926 novel *El Sol de Texas*, author and journalist Conrado Espinoza described the U.S.-Mexican population as "families that that, in terms of appearance, have lost their Mexican identity and are in terms of language (horrible Spanish and horrible English), in terms of their customs (grotesque and licentious), in terms of their desires (futile and fatuous ambition); a hybrid group which adapts itself neither in this country [the U.S.] nor in our own [Mexico]" (48).[2] Espinoza was not alone in his assessment; many other journalists felt similarly. One explained that "few Mexicans who are living in the

United States have the brilliant characteristics and virtues of a true lover of his country . . ." ("Lirismos Absurdos").

Unwittingly, the project of *México de afuera*—creating true patriots and real Mexicans—intersected with the Mexican government's new attempt at *Forjando Patria*—creating a new nation and new citizens—by displacing Mexican belonging from the United States. By 1918 Mexican consuls in the United States started to reach out to the ethnic Mexican population in the U.S again, an effort that only grew in the years afterward (Rosales, 1999, p. 41). By 1921, Consuls in cities like San Antonio, Dallas, and Austin formed patriotic commissions to promote Mexican nationalism and organize *fiestas patrias* (Rosales, 1999, p. 42). In an effort to forge a new national identity and to create belonging for its citizens, the Mexican state was reaching out to its displaced citizens in the United States.

The Mexican state through their bureaucratic control over the legitimate means of belonging and the efforts of its consuls, sponsored lectures, and patriotic festivals in the United States in an effort to make Mexicanness dependent upon citizenship in the 1920s (Arredondo, 2008, p. 172). The Mexican government tried to use the obligations of a new and robust citizenship to ensure political allegiance and economic ties for its citizens living in the United States. While just decades earlier, ethnic Mexicans understood their identity in a primarily cultural context, they could now know for certain they were Mexican because they were Mexican citizens. This had an important effect on ethnic Mexicans and their conceptualizing of belonging. In one article an author condemned U.S.-Mexicans to the darkest corner of hell for not being true citizens: "We have heard that my country is wherever I have a good time. Furthermore, [we have heard] 'I am a Texas-Mexican.' To close, those who do not love their country, do not love god or their homes; they are beings from the darkest corner of hell" (Guzman, 1930).

In 1930, after interviewing ethnic Mexicans in the United States and after his initial call for a new Mexican nationalism and sense of belonging, Mexican anthropologist and public intellectual Manuel Gamio (1930) concluded that U.S.-Mexicans were "semi-mexican[s]" and "[persons] without a country" (pp. 65; 129). He continued by stating that "[the ethnic Mexican] does not find that country a true homeland even when he becomes naturalized" (Gamio, 1930, p. 177). The Mexican consul in San Antonio, Enrique Santibáñez, agreed with Gamio's conclusion. He wrote in his book *Ensayo Acerca de la Inmigración Mexicana en los Estados Unidos*, "Some [U.S.-Mexicans] live conceitedly with the sense of superiority that they are American citizens. I believe that they try to show it off more than they actually feel it." (Santibáñez, 1930, p. 90). In a 1930 editorial in the Spanish-language newspaper *La Prensa*, Santibáñez directed a harsh criticism to U.S.-Mexicans, "allow me to say to the Mexicans, my co-nationals, that they should always remember that they live in a foreign nation, that they came by their own choice to the United States and that they have no right to disturb the existing social conditions here [and] if luck is bad in one place, they should seek their fortune in another or return to their country."

C.R. Escudero described the disdain of U.S.-Mexicans precisely. He called U.S.-Mexicans "a race of white blackbirds, ugly ducklings, without speech, blood, a name, or heritage" ("Americanización y Mexicanización"). They were a race of white blackbirds "who the [Anglos] keep considering Mexicans even though they are citizens of the United States and the Mexicans consider ugly renegades because they do not even know their own language." Perhaps it was journalist and novelist Jorge Ainslie's character José, a *pocho* himself, that best described the feeling of Mexican nationals about U.S.-Mexicans. José described his *pocha* sister by asking her "And you, what are you? You are a sad wannabe American, who does not even come close to a white girl" (Ainslie, 1934, p. 143). Whether they considered U.S.-Mexicans cursed deformed Mexicans, ugly white blackbirds or sad wannabe Americans who were not close to being white, Mexican nationals did not think highly of U.S.-Mexicanness. They had excluded U.S.-Mexicans from belonging in *México de afuera*, they insulted them by labeling them *pochas* and *pochos*, and they disregarded them because they were no longer Mexican citizens. In almost two decades, Mexican nationals had displaced and uprooted U.S.-Mexican belonging. As Gamio concluded in 1930, they were people without a place.

Mexican-Americanism and the New Ideology of Belonging

Thus, within the context of the evolving homeland politics raging in the Southwest and the global changes in the importance of citizenship, U.S.-Mexicans found themselves between nations and with tentative claims of belonging. Mexican nationals believed that U.S.-Mexicans were persons without a country. U.S.-Mexicans were left outside of *México de afuera* and they were marginalized and attacked in the United States. But a group of middling and middle-class U.S.-Mexicans began to call themselves "Mexican-American" in response to both of these forces. They chose citizenship in order to answer the question of U.S.-Mexican belonging. However, this was not without a price. Mexican Americans did not just *acknowledge* citizenship but *understood* it in a particular way. They understood that citizenship was the legitimate mode of belonging and was controlled by the state. Moreover, they understood the racialized nature of citizenship—the connections between being white and being a citizen. Mexican-Americanism chose this form of citizenship over other modes of imagining. Unfortunately, the ideology of middle-class Mexican-Americanism did not *co-opt* the exclusive language of citizenship, but instead *cooperated* in its reproduction. Mexican Americans, like Alonso S. Perales, Andres de Luna, J.T. Canales, and many others helped craft an ideology, a new way of understanding the relationships among people of the world. During the first half of the twentieth century a powerful ideological and intellectual shift was underway in U.S.-Mexican thought.

In 1919, a young World War I veteran named Alonso S. Perales wrote an article in the Laredo paper, *La Evolución*, under the title "Como Inculcan Americanismo en este Pais." In the article he stated that the most important factor in the success of U.S.-Mexican Americanization was recognizing the difference between Mexican nationals and "México Texanos." Mexico-Texans, according to Perales' article, were not "semicitizens" because of the failures of Americanization, but were second-class citizens. The journey of becoming Americans was dependent on becoming full citizens. He described the problem of being abeyant Americans again in the 1920s, "It is now time that we awake from our lethargy and we see the situation how it is . . . Not here nor in Mexico is there anybody who worries about our welfare and our future" (Ts., Alonso S. Perales, "El Porvenir de los Mexico Americanos," n.d., Microfilm 2309, Reel 12).[3] By 1924, Perales was already articulating an emerging imaginary, writing "we who are citizens of this country are just as American as the Americans and no individual who has the blood of other peoples in his veins has the right—he has the audacity—to tell us that we are not 'one hundred percent Americans'" ("La Evolución de los Mexico-Americanos," October 1924, Microfilm 2309, Reel 13).

These were early vocalizations of a new way of understanding U.S.-Mexican belonging, one keyed in on the language of citizenship. Early proponents and shapers of Mexican-Americanism, such as Perales, understood that belonging was now dependent on citizenship, on legal documents, statutes and precedents. Belonging was hinged on publicly accepted performances of allegiance. Citizenship, many Mexican Americans understood, was a legal concept that needed to be defended but also a racial description. They would elaborate on these points throughout the century.

Emphasizing citizenship was a dramatic change (Gutiérrez, 1995, pp. 74-78). Just a decade earlier, ethnic Mexican *mutualistas* operated under different ideas and pursued different goals. The Orden Caballeros de Honor y los Talleres (Order Knights of Honor), with twenty four chapters across Texas in 1911, and the San Antonio chapter of the Alianza Hispano-Americana in 1913, founded in Arizona in the 1880s, were two major ethnic Mexican organizations that were open to both Mexican nationals and U.S. Mexicans regardless of citizenship (Orozco, 2009, p. 67). Their goals differed from the later organizations; they promoted workers and burial insurance, fraternalism, and social life (Orozco, 2009, p. 67). These (mostly) working-class groups did not desire to create an overarching definition of what it meant to be Mexican in the United States like later groups would. The contentious debates over homeland politics forced a wedge between U.S.-Mexicans and Mexican nationals. The new groups of the 1920s were not creating fraternity, but instead constructing their belonging on the claims of a new legal and racial definition. The new groups distinguished themselves from Mexican nationals because they were American citizens.

Alonso S. Perales was not the only one who was thinking about U.S.-Mexican belonging and the concept of citizenship. The 1920s saw the rise of a number of Mexican-American civic organizations that distinctively emphasized citizenship. In 1922, the Order Sons of America was the first major U.S.-Mexican civic organization to make membership dependent on citizenship but it was not the last. "The Order Sons of America was created," stated their constitution in 1922, "with the fixed purpose of changing the channel of events, battling the negligence and slowness of the citizens of this country—of Mexican or Spanish racial origin" (*"Constitucion y Leyes de la Orden Hijos de America*). It went on to explain that "that until today, and never in the past, has [the Mexican-American community] had a single well defined idea of what they should try in their present position and their duties, rights, and prerogatives as citizens of the United States" (*Constitucion y Leyes de la Orden Hijos de America*). They needed to consider themselves Americans and make themselves conscious of the obligations that citizenship entailed. They needed to change their individual and collective ideas to become Americans. According to the OSA constitution, Mexican Americans could not claim citizenship until they established the validity of Mexican-American loyalty to the nation, not to each other. They chose as their motto, "por nuestra patria" (*Constitucion y Leyes de la Orden Hijos de America*). This came during a period when Mexican nationals and U.S.-Mexicans were struggling with the notion of "patria." Mexican nationals were in the midst of trying to deal with the meaning and contradictions of exile and the implications that had on having a country. Indeed by the late 1920s, when the OSA was reaching a critical mass, many Mexican nationals saw U.S.-Mexicans as being a people without a country. Perales hinted at the ideas behind an emerging Mexican-Americanism and the claims of being without a homeland in 1924, writing

> What is the ideal of the Mexican-Americans? Pretend to Americanize ourselves? Do we want to rebel against our people? Do they just ask Anglo-Saxons if they can mix socially with them? These are the answers: conscious Mexican-Americans consider themselves, under a certain point of view, just as American as the most American and we challenge whoever who wants to prove the contrary. ("El Ideal de Los Mexico-Americanos," October 1924, Microfilm 2309, Reel 13)

Mexican-Americanism was an emerging ideology that settled the issue of U.S.-Mexican belonging by rooting it in the United States. In a group mailing in 1926, the OSA president Andres de Luna declared: "for once and for all we want to stop being beggars of a nationality, men without country, an unconscious and disoriented racial element, or pilgrims after many generations who live in an incomplete state of uncertainty in regards to their country and citizenship" ("Orden Hijos de America").

In 1927, members from the Order Sons of America formed a new association called the Order Knights of America (Orozco "Order Knights of America"). They also based their claim of belonging on citizenship. They communicated the goals of the group: "this is exclusively made up of individuals of Mexican origin, and it works for the education of its members in regards to their obligations and rights as citizens of this country" (*OKA News*, Vol. 1 No. 2. December 1927). Another group emerged in 1927 in South Texas called the Latin American Citizens League. The organization's first objective was to "define with clarity and absolute and unequivocal precision our indisputable loyalty to the ideals, principles, and citizenship of the U.S." (*Manual for Use by the League of Latin American Citizens*). Under their "Code," their first obligation was to "Respect your citizenship, preserve it; honor your country" (*Manual for Use by the League of Latin American Citizens*).

In 1929, these three organizations combined to form the League of United Latin American Citizens (LULAC), perhaps the most famous Mexican-American civil rights organization. Its primary aim was to "develop within the members of our race the best, purest, and most perfect type of a true and loyal citizen of the United States of America" (Constitution, League of United Latin American Citizens). The conglomeration of all three organizations into LULAC in 1929 produced some of the most definite statements of Mexican-Americanism and belonging. Wanting to move away from being "beggars of nationality," as the OSA had called Mexican Americans, LULAC wanted to root U.S.-Mexican belonging firmly in the United States. In one article a LULAC member complained that "if the other groups were like us this would be a hodge-podge of little countries: Little Germany, Little England, Little Switzerland, etc., neither of which, much like ourselves, actually form another country" ("Para los que no conocen nuestra [institucion]"). The ideology of Mexican-Americanism shifted the view of U.S.-Mexicans as a diaspora towards an imaginary as bounded ethnic Americans. "While we do not elevate ourselves to the level of citizens we will never be more than conquered people" explained one member ("Para los que no conocen nuestra [institución]").

It seemed that the efforts of Mexican nationals to dislocate U.S.-Mexican belonging had worked. At the 1929 Corpus Christi Conference which created LULAC representative José G. González said in his speech, "I see that we form a conglomerate without country, without prerogatives, and what is ever more sad, with very few hopes of obtaining a betterment of this deplorable condition of parias [sic]." But, Mexican Americans were working to relocate U.S.-Mexican belonging within the U.S. nation-state. González concluded that "perhaps this union [LULAC] will serve to give a country to our children, who otherwise each time they thought of us would say: They lived parias [sic], and they left us this sad inheritance." This sentiment was echoed repeatedly by other members. In April of 1929, one member wrote in *El Paladín* that "our children [are] the vestiges of a great disinherited family and tomorrow, if our apathy permits, they will be begging for a country and even for homes" (*El Paladín* April 12, 1929). Another member commented on the sad fate of being a person without a country, "the only recourse for him is to bow his head and go out of that place and sob out his shame and sadness on finding himself turned into a new Wandering Jew, condemned to travel, a stranger among strangers, and a stranger even in his own land" (*El Paladín* May 24, 1929). The answer that Mexican-Americanism provided was "to seek for ourselves a definite nationality and a country of our own which we are to serve" (*El Paladín* April 12, 1929).

They needed to become Americans inside and out; no longer could they be anything "*de afuera*." In a radio address at the end of the 1930s, LULAC addressed the issue of belonging yet again. The radio address inquired, "Which is our country? Just because we are descendents of Mexicans we can have two countries? This gives us the right to have double citizenship?" ("Respetable Radio-Auditorio"). The answer was a resounding no. The address provided the following answer: "in this shred of land that makes up the border states of the American Union, the tri-colored [Mexican] flag, the glorious insignia of our ancestors, does not reach to cover us" ("Respetable Radio-Auditorio"). The work to be done was to "pedir patria dentro de su propia patria" (Respetable Radio-Auditorio).

By the end of the 1920s Mexican Americans did not just recognize their status as U.S. citizens, but understood that citizenship was the legitimate avenue to claim belonging. They were citizens; no longer were they wayward souls. But by basing their belonging on a racially prescriptive and conservative citizenship, Mexican

Americans did not expand the definition. Instead, they placed their claims of belonging on a concept that was under the control and authority of the state. It was also a term that was increasingly exclusive because of the racial limitations associated with citizenship.

The 1930s were particularly important in the crafting of Mexican-Americanism's case for belonging. One journalist described the goal for the decade in 1930: "we will demonstrate that we do have a country . . . that we love her and we want to endeavor to ennoble her" ("Editorial: Nobles Propositos"). The goals of demonstrating that Mexican Americans had a place to belong would be asserted in the decade by trying to claim Mexican-American whiteness and cooperating in the narration of the nation during the Texas centennial celebration of independence in 1936.

The racial order of early twentieth-century America gave Mexican Americans one of their early strategies. They would ardently claim whiteness. The Johnson-Reed Act had codified the assumption that the United States was a white nation with its origins in a white Europe (Ngai, 2004, p. 27). Whiteness was a prerequisite for citizenship. Being non-white and unfit for citizenship implied social degeneracy and a lack of political values (Haney López, 1996, p. 16). This implication was built on a racial regime that esteemed whiteness and denigrated blackness (Gerstle, 1996, p. 118). As early as 1922, the OSA had made a case for Mexican-American whiteness in their constitution and laws. This effort only increased in later years.

In the 1930 Census, ethnic Mexicans were separated and counted as a non-white group. This struck a blow in the Mexican-American project because they had effectively lost their whiteness (Foley, 1998, p. 61). Mexican Americans tried tirelessly to reclaim their lost status in their writings and actions. They objected to the association of Mexican Americans as "colored" not only in the Census but also in city directories and in social interactions. In one incident in 1936, LULAC Council No. 16 Secretary Gregory R. Salinas complained of racial interaction between black men and Mexican-American women at an event. He wrote angrily in a letter, "let us tell these negroes that we are not going to permit our manhood and womanhood to mingle with them on an equal social basis" (Gregory R. Salinas to Louis Wilmot, 13 August 1936). In 1936, Perales wrote a letter to the editor of *El Democrata*, a Spanish-language newspaper in San Diego, Texas, congratulating a group of Mexican Americans in El Paso for fighting the Department of Health's classification of Mexicans as people of color. He objected to the implication that Mexicans were not white. "In the interest of Genuine Americanism," Perales explained, all Mexicans should be considered white and all Mexican Americans should "energetically and constantly combat all the acts that denigrate" the Mexican-American community as non-white ("Letter to the Editor of *El Democrata*," October 23, 1936, Microfilm 2309, Reel 14). In another incident in Corpus Christi in 1939, the secretary of LULAC Council 1, Robert Meza, complained to the manager of the Corpus Christi Chamber of Commerce for ethnic Mexicans being separated from "Americans," which meant white, in the city directory. He wrote in a letter, "the fact of the matter is that the scheme is nothing more than an unparalleled singularity purporting to discriminate between the Mexicans themselves and other members of the white race when in truth and in fact we are not only a part and parcel but as well the sum and substance of the white race" (Robert Meza to Jeff Bell, 24 November 1939).

Throughout the 1930s Perales wrote extensively on Mexican American exclusion from whiteness. In a 1938 letter to Estelle Ripley Hudson, Perales wrote regarding the Census and the labeling of Mexicans that it was "an error to classify people of Mexican lineage under the [separate] heading 'Mexican'" because "Mexicans belong to the Caucasian race and we should be classified as white" ("Alonso S. Perales to Estelle Ripley Hudson," January 22, 1938, Microfilm 2309, Reel 12). He then gave a list of legal precedents that established Mexican-American whiteness. The list included Article 2900 of the Civil Laws of Texas, which described "colored people" as a group descended from African ancestry; Article 493 of the Texas Criminal Code, which described colored people similarly; Article 1659 of the Texas criminal code, which also described people of color as descendants of African ancestry; and an opinion from the Solicitor General of Texas in 1934 that said Mexicans should be considered white citizens ("Alonso S. Perales to Estelle Ripley Hudson"). Perales reasoned that the separate classification as Mexican was acceptable only if it was "clear, plain, and unequivocally understood as a subclassification of the general classification of 'Whites'" ("Alonso S. Perales to Estelle Ripley Hudson"). In an editorial that same year he explained that being labeled as Mexican in the census was a "grave daño" (a grave danger) to Mexican Americans ("El Negocio del Censo del Estado Unidos," January 22, 1938, Microfilm 2309, Reel 12). He continued, "the point that we want to make clear is that we are white and that is how we are recognized by the law of the United States, including the laws of the state of Texas, and we should be classified as such by the Department of the Census of the United States" ("El Negocio del Censo del Estado Unidos").

The strategy for claiming whiteness as an avenue to make larger claims of belonging was uneven at best. At times, it hurt their chances at receiving fair trials or just redress under the law (Haney López and Olivas, 2008, pp. 280-300). Even though Mexican Americans made boisterous claims that they were white, few Anglos in Texas accepted their arguments. Unfortunately, not only was their strategy complicit in the hierarchical ordering of races in the United States, but condoned it. Belonging based on whiteness only helped harden the color line in the United States and reproduce the ideas that justified it. Whiteness was a Janus-faced reflection for Mexican Americans.

The 1930s witnessed the development of another strategy to establish belonging by Mexican Americans. In order to make themselves part of the nation, Mexican Americans had to add themselves to the narrative of the nation. However, they did not want to challenge the basic premises of the narrative, but only wanted to include themselves in the general plot. This was particularly true in Texas during the centennial celebration in 1936. While Mexicans could not make themselves part of the army at Valley Forge or participants at Lexington and Concord, they could make themselves present at the Alamo or San Jacinto. They could argue that they may not have ridden with Washington but they did fight with Houston.

In 1936, Ruben Rendon Lozano, a San Antonio lawyer and the chairman of LULAC's state education committee, published *Viva Tejas: The Story of the Mexican-born Patriots of the Republic of Texas*. One scholar has written that Lozano's, and Mexican Americans' in general, historiographical interventions were radical in their revisions of the narrative of the nation (González, 2009, pp. 110-119). However, Lozano was adding another facet to the ideology of Mexican-Americanism. Citizenship was an identity that only made sense through the coherence of the nation. Since Mexican-Americanism based belonging on citizenship, the subscribers tried to make the nation more intelligible. It had to make Mexican Americans recognizable to the logic of the nation. Lozano did this by making comparisons of the independence of Texas to the independence of the U.S. Lozano (1936) called the Battle of Gonzalez the "Lexington of Texas" (p. 19). In another section of the book, he made connections between the events in 1836 and the American Revolution by commenting, "exactly sixty-one years after the Battle of Lexington, Houston crossed the Buffalo Bayou" (Lozano, 1936, p. 26). Lozano concluded his book with a paragraph that revealed very much the historicizing side of Mexican-Americanism:

> . . . may the progress made in these one hundred years of Texas freedom carry us even farther in the direction of Americanizing this native population. . . . Today, on the hundredth anniversary of the events which created history, the descendants of those patriots whether Mexican-Texan or American-Texan, share equally the glory of a resplendent ancestry. (pp. 49-50).

LULAC member J.C. Machuca also tried to re-frame ethnic Mexican history in the region to lend coherence to the nation. He wrote in a 1938 letter, "we are *not* United States citizens by conquest. Our forebears fought for the independence of Texas, and most of us were born in this country subsequent to the time Texas was admitted to Union" (J.C. Machuca to Alicia Dickerson Montemayor, 26 January 1938). In yet another letter, he elaborated his understanding of U.S.-Mexicans in Texas history, writing, "Texas was not conquered. There is abundant proof that Texas won its independence from Mexico and it existed as an independent republic for over a decade, before it became a state of the Union. In fighting for its independence many Texas patriots of Mexican extraction participated actively in the Military campaigns" (J.C. Machuca to Mrs. O.N. Lightner, 2 February 1938). Perales contributed to this discussion as well. In a speech he exclaimed:

> Persons of Hispanic descent in Texas should not be discriminated against merely because of their racial lineage. We are members of the Caucasian Race and are so recognized and considered by the Law of our Nation. And speaking of the historical phase of the problem, our Anglo-American friends and fellow citizens would do well to remember always that it was men like Ruiz, Navarro, Seguin, Menchaca and others who made possible the independence of Texas. ("Mr. Chairman Ladies and Gentlemen RE What Kind of Education Do Latin American Citizens Want for their Children," 1940, Microfilm 2309, Reel 13)

He finished his statement by adding that "if there is any such thing as a real dyed-in-the-wood, honest-to-goodness American, we Americans of Hispanic descent are better qualified than anyone else to claim that title" ("Mr. Chairman

Ladies and Gentlemen RE What Kind of Education Do Latin American Citizens Want for their Children").

Lozano's, Machuca's and Perales' writings were illustrative of the contours of Mexican-Americanism; it rooted belonging in the United States, it was associated with whiteness and assimilation, and it tried to include Mexican Americans in the narration of the nation. In other words, Mexican-Americanism contributed to the coherence of the nation-state. It did not disrupt it. Mexican-Americanism did not explicitly challenge racism or imperialism, but turned Mexican Americans into participating white conquerors. This strategy would continue for many more decades.

In 1940, Perales explained in an article that Anglos and Mexicans came together to fight for Texas independence ("Impuesto Electoral y Nuestra Lucha en Pro de Justicia," Juanary 8, 1940, Microfilm 2309, Reel 12). But Perales' recounting of the battles was in a very different context than it had been just a few years earlier. By 1940 the United States was preparing to take part in World War II. Many Mexican Americans saw this as a chance to finally prove they belonged in the nation. They built upon the stories of Anglos and Mexicans fighting for independence in Texas and made connections to Mexicans and Anglos fighting in Europe. Mexican Americans appreciated the opportunity to prove their loyalty as a way of securing belonging. Perales wrote in 1944 that many of the lists of fallen soldiers in Europe included Spanish-surnamed young men. He explained "this is something that gives us pride because it demonstrates that we are citizens conscious of our obligations and we are loyal to our country, the United States of America, and, moreover, that in this global conflict in which we are giving our all in favor of the democracy, [we] are participating in great numbers, in actuality, in a larger proportion than our population" (Hispanoamericana de San Antonio, Texas Mantiene de Batalla los Sagrados Postulados de America," September 1944, Microfilm 2309, Reel 12).

Although Perales recognized that Mexican Americans were dying in disproportionate numbers, he did not complain. Instead, this was a point of pride for Perales because it was further proof that Mexican Americans were good citizens. Perales was not alone in his support of the war. Mrs. Santos V. Lozano of Raymondville, Texas, wrote in a letter to the editor of the *Valley Morning Star* "As for us Latin Americans taking part in past wars, we have done it for generations, and will gladly do it again if necessary . . . because this is our country, our very own, and we defend with our blood what is rightfully ours . . ." ("All Kinds of People," Microfilm 2309, Reel 10). World War II and the shared history of the Texas Revolution contributed to Mexican-Americanism's ideology of belonging. It is important to note that while WWII overwhelmingly provided Mexican Americans a militaristic and masculinist way of securing belonging (Oropeza, 2005, pp. 36-46), it also, through the Good Neighbor Policy, provided an avenue for the language of citizenship to broaden its scope of inclusion through the grammar of Pan-Americanism (Zamora, 2009, p. 17). This avenue, however, was quickly closed to due to the ardent anti-communism of the subsequent decade (Gómez-Quiñones, 1994, p. 45).

By the 1950s, the importance of whiteness, citizenship, and narrating the nation were well-established. This was perhaps best exemplified in J.T. Canales' 1951 radical revision of the Mexicano folk hero, Juan N. Cortina. In 1951, Canales released a publication that showed the maturation of Mexican-Americanism and its project of rewriting ethnic Mexican contributions into the history of the United States. The publication, *Juan N. Cortina: Bandit or Patriot?*, was a short pamphlet with telling revisions.

Juan N. Cortina had shot an Anglo marshal in South Texas and then took the city of Brownsville in protest of the treatment of Mexicans in the nineteenth century (Thompson, 2011). He was regarded as a bandit to most Anglos and as a hero to many ethnic Mexicans living in Texas. However, in Canales' retelling, Cortina was not a bandit but a citizen. Patriotism, not violence, inspired Cortina. He re-wrote the story of Cortina removing him from both the Anglo story of banditry and violence and the Mexicano story of folk heroism and anti-colonial struggle and placed him within the boundaries of an emergent bourgeois Mexican-American worldview.

In Canales' revision, Cortina was not working class or poor but esteemed and honorable. Cortina was white, Spanish, and part of the elite *hacendado* class (Canales, 1951, p. 5). Canales explained that Cortina never stole from anybody; he was only defending the rights of the people (pp. 10-11). If cattle rustling occurred, it was only a few unsavory individuals but definitely not Cortina. The idea that Mexican Americans were not conquered people, but a partner in the conquering, made it into his story. The Treaty of Guadalupe Hidalgo that ended the Mexican-American War, was not a theft of Mexican lands but a document that established U.S.-Mexican citizenship. Because of this, Canales reasoned that Cortina was a U.S. citizen who fought injustice. "There is no record that any of the Cavazos or Cortina [family members] ever formally repudiated their American citizenship; but there is abundant proof that they considered themselves American citizens and acted as such," he wrote (p. 6). Canales also compared Cortina to George Washington in history rendition of the story. He wrote: "whether a man is called a 'bandit' or a 'hero' often depends just upon one word—SUCCESS; for very often a successful bandit turns out to be a real hero and a true patriot, such as our Washington" (p. 7). This was an important historical analogue because it reinforced the idea that Canales was emphasizing: Cortina was not a racialized Mexican *bandit*, but a recognizably American *citizen*. In other words, he was part of the LULAC tradition. Indeed, one of its forerunners.

Canales' focus on Cortina served as an interesting foil to the story of Gregorio Cortez, an early twentieth century *vaquero* and ranch hand. In 1901, Cortez was approached by the Karnes County sheriff and two deputies at his small ranch. There had been a report that there was a Mexican horse thief in the vicinity. The three men approached Cortez and his brother, Romaldo. The sheriff asked through a poor translator if the Cortez brothers had sold a horse recently. They replied they had not sold a *caballo* (horse) but had sold a *yegua* (mare). The sheriff and deputies continued to push the subject and in another miscommunication, Cortez thought he was going to be arrested and the officers thought that Cortez was taunting and threatening them. In the confusion, the sheriff shot Romaldo. Cortez returned fire, killing the sheriff and fled into the brush. Cortez evaded a statewide manhunt that included the notorious Texas Rangers for ten days until he was finally captured. He was tried before a jury of his peers, which comprised an all Anglo jury. He was found guilty (Orozco, 2012). The ethnic Mexican community, however, enshrined Cortez's story in a *corrido* (ballad) and remembered him for his cunning, bravery, and innocence.

Canales was silent about the story of this fellow Tejano. Canales did not award Cortez his posthumous citizenship and notoriety as a LULAC predecessor. However, there was a young U.S.-Mexican scholar by the name of Américo Paredes who would tell Cortez's story only seven years later in 1958. Paredes seemed to think that U.S.-Mexicans shared more in common with the wronged Cortez than with the hagiographic version of Cortina. In Paredes' story, Gregorio Cortez was not a whitened U.S.-citizen. Paredes' Cortez did not need to be rehabilitated as such. He was a border resident who was "not too dark and not too fair . . . [and] he looked just a little bit like me" (Paredes, 1958, p. 34).

By the end of the 1950s and the beginning of the 1960s, Mexican-Americanism was ideologically developed and mature. Mexican-Americanism had spread across the nation; it was no longer limited to Texas. For example, in 1965, the major California Mexican-American organizations (MAPA, LULAC, the CSO, and the G.I. Forum) wrote a resolution to President Johnson asking for aid. It was written in the language pioneered in Texas and it followed the ideological contours of Mexican-Americanism. They wrote, "Over 150 years ago, Spanish-speaking Mexican-Americans stopped the Russian colonial advance and conquest from Siberia and Alaska, and preserved the Western portion of the United States for our country, which at that time consisted of thirteen colonies struggling for their existence, into which nation we and our predecessors became incorporated as loyal citizens and trustworthy participants in its democratic forms of government" (qtd. in Briegel 64). In the resolution's logic, U.S.-Mexicans were loyal citizens even before there was a nation and they had resisted territorial incursions into the United States by the forerunners of the communist USSR. U.S.-Mexicans, then, had been fighting communism on American soil since at least the Spanish colonial period. While their logic was flawed, their ideology was clear.

Unfortunately, Mexican-Americanism was becoming increasingly brittle. By the mid-1960s, it had become a prominent ideology that explained U.S.-Mexican belonging. Mexican-Americanism understood the world, citizenship and belonging in certain ways. It was patriotic, and, at times, blindly so. Around the same time, some young U.S.-Mexican activists in Texas and across the nation were forming an alternative imaginary that explained belonging and the relationship between people of the world differently. Many Mexican Americans ardently disagreed with these young activists. Through their responses the rigidity of the ideology of Mexican-Americanism was revealed. The venerable Texas politician Henry B. González tried to undermine the budding Chicano Movement (Montejano, 2010, pp. 87-98; 228-233). He berated Chicano Movement leaders, ideas, and organizations. In 1969, González described the youth as "new racists" ("The New Racism: Speeches of U.S. Rep Henry B. Gonzalez"). As U.S.-Mexican youth protested inequality, discrimination, and the increasing death of soldiers in Vietnam, González refused to acknowledge that any such problems existed. He proclaimed adamantly "I cannot accept the argument that this is an evil country or that our system does not work. . . . I cannot find evidence that there is any country in the world that matches the progress of this one" ("The New Racism: Speeches of U.S. Rep Henry B. Gonzalez"). He would continue to attack the young activists for their lack of patriotism and their understanding of the community as an internal colony. González was not alone in his criticism; LULAC member Jacob Rodríguez wrote in an essay, "the younger generation doesn't know any better. It still has a lot to learn. . . . Our youngsters' lack of living, practical experience and comprehension is impelling them to 'identify' with something and—unfortunately for them and all the rest of us—they don't even know what with or why. All they feel is that this word is a call to rebellion . . . Imagine burning your own Flag for something like that, and hoisting a foreign, alien, flag in its place! Only the years will teach them better!" ("Mexican? Mexican-American? Chicanos? All Wrong!!"). Older leaders like González and Rodríguez were entrenched in this strain of thought. They had spent the better part of their lives developing this ideology.

Throughout the twentieth century, Mexican Americans had created a new imaginary that explained U.S.-Mexican belonging. Mexican-Americanism rooted U.S.-Mexican belonging firmly within the U.S. Citizenship, whiteness and the nation were central features in Mexican-Americanism. Mexican Americans did not want to re-write the narratives of the nation, but only wanted to include themselves in the plots. Keeping the essential tropes and themes of their amended tales of America helped make the case for their status as citizens while keeping the racial connotations. By never questioning the central premises of the American narrative, they perpetuated the false promises of a romantic fiction. But change was in the air. By the mid-1960s, a new generation of youth was in the process of developing their own alternative imaginary. Its impact too would be felt for many years.

Conclusion

It was the hope of Mexican Americans that by rooting their belonging in the United States and focusing on the legal/racial status of citizenship that they would be accepted wholly into the American social imaginary. Citizenship, unfortunately, was a consciousness concocted by the state and Mexican-Americanism offered an imagined community that gained currency through the increasingly powerful reach of the state apparatus. Only by coming to the state for identity and access could ethnic Mexicans claim a sense of place in the United States. As one historian described it, Mexican-Americanism was a "politics of supplication" (Oropeza, 2005, p. 49). It was an ideology that reified the state and reinforced their dependence on modernist, state-centered notions of belonging. Historian John Chávez explains that their view of the Southwest marked a definite ideological break in the way they perceived their location socially and spatially. Mexican-Americanism saw the region as part of the "'American Southwest,' an integral part of a country whose language and customs were Anglo, a region that was only theirs insofar as they were true U.S. citizens" (*Lost Land* 114). Mexican-American belonging, then, was tenuous at best, and completely dependent on citizenship. The legal historian Ian F. Haney López (1996) explains that "citizenship, easily granted and easily withheld, is a tenuous concept on which to hang social privileges such as the right to attend school or to receive medical care. It is made even more untenable as a basis for social distinctions when one understands . . . that citizenship easily serves as a proxy for race" (p. 35).

The intellectual project of reconceptualizing U.S.-Mexican belonging as American citizens was a departure from previous modes of imagining in U.S.-Mexican thought. This change required a reformulation of the position of U.S.-Mexicans in the region, nation, and world. Calling themselves Mexican American came with a direct intent and entailed an ideological shift. They were responding to the global change in citizenship and the evolving homeland politics in the Southwest in the years after the Mexican Revolution. Many U.S.-Mexicans found themselves outside of the mainstream American social imaginary and excluded from the imagined community of *México de afuera*. This forced many people on a search for belonging. For a group of U.S.-Mexicans, they were Americans—including the exclusive racial, class, and linguistic connotations the word carried with it. They emphasized whiteness and promoted a specific modernist worldview that underwrote racial and social hierarchies. Leaders like Alonso S. Perales and Andres de Luna, as well as organizations like the Order Sons of America and LULAC cooperated in ideas that while not necessarily hegemonic were definitely homogenizing.

It would be impossible, and nearly foolhardy, to argue that citizenship did not provide U.S.-Mexicans with political and material benefits. Being recognized as citizens gave them power to access a legal system that offered avenues of protection and redress. By being citizens, U.S.-Mexicans could claim inclusion into an important imagined community. However, the change towards the emphasis on citizenship did indeed limit the intellectual and ideological possibilities of other human connections between people of the world. It is difficult to criticize Mexican Americans for the social distance they kept from African-Americans during the period, but the ideology of Mexican-Americanism did not co-opt the racial regime of the twentieth century; it cooperated in its reproduction. For that reason and many others, Mexican-Americanism was a limited and, at times, limiting ideology.

Works Cited

Ainslie, J. (1934). *Los pochos: Novela*. Los Angeles: Latin Publishing Co.
Arredondo, G. (2008*). Mexican Chicago: Race, identity, and nation, 1916-1939*. Urbana: University of Illinois Press.
Canales, J. T. (1951). *Juan N. Cortina: Bandit or patriot?*. San Antonio: Artes Gráficas.
Chávez, J. (2009). *Beyond nations: Evolving homelands in the North Atlantic world, 1400-2000*. New York: Cambridge University Press.
Chávez, J. (1984). *The lost land: The Chicano image of the Southwest*. Albuquerque: University of New Mexico Press.
Constitucion y leyes de la Orden Hijos de América. (n.d.). Oliver Douglas Weeks Collection, Box 1 Folder 1, Benson Library, University of Texas at Austin.
Editorial: nobles propósitos. (1930, November 21). *El Defensor*. (n.p).
Escudero, C. R. (1935, December 25). Americanización y Mexicanización. *El Continental* (n.p.).
Espinoza, C. (2007). *El sol de Texas*. Houston: Arte Público Press.
Foley, N. (1998). *Becoming Hispanic: Mexican Americans and the Faustian pact with whiteness*. In Foley, N. (Ed.) Reflexiones: New directions in Mexican Amer-

ican studies (pp. 53-70). Austin: Center for Mexican American Studies, University of Texas.

Gamio, M. (1930). *Mexican immigration to the United States: A study of human migration and adjustment.* Chicago: University of Chicago Press.

García, M. T. (1989). *Mexican Americans: Leadership, ideology, & identity.* New Haven: Yale University Press, 1989.

Gerstle, G. (1996). The working class goes to war. In Erenberg, L. A. & Hirsch, S. E. (Eds.) *The war in American culture: Society and consciousness during World War II* (pp. 105-127). Chicago: University of Chicago Press.

Gómez-Quiñones, J. (1994). *Chicano politics: Reality and promise, 1940-1990.* Albuquerque: University of New Mexico Press.

González, H. B. (1969, May 1). *The new racism: Speeches of U.S. Rep. Henry B. Gonzalez.* [Congressional Record April 3, 15, 16, 22, 28-29]. Joe J. Bernal Collection, Box 18, Henry B. Gonzalez Folder, Benson Library, University of Texas at Austin.

González, J. M. (2009). *Border renaissance: The Texas centennial and the emergence of Mexican American literature.* Austin: University of Texas Press.

Gutiérrez, D. G. (1995). *Walls and mirrors: Mexican Americans, Mexican immigrants, and the politics of ethnicity.* Berkeley: University of California Press.

Gonzalez, J. G. (1929, February 22). *El Paladín.* Oliver Douglas Weeks Collection, Box 1 Folder 10, Benson Library, University of Texas at Austin.

Guzmán, S. G. (1930, May 2). En Edinburg no hay mexicanos. *El Defensor.* (n.p.)

Haney López, I. F. (1996). *White by law: The legal construction of race.* New York: New York University Press.

Haney López, I. F. & Olivas, M. A. (2008). Jim Crow, Mexican Americans, and the Anti-Subordinate Constitution: The story of Hernandez v. Texas. In Moran, R.F. & Carbado, D.W. *Race law stories* (pp. 273-309). St. Paul: Foundation Press.

Jacobson, M. F. (1999). *Whiteness of a different color: European immigrants and the alchemy of race.* Cambridge: Harvard University Press.

Johnson, B. H. (2003). *Revolution in Texas: How a forgotten rebellion and its bloody suppression turned Mexicans into Americans.* New Haven: Yale University Press.

Kanellos, N. (2011). *Hispanic immigrant literature: El sueño del retorno.* Austin: University of Texas Press.

Lee, E. (2003). *At America's gates: Chinese immigration during the Exclusion Era, 1882-1943.* Chapel Hill: University of North Carolina Press.

¡Lirismos Absurdos! (1929, December 22). *El Heraldo Mexicano.* (n.p.)

Lozano, R. R. (1936). *Viva Tejas: The story of the Mexican-born patriots of the Republic of Texas.* San Antonio: Southern Literary Institute.

de Luna, A. (n.d.). *Orden Hijos de America.* Clemente N. Idar Papers, Box 8 Folder 4, Benson Library, University of Texas at Austin.

Machuca, J. C. (1938, January 26). [Letter to Alicia Dickerson Montemayor]. Alicia Dickerson Montemayor Papers, Box 3 Folder 3, Benson Library, University of Texas at Austin.

Machuca, J. C. (1938, February 2). [Letter to Mrs. O. N. Lightner]. Alicia Dickerson Montemayor Papers, Box 3 Folder 6, Benson Library, University of Texas at Austin.

Manual for use by the League of Latin American Citizens. Oliver Douglas Weeks Collection, Box 1 Folder 3, Benson Library, University of Texas at Austin.

México emigrado y México esclavo: El regreso a la patria. (1916, August 6). *Revista mexicana.* San Antonio, Texas. (n.p.).

Meza, R. (1939, November 24). [Letter to Jeff Bell]. Andres de Luna Collection, Box 1 Folder 6, Benson Library, University of Texas at Austin.

Monroy, D. (1999). Rebirth: Mexican Los Angeles from the Great Migration to the Great Depression. Berkeley: University of California Press.

Montejano, D. (2010). *Quixote's soldiers: A local history of the Chicano Movement, 1966-1981.* Austin: University of Texas Press.

Ngai, M. M. (2004). *Impossible subjects: Illegal aliens and the making of modern America.* Princeton: Princeton University Press.

OKA News. (1927 December). Oliver Douglas Weeks Collection, Box 1 Folder 2, Benson Library, University of Texas at Austin.

Oropeza, L. (2005). *¡Raza sí! ¡Guerra no!: Chicano protest and patriotism during the Viet Nam era.* Berkeley: University of California Press.

Orozco, C. E. (n.d.). Cortez Lira, Gregorio. *Handbook of Texas Online.* 15 August 2012. Retrieved 15 August, 2012 from http://www.tshaonline.org/handbook/online/articles/fco94.

Orozco, C. E. (2009). *No Mexicans, women, or dogs allowed: The rise of the Mexican American civil rights movement.* Austin: University of Texas Press.

Orozco, C. E. Order Knights of America. *Handbook of Texas Online.* Retrieved 8 March 2011 from http://www.tshaonline.org/handbook/online/articles/veo02.

Padilla, B. (1919, June 15). Las que tienen novios gringos. *La Evolución.* (n.p.).

El Paladín. (1929, April 12). Oliver Douglas Weeks Collection, Box 1 Folder 10, Benson Library, University of Texas at Austin

El Paladín. (1929, May 24). Oliver Douglas Weeks Collection, Box 1 Folder 10, Benson Library, University of Texas at Austin.

Para los que no conocen nuestra [institución]. (ca. 1920, 1930). Ben Garza Collection, Box 1 Folder 2, Benson Library, University of Texas at Austin.

Paredes, A. (1976). *A Texas-Mexican cancionero: Folksongs of the lower border.* Austin: University of Texas Press.

Paredes, A. (1958). *With his pistol in his hand: A border ballad and its hero.* Austin: University of Texas Press.

Perales, A. S. (1919, November 11). Como inculcan americanismo en este pais: Un Mexico-Americano envía expresiva carta a 'evolucion'. *La Evolucion.* (n.p.).

Quevedo, E. et al. (1967). Open resolution directed to the president of the United States and executive departments and agencies, by national Hispanic and Mexican-American organizations on civil disobedience and riot investigations. In Briegel, K. L. (1971) *The history of political organizations among Mexican-Americans in Los Angeles since the Second World War* (p. 67). Master's thesis, University of Southern California.

Ramírez, J. A. (2009). *To the line of fire: Mexican Texans and World War I.* College Station: Texas A&M University Press.

Respetable Radio-Auditorio. (n.d.). Andres de Luna Collection, Box 1 Folder 9, Benson Library, University of Texas at Austin.

Rodríguez, J. I. (n.d.). *Mexican? Mexican-American? Chicanos? All Wrong!!.* San Antonio: Americanos Period of San Antonio. Jacob I. Rodríguez Collection, Box 7 Folder 12, Benson Library, University of Texas at Austin.

Rosales, F. A. (1999). *¡Pobre raza!: Violence, justice, and mobilization among México lindo immigrants, 1900-1936.* Austin: University of Texas Press.

Salinas, G. R. (1936, August 13). [Letter to Louis Wilmot]. Andres de Luna Collection, Box 1 Folder 6, Benson Library, University of Texas at Austin.

Salyer, L. E. (1995). *Laws harsh as tigers: Chinese immigrants and the shaping of modern immigration law.* Chapel Hill: University of North Carolina Press.

Sánchez, G. J. (1993). *Becoming Mexican American: Ethnicity, culture, and identity in Chicano Los Angeles, 1900-1945.* New York: Oxford University Press.

Santibáñez, E. (1930). *Ensayo acerca de la inmigración Mexicana en los Estados Unidos.* San Antonio: The Clegg Co.

Santibáñez, E. (1930, April 24). Editorial. *La Prensa.* (n.p.)

Taylor, P. S. (1934). *An American-Mexican frontier: Nueces County, Texas.* Chapel Hill: University of North Carolina Press.

Thompson, J. (n.d.). Juan Nepomuceno Cortina. *Handbook of Texas Online.* Retrieved 2011 March 8 from http://www.tshaonline.org/handbook/online/articles/fco73.

Torpey, J. (2000). *The invention of the passport: Surveillance, citizenship, and the state.* New York: Cambridge University Press.

Zamora, E. (2009). *Claiming rights and righting wrongs in Texas: Mexican Workers and job politics during World War II.* College Station: Texas A&M Press.

Zamora, E. (1993). *The world of the Mexican worker in Texas.* College Station: Texas A&M Press.

From the Alonso S. Perales Collection (Transcript form):

Lozano, S. V. (1947). [Letter, *All kinds of people*]. *The Valley Morning Star.* Microfilm 2309, Reel 10.

Perales, A. S. (1924 October). *La evolución de los Mexico Americanos.* Microfilm 2309, Reel 13.

Perales, A. S. (1944 September). *Hispanoamericana de San Antonio, Texas mantiene de batalla los sagrados postulados de América.* Microfilm 2309, Reel 12.

Perales, A. S. (1924 October). *El ideal de los Mexico-Americanos.* Microfilm 2309, Reel 13.

Perales, A. S. (1940, January 8). *Impuesto electoral y nuestra lucha en pro de justicia.* Microfilm 2309, Reel 12.

Perales, A. S. (1940). *Mr. Chairman ladies and gentlemen RE what kind of education do Latin American Citizens want for their children.* Microfilm 2309, Reel 13.

Perales, A. S. (1938, January 22). *El negocio del censo del Estados Unidos.* Microfilm 2309, Reel 12.

Perales, A. S. (n.d.). *El porvenir de los Mexico Americanos.* Microfilm 2309, Reel 12.

Perales, A. S. (1936, October 23). [Letter to the Editor of *El Democrata*]. Microfilm 2309, Reel 14.

Perales, A. S. (1938, January 22). [Letter to Estelle Ripley Hudson]. Microfilm 2309, Reel 12.

Notes

[1] The author would like to thank the Recovering the U.S. Hispanic Literary Heritage Project for providing him research funds through the 2011 Research Grants Program of the Hispanic History of Texas Project.

[2] The translations from Spanish to English are the author's, unless otherwise noted.

[3] Translation from 2007 Arte Público reprint.

[4] All subsequent references to the Alonso S. Perales collection materials will appear in parentheses in the text. The parenthetical references are take from the transcript (ts.) form.

Alonso S. Perales and the Effort to Establish the Civil Rights of Mexican Americans as Seen through the Lens of Contemporary Critical Legal Theory: Post-racialism, Reality Construction, Interest Convergence, and Other Critical Themes

George A. Martínez[1]

INTRODUCTION

Alonso S. Perales was a pioneering antiracist activist who sought to establish the civil rights of Mexican Americans. He was particularly active in his civil rights work during the middle part of the twentieth century. Perales was born on October 17, 1898, in Alice, Texas (Perales, 1974, p. 87). An attorney, Perales received his law degree from National University in Washington, D.C. (now George Washington University) (Perales, 1974, p. 87). He served in the United States Army in World War I (Perales, 1974, p. 87). Over the course of his career, he held a number of positions in the United States government, including in the Department of Commerce and the United States Diplomatic Service (Perales, 1974, p. 87). In addition, he practiced law privately in San Antonio, Texas (Perales, 1974, p. 87). He also represented the interests of Mexican Americans as Chairman of the Committee of 100, Director General of the League of Loyal Americans and as President of the League of United Latin American citizens in 1930 (Perales, 1974, p. 6).

In this chapter, I seek to examine and analyze the efforts of Alonso S. Perales to establish the civil rights of Mexican Americans through the lens of contemporary critical legal theory, which offers an important set of insights and conceptual instruments to analyze issues of race. Toward this end, I consider how Perales dealt with claims of post-racialism—the idea that racism is not a significant factor in the lives of racial minorities—by constructing an alternative reality through subjugated knowledge. I also examine how Perales' efforts to advance the cause of Mexican Americans anticipated the guidelines or framework set out in Derrick Bell's interest convergence theory. Next, I argue that Perales' effort to establish laws to prevent discrimination against Mexican Americans represents an attempt to bring an end to a state of nature-like existence for Mexican Americans. In addition, I argue that Perales is significant because he attempts to establish the rights of Mexican Americans as a distinctive group as opposed to basing such rights on a claim that Mexican Americans are members of the white race. Finally, I close with some thoughts on Alonso S. Perales and fame.

Alonso S. Perales and Critical Theory

A. Alonso S. Perales, Post-racialism and Reality Construction: Proving the Existence of Racism against Mexican Americans.

Recently, and especially in light of the election of America's first black president—Barack Obama—some have asserted that we are living in an era of post-racialism—a time when racism has been overcome and no longer is a significant problem that holds racial minorities back (McWhorter, 2008). As Thomas Sugrue (2010, p. 1) explains:

It is now a commonplace that the election of Barack Obama marks the opening of a new period in America's long racial history. The unlikely rise of a black man to the nation's highest office—someone who was a mostly unknown state senator only five years before he was inaugurated president—confirms the view of many, especially whites, that the United States is a post-tracial society. At last the shackles of discrimination have been broken and individual merit is rewarded, regardless of skin color.

In the face of such a claim, critical race scholars now argue that it is premature to conclude that we are in a post-racial era, and therefore, a central task for race scholars and antiracist activists is to dismantle this ideology or claim of post-racialism (Crenshaw, 2011, pp. 1347-52); (Valdes and Cho, 2011, pp. 1548-1560); (Green, 2012, pp. 373-76); (Cooper, 2010, pp. 31-43); (Cho, 2009, pp. 1593). One way to begin this task is to recognize that there is a long history in the United States of what we might call post-racialism—*i.e.*, the idea that racism is no longer a significant force that shapes the life chances of persons of color. It is worth considering this history to see how earlier scholars and antiracist activists dealt with claims of post-racialism. Two such pioneering activists and scholars are Alonso S. Perales and W.E.B. DuBois.

For instance, in W.E.B. DuBois's classic study entitled *The Philadelphia Negro* published in 1899, W.E.B. DuBois (1899, p. 322) observed that blacks saw racism "as the chief cause of their present unfortunate position." As DuBois (1899, p. 322) explains:

In the Negro's mind, color prejudice in Philadelphia is the widespread feeling of dislike for his blood, which keeps him and his children out of decent employment, from certain public conveniences and amusements, from hiring houses in many sections, and in general, from being recognized as a man.

According to DuBois, the white majority in Philadelphia did not see racism as a significant force in generating the situation for blacks at that time. DuBois (1899, p. 322) observed that:

On the other hand, most white people are quite unconscious of any such powerful and vindictive feeling [of color prejudice]; they regard color prejudice as the easily explicable feeling that intimate social intercourse with a lower race is not only undesirable but impracticable if our present standards of culture are to be maintained; and although they are aware that some persons feel the aversion more intensely than others, they cannot see how such a feeling has much influence on the real situation, or alters the social condition of the mass of Negroes.

According to DuBois (1899, p. 325), most white Philadelphians would deny that racism against blacks existed at that time. DuBois (1899, p. 326) says that whites think as follows:

Everyone knows that in the past color prejudice in the city was deep and passionate; living men can remember when a Negro could not sit in a street car or walk many streets in peace. These times have passed, however, and many imagine that active discrimination against the Negro has passed with them.

Accordingly, in response to the post-racialism of his era, DuBois (1899, p. 326), in *The Philadelphia Negro*, sought to prove the existence of racial discrimination against blacks by describing a number "of actual cases" to "illustrate" various types of racial discrimination against blacks that continued to exist. As to the veracity of these cases, DuBois (1899, p. 326) explains that "so far as possible these have been sifted and only those which seem undoubtedly true have been selected."

In this connection, DuBois (1899, pp. 327-329) describes a number of cases in the "higher vocations" where blacks were unable to secure employment: a kindergarten teacher, a stenographer, pharmacists, a mechanical engineer and a telegraph operator. DuBois (1899, p. 329) then presents a number of cases to show that blacks are unable to find employment "in the world of skilled labor." Here he describes the following persons as unable to secure employment because of race discrimination: a bookbinder, a brush maker, a shoemaker, a bricklayer, a painter, a telegraph lineman, an iron puddler, a cooper, a candy maker and many others (DuBois, 1899, pp. 329-330). DuBois (1899, p. 332) concludes that "without strong effort and special influence it is next to impossible for a Negro in Philadelphia to get regular employment in most of the trades."

DuBois (1899, pp. 344-346) also provides instances where blacks are discriminated against in terms of the wages they receive. Similarly, DuBois (1899, p. 347) provides examples to show that blacks are required to pay higher rents than whites. DuBois (1899, p. 350) concludes by observing:

Such is the tangible form of Negro prejudice in Philadelphia. Possibly some of the particular cases can be proven to have had extenuating circumstances unknown to the investigators; at the same time many not cited would be just as much in point. At any rate no one who has with any diligence studied the situation of the Negro in the city can long doubt but that his opportunities are limited and his ambition circumscribed about as has been shown.

DuBois (1899, pp. 350-351) warns that such racial prejudice generates a cost for the city: crime (pp. 350-351). As DuBois (1899, p. 351) explains: "certainly a great amount of crime can be without doubt traced to the discrimination against Negro boys and girls in the matter of employment." DuBois (1899, pp. 353-354) appeals to the conscience of white Philadelphians to remedy this discrimination against blacks:

> It is high time that the best conscience of Philadelphia awakened to her duty; her negro citizens are here to remain; they can be made good citizens or burdens to the community; if we want them to be sources of wealth and power and not of poverty and weakness then they must be given employment according to their ability and encouraged to train that ability and increase their talents by the hope of reasonable reward. To educate boys and girls and then refuse them work is to train loafers and rogues.

Antiracist activist Alonso S. Perales (1974), in his classic 1948 work, *Are We Good Neighbors?*, also dealt with a claim of post-racialism—this time a claim that racism was not a significant factor affecting the life fortunes of Mexican Americans. The book collects a number of statements and documents which, as Perales (1974, p. 7) explains in his foreword, are designed:

> To publish the facts regarding the problem of discrimination, particularly against Latin Americans, as he knows them, a problem that vitally affects the interests of our country—the United States of America—and which is crying for solution. The reference is to the discrimination practiced by some, against persons of Mexican or Spanish descent in Texas and other states.

Perales (1974, p. 9) offers this evidence of discrimination in order to convince citizens and legislators to support the enactment of "both federal and state legislation forbidding discrimination against persons of Mexican or Spanish extraction . . ." Perales (1974, p. 8) further makes clear that the book is offered as a response to a claim of post-racialism when he states in the foreword that "[a] perusal of this book will disclose to the reader that discrimination does exist, that it is not confined to a few isolated cases as some declare, but that the practice is widespread." Additional evidence that Perales is responding to a claim of post-racialism is found in one of the documents the book collects, a statement by Carlos E. Castañeda, Professor of History at the University of Texas. Castañeda ("The Second Rate Citizen and Democracy," p. 17) writes:

> There are many in high places who feel strongly that the subject of discrimination must not be discussed. If one needs mention it, the only thing one can say with decorum is that the practice has become a thing of the past. It existed, yes; but fortunately it has been eliminated by the good neighbor policy.

Contrary to this claim of post-racialism, Castañeda ("The Second Rate Citizen and Democracy," p. 20) goes on to say that the "concrete cases of discrimination against Mexicans presented in this [*Good Neighbors*] volume illustrate many phases of the problem and the extent of the malady."

Accordingly, the *Good Neighbors* book offers documentary evidence of employment discrimination against Mexican Americans. Professor Carlos Castañeda (Letter to R. Carr, 9 May 1947, p. 58) submitted a letter to the President's Committee on Civil Rights which opines that discrimination against Mexican Americans in the economic context "forms the basis for all other forms of discrimination" against Mexican Americans. Castañeda (Letter to R. Carr, 9 May 1947, pp. 58-59) summarizes the dire situation for Mexican Americans as follows:

> Briefly, the Mexican, be he an American citizen or not, is generally refused employment except in certain types of undesirable jobs. Furthermore once employed, he is refused advancement, generally speaking, regardless of ability. Thus his income is restricted and held below that of the average citizen. As a result, he and his family are forced to live in homes that lack every comfort and sanitary devices, they are ill dressed, ill cared for, and ill fed. They are unable to keep their children in school.

During World War II, Castañeda (Statement on 9 May 1947, 59) served as "assistant to the Chairman of the President's Committee on Fair Employment Practice as regards cases of discrimination against Mexicans throughout the United States." In that capacity, he "investigate[d] numerous cases in Chicago, the states of Texas, New Mexico, Arizona, Colorado, Utah and California . . ." (Castañeda Statement on 9 May 1947, p. 59)

In his testimony presented in 1944, to the United States Senate Hearings on the proposed Fair Employment Practices Act to prohibit race discrimination in employment, Carlos Castañeda (Statement on 8 September 1944, p. 94) gave examples of discrimination in employment against Mexican Americans. For example, he testified that there were 8,000-10,000 Mexican Americans working in the Arizona mining industry but that "their employment is restricted . . . to common labor and semi-skilled jobs . . ." (Statement on 8 September 1944, p. 94). Similarly, Castañeda (Statement on 8 September 1944, p. 94) testified that although there were 315,000 Mexican Americans in Los Angeles, California, "only 5,000 persons of Mexican-Extraction were employed in basic industries." Castañeda (Statement on 8 September 1944, p. 94) further said that only 400 of 16,000 Los Angeles County Civil Service Employees were Mexican American. Castañeda (Statement on 8 September 1944, pp. 94-95) described similar employment discrimination in the Colorado steel industry, the New Mexico mining industry, and various Texas industries.

In his Statement before the Senate Committee or Labor and Education on March 13, 1945, Alonso S. Perales (Statement on 13 March 1945, p. 117) presented evidence of employment discrimination by the federal government in San Antonio, Texas. For instance, he testified that the federal government employs 10,000 people at Kelly Field but that "our men of Mexican descent never could hold a position of a higher category than that of laborer or mechanic's helper" (Perales Statement on 13 March 1945, p. 117). To support this claim of discrimination by the federal government, he produced sworn statements of Mexican-American employees made under oath (Perales Statement on 13 March 1945, pp. 117-118). Perales (Statement on 13 March 1945, p. 121) further produced "a list of 150 towns and cities in Texas where there exist from 1-10 public places of business and amusement, where Mexicans are denied service or entrance." Perales (Statement on 13 March 1945, p. 121) also testified:

In nearly every town and city of Texas the Mexican children are segregated from the Anglo Saxon children in the public schools. In nearly every town and city of Texas there are residential districts where Mexicans are not permitted to reside, regardless of their social position. The purpose, Mr. Chairman, has been to keep the Mexican at arm's length and to treat him as an inferior.

Perales (Statement on 13 March 1945, p. 121) further stated that Mexican-American U.S. military servicemen were also subjected to racial discrimination or were "the victims of these Nazi tactics." As evidence for this claim, he produced sworn affidavits of Mexican-American servicemen which described various incidents of discrimination such as refusals to serve at restaurants and drug stores (Perales Statement on 13 March 1945, pp. 121-124). Perales (Statement on 13 March 1945, pp. 125-126) also produced other sworn affidavits setting out discrimination against Mexican Americans such as exclusion from a public Fourth of July celebration.

Beyond this, in part III of the *Good Neighbors* book, Perales (1974, pp. 139-213) sets out over 70 pages of sworn affidavits by Mexican Americans describing numerous incidents of racial discrimination against Mexican Americans. These sworn affidavits describe many "concrete cases" of discrimination against Mexican Americans in the purchase or rental of homes, refusals to serve at restaurants, segregation in public schools on the basis of race, club membership, admission to theaters, employment discrimination, refusals to serve in barber shops, and so on (Perales, 1974, pp. 139-213). Many of the sworn affidavits are from Mexican-American World War II veterans, including one medal of honor winner, Macario Garcia, who experienced various types of race discrimination (Perales, 1974, pp. 139-213; 156).

In this regard, theorists have recognized that white supremacy "systematically maintained a network of institutions which unjustifiably concentrated power, authority and goods in the hands of white male individuals, and which systematically consigned [racial minorities] to subordinate positions in society." (Wasserstrom, 1982, p. 188) The affidavits supplied by Perales reveal white supremacism at work in the distribution of benefits, burdens, goods and services. Consider a few examples. World War II veteran, Perfecto Solis (Affidavit, 29 April 1948, pp. 139-140) stated that when he and his wife attempted to purchase a home in Texas he was told by the salesman that "he could not sell it to us because of the restrictive clause against the purchase or use by Latin Americans" (Solis Affidavit, 29 April 1948, p. 139). World War II veteran Leopoldo Mancilla (Affidavit, 24 September 1947, p. 143) sought to purchase a home in San Antonio, Texas, in a location with a sign stating "Homes for Veterans Only." The home builder refused to sell Mancilla (Affidavit, 24 September 1947, 143) a home stating "that the homes were not for sale to Latin Americans." Walter Gipprich (Affidavit, 21 July 1947, pp. 144-145) stated that his landlady informed him that Gipprich and his wife would have to move out of their apartment in San Antonio, Texas, since "the neighbors were complaining because my wife is of Mexican descent." World War I veteran Julian Suarez (Affidavit, 4 March 1947, p. 148) stated that "in the public schools our children of Mexican descent are segregated from the Anglo-American children up to and including the fourth grade." World War II veteran and Congressional Medal of Honor winter, Macario Garcia

(Affidavit, 5 October 1946, pp. 156-157) stated that he was refused service "while wearing the uniform of the United States Army" at a café in Richmond, Texas, by a waitress on the ground that "Mexicans were not served at that place." Willie Benavides (Affidavit, 13 September 1943, pp. 190-191) stated that the manager of a beer garden in Bexar County, Texas, informed him that "We do not allow Mexicans in this place." When Benavides (Affidavit, 13 September 1943, p. 190) responded by saying that he "was just as good an American citizen as anyone else . . . [the manager] went behind the counter and brought out either a gun or a stick . . . and without saying anything he struck me on the head with it."

The methodology of Alonso S. Perales in establishing the existence of widespread discrimination against Mexican Americans is consistent with recent critical race theory methodology and epistemology which has advocated "looking to the bottom" and seeking knowledge about issues race "in the particulars of [people of color's] social reality and experience" (Matsuda, 1989, p. 2324). Accordingly, this epistemology has based knowledge on, among other things, "stories from [people of color's] own experiences of life in hierarchically arranged world." (Matsuda, 1989, p. 2324). As Mari Matsuda (1987, p. 324) has explained, this epistemology is based on the idea:

that those who have experienced discrimination speak with a special voice to which we should listen. Looking to the bottom—adopting the perspective of those who have seen and felt the falsity of the liberal promise—can assist critical scholars in the task of fathoming the phenomenology of law and defining the elements of justice.

Accordingly, Perales has looked to the actual experience of Mexican Americans in the United States. He produced numerous sworn affidavits in which Mexican Americans describe experiencing racial discrimination in a wide variety of contexts. The cumulative effect of such sworn affidavits is to generate an overwhelming case which clearly establishes the existence of widespread discrimination against Mexican Americans. Perales showed that any claim of post-racialism with respect to Mexican Americans is without merit.

The fact that Alonso S. Perales gathered sworn affidavits to establish the existence of discrimination against Mexican Americans is remarkable. Indeed, he appears to be the only one at the time who did this. This shows that Perales used the skills that he developed as a lawyer—i.e., taking sworn testimony—to advance his civil rights project. Perhaps only a lawyer would have thought to put people under oath in order to establish and prove the existence of discrimination.

Some detractors of the critical race scholars who seek to base knowledge on the stories or experiences of racial minorities have argued that one should reject such an approach because such stories are not typical experiences of racial minorities or the stories are not true (Farber and Sherry, pp. 74-78, 89, 95-99); (Coughlin, 1995, pp. 1333-34). Alonso S. Perales' methodology provides a powerful response to these sorts of criticisms. Perales (1974, pp. 139-213) has supplied over seventy pages of sworn affidavits of numerous Mexican Americans describing their experiences and encounters with racial discrimination. The large number of individual descriptions of the racism of the day provides strong evidence that such experiences are indeed typical. In addition, the fact that the affidavits are sworn statements given under oath provides good reason to believe that the stories are true and verifiable.

From the perspective of critical theory, we can understand Perales' project as "reality construction." Critical theorists now understand "reality as a social construction" (Torre-MacNeill, 2011, p. 29). In order to establish their rights, racial minorities must first deconstruct "the officially (state sanctioned) accepted reality" (Torre-MacNeill, 2011, p. 29). In its place, persons of color must substitute "a more accurate account of reality" (Torre-MacNeill, 2011, p. 29) Racial minorities construct an alternative reality by describing their experiences of being oppressed which "works to invalidate the culture of white . . . supremacy," which is "the socially constructed reality (of the oppressor)" (Torre-MacNeill, 2011, p. 31). Reality construction operates as follows:

> Experience is a distinct way of knowing truth (and/or reality). When put together, a group of individuals who share similar experiences of being oppressed begin to relate their personal story, or individual experience with the group, the group begins to create a collective reality, or regime of truth, rooted in common experience. This process of consciousness raising could be seen as experiments in the science of reality construction, reflecting the various cultures, or 'ways of knowing' that exist. (Torre-MacNeill, 2011, p. 32)

Given this theoretical approach, we can observe that Perales has sought to invalidate and deconstruct the socially constructed reality of post-racialism—a worldview which holds that racism does not play a significant role in the lives of Mexican Americans. In its place, he substitutes a new more accurate reality based on the actual experiences of Mexican Americans in which they describe an alternative reality that is permeated with racism against Mexican Americans.

It is worth noting that Perales' task of reality construction is a large one. In Perales' day, most people were operating well within a black/white paradigm regarding civil rights—i.e., "the conception that race in America consists, either exclusively or primarily, of only two constituent groups, the Black and the White." (Perea, 1997, p. 1219) Accordingly, civil rights discourse focused primarily on black/white relations (Brooks and Widner, 2010, pp. 109-110). Mexican Americans fell outside of this black/white paradigm (Perea, 1997, p. 1215). This point is highly significant. As philosopher of science Thomas Kuhn (1970, p. 24) has explained, phenomena that do not fit within the prevailing paradigm or "normal science" of the day "are often not seen at all." Accordingly, the phenomena regarding Mexican Americans that Perales was seeking to publicize would generally be invisible or not seen because of the prevailing black/white paradigm (Perea, 1997, pp. 1213-1215).

This alternative reality based on the personal experiences and struggles of Mexican Americans also constitutes what Michel Foucault (1980, p. 82) has called "subjugated knowledge." According to Foucault, there are two categories of subjugated knowledge:

[1.] Those blocks of historical knowledge which were present but disguised [or buried] within the body of . . . systemizing theory and which [meticulous erudite, exact historical knowledge] . . . has been able to reveal . . . and [2.] a whole set of [local, specific and popular] knowledges that have been disqualified as inadequate to their task or insufficiently elaborated: naïve knowledges, located low down on the hierarchy, beneath the required level of cognition or scientificity (Naughton, 2005, p. 82).

These forms of knowledge—the "buried discourses of academic erudition and those popular disqualified discourses of popular experience"—have in common the fact that they "both are essentially concerned with an 'historical knowledge of struggles'" (Naughton, 2005, p. 177) Foucault asserts that we should take note of "the past and ongoing epistemic battles among competing power/knowledge frameworks that try to control a given field" (Medina, 2011, p. 10) According to Foucault, "in the battle among power/knowledge frameworks, some come out on top and become dominant while others are displaced and become subjugated" (Medina, 2011, p. 11). Foucault argues that it is possible to "fight against established and official forms of knowledge" by using subjugated knowledge against them (Medina, 2011, p. 13). Foucault contends that

The critical task of the scholar and the activist is to resurrect subjugated knowledges—that is, to revive hidden or forgotten bodies of experiences and memories—and to help produce insurrections of subjugated knowledges . . . these insurrections . . . are critical interventions that disrupt and interrogate epistemic hegemonies and mainstream perspectives. . . . Such interventions involve the difficult labor of mobilizing scattered, marginalized publics and of tapping into the critical potential of their dejected experiences and memories (Medina, 2011, p. 11).

Given this theoretical framework, it is possible to see that Perales collects and uses this subjugated knowledge—the personal experiences and struggles against racism of Mexican Americans—to challenge the prevailing post-racial worldview and other "established regimes of thought" (Naughton, 2005, p. 177) such as the black/white paradigm.

The Perales project of proving the existence of discrimination against Mexican Americans is also noteworthy because the United States Supreme Court would eventually find the existence of similar proof relevant to establishing a Mexican-American identity and constitutional protection for Mexican Americans. In *Hernandez v. Texas* (1954, pp. 477-79), the United States Supreme Court held that "persons of Mexican descent" are a cognizable or identifiable group and entitled to equal protection under the United States Constitution in areas where they are subject to local discriminatory treatment. The Supreme Court observed:

Throughout our history differences in race and color have defined easily identifiable groups which have at times required the aid of the courts in securing equal treatment under the laws. But community prejudices are not static, and from time to time other differences from the community norm may define other groups which need the same protection. Whether such a group exists within a community is a question of fact. When the existence of a distinct class is demonstrated, and it is further shown that the laws, as written or as applied, single out the class for different treatment not based on some reasonable classification, the guarantees of the constitution have been violated. (Hernandez, 1954, p. 478)

The Court ruled that the Mexican-American petitioner had the burden of proving that Mexican Americans were discriminated against on the basis of race (Hernandez, 1954, p. 479). The Court found that Mexican Americans constituted a distinctive class or group in part because they were discriminated against in that they were segregated in public schools and public accommodations such as restrooms (Hernandez, 1954, pp. 779-800); (Lopez and Olivas, 2008, p. 290). Importantly, where Mexican Americans were unable to establish that they experienced racial discrimination, they did not constitute a distinctive class which would be entitled to constitutional protection (Delgado and Palacios, 1975, p. 395).

Beyond this, Alonso S. Perales and W.E.B. DuBois both provide contemporary race scholars with a lesson on how to confront claims of post-racialism. Their example shows that scholars of race must come forward with evidence to construct an alternative reality to show that race is still a major factor affecting the life prospects of racial minorities. Some recent scholarship on post-racialism shows that some contemporary scholars are suggesting that any claim of post-racialism be met and dispelled with the appropriate facts. For instance, Tanya Hernandez (2011) has recently argued that critical scholars can learn a lesson from the Brazilian experience (Hernandez, p. 1407). There she points out that Brazil has a history of slavery (Hernandez, 2011, p. 1412). As a result, Brazil has a large population of citizens who are of African descent (Hernandez, 2011, pp. 1412-1413). Since the abolition of slavery in Brazil, many have claimed that Brazil constitutes a post-racial society (Hernandez, 2011, pp. 1414-1415). Hernandez (2011, pp. 1420-1431) explains that the claim of Brazilian post-racialism has been effectively challenged by race scholars producing social science evidence of the continuing influence of racism in the lives of Brazilian citizens. Hernandez (2011, p. 1437) suggests that claims of post-racialism in the United States can be challenged in a similar manner.

Similarly, Mario Barnes, Erwin Chemerinsky and Trina Jones (2010, pp. 979-992) have confronted the contemporary claim of post-racialism in the United States with the facts. In this regard, they produce evidence showing "the disparate conditions under which many people of color struggle" (Barnes, Chemerinsky and Jones, 2010, p. 982). They show, among other things, that (1) there continues to be a high poverty rate for racial minorities, (2) "the median net worth of white households is more than ten times that of black households," (3) "African-Americans and Latinos still disproportionately tend to occupy lower paying and lower status jobs," (4) racial minorities "experience significant disparities in educational achievement," and (5) there is "unequal treatment within the U.S. criminal justice system" (Barnes, Chemerinsky and Jones, pp. 983-992).

Likewise, Angela Onwuachi-Willig and Mario Barnes (2012, p. 347) challenge the claim of post-racialism by showing that in the wake of the election of President Obama, "new and increased forms of racial discrimination" have been created in the employment context. In their review of the employment discrimination case law where the word "Obama" appears, they found that "some employees have claimed that their workplaces grew increasingly hostile as a function of Obama's ascendance toward, and assumption of, the presidency" (Onwuachi-Willig and Barnes, p. 340) They also found that some employees claimed "that the very name Obama became a racial slur in the workplace" (Onwuachi-Willig and Barnes, p. 343)

Similarly, Ian Haney Lopez (2010, pp. 1068-69) confronts the claim of post-racialism by arguing that race or racism "will remain a principal means through which our society structures and justifies inequality." In particular, Lopez (2010, p. 1025) points out that "the public security system in the United States produces shocking racial disparities at every level, from stops to arrests to prosecutions to sentencing to rates of incarceration and execution" and that "state prison populations are two-thirds black and Latino." According to Lopez (2010, p. 1072), "the vast racial disparities that mar our society and in particular our criminal system, result from continuing patterns of racism . . ."

There is much at stake in overcoming the claims of post-racialism. For instance, some now argue that because we now live in an allegedly postracial era, there is no longer a need for the Voting Rights Act, which protects the voting rights of racial minorities (Clegg, 2009, pp. 49-50). Similarly, one commentator has proposed that post-racialism requires that the constitutional doctrine of strict scrutiny—which has traditionally been used by courts to carefully examine and strike down laws that invidiously discriminate on the basis of race—must be rethought because it should not "exist in perpetuity" inasmuch as "strict scrutiny elevates race to an exceptional role in American law, one which effectively guarantees we will not 'get beyond' race" (Schraub, 2011, p. 54).

Accordingly, the current debate over the existence of post-racialism in our society is an epistemic dispute between competing power/knowledge frameworks. At issue is which power/knowledge framework will become the dominant or mainstream perspective and which framework will become subjugated and pushed to the margins.

B. Alonso S. Perales and Interest Convergence

Derrick Bell (1980) has developed one of the leading critical insights which is known as interest convergence theory. According to this theory, racial minorities will not make progress in advancing their civil rights unless it is in the interest of the white majority (Bell, 1980, p. 524); (Bell, 1992, p. 44-45). Thus, Bell (1980, p. 524) argues that *Brown v. Board of Education* (1954), which outlawed racial segregation in public schools, was handed down not out of a recognition that it was the morally correct outcome, but because it advanced the foreign policy and domestic interests of the dominant group. At that time, the United States was engaged in a Cold War with the Soviet Union and was struggling for influence around the world, especially in the Third World (Bell, 1980, p. 524). The Soviet Union sought to exploit racial divisions by claiming that the United States was racist as demonstrated in the Jim Crow segregationist laws of the day (Bell, 1980, p. 524). Accordingly, Bell (1980, p. 524) contends that the Supreme Court outlawed segregation in *Brown* to promote the foreign policy interests of the majority in having a positive, non-racist image of the United States. In addition, Bell (1980, pp. 524-525) argues that the Supreme Court outlawed segregation in *Brown* to advance the domestic interests of the majority because it was concerned that racial minorities who had just fought a war opposing the white supremacist policies of the Nazis would not accept a racist society in the United States.

In his *Good Neighbors* book, Alonso S. Perales seems to anticipate the framework of this interest convergence theory in seeking to advance the civil rights of Mexican Americans. In the book, he supports the argument in favor of outlawing discrimination against Mexican Americans by presenting evidence and arguments that doing so would advance the foreign policy and domestic interests of the United States. For instance, Perales provides a Statement by Professor Carlos Castañeda ("The Second Rate Citizen and Democracy," p. 20) which observes that it is important to deal with the oppressive situation of Mexican Americans truthfully in order to preserve American democracy and reject the white supremacist ideology of the axis powers:

> Failure to reveal the true facts in regard to our second rate citizens [i.e., Mexican Americans] can lead only to the ultimate destruction of the basic principles of democracy. If we admit the damning theory of racial superiority implied in such a condition, we are no better than the Nazis.

Similarly, Perales includes a Statement on Racial Discrimination by Jack Danciger (Statement on 15 November 1947, pp. 21-28) which observes that racial discrimination against Mexican Americans in the United States is disrupting foreign relations in Latin America—especially in Mexico. Danciger (Statement on 15 November 1947, p. 23) writes that such racial discrimination "places some in a position to question the right of the United States of America to assume postwar leadership . . ." He further observes:

> When newspapers in the United States . . . published detailed reports of all kinds of discrimination and indignities practiced against Mexicans or Latin Americans in Texas, these articles were reproduced in the newspaper and magazines in all the countries of Latin America and often enlarged upon, doing great damage to the prestige of all North Americans thus engendering a bad feeling that will take decades to overcome. (Dancinger Statement on 15 November 1947, pp. 25-26)

Likewise, in his statement in the Fair Employment Practices Act Hearings in the United States Senate in 1944, Alonso S. Perales (Statement on 30, 31 August and 6, 7 and 8 September 1944, p. 89) testified that federal legislation should be passed outlawing discrimination against Mexican Americans in order to build the unity necessary to win World War II in light of the fact that "more than a quarter of a million soldiers of Mexican descent are giving their blood for democracy." Perales (Statement on 30, 31 August and 6, 7 and 8 September 1944, p. 89) observed:

We are at war and in order to win it, we need unity among the peoples of the Americas. The best way to show all the inhabitants of Hispanic America that they are respected in our country is to pass a federal law making it unlawful for anyone to humiliate them here. The citizens of Venezuela, Honduras, Argentina and the other Hispanic American Republics feel just as deeply hurt as the citizens of Mexico when they learn there are places in the United States where members of their race, and above all their fellow citizens, are humiliated.

With respect to advancing the American war effort during the Second World War through the brave efforts of Mexican Americans who were fighting on the front lines, Perales (Statement on 30, 31 August and 6, 7 and 8 September 1944, p. 90) further stated:

In regards the thousands of American citizens of Mexican descent who are fighting in the battle fronts, the best way to encourage them to continue fighting with enthusiasm is to pass a Federal law that will assure them that our Federal Government does not intend to permit anyone to humiliate them or any member of their families, either in Texas or in any other state of the Union, merely because they are Mexicans by blood. Incidentally, it might be said in passing that the casualty lists published in the local newspapers show that from 50-75 percent of those from south Texas who are falling, either dead or wounded, are soldiers of Mexican descent. Our Federal Government owes it to these boys to make sure that when they return to the United States they will find the kind of democracy that they have been given to understand they are fighting for. It would be a great disappointment to them, to say the least, to find upon their return that they could not secure employment or that if they found it they could not receive equal wages for equal work merely because of their racial origin, or that the owner of any restaurant, barber shop, or theater could continue to humiliate them as he saw fit just because they were of Mexican descent.

Perales' arguments regarding the negative impact of racism practiced against Mexican Americans on the foreign policy interests of the United States are powerful and well-taken. This is confirmed by United States Secretary of State Dean Acheson's 1946 letter to the Chief of the Fair Employment Practices Committee where he described the impact of American racism on American foreign policy:

The existence of discrimination against minority groups in this country has an adverse effect on our relations with other countries. We are reminded over and over by some foreign newspapers and spokesmen that our treatment of various minorities leaves much to be desired . . . Frequently we find it next to impossible to formulate a satisfactory answer to our critics in other countries . . .
An atmosphere of suspicion and resentment in a country over the way a minority is treated in the United States is a formidable obstacle to the development of mutual understanding and trust between the two countries. We will have better international relations when these reasons for suspicion and resentment have been removed. (Dudziak, 1988, p. 101)

C. Alonso S. Perales and the State of Nature

In a recent article, I have argued that there is a tendency for the dominant group to relate to racial minorities as if they were in what philosophers have described as the state of nature—i.e., there is or has been a tendency for the majority to act without legal or moral constraints on their actions (Martínez, 2010, pp. 806-833). This state of nature is a very dangerous situation in that it leads to the denial of the human rights of racial minorities and presents the dominant group with too much temptation to do wrong (Martínez, 2010, pp. 806-837). In light of this state of nature theory, we can understand Alonso S. Perales' efforts to convince legislators to enact federal legislation to protect Mexican Americans from racial discrimination as an effort to place legal constraints on the dominant group and lift Mexican Americans out of the state of nature.

Perales presents evidence of the state of nature existence of Mexican Americans where there was no law to protect them. As discussed, Perales (1974, pp. 139-213) provides powerful evidence that Mexican Americans are subject to widespread discrimination in, among other things, housing, employment, public accommodations and segregation in public schools. The sworn affidavits of a number of persons explain the failure of the law to protect Mexican Americans. For instance, World War II disabled veteran José García (Affidavit, 18 October 1947, pp. 141-142) describes an incident where he was denied service at a restaurant in Hamlin City, Texas. The owner told him, "I am the owner of this place and I won't serve any Mexicans, regardless of who you are" (García Affidavit, 18 October 1947, p. 142). García (Affidavit 18 October 1947, p. 142) went to seek help from the City Marshall who told him "there was nothing he could do about it." Horacio Guerra (Affidavit, 3 May 1946, p. 163), a World War II veteran, also stated that he was refused service at a restaurant in Uvalde, Texas, where the waitress informed him that "she does not serve Mexicans." Guerra (Affidavit, 3 May 1946, p. 163) then sought relief from the "County Judge" who "told [Guerra] he could not do a thing about it." While wearing his United States Army uniform, Dionicio Ortíz (Affidavit, 3 December 1943, p. 187) was refused service at a restaurant in Lockhart, Texas. Ortíz (Affidavit, 3 December 1943, p. 187) then went to complain to the Sheriff who responded by saying "you were not born in that restaurant." The Sheriff then "slapped [Ortíz] (Affidavit, 3 December 1943, p. 187) and told [Ortíz] to get out." Similarly, United States Army veteran David Rodriguez (Affidavit, 11 October 1945, p. 171), in his sworn affidavit, describes being denied service at a barber shop in San Marcos, Texas. Rodriguez (Affidavit 11 October 1945, p. 171) complained to the Sheriff of Hays County "but he said he could not do anything about it." Likewise, the sworn affidavit of Leonardo Rodriguez (Affidavit, 7 March 1944, pp. 185-186) describes a situation where the manager of a theatre attempted to relegate him to segregated seating for Mexicans. Rodriguez (Affidavit, 7 March 1944, p. 185) refused to be seated in the segregated section and demanded his money back. Rodriguez (Affidavit, 7 March 1944, p. 185) then states that the manager:

> went and got the money and brought it to me, but he also brought with him a stick about two and one-half feet long, one inch thick and two inches wide. He

handed me the money and he punched my ribs with the stick and told me to get out. I told him it was not necessary for him to get angry about it, and as I turned around to get out he struck me on the head with the stick and fell me to the floor and while I was lying down, he struck me in the back with the stick. When he stuck me on the head he broke my glasses. As soon as I got up he struck me on the left cheek with the same stick. He also struck me on my right hand and in the mouth . . . I reported the case to Sheriff Sidney F. Edge of Kendall County but he said there was nothing he could do about it.

In these examples, the Mexican Americans find themselves in the state of nature as they are unable to appeal to official authority or the law to give them relief. This is precisely the state of nature imagined by the philosopher Thomas Hobbes:

The state of nature is . . . [a situation where there is] no common authority to which [men] could turn to settle their disputes, or on which they could rely to give stability to their expectations of how other men would act towards them. (Malcolm, 2002, p. 35)

Perales insisted that it was necessary to impose legal constraints on the dominant group to bring an end to racial discrimination against Mexican Americans. Perales (Statement on 30, 31 August and 6, 7 and 8 September 1944, p. 89) explained:

There are some people who opine that the solution of this problem rests in waging an educational campaign among the Anglo-American element designed to show them the merits and qualities of Mexicans and of the His-panic race generally, but the overwhelming majority of us contend that in addition to such an educational program there is need for a Federal law pro-hibiting the humiliation of Mexicans and persons of Hispanic descent gen-erally in any part of our country. A Federal law is necessary to put an end to this painful situation immediately.

D. Alonso S. Perales and Mexican-American Whiteness

Critical theory has established that the race of Mexican Americans has been legally constructed or categorized as white (Martínez, 1997). As a result, some Mex-ican Americans thought that the best way to establish their civil rights was to claim the traditional rights and privileges normally associated with a white racial identity (Martínez, 1997, pp. 322-23); (Foley, 2005, p. 140). Accordingly, at certain points in history some Mexican Americans pursued an "other white" strategy in seeking relief from racial discrimination—i.e., they claimed that although they were not Anglo Saxons, Mexican Americans were still white, and, therefore, Anglo Saxon whites should not discriminate against them (Behnken, 2011, p. 27); (Wilson, 2003, p. 148). For instance, some argued that Mexican Americans could not be segregated from whites in the public schools because Mexican Americans were also white (Behnken, 2911, p. 42). In any event, some contend that during the first half of the twentieth century "Mexican-Americans primarily fought for rights by positioning themselves as members of the white race in order to avoid Jim Crow" (Behnken, 2011, p. 14).

Ultimately, the strategy of seeking to base Mexican-American civil rights on a claim of whiteness was a failure (Behnken, 2011, p. 38); (Martínez, 1997, pp. 335-338). The affidavits supplied by Perales show how the claim of whiteness did not prevent racial discrimination against Mexican Americans. For instance, Ernesto Perez (Affidavit, 24 June 1943, p. 194) stated that he was told by the usher at a movie theatre in Hondo, Texas, that he could not sit in a particular section of the theatre because it "was for white people only." Perez (Affidavit, 24 June 1943, p. 194) told the usher that "[Perez] was classified as white by the United States Government in Washington . . . ." Perez (Affidavit, 24 June 1943, 194) then went to the manager who informed Perez that, "No, you are not white; you are a Mexican." Jesús Valdez (Affidavit, 26 June 1941, p. 211) worked at a construction site where "drinking water pails" were designated "as follows: 'For Whites;' 'For Mexicans;' and 'For Negroes.'" When Valdez (Affidavit, 26 June 1941, 211) drank water out of the pail marked "For Whites," the foreman fired him "because [Valdez] had drunk water out of the pail marked 'For Whites.'" In response, Valdez (Affidavit, 26 June 1941, p. 211) told the foreman that:

I considered myself as white as he or any other white person. He then said substantially, the following: "You are discharged, and any other person of Mexican or African descent who drinks water out of the pails marked 'For Whites' will be discharged also."

These affidavits are consistent with the case law of the time which shows that the legal whiteness of Mexican Americans failed to provide them with rights or protection in Texas even when the Texas legislature passed, in 1943, House Concurrent Resolution 105 which was approved and proclaimed by the Texas Governor, Coke Stevenson, and that declared that it was Texas policy that

all persons of the Caucasian race within the jurisdiction of the State are entitled to full and equal accommodations, advantages, facilities and privileges of all public places of business or amusement. (*Terrell Wells Swimming Pool*, 1944, p. 826)

When a Mexican American was refused entry to a swimming pool because he was of "Mexican descent," he brought a lawsuit, *Terrell Wells Swimming Pool v. Rodriguez* (1944, p. 826); (Martínez, 1994, p. 563-64), and sought to rely on the House Concurrent Resolution 105 to establish that since Mexican Americans are legally white or Caucasian, he had a right to use the swimming pool. The Texas court of appeals denied his claim holding that the resolution did "not have the effect of a statute" or the force of law (*Terrell Wells Swimming Pool*, p. 826). As a result, the resolution could not change the law which existed prior to the resolution to the effect that "the proprietor of the Terrell Wells Swimming Pool had the legal right to admit to his place of amusement only such persons as he desired" (*Terrell Wells Swimming Pool*, p. 826).

Similarly, the case law from that general time period shows that a white racial identity did not protect Mexican Americans from being excluded from juries. In *Hernandez v. Texas* (1952), a Mexican-American defendant, Pedro ("Pete") Hernandez, sought to reverse his murder conviction on the ground that Mexican Americans had been systematically excluded from the jury in violation of the equal protection clause of the Fourteenth Amendment. In seeking to establish a constitutional violation, Hernandez constructed an argument from analogy. He argued that the case law established that the exclusion of African-Americans from juries constituted a constitutional violation. In the same way, he contended that the exclusion of Mexican Americans was similarly constitutionally impermissible. The Court of Criminal Appeals of Texas held that the Fourteenth Amendment protected only whites and blacks and that Mexican Americans were white as a matter of law (*Hernandez*, 1952, p. 535). As a result, the Court also held that there was no denial of equal protection since the juries that indicted and convicted Hernandez were made up of white people (*Hernandez*, 1952, p. 536).

Given this background, Alonso S. Perales is important because he sought to establish in the 1940s the rights of Mexican Americans by seeking laws to prevent discrimination against Mexican Americans as a distinctive group. He did not seek to establish that Mexican Americans were white and therefore could not be discriminated against. His testimony before the United States Congress does not attempt to establish rights on the basis of a claim of whiteness. He simply sought legislation to outlaw discrimination against Mexican Americans as Mexican Americans (Perales, Statement on 30, 31 August and 6, 7 and 8 September 1944, p. 89).

In light of this discussion, it is possible to see that it is a mistake for some to assert that in the first half of the twentieth century Mexican Americans primarily sought to base their rights on a claim to whiteness. As demonstrated by the sworn affidavits and the case law of the time, Alonso S. Perales—one of the major civil rights leaders of the era—and others were well aware that seeking to base Mexican-American civil rights on a claim to whiteness was misguided. Perales rejected the whiteness strategy in his efforts to secure anti-discrimination legislation. Perales' approach made sense since in that era where Mexican Americans were generally seen by society as an inferior, non-white race (Lopez and Olivas, 2008, pp. 293-94). These conclusions also are consistent with Neil Foley's (2008, pp. 61-62) observation that there are "numerous examples" of Mexican Americans who did not seek to base their civil rights on a claim to a white racial identity.

E. Alonso S. Perales and Fame

For some reason, Alonso S. Perales has not achieved the fame of other Mexican Americans who have been important in the effort to secure the rights of Mexican Americans. For instance, one recent book on the history of the Mexican-American struggle for civil rights contains no entry for Alonso S. Perales in its index (Behnken, 2011, pp. 333-347). This chapter was written for a symposium and book about the civil rights work of Alonso S. Perales and these efforts will help Perales achieve the fame that he deserves as a major figure in Mexican-American civil rights history. In reaching this conclusion, one is reminded of the philosopher Arthur Schopenhauer's (1901, p. 88) observations on fame:

Whether authors ever live to see the dawn of their fame depends on the chance of circumstance; and the higher and more important their works are, the less likelihood there is of their doing so. That was an incomparably fine saying of Seneca's, that fame follows merit as surely as the body casts a shadow; sometimes falling in front, and sometimes behind . . .

As a general rule, the longer a man's fame is likely to last, the later it will be in coming; for all excellent products require time for their development . . .

It is time to recognize the importance of Alonso S. Perales.

Conclusion

Alonso S. Perales was a pioneering antiracist activist who sought to establish the civil rights of Mexican Americans. Based in Texas, he was particularly engaged in civil rights work during the middle part of the twentieth century. This chapter has sought to analyze the efforts of Alonso S. Perales to establish the civil rights of Mexican Americans through the lens of contemporary critical legal theory, which offers an important set of insights and concepts to analyze issues of race. Examining the civil rights work of Alonso S. Perales through the lens of critical theory reveals that, in many ways, Perales was ahead of his time in that contemporary critical race theorists would recognize that his work employs modern critical techniques and deals with issues at the heart of today's critical race theory. Accordingly, the chapter has considered how Perales addressed claims of post-racialism—the idea that race is not an important factor in the lives of people of color—by constructing what critical theorists would now describe as an alternative reality with subjugated knowledge. The chapter shows how Perales' work is relevant to the contemporary debate in critical race theory over whether America now constitutes a post-racial society. The chapter also has considered how Perales' efforts to advance the cause of Mexican Americans anticipated the framework and the strategy for establishing civil rights for racial minorities as set out and elaborated by leading critical race theorist Derrick Bell in his well-known interest convergence theory. Next, the chapter has argued that Perales' effort to outlaw discrimination against Mexican Americans constitutes an attempt to lift Mexican Americans out of what contemporary critical race theory now characterizes as a state of nature existence. In addition, the chapter has contended that Perales is important because he sought to establish the rights of Mexican Americans as a distinctive group as opposed to founding such rights on a claim that Mexican Americans were members of the white race. Finally, the chapter suggests that it is time to give Alonso S. Perales the recognition and fame that he deserves as an important figure in Mexican-American civil rights history.

Works Cited

Barnes, M., Chemerinsky, E. & Jones, T. (2010) A post-race equal protection? *Georgetown Law Journal 98,* 967-1004.
Behnken, B. D. (2011). *Fighting their own battles: Mexican Americans, African Americans and the struggle for civil rights in Texas.* Chapel Hill: University of North Carolina Press. ell, D. (1980). Brown v. Board of Education and the interest convergence dilemma. *Harvard Law Review 93,* 518-533.

Bell, D. (1992). *Race, racism and American law,* 3rd ed. Boston: Little, Brown and Company.

Benavides, W. (1974). Affidavit, 13 September 1943. In Perales, A. (Ed.), *Are We Good Neighbors?* (pp. 190-191). New York: Arno Press.

Brooks, R. & Widner, K. (2010). In defense of the black/white binary: Reclaiming a tradition of civil rights scholarship. *Berkley Journal of African-American Law and Policy 12,* 107-144.

Brown v. Board of Education. 347 U.S. 483 (1954).

Castañeda, C. E. (1974). Letter from Carlos Castañeda to Robert K. Carr, 9 May, 1947. In Perales, A. (Ed.), *Are we good neighbors?* (pp. 58-59). New York: Arno Press.

Castañeda, C. E. (1974). The second rate citizen and democracy. In Perales, A. (Ed.), *Are we good neighbors?* (pp. 17-20). New York: Arno Press, 1974 .

Castañeda, C. E. (1974). Statement on discrimination against Mexican-Americans in employment, 9 May 1947. In Perales, A. (Ed.), *Are we good neighbors?* (pp. 59-63). New York: Arno Press.

Castañeda, C. E. (1974). Statement of Carlos Castañeda at fair employment practices hearing in U.S. Senate, 8 September, 1944. In Perales, A. (Ed.), *Are we good neighbors?* (pp. 92-98). New York: Arno Press.

Cho, S. (2009). Post-racialism. *Iowa Law Review 94,* 1589-1649.

Clegg, R. (2009). The future of the Voting Rights Act after *Bartlett* and *Namudno. Cato Supreme Court Review 2009,* 35-51.

Cooper, F. R. (2010). Masculinities, post-racialism and the Gates controversy: The false equivalence between officer and civilian. *Nevada Law Journal 11,* 1-43.

Coughlin, A. M. (1995). Regulating the self: Autobiographical performances in outsider scholarship. *Virginia Law Review 81,* 1229-1340.

Crenshaw, K. W. (2011). Twenty years of critical race theory: Looking back to move forward. *Connecticut Law Review 43,* 1253-1352.

Danciger, J. (1974). Statement on racial discrimination, 15 November, 1947. In Perales, A. (Ed.), *Are we good neighbors?* (pp. 21-28). New York: Arno Press.

De La Torre-MacNeill, J. (2011). Consciousness raising and reality construction within oppressed groups: Bridging the gap between feminist theory and critical race theory. *Res Cogitans 2,* 29-36, 29.

Delgado, R. and Palacios, V. (1975). Mexican-Americans as a legally cognizable class under rule 23 and the equal protection clause. *Notre Dame Law Review 50,* 393.

Dubois, W.E.B. & Eaton, I. (1899). *The Philadelphia negro: A social study.* Boston, Mass.: Ginn & Co.

Dudziak, M. L. (1988). Desegregation as a Cold War imperative. *Stanford Law Review 41* (1088), 61-120.

Farber, D. A. & Sherry, S. (1997). *Beyond all reason: The radical assault on truth in American law.* New York: Oxford University Press.

Foley, N. (2005) Over the rainbow: Hernandez v. Texas, Brown v. Board of Education, and Black v. Brown. *Chicano-Latino Law Review 25,* 139-152.

Foley, N. (2008). Becoming Hispanic: Mexican-Americans and whiteness. In Rothenberg, P. S. (Ed.), *White Privilege* (pp. 55-65). New York: Worth Publishers.

Foucault, M. (1980). *Power/knowledge: Selected interviews and other writings 1972-1977* (C. Gordon, Ed.). New York: Pantheon Books.

Garcia, J. (1974). Affidavit, 18 October, 1947. In Perales, A. (Ed.), *Are we good neighbors?* (pp. 141-142). New York: Arno Press.

Garcia, M. (1974). Affidavit, 5 October 1946. In Perales, A. (Ed.), *Are we good neighbors?* (pp. 156-157). New York: Arno Press.

Gipprich, W. (1974). Affidavit, 21 July 1947. In Perales, A. (Ed.), *Are we good neighbors?* (pp. 144-145). New York: Arno Press.

Green, M. Z. (2012). Reading Ricci and Pyett to provide racial justice through union arbitration. *Indiana Law Journal 87*, 367-419.

Guerra, H. (1974). Affidavit, 3 May 1946. In Perales, A. (Ed.), *Are we good neighbors?* (pp. 163-164). New York: Arno Press, 1974.

Haney López, I. H. and Olivas M. A. (2008). Jim Crow, Mexican-Americans, and the Anti-Subordination Constitution: The story of Hernandez v. Texas. In Moran, R.F. & Carbado, D.W. (Eds.), *Race Law Stories* (pp. 273-310). New York: Foundation Press.

Haney López, I. H. (2010) Post-racial racism: Racial stratification and mass incarceration in the age of Obama. *California Law Review 98*, 1023-1073.

Hernandez v. Texas. 251 S.W.2d 531 (1952).

Hernandez v. Texas. 347 U.S. 475 (1954).

Hernandez, T. K. (2011) The value of intersectional comparative analysis to the "post-racial" future of critical race theory: a Brazil-U.S. comparative case study. *Connecticut Law Review 43*, 1407-1437.

Kuhn, T. (1970). *The structure of scientific revolutions*, 2nd ed. Chicago: The University of Chicago Press.

Malcolm, N. (2002). *Aspects of Hobbes.* Oxford: Clarendon Press.

Mancilla, L. (1974). Affidavit, 24 September 1947. In Perales, A. (Ed.), *Are we good neighbors?* (pp. 142-143). New York: Arno Press.

Martínez, G. A. (1994). Legal indeterminacy, judicial discretion and the Mexican-American litigation experience: 1930-1980. *University of California at Davis Law Review 27*, 555-618.

Martínez, G. A. (1997). The legal construction of race: Mexican-Americans and whiteness. *Harvard Latino Law Review 2*, 321-347.

Martínez, G. A. (2010). Race, American law and the state of nature. *West Virginia Law Review 112*, 799-838.

Matsuda, M. J. (1987). Looking to the bottom: critical legal studies and reparations. *Harvard Civil Rights-Civil Liberties Law Review 22*, 323-399.

Matsuda, M. J. (1989). Public response to racist speech: considering the victim's story. *Michigan Law Review 87*(8), 2320-2381.

McWhorter, J. (2008, December 30). Racism in America is over. *Forbes.* 30 December 2008, Retrieved from http://www.forbes.com/2008/12/30/end-of-racism-oped-cx_jm_1230mcwhorter.html.

Medina, J. (2011). Toward a Foucaultian epistemology of resistance: Counter-memory, epistemic friction, and guerilla pluralism. *Foucault Studies 12*, 9-35.

Naughton, M. (2005). Redefining miscarriages of justice: A revived human-rights approach to unearth subjugated discourses of wrongful criminal conviction. *British Journal of Criminology 45*(2), 165-182.

Onwuachi-Willig, A. & Barnes, M. (2012). The Obama effect: Understanding emerging meanings of 'Obama' in anti-discrimination law. *Indiana Law Journal 87*(1), 325-348.

Ortiz, D. (1974). Affidavit, 3 December 1943. In Perales, A. S. (Ed.), *Are we good neighbors?* (pp. 186-187). New York: Arno Press.

Perales, A. S. (1974). *Are We Good Neighbors?* New York: Arno Press.

Perales, A. S. (1974). Statement at Fair Employment Practices Act Hearings on 30, 31 August and 6, 7 and 8 September, 1944. In Perales, A. S. (Ed.), *Are we good neighbors?* (pp. 88-91). New York: Arno Press.

Perales, A. S. (1974). "Statement before Senate Committee on Labor and Education on 13 March, 1945." In Perales, A. S. (Ed.), *Are we good neighbors?* (pp. 114-132). New York: Arno Press.

Perea, J. (1997). The black/white binary paradigm of race: The 'normal science' of American racial thought. *California Law Review 85*(5), 1213-1258.

Perez, E. (1974). Affidavit, 24 June 1943. In Perales, A. S. (Ed.), *Are we good neighbors?* (p. 194). New York: Arno Press.

Rodriguez, D. P. (1974). Affidavit, 11 October, 1945. In Perales, A. S. (Ed.), *Are we good neighbors?* (p. 171). New York: Arno Press.

Rodriguez, L. (1974). Affidavit, 7 March, 1944. In Perales, A. S. (Ed.), *Are we good neighbors?* (pp. 185-186). New York: Arno Press.

Schopenhauer, A. (1901). *The wisdom of life and other essays.* Washington & London: M. Walter Dunne, Publisher.

Schraub, D. H. (2011) Post-racialism and the end of strict scrutiny. *Illinois Public Law Research Paper* No. 11-09. Retrieved from SSRN: http://ssrn.com/abstract= 1960015.

Solis, P. (1974). Affidavit, 29 April 1948. In Perales, A. S. (Ed.), *Are we good neighbors?* (pp. 139-140). New York: Arno Press.

Suarez, J. (1974). Affidavit, 4 March 1947. In Perales, A. S. (Ed.), *Are we good neighbors?* (p. 148). New York: Arno Press.

Sugrue, T. J. (1944). Not even past: Barack Obama and the burden of race. *Terrell Wells Swimming Pool v. Rodriguez.* 182 S.W.2d 824.

Valdes, F. & Cho, S. (2011). Critical race materialism: Theorizing justice in the wake of global neoliberalism. *Connecticut Law Review 43*(5), 1513-1572.

Valdez, J. (1974). Affidavit, 26 June 1941. In Perales, A. S. (Ed.), *Are we good neighbors?* (p. 211). New York: Arno Press.

Wasserstrom, R. (1982). A defense of programs of preferential treatment. In Mappes, T.A. & Zembaty, J. S. (Eds.), *Social ethics: Morality and social policy* 2nd ed, (pp. 187-191). New York: McGraw Hill Book Company.

Wilson, S. H. (2003). Brown over 'other white': Mexican-Americans legal arguments and litigation strategy in school desegregation lawsuits. *Law and History Review* 21(1), 145-194.

Notes

[1]This chapter has been prepared for the conference "In Defense of My People: Alonso S. Perales and the Development of Mexican-American Public Intellectuals," January 13, 2012, at the University of Houston Law Center. I would like to thank Professor Michael Olivas for inviting me to participate in the Conference and for his comments on a draft of this chapter. I also would like to thank Dean John Attanasio, the Law Faculty Excellence Fund and Southern Methodist University for providing a research grant to support this project.

Young Alonso S. Perales.

Alonso S. Perales in Army uniform, 1919.

Alonso and Marta Pérez de Perales walking on Houston Street in San Antonio, TX [ca. 1940s].

Alonso S. Perales at a Pan American Round Table of Texas (PARTT) event [ca. 1940s].

International Conference of Attorneys in Mexico City. Alonso S. Perales in the back.

Alonso S. Perales, Henry Guerra, Leonidas Gonzalez and others.

Inauguration of courses in San Antonio, Texas, in partnership with the Universidad Autónoma de México. Alonso S. Perales to the left.

Alonso S. Perales awarded the Medal of Civil Merit by the Spanish Government. March 20, 1952. Also pictured, from left, Dr. Carlos E. Castañeda, the diplomat from the Spanish Consul in Galveston, Texas, and the Archbishop of the Archdiocese of San Antonio, the Most Rev. Robert E. Lucey.

Alonso S. Perales and José de la Luz Saenz.

Founding of the United Nations, Alonso S. Perales and his wife, Marta Pérez de Perales, with the Nicaraguan Delegation (June 1945).

Alonso S. Perales official portrait with the Medal of Civil Merit awarded by the Spanish Government, 1952.

Religion and Race

Alonso S. Perales and the Catholic Imaginary: Religion and the Mexican-American Mind

Mario T. García

Alonso S. Perales, although not as well known historically as other Mexican-American leaders, is one of the giants in Chicano history. Although he himself did not care for the term "Chicano," in my estimation he needs to be incorporated into the field of Chicano history that has exceeded the more strict definition of the term set by the Chicano Movement of the late 1960s and 1970s. Part of this redefinition and revision is the correct recognition that many pre-Movement figures and groups, although not using the term "Chicano," nevertheless are part of what we as historians call Chicano history which is the history of Mexican-descent people in the United States. As such, Perales, through his role as one of the key founders of LULAC and his long history as a civil rights leader in Texas, including his vast writings on the pursuit of civil rights for Mexican Americans, clearly qualifies as one of the leading Mexican-American leaders of the twentieth-century.

But Perales' leadership and his role as an activist was not just the product of secular ideological influences. Perales, first of all, as did other Mexican-American leaders of his time, reacted to the objective and lived reality of their Texas environment that was unfortunately steeped in a historic racism by whites or Anglos against Mexicans beginning with the Texas Revolution of 1836. Such racial hostility and the racialization of Mexicans included not only U.S.-born Mexican Americans such as Perales, but the thousands of Mexican immigrants who entered Texas and the Southwest in the early part of the twentieth-century, pulled in by the demand for cheap and manageable labor by the railroads, agri-business, mining and other developing industries in what had once been New Spain and Mexico's El Norte. Racialization turned the very term "Mexican" into a stigma of racial inferiority. This resulted in "Mexican jobs," "Mexican wages" and the infamous "Mexican schools." This institutionalized racism or "internal colonization," further included discrimination and exclusion or marginalization in public facilities such as restaurants, theaters, swimming pools, parks, etc. Such segregation, and discrimination rankled especially proud and educated Mexican-American leaders such as attorney and diplomat Perales. It not only limited their economic opportunities but it insulted their honor. Conditions on the ground laid the foundation for Perales' and that of other early Mexican-American leaders civil rights struggles commencing, as Cynthia Orozco so well documents, in the 1910s and 1920s before LULAC was formed in 1929 (Orozco, 2009).

At the same time, it seems to me that Perales and other Mexican-American leaders of this era were likewise affected by American liberalism and its concretization in President Franklin Roosevelt's New Deal. Liberalism in this context argued for the federal government's active role in assuring a social safety net for all Americans and for a revitalization of the full promises of the U.S. Constitution for all Americans, including minorities such as Mexican Americans. While Perales' political engagements predate the New Deal, it appears that from a secular position many of his evolving political views in time coincide with New Deal Liberalism.

However, racialized conditions in Texas and the influence of American liberalism are not enough to explain the worldview of Alonso S. Perales. There is a statement made many years later by César Chávez that is very apropos to Perales. After many years of struggling on behalf of the dignity and rights of farm workers, César was asked: "What has kept you going all of these years?" César responded: "Today I don't think I could base my will to struggle on cold economics or on some political doctrine. I don't think there would be enough to sustain me. For me the base must be faith" (García, 2007, p. 31). The same, I maintain, applies to Alonso S. Perales. As with César Chávez, you cannot fully understand Perales without understanding the central role that his faith, Catholicism, played in his personal, social, and political formation and mind set. It is his Catholic imaginary—his imagining his world and the new world he sought for Mexican Americans through his Catholic faith— that envelops his life and career. I first asserted this contention in my chapter on Perales and his contemporary Cleofas Calleros as part of my 2008 book *Católicos: Resistance and Affirmation in Chicano Catholic History* in which I argued that both Mexican-American civil rights leaders, Perales in San Antonio and Calleros in El Paso, were significantly influenced by Catholic Social Doctrine as defined by important papal encyclicals such as *Rerum Novarum* (1891) and *Quadragesimo Anno* (1931). Catholic social doctrine "recognizes the human dimension of people—the incarnational—and, as such, further recognizes the social and political in human beings" (García, 2008, p. 55). It stresses human dignity, truth, justice, charity, freedom, and civil and political as well as social and economic human rights. In their many writings in both Spanish- and English-language newspaper columns, in their correspondence, and in their praxis as civil rights leaders, Perales and Calleros identified with the principles of Catholic social doctrine.

But if Catholic social doctrine represented the more public face of Perales' Catholicism, his "foreign policy" if you will, there is another and more personal side to his Catholicism that represents his "domestic policy" aimed not at an outside non-Mexican-American audience but at Mexican Americans themselves. That is, Perales employed Catholic social doctrine as a way of influencing Anglos, especially policy-makers about the civil rights concerns of Mexican Americans in a way that gave his views more credibility because they coincided with those of the Catholic Church itself. At the same time, he employed his more personal Catholicism and faith to socialize or attempt to socialize Mexican Americans in Texas or his part of Texas to observe, respect, and practice their Catholic faith not only for their own redemption, but to show the outside world that Mexican Americans represented a strong and observant religious American people who as such should be fully accepted and integrated by other God-fearing Americans. In order for Perales to convincingly argue for integration and equal opportunities for Mexican Americans, he needed to also display that Mexican Americans were worthy of such inclusion by showing that they constituted a strong Christian community based, as with other Americans, on solid Christian family values. This domestic side of Perales' Catholicism is especially observed in his many personal advice columns and other writing in the San Antonio Spanish-language Catholic newspaper *La Voz* during the 1950s. These writings are found in the now available Alonso S. Perales Papers, 1898-1991, at the University of Houston. My chapter is based on the Microfilm Collection of the Perales Papers, specifically reels 5 and 6 that contain Perales' Spanish-language typescripts of his column "Por Mi Religión" published in *La Voz* (San Antonio) from 1951 to 1960, the year he died. In quoting Perales, I have translated his writing into English.

While I want to stress the central role of religion and faith in Perales' worldview, I also want to approach what represent his pious sentiments with a critical perspective. That is, Perales' almost authoritarian pronouncements on how Mexican Americans should spiritually comport themselves based on his interpretation of Catholicism in many cases, it seems to me, displayed contradictions and disparities with the reality of Mexican-American life and with the context of their social position in Texas as well as elsewhere. This critical perspective does not take away from Perales' Catholic imaginary, but only helps to bring out its complexities that Perales, himself, seems to have been unaware of.

In his advice columns, Perales functioned almost as a secular priest and confessor. Fellow-Catholic and Mexican-American leader, Professor Carlos E. Castañeda, referred to Perales as possessing "una visión de profeta" (a vision of a prophet) (García, 2008). He also represented what Archbishop Robert E. Lucey of San Antonio called the "priesthood of the laity" (García, 2008). Based on his own religious training and studies as well as his deep faith and as a practicing Catholic, Perales comfortably counseled and even admonished those who wrote to him asking him to address their particular personal and family problems. He titled his column "Por Mi Religión." Throughout all of his many columns that represent a significant addition to his more secular writings, Perales consistently stressed that family and personal problems could only in the end be addressed by people—in this case Mexican Americans—practicing their Catholic faith. For Perales, embracing God was the only way not only to be saved in Heaven, but for happiness and goodness in this world. But, as noted, Perales' advice did not just have, in my opinion, a personal objective but a political or quasi-political one. That is, Mexican Americans by being good Catholics were also asserting that they were good American citizens. As such, Perales' columns represented a form of Mexican-American jeremiad or "political sermon" (Bercovitch, 1978, p. xiv).

The difficulty, however, in Perales' approach was that the problems of Mexican Americans based on racial discrimination and working-class exploitation could not just be addressed by a spiritual uplifting as Perales seemed to suggest. Perales surely must have understood this since much of his life had been devoted to civil rights struggles against such oppression. However, in his spiritual writings he failed to bring the spiritual and the profane together in a way that would lead to creative faith-based struggles.

I

   One of the themes that he focused on in some of his columns had to do with faith and citizenship. But for Mexican Americans to be good citizens, they first had to know their faith. In October 1951, Perales encouraged attendance at the procession in honor of Cristo Rey or Christ the King. In calling on Mexican Americans in San Antonio to practice their faith, he stressed that one could not be neutral on one's faith. You had to embrace it, but you embraced it by knowing it and practicing it (Typescript; hereinafter cited as Ts, Oct. 23, 1951, p. 2, Reel 5; hereinafter cited as Reel). On another occasion, he directed his readers to take advantage of a new correspondence course on Catholicism sponsored by the Confraternity of Christian Doctrine. Only by knowing one's religion, Perales noted, could one defend it suggesting that too many other Americans still had suspicions and doubts about the loyalty of American Catholics into the 1950s and that as good and loyal American citizens, Mexican Americans had to uphold their faith as an American religion (Ts, Sept. 11, 1953, Reel 5). But one could not just be an armchair Catholic, one had to be a practicing Catholic and, among other things, attend weekly Sunday Mass. Perales emphasized this when one reader wrote in: "I am a Catholic, but I don't go to church because I don't think it's necessary since God is everywhere not just in church." Perales responded that it was one thing to be a Catholic in name and another to be a Catholic in practice. As far as he was concerned, the reader was in fact not a Catholic because he/she didn't attend Mass and obviously also did not observe the other sacraments or the teachings of God and the Church. Only practicing Catholics, according to Perales, were true Catholics. Being so was also necessary to be good citizens (Ts., Oct. 31, 1953, p. 1, Reel 5). He admonished still another reader who questioned the authority of priests to hear confessions since they were only human beings. Perales strongly demurred because priests were sacramental representatives of God and as such ordained to hear confessions. "When we confess to them, it is the same as confessing to God." Going to confession, he reminded his readers was an obligation that good Catholics had to observe (Ts.,no date, Reel 5). Knowing one's faith, moreover, was a continuing practice and as such Perales called attention to opportunities for Mexican-American Catholics to learn more about their religion through such things as special instructional missions offered in the different parishes at different times of the year (Ts., Jan. 23, 1954, p. 2, Reel 5). While the subtext of Perales' unofficial preaching or his political unconsciousness linked faith to citizenship, he did not in any way suggest that all faiths were equal. Quite the contrary, he maintained that Catholicism was the only true religion and that only Catholics were entitled to participate in Catholic services. For Perales, his faith was as enviable as his ethnicity (Ts., Feb. 24, 1955, Reel 5).

   Being a good citizen and ameliorating social problems, according to Perales, were also tied in to being a good Catholic. Only by turning to God and his guidance and living a good Christian life could Mexican Americans hope to solve not only their personal and family problems, but social problems of poverty, prejudice, and issues of war and peace in the world. "The entire world needs God's help in solving our many problems." Human beings had it within their hands to address their human problems, but they could not do it without God. For Perales, Christianity and citizenship were tied together. "The day that we come closer to God and give him the love and respect that He deserves, that day we will become better citizens and better Christians" (Ts., no date, Reel 5). Moreover, for Mexican-American Catholics, the Church itself possessed the correct positions on addressing many of the social ills facing not only Mexican Americans but also the country as a whole. In one of his columns, Perales praised his good friend, Archbishop Lucey, who at a conference in Albuquerque condemned the maltreatment and racism toward the Bracero workers in Texas and other southwestern states and that received wide coverage in Mexico. Perales not only noted that Archbishop Lucey was a strong friend and supporter of Mexican Americans, but that his leadership on social issues reflected how the Catholic Church did not separate its spiritual concerns from its temporal ones. For Perales, this was a good example that Mexican-American Catholics should emulate (Ts., no date, Reel 5). Unfortunately, Perales, himself, did not do this in his spiritual writings where he almost exclusively focused on inner moral conversion.

Writing in the early and tense years of the Cold War and the Red Scare in the United States, Perales stressed faith and citizenship for Mexican Americans as a way of also emphasizing that they were anti-Communist and loyal Americans. He incorrectly suggested that countries such as the United States that believed in God and practiced the Ten Commandments were nations, unlike the Soviet Union, that did not invade, conquer and deprive others of their liberties including their right to love God. Moreover, Mexican Americans had to link their faith with their rights for others by honoring the Ten Commandments. Perales stressed that with the threat of atomic weapons that the stakes were even higher for people including Mexican Americans to practice their faith to prevent the destruction of the world. "Staying close to God," Perales urged his readers, "is the way to prevent the destruction of humanity" (Ts., Dec. 13, 1951, p. 3, Reel 5). Here, Perales' role as an American diplomat in his early career and his support for American imperialist intervention in Latin America and, in particular, Central America undoubtedly influenced these later views.

Perales, however, feared that in the new atomic age and the threat of Communism that a new world war might still be inevitable. He observed that in this Cold War that could at any time turn into another world war that Mexican Americans had to express their commitment to the United States and to democracy in order not to be perceived as less than loyal Americans. They could do this by linking their faith with their citizenship. "In this growing conflict that will be the biggest and most destructive in world history, on one side there will be those of us who will be soldiers of Christ and of our country, and on the other side will be those who are not." Mexican Americans had to be soldiers on Christ's side and that of the United States (Ts., no date, Reel 5). In this conflict, Perales went so far to criticize the United Nations for being ineffective in lessening the tensions of the Cold War and the reason for this, he preached to his readers, was because that international body did not reflect the Christian faith or embrace Jesus. For Perales as a fundamentalist Catholic there was no such thing as separation of church and state both nationally and internationally (Ts., Oct. 23, 1953, p.2, Reel 5).

Yet Perales' position on the UN was curiously in direct contradiction when as a diplomat he first supported the League of Nations in the 1920s and later represented Nicaragua at the UN after World War II. In these experiences, he did not appear to doubt the efficacy of these international bodies. Clearly, his strong and growing anti-Communism seemed to be influenced by those on the American political right who, in the early 1950s through McCarthyism, attacked the UN as a front for international Communism.

Finally, Perales linked faith and citizenship by stressing that first and foremost Mexican Americans had to be good practicing Catholics and being people of truthfulness or "hombres de veras." In a way, what Perales was telling his readers was that to be a good Catholic was to be a good person and being a good person also translated into being a good citizen. While Perales did not directly link faith and citizenship, his references seem to clearly suggest that if Mexican Americans were insisting that they be treated as first-class American citizens, then it was incumbent on them to show other Americans that they possessed good Christian values that made them good citizens. All they needed to do was to fall back on their Catholic faith and to observe it to the fullest (Ts., no date, Reel 5). Unfortunately, Perales did not take these occasions to link the need for faith with utilizing that faith as a basis for political struggles against discrimination rather than making it appear that faith alone, as the Church too often preached, would ameliorate people's sufferings if not in this world than in the next.

II

Yet good citizenship depended on strong Catholic families. In his advice column, Perales often addressed "Problemas del Hogar" [Problems of the Home]. For Perales, the family represented the foundation of society and the nation. Strong Mexican-American Catholic families resulted from an understanding of one's faith and, second, an understanding of the true meaning of marriage. "It has been my experience as a professional," Perales wrote in 1952, "that marital problems are directly tied to couples not knowing their faith and, therefore, not being close to God" (Ts., Dec. 26, 1952, p.1, Reel 5). But strong Catholic families meant also practicing one's faith. One reader wrote to Perales that she and her husband had been married for several years and had five children, but that her husband liked to drink and when he did he could become abusive at home. She noted that her husband did not go to church and that she went when she could. She further informed that they had been married in the Catholic Church. She wrote to Perales, as did many other readers on similar situations, for his advice on what to do. Perales took this, and other occasions, to stress that the problem in their family was that her husband no longer practiced his religion and he observed that the only solution was for him to return to the Church, go to Mass each Sunday, and to observe the Ten Commandments. He also advised her to attend church regularly (Ts., Oct. 3, 1952, Reel 5). In other columns, Perales noted that homes that exhibited family problems were homes where God was excluded. "In other words, these homes omit the principal figure of the home that is God and this is why there is a lack of harmony and happiness in that home" [Ts., Feb. 20, 1953, Reel 5).

Strong Catholic families also needed to eschew divorce and marital infidelity. One woman wrote to Perales that her husband of twenty-one years and after nine children wanted a divorce because he believed that she was not being faithful to him. She denied this and noted that they had been married in the Catholic Church. Perales' "respuesta" or response was to remind his reader that having been married in the Church meant that they were married for life and divorce, therefore, was not an option. He advised her to work for reconciliation with her husband if not for their sake for that of their children. To divorce would be to offend God and a disservice to their children (Ts., Nov. 13, 1952, Reel 5). On another occasion, an elderly woman wrote in that after many years of marriage, that she and her husband were thinking of divorcing because they were always fighting. Because they too had been married in the Church, Perales reminded her that they were prohibited from divorcing but also that they had no basis for divorce. "All couples have differences and disagreements," he told them, "but this is part of life and no one is perfect" (Ts., Sept. 3, 1954, Reel 5).

Infidelity was totally unacceptable to Perales. He often severely criticized married men and even married women who told him about such infidelities. In writing to one woman who informed him of her husband's extramarital deviation, Perales exposed a contradiction when he stated: "No woman likes her husband to be unfaithful; the only exception being when the woman herself is unfaithful to her husband." Despite this contradiction, Perales, for the most part, counseled against unfaithfulness in marriage since it weakened the family (Ts., July 10, 1953, Reel 5). Irresponsible husbands who did not adequately provide for their families also brought on Perales' condemnation. To help healing in these troubled families, besides strongly calling for such families to practice their Catholic faith, Perales encouraged them to read what seemed to be his "bible" with respect to issues of the family and marriage, Bishop Fulton J. Sheen's book *Three to Get Married*. This, of course, assumed that some of his readers, like him, were U.S. born-Mexican Americans who could read English (Ts., Feb. 6, 1953, Reel 5).

Above all, Perales consistently called upon Mexican-American Catholics to marry in the Church. Only by so doing could they guarantee that God would bless their marriage and resulting family and prevent "Satanás" or Satan from infiltrating their home (Ts., March 20, 1953, Reel 5). His repetitive advice to those who wrote to him about their family problems but who also noted that they had not been married in the Church was to first and foremost urge them to remarry in the Church as the first step toward dealing with their conflicts (Ts., Sept. 25, 1954, Reel 5).

In his advocacy for strong Mexican-American Catholic families, Perales, in my opinion, not only had in mind the spiritual aspects of such unions, but also the fact that he wanted to eliminate as much as possible the dysfunctions of the Mexican-American family that he observed through those who wrote to him about such problems. Mexican Americans, no doubt Perales believed, could not be readily accepted into American society if they exhibited weak family structures. Mexican Americans, according to this view, meant that they had to prove themselves worthy of integration by exhibiting strong family values that for Perales meant strong Catholic values. While Perales was certainly correct in advocating strong family values and a strengthening of the family unit among Mexican Americans, he, at the same time, failed to link the weakening of the family, as he perceived it, with poverty, racism and a lack of opportunities for Mexican Americans that certainly also affected family culture.

III

But strong Catholic families depended on good Catholic parents. Parents not only had to be married in the Church, but they had to know their faith and practice it. Perales many times in his column admonished parents who did not conduct themselves in exemplary fashion for their children. In one case, he condemned a couple that instead of properly caring for their children went out drinking. The husband did so with his friends and neglected his family and in retaliation so too did the wife. Revealing a patriarchic view of marriage, Perales supported an idealized situation where the husband was the breadwinner and the wife and mother did not work outside the home, but instead stayed at home and took care of the children (Ts., April 10, 1952, Reel 5). Of course, the reality was that given the weak economic conditions of many Mexican Americans, many wives and mothers had to find jobs outside the home. Many did not have the choice of simply being housewives.

Parents also needed to be vigilant about their children. This especially included their daughters. One woman wrote in that she and her husband had allowed their daughter to date a young man who then got their daughter pregnant. Perales responded by first criticizing the daughter for being reckless and dishonoring her family. However, he also criticized the parents for allowing their daughter to date unsupervised "because humanity being what it is this is often dangerous." The proof of this was what happened to their daughter. The young man might not be legally prosecuted because of the consensual nature of the relationship and because their daughter was over twenty-one, but Perales promised, God would punish him (Ts., July 17, 1953, Reel 5). Perales further blamed those Mexican-American parents who did not supervise their sons and allowed them to join gangs and to become juvenile delinquents. Such behavior and delinquency was, of course, quite prevalent in the barrios in the 1950s. One reader wrote in that it seemed to be the case that boys were receiving the brunt of blame for such delinquency, but she wanted to know if Perales believed that the parents should also be blamed. As if on cue, this gave Perales the opportunity to provide his own homily on this issue:

"I agree that both the sons and the parents are to blame for many cases of juvenile delinquency. The parents are especially to blame because the fathers are not good examples to their children. The father who gets drunk, who fails to go to church, and whose behavior leaves much to be desired cannot expect his children to respect him and obey him. We need to set good examples for our children. Give me a family who practices its faith, beginning with the parents, and I will give you a harmonious and happy family blessed by God and whose children honor and obey their parents. (Ts., no date, Reel 5)

For Perales, good Catholic parents were indispensable for strong Catholic families who, in turn, would provide the foundation for functional communities as Mexican Americans struggled for their full civil rights. Mexican Americans could not effectively argue for inclusion if they exhibited weak parenthood and weak family structures. All this was true; however, given Perales' concerns over the lack of education for Mexican Americans, he might have also brought attention in his columns to the failures of the infamous "Mexican schools," that for years as segregated and inferior public schools in the barrios had been responsible for high drop-out rates among Mexican-American students as well as providing limited education that in turn limited economic opportunities for young Mexican Americans, many of whom unfortunately turned to gangs and crime.

IV

But if it was necessary to have a strong Catholic family and good and practicing Mexican-American Catholic parents, it all began with marriage. Perales insisted that marriage represented the foundation of the home culture. But it also transcended the home. He noted that a peaceful world and society was unachievable without a strong family and that, in turn, was based on a Christian marriage (Ts., Nov. 2, 1951, Reel 5). In such a marriage, it was also vital that both partners be religious. In addressing one reader who wrote to Perales that while she was a practicing Catholic, her fiancé was not, but that he was a good person and, therefore, she believed that their marriage would be a good one. Nevertheless, she wanted to know what Perales thought. He responded that he did not believe their marriage would succeed unless her fiancé returned to his Catholic faith and they were married in the Church. If he did not do this, they should not even marry since, in his opinion, their relationship in time would deteriorate without this spiritual bond (Ts., March 7, 1952, Reel 5).

Throughout his columns, Perales consistently insisted on the importance of Mexican-American Catholics marrying in the Church. It was the only way for God to bless their union (Ts., Nov. 5, 1962, Reel 5). In addressing one reader who told him of the debauchery of her husband and that they had not been married in the Church, Perales, assuming the role of confessor, told the woman that there was no alternative but to get married in the Church if she wanted to save her husband from his drinking and womanizing. In the meantime, he told her to say the rosary every day with her family, go to Mass each Sunday, and to obey the Ten Commandments, the traditional Catholic pieties (Ts, March 27, 1952, Reel 5).

Based on such letters by readers, one of the things that concerned Perales was that too many Mexican Americans did not receive pre-marital instructions prior to getting married. People had to know the meaning of a Catholic marriage and their obligations as married Catholics. He informed his readers that those thinking of getting married should seek to enroll in Church-sponsored marriage classes or at least read books on marriage written by Catholic priests such as Bishop Sheen (Ts., Nov. 2, 1951, Reel 5). By getting such instructions, couples would be able to avoid future marital difficulties that would lead to various family problems even after they had children. "Here lies the problem," Perales lamented. "Too many get married, but very few in reality know what marriage is really all about. We all know that to become a lawyer, a doctor, or a mechanic, you have to study and be trained. The same is true for marriage" (Ts., no date, Reel 5). Possessing such strong views on pre-marital education, Perales went so far to advocate that all high schools and colleges have a requirement that in order for students to graduate, they had to first take a class on marriage, presumably he meant on Catholic marriage, before they could get their diplomas (Ts., no date, Reel 5). He reminded his audience that marriage next to the priesthood was the highest and most important vocation (Ts., no date, Reel 5).

As with the family and parenthood, Perales clearly was concerned that too many Mexican Americans exhibited failed or dysfunctional marriages, and that this was not acceptable at the same time that Mexican-American leaders such as he were arguing outside the barrios that Mexican Americans were respectful citizens with strong family values that should be fully integrated into the mainstream of American society. Mexican Americans, Perales seemed to be saying, had to clean up their marriage and family act if they expected to be accepted alongside other Americans. He might also have added that strong marriages could likewise be aided by addressing economic tensions, in particular, that often negatively affected marriages.

V

But marriage, parenthood and family could not succeed without the active participation of men. Perales especially focused on those Mexican-American men who were not good husbands and fathers although again not contextualizing this with larger socio-economic conditions facing all Mexican Americans especially men. Many of the letters written to him for advice concerned such men. They posed for Perales the most critical threat to his efforts to encourage exemplary Mexican-American families as a showcase for his integrationist efforts. Men had to be the leaders in displaying to the Anglo world that Mexican Americans qualified as good and loyal citizens. They and they alone needed to challenge and dispel the stereotype of the drunken and unfaithful husband and father that too many non-Mexican Americans believed characterized Mexican-American families. Good and decent Mexican-American men, for Perales, equaled good citizenship.

Perales identified the root of the problem related to Mexican-American men in too many of them not practicing their Catholic faith. Many of his female readers appealed to him as to what to do about their faithless husbands. They noted that their husbands did not attend Sunday Mass or practice any of their religion, thus giving bad example to their children. As one reader put it:

Here in my church for Mass or for Rosary Hour, you rarely see men. However, if you go to the cantinas, billiard halls, nightclubs, and street corners, there you see the men. It looks like they are afraid to go to church. And when you encourage them to go to confession or to pray the rosary in church, they say that they are not willing to do so because other men don't do this. They believe if they go to confession or go pray the rosary, that other men will make fun of them. They say that church is only for women and for old men. (Ts., Sept. 19, 1952, p. 2, Reel 5)

In addition to not practicing their faith, many Mexican-American men also, as noted earlier, engaged in drunkenness as well as being unfaithful to their wives. This behavior too often led to wife and child abuse. Perales preached against such behavior and in one very angry response to a woman whose husband behaved this way, stated: "Señora, what has occurred with your husband is that he is under Satan's control and because of your husband's acts, Satan has come into your home. Instead of hosting Jesus and Mary, you are hosting Satan" (Ts., no date, Reel 5).

Perales attacked this male problem by going right at the masculinity of the men and their machismo. He asserted that it was not masculine for men to behave in these fallen ways and to have strayed from their Catholic faith. A real man did not act this way. A real man was a good husband and father, but this came from being a good and practicing Catholic. Masculinity meant being a man of the Church. The macho did not go to the cantina; he went to Mass. He pointed out that a man could not function as a man without God. "I have always maintained," Perales wrote, "that to be a Catholic it is necessary to be a complete man" (Ts., no date, Reel 5). One man wrote to him that while he attempted to be a good Catholic, too many other Mexican-American men believed that religion was only for women. He wanted to know what Perales felt about this. Of course, Perales responded that this idea was wrong. He praised this man for being a practicing Catholic and one that did not pay attention to the stupidities of those other men who criticized him and other men for being churchgoers. In effect, Perales challenged the notion that it was not masculine for men to attend church. "On the contrary," he wrote, "the Catholic man who knows and practices his faith and lives his life as God wants him to does not concern himself as to what others think" (Ts., no date, Reel 5). "A true man," Perales suggested, "is a true Catholic." Good Mexican-American Catholic men rejected the popular Mexican song with the lyrics "La cantina es para los hombres y la iglesia es para las mujeres" [The bar is for men and the church is for women]. (Ts., no date, Reel 5).

What particularly disturbed Perales was the unfaithfulness of married men. This was not only scandalous but also threatening to Mexican-American civic culture. It exposed and contradicted the efforts by him and other Mexican-American leaders to propose that the family—la familia—was the bedrock of the culture. The behavior of unfaithful husbands was in fact embarrassing to Perales' middle-class values. It was a part of barrio culture and working-class Mexican-American culture that he believed needed to be cleaned up and eradicated. In one of his columns, Perales provided an entire discourse on the sanctity of marriage and the violation of it by some men:

What is matrimony? Is it just a civil contract as some say? Yes, it is a civil contract made by men, but under God it is much more than that. It is a sacrament especially when it is contracted by the representatives of God on earth. What is marriage? Is it just a ceremony that permits one to get married one day and then abandon it the next? What rights and obligations does marriage entail? Does marriage allow a man to treat his wife like a slave and that she has the obligation to accept this treatment, injustices, and shame (*sinverguensas*) [sic]. Does it mean that a husband can spend all his earnings at the cantina? Does it mean that a man can come home drunk and abuse his wife and children without them protesting? Does it mean that a husband can have extramarital affairs? Does it mean that a husband can hit his wife and suffer no consequences? Does it mean that a husband can be an absolute tyrant at home and that his wife has to accept this?" (Ts., no date, Reel 5).

Clearly, Perales disputed that marriage allowed such conduct on the part of men. This type of behavior was what needed to be expunged.

Yet many married woman continued to write to Perales detailing their husband's unfaithfulness. One woman wrote that she and her husband had four children. She noted that they fought a great deal especially since her husband began to see another woman. Instead of going home right after work, he, instead, went to see his mistress (May 30, 1953, p. 2, Reel 5). Another woman wrote in that she and her husband had been married for several years and had six children. They had been married in the Church and were quite happy until her husband "se enamoró de otra mujer" [fell in love with another woman]. Now, her husband arrived home cranky and constantly criticized her for everything (Ts., Aug. 21, 1952, Reel 5). In all of his responses to such letters, Perales maintained that a husband had an obligation to his wife and children and that such wayward behavior was not to be tolerated. But how to deal with such improper behavior and violations of the marriage vow? For Perales, there was only one answer and that was that the couple and especially the men had to return to the Church and practice their faith. He also advised the women to pray for their husbands (Ts., Nov. 21, 1952, p. 2, Reel 5). Only in this way, could a good Catholic marriage work.

While one can appreciate Perales' pious belief that men could and should practice self-control and that they had to be personally responsible for their behavior, at the same time, his piety was not necessarily efficacious. Certainly given his awareness of racism and discrimination against Mexican Americans, Perales might have balanced his condemnation of male comportment with a condemnation of the Texas race/class structure that relegated Mexican-American men to the lower-rung of jobs and limited economic mobility, all of which undoubtedly affected their unfortunate and unacceptable behavior toward their families.

What was needed was a New Man—a new Mexican-American man. Perales did what he could to foster this new male subject. But this new subject had to be also linked to new male leadership. Advocating agency in creating lay leadership, Perales especially stressed the importance of spiritual retreats in fostering lay leadership in particular for men. Beginning in the early 1950s, he in his column encouraged lay Catholic men to participate in the various retreats that he announced. Prior to the more popular and better-known *cursillos* that began to operate by the end of that decade and increased in importance into the next several years, Perales was, in a sense, ahead of his time by linking male lay leadership in the Church with retreats. A spiritual retreat was usually a two-day affair held in the parish, he explained, "and was an opportunity for us to *come speak with God* [Perales' emphasis]. We meditate and reflect over our past lives and to form resolutions for our future ones. A retreat is a place where we can recharge our spiritual batteries. It is certain that after this experience we will return to our homes as better men focused on living within God's laws" (Ts., no date, Reel 5).

Perales noted that retreats were also held for women but that the great need was for men to participate in them. He observed that women by far greater numbers attended retreats compared to men and he lamented this lack of male involvement. While this, in a sense, proved, he admitted, that women in religious traditions were superior to men, still this should not be the case. "When Jesus Christ founded his Church almost two thousand years ago," he wrote, "he established it for everyone not just women. I want to stress that we men are even more obligated than women to demonstrate our *religiosity* [Perales' emphasis] given that the deplorable state of the world has been created by *us men* [Perales' emphasis] and not by the women" (Ts., no date, Reel 5).

The Church desperately needed male lay leadership, including Mexican-American men, and Perales strongly encouraged it by promoting the spiritual rejuvenation of the men. At the same time, Perales understood that strong Catholic lay leadership among the men would likewise benefit the Mexican-American community as a whole by creating new leadership in the struggle for the integration and full civil rights for his people.

To further counter dysfunctional Mexican-American men, Perales called on other Mexican-American men to display strong lay Catholic leadership. No better example of such leadership was Perales himself. Indeed, he signaled out professionals like himself as well as prominent businessmen to openly display their Catholic allegiance and to become role models for other men. "Businessmen, professionals, and the well-to-do are more obligated than others to show a good example" (Ts., Feb. 25, 1952, p. 4, Reel 5). One way to do this was to become active, as Perales was, in Church-related groups and activities. He particularly signaled out Mexican-American men who belonged to the Knights of Columbus (Caballeros de Colón). Men could also participate in Bible groups and conferences or be active in parish and archdiocesan Catholic lay meetings (Ts., Nov. 12, 1954, p. 2, Reel 5). The clergy faced many pressures due to a lack of vocations and priests and, according to Perales, laymen had to fill the void as much as possible. They could do this by helping in organizing religion classes or spiritual discussion groups, and by reading Catholic magazines or newspapers to prepare them to serve the Church. "Our clergy is facing a huge problem," Perales observed, "but they cannot do it alone. We have to help them" (Ts., Nov. 12, 1954, p. 2, Reel 5). By so doing, Mexican-American lay leaders would represent role models for other Mexican-American men and help in the crisis, as Perales saw it, among many men.

VI

Into the 1950s, the issues of youth in particular juvenile delinquency occupied Perales' attention. He received many letters from mothers about their problems with their teenage children, especially their boys. "Much has been said and written over the problem of juvenile delinquency," Perales wrote. "We are all in agreement that this problem has taken on gigantic proportions and grows more and more each day" (Ts., no date, Reel 5). Perales lamented that such delinquency involving gangs affected specifically the Mexican-American community. Youth crime was a barrio issue. In one case that Perales brought to his readers' attention, a young woman was offered a ride home by her cousin and his friend who then instead of taking her home drove her to an isolated rural area where they and some other friends attempted to rape her. Fortunately, the young woman fought back and somehow escaped. Perales observed that decent young gentlemen did not behave this way and, at the same time, lectured young women to also fight back if they found themselves in a similar situation (Ts., no date, Reel 5). This and other incidents of juvenile delinquency only further accelerated Perales' effort to attack the social problems among Mexican Americans in order to better prepare them for full civic participation. However, Perales only approached the issues of delinquency from a moral perspective but not from a social one. Morality, and specifically Catholic morality, might be useful in combating delinquency, but without attention also to the educational, economic and cultural discrimination and segregation facing Mexican Americans, delinquency could not be adequately addressed.

Combating juvenile delinquency for Perales began at home. Parents had to take the primary responsibility of raising their children in a moral and Catholic environment as a way of preventing them from getting into trouble. Many parents, however, did not foster such a family climate as witnessed by those who wrote in to Perales asking advice on how to deal with their teenage children. One woman, for example, wrote that she and her husband had a serious problem with their two sons, ages 13 and 15. Both refused to obey their parents and after their school instead of going home they hang around the streets. When their father threatened to punish them, they, in turn, threatened physical harm if their father attempted to do so. The mother also noted that neither she nor her husband went to church and neither did their sons. Perales responded that unfortunately the same problems seemed to be afflicting many other parents. However, he reminded them of the importance of the Fourth Commandment of children obeying their parents and stressed that their problems with their children could only be attenuated through spiritual and moral means beginning by their attendance at church and by their instructing their sons on their Catholic faith. If they did this, Perales promised, they would see positive results (Ts., May 16, 1952, Reel 5).

Parents, according to Perales, had to be the primary role models for their children. This began by the parents practicing their faith and by being good partners and parents. Children did not turn to delinquency, he noted, if they had a father who did not drink or womanize or abuse his wife. They further did not turn to delinquency if they had a mother who made sure that her home reflected Catholic principles. "The parents who are religious," Perales concluded, "and who insist that their children also be religious have prosperous and happy homes" (Ts., Dec. 6, 1951, p.2, Reel 5).

But boys getting into trouble were not all that antagonized Perales with respect to youth. He also expressed concern over young women getting into difficulties. In particular, he paid attention to young women wrongfully seduced by men and warned parents about dating with respect to their daughters. One young woman wrote to him that she began seeing a young man who seemed very honorable and proper and who at first only visited her at home with her parents present. In time, her parents grew to like him and have confidence in him and began to allow him to date their daughter, including going out in his car. Unfortunately, the young woman informed Perales, her boyfriend took advantage of her and got her pregnant, but refused to marry her. Perales observed that she was to blame as were her parents for trusting this young man who turned out to be a scoundrel. He noted that this was not an isolated incident and that he knew of too many other similar cases. The only solution, he advised, was for Mexican-American girls not to go out on dates in their boyfriend's car and that parents should be vigilant about this (Ts., Dec. 19, 1952, p. 2, Reel 5). On another occasion, some parents wrote to him about their daughters insisting that they be allowed to go out on car rides with their boyfriends. The parents told Perales that they understood that Anglo parents permitted this and wanted to know his advice as to whether this was also acceptable for Mexican-American girls. Absolutely not, Perales replied. Anglos had their own more permissive culture, but Mexican Americans had their more restrictive one and on this issue, Mexican Americans had the correct view of not allowing their daughters to date in their boyfriend's cars (Ts., May 3, 1952, Reel 5).

As he advised with respect to boys, Perales instructed parents that they could avoid problems with their girls including teenage pregnancies by raising them in a strict Catholic household and making sure that their daughters also attended church and practiced their faith. Young Catholic girls who knew their religion and honored it did not get into problems. He praised, for example, young girls who he saw celebrating their "quinceañeras" [15th birthday] not just as a party, but as a religious event. He observed that such girls went to church with their escorts and all received Communion. This, to Perales, was impressive (Ts., July 24, 1952, Reel 5).

In addition to parent's role in guiding their children away from delinquency, Perales strongly advocated that for those children not attending parochial schools where they received religious instruction that they attend after schools classes provided by the Confraternity of Christian Doctrine (CCD). "It is very important that our children and teenagers learn at least the rudiments of our Catholic religion," he stressed, "and above all the Ten Commandments in which they learn the one about HONORING OUR PARENTS [Perales' emphasis]." Perales observed that a youth who knew about his religion including the Commandments was not a problem for anyone, obeyed his parents, avoided issues with the police and the courts, and went on to become a good Christian, and excellent citizen, and was proud of his parents (Ts., Dec. 6, 1951, p. 2, Reel 5). Perales made it a point in his columns to notify parents of the location and information on CCD classes. He especially observed the importance of this instruction due to the growing immorality of American popular culture noticeable in the new media of television. He believed that too many TV programs conveyed the wrong moral message, especially for youth. Consequently, Perales announced his support for an effort by some in the San Antonio community to establish an educational television station. He likewise called on other Mexican Americans to support this. "In this way we will be assured of having sane, moral, and educational television programs for our children and youth," he advocated. "But in the meantime, we need to not watch those immoral programs that come into our homes through television, and we need to tell the owners of the stations that we will not watch such programs" (Ts., June 20, 1954, p. 2, Reel 5). Finally, as a way of further promoting religious instruction for youth to combat delinquency, Perales proposed that such instruction be carried out in the public schools. He proposed that all religions, not just Catholicism, be taught depending on the children's faiths. It was a right for parents to insist on this since their tax dollars funded the public schools and the schools needed to reflect the wishes of parents. "It is not by expelling God from the public schools," Perales added, "that we can best combat juvenile delinquency" (Ts., no date, Reel 5).

As is obvious in any community, the youth represent the future, and for Perales this meant that one additional area needed to be attended to from a spiritual approach: the growing problem of juvenile delinquency. Mexican Americans could not make their case for full social inclusion in American society if their children represented gangsters rather than future upstanding citizens. Yet how this problem could be alleviated without also focusing on socio-economic issues, Perales, at least in these columns, failed to address.

VII

Religious education represented a major cause for Perales. First and foremost, he praised the efforts of the parochial schools for doing this and specifically through the Catholic faith. Children and youth needed religious training and the best option was for parents to send them to Catholic schools, although Perales failed to note the additional expenses of a parochial education that made it unrealistic for many, if not most, Mexican Americans. He opined:

This is precisely why the parochial schools are superior to the public schools, . . . because in the parochial ones the students are taught Sacred Law and the love and fear of God whereas in the public schools it is strictly forbidden to teach God's Law. . . . Parents who send their children to parochial schools possess a strong hand in the intellectual and spiritual education of their children who in the future will not only become model children of God but also of their country. (Ts., Aug. 28, 1952, Reel 5)

Linking Catholic education with good citizenship, Perales consistently encouraged Mexican-American parents to send their children to the parochial schools. It was not enough, he pronounced, for children to attend weekly Mass or even to participate in CCD classes, but it was preferable if they attended Catholic schools. "The public schools are good and they belong to us because of our taxes," he observed, "but unfortunately they do not teach students the word of God" (Ts., Oct. 16, 1954, Reel 5).

While Perales supported the public schools in as much as the majority of Mexican-American students attended them, still he did not fail to criticize them for not incorporating religious instruction. Clearly, Perales did not believe in the separation of church and state and would argue that this only forbade the state endorsing one set religion over another, but that it did not forbid the public schools teaching a variety of religious beliefs to children of varied faiths. In other words, the schools should teach Catholicism to Catholic students and Protestantism to Protestant students, etc. From this position, Perales stressed that the failure of the public schools to teach religion only added to the worsening of not only domestic social problems but world problems as well. In 1951, he wrote

> The world needs as much religious instruction as possible and the sooner the nations of the world take the necessary steps of making sure that all schools, public and private, teach religion the sooner will humankind benefit from this. Because of the ignorance of God and His kingdom and of the Ten Commandments, the world is in the dire situation that it finds itself in. Can the world be worse off than it is today? We are on the brink of a third world war that can lead to the final destruction of the world; we have family problems in the homes between couples, between parents and children, between brothers; we have neighbors fighting each other; we have growing killings and injuries in our cities, in our countries, and in the battlefields, etc. Can we honestly say that the situation is not dire? It would be difficult to argue otherwise. But there is only one remedy and that is for the nations of the world for once and for all to choose the Kingdom of God over that of men. (Ts., Dec. 19, 1951, p.1, Reel 5)

One solution for this myriad of problems, Perales advanced, was to inculcate religious instruction in all schools. He noted recent efforts in Mexico to get religious education in the schools where law prohibited any teaching of religion whether in public or even private schools. He noted that the situation was different in the United States, where at least religion could be taught in religious schools unlike the case in Mexico. However, Perales decried the fact that religion was prohibited in American public schools. "This is causing much damage to our country," he noted, "and is in part the result of our moral descent" (Ts., Dec. 19, 1951, p. 2, Reel 5). Perales in particular lamented and condemned a recent Supreme Court decision, the Scotus Case, that overturned a ruling by Illinois courts that allowed the teaching of religion in the public schools of that state. The Court did so on the basis that the Constitution insisted on the separation of church and state. By this decision, the Supreme Court, according to Perales, "had expelled God, whom we so dearly need, from the public schools." He called on his readers to join the struggle to get religion into the public schools (Ts., Dec. 19, 1951, p.2, Reel 5). He vowed personally to continue that effort that he hoped would succeed before he died (Ts., Aug. 22, 1953, Reel 5).

Interestingly but contradictory, while Perales denounced the U.S. Supreme Court for not allowing religious instruction in the public school, he a few years later applauded the Court for its rulings in desegregating the public schools and also praised President Dwight D. Eisenhower for sending federal troops into Little Rock Arkansas in 1957 to carry out the Court's desegregation ruling (Ts., no date, Reel 5). The weight of the latter as based on the Brown Case, however, far outweighed the importance of the former although Perales seemed to suggest a symmetry.

VIII

While Perales paid lip service to the Christian background of most Americans, he was first and foremost a Catholic. For him Christianity was Catholicism. He believed that it was the one true faith and he constantly reminded his readers of this. But in doing so, he also warned about the Protestant threat and efforts by Protestant denominations and groups to make inroads into the Mexican-American community. In this, Perales was in tune with the pre-ecumenical ethos of the Catholic Church that viewed Protestantism, in particular, as a feared rival that needed to be combated. In responding to one reader who asked his advice about her husband wanting her to attend with him a Protestant healing revival, Perales did not mince words as to the unacceptability of such a decision. Only God through Jesus could cure people, he told her, and obviously for Perales, God and Jesus were Catholic. Instead of going to such heretical events, Perales instructed this woman to attend Mass and to take her husband with her (Ts., June 10, 1952, Reel 5). Another reader wrote to him that he was invited to attend a Mason service and that when he stated that he was Catholic, he was told that there was no contradiction for a Catholic to attend a Mason event. Perales, of course, strongly disagreed. He warned the reader that if he joined the Masons, he would be excommunicated from the Catholic Church. He noted that the Masons represented not only a secret society, but also an immoral one. According to Perales, it was impossible to be both a Catholic and a Mason (Ts., no date, Reel 5). Still another reader informed Perales that her son wanted to join the Y.M.C.A. and that her husband felt that it was fine for him to do so even though they were Catholics. She, however, felt otherwise. Perales congratulated her for taking the correct position. "The Y.M.C.A. constitutes a danger to the Catholic faith of our youth," he responded, "because it teaches a vague and wrong view of religion." Perales concluded by warning that the Y further taught that one religion was as good as the next. "This is a view that we as Catholics cannot accept" (Ts., June 26, 1952, Reel 5).

Clearly Perales linked citizenship with Christianity, but it had to be Catholic Christianity. A strong Catholic community equaled, in his eyes, a strong citizenry (Ts., Jan. 23, 1953, Reel 5).

IX

I conclude by coming back to my point that you cannot fully understand Alonso S. Perales without understanding the centrality of his Catholic faith. Like César Chávez, it was not just Catholicism but Mexican-American Catholicism that enveloped Perales' private and public life. For him, personal and public issues had to be seen in spiritual terms. You could not achieve personal redemption without faith and this also applied to society. By examining Perales' religious writings in particular his Catholic essays and advice column in *La Voz*, you come to understand the magnitude of what we might call the "Gospel of Alonso S. Perales." What I am advancing is that Perales' Catholicism possessed a dual character. One aspect was his identification with Catholic Social Doctrine that argued that Mexican Americans as children of God should be treated humanely and deserved social justice. He filtered his civil rights agenda through this prism that had the advantage of positioning the Mexican-American struggle alongside the Church's social teachings. This linkage I refer to as Perales' foreign policy in that it is outer directed and aimed at an Anglo audience in Texas. It is the message intended to ideologically both sustain the Mexican-American civil rights movement of his era as well as to convince Anglos to the just cause of Mexican Americans.

At the same time, the other side of Perales' Catholicism was an inner-directed one or his domestic policy that was aimed at a dual objective, although interconnected. As noted, Perales, almost as a secular priest and confessor and even missionary, sought to convert or re-convert wayward Mexican-American Catholics back to their faith because this was God's will and because one could not have happiness in this world or the next without God. Yet, this interior Catholicism had, I argue, another although less obvious intent. Perales understood that if his civil rights efforts and that of other Mexican-American leaders were to succeed Mexican Americans had to display that they qualified as Americans who should be thoroughly integrated into U.S. society, not just from a legal perspective, but also from a social and cultural one. Legal citizenship had to be complemented by cultural citizenship. For Perales, this meant that Mexican Americans had to display that they were, like other ethnic Americans, God-loving and God-fearing people who were sustained by their faith. They, as predominantly Catholics, were an American Christian people and who as Catholic Christians further qualified to be fully accepted as Americans. But this cultural citizenship could only succeed if, in fact, Mexican Americans practiced their faith. They had to come to God and abandon the types of un-Christian behavior that Perales railed against in his columns in the form of dysfunctional families, marriages, parenthood, juvenile delinquency, teenage pregnancies, and the debauchery of too many men.

The problem for Perales, however, was that his almost exclusive attention, at least in these religious writings, on individual redemption neglected or marginalized the race/class conditions that affected Mexican Americans that likewise had to be transformed. Spiritual conversion was not enough.

Still, Perales' inner Catholic agenda was to, in effect, re-Christianize Mexican Americans to better complement the outer agenda of the civil rights struggles. Only a faith-based community could achieve full rights and acceptance in the United States and Alonso S. Perales aimed to accomplish this guided by his own faith.

Bibliography

Bercovitch, S. (1978). *The American jeremiad*. Madison: University of Wisconsin Press.

García, M. T. (2007). *The gospel of César Chávez: My faith in action*. Lanham: Sheed & Ward.

García, M. T. (2008). *Catolicos: Resistance and affirmation in Chicano Catholic history*. Austin: University of Texas Press.

Orozco, C. E. (2009). *No Mexicans, women, or dogs allowed: The rise of the Mexican American civil rights movement*. Austin, Texas: University of Texas Press.

Faithful Dissident: Alonso S. Perales, Discrimination, and the Catholic Church

Virginia Marie Raymond

Introduction

Alonso S. Perales distinguished himself by advocating for Mexicans and Mexican Americans[1] in the United States as an individual and through numerous organizations, by writing, public speaking, organizing, personally appealing to potential allies as well as adversaries, running for the school board in San Antonio and practicing law. He also represented the United States as a diplomat early in his career, and used his considerable talents to study and propagate Catholicism through his writings and a radio show, especially during the last years of his life. In his own words, Perales worked "in defense of [his] people."

At different moments, Perales found common ground with Robert E. Lucey, Archbishop of the Roman Catholic Diocese of San Antonio from 1941 to 1969, and Allan Shivers, Governor of Texas from 1949 to 1957, two powerful leaders between whom no love was lost. Perales' political and religious commitments may confound those in our day who accept facile categories such as "left" and "right" or "progressive" and "conservative," as if political beliefs were one-dimensional and linear in nature, lining up as definitively as points on a ruler. Perales, Lucey, and Shivers, as different as they were, shared the ferocious anti-communism dominant in their time and place.

Perales was an outsider in the secular as well as the religious worlds in which he circulated. Both as a Mexican American and a layperson, he found himself at the margins of the Catholic Church. He was also outside some secular political circles as a Mexican American, a Catholic, or a social conservative.

From one point of view, Perales' religious and political commitments might seem complicated: sometimes overlapping or identical and at other times tense. Even to assign "religion" and "politics" to separate categories, however, might betray and mislead us. This paper will focus on the dual political aspects of Perales' Catholicism. I mean "political" in the broadest sense, that is, having to do with *power relations* between and among people.

On the one hand, Perales forcefully advocated for Mexicans and Mexican Americans *within* the Catholic Church during the last two decades of his life. Specifically, this paper discusses three incidents in which Perales made complaints to the

Catholic hierarchy about the segregation of Mexican-origin people in Catholic institutions. One narrow goal of this paper is explore these instances in order to understand what happened and why.

On the other, Perales' adherence to conservative and anti-communist strains, dominant in the United States generally, but perhaps especially fierce within the U.S. Catholic Church, set him apart from, and at odds with, political activists in the secular realm with whom he might otherwise found common cause. Our protagonist was a sometime ally of both the highest-ranking secular executive and the highest-ranking member of the Catholic hierarchy in Texas. To be a Mexican-American civil rights advocate politically positioned uncomfortably between Governor Allan Shivers and Archbishop Robert E. Lucey is the essence of the Perales paradox. The trajectories of Perales' anti-communism, and the relationship of his anti-communism to his Catholicism, warrant close attention.

Discrimination against Mexican Americans within the Catholic Church in Texas

This paper will not provide anything close to a comprehensive look at anti-Mexican segregation within the Catholic Church in Texas, even within the short period of Perales' lifetime. It will instead recall three historical facts and warn of two grave challenges to understanding the segregation of Mexicans and Mexican Americans from other people within the Church. First, Mexican Americans have always opposed forced segregation, especially in schools, and second, they have always sought both excellence and equity of education for their children (San Miguel, Donato, Cárdenas). Third, while some Mexicans and Mexican Americans have at time adopted strategies to make themselves seem less "Mexican" and more "American" (in a misleading and restrictive sense of "American" as "Anglo American"), the Spanish language and its literature, as well as Mexican practices and modes of being, have endured. In other words, Mexican Americans have sought access, equity, and excellence, in education, while also seeking to preserve distinct identities as Mexicans, Mexican Americans, Chicanas, Chicanos, Tejanas, Tejanos, or Latinas and Latinos or Hispanics. A desire to end forced segregation is different from a desire to assimilate, which is why it is possible for people both to work *against* segregation and *for* Mexican spaces and institutions.

Our first challenge is to define segregation: whether segregation means only the intentional act of causing forced segregation, or also include all circumstances in which people are separated (deliberately or not, voluntarily or not) by ethnicity or "race." Shall we deem segregated those institutions that do not practice explicitly anti-Mexican segregation, but operate in ways with disparate impacts? Practices that disproportionately exclude Mexicans are common: charging very costly tuition, opening parks or schools only to residents of given neighborhoods, posting exclusively English signs in ostensibly public spaces, or excluding from cemeteries glass, candles, flowers that don't come from specified florists, and food. Measurement is necessarily difficult both because people don't agree on the definition of segregation, and because at times segregation has been fixed and at other times fluid.

Catholics, like most of the United States outside the Southwest, tended to think of racial segregation in black and white terms. Moreover, at least in the U.S. Southwest, Mexicans and Mexican Americans were legally "white" or members of the "Caucasian race" (In *Re: Ricardo Rodriguez*, 81 F. Supp. 337, W.D. Tex. 1897; H.C.R. No. 105, "Caucasian Race—Equal Privileges," Texas House of Representatives, 1943). Thus, when Rev. John LaFarge, a Jesuit priest and associate editor of the national weekly *America* wrote *Interracial Justice: A Study of the Catholic Doctrine of Race Relations* in 1937, he focused solely on "Negro and white relations," even though he asked his audience "to bear in mind that the principles and modes of action herein discussed are by no means confined their application to the Negro-white solution alone . . . [and] that the Negro-white problem is only one of a multitude of similar interracial problems in this country, and, indeed, throughout the world" (v-vi).[2]

When Mexican-origin people spoke of racial discrimination, in contrast, they sometimes were referring mainly or exclusively to *intra*-racial racial discrimination, because the law until *Hernandez v. Texas* (1954) recognized only state (which is to also to say "white") discrimination against people of a different ("non-white") "race" (see Olivas 2006 on the importance of *Hernandez*). For instance, in 1941, Perales attempted to persuade Paul Kilday, Congressional representative from San Antonio from 1939-01962 (http://bioguide.congress.gov/biosearch/biosearch1.asp), of the necessity and feasibility of a federal "Anti-Race Hatred Law," modeled after a state law in New Jersey. Perales argued that Congress had the power to adopt such a law under its general powers to "provide for the common defense [and] promote the general welfare." The intent of his proposal was limited to "put[ting] an end to the fomenting of racial prejudice against members of the Caucasian Race in the United States" (Perales to Kilday, February 8, 1941).[3]

A second challenge is that people may not recognize segregation even when they are looking right at it, if it is not *de jure* segregation. In addition to the *de facto* segregation in schools and churches that took place by virtue of residential segregation, segregation of Mexicans and Mexican Americans also went under other names, including "missions" and "national parishes." The deliberate exclusion of ethnic or racial minorities was not among the canonical justifications for the creation or maintenance of separate congregations, as will become clear below.

1. Discrimination, including segregation, was widespread and varied[4]

Leo Tolstoy opened Ana Karenina with the observation that "happy families are all alike; every unhappy family is unhappy in each own way." Similarly, *de jure* discrimination worked in predictably dismal patterns across Texas, but each instance of *de facto* discrimination was miserable in its own way. Anti-Mexican discrimination, including segregation, in Texas, precisely because it was *not* written into the law, took many diverse forms. Not only was anti-Mexican discrimination not prescribed in the Catholic Church, but it also actually ran counter to Catholic teaching. For this reason, anti-Mexican discrimination manifested itself in diverse ways, many of which were blatant but some of which were somewhat covert. Thick blankets of evasive language, excuses and rationalizations accompanied this discrimination.

Mexicans and Mexican Americans were frequently unwelcome at Catholic churches dominated by Anglos. In San Antonio, according to Timothy Matovina (2005), "people attended San Fernando because they were rebuffed at Anglo American parishes and told to attend the 'Mexican church' where they 'belonged'" (*Guadalupe and Her Faithful* p. 100). "In some towns," writes Moises Sandoval (1983), "there was a parish church for Anglos and one for Mexican Americans and woe to those who went to the wrong one!" (p. 26). Richard Martínez (2005) reports that *de facto* segregation of Mexicans was common, especially in large towns, during the first part of the twentieth century. "Whites" attended the well-maintained churches, while Mexicans were relegated to "run-down" facilities (pp. 5-6).

As he documented places that discriminated against Mexicans and Mexican Americans, Alonso S. Perales included the Catholic Church in Midland. There, he reported,

> Persons of Mexican descent are not permitted to attend the Catholic Church when services are being held for the Anglo-Americans. On Sunday, May 7, 1944, about 9:00 A.M., two Mexican boys were requested to leave Church. The usher informed them that that was a mass for "White" people only. ("Some places . . ." at 2)

Subjecting Mexicans to the humiliation of being asked to leave Mass was an intolerable affront to the dignified Perales. Unfortunately, Midland was not unique. Robert Treviño cites a Sister Agnes Rita Rodríguez, who "remembered her father's anguish at being escorted out of Annunciation Church, the premier Anglo Catholic church and an architectural showcase in downtown Houston" (Treviño, 2003, p. 143).

Moises Sandoval (1983) reports that some parishes practiced segregation of Mexicans and Anglos within a given church building. "Mexican Americans were welcome at one Mass but not at any of the others. Some parishes made the Hispanic newcomers [migrant workers] sit in the back pews, allowing them to approach the altar for communion only *after* Anglos had received" (p. 26). Carlos Castañeda noted that Mexicans were made to sit in the back of the church (though he did not call this practice segregation) and Jennifer Nájera reports the practice of having Mexicans sit on a different side of the church. Ana María Díaz-Stevens writes that Catholic Hispanics were often relegated to "basement churches," although these last were less common in Texas than in the parts of the U.S. where soil conditions facilitated basement building (see also Richard Edward Martínez at 6).[5]

Writing of the conditions that gave rise to the organization of PADRES, Richard Edward Martínez (2005) identified several variants of discrimination.

> [I]t was common for Mexicans to be denied access to white Masses or to be relegated to the back pews. Where only one church existed, separate Masses were often held for Mexicans . . . In the 1950s in Floresville, Texas, where there was only one Catholic church, the Masses themselves were segregated. Mexicans sat on one side and whites on the other. The homily was partially bilingual, fifteen minutes in English and five minutes in Spanish. In addition, throughout the Southwest it was common for Catholic clergy to publicly

express anti-Mexican attitudes and for Mexicans to be denied access to white cemeteries. (p. 6)

The Catholic churches, in other words, reinforced the racist practices of the secular community.

Even when Mexicans attended integrated churches, they experienced discrimination. "Like other immigrant communities (69-70), Italians in New York and Chicago, for example, Mexican Catholics in Houston felt pressured to change their style of Catholicism to conform to the Irish American model that set the standard for 'acceptable' Catholicism in America" (Treviño, 2003, p. 70). Jennifer Nájera (2009) provides a poignant example from La Feria, in the Río Grande Valley of Texas. In the 1940s, pious Mexican and Mexican-American families were accustomed to walking to church barefoot, and then entering the church building and approaching the altar on their knees, "al uso de antes" or "the way it used to be done" (p. 11). Men in many of these families were serving in the U.S. Armed Forces. Expressions of religious devotion, explains Nájera (2009), were particularly important to people who had no other way to protect their loved ones fighting on three other continents. Anglo Catholics, however, mocked the rituals (p. 11).

Rather than let the Mexican members of the congregation worship as was their custom. Anglo parishioners would literally lift up Mexican people from their knees, establishing—and, actually, policing—the boundaries of what was acceptable behavior in the church. (Nájera, 2009, p. 12)

Under this ridicule and pressure, "poco a poco ya la gente no se usaba éso" (Nájera, 2009, p. 11). Little by little, the people gave up their rituals.

Not only churches, but schools, as well, were often segregated. Carlos E. Castañeda devoted a chapter of the last volume of his encyclopedic *Our Catholic Heritage in Texas* to "educational endeavors." In between his account of how the Ursuline nuns created their academy in San Antonio, and his assessment of the Ursuline Academy's enduring contribution, he spent about a paragraph describing these nuns' extra project.

In addition to the Academy, the zealous daughters of St. Ursula had opened and maintained a free day school principally for the benefit of Mexican children. (Castañeda, 1976, p. 293)

The Mexican school opened by the Ursulines was doomed, however. Castañeda explained that, in 1874, a new bishop "was anxious to promote parochial schools for which the need was great. But the Uruslines, being a cloistered order, were not prepared to help in parochial educational work at this time" (p. 294). So the Academy was assigned to the care of the Sisters of the Incarnate Word, the Sisters of Mercy, and the Sisters of Divine Providence. "With aching heart[s]" the Ursulines watched "the 300 Mexican children of their free school . . . pass from their care to that of the Sisters of the Incarnate Word" (p. 294).

Losing their free school was not the only blow to the Ursuline sisters. "After Reconstruction," on a day that Castañeda did not specify, the Ursuline school—both

its day and boarding components—became restricted to English-speaking students"
(294). Castañeda does not address the question of whether English-speaking students
of Mexican descent were equally as welcome as their Anglo counterparts. What is
clear from this history is that the education of Spanish-speaking Mexican children
was, at that time, a lesser priority in the eyes of these four religious orders as well as
the Diocese. Accounts of the contributions of Catholic educators, as well as their
ambivalent effects in reinforcing, resisting, and overcoming segregation, would over-
whelm this chapter. Segregated hospitals were also common (Castañeda, 1976, pp.
359-421) as was discrimination at non-segregated hospitals (Treviño, 2003, 144).

The index for Castañeda's seventh volume of *Our Catholic Heritage,* which
covers the period from 1836 to 1950, does not contain listings for the terms "segregation," "race," "ethnicity," "Spanish-speaking" (with or without a hyphen), "Mexican American" (with or without a hyphen), or "Hispanics." Neither does this volume
index "national parishes." An entry on "Bigotry" refers to a description of persecu-
tion of nuns in Marshall, Texas, and on "Eradication of Prejudice and Correction of
Errors," to a history of anti-Catholicism and efforts by the Knights of Columbus to
respond by disseminating information. Castañeda does use the word "prejudice"
referring to the racial kind, but he does not make it easy to find examples by including the category of racial prejudice in his index. Twice in two pages, he identifies
Holy Cross Hospital in Austin, founded in 1940, as originally designed for Negroes
("particularly" and later "exclusively"), but since "thrown open to all patients
regardless of race or creed" (Castañeda, 1976, pp. 410-411). He proudly reports the
success of Sister Celline Heitzman, a "Medical Doctor and resident physician" in
"breaking down prejudice and organizing a mixed staff of White and Negro doctors"
(p. 411). In its index, Castañeda's Volume VII does contain the following listings for
"Mexicans; school for by Ursulines in S.A.," "Spanish children," Negro Children
(capital "C" here, though not in "Spanish children"), "Negro Education," and
"Negroes; spiritual welfare of; hospital for in Austin." These topics arise particularly in the chapters entitled "Religious Communities of Men in Texas," "Catholic Educational Endeavors," and "Public Health and Social Welfare Work," in which Castañeda describes the work of particular religious orders (female and male) in serving
specific populations and in creating institutions "for" those populations.

These assignments and special projects recognize in an apparently neutral,
matter-of-face matter, the existence of separate spheres. Castañeda's acknowledgement
in the text, but partial omission from the index, of the existence of racial prejudice, suggests the sensitive and controversial nature of the subject. After all, the Catholic censor
in Houston and all the Catholic bishops in the state approved the history.

3. Segregation versus self-determination

Because widespread segregation of Mexicans was rarely labeled as such, it is
appropriate to pause to ask what "segregation" means in this exploration. Segregation, in this paper, means exclusion and involuntary separation. It does not include
churches, religious orders, and other organizations and institutions, created by Mexican-origin laity and clergy, oriented to Mexican and Mexican-American congrega-

tions specifically. The Missionary Catechists of Divine Providence (MCDP) emerged from the work of Mexican-American women with Sister Mary Benitia Vermeersch, a member of the Congregation of Divine Providence (CDP), first in Houston in the late 1920 and then continuing through the 1930s and 1940s in San Antonio as well (De Luna, 2002, pp. 56-58). Other institutions emerged, according to Ana María Díaz-Stevens (1998), "roughly" between 1967 and 1981, during what she terms "The Period of the Latino Religious Resurgence" (p. 157).

Mexican-centered practices go far beyond speaking Spanish. Numerous practitioners and scholars have written about the many benefits of developing Mexican and Mexican-American clergy, such as the MCPDs and much later PADRES and Las Hermanas, as well as lay leadership (National Association of Hispanic Deacons). Virgilio Elizondo has developed theology that centered the Mexican experience (*The Future is Mestizo, Galilean Journey*). Richard Reyes Flores (1984) advocated liturgy and practices that respect and incorporated the "lived faith experiences of the people" and that "allow[ed] people to theologize out of their own experience" (pp. 1, 4). The Mexican American Cultural Center (MACC) first designed programs specifically for Mexican-origin or Latino congregants or at least centering their experience (Matovina, 2003; Mexican American Cultural Center; Icaza, 2003). Soon, MACC was recruiting Anglo priests to its trainings, so that they, too, could more effectively serve Spanish-speaking congregants (Proposal, Regional Mexican American Cultural Center). The idea of creating services that cater to Spanish-speaking parishioners with powerful affective bonds to particular songs and practices was never motivated by a desire to exclude Anglos. Majority-Mexican programming is not "segregation" as used in this chapter, if such services are designed and controlled by people of Mexican descent, and if participation open to all. Mandatory separation imposed by the dominant authorities is segregation: an entirely different beast.

3. The agents and mechanisms of segregation

Influential Jesuit writer and editor John LaFarge, in both his 1937 book on "race relations" and more accurately titled 1943 book on "Negro-white" relations, alerted readers to the fact that other marginalized peoples, in addition to Negroes, were targeted for racial discrimination. That was helpful. The comparison may have also caused confusion, however, because the "modes" of discrimination against Mexican Americans (and Asians, indigenous people, women, sexual minorities, people with disabilities, none of whom Perales wrote about) did not look like anti-Negro discrimination.

In the secular realm, discrimination against African Americans was not only permitted, but also actually required, by the law throughout most of Perales' lifetime. *De jure* discrimination remained in force as a national policy until at least 1967, when the U.S. Supreme Court struck anti-miscegenation laws in *Loving v. Virginia*, and continued to exist in local ordinances and state laws until the 1970s. From Emancipation through 1954, the Catholic Church maintained "Jim Crow" churches for African Americans (Ciesluk, 1944, p. 99): this history is clear and unambiguous.

Customs, traditions, economics, ignorance and bigotry—but for the most part, not the law—provided the basis for *de facto* discrimination against Mexicans and

Mexican Americans in Texas. At least in the U.S. Southwest, Mexicans and Mexican Americans were legally "white" or members of the "Caucasian race" (*In Re: Ricardo Rodriguez*, 81 F. Supp. 337, W.D. Tex. 1897; H.C.R. No. 105, "Caucasian Race—Equal Privileges," Texas House of Representatives, 1943).

The Catholic Church's distinct treatment of African Americans and Mexican Americans follows the distinct trajectories of each group in U.S. history. The Spanish colonized the Americas before the English did. Mexicans are mestizos, products of mixing between among indigenous, Spanish, African and often other peoples. The Spanish colonizers were predominantly Catholics (or posing as Catholics), and despite its anti-clerical history, Mexico has been predominantly a Catholic country for centuries. When Anglos came to Texas, Mexicans were already here and already Catholic. They were also, initially, the majority population. Catholics from the Canary Islands were the first non-indigenous settlers of San Antonio.

In contrast, the Africans who were forcibly brought to what is now the United States as slaves principally (but not exclusively) acquired their predominantly Protestant Christianity in this country. African Americans were a dominated population and a numerical minority. Black Catholics were few; they constituted a minority religious group within a minority "racial" category. According to Richard A. Lamanna and Jay J. Coakley

It has been estimated that not more than 5 per cent of the nearly 4.5 million Negroes in the United States were Catholic at the time of emancipation. The fact that a large number of these left the Church after the bonds tying them to their Catholic masters has led to the conclusion that in spite of 'the fact that in many instances Catholic masters watched over the religious interest of their slaves, the majority of Catholic slaves were Catholic in little more than name. (p. 149, quoting John T. Gillard, *The Catholic Church and the American Negro*: Baltimore 1929, at 260)

"In one section of Louisiana," the state with the largest Catholic population in the Confederacy, "an estimated 65,000 Negroes left the Catholic religion in the years immediately following the Civil War" (Lamanna and Coakley, p. 149, n.5, again citing Gillard).

While elements of the following discussion apply, to some degree, to both African Americans and Mexican Americans, it is important to keep in mind the profound differences in the histories of these two peoples. Likewise, I have used sources primarily from or about Texas; I am not making any claims about anti-Black or anti-Latino segregation outside of the state, or, in some cases, the U.S. Southwest. Finally, this discussion does not go beyond 1960; it does not address Catholic Church policy or significant activities concerning Southeast Asian refugees.

From the mid-nineteenth century through Perales' lifetime, one convenient fiction, and two ostensibly benevolent forces, facilitated segregation.

    a) The fiction was that "national parishes" for "Negroes" or Mexicans were akin to national parishes for people of European descent.

b) The first force was the creation and flourishing of religious orders dedicated to serving particular populations, especially distinct ethnic or "racial" groups: Negroes, Mexicans, and Indians.

c) The second force, beginning in 1907, was the Catholic Extension Society.

Religious orders provided the labor, and the Extension Society, the material support, to create and maintain separate institutions for racialized peoples in Texas, typically in "missions." Regular, or "territorial" parishes, served the politically dominant group in any given region; missions served the racial or ethnic marginalized.

a) National Parishes

"Immigrants," wrote Joseph Ciesluk (1944), "came to the shores of this friendly country [possessing] little if any knowledge of its language; they were cut off from communication with home, family, and friends, and they needed to be with people who spoke their language" (p. 52). "The national churches," Ciesluk explained, "are a testimony of [immigrants'] faith and devotion during a time when they were very much exposed to the danger of losing their faith, as did many who came to this country" (p. 53). Ciesluk and other Catholic scholars addressing the issue of separate parishes for immigrant populations in the United States typically referred to European populations. Clearly immigrants from Eastern Europe, Southern Europe, and Ireland suffered discrimination, but the racialization of these populations diminished as generations of once-immigrant populations became more fully integrated and assimilated into "American" and "white" identities (see, for example, Ignatiev 1995; Guglemio and Salerno 2003).

According to Catholic canon law, the four elements of a parish are: 1) a congregation or community of the faithful; 2) defined boundaries, usually but not always territorial but sometimes via a classification; 3) a priest "with rights and duties involving the care of souls among the faithful in the Christian community; and 4) a parish church (Connolly, 1938, p. 3). It is also necessary that the parish be canonically established as such (Connolly, 1938, p. 3). None of the first four requirements is or was an "inherent requisite" as a parish could be created even if one element was missing (Ciesluk, 1944, p. 3), especially if the missing element was absent only temporarily. A priest could be away, or be removed or die (Ciesluk, 1944, p. 5); a congregation might need to leave (in case of natural disaster, for example) or war (Ciesluk, 1944, p. 5); a church might be destroyed (as by fire). The only absolute requirement had been the erection or formation of a parish by the proper church authority (Ciesluk, 1944, p. 5), normally a bishop or archbishop of a diocese or archdiocese (Ciesluk, 1944, pp. 5-6), although even that requirement had recently been called into question (Ciesluk, 1944, p. 6 at note 20).

Most parishes are territorial, but canon law provided for non-territorial parishes long before Catholics came to the Americas. These might be "personal" parishes, such as parishes for those "of noble birth" or distinct parishes for Catholics observing different rites. The existence of two parishes in one territory was not common and had been "considered . . . somewhat abnormal in the organization of the Church" before the nineteenth century, but they became numerous in the United States as "language parishes" (Connolly, 1938, p. 10). In 1884, the Third Plenary Council encouraged the assigning of "prudent priests . . . who were familiar with European languages to assist and advise" immigrants from diverse nations in large cities on the eastern seaboard (Connolly, 1938, p. 105). Richard Martínez (2005) explains:

> During the late nineteenth and early twentieth century, large waves of Catholics immigrated to the United States from Ireland, Italy, Germany, and Poland. Each group arrived with its own priests and religious leaders who established parishes, schools, and hospitals, which serviced the respective ethnic enclaves. (p. 4)

Most of the money for national parish churches in the United States came from the immigrants' home countries Europe in the 1900s (Castañeda, 1976, pp. 165-205).

In Texas, such churches include St. Mary's Catholic Church in Fredericksburg (German, 1862); Guardian Angel Catholic Church in Wallis, (Czech, 1892); and San Francesco di Paolo (Italian, 1927). The Archdiocese of San Antonio describes San Francesco di Paola with pride:

> Annually, the first Sunday of May is a day dear to the hearts of all Italo-Americans of San Antonio. It was on that day, in 1927, that their church . . . was solemnly solemnly blessed and dedicated by his Excellency, the Most Reverend Archbishop Drossaerts (Archdiocese of San Antonio 25).

This wholly celebratory, proud description, published in 1949, is typical of the period in its view of national parishes.

Membership in national parishes was supposed to be entirely voluntary (Ciesluk, 1944, pp. 102-109). If Catholics originally joined a "national parish" because of language, they were free to join the territorial parish when they learned English. Foreign-born Catholics "[were neither] bound to remain in the national parish once they [had] learned English, [nor were] they obligated to leave it, even after the immediate necessity of the use of their native language [had] passed" (Ciesluk, 1944, pp. 105). Children of foreign-born parents whose native languages were other than English were to stay in their parents' parishes until these children reached adulthood. At the age of majority, they could decide to join a territorial (English-speaking) parish or stay in their parents' "national" parish (Ciesluk, 1944, pp. 107-108). Similarly, in 1944, a woman who married was "considered as one with [her husband's] person" and thus would become part of his parish, although she retained the right to return to her home parish on dissolution of the marriage (Ciesluk, 1944, p. 109).

The question of membership in a particular parish, within these general rules, was supposed to be up to the individual layperson's preference.

> [T]he greatest liberty is given by the Sacred Congregation to those parishioners of a national parish who speak English to make this change [to a territorial parish] themselves, . . . [T]he authority of both the territorial and the national pastor is restricted. *No pastor may determine in this respect who shall or shall not be a member of his parish.* If a parishioner of a national parish

chooses to affiliate himself with a territorial parish in which he has domicile, the pastor of the national parish cannot oblige him to remain, nor can the pastor of the English-speaking territorial parish refuse admittance. (Ciesluk, 1944, pp. 106-107, emphasis added)

This discussion speaks to the rights of individual parishioners to choose affiliation with a territorial or national parish. It does not address the issue of creation of "national"—that is, segregated—parishes or missions in the first place.

Moreover, the discussion eludes the question of how territories come into being in the first place. Who designates the borders and boundaries of parishes? The political nature of the process could hardly be clearer to those of us living in Texas in 2011 without knowing to which congressional district we might belong next year, even if we're planning on living in the same place. Rivers, at least if not dammed, and mountains, at least before mining, are natural features. There is nothing "natural" about electoral districts or parish lines.

There is a simple way to distinguish between real "national parishes" and segregated faux-"national parishes." The former were voluntary; the latter mandatory. "Separate nationality parishes existed for the various European immigrant groups as a rule, but if they lacked churches of their own, European ethnics could attend any white Catholic church, unlike Mexicans and blacks" (Treviño, 2006, p. 33).

A second way to distinguish between true national churches and segregated institutions is to "follow the money." Knowing the financial basis for an institution can reveal its probable purpose. Carlos E. Castañeda (1976) elaborated at length on this subject in a chapter entitled "Financial Support for the Church in Texas" (pp. 165-205). If a Czech, German, Bavarian, or other European group provided the resources to serve its own national emigrants, the parish was a national one. The European branches of the Society for the Propagation of Faith, which started in Lyons, France, funded many churches for then-impoverished Catholic immigrant communities in the nineteenth-century United States. If the Catholic Extension Society paid for the mission, it was most likely segregated (although Castañeda did not use that word).

Institutionalized, historical, deeply engrained, and dominant practices of racism in the United States posed a quandary for Catholic scholars and theologians in the 1930s and 1940s. These men in the mid-twentieth century wrestled mightily with the definition of "parish" and the question of when "non-territorial" parishes were permitted. How it could be that two (or more) Catholic parishes could exist within the same or overlapping geographical boundaries, especially when the ostensibly "national" parish did not appear to meet the criteria for that category? Nicholas P. Connolly, a San Francisco priest whose doctoral dissertation at Catholic University on the canonical erection of parishes was published in 1938, considered "lingual, national, **and racial** parishes" to be "natural" (p. 107, emphasis added). By 1944, however, the Grand Rapids priest and Catholic University doctoral candidate Joseph E. Ciesluk apparently felt that the existence of "national parishes" for "Negroes" required at least some explanation.

According to Connolly (1938), in 1868, the Second Plenary Council at Baltimore "recognized,"

[t]he need of special zeal for the spiritual welfare of Negroes in the United States . . . The Second Council left it to the judgment of each bishop to decide whether or not to found separate churches for them. It was thought unwise to issue a general decree probably because the work of caring for the newly liberated colored race was in a formative stage. (p. 106, citing II Plenary Council of Baltimore at note 485)

Connolly depicts the Catholic Church as taking a "wait and see" approach about whether or not to segregate "Negroes." Lamanna and Coakley paint a still more damning picture.

Nine degrees on the Negro apostolate were enacted by the [Second] Plenary Counil, among which was one accepting the principle of segregation in those regions where it was in vogue. The extent of this acceptance is reflected in the action of Peter Richard Kenrick, Archbishop of St. Louis, who gave the St. Louis Jesuits permission to open a church for Negroes but on condition that no sacraments were ever to be administered in the church to whites. (p. 151, citing an undated pamphlet by John Tracy Ellis published in Huntington, Indiana, at p. 4)

Catholic clergy, the Council appeared to say, were to "render unto Caesar" the segregation that "Caesar" demanded; nowhere in the work cited by Connolly, Ciesluk, or Lamanna and Coakley does there appear any mention of dissenting views within the church hierarchy.

Connolly's reports of the Third Plenary Council at Baltimore, held in 1884, are more confusing.

the time was opportune for the widespread practice of establishing parishes for the Negroes. A mandatory note was injected into the legislation. (p. 106)

Here, Connolly appears to be saying that the Catholic Church in the United States actually decreed, in 1884, that Negroes parishes be separated from the territorial parishes. On the next page, however, Connolly seems to imply that the local bishop could decide what to do. The question is important enough to justify citing Connolly at length.

It is possible that the problem of parishes for Negroes and Indians in the United States is one which, because of its local and more or less temporary nature, was left untouched by the compilers of the Code. These are certainly not family parishes. They can hardly be called personal in the limited sense in which that word is used in this place, because membership in them embraces a whole class of people, and is generic: whereas the personal type of parishes seem to embrace a more specific and individual membership. They are not based upon diversity of language, because frequently the vernacular is used.

Probably they can be included under the wording *pro diversitate nationis* which is general enough to include race. It is true that the wording of the Code seems to be primarily concerned with diversity of language when it deals with lingual and national parishes, but on the other hand it seems also to have intend to require an indult for all kinds except those that are solely territorial. The parity between lingual, national, and racial parishes is so natural that it would seem most reasonable . . . to seek an indult in every case. (Connolly, 1938, p. 107)

An "indult," in this context, means an exemption from the general law.

Without admitting to doing so, Connolly outlined three possible answers: 1) separate churches were mandatory; 2) separate churches were permissible if the bishop so decided; or 3) separate churches were permissible if the bishop requested an indult, which—Connolly implies—would be automatically granted. Which was it: mandatory or discretionary segregation? One might wonder what exactly Connolly meant by "a mandatory note was inserted into the legislation." Who inserted the "note" and was the "note" actually part of the legislation? Was a "note" analogous to "legislative intent" or akin to legislative dicta? At this point it is well to consider that Connolly's inconclusive parsing came in a doctoral dissertation; in practice, the Catholic Church followed Jim Crow.

Ciesluk clarified that the bishops had discretion to decide whether to create separate parishes or services or not, depending on "conditions" in their areas, and without having to consult the Vatican every time. These conditions included "political animosities along with racial and religious prejudice [that] made it especially difficult to make any general provision for the whole country" (Ciesluk, 1944, p. 97). Perhaps clerical consciences were also relieved to note that separate churches for Negroes and whites pre-existed the Second and Third/Plenary Councils.

Even before the II Plenary Council of Baltimore there existed separate churches for the colored people . . . The III Plenary Council . . . approved the decrees of the II Plenary Council, and noted that a number of separate churches and schools had been built [while] in other places the spiritual needs of the colored people were provided for together with the rest of the members of the congregation at the church they attended. (Ciesluk, 1944, pp. 97-98)

The Church hierarchy could claim that it was merely leaving existing churches alone, rather than itself introducing the segregation it could not canonically justify.

The Third Plenary Council of 1884 also expressed a weakly positive statement about inclusion or integration. Its participants, according to Ciesluk,

decreed that **wherever possible** the bishops should erect churches, schools, orphanages and poor-home for the use of the Negroes. In other places, the Negroes were to be accommodated in the local church, and were to be permitted to receive the Sacraments without any discrimination against them. (Ciesluk, 1944, pp. 97-98, emphasis added)

"Wherever possible" seems to have been an even less effective directive than the U.S. Supreme Court's "all deliberate speed" in *Brown v. Board of Education* (1954). At the time he wrote, Ciesluk (1944) acknowledged, "about half the Negro Catholics in the United States worship in churches that can be designated as exclusively for the colored" (p. 99).

Ciesluk admitted that the normal rationales for creating "national parishes" did not apply to "Negro" Catholics, as they spoke English and were U.S. citizens. He also "unquestionably" understood that "the mind of the Church is that no distinction be made as to racial differences in the common bond of faith" (p. 99).

Nevertheless, Ciesluk defended segregation. In the first place, he reasoned,

> the United States is not a Catholic country. Bi-racial problems are the cause of situations that, humanly viewed, are difficult to overcome. The Church has to accept human nature as it is and seek to mold it in the pattern of Christ. If the Church has found it necessary to erect separate churches for these people, one can only interpret this arrangement as being equally advantageous for all concerned. (p. 99)

In other words, if the Catholic Church practiced segregation, it must be a good thing. Moreover, Ciesluk explained that separate churches could be classified as "national parishes"

> by reason of the racial origin of the members. In the first case nationality is considered from the standpoint of political unity, and in the second as a characteristic of people of a common origin. (p. 100)

Membership in "national parishes," as we have seen, was supposed to be entirely voluntary. The exclusion of African Americans from "regular" territorial parishes and their relegation to "colored" parishes or missions was not voluntary. Nor did membership in a segregated Negro church necessarily provide a congregant with a priest who shared her background or cultural practices. The Catholic Church fathers contradicted themselves with respect to national parishes.

The "national parishes" as applied to Mexican-origin populations often relied on an argument often repeated in the context of secular education: Anglos and Mexicans should be separated for everybody's linguistic comfort and convenience. That argument soundly rejected by Mexican-American advocates, including Perales, was no more persuasive in the religious sphere. Separate English and Spanish masses may seem normal today, but the rational for linguistic segregation was a weak one indeed, up until Vatican II. During Perales' lifetime, priests conducted masses in Latin, a foreign language to Anglos and Mexicans alike, although they preached in the vernacular languages of the people. Few priests assigned to Mexican congregations in the first two-thirds of the twentieth century spoke Spanish; fewer still were ethnic Mexicans themselves (Hurtado, 1975, p. 52). Thus, Mexicans attending segregated churches were, for the most part, no more likely to benefit from preaching and pastoral counseling in Spanish than were Mexicans attending territorial parishes.

b) Religious orders, missions, and the Catholic Extension Society

Diocesan histories or clerical biographies emphasize accomplishments in numbers and dates. They record successes enthusiastically: churches built, missions opened, schools in operation, Masses offered and confessions heard, baptisms, First Communions, confirmations, ordinations, and weddings, the existence of well-attended lay groups, retreats. For instance, the *Journey of the Diocese of Amarillo* reports that San Angelo saw its first Catholic priest in 1871; the church first known as Immaculate Conception was constructed in 1879 and a newer church named Sacred Heart replaced it in 1906 (Diocese of Amarillo, *Journey*, p. 67). San Angelo erected another church, St. Mary's, in 1906 (Diocese of Amarillo, *Journey*, p. 72). Yet San Angelo saw the creation of a San José, specifically for Mexicans, in the late 1930s (1936 according to Regina Foppe at 92) or early 1940s (Diocese of Amarillo, *Journey*, p. 72).

Similarly, Castañeda (1976) describes Rudolph Aloysius Gerken by listing his dates and accomplishments. Gerken received his first pastoral assignment to Abilene in 1917:

Here [Gerken] had the care not only of the parish but its missions scattered in six counties. He, like many missionaries, took a deep interest in the candid faith of the Mexicans. Moved by their plight, he built in 1918 a church and parochial school for them in Abilene. During the next two years he founded missions at Ranger and Cisco and built two new churches. (p. 159)

Gerken also started a parochial school for Mexicans in Ranger in 1924 (Castañeda, 1976, p. 160).

Beginning in the early 1900s, the Catholic Extension Society fueled the growth and spread of Catholic institutions in the U.S. Southwest. It underwrote missions within the U.S. for "Negroes, Mexicans, and Native Americans" as well as for people living in remote rural areas. If one's goal is to evangelize, then building and staffing churches where none exist is a logical goal. The Extension Society, however, frequently underwrote the building of missions "for Mexicans" in places with established Catholic churches. In so doing, the organization reinforced and even sometimes introduced racial segregation.

Religious orders of women and men, rather than diocesan clergy, have typically staffed missions. These missions were congregations of primarily "minority" populations. Like their members, missions typically enjoy less status, less autonomy, and fewer resources than regular or territorial parishes. A religious Catholic who desires the propagation of that faith as well as equality of all people might feel ambivalence towards religious orders dedicated to serving specific ethnic or "racial" populations in missions: colonialism, in a word.

On the one hand, missions and dedicated religious orders served the spiritual needs, and frequently provided material goods as well as education to people who might not otherwise have had access to these resources.[6] On the other hand, the existence of clergy dedicated to a particular people made it easier to segregate that group of people during the late nineteenth century into the twentieth. The Josephites, founded in 1871, served African Americans; the Oblates, as well as the Congregation of the Divine Providence, and later the Missionary Catechists of Divine Providence (MCDP), primarily served Mexican congregations. Other orders—for instance, Jesuits, Holy Cross fathers and sisters, Victory Knoll Sisters and Sisters of the Incarnate Word—would also devote their efforts to a particular group at a given time or place, but they had other callings, as well (Castañeda, 1976; ReligiousMinisteries.com). As the Josephites, CDP, and MCDP recruited more clergy from among those they served, the justification for their existence shifted from serving people who could not participate in territorial congregations or schools. Instead they could offer more "culturally sensitive" spiritual guidance and education.

San José

The case of St. Anthony's Church in Hereford, and San José mission, just outside the Deaf Smith County seat in the Texas Panhandle, demonstrates the ambiguous role of religious orders. The first Franciscan Sisters of the Atonement, an order founded in 1898 in Graymoor, New York, came to Hereford, Texas, shortly after the establishment of a chapel named after St. Anthony. In 1917, these sisters and a local priest established the first Catholic school in Hereford (St. Anthony's Parish History). At the time, the Catholic population of the Texas Panhandle was primarily of German origin. In 1920, the first two Friars of the Atonement—also from Graymoor—arrived in Hereford. The parish of St. Anthony grew, served by these Franciscans.

In 1947, with the arrival of Mexican laborers in Deaf Smith County, local growers supplied workers with former P.O.W. barracks for housing just outside the city limits of Hereford. That labor camp housed, and the San José mission served, thousands of migrants a year ("Mexican Migrant Labor in Amarillo Diocese" p. 3). Hereford city leaders were careful to keep Mexicans from living in the city itself, and to keep the city lines away from the labor camp, so as to avoid providing water to the thirsty workers and families. Fr. Raymond Gillis, an Atonement Friar from Graymoor, moved out to the labor camp to be with the workers. Later, so did Dr. Lena Edwards, a Catholic lay physician under whose leadership workers constructed a hospital, Our Lady of Guadalupe Maternity Clinic (Parish files; Moorland-Spingarn Manuscript Collection at Howard University). The new mission acquired the name "San José" (Parish History files, Diocese of Amarillo; Raymond, 2007, pp. 337-342, 431).

Lubbock

Sometimes primarily Mexicans, Mexican Americans, or both populated the first Catholic church in an area; later-arriving Anglo Catholics disliked these missions or parishes and sought to create their own. Such was the case in Lubbock, where the first Catholic Church was St. Joseph's. A parish between 1924 and 1939, St. Joseph's *lost* its status as an independent entity not long after the construction of the new, Anglo, St. Elizabeth's, in 1939. St. Joseph's was downgraded to a mission of St. Elizabeth's, and did not regain its designation as a parish in its own right until 1961 (Diocese of Amarillo, *Journey*, p. 71).

La Feria

Of course, sometimes missions were created, either by Dioceses or independent orders (the Oblates of Mary Immaculate, for instance), in areas in which there had been no Catholic churches at all. In these instances, ethnic or racial segregation might not have been intentional or even taken place *within* the Catholic institutions. Jennifer Nájera's case study of St. Francis Xavier church La Feria reveals both of these phenomena.

> The Catholic Church in La Feria benefited from the faith practices of one of the town's early land speculators as well as the French missionaries whose ministry was prevalent in South Texas . . . In 1907, S. J. Schnorenberg [a Catholic] donated land for the construction of a Catholic church . . . A wooden mission was constructed on the site, dedicated in 1912, [and] served by the Oblate Fathers, the order that had been sent to evangelize South Texas in the middle of the 18th Century. (2009, p. 10)

Non-Mexican Catholics were a minority in Cameron County in the earliest years of the twentieth century, but by 1930 the Catholic population had grown and included whites. The Oblates left; the La Feria mission was promoted to a parish. With the help of the Catholic Extension Society, the new St. Francis Xavier Parish established its own mission for the Mexicans in nearby Santa Rosa (Nájera, 2009, p. 10; St. Francis Xavier—La Feria webpage, http://www.cdob.org/ parishes/st-francis-xavier-la-feria). Though the now integrated St. Francis Xavier church had initially served primarily Mexicans, the Anglos established control and set about to change the parish into their own image. "Though the ..church..served both Anglos and Mexicans," observes Nájera (2009), "it was still marked by an ethos of segregation and racial dominance" (p. 11).

Austin

The history of Our Lady of Guadalupe Church in Austin provides another case study in segregation.

> Until 1907, the Spanish-speaking of Austin attended St. Mary's Church [now Cathedral]. The steady increase in numbers and the deep interest of Reverend P.J. O'Reilly, C.S.C., in their peculiar problems, resulted in the organization of a separate parish, which was erected under the advocation of Our Lady of Guadalupe and placed under Father J. McDonald, C.S.C., the first pastor. (Castañeda, 1976, pp. 225-226)

Austin's Guadalupe Church stood at Fifth[th] and Guadalupe Streets from its establishment in 1907 (Our Lady of Guadalupe Parish History)[7] until approximately twenty years later. Fifth Street, which runs north of and roughly parallel to the river in what is now downtown Austin, also ran along the railroad tracks. Austin owed its railroad, which arrived in 1871, primarily to the labor of Mexican workers. These laborers then built their homes near their work, as they did in many parts of Texas and the U.S. Southwest ("South Colton").[8] By 1875, about three hundred people lived in a neighborhood near the railroad tracks and river. "Mexico," as the neighborhood was called, was bounded by Shoal Creek, Cyprus (now Third Street) and Live Oak (Tyler, http://www.birdseyeviews.org/zoom.php?city=Austin&year=1873&extra_info).

On January 14, 1925, the Holy Cross fathers turned this "work among the Spanish-speaking" to the Oblates (Castañeda, 1976, p. 226). The arrival of the Oblates roughly coincided with the church's move to east. The parish history blandly notes "the new families that were coming in, were located mostly to the east of the city (Our Lady of Guadalupe Parish History).

Guadalupe's parish history does not explain that Mexicans and Mexican Americans (or "Spanish") people were moving to the eastern part of the city, between the river and Seventh Street, because that neighborhood, already primarily Mexican, was in the process of becoming one of the officially designated residential areas for Mexican-origin Austinites (Koch and Fowler, City Plan). Mexicans continued to live in other parts of the city, especially along the railroad tracks near Fifth Street and parts of south Austin. "Negroes" were assigned to live on the east side of the city between Seventh[th] Street and Manor Road, although a small number were also allowed to stay in the well-established Black neighborhood of Clarksville (Koch and Fowler). The City Plan of 1928 codified these districts and induced people to live in their ethnically assigned areas by placing segregated schools, cemeteries, parks, playgrounds, libraries, and swimming pools east of East Avenue (Koch and Fowler). Jim Crow stores, doctors, funeral services, and restrictive covenants enforced segregation in privately owned properties.

Secular authorities had dictated neighborhood and ethnic boundaries, thus pushing Mexicans to the east side, and the church had followed. Guadalupe Church itself, however, was not bound by territorial limits. The second Catholic Church in Austin was "a national parish," a category described in glowing terms in an article honoring the parish's one-hundredth anniversary.

> Our Lady of Guadalupe is a national parish, which is a parish established to care for people of a particular nationality. It has no geographic boundaries and in fact, a recent survey of membership showed that parishioners at Our Lady of Guadalupe come from more than 50 zip codes. About half are from 78702, the local neighborhood.
>
> Many other parishioners, such as administrative assistant Sylvia de la Rosa, were initially from the neighborhood and have moved to other parts of the city but still consider Our Lady of Guadalupe home. Oblate Father J. C. Cain, the current pastor, said people choose Our Lady of Guadalupe for many reasons. Some are "church shopping" while the church's name attracts others (Alfredo Cárdenas).

The Oblates remained in charge of Our Lady of Guadalupe in Austin from 1925 until very recently.[9]

Perales' protests and the Church's official responses

Alonso S. Perales' passionate work on behalf of Mexican or "Latin American" communities, as well as his profound investment in Catholicism and involvement in Catholic organizations, enabled him to notice when injustices against Mexicans and Mexican Americans, principally segregation, took place within the Church itself. In his list, "Some places where Mexicans are discriminated against in Texas either by denying them service or by segregating them from Anglo-Americans," Perales noted that such discrimination existed within the Catholic Church itself. Calling attention to the fact that segregation took place within the religious as well as the secular sphere was only his first step. In the 1940s and 1950s, he directly confronted Catholic authorities about the "embarrassment and humiliation" that segregated churches and parochial schools caused Mexican Americans. His papers contain evidence of several such instances.

In the early 1940s, a Father Smith in Raymondville attempted to segregate the Mexican-origin and Anglo parishioners in Raymondville by building a new church. Protesting the plan, Perales wrote forcefully to Bishop Ledvina of the Diocese of Corpus Christi[10] on behalf of aggrieved Mexican-American Catholics in Corpus Christi.

> . . . The position assumed by the petitioners I represent, and which I am sure is shared by the entire population of Mexican or Hispanic descent of the United States, is, FIRST that there never should be any segregation of the Latin Americans from the Anglo Americans anywhere merely because of race, and, SECONDLY, that the present time, more than at any time in the history of our Nation—the United States of America—the interests of our country require that there be no discrimination against persons of Mexican or Hispanic lineage anywhere, not even in the churches . . . (AP letter to Emanuel B. Ledvina, July 5, 1944).

Perales was unmoved by the unwanted "generosity" of donors who supported building a new, segregated church.

> As for the money of which Your Excellency states has been donated by good people of other extractions in other parts of the country for building the particular church Father Smith has in mind, I will say that we Americans of Mexican descent, and all inhabitants of Mexican lineage generally, prefer not to have any Church at all than to have a Church which has built with money contributed by the understanding that it is to be "A CHURCH FOR MEXICANS ONLY" . . . [T]he segregation of our people at any time and place, merely because of race is un-Christian, undemocratic and un-American, and, therefore all thought of continuing its practice must be given up by all of us NOW for all time to come. . . . (AP letter to Emanuel B. Ledvina, July 5, 1944)

Canon law was on the side of the Mexican Americans of Raymondville; if they lived within the boundaries of the territorially defined parishes, no pastor should have been able to force them to join a segregated or national parish. There is no reply from Bishop Ledvina in Perales' papers; it's impossible to determine, from that source alone, whether the bishop responded.[11] In any event, Perales wrote to Archbishop Lucey on July 8.

Lucey replied that his position as archbishop did not give him direct authority over bishops within the archdiocese "in the matter of church building." (Robert E. Lucey to AP, July 8, 1944, Box 7, Folder 14). Surely the cleric's characterization of segregation as a "matter of church building," as if an administrative matter of little import, could have provoked great frustration for Perales. Perhaps Lucey might have exerted some measure of moral influence or pressure; his actions over the next two decades betrayed no reluctance to speak frankly and forcefully. In the summer of 1944, however, Lucey was still relatively new to south Texas. Ledvina was almost seventy-six years old and had been a bishop for over twenty-three years (Goldapp, 2006, p. 63). Perhaps the archbishop, despite his superior position within the Catholic hierarchy, deferred to the older and more experienced Ledvina out of respect or a distaste for a direct challenge. It is also true, however, that Lucey had not yet—at this point—taken a firm public stand against segregation of Mexican-origin or "Hispanic" Catholics.

Today in Raymondville, there are two Catholic parishes: Saint Anthony, founded in 1907, and Our Lady of Guadalupe, established in 1927. As far as I have been able to determine, the plan to build a separate "Mexican only" church in the 1940s did not come to fruition. Perhaps the Archbishop exerted quiet personal influence behind the scenes with Bishop Ledvina, prospective funders or others; his correspondence with Perales only reveals part of the story.[12] What we do know is that a critical mass of Mexican-American Catholics opposed the building of a separate church, and that their complaints reached both the bishop and archbishop. The organized opposition of would-be congregants was key. The Extension Society, faced with many compelling needs and demands, would have been foolish to spend scarce resources building an unwanted and vexatious church.

The first Catholic church in San Antonio—other than the sanctuary inside the Alamo Mission—was the San Fernando Cathedral, established in 1738 (Archdiocese of San Antonio, 1949, p. 24). Because Mexicans and Mexican Americans mostly populated the Cathedral parish, the Catholic Church created St. Mary's for Anglos in 1910 (Archdiocese of San Antonio, 1949); as we have seen, non-Mexican priests and congregations pushed Mexican Americans out of local, territorial parishes and towards San Fernando (Matovina, 2003, *Guadalupe and Her Faithful*, pp. 100, 136). In the 1940s, both St. Mary's and San Fernando parishes had schools.

In 1947, Gregory Gaytan of San Antonio asked for Alonso Perales' help. Gaytan wanted his son, a fifth grader, to attend the parochial school long attached to St. Mary's Church on North St. Mary's Street. Gaytan believed that the school refused admission to his son because of his ethnicity. Perales prepared an affidavit for Gaytan's signature and submitted it to Archbishop Lucey. The Archbishop took the complaint seriously enough to write a very emotional letter to Father Sammon.

You are quoted as stating to Mr. Gaytan that I have made a rule excluding Latin-American children from certain parish schools, presumably among others, that of St. Mary's Parish. I am described as entertaining the thought that St. Mary's Parochial School is for a class of people higher than our beloved Latin-Americans.

I can hardly believe that you ever made such a statement directly or indirectly although I must point out that Mr. Gaytan . . . swears that you did . . . It seems to me that anyone who has reached the age of seven years in this archdiocese would know where I stand regarding discrimination against all minority groups. I have suffered a great deal because I have stood for social justice and it is certainly news to me that I have ever given directions of any kind at any time looking to the exclusion of Latin-Americans from our parochial schools. The truth is that I am gradually forcing all Pastors and all Sisters to accept Latin-American children everywhere. (Robert E. Lucey to Joseph P. Sammon, September 23, 1947)

Sammon vehemently denied the allegation of discrimination (Joseph P. Sammon to Robert E. Lucey, September 25, 1947).

Gaytan's child was denied admission to St. Mary's School, Sammon explained, because he lived within the San Fernando Cathedral parish boundaries, which had a parochial school open to him. Sammon expressed the suspicion that "we were being baited on this issue and that [Gaytan] is either lying, unable to understand English or ignorant of the facts governing parochial territories."

Any and every Catholic child within our boundaries is welcome to attend their parochial school. Those not now attending are being sought after. The next in line are those children attending public schools because there is not a school attached to their parish. Lastly, those children in parishes where the parochial school is filled to capacity, and then only with the permission of the pastor. (Joseph P. Sammon to Robert E. Lucey, September 25, 1947)

Sammon told the Lucey that 125 children of Mexican descent attended St. Mary's School, and that their parents were "all good, humble, hardworking people, willing to make sacrifices that their children might get the best" (Joseph P. Sammon to Robert E. Lucey, September 25, 1947).

The Archbishop forwarded a copy of Father Sammon's letter to Perales, characterizing the controversy as a "misunderstanding" and affirming the idea of Gaytan's son going to the San Fernando School (Robert E. Lucey to AP, September 26). The fact that both Archbishop Lucey and Father Sammon voiced shock at the allegation of race segregation is a sign of significant change.

On the other hand, there is no discussion in the correspondence of why Gaytan may have wished his son to attend school at St. Mary's rather than San Fernando. What if Sammon specifically meant St. Mary's, rather than Catholic education generally, as "the best," and what if the characterization of St. Mary's as "the best" was based on objective factors? Gaytan might have wanted his son to attend St. Mary's for reasons of convenience, but it is more likely that he sought admission because he perceived St. Mary's to be a better school, or a better-equipped school, than San Fernando's. Gaytan's attempts on behalf of his son's education, and implicit comparison between a largely Anglo school and a predominantly Mexican one, foreshadow the actions of Edgewood parents twenty-one years later (Cárdenas, 1997; Scracic, 2006; Raymond. 2007, p.p. 498-595).

Moreover, from this distance, both Sammon and Lucey letters seem disingenuous in their rigid allegiance to territorial boundaries. There were no geographical limits to attendance at the San Fernando Cathedral; in contrast, Catholics of Mexican descent from all over the city were encouraged to go there. Perhaps Gaytan found it hypocritical for the clergy to be insisting on adherence to territorial boundaries when it came to keeping his son out of St. Mary's, at the same time that they freely ignored such rules when it came to excluding Mexicans from "regular" territorial parishes and directing all Mexicans to a single "Mexican" church. The paper record does not reveal whether Lucey commented on Sammon's unkind remarks about Gaytan. Sammon insulted Gaytan by implicitly equating the inability to understand English with immoral deeds such as "baiting" and "lying," and the unflattering attribute of "ignorance."

On April 25, 1952, Alonso S. Perales went to an ill-fated meeting in Austin, planning to address the gathering about discrimination within Catholic schools. Father Theodore Radtke, then the executive secretary of the Bishops' Committee for the Spanish Speaking (BCSS, later, the Bishops' Committee for Hispanic Affairs) had convened the meeting, so the gathering was significant. Perales had addressed BCSS before (Carlos Castañeda to AP, letters of October 2, October 22, and October 30), but the Austin meeting had been very important to him. He later wrote that

> the Holy Spirit [had] prompted me to raise my voice to protest in behalf of our school children and their parents against the humiliations to which they are often subjected in their endeavor to acquire an education in parochial schools. (Perales to Frederick A. Schmidt, April 28, 1952)

Convincing the Bishops' Committee to root out discrimination within Catholic institutions would have been a great accomplishment. The attempt failed when Father Radtke denied Perales the opportunity to speak at the April 1952 meeting.

A priest from Georgetown, Father Frederick A. Schmidt, wrote Perales a letter of commiseration in which he expressed his sorrow at the treatment Perales received even as he rationalized both Radtke's actions and those of the Church.

> I was at the meeting yesterday afternoon, and I know you must have felt badly after what happened there. I think everyone especially Father Radtke was quite tired and wanted the meeting to end. (Frederick A. Schmidt to AP, April 26, 1952)

While Schmidt tried to soften the blow, making it appear that the termination of the meeting was not a personal affront, Perales knew better. In his answer to Schmidt, Perales revealed that Radtke acknowledged the real reason for ending the meeting: "he had done what he did because the meeting was too public" (AP to Frederick A. Schmidt, April 28, 1952).

The rebuke stung. Schmidt's superficially friendly but deeply condescending letter could not have provided much comfort and Perales responded cordially but coolly. Even Schmidt's letterhead—St. Helen's Mexican Missions—must have irked Perales, who addressed the letter to Schmidt at "St. Helen Church." Schmidt misspelled Perales' first name as "Alonzo"; Perales wrote back to "Fredrick" rather than "Frederick." Schmidt began with the overly warm "Muy querido amigo" followed by a comma. Perales responded with "Dear Father Schmidt," followed by a business-like colon. Schmidt closed his comments with an invitation to "stop in whenever you like" and an ungrammatical as well as presumptuous "tu" construction ("aquí tiene tu casa"). Schmidt signed his letter "Padre Federico."

Schmidt's letter revealed tone-deafness, but the real problem was its content.

Since you did not get a chance to say your piece, I do not know its full import. I know it must hurt you deeply that some who want a Catholic education are denied it and turned away from Catholic schools. 'Language parishes' have to take their share of building parochial schools. Predominant English speaking may want their own anglos for several reasons. Correct me if I am wrong: Anglos ease the headache of financial support a little better because there are more of them in the middle class; then the pastor of anglos has to buck the prejudices of the people which could close his school; his hands seem tied. A pastor is responsible for his parish and not for the flock of his neighboring Spanish speaking pastor. (Frederick A. Schmidt to Alonso S. Perales, April 26, 1952)

Schmidt's missive is not completely coherent. He seems to take for granted the existence, and appropriateness, of separate parishes for Anglos and Spanish-speaking persons. Given that assumption, he finds Anglo pastors' and parishioners' reluctance to take responsibility for a neighboring parish reasonable. This circular reasoning seems to ignore the possibility of a "flock" with both Anglos and Mexicans, English and Spanish-speakers, but in a post-script typed sideways on the page Schmidt not only acknowledges but boasts of an integrated school. In an obvious attempt to prove his personal freedom from bias to Perales, Schmidt wrote, "Father Dore and I built a parochial school in Lampasas for ALL who come, and it's doing fine under Father Healy."

Schmidt's condescension, intentional or not, continued:

Canon law comes in there. Since you are a lawyer I think you would appreciate looking into what canon law has to say. It gets a great deal of praise from the legal profession.

Schmidt appears not to have considered the possibility that Perales might already have researched canon law.

Perales adopts several different tones in his letter to Schmidt. At first he refers to the incident as "a temporary setback" in a noble and worthy cause. Then he sounds bitter, remarking that he "accepted [Radtke's] explanation [for ending the meeting], but in the future [he would] make [his] views known to the Clergy only at such times and places as [he might] be permitted to do so." Determination follows, "I am fully determined to aid our Clergy in bringing all Spanish speaking Catholics of the Southwest closer to God," as well as firmness: "it will be absolutely necessary that all those practices which cause [Spanish-speaking Catholics] embarrassment and humiliation be done away with." Finally, Perales speaks as if he had little or no faith in Catholic clergy to do the right thing. "I hope and pray to God that I may someday have the money (or that I may be able to find a good soul who has it) to built [sic] Churches and Parochial Schools to which everybody will be perfectly welcome regardless of race, color, or creed" (Alonso S. Perales to Frederick A. Schmidt, April 28, 1952). If the Church would not behave justly, it would be up to righteous individual Catholics to personally make changes.

This letter leads its readers on a tour through the emotions of a civil rights lawyer, or perhaps any social justice advocate, emotions that exist simultaneously in tension with each other. They also reveal the Perales' stance as a critic, advocate, loyal member of the Catholic Church, and deeply religious man. Referencing "the Holy Spirit," he implicitly argues that his position is morally superior to those of the Catholic authorities who dismiss him, but he does not directly criticize any individual person. He does not plead, warn, threaten, or even reference the strength of all the people who agree with him, as he had in letters to Bishop Ledvina, Archbishop Lucey, and secular authorities. Rather he emphasizes, albeit with bitterness, that he will speak only when spoken to. This backhanded way of complaining about being treated disrespectfully serves to emphasize his low status in the Church as a layperson compared to his higher status in the broader community as a lawyer and public speaker. Perales' correspondence could be flowery, deferential, and effusively deferential. None of those qualities are present here. He must have been deeply disappointed and angry.

Perales' papers reveal a third specific complaint about segregation within the Catholic Church. His target in 1953 was St. Anthony's Church, a church in Runge in the southeastern part of Karnes County, founded in 1901 (Archdiocese of San Antonio Parish Locator). In 1953, Perales first wrote a polite letter to the parish priest of St. Anthony's Church, Reverend Rudolph C. Hoffman.

> The people of Mexican descent of Runge, Texas, are very unhappy because they are segregated from the parishioners of other extractions in the Catholic (St. Anthony's Church) in Runge. I am wondering whether anything could be done to end such segregation. Is there something I could do to help, Father Hoffman. I am certain you are not at fault in any way and that is the general feeling among the offended ones. They do feel, however, that you are the boss in your Church. (Perales to Rudolph C. Hoffman, January 13, 1953)

Receiving no answer, Perales forwarded a copy of his letter to Hoffman to Lucey, but without any specific appeal for Lucey to do anything (AP to Robert E. Lucey, February 14, 1953). It has the feel more of "for your information" correspondence than Perales' earlier ardent advocacy, and I have not found evidence of Perales' pursuing the issue.

Perales' efforts to improve the status of Mexicans and Mexican Americans in the U.S. Catholic Church did not meet with success during his lifetime, a frustration that in no way diminishes the valor or value of his efforts. The apparent lack of progress within the Church is striking, however, given both the modest but steady civil rights advances Mexican Americans were making during the mid-twentieth century, and the presence of a powerful ally in the Church hierarchy, particularly in Texas, during Perales' lifetime.

Alonso S. Perales and Archbishop Robert E. Lucey

Perales' life and work intersected with that of the Reverend Robert E. Lucey, who served as the Archbishop of the Archdiocese of San Antonio from 1940 and until Lucey's 1969 retirement. Archbishop Lucey was the highest-ranking member of the Catholic hierarchy in Texas during the last two decades of Perales' life, as Perales practiced law and advocated for the rights of Mexicans and Mexican Americans. The title for Perales' second book, *Are We Good Neighbors?* (1948) came from an address by Archbishop Lucey with Lucey's permission; the speech itself is the first testimony in the collection (Alonso S. Perales letter to Robert E. Lucey, March 20, 1947;[13] Robert E. Lucey letter to AP, March 24, 1947; Alonso S. Perales, *Are We Good Neighbors?*).

During the 1940s and 1950s, Archbishop Lucey was arguably also the highest-ranking member of the Catholic hierarchy in the United States who took a sympathetic interest in Mexicans and Mexican Americans, although beginning in the 1940s Midwestern Catholic leaders also attended to the spiritual needs of Mexican migrant laborers via the Bishops Committee on the Spanish Speaking as well as their own local efforts (Badillo, 2003, pp. 37-40).

The lawyer Perales and Archbishop Lucey, Catholic and committed to the rights of Mexicans and Mexican Americans in Texas, had significant interests in common. The differences in their political trajectories and priorities were also clear. Archbishop Lucey and Alonso S. Perales came to their advocacy for Mexicans and Mexican Americans from different backgrounds and with different priorities. While Perales was primarily concerned with civil rights, Lucey was a labor advocate, more passionate about what have been variously called "human needs," "human rights," or "economic rights"—that is, not so much liberty and equality but humane working and living conditions. Perales was a Mexican American first; he saw anti-Mexican racism as the cause of Mexican and Mexican-American poverty in the United States Perales and Lucey both supported the Fair Employment Practices Committee (FEPC) established by President Franklin Delano Roosevelt in 1941 (Zamora, 2009, p. 137; Perales, *Are We Good Neighbors?*), but the FEPC complainants tended to be refinery workers, government office employees, or members of labor unions. The FEPC did not concern itself with (so-called) "unskilled" agricultural workers or migrants (pp. 229-238); in this omission, it followed the exclusions of the National Labor Relation Act (N.L.R.A.).[14]

Perales, a lawyer and diplomat, did not readily identify with the working class (or even use such terminology). Cynthia E. Orozco has noted that the LULAC constitution of 1929, compared to the constitution of the Order of Sons of America (OSA),

. . . reflected the influence of new leadership, with Canales, Perales, Eduardo Idar Sr., and Saénz as its major authors. It embodied the ideas of the new middle class and lawyers Perales and Canales . . . [It] exhibited a new middle-class ethos. Little mention was made of the workplace as a site of struggle. Race and citizenship, not class or gender, became primary. (Orozco, 2009, p. 180)

Perales' writings, moreover, provide abundant evidence that he wielded his elite status, a status he earned rather than inherited, strategically as he advocated for Mexicans and Mexican Americans. While according full dignity to other people regardless of their social status, he did not hesitate to highlight his own education and standing, or that of other Mexicans and Mexican Americans. Perales was, at least in public, an elitist. He did not allow Anglos or anyone else to mistake him for a laborer.

Archbishop Lucey, in contrast, was first committed to rights of workers; his interest in Mexicans and Mexican Americans was founded in his horror at the low wages and horrific working conditions of Mexican-origin laborers specifically. Lucey, whose own father had died in a preventable railroad accident in 1900, when the future archbishop was only nine years old (Bronder, 1982, p. 6), grew up steeped in pride in working people and disgusted by employers' disregard for their laborers. As an adult, Lucey recalled, "It was barbaric how companies treated their workers in those days, just barbaric" (Bronder 7). When President Lyndon B. Johnson attended services at San Fernando Cathedral in 1966 (the first president to do so), he recalled, according to one report "that his acquaintance with Archbishop Robert E. Lucey . . . dates back [to] when both men were eating the grapes of wrath":

"I remember Archbishop Lucey (in the 30s) and he wasn't nearly as respectable [sic] then as he is now—he was kind of a Bolshevik in the minds of a lot of people when he came down here," the President said.

"I remember his writing me and quarreling and fussing and just doing everything that he could do to try to help do something for people who were picking pecans in San Antonio for eight cents an hour." ("LBJ recalls archbishop as 'bolshevik'")

His support of organized labor was a constant in Lucey's life. As bishop of the Diocese of Amarillo between 1934 and 1940, Lucey had insisted that parishes building churches should do so by employing union labor and paying prevailing wages (Bronder, 1982, pp. 53-55). As Archbishop of San Antonio, Lucey continued to insist on fair wages for construction workers and maintained close ties to organized labor (Rendón).

Lucey moved from Amarillo to San Antonio in 1940, where he was officially installed as Archbishop in 1941 (Catholic Archives of Texas Episcopal files). He left the Panhandle before the great post-World War II migration of Mexican and Mexican-American workers to Castro and Deaf Smith Counties, and into the Diocese of Amarillo more generally (Foppe, 1976, pp. 117-139; Catholic Diocese of Amarillo, *The Journey of the Diocese of Amarillo*, 2001, pp. 38-44; Catholic Diocese of Amarillo Parish files; Tijerina).[15] Nevertheless, Lucey stayed attentive to and was moved by the hardships faced by Mexican-origin laborers in Texas (Catholic Diocese of Amarillo, 1959). Lucey's concern for migrant agricultural workers fueled his creation of BCSS (Bronder, 1982, 77). Beginning the enterprise soon after his arrival in San Antonio (Acosta), Lucey saw the successful launch of BCSS in 1945. According to his biographer, Saul Bronder (1982), Lucey "divided his efforts on behalf of migrant farm workers between public opposition to their exploitation and practical program of assistance (p. 79).

Alonso S. Perales admired Archbishop Lucey's efforts with respect to agricultural laborers. In particular, Perales was pleased that Lucey, as well as representatives of the National Catholic Welfare Conference, the National Catholic Rural Life Conference and other Catholic organizations, testified and lobbied against the Bracero program in Congress (Vento 34-37), as Perales did. These allies all pointed to the deleterious effects that the availability of a huge force of poorly paid and exploited Mexican nationals had on Mexican Americans, depressing their wages and forcing them into migrant labor to survive. Perales wrote Adela Sloss-Vento, "I believe Archbishop Lucey deserves credit for championing our cause in the midst of such opposition on the part of the Southern Growers and the Texas Congressman" (Sloss-Vento, 1977, p. 36). Perales cared for Mexican-origin laborers, both Mexican nationals and U.S. citizens, but they were not his primary focus. Archbishop Lucey's concerns for Mexican-origin peoples did extend beyond the workplace. Early in his appointment, he reported to the Vatican liaison that Mexican Catholics in the archdiocese were

> a people, ostracized and held in social and economic subjugation . . . they are paid frightfully low wages . . . and barely manage to exist in poverty, disease and squalor. If a Mexican is murdered, the officials do little or nothing about it. The Mexicans in Texas, even if born here, are classed with Negroes. (Bronder, 1982, pp. 63-64)

Apparently, the standard for atrocious treatment and low status was that of the Negro; to say Mexicans were classified as such was a damning indictment in itself.

Yet Lucey had to be converted to the cause of equal rights for Mexicans and Mexican Americans *within* the Catholic Church. Ethnic and racial segregation within Catholic populations was the norm during Perales' and Lucey's lives. Sr. Regina Foppe, writing in 1976, was still tiptoeing as she wrote about Catholic West Texas of the 1930s.

> A number of communities, some large, others smaller, appear to have set up congregations with segregation patterns, separating the English-speaking from the Spanish-speaking. Among them were Amarillo, Big Spring, Hereford, Lamesa, Lubbock, Midland, Plainview, San Angelo, and Slaton. While the language barrier may have been the primary reason in the majority of the cases, distance and a lack of transportation may have been a deciding factor in building or moving a church structure into the barrio. However, it seems that in some situations there may have existed racial-cultural discrimination within Catholic communities . . . While no explicit reasons for this segregation have been discovered in documents, it may have been unrecognized prejudice of the Anglo communicants. (pp. 89-91)

Lucey, at least early in his career, did not dissent. He accepted the assumption that Anglos and Mexicans should not only worship separately (for instance, with Spanish masses at one time and English masses at another), but also that they should have separate church buildings.

As Lucey prepared to move from California, he received a letter from an Anglo Catholic in Lubbock. B.W. Kieran wrote to the incoming bishop that "[a]t present, we [the Anglos] have no place to worship, other than the Mexican Church, situated on the outskirts of the city, a very undesirable location . . . We have forty to sixty white families, who are reasonably well fixed and outstanding business people" (Foppe, 1976, 90). The "outstanding [Catholic] business people" of Lubbock built their new, segregated church, St. Elizabeth's, in 1935, dedicating it in 1936 (Diocese of Amarillo, 2001, *Journey*, p. 72; St. Elizabeth's Catholic University Parish).[16] They no longer needed to go to the Guadalupe barrio to pray. Under then-Bishop Lucey's direction, no other churches were built in the Amarillo Diocese.

When Lucey addressed the question of "Democracy and Church-Related Schools" in a major 1948 address at Our Lady of the Lake University, he did not mention segregation. Perales (1974) included the presentation in print in *Are We Good Neighbors?* (pp. 45-52). In 1948, Lucey's principal message was that democratic institutions would wither without religion. "Society," he argued, "cannot live of relative morality . . . without a divine legislator there is no test, no standard, no measure of right and wrong; everything is futility and frustration" (Perales, 1974, 51). The function of Christian colleges was to imbue its students with the Church's immutable values so they might go forth and "rebuild a broken world" (p. 52).

The Archbishop's only reference to ethnic Mexicans in "Democracy and Church-Related Schools" was to note their frequent absence in schools of any kind, observing that "[w]e believe a good education is necessary for every American child and Dr. George I. Sanchez . . . has just declared that one half of the children of Texas who have Spanish names do not spend even one day in school throughout the year" (p. 49). Lucey had been concerned about Mexican children's school attendance for some time. In the 1943 address that gave Perales' volume its title, and that begins Part I of *Are We Good Neighbors?*, Lucey had apparently seen the solution to Mexican education in truant officers, criticizing a

> type of false economy is the refusal to employ truant officers for the compulsory education of our children in public or private schools. A study of school enrollment in the city of Dallas was made recently and it was found that 3800 children were not even registered in school. Many of them were Latin Americans. In this Archdiocese we estimate that there are 10,000 children of grammar school age not enrolled in any school. Most of them are Spanish-Americans. By refusing to employ attendance officers we may save a few hundred dollars annually but we spend all of that and much more to provide jails, juvenile courts and probation officers for delinquent youth; and the loss in social values is beyond estimation. (Lucey in Perales 1948, p. 14)

Decades later, Timothy Matovina (2003) would describe "a fundamental gap" between Hispanic and Anglo Catholics ("A Fundamental Gap"). The gap between Lucey and Mexican Americans with respect to their understanding of problems in education is difficult to fathom. Lucey's oddly discordant contribution appears in a volume condemning anti-Mexican discrimination. It is hard to fathom his insensitivity to the problem—especially since he had asserted his firm opposition to segregation within the Catholic schools of the Archdiocese the previous year (Robert E. Lucey to Joseph P. Sammon, September 23, 1947).

Rev. John J. Birch,[17] Executive Secretary of the Bishops Committee for the Spanish Speaking, seemed to have a fuller understanding of the extensive challenges ethnic Mexicans faced in Texas. Birch's testimony before the President's Committee on Civil Rights in 1947 cited multiple problems. These included the exploitation of ethnic Mexicans in the work place; their exclusion from many residential areas; lack of water, playgrounds, street lights in Mexican neighborhoods; inadequate school buildings and badly trained teachers; widespread discrimination in public accommodations; exclusion from membership in organizations; exclusion from jury service; and the economic conditions that compelled migration and child labor ("The Spanish Speaking People of the United States" pp. 53-57).

Moreover, Timothy Matovina (2003) reports that Lucey deplored segregation, including the segregation of Mexicans and Mexican Americans.

Shortly after his arrival in San Antonio, he had noted that many Catholic pastors induced Spanish-speaking Catholics who lived within their parish boundaries to attend San Fernando. He deemed this a segregationist practice, called it his "special headache," and subsequently fought to integrate parishes. (p. 136)

Nevertheless, Lucey never spoke out as consistently ferociously against anti-Mexican segregation within the Catholic Church as he did on labor issues, or, after 1954 and especially during his retirement, against segregation of Negroes (numerous clippings in the Catholic Archives of Texas Episcopal files).

Priest and theologian Virgilio Elizondo (1997) has critiqued an image of Mexicans and Mexican-American workers:

Mexican help is good to have around because Mexicans are always happy and docile. They never give any problems to the Anglo-Saxon masters. They have a quick smile as they respond with a polite,'Yes, Sir,' or 'Yes, Ma'am,' as if it were a great privilege to be in the presence of their Anglo lords. They appear to be satisfied with so little. (pp. 29-30)

It is the saintly and dignified worker for whom Archbishop Lucey felt great sympathy and on whose behalf he exerted his considerable influence. Perhaps it is not too great a stretch to suggest that many Anglos who worked with and supported the Bishops' Committee on the Spanish-Speaking shared Lucey's perspective to one degree or another.

What I mean by that is that it is one thing for Anglos to see impoverished Mexican workers as children of God, as worthy of spiritual instruction, and as deserving of food, shelter, and kind and dignified treatment. It was (and perhaps to some degree still is) another thing for Anglos to accept Mexican-origin people as full equals, not to mention leaders. Archbishop Robert E. Lucy offered paternalistic care in both the material and spiritual realms—and that material support may have indeed saved lives. Alonso S. Perales sought something different: equality and respect.

Anti-communism and its effects

The political evolution of Alonso S. Perales took a turn in the 1950s, as did that of Archbishop Lucey and the Catholic Church. Two powerful political currents, anti-communist fervor and the civil rights movement, characterized the United States during the late 1940s and early 1950s; at moments these movements conflicted, and at other moments fed one another. In Perales, they clashed, exacerbating pre-existing differences between Perales and his contemporary Mexican American advocates and would-be allies.

Of the many civil rights landmarks of the 1950s, two are particularly salient here, as they demonstrate both progress on a large scale, and Perales' personal status as odd-man-out during this period. In the secular realm, the U.S. Supreme Court ruled with civil rights advocates in both *Hernandez v. Texas* and *Brown v. Board of Education* in 1954. As Michael Olivas (2006) and his colleagues have demonstrated, Mexican-American advocates achieved a significant victory as the U.S. Supreme Court acknowledged in *Hernandez* that Mexican Americans lived as "a separate class" in Texas, and were thus entitled to Fourteenth Amendment equal protection (*Colored Men and "Hombres Aquí"*). This milestone was the result of a coordinated effort of Mexican-American lawyers including John (Johnny) Herrera, James DeAnda, Gustavo C. García and Carlos Cadena (Oliva 213-218). In 1948, Perales had supported García in the latter's race for the San Antonio ISD school board and praised García's victory against school segregation in *Delgado v. Bastrop ISD* to his friend Carlos Castañeda. Perales had also successfully tried *Clifton v. Puente*, striking a racially restrictive covenant, with Carlos Cadena in the same year ("Equal Protection and the Racial Restrictive Covenant" p. 369; AP to Castañeda, June 30, 1948).[18] Nevertheless, Perales was seriously at odds with at least García and Herrera and was not part of this group.

In April 1954, Archbishop Lucey denounced racial segregation, as his biographer and the Archdiocese of San Antonio repeat with pleasure, a month before *Brown v. Board of Education.* Lucey, as other social-justice oriented clergy, became increasingly active in condemning racial discrimination and segregation, although all indications are that these clergy were talking about discrimination against African Americans. The Catholic Church, just as the secular authorities in Texas, practiced discrimination against Mexicans and Mexican Americans, but refused to acknowledge doing so. Such acknowledgement, it would appear, was a pre-requisite for addressing segregation, but Church personnel had rebuked Perales for even raising the subject.

Meanwhile, Perales was increasingly spending his time studying, thinking, writing, and speaking about Catholic theology. In the secular realm, Perales' anti-communism, heretofore most salient in his diplomatic career and personal life as a friend of Anastocio Somoza García, for example, began to shape his political work locally and in Texas. Caught up in the furor of the times, Perales even courted, with flattering correspondence and participation in electoral politics, a new and powerful ally in Texas—Governor Allan Shivers—on account of Shivers' ferocious anti-commu-nism. In February 1954, Shivers had declared that because "[m]embership in the Communist Party is..mass murder," he would seek legislation making such mem-bership punishable by electrocution (Carleton, 1985, p. 259). Perhaps he had been inspired by the execution of Ethel and Julius Rosenberg eight months earlier.

Shivers also accused his challenger, former Judge Ralph Yarborough, of both being a Communist and an integrationist (Odintz). Perales agreed, writing to Gover-nor Shivers that in his opinion, both Yarborough and State Representative Maury Maverick, Jr., were "soft" on communism. Maverick, Jr., had opposed Shivers' attempt to make membership in the Community Party a capital offense (Maverick, 1997, p. 60). Perales wrote admiringly to the governor.

. . . [Y]ou jumped the fence and declared yourself unequivocally against com-munism, and that is exactly what we Americans must insist that each and every candidate do in determining whether [sic] or not we are going to support him; and that any candidate who refuses to do that is not deserving of our considera-tion at the polls. (AP letter to Allan Shivers, August 19, 1954. Box 2, Folder 20)

Perales also wrote to a lawyer, Elmer Stahl, complaining of handbills circulated on behalf of Yarborough that called Shivers a "cabrón. Perales identified the printer, the distributors, and "the man behind" the handbill by name (AP to Stahl, September 2, 1954).

In endorsing Shivers, Perales departed from many Mexican American activists and advocates who supported Yarborough. The elder Maury Maverick had even played a supporting role in *Hernandez v. Texas*, encouraging Hernandez's lawyers to "press on with jury selection challenges" and signing the U.S. Supreme Court brief (Olivas, 2006, p. 214 and n. 30). Perales wrote an article in *La Prensa* and campaigned for Shivers in South Texas, boasting later that Shivers had done better in those counties where Perales had campaigned. Perales also denounced other Mexican-American leaders to Shivers:

Here are the names of some persons who campaigned against Your Excellen-cy recently: Gus C. Garcia, Dr. George I. Sanchez, D,. [sic] Hector Garcia, J. J. Herrera, Ed. Idar, Jr., Virgilio C. Rosel, Tomas M. Rodriguez. (AP to Allan Shivers, September 13, 1954)

Perales did not include Carlos Cadena in his condemnation. (Note that Perales addressed the governor as "Excellency," the honorific used to address bishops and archbishops.)

In supporting Shivers, Perales made clear that his political priority was anti-communism. Such a view was consistent with that of the dominant Catholic Church hierarchy in the United States of the time, which was also passionately committed to anti-Communism. Archbishop Lucey, though a target of red-baiters, including Shiv-ers, because of his support of workers and organized labor, was in fact fiercely anti-communist himself.[19] Writing about the "Catholic counterculture," historian James Fisher notes, "no one in the American church of the 1940s and early 1950s believed it was possible to be at once a Catholic and a Communist, socialist or self-styled Marxist of any flavor" (Ellwood, 1997, p. 35). Richard Gid Powers (2004) has written persuasively about the reasons for the rise and fall of Catholic anti-communism, an important facet of Perales' life and work that deserves a separate article, but it is sufficient here to note Powers' observation that "[a]nti-Communism was for many American Catholics the bond between their piety and their patriotism" (p. 31). Indeed, both Catholics and Mexican-origin people were already the targets of discrimination and subject to suspicion as "outsiders." Bigots doubted the "Americanness," loyalty, and patriotism of both Mexicans and Catholics. For some Mexican Americans, and some Catholics, their vulnerability to accusations of being un-American, could fuel extreme displays of anti-communism. If we look only at their shared anti-Communist fervor, Shivers' attraction for Perales makes sense.

Shivers, however, was consumed with another passion as well, and that was his fierce opposition to desegregation, an issue that became increasingly salient after the Supreme Court ruled in *Brown*. Shivers argued for state supremacy and rejection of the Supreme Court's ruling. In 1956, he supported the segregationists in Mansfield, Texas, who threatened violence against the African American students who had planned to integrate the high school; Shivers' very flagrant disobedience of federal law was a direct precursor to the confrontation of segregationists and federal troops in Little Rock, Arkansas (Duff). Shivers was most vehemently opposed to the integration of Black and white people, and associated integrationists with Communists. Perales, though in favor of the integration of African Americans (as his correspondence with Castañeda makes clear) however, has not publicly opposed this segregation. Neither had many of his contemporary advocates for Mexican-American rights. As Neil Foley (2010) has observed, despite correspondence between Thurgood Marshall and University of Texas professor, George I. Sánchez, about ending school segregation, "Mexicans and African Americans pursued their struggles for equality..in largely parallel universes" (p. 20).[20] African Americans were subject to *de jure* discrimination; Mexican Americans to *de facto* discrimination. Foley (2010) observes that

> many European immigrant groups, whether Russian Jews, Sicilian Catholics, Irish, or Germans, sought to shed the stigma of their Old World roots by reconstituting their identities as white Americans. They would have been crazy not to. (p. 14)

Some, but (as Foley takes pains to note) not all, Mexicans claimed white identities (p. 14).

Perales' anti-communism increasingly took him away from causes and strategies that he had embraced in the 1940s. For instance, Perales had participated in hearings during the formation of the U.N. and promoted the idea of using international forums in the fight against discrimination within the United States, as the NAACP and the American Committee for the Protection of the Foreign Born would each later do (Anderson, American Committee). In contrast, Shivers and other anti-Communists that fomented Texas' Red Scare opposed the United Nations. In *Cold War Civil Rights,* Mary Dudziak provides compelling evidence that anti-communism and civil rights activism often went hand in hand in the early 1950s; some of the most important civil rights advances courts, executive branch, and legislatures of the United States were due, in part, to the fear that racism in the United States provided "ammunition" and "propaganda" to Communists. For Shivers and the segregationist Shivercrats with whom Perales began to associate, civil rights advocacy was akin to, or the same as, communism. It might have been possible for Alonso S. Perales to have worked—in harmony with other Mexican-American advocates—simultaneously for civil rights, against what he saw as the evils of communism, and within the Catholic Church until his death. His new political alliances as well as his denunciation of other Mexican-American civil rights lawyers, complicated that possibility.

The last deferential rebel?

Perales was ferociously defensive of his Catholic faith and the Catholic Church, so much so that he could not tolerate people who lambasted the Church or its clergy in public. In one letter to Carlos Castañeda, he imagined "a conspiracy, perhaps based in Mexico City," that included "los protestantes y masones" as well as fellow Catholics, out to "ridicule and bring our Church into disrepute" (AP to Carlos Castañeda, February 28, 1948; see also AP to Carlos Castañeda, March 9, 1949). As an official in the Knight of Columbus who took his membership and position very seriously, he felt a duty to protect the Catholic Church against its critics.[21] His repugnance for those who criticized the Catholic Church must have caused him great cognitive dissonance, at the least, when he found himself disappointed at the Church's dismissal of his complaints of anti-Mexican discrimination.

Perales accorded Archbishop Lucey and other Catholic authorities not only the *respect* that they demanded but did not reciprocate to this lay leader, but also deference. When he could no longer maintain his deferential tone, he ceased to confront the Catholic Church about its inequities. Rather, he turned his attention away from internal Church politics and increasingly toward the personal spiritual realm. Several factors—his inherently conservative personal nature, his conservative politics, his religiosity, and the spirit of the times—likely combined to result in such discomfort with challenging ecclesiastical authority. In this aspect, Perales epitomizes a man of the 1950s, to whom the challenges and disruptions that were to emerge in the coming decade would have been unthinkable—even though their roots, in national liberation movements around the world, and in the African American and Mexican-American civil rights movements, became evident immediately following World War II.

Within the Catholic Church, discontent and the spirit of change found expression in the Second Vatican Council, taking that vehicle in directions no one—least of all Pope John XXIII—had predicted. Perales did not live to see, for example, the publication by John L. McKenzie of *Authority in the Church*, or the Catholic Theological Society's awarding of a prestigious prize to the book in 1967 ("Archbishop labels Bible scholar's views 'heretical' "). McKenzie, a Jesuit priest at the time he wrote his most influential books, argued that the authority of the Catholic Church inhered in its service; that authority belonged to the whole Church, not just the hierarchy; and that the New Testament recognized love as the only real power: views that

Archbishop Lucey deemed "heretical" ("Archbishop labels Bible scholar's views 'heretical'"; "Rev. John L. McKenzie, 80, Dies; Leader in Catholic Bible Research"). Around the country, a critical mass of priests and nuns confronted the U.S. Catholic Church for its support of the Vietnam War and perceived lack of energy in addressing other social ills; clergy and lay people alike challenged the requirement of priestly celibacy and Humanae Vita, Pope Paul VI's encyclical on birth control. In Los Angeles and San Antonio, Mexicans and Mexican Americans would challenge the Church about anti-Mexican discrimination within the Church and inattention of the Church to the needs of the community, especially via groups such as Católicos por La Raza, Padres Asociados para Derechos Religiosos, Educativos y Sociales (PADRES), and Las Hermanas.

In the San Antonio Diocese, Lucey found himself locked in battle with a group of priests, partially over substantive issues such as the priests' involvement in anti-war protests and pro-farm worker protests, but chiefly over the question of his authority itself ("Archbishop says all Catholics bound to follow Pope's teaching"; "San Antonio archbishop asks priests to renew their ideals"; "Prelate defends Church authority, rebukes critics"; "Archbishop Lucey Still Anti-Rebel").

Many Mexicans and Mexican Americans were appreciative of the Archbishop's efforts on their behalf, especially in the realm of social services. Lucey had consistently supported Mexican and Mexican-American laborers on workplace issues, including fair wages and living conditions. Mexicans and Mexican-American priests, moreover, were few in number. Nor did Lucey's consistent support of organized labor no longer counted for as much among "liberals." By the mid-1960s, the primarily Anglo left wing of the Democratic Party split with organized labor over the war in Vietnam. Construction workers (represented as primarily Anglo, an image that may have been accurate in other parts of the United States) were described derisively as "hard hats" and associated with the right wing, pro-war "hawks." Thus, whatever good will Lucey had engendered among organized labor, or within Mexican communities in Texas, counted for little in the battles to come. Lucey was, in fact, a hard-line ecclesiastical conservative who viewed claims of equality as preposterous and belittled the "little theologians" who had

> [begun] to shout, 'Every man is allowed to follow his own conscious. Freedom of conscience is a gift of God.' . . . These arguments are specious. In Texas we call them hogwash ("Archbishop says all Catholics bound to follow Pope's teaching").

The portrait of Lucey as benevolent dispenser of social goods lost out, at least in the short-term, to the portrait of Lucey as a relic and tyrant.

In September, 1968, a substantial number of dissident priests in the Diocese of San Antonio openly rebelled against Archbishop Lucey.[22] They wrote directly to Pope Paul VI; Amleto Cardinal Cicognani, papal secretary of state; Carlo Cardinal Confalonieri, prefect, Vatican Congregation for Bishops; Archbishop John F. Dearden, of Detroit, president, National Conference of Catholic Bishops; and Archbishop Luigi Raimondi, Apostolic Delegate to the United Sates, requesting Lucey's resignation. In doing so, they complained of "a spirit of fear and intimidation in the archdiocese;" "atmosphere of fear, alienation and dissatisfaction;" and a breakdown of communication between the priests and Lucey ("San Antonio archbishop asks priests to renew their ideals"). Lucey's biographer, Saul E. Bronder (1982), gives an account of the result.

Pope Paul did not reply immediately but finally sent a representative to investigate the matter. By the time he arrived, however, the papal delegate to the United States had sent a letter to the archbishop reminding him that the Second Vatican Council had stated that prelates should resign their offices at the age of seventy-five. Lucey was seventy-seven. After much deliberation, he submitted his resignation, with the request that it be effective several months later, so as to avoid suggesting any connection with the events of the previous two years. Mindful of the great contributions Lucey had made to the church, the Pope acceded to Lucey's request. (Lucey, Robert Emmett)

Lucey's fall came at about the same time, and for some of the same reasons, as his friend Lyndon B. Johnson, also a "social liberal" and authoritarian, anti-communist "hawk."

Father Patrick (Patricio) Flores, who would later become the Archbishop of San Antonio, described a sense of abandonment by the Catholic Church as he gave the keynote address at the First National Hispanic Pastoral Encuentro, which took place in Washington, D.C., in 1972. "We have appealed to the church, and have been abused, and the church has remained silent" (Matovina (2003), citing Richard Edward Martínez at p. 113, in Matovina's review of PADRES). Two decades had passed between Perales' most poignant appeal to an Anglo apologist for the Catholic Church, and Flores' call to action. Over those twenty years, despite Mexican-American appreciation for Lucey's support for migrant workers, the taken-for-granted deference of Mexican Catholics had dissipated.

Conclusion

Using Perales' own writings, this chapter has begun to investigate Perales' work against discrimination and segregation within the Catholic Church. Many questions about the specific episodes in Raymondville, San Antonio, Runge, and Austin, remain. So does a broader question: Alonso S. Perales' deep commitments to Catholicism not only inspired him to seek justice, but also created opportunities and fostered certain alliance. At the same time, however, there were ways in which the nature of Perales' Catholic practice hindered, complicated, or foreclosed other alliances and opportunities, in the context of mid-twentieth century Texas: a Texas deeply steeped in both anti-Mexican racism and anti-Catholicism. I look forward to continued conversations about the ways in which Perales' Catholicism served his civil rights work, and it what ways the fact that he was a Catholic—in this particular historical juncture and this place—politically complicated his advocacy for Mexicans and Mexican Americans in both the secular and religious spheres.

It must have been difficult to be Alonso S. Perales; I also imagine it must have been difficult to be in a close but non-familial relationship with him. His papers leave no doubt that he worked obsessively as an advocate, accomplishing much but also experiencing many bitter disappointments. By his own account, he had a bad temper (Perales to Castañeda, August 29, 1946). He made enemies and those enemies mocked him cruelly (The Committee, "The Circus Perales"). Perales remained an outsider in the very communities—Mexican American and Catholic—to which he had devoted his life. His passion for righteousness, as he saw it, cost him dearly.

Perales displayed extraordinary personal, political, emotional, and indeed spiritual courage. When Perales called attention to the existence of discrimination, and more specifically segregation, within Catholic institutions, he was using words that others had avoided applying to the treatment of Mexican Americans.

Even historian Carlos E. Castañeda (1976) was elusive on the subject: that anti-Mexican discrimination, including segregation, was widespread, is clear in *Our Catholic Heritage*, but Castañeda did not name it as such. Castañeda, born in Mexico in 1896 and resident of the United States since 1906 (Almaráz), was more than a formidable scholar. He had also wrestled in the muddy realpolitik of both academia, where he was the target of racism and the victim of factionalism, and public service, as superintendent of schools in Del Rio and as regional director of the Fair Employment Practices Committee (FEPC) (Almaráz, 1998, pp. 69-70; 105-145; 216-252).

Castañeda was deeply, broadly, intimately, and acutely aware of anti-Mexican discrimination in Texas and in the U.S. Southwest. A passionate advocate for the rights of Mexicans and Mexican Americans alike, Castañeda told the U.S. Senate Labor Committee on Labor and Education that, "if a workers name is a Spanish one, he is considered as Mexican and treated as such." He testified that relief agencies apparently believed that "anybody with a Spanish name" did not "have to eat so much" or as well as Anglos (Almaráz, 1998, p. 258). Castañeda enthusiastically celebrated litigation to end anti-Mexican discrimination in the public schools and encouraged Perales to even as he also embraced electoral strategies and lamented Perales' loss in his own school board race (CEC to AP, April 17, 1946).[23] Likewise, Castañeda protested discrimination against African Americans and Native Americans (Almaráz, 1998, pp. 260-261; 244-245).

Perales was Castañeda's contemporary, lawyer, and friend. The men corresponded with each other about local, state, national, and church politics; activities of the Knights of Columbus, Holy Name Society, and other Catholic organizations; the comings and goings of priests; their research, public addresses, and their families. In their extensive letters, Castañeda and Perales asked for each others' assistance in locating employment for young people—mostly men—they had mentored; they gossiped about rivals and overrated (in their view) ostensible allies such as Paula Kibbe and George Sánchez; they asked for and dispensed advice; and they dined together with their families (Castañeda papers, Box 34, Folders 1, 2, and 3). Perales and Castañeda had much in common, but their shared devotion to Catholicism, reflected in the majority of their letters, was their deepest bond (Castañeda papers, Box 33, Folders 10, 11, and 12; Box 34, Folders 1, 2, and 3).

To criticize the government and political adversaries is difficult and often dangerous. To confront admired, revered—and even beloved—authorities, and to call attention to the contradictions and failings in one's own spiritual community: that is wrenching. If there were other Texas-Mexican public intellectuals who criticized anti-Mexican racism within the Catholic Church before 1950, I have yet to learn about them. Even Carlos E. Castañeda, outstanding academic, well-regarded public servant, the indisputable expert on Catholic history in Texas and target of bigotry himself, refrained from calling attention to the anti-Mexican discrimination rampant within the Catholic Church. That painful but understandable fact does not diminish Castañeda's contributions as advocate and historian. It does, however, serve to highlight the unique and courageous nature of Perales' work.

Works Cited

Published Materials

About us. (n.d.). *Catholic Diocese of Brownsville*. Retrieved from http://www.cdob.org/about-us/about-the-diocese.

Acosta, T. P. (n.d.). Bishops' Committee for Hispanic Affairs. *Handbook of Texas Online*. The Texas State Historical Association. Retrieved from http://www.tshaonline.org/handbook/online/articles/icb05.

Ainslie, R. (1995). No dancin' in Anson: An American story of race and social change. Northvale, New Jersey: J. Aronson.

Almaráz Jr., F. D. (1998). *Knight without armor: Carlos Eduardo Castañeda, 1896-1958*. College Station: Texas A & M Press.

Almaráz Jr., F. D. Carlos Eduardo Castañeda. (n.d.). *The Handbook of Texas Online*. Retrieved from http://www.tshaonline.org/handbook/online/articles/fca85.

Anderson, C. (2003). Eyes off the prize: The United Nations and the African American struggle for human rights, 1944-1955. Cambridge: University of Cambridge Press.

Archbishop labels Bible scholar's views 'heretical' [Clipping from an unknown newspaper in ecclesiastical files]. (1967, December 3). Catholic Archives of Texas.

Archbishop says all Catholics bound to follow Pope's teaching [Clipping from an unknown newspaper in ecclesiastical files]. (1968, August 16). Catholic Archives of Texas.

Archbishop Lucey still anti-rebel. [Clipping in ecclesiastical files]. (1969, June 6). *Austin American-Statesman*. Catholic Archives of Texas.

Archdiocese of San Antonio (n.d.). Parish Locator. Retrieved from http://www.arch-sa.org/ParishLocator/.

Badillo, D. A. (2003). *Latinos in Michigan*. East Lansing, Mich.: Michigan State University Press.

Barnes, S. J. (1948). Bitterness on our border. In Perales, A. S. (Ed.) *Are we good neighbors?* (pp. 78-86). San Antonio: Artes Gráficas.

Barton, P. (2006). *Hispanic Methodists, Presbyterians, and Baptists in Texas*. Austin: University of Texas Press.

Birch, J. J. (1947, May 14). The Spanish speaking people of the United States, testimony before the President's Committee on Civil Rights, May 14, 1947, Washington, D.C. In Perales, A. S. (Ed.) *Are we good neighbors?* (pp. 53-57). San Antonio: Artes Gráficas.

Bronder, S. E. (1982). Social justice and church authority: The public life of archbishop Robert E. Lucey. Philadelphia: Temple University Press.

Bronder, S. E. (n.d.). Lucey, Robert Emmett. *The Handbook of Texas Online*. Retrieved from http://www.tshaonline.org/handbook/online/articles/flu14.

Cárdenas, A. (2007). Our Lady of Guadalupe parish celebrates 100 years. *Catholic spirit: In our parish*. Diocese of Austin. Retrieved from http://www.austindiocese.org/newsletter_article_view.php?id=1445.

Cárdenas, J. A. (1997). *Texas school finance reform: An IDRA perspective*. San Antonio: Intercultural Development Research Association.

Carleton, D. E. (1985). Red scare!: Right-wing hysteria, fifties fanaticism, and their legacy in Texas. Austin, Texas: Texas Monthly Press.

Castañeda, C. E. (1976). Our Catholic Heritage in Texas, in seven volumes, 1519-1936, volume VII, 1836-1950. New York: Arno Press.

Castillo, A. (1996). Goddess of the Americas: Writings on the virgin of Guadalupe. New York: Riverhead Books.

Catholic Church & Gilbert, M. J. (1949). Archdiocese of San Antonio, 1874-1949: An illustrated record of the foundation and growth of parishes, missions, and religious institutions in that part of Texas under the spiritual jurisdiction of the See of San Antonio. San Antonio: Schneider Printing Company.

Catholic News Publishing Company. (2005). *A Guide to religious ministries for Catholic men and women*. New Rochelle, NY: Catholic News Pub. Co.

Christian, C. E. (n.d.). Herrera John J. *Handbook of Texas Online*. Retrieved from http://www.tshaonline.org/handbook/online/articles/fhe63.

Ciesluk, J. E. (1944). National Parishes in the United States. (Doctoral dissertation). Available from ProQuest Dissertations & Theses database. (UMI No. 0165965).

Connolly, N. P. (1938). *The canonical erection of parishes: An historical synopsis and commentary*. Washington, D.C.: Catholic University of America Press.

Cruz, G. R. (n.d.). San Antonio, Catholic archdiocese of. *Handbook of Texas Online*. Retrieved from http://www.tshaonline.org/handbook/online/articles/ics01).

De Luna, A. (2002). *Faith formation and popular religion: Lessons from the Tejano experience*. Lanham, Boulder, New York, Oxford: Rowman & Littlefield.

Díaz-Stephens, A. M. (1998). The Hispanic challenge to U.S. Catholicism. In Casarella, P., and Gómez, R. (Eds.) *El cuerpo de Cristo: The Hispanic presence in the U.S. Catholic church* (pp. 157-179). New York: Crossroad Publishing.

Diocese of Amarillo (2001). The journey of the Diocese of Amarillo: 75 Years on the Llano Estacado, 1926-2001. Amarillo: Diocese of Amarillo

Dripping Springs, Texas. (n.d.). In *Black City Info*. Retrieved from http://www.blackcityinfo.com/texas/texas-dripping-springs.html.

Diocese of Corpus Christi. http://www.diocesece.org/

Dudziak, M. L. (2000). *Cold War civil rights: Race and the image of American democracy*. Princeton: Princeton University Press.

Elizondo, V. P. (1997). *Guadalupe: Mother of the new creation*. Maryknoll, New York: Orbis.

Elizondo, V. P. (2000). *The future is mestizo: Life where cultures meet* (Revised edition). Boulder: University of Colorado Press.

Elizondo, V. P. (2003). *Galilean journey: The Mexican-American promise*. Maryknoll, New York: Orbis.

Ellwood, R. S. (1997). The fifties spiritual marketplace: American religion in a decade of conflict. New Brunswick, N.J.: Rutgers University Press.

Evangelizadoras del barrio: The rise of the missionary catechists of divine providence. *U.S. Catholic Historian 21*(1), 53-71.

Father John L. McKenzie, 80; biblical scholar. (1991, March 8). *Los Angeles Times.* Retrieved from http://articles.latimes.com/print/1991-03-08/news/mn-2615_1_roman-catholic-church.

Flores, L. (1948). Discrimination in Texas. In Perales, A. S. (Ed.) *Are we good neighbors?* (pp. 40-44). San Antonio: Artes Gráficas.

Flores, R. R. (1984). *Popular fiestas and evangelization* (Unpublished Master's thesis). University of the Incarnate Word, San Antonio, TX.

Flores, R. R. (2002). Remembering the Alamo: Memory, modernity, and the master symbol. Austin: University of Texas Press.

Foley, N. F. (2010). *Quest for equality: The failed promise of black-brown solidarity.* Cambridge, Mass: Harvard University Press.

Foppe, R. E. (1976). The response of the Roman Catholic church to the Mexican Americans in west Texas, 1839 into post-Vatican II (Unpublished Master's thesis). Texas Tech University, Lubbock, Texas.

García, M. T. (1998). Catholic social doctrine and Mexican American political thought. In Casarella, P. and Gómez, R. (Eds.) *El cuerpo de Cristo: The Hispanic presence in the U.S. Catholic Church* (pp. 292-311). New York: Crossword Publishing Company.

García, M. T. (2008). *Católicos: Resistance and affirmation in Chicano Catholic history.* Austin: University of Texas Press.

General description. Retrieved July 17, 2012 from the American Catholic History Research Center and University Archives, Catholic University of America website: http://archives.lib.cua.edu/ncwc.cfm.

Gleason, P. & Coakley, J. J. (1969). Contemporary Catholicism in the United States. Notre Dame: University of Notre Dame Press.

Goldapp, P. (Ed.). (2006). Becoming the body of Christ: A history of the Diocese of Corpus Christi. Strasbourg, France: Éditions du Signe.

Green, G. N. (1979). *The establishment in Texas politics: The primitive years, 1938-1957.* Norman and London: University of Oklahoma Press.

Guglielmo, J. & Salerno S. (2003). *Are Italians white? How race is made in America.* London and New York: Routledge, 2003.

Guglielmo, T. A. (2006). Fighting for Caucasian rights: Mexicans, Mexican Americans, and the transnational struggle for civil rights in World War II Texas. *Journal of American History 92*, 1212-1237.

Hurtado, J. (1976). *An attitudinal study of social distance between the Mexican American and the church* (Doctoral dissertation). Available from ProQuest Dissertations & Theses database. (UMI No. 7610588).

Icasa, R. M. (2003). *Faith expressions of the Hispanics in the Southwest.* San Antonio: Mexican American Cultural Center.

Ignatiev, N. (1995). *How the Irish became white.* London and New York: Routledge.

Jacobson, M. F. (1998). *Whiteness of a different color: European immigrants and the alchemy of race*. Cambridge, Massachusetts: Harvard University Press.

John Birch Society. (n.d.). John Birch. Retrieved from http://www.jbs.org/john-birch.

Knopp, K. (2009). A short history of new St. Mary's Church. *KLRU*. Retrieved from http://www.klru.org/paintedchurches/fredericksburg.html.

Knopp, K. (2009). The painted churches of Texas: Echoes of the homeland. *KLRU*. Retrieved from http://www.klru.org/paintedchurches/fredericksburg.html.

Ladino, R. D. (1996). Desegregating Texas schools: Eisenhower, Shivers, and the crisis at Mansfield High. Austin: University of Texas Press, 1996.

LaFarge, J. (1937). Interracial justice: A study of the Catholic doctrine of race relations. New York: America Press, 1937. Print.

LaFarge, J. (1943). *The race question and the negro*. New York: Longmans, Green & Co.

LBJ recalls archbishop as 'Bolshevik' [Clipping from Episcopal Collection of Robert E. Lucey]. (1966, April 22). *Catholic Herald*. Catholic Archives of Texas.

Lamanna, R. A. & Coakley J. J. (1969). The Catholic church and the negro. In Gleason, P. (Ed.) *Contemporary Catholicism in the United States* (pp. 147-193). Notre Dame: University of Notre Dame.

Lucey, R. E. (1948). Democracy in church related schools. In Perales, A. S. (Ed.) *Are we good neighbors?* (pp. 46-52). San Antonio: Artes Gráficas.

Márquez, B. (2006). *Mexican Americans break the color line in Texas politics, 1950-1970*. Retrieved from http://users.polisci.wisc.edu/apw/archives/marquez.pdf.

Martínez, R. E. (2005). *PADRES: The National Chicano Priest Movement*. Austin: University of Texas Press.

Matovina, T. (2003, March 17). A fundamental gap. *America: The National Catholic Weekly*. Retrieved from http.americamagazine.org/gettext.cfm?articleTupeID=1&textID=2855&issueID=426.

Matovina, T. (2005). Guadalupe and her faithful: Latino Catholics in San Antonio, from colonial origins to the present. Baltimore: Johns Hopkins University Press.

Matovina, T. (2006). Review of *PADRES: The National Chicano Priest Movement (2005)*. *Spiritus 6*(1). Baltimore: Johns Hopkins University Press/Society for the Study of Christian Spirituality (SSCS), 137-140.

Maurer School of Law. (1955). Equal protection and the racial restrictive covenant: A reevaluation. *Indiana Law Journal 30*(3). Retrieved from http://www.repository.law.indiana.edu/cgi/viewcontent.cgi?article=2622&context=ilj.

Maverick Jr., M. & Kownslar, A. O. (Eds.). (1997). *Texas iconoclast*. Fort Worth, Texas: Texas Christian University Press.

McCaslin, E. P. (1944). *The division of parishes: A historical synopsis and a commentary*. (Doctoral dissertation). Washington, D.C.: Catholic University of America Press.

Meyer, J. A. & Southern, R. (Trans.). (2008). *The Cristero rebellion: The Mexican people between church and state, 1926-1929*. Cambridge: University of Cambridge Press.

Mickells, A. B. (1950). *The constitutive elements of parishes: A historical synopsis and a commentary*. (Doctoral dissertation). Washington, D.C.: Catholic University of America Press.

Najera, J. (2009). Practices of faith and racial integration in South Texas: A case study of Mexican segregation. *Cultural Dynamics 21*(1), 5-28.

Odintz, M. (n.d.). Yarborough, Ralph Webster. *Handbook of Texas Online.* Retrieved from http://www.tshaonline.org/handbook/online/articles/fyags

Olivas, M. A. (Ed.). (2006). 'Colored men" and 'hombres aquí': Hernandez v. Texas and the rise of Mexican American lawyering. Houston: Arte Público Press.

Olivas, M. A. (2006). Hernandez v. Texas: A Litigation History. In Olivas, M. A. (Ed)., *'Colored men" and 'hombres aquí': Hernandez v. Texas and the rise of Mexican American lawyering.* Houston: Arte Público Press.

Orozco, C. E. (2009). No Mexicans, women, or dogs allowed: the rise of the Mexican American civil rights movement. Austin: University of Texas Press.

Orozco, C. E. (n.d.). Del Rio ISD v. Salvatierra. Handbook of Texas Online. Retrieved from http://www.tshaonline.org/handbook/online/articles/jrd02.

Orozco, C. E. (n.d.). Texas Council on Human Relations. *Handbook of Texas Online.* Retrieved from http://www.tshaonline.org/handbook/online/articles/pqtda

Parish listing. (n.d.). *Catholic Diocese of Brownsville.* Retrieved from http://www.cdob.org/.

Paulist Fathers. (n.d.). The Paulists and the First World War. Retrieved July 17, 2012 from http://www.paulist.org/associates/paulists-and-first-world-war.

Perales, A. S. (1974) *Are we good neighbors?* Reprint. New York: Arno.

Prelate defends Church authority, rebukes critics. [Clipping in ecclesiastical files from an unknown newspaper]. (1968, May 17). Catholic Archives of Texas.

Pius IX. (1870, December 8). *Quemadmodum Deus, Joseph In Magisterium.* Retrieved from http://www.osjoseph.org/stjoseph/magisterium/QuemadmodumDeus.php.

Pius XI. (1937, March 19). *Divini redemptoris, encyclical of Pope Pius XI on atheistic communism, to the patriarchs, primates, archbishops, bishops, and other ordinaries in peace and communion with the Apostolic See.* Retrieved from http://www.vatican.va/holy_father/pius_xi/encyclicals/documents/hf_p-xi_enc_19031937_divini-redemptoris_en.html.

Powers, R. G. (2004). American Catholics and Catholic Americans: The rise and fall of Catholic anticommunism. *U.S. Catholic Historian 22*(4), 17 – 35.

Quiroz, A. (2005). Claiming citizenship: Mexican Americans in Victoria, Texas. College Station: Texas A & M.

Raymond, V. M. (2007). *Mexican Americans write toward justice in Texas, 1973 – 1982.* (Doctoral dissertation). Retrieved from http://repositories.lib.utexas.edu/handle/2152/6260.

Religious Ministries.com (n.d.). *A guide to religious ministries for Catholic men and women: Listing of the religious communities of priests, brothers, and sisters active in the United States.* 26th Ed.

Rendón, J. M. (n.d.). Archbishop Robert E. Lucey and Organized Labor in San Antonio, 1960 – 1968. *The Journal of Life and Culture of San Antonio.* Retrieved from http://www.uiw.edu/sanantonio/Lucey.html

Rodríguez, J. (1994). *Our Lady of Guadalupe: Faith and empowerment among Mexican-American women.* Austin: University of Texas Press.

Roediger, D. R. (2005). *Working toward whiteness: How America's immigrants became white: The strange journey from Ellis Island to the suburbs.* Cambridge, Mass.: Perseus.

salinas, r. (1999). Un trip through the mind jail. In salinas, r. r. *Un trip through the mind jail y otras excursions,* 2nd edition (pp. 55-60). Arte Público Press.

Sandoval, M. (Ed.), Mexican American Cultural Center (San Antonio, Tex.), & Mexican American Cultural Center Tenth Anniversary Forum. (1983). *The Mexican American experience in the church: Reflections on identity and mission : Mexican American Cultural Center Tenth Anniversary Forum.* New York: Sadlier.

Steinfels, P. (1991, March 6). Rev. John L. McKenzie, 80, Dies; Leader in Catholic Bible Research. *New York Times.* Retrieved from http://www.nytimes.com/ 1991/03/06/obituaries/rev-john-l-mckenzie-80-dies-leader-in-catholic-bible-research.html?pagewanted=all&src=pm.

Treviño, R. R. (2003). Facing Jim Crow: Catholic sisters and the 'Mexican Problem in Texas'. *The Western Historical Quarterly 32*(2), 139-164.

Treviño, R. R. (2006). *The church in the barrio: Mexican American ethno-Catholicism in Houston.* Chapel Hill: University of North Carolina Press.

San Miguel Jr., G. (1987). 'Let all of them take heed': Mexican American and the campaign for educational equality in Texas, 1910 – 1981. Austin: University of Texas Press.

St. Anthony's Parish History. Retrieved from St. Anthony's Church and School website: http://www.herefordstanthonys.com/html%20pages/church/History.htm.

St. Elizabeth's Catholic University Church. Retrieved from St. Elizabeth's Catholic University Parish website: http://www.stelizabethslubbock.com/pages/history.html.

St. Francis Xavier – La Feria. Retrieved from St. Francis Xavier Church in La Feria on the Catholic Diocese of Brownsville website: http://www.cdob.org/parishes/st-francis-xavier-la-feria.

St. Joseph Catholic Church, Donna. Retrieved from http://stjosephdonna.com/ default.aspx

Scracic, P. (2006). *San Antonio v. Rodríguez and the pursuit of equal education: The debate over discrimination and school funding.* Lawrence, Kansas: University of Kansas Press.

Sloss-Vento, A. (1977). *Alonso S. Perales: His struggle for the rights of Mexican-Americans.* San Antonio: Artes Gráficas.

South, C. (n.d.). A History of Mexican Americans in California: Historic Sites. *Five Views: An Ethnic History Site Survey for California.* Retrieved fromhttp://www.cr.nps.gov/history/online_books/5views/5views5h84.htm

St. Joseph. (n.d.). *Catholic Online.* Retrieved from http://www.catholic.org/saints/ saint.php?saint_id=4

Thonhoff, R. H. (n.d.). Runge. *The Handbook of Texas Online.* Retrieved from http://www.tshaonline.org/handbook/online/articles/hjr16

Tijerina, A. A. (1979). *History of Mexican Americans in Lubbock County, Texas.* (MA report). Graduate Studies Texas Tech University. Lubbock: Texas Tech Press.

Tyler, Ron. (n.d.). Texas Bird's-Eye Views. Retrieved from http://www.birdseye-views.org/.

U.S. Congress. (n.d.). *Biographical Directory of the United States Congress, 1774 – present.* Retrieved from http://bioguide.congress.gov/biosearch/biosearch.asp.
Watras, J. (1997). *Politics, race, and schools: Racial integration, 1954-1994.* New York and London: Garland Publishing.
Zamora, E. (2009). *Claiming rights and righting wrongs in Texas: Mexican workers and job politics during World War II.* College Station: Texas A & M University Press.

Published legislative and court materials

Brown v. Board of Education, 347 U.S. 483 (1954)
Hernández v. Texas, 347 U.S. 475 (1954)
In *Re: Ricardo Rodriguez*, 81 F. Supp. 337, W.D. Texas 1897
"Caucasian Race – Equal Privileges," Texas House of Representatives, 1943. Adopted by the House, April 15, 1943; adopted by the Senate, May 5, 1943, by a viva voce vote. *General and Special Laws of the State of Texas Passed by the Regular Session of the Forty-Eighth Legislature (48th Legislature)*, Convened at the City of Austin, January 12, 1943, and Adjourned May 11, 1943, published under the Authority of the State of Texas, Sidney Latham, Secretary of State, Claude Isbell, Assistant Secretary of State, page 1119.

Archives

Alonso S. Perales Collection, University of Houston Libraries, Houston, Texas

"Better Schools Committee," mimeographed flyer, March 24, 1948, Box 10, Folder 1
The Committee. "The Circus Perales of San Antonio, Texas." One typewritten page in English, n.d., Box 10, Folder 2.
Paul J. Kilday letter to AP, Box 2, Folder 2
Robert E. Lucey letter to AP, March 24, 1947
Robert E. Lucey to AP, July 8, 1944, Box 7, Folder 14
Robert E. Lucey letter to AP, September 26, 1947, Box 7, Folder 14
Robert E. Lucey letter to Joseph P. Sammon, September 23, 1947, Box 7, Folder 14
Alonso S. Perales (hereinafter "AP") letter to Rudolph C. Hoffman, January 13, 1953, Box 7, Folder 14
AP to Paul J. Kilday, February 8, 1941, 2 pp., Box 2, Folder 2
AP to Emanuel B. Ledvina, July 5, 1944, Box 7, Folder 14
AP to Robert E. Lucey, July 5, 1944, Box 7, Folder 14
AP to Robert E. Lucey, March 20, 1947, Box 7, Folder 14
AP to Robert E. Lucey, February 14, 1953, Box 7, Folder 14
AP to Allan Shivers, August 19, 1954, Box 2, Folder 20
AP to Elmer Stahl, September 2, 1954, Box 2, Folder 20
Ts. AP. "Power at the Polls," Tr., Catholic Conference on the Spanish Speaking of People of Texas, Austin, Texas, April 23-25, 1952.

"Some Places Where Mexicans Are Discriminated Against in Texas either by Denying Them Service or by Segregating Them from Anglo-Americans." Typed,
mimeographed, seven (7) legal-sized pages, page 2, n.d., Box 10, Folder 8
Joseph P. Sammon letter to Robert E. Lucey, September 25, 1947, Box 7, Folder 14

Archives of the Catholic Diocese of Amarillo, Amarillo, Texas

"Mexican Migrant Labor in Amarillo Diocese," Report of November 1959
Parish files
Proposal, Regional Mexican American Cultural Center, San Antonio, Texas, submit-
ted to the Campaign for Human Development, United States Catholic Confer-
ence, Washington, E.C., February 1972. Box: "Hispanic Ministry." Folder:
MACC 1971-1975

Austin History Center

Koch and Fowler. "A Plan for the City of Austin." 1928.

Nettie Lee Benson Latin American Collection, University of Texas at Austin

Carlos E. Castañeda Papers, 1497-1958. For this list, I will refer to Carlos E. Cas-
tañeda as "CEC" Boxes 33, Folders 10, 11, and 12 Box 34, Folders 1, 2, and 3
CEC to AP, April 3, 1946, Box 34, Folder 2
CEC to AP, April 17, 1946, Box 34, Folder 2
AP to CEC, August 29, 1946, Box 34, Folder 2
CEC to AP, October 13, 1947, Box 34, Folder 2
AP to CEC, February 28, 1948, Box 34, Folder 2
AP to CEC, June 30, 1948, Box 34, Folder 2
CEC to AP, October 2, 1948, Box 34, Folder 2
CEC to AP, October 22, 1948, Box 34, Folder 2
CEC to AP, October 30, 1948, Box 34, Folder 2
AP to CEC, March 9, 1949, Box 34, Folder 2

Catholic Archives of Texas, Austin, Texas
Episcopal Files, Archbishop Robert E. Lucey folders (Incomplete, consisting prima-
rily of clippings, programs, and other published documents. Archives at Notre
Dame University hold an extensive collection of Archbishop Lucey's papers.)

Moorland-Spingarn Research Center at Howard University
Online entry for Edwards, Lena, 1900 – 1986, listing of processed collections.
Retrieved from http://www.howard.edu/msrc/manuscripts_processed_listings.
html#e

Notes

[1] A note on terminology: for the most part, I use the noun "Mexican" to refer to any person of Mexican descent and "Mexican American" to any person of Mexican descent living in the United States. Exceptions will be clear from the context. At times, the adjective "Mexican" will refer specifically to *people or institutions* from, of, or pertaining, to the nation of Mexico: Mexican exiles, Mexican authorities, Mexican citizens. When modifying *practices*, the adjective "Mexican" means from or pertaining to "Greater Mexico" in the broad sense used by Américo Paredes and José E. Limón. Mexican churches, for example, are those churches in which the congregants are primarily or exclusively of Mexican descent. Mexican rituals or religious practices are those particular to, or especially associated with, people of Mexican descent, wherever they are.

[2] LaFarge revised his book for publication in 1943, giving it a more precise title: *The Race Question and The Negro,* and providing specific reasons for his decision to focus on "Negro and white relations," rather than on other racial disputes. These reasons included the simple fact that he had more experience with "Negro and white" relations than with other inter-ethnic or interracial encounters.

[3] Kilday assured Perales that he, Kilday, "thoroughly disapprove[d]" of conduct motivated by racial discrimination, but disagreed with Perales about whether the U.S. Congress had the power to make such a law. Kilday invited Perales to propose a draft and a strategy for ensuring its compliance with the constitution, but strongly advised Perales to work for a state law rather than a federal one (Kilday to AP, January 31, 1941).

[4] This chapter addresses the time period roughly between the Civil War and Perales' death in 1960.

[5] As viewers of "Pee Wee's Great Adventure" (1985) may remember, "there's no basement in the Alamo."

[6] The Diocese of Amarillo parish files for Muleshoe, Plainview, Hereford, and Tahoka provide detailed information about the funding and staffing of missions and summer school for Mexicans. Of course I have not attempted to look at the archives of all the Catholic dioceses in Texas, but my requests to conduct research were denied in all dioceses but Amarillo.

[7] The street had been named "Guadalupe" since about 1839; all north-south streets in what is now "downtown Austin" were named after Texas rivers (Austin History Center).

[8] "Begun as a railroad labor camp adjacent to the railroad tracks, South Colton developed in the same way as many Chicano barrios and colonias throughout the southwest and the midwest. In most cases, Mexican labor came in with the railroads and established lasting communities from what were originally railroad labor camps. These communities were founded next to the tracks because that was often marginal land, affordable and close to work, and because *de facto* segregation existed. In Colton, the Chicano community established itself on an open section of land southeast of the Southern Pacific Railroad tracks where most of the Mexicanos worked" ("South Colton"). See also Tijerina.

[9] An Oblate priest still served Guadalupe as of April 2007, when Alfredo Cárdenas wrote "Our Lady of Guadalupe Parish Celebrates 100 Years."

[10] Raymondville was part of the Diocese of Corpus Christi between and 1965. In 1965, the Vatican created the Diocese of Brownsville by separating Cameron, Willacy, Hidalgo, and Starr Counties from the Diocese of Corpus Christi (Catholic Diocese of Brownsville).

[11] The archives of the Diocese of Corpus Christi are closed; my request for permission to look at Ledvina's correspondence for this limited purpose was rebuffed. My request for information about any correspondence between Perales and Ledvina was also unsuccessful. (Phone conversation with Cyrus Richards, archivist of the Diocese of Corpus Christi, on July 13, 2012.)

[12] I have not reviewed Archbishop Lucey's papers. Those at the Archdiocese of San Antonio were not public at the time of this research. There is also a significant collection of Lucey's manuscripts at Notre Dame University that I have not visited.

[13] In-text citations to future correspondence to or from Alonso S. Perales will indentify him only as "AP."

[14] The definition of "employee" at 29 U.S.C. § 152 excludes "any individual employed as an agricultural laborer, or in the domestic service of any family or person at his home, or any individual employed by his parent or spouse, or any individual having the status of an independent contractor, or any individual employed as a supervisor, or any individual employed by an employer subject to the Railway Labor Act."

[15] Andrés Tijerina and Regina Foppe focused much of their work on Lubbock, which was part of the Diocese of Amarillo until 1983 (Diocese of Amarillo 2001, 57).

[16] St. Elizabeth's was designated "St. Elizabeth's University Parish" in 1980 (Diocese of Amarillo 2001, 72).

[17] Not to be confused with John Birch, the Army Captain and fundamentalist Baptist missionary after whom the John Birch Society was named (John Birch Society). Rev. Birch should also not be confused with the Rev. John J. Burke, CPC, (a Paulist priest), who was General Secretary of the NCWA (García 305). I violate the practice of referring to an organization by its full name before using its acronym for a son purpose. The NCWA, founded as the National Catholic War Conference during World War I, changed its name but not its acronym to the National Catholic Welfare Conference in 1922. Birch was a crucial figure in both incarnations of the NCWC. After the events described in this chapter, in 1966, the NCWC divided into two separate entities: the National Council of Catholic Bishops (NCCB) and the United States Catholic Conference (USCC) (Paulist Fathers, American Catholic History Research Center and University Archives). There are ample grounds for confusion of the priests Birch and Burke. John J. Birch of the Bishops' Committee in Texas, and John J. Burke of the NCWC, later rector of Catholic University, were both interested in Mexicans. Monsignor Burke was particularly interested in the Cristero Revolution and the refugees who fled after its failure. The national figure Burke, of Catholic University, died in 1936, well before the founding of the Bishops' Committee in Texas.

[18] Thank you to Michael Olivas for this observation.

[19]Lucey's support of President Lyndon B. Johnson and the war in Vietnam was based on Lucey's anti-communism, and reinforced by Johnson's appointment of Lucey to a 1967 delegation to observe elections in South Viet Nam.

[20]Mexican-American advocates—including John J. Herrera and Carlos Castañeda—apparently made attempts, not always successful, to join forces the "Negroes" with in electoral politics (CEC to AP, April 11, 1947, on Herrera's letterhead and concerning Herrera's campaign to fill a state senate seat in a special election). The Anglo political elite in San Antonio exercised its considerable muscle against both Mexican Americans and African American school board candidates in the 1940s (AP to CEC, April 9, 1946; Better Schools Committee, March 24, 1948).

[21]See Castañeda, Vol. 7, Chapter X, "Columbianism in Texas," which is a very detailed account of the efforts by the Knights of Columbus to counter anti-Catholic rumors and bigotry.

[22]The article, "Archbishop Lucey Still Anti-Rebel," gives the number of priests as sixty-seven; the article entitled "San Antonio archbishop asks priests to renew their ideals" provides a count of fifty-one (51) priests.

[23]Castañeda sent Perales a copy of the district court decision in *Mendez v. Westminster*, perhaps twice (April 3, 1946 and April 17, 1946). "I have marked with red pencil certain sections, but I think you will enjoy reading the whole thing. You really ought to. Now, then, why can't we get a similar case here? Lets [sic] get busy and work up a good case. I can get the money to fight it to the better end and take it t the Supreme Vourt [sic] of the U.S. if necessary. Lets [sic] think the matter over. Sanchez says he is doing something, but I doubt it" (April 17, 1946).

Letters, Piety, and Politics

Changing Voices: Approaching Modernity from Mexican to Mexican American to Chicano in the Epistolary Archives of Alonso S. Perales

Norma Adelfa Mouton

This study of the epistolary archives of the Alonso S. Perales Collection housed at the University of Houston draws upon a paper presented by José F. Aranda, Jr., in 2010[1], entitled "Origins of the 'Transnational' Character of Mexican-American Literature." In his presentation Aranda coins the phrase "modernity of subtraction" to describe the way that Mexican Americans after 1848 have been required to accept the limitations placed upon them by the dominant Anglo-Saxon culture. A modernity of subtraction is one that requires the Mexican American to subtract elements of his culture from his nature in order to be accepted by the Anglo Americans around him (Aranda, pp. 15-16). This can be anything from not being allowed to speak Spanish in public forums to being expected to perform well in school without the same advantages that the Anglo-Saxon children have in the way of books and materials to actually changing the spelling of one's name to make it more acceptable to the English speaker.

Letters in the Perales archives written by Mexican Americans, with a few written by Anglo Saxons on behalf of Mexican Americans, have been analyzed in this study to determine how a modernity of subtraction is expressed and to determine if the expression of that subtraction has changed specifically before and after World War II. While this study supports Aranda's premise, many letters point to a more complex issue in the discrimination experienced by the writers. Most of the early letters demonstrate how the hegemony tended to exclude the subaltern completely whenever possible; applying a subtraction of individual characteristics only when complete exclusion was not possible or desirable because of laws like the Civil Rights Act of 1964[2] that prohibited it and exacted punishment upon the representative of the hegemony responsible for the discrimination.

Enrique Dussel (1993) defines modernity as a European phenomenon and argues that the "periphery . . . [is] . . . consequently part of its self-definition" (p. 65). Thus the term "transnationalism" is less easily associated with "Mexican-American literature prior to the Chicano/a Movement . . . [of] the late 1960s/early 1970s" (Aranda, 2010). Understanding the term "transnationalism" in the context of literature before the Chicano/a Movement is complicated by "the role that coloniality played in the territories ceded to the United States after the Mexican American War" (Aranda, 2010). The prefix "trans" is associated with

the transitions that occurred when one colonial matrix gave way to yet a more powerful one; . . . the transitory promises of a modernity that accompanied the Anglo-American colonial matrix . . . [and] the sense of betrayal and confusion . . . [engendered by the vulnerability of] the prior Spanish-Mexican order . . . [as well as] the transparency of the raw naked power of the nation-state. (Aranda, 2010, p. 3)

So it is that "transnationalism is linked to an analysis of modernity that posits its rise not just with capitalism and racism, but as an invention that arose from Europe's colonization of the Americas" (Aranda, 2010, p. 3). Further, the 'coloniality of power' reflected in these texts written before the Chicano/a Movement but after 1848 is often representative of not only the hegemony of the Anglo American political force, but also of the Mexican subversion of the social capital of those Mexicans living in the north (Aranda, 2003, p. 16).

In order to understand what "this dual focus on modernity and a 'coloniality of power'" offers to a study of U.S. literature, one must turn to the work of Enrique Dussel, Anibal Quijano and Walter Mignolo who define this perspective in Latin American Studies (Aranda, 2010 p. 5). Mignolo also uses the expression of "colonial difference" (Mignolo, 2010, x) in seeking to name "the kind of modernity that was visited on a 'territory' conquered by war and words in the mid-nineteenth century" (Aranda, 2010, p. 6). The fluctuations of a changing nation-state felt by the community of Mexican Americans caught up with the changing geopolitical border between 1848 and 1960 resulted in that community existing "outside the state sanctioned narratives of nation-building" (Aranda, 2010, p. 4). Hence they lived in a "modernity lodged between the United States and Mexico" (Aranda, 2010, p. 5).

Only after the Constitution of 1824, when Mexico had broken all ties with Spain did they turn to colonizing their northern territories. A short twelve years later, in 1836, the Battle of the Alamo and the subsequent Battle of San Jacinto caused Mexico to lose its northern territories leading eventually to the Treaty of Guadalupe-Hidalgo in 1848. The communities established in Mexico's northern states had only barely begun to take on a Mexican national identity when they had to accommodate themselves to the Anglo-Saxon national identity of the United States (Aranda, 2010, pp. 8-10). This was a national identity that brought with it the narrative of Manifest Destiny. Such changes could not be effected overnight (Aranda, 2010, p. 9). Those who were unable or unwilling to adapt and accept the changes found themselves "discipline[d], punish[ed], and alienate[d]" (Aranda, 2010, p. 10).

This expression of modernity Aranda calls a "modernity of subtraction," a phrase he has borrowed and modified from a sociological study by Angela Valenzuela. While Valenzuela's study focuses on Mexican-American school children during the last twenty years, Aranda argues that its conceptual model "would hold true for any period after 1848." Aranda has synthesized Valenzuela's work that shows that the American education system subtracts resources from Mexican-American youth in two ways: "it dismisses their definition of education which is . . . grounded in Mexican culture . . . [and it] encompasses subtractively assimilationist policies and practices designed to divest Mexican students of their culture and language" (Valenzuela, 1999, p. 20). In the first instance, Valenzuela's example focuses on the cognates "education" and *educación* and demonstrates that misconceptions concerning the meaning of the Spanish term and its Mexican cultural content lead to a fatal misinterpretation of Mexican and Mexican-American conceptual orientation on the part of the educational institution and its representatives. As Valenzuela (1999) states, "although *educación* has implications for pedagogy, it is first a foundational cultural construct that provide instructions on how one should live in the world. With its emphasis on respect, responsibility, and sociality, it provides a benchmark against which all humans are to be judged, formally educated or not" (p. 21). Rejection of the Mexican definition of *educación* "constitutes a dismissal of [the] culture as well (Valenzuela, 1999, p. 23).

In the second instance, Valenzuela (1999) points out how it is that while rules that require students to speak English at all times have been abolished, "Mexican youth continue to be subjected on a daily basis to subtle, negative messages that undermine the worth of their unique culture and history" (p. 172). Valenzuela also points out that apart from denigrating the use of Spanish, names and surnames are often mispronounced out of ignorance of the rules of Spanish pronunciation (p. 173). These are only two examples of the subtractive practices that Valenzuela observed. In this study, subtractive practices range from the most blatant elimination of the person from the public sphere to the more subtle such as discrimination through false assumptions concerning Mexican American's capacity for education. According to Valenzuela, "mainstream institutions strip away students' identities, thus weakening or precluding supportive social ties and draining resources important to academic success" (p. 10). The same can be said for any institution dominated by the hegemony.

This analysis, in considering how a "modernity of subtraction" functions, looks precisely at how the subaltern is disciplined, punished, and/or alienated by the dominant culture. The shift from total separation or alienation from the dominant culture to discipline or punishment for being unable or unwilling to accept the changes required by the dominant culture demonstrate the subtle changes that went into setting the stage for the civil actions of the Chicano/a Movement mentioned above.

All but a few[3] of the letters analyzed were written in response to a request made by Alonso S. Perales in his weekly commentary in *La Prensa* of San Antonio. In that article Perales requested that his readers send in specific information detailing incidents of discrimination experienced by them or their family or friends. He not only requested details of the experience, but also specific information as to the perpetrator and location of the event. The majority of the letters reporting such events are dated 1944 and 1945. Letters written before 1944 either tended to describe specific incidents of discrimination or discrimination in more general terms. Letters after 1945 and through 1964 were fewer in number, but also described incidents of discrimination with the details that Perales requested. There were three letters that were missing the first page, that had not been dated or the dates for which were illegible but that contained details of discrimination.

The first letter dated March 8, 1932 is written in English and is a copy of a letter written by a Hispanic naturalized citizen to a Mr. D. E. Kirgan. This copy has a note in perfect Spanish to Perales asking his opinion (AP letter from D.E. Kirgan, March 8, 1932, Box 2, Folder 1).[4] The writer, Mr. R. Austin (AP letter from R. Austin, January 13, 1932, Box 1, Folder 23), is apparently perfectly bilingual and so has already surpassed one of the major hurdles to acceptance by the dominant culture. His letter is a plea for improvement of classroom facilities for the Mexican community in Mission, Texas (AP letter from R. Austin, January 13, 1932, Box 1, Folder 23). The letter is written in a formal register and a straightforward tone. While this letter is meant to represent the plight of the Mexican-American community to a prominent Anglo leader it cannot be considered typical of the majority of the expressions of discrimination found in the collection because the writer appears to be better educated than most of the people for whom he is advocating.

On November 30, 1936, Pedro Fernández wrote a letter in Spanish to Perales concerning the classification of Mexican Americans as other than white on forms required by the Social Security Administration. The issue of *mestizaje* had long been one used to separate Mexican Americans from Anglo Americans, but it was an issue that had recently been fought and won in Congress. Still because the public had not yet been made fully aware of the laws, many continued to classify Mexican Americans as "colored" based on their Hispanic surnames. The letter asked that Perales translate the missive into English so that it could be published in the *Victoria Advocate* and so bring the issue to the attention of the English-speaking public (AP letter from Pedro Fernández, November 30, 1936, Box 1, Folder 31). In a subsequent letter by Pedro Fernández dated December 11, 1936, he notifies Perales that a local Anglo-American lawyer has been quoted in the local newspapers as stating that all Mexican Americans should be classified as white. Fernández then goes on to state that while officials at the post office are now allowing people to specify "white" on official documents, they are later adding the term "Mexican" and passing it off saying that they need to clarify nationality when no nationality is requested on the form. In this way, some of the people whose forms are amended are not of Mexican nationality but Americans. This is an example of tying to separate out the Mexican Americans from the greater pool of Americans and thus subtract them from the pool.

Essiquio Garza wrote a letter in Spanish dated November 2, 1937, in response to an encounter with Perales. Garza relates an incident that occurred in front of the Luna Bar on October 27, 1937, at 7:30 p.m. A car pulled up and stopped in front of the bar with two men in the front seat (AP letter from Essiquio Garza, November 2, 1937, Box 1, Folder 34). A second car pulled up and a man got out (AP letter from Essiquio Garza, November 2, 1937, Box 1, Folder 34). The owner of the bar poked her head out of the door and commented that it was the constable of Sinton, Texas (AP letter from Essiquio Garza, November 2, 1937, Box 1, Folder 34). The constable came around to open the driver's side door of the other car, took out his gun and hit the driver on the head then yanked him out of the car (AP letter from Essiquio Garza, November 2, 1937, Box 1, Folder 34). The passenger tried to run off and the constable fired his gun at him (AP letter from Essiquio Garza, November 2, 1937, Box 1, Folder 34). This shot came so close to Garza that he temporarily lost hearing in one ear (AP letter from Essiquio Garza, November 2, 1937, Box 1, Folder 34). All this was done without one word from the constable (AP letter from Essiquio Garza, November 2, 1937, Box 1, Folder 34). The letter does not explain if there was any justification for the actions of the constable, but that an officer of the law should fire his weapon without uttering a word when innocent bystanders were in the line of fire was apparently the reason for the letter. The letter does not ask Perales to take any specific action nor does it contain any expressions of outrage or surprise. Without further details of the incident, one cannot speak to the interactions between the constable and the two men who were in the car he stopped. But that an Anglo police officer should fire his weapon at someone without any warning when innocent bystanders could have been hit speaks to how Mexican Americans were subtracted in the eyes of those who represented the authorities among the Anglo-Saxon population. Constable McNeil acted as if Garza and his companion weren't even present.

On October 23, 1939, Octavio R. García wrote to Perales concerning the poor conditions of the Navarro School for Mexican Americans in Lockhart, Texas. Members of the Mexican-American Parent-Teacher Association had been promised improvements in the form of two additional classrooms, two more teachers and a janitor (AP letter from Octavio R. García, July 23, 1939, Box 1, Folder 33). The letter also stated that these improvements were only a stopgap measure while a new building was being constructed (AP letter from Octavio R. García, July 23, 1939, Box 1, Folder 33). One week later the response they received from the School Board was that they would be given two more classrooms and two more teachers, but no janitor since the Board was not concerned with the sanitary conditions of the Navarro School (AP letter from Octavio R. García, July 23, 1939, Box 1, Folder 33). The letter goes on to seek Perales' advice on how to proceed with obtaining the improvements that the parents consider necessary for their children (AP letter from Octavio R. García, July 23, 1939, Box 1, Folder 33). While the tone of the letter is generally straightforward and businesslike, in the last paragraph García refers to "esta clase de personas" ("this sort of people" AP letter from Octavio R. García, July 23, 1939, Box 1, Folder 33)[5] and states that it is "imposible tener ningún [sic] arreglo, pues se consideran demasiado superiores a sus conciudadanos de origen México-Americanos" ("impossible to come to any agreement because they consider themselves too superior to their fellow Mexican-American countrymen " AP letter from Octavio R. García, July 23, 1939, Box 1, Folder 33). The bitterness in the tone of this statement is prompted by the perceived subtraction that does not consider the Mexican-American children worthy of a clean and safe learning environment.

Perales' response to García in a letter dated August 25, 1939, is very telling for the patience with which he suggests that the P.T.A. proceed. He gives the School Board the benefit of the doubt stating that "dichos señores no se rehusan a remediar la situación" ("said gentlemen do not refuse to remedy the situation" AP letter to Octavio R. García, August 25, 1939, Box 1, Folder 33). To suggest proceeding with such caution demonstrates an unwillingness to provoke political action or the ire of the School Board. Perales further suggests that the P.T.A. representatives schedule a meeting with the entire School Board bringing sufficient numbers to bear witness to the proceedings. Only then if no satisfaction is accorded does he suggest that steps be taken to present the grievance to the State Superintendent of Schools in Austin, Texas (AP letter to Octavio R. García, August 25, 1939, Box 1, Folder 33). The rhetoric at this point demonstrates restraint and lacks the militancy of the Chicano/a Movement of the 1960s/1970s.

There were few letters written by women. María Antonia Chávez Saldaña penned the first one encountered in the collection. It was dated March 6, 1940. A mother wrote this letter about her two sons expressing to Perales how difficult it is to motivate children who see no future for themselves because they are discriminated against (AP letter from María Antonia Chávez Saldaña, March 6, 1940, Box 1, Folder 25). Chávez Saldaña takes great pains to explain her lineage stating that her ancestors first came to Texas in 1715. She mentions this because she cannot understand how those Anglo Saxons who may have only recently moved to Texas can claim to be entitled to more than those like herself whose families founded and first settled the territory (AP letter from María Antonia Chávez Saldaña, March 6, 1940, Box 1, Folder 25). The letter is written in excellent English, but while she presents a lot of facts in a straightforward manner the underlying tone is pleading and supplicating. Chávez Saldaña never refers to a specific incident of discrimination, rather just to a sentiment perceived by herself and her sons.

Another letter written by a woman, Florencia Sáenz de Acosta, and dated October 7, 1940, takes a more militant tone when advocating for integration of future military camps at the start of World War II. Sáenz de Acosta uses phrases such as: ". . . ante la injusta y humillante diferencia con que se quiere distinguir al méxico-tejano" (". . . in view of the unjust and humiliating difference with which they want to characterize the Mexican-Texan" AP letter from Florencia Sáenz de Acosta, October 7, 1940, Box 2, Folder 18). She goes on to refer to this segregation of the troops as a "¡Maldita calamidad [sic] nacional!" ("Damned national calamity!" AP letter from Florencia Sáenz de Acosta, October 7, 1940, Box 2, Folder 18). Sáenz de Acosta also makes an atypical reference to the hegemony when she refers to "¡El yo! ¡El Colosal! ¡El angloamericano! ("The 'I'! The Colossal! The Angloamerican!" AP letter from Florencia Sáenz de Acosta, October 7, 1940, Box 2, Folder 18). In a postscript, Sáenz de Acosta makes another reference that was not typical for 1940 when she alludes to a separate Mexican-American "nation": "Felicito á [sic] Ud. en nombre de todos los mexicanos y mexicoamerica [sic] y en nombre mio, por la héroica [sic] defensa á [sic] nuestros connacionales [sic]" ("I congratulate you in the name of all Mexicans and Mexican America and in my own name for your heroic defense of our fellow countrymen" AP letter from Florencia Sáenz de Acosta, October 7, 1940, Box 2, Folder 18). This reference to "mexicoamérica" as a separate country or nation state with its own unique population was later made more forthrightly and forcefully when the Chicano/a Movement of the 1960s/1970s popularized the name "Aztlan" to refer to the American Southwest with its predominantly Hispanic population and distinct Mexican heritage. In this letter, Sáenz de Acosta presages much of the rhetoric adopted by the Movement twenty to thirty years later. This is the first letter in the collection to use the militant rhetoric that would later characterize the Chicano/a Movement and signals a change in expression brought on by the conditions that the hegemony tried to impose upon U.S. Hispanics that were prepared to give their very lives for the United States. The U.S. government attempted to subtract the Mexican Americans from the mainstream military environment while availing itself of their services and possibly their lives.

A letter written on February 16, 1941, by George Reid, a Baptist preacher, speaks in defense of Mexican Americans working at a mining camp in Malakoff, Texas. Reid tells of a fraud perpetrated by Anglo-American doctors on the Mexican-American miners. The miners had pooled their funds to care for those among them who might need medical attention and the doctors contrived to undertake unnecessary operations and other procedures and charged sums that continually left the funds depleted (AP letter from George Reid, February 16, 1941, Box 2, Folder 15). Reid states that these doctors "seemed to be [charging] much higher than others had to pay on the average." Reid then goes on to advocate for a "state-wide movement for medical insurance among the Mexicans and [to] set up Mexican institutions to care for their sick." Militant as this stance may appear to be, Reid assures his reader that he does "not wish to try to stir up any more strife." Reid writes this letter on letterhead bearing the name of the Sociedad Mutualista Mexicana of Malakoff, Texas. He also gives the name of Jesus García, secretary of the society, as a reference (AP letter from George Reid, February 16, 1941, Box 2, Folder 15).

By mid-1941, letters with more specific details of incidents experienced by the authors begin to appear in the collection. The first of these is dated July 15, 1941, and is written by Eduardo Cázares. In this letter, Cázares apprises Perales of a personal experience in McAllen, Texas, when he attempted to get a drink of water from a public fountain at a service station. The attendant told him he could not drink there and had to leave (AP letter from Eduardo Cázares, July 15, 1941, Box 1, Folder 25). The attendant was subtracting Mexican Americans from the greater population allowed to drink at the water fountain. Cázares goes on to provide the name and address of the station. He also states that this is not the first time similar events have occurred (AP letter from Eduardo Cázares, July 15, 1941, Box 1, Folder 25).

Francisco González wrote a similar letter on September 22, 1941, complaining of having been ejected from a restaurant just because he was a Mexican. While a U.S. citizen and willing to serve in the military, he had not yet been called up because he had a family (AP letter from Francisco González, September 22, 1941, Box 1, Folder 34). González mentions exclusion from most public places including swimming pools and public restrooms. While the tone of his letter is emotional and heartfelt, it lacks the militant rhetoric seen in the Sáenz de Acosta letter above. The man is obviously tired of being subtracted from public life when he is willing to serve the nation he loves.

A letter dated October 14,1942, and written by Donald G. Kobler cited a telegram sent to him by an unnamed Mexican field worker who stated that ". . . I find a lot of places where the Mexican people is [sic] discriminated . . . this is dangerous . . . , because there are a lot of Spanish speaking people that thinks [sic] that don't worth a while [sic] to fight for a Country [sic] where they are not considered as civilized people." Kobler advocated for rectifying such discriminatory practices when he called such cases "undemocratic and Nazi-like discriminations." This letter demonstrates the awareness by some Anglo Saxons of the increased unwillingness on the part of Mexican Americans to continue tolerating the discrimination to which they have been subjected.

On April 28, 1943, Carlos Reyes B. wrote to Perales wanting to find an end to the discrimination suffered by Mexican Americans in Goliad, Texas. Reyes does not give specific cases of discrimination except to say that restaurants in Goliad display signs stating that "aquí no servimos a los Mexicanos" ("no service to Mexicans" AP letter from Carlos Reyes B., April 28, 1943, Box 2, Folder 15).[5] The focus of his letter is to request assistance in expanding a local organization of parents and family of Latino servicemen to the state level (AP letter from Carlos Reyes B., April 28, 1943, Box 2, Folder 15). While the rhetoric here is restrained the call to action is clear.

In a letter dated May 5, 1943, Ramón Galindo writes about the discriminatory real estate practices in San Antonio. He lists the names of several agents, all Anglo Saxon, who persist in promulgating discrimination in real estate sales and purchases (AP letter from Ramón Galindo, May 5, 1943, Box 1, Folder 33). The letter is short and direct and does not refer to a specific incident in detail, but the fact that it lists the names of several agents demonstrates boldness beyond the mention of one specific incident.

A second letter with the same date written by Christino D. Pérez from San Antonio, Texas, presents three specific cases of discrimination in the workplace. The first two involve incidents in civil service positions at a local Air Force Base, Kelly Field, while the third is in a local cement factory (AP letter from Christino D. Pérez, May 5, 1943, Box 2, Folder 12). In all three cases, the Mexican Americans who experience the discrimination are either replaced by Anglo Saxons or asked to take a lower paying position so that an Anglo Saxon without any experience can be given the higher paying job (AP letter from Christino D. Pérez, May 5, 1943, Box 2, Folder 12). These are examples of either subtraction by complete elimination or subtraction by denigration since the more qualified worker is replaced by the less qualified.

On September 10, 1943, Cpl. F.S. Treviño responded to a request by Perales and wrote about cases of discrimination in Midland, Texas. This letter is not unique because it is written by an active duty serviceman nor because it describes several cases of discrimination, but because in one instance where a restaurant displayed a sign stating "no Mexicans allowed," the letter states that the author returned to the establishment with the military police after having been refused service because he was Latino (AP letter from F.S. Treviño, September 10, 1943, Box 2, Folder 23). He had the military police officer tear down the sign and declare the establishment off-limits to military personnel (AP letter from F.S. Treviño, September 10, 1943, Box 2, Folder 23). This is the first expression of political activism in the Perales collection. Treviño's actions squarely confronted the problem and made those perpetrating discrimination suffer by losing the business of all servicemen no matter what their race. Treviño's letter goes on to close by stating that it "looks like we got to [sic] wars to win, one with the Japs and Germans and the other against the people that is [sic] still fighting the civil war [sic]." The clearly militant rhetoric used here followed by the direct action taken by Treviño presaged the Chicano/a Movement that finally erupted twenty years later.

A young sailor, Ricardo Ogas, assigned to the U.S.S. *Honolulu* wrote to the then Texas Governor, Coke Stevenson, in a letter dated September 18, 1943, giving the name of his commanding officer and outlining an incident he experienced while on leave in his hometown of Alpine, Texas. While invited into a local pool hall by a fellow Anglo-Saxon sailor, Ogas was invited to play pool by a civilian who was also Anglo Saxon. When they had just undertaken to play, the manager approached them and told them that Ogas was not welcome to play pool (AP letter from Ricardo Ogas, September 18, 1943, Box 2, Folder 8). When questioned, the manager stated that if he "played the Negroes would also like to come and play there" (AP letter from Ricarado Ogas, September 18, 1943, Box 2, Folder 8). While the tone of the letter is very formal and restrained, it is unequivocal in stating the discrimination endured and requesting that the governor obtain a formal apology from the manager (AP letter from Ricardo Ogas, September 18, 1943, Box 2, Folder 8).

On September 30, 1943, Lorenzo G. Lafarelle also wrote to then Texas Governor, Coke Stevenson, formally filing a complaint against Mr. C.W. Davis, Manager of the Granada Theater in Alpine, Texas, for an incident he experienced on September 15, 1943. Lafarelle tried to purchase downstairs tickets for a show and was told that he could only be allowed to purchase balcony tickets. This is typical of the discriminatory practices of the era, but Lafarelle goes on to question how it is that a "Latin American [can be] expected to fight against Hitler's and the Japs' ideas of a superior race, when he sees those principles against which [he is] fighting practiced against him by many Anglo Americans." Mr. Lafarelle, a nineteen-year-old native of Alpine, Texas, and a sergeant in the Texas State Guard begins his letter by citing the recently passed "House Concurrent Resolution No. 105" as well as an open letter by the Governor to peace officers in Texas and demands that the Governor obtain an apology from the theater owner on his behalf. This young man whose brother had been recently called into active duty service in the U.S. Army (AP letter from Lorenzo G. Lafarelle, September 15, 1943, Box 2, Folder 4) used strong rhetoric and as with the previous letter had no trouble addressing the highest authority in the state. Lafarelle was forceful but respectful and fully expected the governor to take action on his behalf.

While both these letters use bold and forthright rhetoric, the fact that they were written to the governor of the state by young Latino servicemen is unique. In both cases these writers were being removed or ejected from otherwise public venues because of their race. The bold rhetoric employed by both came about as a result of the service that both men had given to their state and country. The letter by Lafarelle above is bolder yet for its comparison of the treatment he received to that being exercised by the Fascist regimes of Germany and Japan. At this point in history, the Latino was not merely being required to subtract facets of his culture from his personality and being, but rather was usually required to remove himself from the public realms reserved for the hegemony.

Eloísa Galán wrote several letters, but two letters, one dated February 14, 1944, and a second dated February 27, 1944, stand out. She writes from Eagle Pass, Texas, and in the first letter she gives suggestions as to who Perales should contact to obtain details of cases of discrimination; in the second she expresses outrage at a series of articles that appeared in Time Magazine on February 7 and 28 (?), 1944 (AP letters from Eloísa Galán, February 14, and February 27, 1944, Box 1, Folder 33). These articles apparently ridiculed Mexican Americans and caused deep resentment among the local Mexican-American community (AP letters from Eloísa Galán, February 14, and February 27, 1944, Box 1, Folder 33). The letter indeed expresses outrage, but Miss Galán seeks to redress this issue by approaching people in power with the aid of Perales rather than through advocating political action. The earlier letter is also lacking the militant rhetoric seen in the letters above written by those serving in the military and by Sáenz de Acosta.

Francisco Echavarría wrote on February 18, 1944, from Cameron, Texas, and explained how the children were segregated in the schools but also pointed out that those children unfortunate enough to have had to attend rural schools were often only schooled from January through March with the excuse that their labor was needed in the fields. He also told about segregation in the cinemas and stores of the town (AP letter from Francisco Echavarría, February 18, 1944, Box 1, Folder 30). In the stores Mexican Americans were allowed to enter and shop, but they were not allowed to try on clothes before buying them (AP letter from Francisco Echavarría, February 18, 1944, Box 1, Folder 30). Echavarría then made an emotional plea for change because it seemed to him unfair that "nuestra sangre se derrama atorrentes [sic] en el campo de batalla" ("our blood is spilled in torrents on the battle field" AP letter from Francisco Echavarría, February 18, 1944, Box 1, Folder 30), but our children were discriminated against.

On February 16, 1944, Fidencia Estrello wrote about the discrimination against her children in the school of Ganado, Texas. She clarified to Perales that she and her husband were Mexican nationals, but that their children were all born in Texas (AP letter from Fidencia Estrello, February 16, 1944, Box 1, Folder 30). In Jackson County, apparently the schools had a larger number of Mexican-American children than Anglo and even so, one day all her children were sent home because they would not keep their lunches and coats separate from those of the Anglo-Saxon students as had been requested (AP letter from Fidencia Estrello, February 16, 1944, Box 1, Folder 30). That afternoon, her husband went to all the other Mexican-American parents explaining to them what had happened and they all decided to keep their children home from school the next day (AP letter from Fidencia Estrello, February 16, 1944, Box 1, Folder 30). When only the twenty Anglo-Saxon children showed up for school the next day, the principal went to beg the Mexican-American parents to return their children to school (AP letter from Fidencia Estrello, February 16, 1944, Box 1, Folder 30). She went on to explain that Mexican-American children in Ganado were kept apart from the Anglo-Saxon children for their first three years of school "para que no se junten con los americanos como son muchos mexicanos en esos grados" ("so that they won't associate with the Americans since there are many Mexicans in those grades" AP letter from Fidencia Estrello, February 16, 1944, Box 1, Folder 30). Estrello also related that in the coming year the older Mexican-American children would be separated from the Anglo Saxons. The tone of the letter is slightly emotional, but far from militant.

Faustino Capiedra and Nasirio Castillo wrote on February 17, 1944, from Strawn, Texas. Their letter mentioned incidents of discrimination in the local restaurants and cinema. This information they provided "con mucho gusto y anciedad [sic]" ("with great pleasure and anxiety" AP letter from Faustino Capiedra and Nasirio Castillo, February 17, 1944, Box 1, Folder 25). These men had already contacted the Mexican Consul in Dallas, Texas, with only the assurance that their case would be presented to the Mexican Consul in Austin, Texas (AP letter from Faustino Capiedra and Nasirio Castillo, February 17, 1944, Box 1, Folder 25). They wrote Perales in response to his article in *La Prensa* of San Antonio, seeking a more immediate response (AP letter from Faustino Capiedra and Nasirio Castillo, February 17, 1944, Box 1, Folder 25).

A letter written on February 19, 1944, by Silvestre M. Zepeda from Forth Worth, Texas, is notable because in the postscript it cites the case of an active duty serviceman who took his complaint to the military authorities and the only satisfaction he was given was to be told that the business would be placed off limits. This was the standard practice for such cases. Unfortunately, it seemed that the process was so delayed that nothing was eventually done (AP letter from Silvestre M. Zepeda, February 19, 1944, Box 2, Folder 29). Zepeda indeed complained that no matter whether Mexican Americans and Mexican nationals submitted their complaints to American authorities or Mexican authorities (Mexican Consuls) "el resultado siempre es el mismo, NADA" ("the result is always the same, NOTHING" AP letter from Silvestre M. Zepeda, February 19, 1944, Box 2, Folder 29). Zepeda went on to say that he therefore expected to see definitive action from Perales on these matters. The tone of the rhetoric, especially in the postscript, is aggressive.

Carmen Cedillo and Jacobo M. Ancira wrote to Perales from Hutto, Texas, on February 28, 1944, concerning the situation at the local bus station cafe. At this establishment, the local Mexican Americans who wanted to patronize the establishment were made to go to the window at the side reserved for people of color (AP letter from Carmen Cedillo and Jacobo M. Ancira, February 28, 1944, Box 1, Folder 25). Interestingly, active duty military travelers in uniform who happened to be Mexican American were served with Anglo-Saxon patrons in the coffee shop (AP letter from Carmen Cedillo and Jacobo M. Ancira, February 28, 1944, Box 1, Folder 25). The discrimination was aimed only at the local civilian population (AP letter from Carmen Cedillo and Jacobo M. Ancira, February 28, 1944, Box 1, Folder 25). This letter was written on behalf of the entire Mexican-American community of Hutto, Texas (AP letter from Carmen Cedillo and Jacobo M. Ancira, February 28, 1944, Box 1, Folder 25). Cedillo and Ancira sought an explanation and were willing to accept that should this discrimination be aimed at the local populace because they presented themselves improperly dressed to enter "un establecimiento de lujo" ("a luxury establishment" AP letter from Carmen Cedillo and Jacobo M. Ancira, February 28 1944, Box 1, Folder 25), they could understand. This willingness to accept an explanation for the segregation demonstrates the lengths to which people were willing to go to avoid a confrontation.

A letter dated April 17, 1944, written by Mrs. Felix H. Morales of Houston, Texas, is unique in that she describes incidents experienced in Dodge City, Kansas, by two active duty servicemen. Both men on separate occasions while in uniform were asked to either sit in the balcony of the Dodge Theatre with the "Negroes" or leave (AP letter from Mrs. Felix H. Morales, April 17, 1944, Box 2, Folder 7). Both chose to leave rather than be humiliated (AP letter from Mrs. Felix H. Morales, April 17, 1944, Box 2, Folder 7). Morales was so upset by the incidents that she wanted to "put these infernal nazis [sic] where they belong" (AP letter from Angelina Morales, April 17, 1944, Box 2, Folder 7). The rhetoric is strong and emotional and the writer seeks advice from Perales on how to proceed to redress the situation.

Agustín Delgado wrote two letters, one dated June 20, 1944 to which it seems that Perales responded because the second letter dated July 5, 1944, makes reference to Perales' response. These letters refer to incidents of discrimination in Victoria, Texas (AP letter from Agustín Delgado, June 29 and July 5, 1944, Box 1, Folder 28). While the first letter is merely a short request for counsel, the second letter contains specifics and mentions that at some of the establishments listed, even Mexican Americans in uniform and on active duty with the military have been refused service (AP letter from Agustín Delgado, June 29 and July 5, 1944, Box 1, Folder 28). Delgado pleads that Perales "nos ayude a poner fin a tan degradante idea de parte de estos propietarios" ("help us put an end to such a degrading idea on the part of these proprietors" AP letter from Agustin Delgado, June 20, 1944, Box 1, Folder 28).

There are approximately thirty-six more letters written in 1944-1945, all citing examples of discrimination in Texas. Taken together these letters form a distressing picture of the discrimination endured by Mexican Americans in those years. All these letters present details in a straightforward manner and none contain militant rhetoric although some are emotional. Some letters take a pleading tone wanting Perales to do something to redress the situations faced. The boldest letters are written either by active duty servicemen themselves or on their behalf by their relatives and compare the discrimination meted out to Mexican Americans to the attitude of Hitler and his minions toward anyone they considered to be outside the mold of the superior race they tried to achieve. Men wrote most of these letters, but women wrote at least two.

Another six letters were written between 1946 and 1949. Women wrote two of these letters. The tone of these post-war letters was more insistent and more demanding, even sometimes militant. In a letter dated January 25, 1946, Felix Garza Jr. writes "pues sepa . . . que nosotros los Latino-Americanos [sic] tenemos todo el derecho igual que cualquier otro ciudadano Americano. Somos verdaderos Americanos, peleamos por nuestras libertades . . ." ("well know . . . that we the Latin Americans have every right just as any other American citizen. We are true Americans, we fought for our liberties . . ."). Militancy is reflected in the following: "ya porque . . . no le gustan las actividades de los Latino-Americanos [sic] nos vallan [sic] a poner en el Periodico [sic] como si se tratara de cualquier cosa (AP letter from Felix Garza, Jr., January 25, 1946, Box 1, Folder 34)" ("now because . . . some don't like the activities of Latin Americans [there's no cause] for them to write about us in the newspaper as if it were about some 'no account'" AP letter from Felix Garza, Jr., January 25, 1946, Box 1, Folder 34). This rhetoric demonstrates an unwillingness to continue tolerating the disdain commonly used by the hegemony when dealing with the subaltern.

C. Arturo Ortiz writes on March 1, 1946 on behalf of several World War II veterans who were denied service in a restaurant in Abilene, Texas, and who would like to take the matter to court. Ortiz gives details of the incident and states that the establishment in question denies service to all Mexican Americans. This is the first time that a group of Mexican Americans expresses an interest in seeking legal action against an act of discrimination.

On June 9, 1947, Jose Caballero writes from Grafton, North Dakota, where he had gone from Texas to work for a beet sugar company that recruited workers from San Antonio. Caballero refers to the treatment of Mexican Americans in many towns of North Dakota as "mucho más [sic] peor que a los negros en Texas" ("much worse than [the treatment] of Afro Americans in Texas") since in Texas at least "les venden en la cocina, pues, [sic] a nosotros en este Estado [sic] de North Dakota ni en la cocina" ("they sell to them in the kitchen, but to us in this state of North Dakota not even in the kitchen [will they sell food to us]"). As contrast, a letter dated November 14, 1946, written by David M. Ortiz notes an incident where veterans would not be served in a restaurant in Uvalde, Texas, except in a back room. The letter goes on to point out how these men had served their country during the recent war and yet were humiliated in such a degrading fashion (AP letter from David M. Ortiz, November 14, 1946, Box 2, Folder 8). Ortiz states that this incident attempted to "robarnos de nuestros derechos que con nuestra sangre obtuvimos" ("rob us of our rights that we won with our blood"). In the letter from North Dakota, the tone is pleading and desperate while in the Texas letter written on behalf of veterans the tone is demanding.

In response to the demanding tone of the letter by Ortiz, Perales writes that they should be patient and "no hagan nada ustedes sobre el incidente que les pasó, hasta que reciban nuevas noticias mías. Déjenme ver que puedo hacer yo" ("not do anything yourselves concerning this incident until you hear from me again. Allow me to see what I can do"). Perales was advocating against a direct confrontation, preferring to go through those established channels he knew to be sympathetic with the plight of Mexican Americans. He did not encourage people to be confrontational but to keep track of situations recording the details and sending them to him.

After 1946, some letters in the Perales collection reflect a stronger tone against discrimination demanding that incidents of public slander and discrimination be redressed with either personal or public apologies. One letter written by the Lay Council for the Spanish Speaking of the Archdiocese of San Antonio dated February 28, 1947, "vigorously protests" an act of discrimination at a restaurant in New Braunfels, Texas, and refers to one of those who suffered the discrimination as the sister of one who died in the service of his country during WWII. Another is the mother of an active duty serviceman and the third has a "brother and seventeen close relatives . . . in the armed forces (AP letter from Henry B. González, February 28, 1947, Box 1, Folder 34)." A second letter dated April 13, 1948, written by Efraín Domínguez, expresses outrage at comments made by a key speaker at a Mission Chamber of Commerce dinner in Mission, Texas, and demands a public apology from the Chamber of Commerce. Of the speaker Domínguez states "such persons . . . keep alive a 'race' consciousness, and sow the seeds of hatred among us."

Mary L. Martínez wrote a response to a "Letter to the Editor" (newspaper unknown) published February 11, 1947, written by an Anglo Saxon woman. Apparently, this woman was complaining of not being able to obtain adequate housing in

Edinburg, Texas, due to the housing shortage after the war and she blamed the situation on Mexican Americans (Ms., AP copy of newspaper article, no date, Box 2, Folder 6). Martínez reminds this woman that Mexican Americans "fought in this war side by side with Anglo Americans . . . and there were no restricted areas for them in the battle fields." The tone of the response is measured and conciliatory, but to make this a response published in an English-language newspaper makes it noteworthy.

A letter written by Marta M. González and dated July 12, 1949, states in no uncertain terms that she is willing to go to jail if justice in the school system is not achieved for her children. She is a mother of fifteen, the elder six of whom served in the military during WWII, and now the younger ones are forced to study in a garage because they are not allowed to attend the regular classroom in Cuero, Texas (AP letter from Marta M. González, July 12, 1949, Box 1, Folder 34). Her Spanish is poor and the rambling nature of her narrative reflects the little education she received, but she is determined that her American-born children will receive better treatment and a proper education (AP letter from Marta M. González, July 12, 1949, Box 1, Folder 34). Her husband, Rafael C. González, writes a letter dated April 20, 1950, relating an incident of discrimination. He states that he was born in Yorktown, Texas, and had six sons and daughters who served in the military during WWII (AP letter from Rafael C. González, April 20, 1950, Box 1, Folder 34). At a local bar in Cuero, Texas, he was refused service and not allowed to buy a Coca-Cola (AP letter from Rafael C. González, April 20, 1950, Box 1, Folder 34). González even took the case to court and was told there was nothing that could be done. Both letters reflect a willingness to take political action.

H. García writes on November 28, 1949, concerning discrimination against Mexican Americans working in the San Antonio City Water Department. Not only are workers denied paid vacations, they are also denied overtime pay and the wages are extremely low (AP letter from H. García, November 28, 1949, Box 1, Folder 33). These same workers were denied the Social Security contributions due them on the part of their employer (AP letter from H. García, November 28, 1949, Box 1, Folder 33). All these injustices were mentioned because in a different department of the same agency, African Americans suffered no such indignities (AP letter from H. García, November 28, 1949, Box 1, Folder 33). García does request that Perales omit any reference to him/her by name in order to avoid retaliation for blowing the whistle on these discriminatory practices.

Between 1950 and 1964 there were only seven letters written and one was by a woman. A letter dated February 3, 1950, was written and signed by a group of Mexican Americans from Moore, Texas, on behalf of discrimination suffered at a restaurant in Lockhart, Texas, by five young Mexican-American women from Maxwell, Texas. It petitioned Perales to write to the owner of the establishment where the incident occurred (AP letter from F. M. Maldonado, et al, February 3, 1950, Box 2, Folder 6). Moore, Texas is located southwest of San Antonio, Texas, while both Maxwell and Lockhart are located northeast of San Antonio. It is unclear what connection the writers have to the aggrieved. They merely state that they have read about the case (AP letter from F. M. Maldonado, et al, February 3, 1950, Box 2, Folder 6), yet it is interesting that they would take such pains to defend these young women in a situation that occurred so far away. Where up to this point, letters had all addressed incidents of which the writers were either personally aware or of which they had been made aware by family members, this letter defends seemingly unknown victims of discrimination.

Feliciano Garza from Kenedy, Texas, wrote on January 16, 1952, complaining of the treatment of Mexican Americans by immigration officials that he had witnessed in Arizona. He related that Mexican Americans were singled out and harassed about their documentation when those he knew to be Europeans standing next to them were not even questioned (AP letter from Feliciano Garza, January 16, 1952, Box 1, Folder 34). He also mentioned that the post office required Mexican Americans to renew their residency registration every two years while no other ethnic group was required to do so (AP letter from Feliciano Garza, January 16, 1952, Box 1, Folder 34). This second case demonstrates a modernity of subtraction imposed upon Mexican Americans by officials of the government. They are not denied service as long as they comply with the extra requirement. This singles them out from the rest of the community instead of acknowledging them as equal citizens.

A letter dated March 29, 1953, written by Irene C. de Estrada, tells of an incident suffered by her daughter in-law at the hands of government officials who administered death benefits to two of the children left to her daughter-in-law by her first husband who died while serving in WWII. These officials did not deny her the benefits, but took it upon themselves to criticize her for having a third child by her present husband saying that she should practice birth control because "no tenía ningunos negocios de traer niños al mundo que no podia [sic] sostener (AP letter from Irene Estrada, March 29, 1953, Box 1, Folder 30)" (she had no business bringing children into the world that she couldn't support). A second person in the same office later told her that she should send her children to public school instead of to the private Catholic school they had always attended and threatened to get her benefits canceled on the pretext that government money should not be used to pay for Catholic schooling (AP letter from Irene C. de Estrada, March 29, 1953, Box 1, Folder 30). These attempts to force a person to observe the cultural practices and standards of the Anglo-Saxon community and to denigrate her for her focus on family and church were clearly expressions of a modernity of subtraction.

The letters in the collection, when taken together chronologically, whether written by men or by women, present an increasingly bolder voice over time. The letters written before 1941 and making no reference to the military service rendered by Mexican Americans during World War II tend to acknowledge a total separation or isolation from the dominant Anglo-Saxon culture. This reflects a complete subtraction not only of the individual, but also of the entire Mexican-American culture and language. Letters written during and after 1941, or those earlier letters mentioning military service during the war, tend to make clearer reference to ways in which individuals are expected to suppress or eliminate their Mexican culture in order to be accepted by the Anglo Saxons around them. It is at this point that the modernity of subtraction begins to focus on specific characteristics of the Mexican-American culture with a view to erase or at least suppress those aspects considered foreign to the hegemony.

The cases of discrimination also change after World War II and after laws begin to be enacted that change the political status of the Mexican American by law if not by practice. Prior to 1946 most of the letters relate incidents of discrimination that tend to attempt to eliminate the Mexican American from establishments reserved for "whites" or Anglo Saxons. During World War II, Mexican Americans begin to voice their displeasure at having to send their boys to war while being discriminated against at home. When those same servicemen and women return home either after the war or while on leave, they too complain, and more vehemently, at the discrimination they must endure at home while fighting in the same trenches with Anglo Saxons at the battlefront. After World War II and especially after the 1960s, when the few laws that have been passed to protect against discrimination gain wider recognition, the nature of the discrimination begins to change. No longer can Mexican Americans be eliminated from participating in public forums and patronizing public establishments, so Anglo Saxons begin to point out the cultural differences that separate the two ethnic groups and belittle those values dear to the Mexican-American traditions. In all cases a "modernity of subtraction" applies. In the earlier letters it is a complete subtraction of the individual subaltern from the dominant culture, while in the later letters it is the subtraction of specific cultural traits of the subaltern that do not fit into the framework of the dominant culture. Just as the nature of the discrimination changes from subtraction of the person to subtraction of cultural characteristics, so the voice of the Mexican-American protest changes from acquiescent and accepting to questioning and finally militant. Letters written after 1950 also begin to reflect a tendency to defend unknown victims as seen in the letter from F. M. Maldonado, et al. This change has taken the focus from defense of the individual to defense of the community. The stage is now set for the Chicano/a Movement of the 1960s/70s.

The progression in the changing attitudes of the Mexican-American community brought all the resentment and injustices of the discrimination practiced in Texas and the Southwest to a head and led to the logical point of civil action. Without a coalescing event like WWII this progression very likely would not have advanced as quickly as it did. World War II demonstrated to the Mexican-American community that its young men and women were necessary for the protection of the nation as a whole. It also showed the Anglo Saxon community that Mexican Americans were just as "American" as they were and so were worthy to participate in the freedoms previously accorded only to whites. While the process of advancing the social position of the Mexican American vis-à-vis discrimination continues, WWII made it no longer possible to ignore the presence and contributions of an entire ethnic group.

Alonso S. Perales and others like him who worked diligently to advance the cause of the Mexican-American community in Texas and the Southwest facilitated the political process of acknowledging the rights and privileges to which Mexican Americans as U.S. citizens were entitled. By collecting the cases of discriminatory practices directly from those who had experienced them and later bringing the worst cases to the attention of the public whether through his weekly column or through his political contacts in Washington, D.C., Perales was instrumental in gaining recognition for the plight of the Mexican American in Texas and elsewhere and so ameliorating the social condition of his community.

TABLE OF LETTERS TO ALONSO S. PERALES 1923-1964

1923-1940	1941-1943	1944-1945	1946-1964	Date unknown
Austin, R.E.	Cázares, Eduardo	Capiedra, Faustino and Nasirio Castillo	Caballero, José	Martínez, Mary L.
Chávez Saldaña, Maria Antonia	Galindo, Ramón	Cedillo, Carmen and Jacobo M. Ancira	Domínguez, Efraín	Peña, Nieves
Fernández, Pedro (2 letters)	González, Francisco	Delgado, Agustín (2 letters)	Estrada, Irene C.	Gutiérrez, Amado
García, Octavio R.	Kobler, Donald G.	Echavarría, Francisco	Garza, Feliciano	
Garza, Essiquio	Lafarelle, Lorenzo G.	Estrello, Fidencia	Garza, Félix, Jr.	
Sáenz de Acosta, Florencia	Ogas, Ricardo	Galán, Eloisa (2 letters)	González, Henry B., et al	
	Pérez, Christino D.	Gallegos, José Gutiérrez, Isabel G. de	González, Marta M.	
	Reid, George	Guzmán, Vicente	González, Rafael C.	
	Reyes B., Carlos	Harris, Grace G., Lillie M.	Ibarra, Alfredo M.	
	Treviño, Cpl. F.S.	González and María M. González	Maldonado, F.M., et al	
		Jaramillo, Alejandro	Martínez, Paz G.	
		Laurel, Serbando C.	Ortiz, C. Arturo	
		Mendoza, Felipe	Ortiz, David M	
		Montero, F.		
		Montoya, A.D.		
		Morales, Angelina		
		Nevarez, Guadalupe And Jesus Villarreal		
		Padilla Jasso, José		
		R. Riojas, G. (2 letters)		
		Ramírez Pérez, Manuel (2 letters)		
		Rivera, Alfonso		
		Rodríguez, Graciela		
		Rodríguez, Jacob I. (2 letters)		
		Silvas, Julio		
		Treviño, Carlos		
		Valadez, Joel (2 letters)		
		Valadez, Petra (2 letters)		
		Vargas, D.		
		Zepeda, Silvestre M.		

Works Cited

Aranda Jr., J. F. (2013). *The Latino nineteenth century* (Lazo, R. & Aleman, J., Eds.). New York: New York University Press.

Aranda Jr., J. F. (2010, December 1). *Origins of the 'transnational' character of Mexican American literature.* Lecture conducted from Chao Center, Rice University, Houston, Texas.

Austin, R.E. (1932, March 8). [Letter to D. E. Kirgan]. Alonso S. Perales Collection, M. D. Anderson Library, Houston, Texas.

Caballero, J. (1947, June 9). [Letter to Alonso S. Perales]. Alonso S. Perales Collection, M. D. Anderson Library, Houston, Texas.

Capiedra, F. & Castillo, N. (1944, February 17). [Letter to Alonso S. Perales]. Alonso S. Perales Collection, M. D. Anderson Library, Houston, Texas.

Cazares, E. (1941, July 15). [Letter to Alonso S. Perales]. Alonso S. Perales Collection, M. D. Anderson Library, Houston, Texas.

Cedillo, C. & Ancira, J. M. (1944, 28 February). [Letter to Alonso S. Perales]. Alonso S. Perales Collection, M. D. Anderson Library, Houston, Texas.

Chávez Saldaña, M. A. (1940, March 6). [Letter to Alonso S. Perales]. Alonso S. Perales Collection, M. D. Anderson Library, Houston, Texas.

Delgado, A. (1944, June 29). [Letter to Alonso S. Perales]. Alonso S. Perales Collection, M. D. Anderson Library, Houston, Texas.

Delgado, A. (1944, July 5). [Letter to Alonso S. Perales]. Alonso S. Perales Collection, M. D. Anderson Library, Houston, Texas.

Domínguez, E. (1948, April 13). [Letter to Alonso S. Perales]. Alonso S. Perales Collection, M. D. Anderson Library, Houston, Texas.

Dussel, E. D. (1993). Eurocentrism and modernity: Introduction to the Frankfurt lectures. *Boundary 2*(20), 65-76.

Echavarría, F. (1944, February 18). [Letter to Alonso S. Perales]. Alonso S. Perales Collection, M. D. Anderson Library, Houston, Texas.

Estrada, I. C. (1953, March 29). [Letter to Alonso S. Perales]. Alonso S. Perales Collection, M. D. Anderson Library, Houston, Texas.

Estrello, F. (1944, Febrary 16). [Letter to Alonso S. Perales]. Alonso S. Perales Collection, M. D. Anderson Library, Houston, Texas.

Fernández, P. (1936, November 30). [Letter to Alonso S. Perales]. Alonso S. Perales Collection. M. D. Anderson Library, Houston, Texas.

Fernández, P. (1936, December 11). [Letter to Alonso S. Perales]. Alonso S. Perales Collection, M. D. Anderson Library, Houston, Texas.

Galán, E. (1944, February 14). [Letter to Alonso S. Perales]. Alonso S. Perales Collection, M. D. Anderson Library, Houston, Texas.

Galán, E. (1944, February 27). [Letter to Alonso S. Perales]. Alonso S. Perales Collection, M. D. Anderson Library, Houston, Texas.

Galindo, R. (1943, May 5). [Letter to Alonso S. Perales]. Alonso S. Perales Collection, M. D. Anderson Library, Houston, Texas.

García, O. R. (1939, July 23). [Letter to Alonso S. Perales]. Alonso S. Perales Collection, M. D. Anderson Library, Houston, Texas.

Garza, E. (1937, November 2). [Letter to Alonso S. Perales]. Alonso S. Perales Collection, M. D. Anderson Library, Houston, Texas.

Garza, F. (1952, January 16). [Letter to Alonso S. Perales]. 16 Jan. 1952. Alonso S. Perales Collection, M. D. Anderson Library, Houston, Texas.

Garza Jr., F. (1946, January 25). [Letter to Alonso S. Perales]. Alonso S. Perales Collection, M. D. Anderson Library, Houston, Texas.

González, F. (1941, September 22). [Letter to Alonso S. Perales]. Alonso S. Perales Collection, M. D. Anderson Library, Houston, Texas.

González, H. B., et al. (1947, February 28). [Letter]. Alonso S. Perales Collection, M. D. Anderson Library, Houston, Texas.

González, M. M. (1949, July 12). [Letter to Alonso S. Perales]. Alonso S. Perales Collection, M. D. Anderson Library, Houston, Texas.

González, R. C. (1950, April 20). [Letter to Alonso S. Perales]. Alonso S. Perales Collection, M. D. Anderson Library, Houston, Texas.

Kirgan, D. E. (1932, March 8). [Letter to R. Austin]. Alonso S. Perales Collection. M. D. Anderson Library, Houston, Texas.

Kobler, D. G. (1942, October 14). [Letter to Will W. Alexander]. Alonso S. Perales Collection, M. D. Anderson Library, Houston, Texas.

Lafarelle, L. G. (1943, September 30). [Letter to Coke Stevenson]. Alonso S. Perales. M. D. Anderson Library, Houston, Texas.

Maldonado, F. M., et al. (1950, February 3). [Letter to Alonso S. Perales]. Alonso S. Perales Collection. M. D. Anderson Library, Houston, Texas.

Martínez, M. L. (n.d.). [A response to a "letter to the Editor," newspaper unknown]. Alonso S. Perales Collection, M. D. Anderson Library, Houston, Texas.

Mignolo, W. (1995). Afterword: Human understanding and (Latin) American interests—the politics and sensibilities of geocultural location. *Poetics Today 16*(1), 171-214.

Mignolo, W. (2000). *Local histories/global designs: Coloniality, subaltern knowledges, and border thinking.* Princeton, N.J.: Princeton University Press.

Morales, A. (1944, April 17). [Letter to Alonso S. Perales]. Alonso S. Perales Collection, M. D. Anderson Library, Houston, Texas.

Ogas, R. (1943, September 18). [Letter to Coke Stevenson]. Alonso S. Perales, M. D. Anderson Library, Houston, Texas.

Orozco, C. E. (1999). *No Mexicans, women or dogs allowed: The rise of the Mexican American civil rights movement.* Austin, Texas: University of Texas Press, 1999.

Ortiz, C. A. (1946, March 1). [Letter to Alonso S. Perales]. Alonso S. Perales Collection, M. D. Anderson Library, Houston, Texas.

Ortiz, D. M. (1946, November 14). [Letter to Alonso S. Perales]. Alonso S. Perales Collection, M. D. Anderson Library, Houston, Texas.

Perales, A. S. (1946, November 27). [Letter to David M. Ortiz]. Alonso S. Perales Collection, M. D. Anderson Library, Houston, Texas.

Perales, A. S. (1939, August 25). [Letter to Octavio R. García]. Alonso S. Perales Collection, M. D. Anderson Library, Houston, Texas.

Pérez, C. D. (1943, May 5). [Letter to Alonso S. Perales]. Alonso S. Perales Collection, M. D. Anderson Library, Houston, Texas.

Quijano, A. (2000). Coloniality of power, Eurocentrism, and Latin America. *Nepantla: View from South 1*(3), 533-580.

Reid, G. (1941, February 16). [Letter to Alonso S. Perales]. Alonso S. Perales Collection, M. D. Anderson Library, Houston, Texas.

Reyes, C. B. (1943, April 28). [Letter to Alonso S. Perales]. Alonso S. Perales Collection, M. D. Anderson Library, Houston, Texas.

Sáenz de Acosta, F. (1940, October 7). [Letter to Alonso S. Perales]. Alonso S. Perales Collection, M. D. Anderson Library, Houston, Texas.

Treviño, F. S. (1943, September 10). [Letter to Alonso S. Perales]. Alonso S. Perales Collection, M. D. Anderson Library, Houston, Texas.

Valenzuela, A. (1999). *Subtractive schooling: U.S.-Mexican youth and the politics of caring*. Albany, N.Y.: State University of New York Press.

Zepeda, S. M. (1944, February 19). [Letter to Alonso S. Perales]. Alonso S. Perales Collection, M. D. Anderson Library, Houston, Texas.

Notes

[1]While this study cites the lecture mentioned, a version of this lecture will be available in the forthcoming publication listed in the works cited list.

[2]Prior to that, in March of 1961, President Kennedy signed Executive Order 10925 to promote actions that achieve non-discrimination. It was the first time that the term "affirmative action" was used.

[3]A letter written by R. Austin on Jan. 13, 1932 to D.E. Kirgan and forwarded by Kirgan to Perales was not written as a response to a plea by Perales. A letter by Essiqio Garza dated Nov. 2, 1937, was written as a response to a personal encounter with Perales who requested that the writer send him a written record of the discrimination suffered. Unless there was a third party involved in forwarding a letter like Austin's 1932 letter, the rest of the letters analyzed all were sent as a response to the plea from Perales printed in his weekly commentary.

[4]All subsequent references to the collection materials will appear in parentheses in the text.

[5]This and all subsequent translations are by the author.

[6]For elaboration on this practice see Orozco, *No Mexicans, Women or Dogs Allowed: The Rise of the Mexican American Civil Rights Movement*, pp. 29-30.

Self-Writing and Collective Representation: The Literary Enunciation of Historical Reality and Cultural Values

Donna M. Kabalen de Bichara

So as to contextualize the contributions of Alonso S. Perales during his lifetime regarding the situation of Mexican Americans as well as those Mexicans who resided in the United States, we must point to his many roles; that is, as husband, father, practicing Catholic, civil rights lawyer, diplomat, defender of the *raza,* writer, and mentor. Born in Alice, Texas in 1898, he is most famous for his defense of Mexican Texans whom he described as "one hundred percent Americans," and it was his firm belief that they should partake in all the rights and privileges enjoyed by those Americans of Anglo descent. This lifelong conviction involved his participation as one of the founding members of the League of United Latin American Citizens. Indeed, his contributions to the defense of Mexican-American citizens as well as Mexican laborers living in the United States is clearly documented in a myriad of newspaper articles he wrote as well as in speeches and his epistolary exchanges with members of congress, governors, U.S. presidents, his collaborators, and those with whom he heartily disagreed. Perales' writings are documented in two volumes of his text, *En Defensa de mi Raza / In Defense of My People* as well as in the large collection of papers and archives acquired by the University of Houston and Arte Público Press, through the Recovering the U.S. Hispanic Literary Heritage Project.

As I argue in this chapter, *En Defensa de mi Raza / In Defense of My People*, provides the reader with information that serves as a starting point for coming to a more clear understanding of various aspects of Alonso S. Perales' life project that involves deconstructing systems of thought that attempt to radically limit the rights of Mexican Americans as citizens of the United States. This project takes on larger dimensions over time as it includes the support of those Mexicans residing in the United States as well. So as to broaden this initial focus, the corpus of my study also focuses on letters exchanged between Alonso S. Perales and Adela Sloss Vento, those exchanged between Marta Perales and Adela Sloss Vento, as well as those letters written by Marta Perales. I suggest that these letters can be seen as literary artifacts embedded within a specific historical reality.

My intention in this direction is a critical reading of a select number of letters so as to highlight the type of discourse production evident within these texts. Although literary theorists have tended to marginalize letters as a sub-genre of autobiography, I propose that they clearly involve a type of self-writing that reveals elements that contribute to a cultural understanding of the writer and his life project. My major goal, therefore, is to demonstrate that the content of these letters presents self-writing that emanates from a cultural community; that is, these letters reflect the concerns of a collectivity of men and women of Mexican descent living in the United States.

In discussing the corpus of letters written by Alonso S. Perales, Marta Perales and Adela Sloss Vento, it is important to consider Wilhelm Dilthey's (1962) definition of autobiography and biography as literary expressions that can be understood as "the germinal cell of history," (p. 85) where the outstanding course of a life is set before the reader. In the discussion that follows, I argue that the epistolary exchanges that form part of the Alonso S. Perales Papers present the reader with evidence that demonstrates the outstanding endeavors undertaken by Alonso S. Perales. Furthermore, his wife Marta, as well as collaborators such as Adela Sloss Vento, were clearly affected by the perspective of this historical figure. Therefore, the letters analyzed as part of the present discussion not only document specific moments of the life experiences of the writers in question, but also the historical struggles on which they chose to focus. I ultimately discuss these texts in terms of what Lefebvre (1992) has defined as "spaces of representation." I argue that they express counter-hegemonic cultural politics that are situated within a Third-space that can be understood as a site of struggle or alternative space of enunciation that emphasizes a sense of identity as well as the transmission of specific cultural politics and values.

Letters and the Process of Self Writing

A major element of self-writing has to do with memory as it is registered within the text. In *Memory, History, Forgetting*, Paul Ricoeur (2004) asserts that a distinctive feature of memory is the presence of those " 'marks', [or] *sēmeia*, in which the affections of the body and the soul to which memory is attached are signified" (p. 12). In general, autobiographical writing can be understood as a type of self-referential writing that signifies different types of memory; therefore, it is pertinent to consider two questions that Ricoeur sets before the reader: "Of what are these memories? Whose memory is it?" (p. 3). In terms of the present corpus, and building on Ricouer's questions, several others guide my discussion here: In what way can the letter as a narrative form be considered as a type of life writing? How does this type of narrative form present us with information regarding the scope of the writer's life project? In what way is a particular life view represented discursively in the letters of each of the writers discussed here? Finally, in what way do these documents shed light on our understanding of personal and collective spaces of representation related to a particular historical period?

In his discussion of autobiographical writing Wilhelm Dilthey (1962) has noted that the great feat of the autobiographer is his capacity to find the "threads" of his life and set them down in writing as a coherent whole. In its strictest sense, autobiographical writing involves a process of retrospective life writing. Letters, however, are forms of autobiographical writing, and as suggested by Dilthey, they "reveal the writer's life at the time of writing . . . These documents show the individual as a centre of forces which act on him and proceed from him. But the meaning of his life in the historical context can only be ascertained if we can establish a general pattern which can be separated from the individual person" (p. 91). My study, then, is clearly concerned with the discovery of this pattern as it provides us with information regarding a specific historical period. Furthermore, as suggested by Julia Swindells (1985), autobiography can be understood as "the text of the oppressed" (p. 7). In this sense, the letter as a type of autobiographical writing can function as a vehicle through which the writer is able to testify against the oppression experienced by marginalized groups, in certain circumstances.

The autobiographical form, however, can be understood as more than simply a narration of the "I." For example, François Lionnet's *Autobiographical Voices: Race, Gender, Self-Portraiture* (1989) points to "self-reading" and "self-writing" as an attempt to represent life, particularly in terms of those elements that point to "deep symbolic and cultural value" (p. 112). Indeed, from her frame of reference, the autobiographical subject can take on the role of cultural observer, one who is involved in autoethnography and writing that takes on anthropological dimensions concerned with the preservation of culture through the written word. Complementing this idea is Avrom Fleishman's position (1983) regarding the various forms of autobiographical writing: "Where does the language of self writing come from? From the community's narrative discourse . . ." (p. 479). Interestingly, Alonso S. Perales chose not to focus on the personal "I" but rather to document the "threads" of his life project through the conservation of letters, articles and other types of writing that point to the narrative and argumentative discourse related to a community of people of Mexican descent; that is, his endeavors focus on "mi raza"/ 'my people' and he clearly situates himself as a member of this cultural group. Thus, as suggested by Paul John Eakin (1992), self writing "must be conceptualized not as some absolute literary essence but instead as historically variable, belonging to constantly changing networks of social practice in which the life of the individual receives articulation" (p. 94). It is through the letters written by Alonso S. Perales, then, that we find a type of life writing which, as noted by Genaro Padilla (1993), "transforms life history into textual permanence" in the form of "diaries, family histories, personal poetry and collections of self-disclosing correspondence" (p. 4). It is precisely through "self-disclosing correspondence" that the reader encounters information that focuses on specific dates and types of information that functions as a historical inscription of facts that represent "a major articulation of resistance to American social and cultural hegemony" (Padilla, 1993, p. 6).

It is relevant to note that the letters and articles written by Alfonso S. Perales are in no way meant to be used as a space for the purpose of self-agrandizement. Rather his writing, which enunciates a particular social and historical reality, is intended to function as a forum for giving testimony, for documenting his own experience and that of others of Mexican descent living within the United States. Indeed, in discussing the genre of testimony, Rosaura Sánchez (1997) argues that "testimonials interpellate not an individual subjectivity but a collective identity, a "We" engaged in political struggle within a diversity of social spaces . . . [they] are spaces for resistance, refutation, and disavowal, counterspaces for recentering collective subjectivity" (pp. 8, 13). Perales' letters and articles can definitely be understood as forms of "resistance, refutation, and disavowal;" that is, he uses them as a means for entering into a critical discussion with those members of his community, and American society in general, who are guilty of discrimination and the marginalization of people of color, particularly those of Mexican descent. Along these lines Frans H. van Eemeren (2010) suggests that "[i]deally, participation in democracy amounts first and foremost to an engagement of the members of the community, or society at large, in a continual and public discourse about common interests, policies to be developed, and decisions to be taken" (p. 1). Perales' writing demonstrates his capacity for using argumentative discourse as a means of fomenting a dialectical exchange that focuses on democratic ideals, ideals which he believes, are not to be understood as the right of white Americans only. Furthermore, his writing presents the voice of an intellectual who works toward constructing a public record intended to stand as a permanent fixing of discourse so as to formalize and verify what is true regarding the daily life experiences of his people. Perales makes use of a variety of venues to move his project forward, speaking deliberately and untiringly to promote his vision that focuses on the advancement of the *raza*. As we shall see in the discussion that follows, the various types of texts created by Alonso S. Perales, as well as those written by Marta Perales and Adela Sloss Vento, provide key information regarding the complex problems surrounding the individual and collective experience of people of Mexican origin in the United States.

Seeking Justice for His People

As part of a historiographical project, Volumes I and II of *En Defensa de mi Raza / In Defense of My People* provide information regarding dates, places and proper names related to a number of social issues concerning Mexican Americans and Mexican nationals. The author's introduction states that Mexican Americans must be committed to complying with their civic responsibilities, and at the same time they must insist on their inalienable rights of life, progress and happiness. He notes that the purpose of his own work in this direction began in 1919. He then alludes to the founders and heroes of the United States who made sacrifices in favor of the ideals of the country. Ultimately he focuses on the importance of continuing to fight for these rights within the framework of "la razón y el derecho"/ 'reason and the law" (Volume I, Introduction).

In Volume I of his text, the very first piece of writing entitled, "Principios Contraproducentes para la Americanización en Estados Unidos,"/'Counterproductive Principles for Americanization in the United States,' is a letter written by Perales and it is addressed to Mr. Nat M. Washer, President of the Americanization Committee of Bexar County (1). Dated November 4, 1919, it is important to note that this letter is a response to what was ultimately a national effort intended to deal with the huge increase in immigrant population in the United States between 1895 and 1924. That is, "[b]etween 1900 and 1910, the Mexican population of Texas and New Mexico nearly doubled . . . it doubled again between 1910 and 1920" (Divine et al., 1999, p.

686). Therefore, the social politics of this period attempted to "erase differences through English classes and deliberate 'Americanization' programs" (Divine et al., 1999, p. 683).

The letter written by Perales makes reference to an article entitled, "Inculcando Americanismo para cultivar mejores Ciudadanos" / 'Inculcating Americanism to cultivate better Citizens,' published in the "Express." Perales begins his letter by clearly identifying himself: "El que ésta escribe, ciudadano Americano de nacimiento y miembo del ejercito de este país, es de origen mexicano"/ 'He who writes this [letter], an American citizen by birth and a member of the armed services of this country, is of Mexican origin' (1). It is important to note that this letter begins by focusing on the author's own national and racial identity, while at the same time stating that he is an American citizen. He further points out that "Cuando aún no prestaba mis servicios a este gobierno en calidad de militar, a menudo se me dificultaba conseguir un lugar donde hospedarme debido simplemente al hecho de ser mexicano, aunque ciudadano Americano"/ 'Even before I served this government as a member of the military, it was often difficult to find a place to stay simply because I was Mexican, though an American citizen' (pp. 1-2). He then focuses on the example of a professor, also of Mexican origin, who had fought for the United States in World War I and was denied the possibility of staying at a hotel because the "hotel no se admitían mexicanos, fueran o no ciudadanos americanos"/ 'hotel did not admit Mexicans, whether they were American citizens or not (p. 2). Ultimately, he argues that "[e]l extinto Coronel y Ex-Presidente Teodoro Roosevelt dijo en su discurso pronunciado el dia [sic] 27 de Enero de 1917, que la ciudadanía Americana consistía en lealtad absoluta hacia los Estados Unidos de América y que por lo tanto no podia haber semi-ciudadanos; es decir, ciudadanos que fueron mitad americanos y mitad extranjeros"/ 'the now deceased Coronel and Ex-President Theodore Roosevelt said in his speech delivered on January 27 of 1917, that being an American citizen consisted in absolute loyalty toward the United States of America and that therefore there could be no semi-citizens; that is, citizens who were half American and half foreign' (p. 2). Perales' claim is that "no deberían hacerse distinciones desfavorables colectivos contra una raza cuya descendencia histórica es intachable,"/ 'no disfavorable distinctions should be made against a race whose historical descendency is irreproachable' (p. 3), and he points to the constitutional rights that should be accorded to all American citizens. He ends the letter by referring to "Las humillaciones de que algunas personas nos han hecho víctimas lesionan nuestros sentimientos como descendientes que somos de una raza noble y digna"/ 'The humiliation that some people have made us victims of have damaged our feelings, we who are descendents of a noble and worthy race' (3). Through the use of discourse that points to the injustices he and others have suffered because they are of Mexican descent, Perales clearly contests the confines of social configurations that impose "disfavorable distinctions" intended to humiliate those, who like himself, must be considered as "noble and worthy" members of American society.

The relevance of this text first of all has to do with Perales' choice to begin the volume by making reference to a personal experience regarding segregation. That is, he chooses to situate himself as part of the Mexican-American collectivity, as a person who is one with his people, as someone who suffers their humiliation. Further-more, by commenting on the case of an American citizen of Mexican descent who fought for the United States during World War I, and then by making reference to Theodore Roosevelt's statement that American citizenship consisted in "lealtad absoluta hacia los Estados Unidos,"/ 'absolute loyalty to the United States,' Perales places this citizen on equal ground with all American citizens who fought in World War I. The tone of the final paragraph of the letter is clear: "Finalmente me permito decir a usted que a menos que se tomen medidas precautorias tendientes a contrar-restar la injustificada mala voluntad que algunas personas guarden hacia los méxi-co-americanos, todo esfuerzo en pro del susodicho proyecto de americanization resultará estéril en lo que se refiere a la americanización de mexicanos"/ 'Finally let me to tell you that unless precautionary measures are taken in an attempt to coun-teract the unjustified ill will that some people harbor against Mexican Americans, all efforts in favor of the so-called project of the Americanization of Mexicans will be fruitless' (p. 3). Discursively, Perales strongly voices his own agenda in this final statement; his intention is to "decir a usted," / 'to tell you,' to speak out against the Americanization project unless measures are taken against the "injustificada mala voluntad"/ 'unjustified ill will' that is focused on people of Mexican descent in the United States. The reader must necessarily question the meaning of the 'unjustified ill will,' referred to in this letter. The history of discrimination and racial segregation in the United States is complex and in terms of people of Mexican descent, and it is important to recall American perspectives regarding those of mixed blood. Frederick Merk, for example, asserts that during the Mexican-American War, those who favored the annexation of all of Mexico proposed in 1847 that American democrat-ic institutions would take responsibility for the "regeneration" of nonwhite races. He suggests that "in the case of Mexico, a *people* was to be saved from cruel and self-ish rulers, a community was to be lifted, and was to have bestowed on it the bless-ings of American order and peace and freedom" (pp. 121-122). There were those, however, who opposed the total annexation of Mexico as it would mean the incor-poration of a nonwhite populaton; therefore, they asserted that only those areas that bordered the United States and were sparsely populated should be incorporated into national domain. Indeed, John C. Calhoun (2008) was one of the outspoken oppo-nents of the plan for complete annexation of Mexico:

> Nor have we ever incorporated into the Union any but the Caucasian race. To incorporate Mexico, would be the first departure of the kind; for more than half of its population are pure Indians, and by far the larger portion of the residue mixed blood. I protest against the incorporation of such a people. Ours is the Government of the white man. The great misfortune of what was for-merly Spanish America, is to be traced to the fatal error of placing the colored race on an equality with the white. (pp. 410-411)

Calhoun's reference to Spanish America's "fatal error" corresponds to the prejudices and propaganda of the "Black Legend" which points to the bigotry that has been applied historically "not only to Spain, but to Spanish Americans and all Hispanics,

not only to the conquistadores but to their mixed-blood descendants—for misce-
genation has also been anathema to Anglo and northern European peoples" (Kanellos, 1998, p. 48). Ultimately, then, as Merk (1995) notes, "the disintegration of the
All Mexico crusade seemed to mean that the Southerner and his ideals had tri-
umphed" (p. 192). This type of ideological discourse that considers those of "mixed
blood" and "the colored race" as unacceptable and outside the national project, circulated in the United States prior to 1848 and afterwards. Indeed, in his text, *Anglos
and Mexicans in the Making of Texas, 1836-1986,* David Montejano (1987) discusses the culture of segregation in Texas during the period from 1920 to 1940 and he
contends that:

> Few settlers described their divided society solely in the pragmatic language
> of economic interest or political control. Most mixed their views and explana-
> tions with ethical statements, superstitions, biblical sayings, historical lessons,
> or just plain 'gut feelings' about the proper place of colored people. In the
> minds of most Anglos, there was no question that Mexicans were an inferior
> people. (p. 220)

Along these same lines Alfred Arteaga (1994), argues that "the Other can be relegated to anything beyond the borders of Self : the Other is colored, pagan, super-
stitious, the Other is primitive, savage, beast" (p. 1). It is precisely Alonso S. Perales'
refusal to accept discriminatory ideas regarding the inferior position assigned to people of Mexican origin in the United States, as well as his progressive sense of the
need for social justice and responsibility, that formed the basis of his social action.
Indeed, if, as suggested by Ramón Saldivar (1998), we can "understand ideology as
the ways a culture links social action with fundamental beliefs, a collective identity
with the course of history" (p. 13), then Perales' text contests those beliefs regarding
the nonwhite, Hispanic population of the United States and his writing stands as an
expression of counter-hegemonic discourse, or what Göran Therborn has defined as
"alter-ideology" (qtd in Saldivar p. 17).

Writings in the first volume of *En Defensa de mi Raza / In Defense of My People,* a collection of letters and articles written by Perales from 1919 through 1929,
contest these ideological perspectives. Furthermore, the images on the cover of the
text include key concepts that underlie his vision: "Cuidadano bueno y progresista" /
Good and progressive citizen;' "Comprensión mutual" / 'Mutual Comprehension;'"Educación" / 'Education;' "Justicia" / 'Justice.' These are the ideas that form
the basis of his worldview expressed during the 1920s, which as suggested by Adri-
ana Ayala (2005), are not simply the years of the Jazz age, but rather "a period filled
with popular media images of social and cultural progress at the same time that racial
conflicts became evident throughout the United States" (p. 4).

Much of Perales' early writing is concerned with projecting an image of Mexicans
as "trabajadores fieles y honrados" / 'faithful and honest workers' (Ayala, 2005, p. 5).
For example, on January 7, 1921, *La Prensa* published an article entitled "Protesta
Contra lo Aseverado por James E. Ferguson" / 'Protest Against the Declaration of
James E. Ferguson.' The publication is based on a letter of protest, dated January 3,

1921, and written by Alonso S. Perales to ex-governor James E. Ferguson who is quoted as saying: "Proclamamos ante el mundo que no tenemos el propósito de reconocer al mexicano como a nuestro igual; ni socialmente ni en ninguna otra forma"/ 'We proclaim before the world that we have no intention of recognizing the Mexican as our equal; neither socially nor in any other form' (p. 6). In his letter, Perales contests this blatantly discriminatory view: "Mi creencia en la justicia me inspira a dirigirme a usted con el único y exclusivo objeto de reprobar vuestra actitud y de refutar de la manera más enfática las aseveraciones asentados por usted . . . "/ 'My belief in justice inspires me to address you for the sole and exclusive purpose of reproving your attitude and to refute in a most emphatic way those statements you have asserted' (p. 6). Perales' reference to his "belief in justice" stands as a linguistic marker that focuses on the writer's life view. As a means of defending his perspective regarding the "verdaderos méritos de la raza mexicana"/ 'true merits of the Mexican race' (pp. 6-7), he points to the achievements of prominent Mexicans such as León de la Barra "recientemente nombrado president de la commision de arbitraje Franco-Austriaco establecido por el tratado de San Germain"/ 'recently named president of the Franco-Austrian Arbitration Commission established by the Treaty of Saint-Germain' (7). Just as he has previously recalled the service of men of Mexican descent who fought for the United States in World War I, Perales vehemently contests Ferguson by referring to Francisco León de la Barra s appointment to an international arbitration commission involved in bringing the war to an end. Indeed, as noted at the beginning of the article, Perales himself chose to send a translation of his letter to Ferguson to *La Prensa* thereby taking a public stand regarding Ferguson's claim that, in keeping with the law, Mexicans, like Blacks, must be separated from the white population.

Outstanding in Perales' project is his defense of Mexican Americans and Mexican nationals; however, he is also critical of the shortcomings of his people. In an article entitled "Problemas de Nuestra Raza en Estados Unidos" written in Managua, Nicaragua, dated August 2, 1928 and published in "Diogenes" in McAllen Texas on September 8, 1928, Perales argues: "ha llegado el momento de que los méxico-americanos y mexicanos radicados en estados unidos despertarnos de nuestra letargo y resueltamente procuremos redimirnos"/ 'the moment has come for Mexican-Americans and Mexicans residing in the United States to awaken from our lethargy and resolutely try to redeem ourselves' (p. 7). He further comments that "Urge, pues, dicidirnos a evolucionar a igualar al anglo-sajón. De esta manera probaremos que, aun cuando es cierto que hasta hoy no hemos demostrado ser progresistas, no somos fundamentalmente inferiores"/ 'It is urgent, then, that we decide to evolve and become equal to the Anglo Saxon. In this way we will prove that, even though it is true that until now we have not demonstrated that we are progressives, we are not fundamentally inferior' (p. 7). In contrast to praising the accomplishments of León de la Barra, here the reader encounters linguistic markers such as "redimirnos," "evolucionar," "ser progresistas." Perales makes obvious reference to thinking that emanates from the spirit of Progressivism which focused on beliefs such as the following: "a better world and in the ability of people to achieve it . . . progress depended on knowledge . . . individual morality and collective action, the scientific method . . ." (Divine, Breen, Fredrickson, Williams, 1999, p. 705). He further asserts that both Mexicans and Mexican

Americans must "proceder activa y firmamente a realizar nuestra redención"/ 'proceed actively and firmly to bring about our redemption' (p. 8). This article emphasizes the reality of people of Mexican descent who are considered by Anglo Americans as inferior and Perales further mentions a San Antonio news article as evidence: "El Dr. Max Handman, director del departamento de sociología de la Universidad de Texas, declaró . . . que la condición social y económica de los mexicanos en San Antonio es penosa y requiere cambios radicales" / 'Dr. Max Handman, director of the department of Sociology at the University of Texas, declared . . . that the social and economic condition of Mexicans in San Antonio is embarrassing and requires radical changes' (p. 8). In response Perales points to the importance of "[l]a elevación del nivel intelectual, económico y social de los méxico-americanos y mexicanos no solamente asegurarían nuestro bienestar sino que también nos pondría en condiciones de reconquistarnos el respeto del anglo-sajón. Solo esta circunstancia bastaría para justificar cualquier esfuerzo o sacrificio que hiciéramos tendente a evolucionar" / 'the elevation of the intellectual, economic and social level of Mexican Americans and Mexicans would not only assure our well-being but would also put us in a condition to re-conquer the respect of the Anglo Saxon. Only this circumstance would be sufficient to justify whatever effort or sacrifice we might make toward evolution' (p. 10). These lines point clearly to Alonso Perales' declaration of resolve that must be taken to heart by his own people in order to achieve progress through "la capacidad latente de nuestra raza" / 'the latent capacity of our race' (p. 10). Indeed, he exemplifies this latent capacity regarding the evolution and progress of Mexican Americans and Mexicans by referring to the importance of achieving the stature of men such as Captain Emilio Carranza, a hero of the Mexican Revolution. By following in the footsteps of this type of man, people of Mexican origin would be able to conquer the respect of Anglo Americans, a necessary step toward eventual racial equality. The examples of the lives of Francisco León de la Barra and Emilio Carranza, then, are used discursively to contest racist attitudes such as those expressed by James E. Ferguson and Max Handman.

During his diplomatic post in Nicaragua, Perales continued to write for the "Diogenes" in McAllen. In an article published on September 8, 1928 he emphasizes his civic project once again as he argues: "Repito que, en mi concepto, la evolución de los méxico-americanos depende de instruction, organización, e inteligente y consciente ejercicio del derecho del sufragio . . ." / 'I repeat that, in my conception, the evolution of Mexican Americans depends on instruction, organization, and intelligent and conscious exercise of the right to vote . . .' (p. 11). Of particular interest in this fragment is the discursive representation of the author as he writes in the first person singular and emphasizes "mi concepto" / 'my conception' which focuses once again on the idea of evolution and the need for instruction and organization. Education, then, becomes a key factor for bringing about what he terms as "redención social" / 'social redemption' (p. 12).

In another article entitled, "Lo Que Significa Para Nosotros Las Escuelas Para Adultos" / 'What Schools for Adults Mean for Us,' published in *El Porvenir* in San Antonio on May 28, 1934, Perales further emphasizes the importance of education: "Indiscutiblemente, la educación para adultos es la llave para la rápida solución de nuestros problemas cívico-sociales, puesto que nuestros conciudadanos adultos estarán major preparados, para participar con actividad e inteligencia en sociedades que tienen por objeto promover fases de actividad social" / 'Education for adults is undeniably the key to a rapid solution of our social-civic problems, since our adult fellow citizens will be better prepared to participate actively and intelligently in societies that have as an objective the promotion of phases of social activity' (p. 21). In this direction he refers specifically to the following organizations: "la Liga de Ciudadanos Unidos Latinoamericanos, las Sociedades de Padres y Maestros, las Sociedades Anti-Tuberculosis . . . la organización de Jóvenes Exploradores de America" / 'the League of United Latin American Citizens, Parent and Teacher Associations, the Anti-Tuberculosis Society . . . the organization of Young American Explorers' (p. 21). These references, in addition to an emphasis on education and progress, further highlight a life project that focuses on personal and collective improvement. It is important to note here that mention of these organizations coincides with Arnoldo Carlos Vento's assertion that, "[b]y the twenties, second generation Mexican American/Chicanos began to move away from the more "Mexican" mutualistic societies and created a number of organizations that were oriented toward citizenship and civil rights" (vii). Based on his conviction that associations of this sort were a necessary format for promoting social activity, Alonso Perales, together with other forward-thinking figures, contributed to the creation of the League of United Latin American Citizens in August of 1927. In "El Verdadero Origen de la Liga de Ciudadanos Unidos Latinoamericanos" / 'The True Origin of the League of United Latin American Citizens' published in the *Diógenes* in McAllen, Texas and *El Fronterizo* of Rio Grande City, Texas on July 2, 1927, Perales clarifies his perspective regarding the organization: "una fuerte entidad de ciudadanos americanos de origen mexicano cuyo exclusive objeto será laborar sinceramente en pro del mejoramiento intelectual, economico, social y politico de los méxico-americanos en lo particular y de la raza mexicana en general" / 'a strong entity of American citizens of Mexican origin whose exclusive objective was to labor sincerely in favor of the intellectual, economic, social and political improvement of Mexican Americans in particular and of the Mexican people in general" (p. 103). The objective evident in this fragment stands as a testament of Perales' life's work. However, as I will discuss in the following section, his commitment to this cause would eventually involve those close to him, especially his wife, Marta as well as Adela Sloss Vento, a close family friend.

The Scope and Effect of Alonso Perales' Life Project

As I have noted, Alonso S. Perales' life project as evidenced in his correspondence and select articles and writings, reflect his commitment to people of his own race. A great deal of his writing was published in newspapers such as the *Washington Post*, *La Prensa* of San Antonio, Texas, *El Monitor* of Falfurrias, Texas, *El Fronterizo* of Rio Grande City, Texas, *Diogenes* of McAllen, Texas , as well as *Las Novedades* of Kingsville, Texas. He also wrote from places such as Managua, Nicaragua where he served in a diplomatic capacity. Indeed, in reviewing the material that makes up the Alonso S. Perales collection, the reader is confronted with the words and actions of an indiviual in relation to a community, especially in terms of those forces that would attempt to exercise power over him and his people. Here we find information regarding the life of a man who is immersed in what Marcel Lefebvre (1992) has called a "representational space," one that can be understood as a space that "is alive, it speaks. It has an affective kermel (*noyau*) or centre: Ego, bed, bedroom, dwelling, house or square, church, graveyard. It embraces the loci of passion, of action, of lived situations . . . it may be directional, situational or relational, because it is essentially qualitative, fluid, and dynamic" (p. 42). Alonso S. Perales' life project is most certainly one that passionately and dynamically embraces a cause that is at once at the center of his own life and that of his cultural community. Furthermore, the spaces from which he writes and speaks involve what Bhabha (1990) has defined as a "'third space' which enables other positions to emerge. The third space displaces the histories that constitute it, and sets up new structures of authority, new political initiatives . . ." (p. 211). Alonso S. Perales speaks of specific "lived situations" where his voice stands out in an effort to bring about important changes in the hegemonic structures intent on silencing Mexican Americans in Texas. His writing, therefore, represents a third space of resistance that focuses on presenting "new political initiatives" that focus on Mexican-American citizens who occupied a marginal position within the United States.

Perales' view is clearly evident in a handwritten text by Marta Perales in which she asserts:

> Yo que fuí la esposa y compañera de Alonso por 38 años, soy testiga de su ardúa lucha de sus tristezas y desilusiones para realizar la obra de formar la Liga [sic] (Lulac) el día 14 de Agosto de 1927 en Harlingen, Texas. Antes de 1925 salieron él y el Profesor José Luz Saens [sic] en una gira por el estado de Texas dando conferencias de orientación, sobre derechos constitucionales [y] sobre educasion, [sic] y de Americanision [sic] para hacer sentir a los nacionales Latino Americano cómo [sic] verdaderos americanos, qué [sic] es lo que somos . . . / I who was the wife and companion of Alonso for 38 years, am a witness of his arduous fight of his sadness and disillusions of trying to bring about the work of forming the League (LULAC) on August 14, 1927 in Harlingen, Texas. Prior to 1925 he and Professor José Luz Saens [sic[left on a trip through the state of Texas giving orientation conferences, about constitutional rights [and] about education, and Americanization so as to make Latin American nationals feel like true Americans, that is what we are . . . (Ts. MP, "Yo que fui la esposa . . ." 12 April 1977, Box 10).[1]

As I have mentioned previously, Perales chose to document his life experience through his articles, speeches and letters, yet the "arduous fight" that marked his life project was clearly a collective one. Marta Perales mentions the work of José Luz Saens [sic], but in "El Verdadero Origen de la Liga de Ciudadanos Unidos Latinoamericanos" Alonso S. Perales also mentions the support of people such as Pablo González, Filiberto Galván, Professor J. Luz Saenz, José T. Canales, Juan B. Lozano, and Bernardo Garza (*En Defensa de mi Raza / In Defense of My People, Tomo Dos* / Volume Two, pp. 101-105).

In addition to the activities of these men who worked toward the organization of LULAC, it is pertinent to examine the role of Adela Sloss Vento in relation to Alonso Perales' activities which were intended to assure the progress and "el bienestar de nuestro pueblo" / 'the welfare of our people' (p. 102). In her text, *Alonso S. Perales: His Struggles for the Rights of Mexican Americans*, Sloss Vento (1977) notes that:

> It was in 1927, when I became an enthusiastic corroborator on behalf of the the cause of the Mexican American.
>
> Collaboration and investigation into the problems of our people was very difficult during these years for many reasons. Among them included a people who were impoverished, disunited and discouraged, due to the many years of persecution and injustice. My collaboration with Alonso S. Perales regarding Mexican-American problems, in addition to the correspondence between our leaders and myself for more than thirty years, as well as the role played by other patriotic Americans of Mexican descent, all contributed to make the present struggle less difficult. (p. 1)

This text is also autobiographical, but like *En Defensa de mi Raza / In Defense of My People* where the author situates himself as a member of the community of Mexican Americans, in the Introduction to Sloss Vento's book, her son introduces the reader to her participation as "an active defender of the *Raza* in their struggle for economoic, political and cultural freedom" (Vento, 1977, ix). However, as Sloss Vento states, the major objective of her text is to focus on the efforts of Alonso S. Perales, J. Luz Saenz and J.T. Canales in favor of the Mexican Americans. Thus, just as Marta Perales presents herself as a witness to her husband's "ardúa [sic] lucha" / 'arduous struggle', Sloss Vento describes herself as "an enthusiastic corroborator" and she points to her correspondence with "leaders" for a period of thirty years. Later in her text she explains that she also met "Prof. J. Luz Saenz, and Mrs. Marta Engracia Perez de Perales in 1927" (Vento, 1977, p. 6). She then recalls that after reading an article written by Alonso S. Perales in "El Fronterizo," she wrote to him "congratulating him for his efforts on our behalf" (Vento, 1977, p. 6). In addition to this letter, Sloss Vento would exchange an important number of letters with Alonso S. Perales dated from November, 1927 through March, 1960; the letters dealt with comments on newspaper articles, issues concerning legal processes, discrimination and other types of organizational activities related to the situation of Mexican Americans. During this time Perales would assume the role of mentor and friend. The letters she exchanged with Marta Perales from February 1968 through February 1984 focused on issues concerning Mexican Americans in Texas as well as the efforts of both women to give testimony regarding the founding of LULAC and the prominent role played by Alonso S. Perales.

Alonso S. Perales responded to Sloss Vento's first letter from the Law Office of Canales & Mckay and Alonso S. Perales in McAllen, Texas. He thanks her for "encouraging remarks with reference to our Organization—The League of American

Citizens of Latin Decent." Here he speaks of his purpose: "to bring about the rapid intellectual, economic, social and political evolution of American citizens of Latin descent, and as far as posible, promote the general welfare of all other latin people residing in Texas. We want to evolve into and to produce the highest type of American citizen attainable." In keeping with this view, he congratulates her for having graduated from high school as well as for her "firm determination to improve your mind" (AP letter to Adela Sloss Vento, 7 November 1927, Microfilm 2309, Reel 27). Evident in Perales' response are references to those aspects of his life view concerning the importance of education and continued intellectual progress for people of Mexican origin.

This view regarding "American citizens of Latin descent" is also reiterated by Sloss Vento in an article published in the *Diogenes* of McAllen, Texas four years later. The article entitled, "Nuestra Gratitud y Estimación Hacia el Autor de la Liga de Ciudadanos Unidos Latino-Americanos" / 'Our Gratitude and Esteem Toward the Author of the League of United Latin-American Citizens', focuses on Perales' efforts in favor of "los nuestros" / 'our people,' and it employs a type of discourse that is adulatory in tone:

> Como una estrella radiante que ha sembrado y sigue sembrando el camino del México Americano . . . Es el Ciudadano quien ocupa en el corazón de tantos pueblos una gratitud tan honda y una estimación tan grande que la mayoría de los Latino Americanos no podemos menos de exclamar que es el México Americano que se alza por encima de todos. Es EL quien siempre ha probado su SINCERIDAD y su GRANDEZA DE ALMA hacia nosotros / Like a radiant star that has sown and continues to sow the way for the Mexican American . . . He is the Citizen who in the heart of so many people deserves such deep gratitude and esteem that the majority of Latin Americans cannot but least of all exclaim that he is the Mexican American who stands above everyone. It is HE who has always proven his SINCERITY and his GREATNESS OF SOUL towards us. (ASV article, 7 May 1931, Microfilm 2309, Reel 27)

She then asks the following questions: "¿Hay algo más noble en un Ciudadano como el esfuerzo de crear entre los nuestros, Ciudadanos leales a nuestro país? ¿Hay algo más noble como el de reclamar la justicia misma, la justicia que corresponde a los nuestros?" / 'Is there anything more noble in a Citizen than the effort to create among our people, loyal Citizens of our country? Is there anything more noble than reclaiming justice, the justice that corresponds to our people?' She then quotes the words of Perales as author of LULAC: "Urge que se nos den los derechos que nos corresponden, pues de lo contrario, una mayoría de los nuestros no podrán llegar nunca a ser los Ciudadanos ideales de nuestro país" / 'It is urgent that we be given the rights that are ours, for if not, a majority of our people will never be able to become the ideal Citizens of our country' (Article ASV, 7 May 1931, Microfilm 2309, Reel 27).

In her texts, Sloss Vento writes in favor of the cause of Mexican-American citizens and she chooses to use the words of Alonso S. Perales as a means of promoting what she has adopted as her own project. In describing Perales as a radiant star she highlights his life project, the project of loyal citizens of "nuestro país" / 'our country.' She thus situates herself as one of those loyal citizens who adheres to a project focused on procuring justice.

In an undated and unsigned document "Los Hechos"we find an extremely detailed description regarding the cruel and unjust treatment of men of Mexican descent in Texas. The essay refers to the October 2, 1934 case of men who were arrested on suspicion of the murder of Homer and Virgil Dobbs in Live Oak County in George West, Texas. The text is seemingly written with the purpose of presenting evidence against the Texas Rangers who took part in the beating and cruel treatment of suspects Teodoro Sáenz and Santiago Alanís: "El joven Santiago Alanis fue gopeado [sic] de una manera criminal . . . Se cree que el joven Alanis no viva, pues su cuerpo está todo negro . . . El Sr. Sáenz estubo [sic] una noche y un día sin conocimiento" / 'The young man Santiago Alanis was beaten in a cruel manner . . . It is believed that the young Alanis is not alive, since his body is all black . . . for one night and a day Mr. Sáenz was unconscious.' The text does not clarify the source of this information, and the reader only finds references such as "Según todos" / 'according to everyone' and "las familias de estos ciudadanos y demás habitantes de este lugar" / 'the families of these citizens and the rest of the inhabitants of this place.' On page two of the essay, the writer notes that she intends to record this information provided by citizens on a separate page, and it will be entitled, "Facts of the Record of the Citizens That Are Held by Suspicion in the Dobbs Brothers Murder Case" (Ms., ASV, "Los Hechos," Microfilm 2309, Reel 27).

We can asume that the essay was written by Adela Sloss Vento because a letter written to her by Alonso S. Perales makes specific reference to "the enclosure regarding the Alanis-Saenz case." In his letter Perales first of all expresses his "outrage." He then indicates that because the case concerns Mexican citizens, the men should report the case to the Consul General of Mexico. He also states his agreement regarding the importance of publicizing the incident, but he cautions her to wait until defense attorney Kelly is sure that the case will not be jeopardized through publicity. Interestingly, in a post script he asks about the existence of an adult night school program in her home town of San Juan, Texas. He points out that if one does not exist, then she should tell the school superintendent that she wants one. Again, in keeping with the overall tone of an elder who guides a novice, he proceeds to give more specific guidelines. He tells her to "get busy" as the U.S. government pays the teachers' salaries and the school board should furnish the building, as well as light and fuel (Letter, AP to ASV, 17 October 1934, Microfilm 2309, Reel 27).

Of particular interest in this exchange is the very brief response offered by Alonso Perales. If indeed he is referring to the six-page essay which is a compilation of what the writer intends to offer as evidence regarding the cruel and unjust treatment of Mexican citizens in Texas, his response is extremely mild when compared to the vehement tone of the essay. The discursive tone of his letter, with the final instructions to "get busy," seems to suggest that he believes Sloss Vento should more appropriately concern herself with adult education classes in her community rather than becoming involved in compiling evidence for a murder case. That is, she is speaking outside the limits that were culturally imposed upon women during this time period. Furthermore, Perales' instructions point clearly to his insistence on using every forum available to improve the situation of Mexican Americans.

A number of letters exchanged between both Alonso S. Perales and Adela Sloss Vento in 1947 point to the continuation of life experiences of two people immersed in activities concerned with the marginalization and bigotry suffered by Mexican Americans in Texas. This series of letters sheds light on the history of a struggle that is difficult to overcome at this time in history. For example, in one letter Perales lauds the work undertaken by Sloss Vento, that is, "su bella y noble labor" / 'your beautiful and noble work. He also expresses his gratutude for her participation in the issues that concern them both: "gracias al ser supremo por habernos dado personas como usted que sincera y desinteresadamente se preocupen por el progreso y bien-estar de nuestro pueblo" / '[I give] thanks to the supreme being for having given us people like you who have sincerely and unselfishly been concerned about the progress and well-being of our people.' To some degree, his praise echoes feelings that Sloss Vento has expressed regarding Perales' own project. He speaks of going to Los Angeles to "una gran Conferencia Nacional Católica" / 'a large National Catholic Conference.' He also refers to "nuestro problema" / 'our problema,' that is, the problem of continued discrimination that is not just a problema in Texas, but one that affects "los nuestros en California" / 'our people in California.' Along these same lines he mentions the book he intends to publish, *Are We Good Neighbors?*, which focuses on the problem of discrimination in Texas. Of particular interest, how-ever, is the final portion of his letter: "la ruego no se desanime. Debemos seguir luchando. Mientras Dios nos da vida y salud habrá esperanza" / 'I beg you not to be disheartened. We must keep fighting. As long as God gives us life and health there is hope' (AP letter to ASV, 11 August 1947, Microfilm 2309, Reel 27). At this point the reader cannot help but sense the extreme limitations that surround this cause. It is relevant to recall that Sloss Vento wrote her first letter to Perales in 1927, and in Perales' letter to her nearly twenty years later, it becomes evident that it is only through the close and longstanding contact of those involved in this fight for equal-ity and justice that they are able to continue to move forward.

We find further evidence regarding setbacks in another of Sloss Vento's letters addressed to Perales. Although the utopic vision of LULAC concerned unity in fight-ing for the cause of Latin American Citizens, and although both Perales and Sloss Vento were inclusive in their view concerning not only the defense of Mexican Americans, but also those of Mexican descent residing in the United States, Sloss Vento presents another viewpoint as well:

Creo que estamos tan mal o peor que antes en lo que respecta a nuestro prob-lema, porque cuando estábamos para dar un paso hacia adelante con el hecho de que los nuestros exijían [sic] mejores sueldos, México se puso a enviar miles de braceros a Texas por sueldos de hambre para enriquecer más al Anglosajon [sic] que nos trata con odio y no tiene otro propósito nomás de acumular riquezas con el trabajo de los Mexicanos, y que el servilismo sigue / I believe we are as bad off or worse than before with respect to our problem, because

when we were about to move forward with the demands of our [people] for better wages, Mexico decided to send thousands of temporary workers to Texas for
starvation wages so as to make the Anglo-Saxon even wealthier and they treat
us with hate and they have no other purpose than to accumulate wealth through
the labor of Mexicans, and that servility continue. (ASV letter to AP, 8 September 1947, Microfilm 2309, Reel 27)

Evident in this fragment of her text is Sloss Vento's criticism of the Mexican government for sending braceros to labor in the United States in spite of the fact that the
Camacho and Cardenas governments had defended a policy of not sending braceros
until racial descrimination and exploitation ceased. She then mentions that over
30,000 new braceros had arrived in additon to those who entered the country illegaly.
She ends her letter by stating her desire that they continue to fight for "nuestros
Problemas" / 'our Problems.' It is within this text that we detect the magnitude of
what the writer has defined as 'our Problem,' one that concerned her deeply, but
which she feels helpless to solve. Furthermore, although the vision of LULAC was
meant to include defense of Mexicans residing in the United States, by the end of the
1940's the influx of large numbers of braceros negatively affected the ongoing
"Problem" of fair wages for Mexican Americans in Texas. This particular problem
was affected by the fact that at this time in U.S. history there was no law making it
illegal for an employer to hire undocumented immigrants. Indeed, even with the passage of the Texas Proviso in 1952 which made it "illegal for any American to "harbor" an undocumented individual, Congress stated that it was specifically *not* illegal
to hire such an individual" (Yale-Loehr, 2007, p. 2).

    In a letter dated seven days later, Perales thanks Sloss Vento her for her "inter-
esting letter of recent date" and he invites her and "other ladies from the Valley who
are interested in our problem . . . to attend a conference to be held in El Paso, Texas."
He then suggests that she and other women who are interested in the problem "get
lined up with the National Council for Catholic Women" (AP Letter to ASV, 15 September 1947, Microfilm 2309, Reel 27). We can assume that this letter is a response
to the extensive three-page letter written by Sloss Vento; but because Perales' vision
was based on the organization of citizens and non-citizens of Mexican descent as a
key factor for bringing about change within U.S. society, it is not surprising that he
is silent regarding the distinctions she makes between "los nuestros" / "our people"
and the "braceros" / "temporary workers." He instead invites Sloss Vento to the El
Paso conference. However, in a later letter, Sloss Vento explains that she is unable to
attend the conference because she must take her two children, ages nine and ten to a
Catholic school in a nearby town. Her letter also refers to a conflict related to
whether children who attend Catholic schools should be permitted to ride on public
school buses. She further emphasizes that Mexico must be responsible and not allow
"braceros" and Mexicans to emigrate illegally into the border regions (ASV letter to
AP, 25 September 1947). It would seem, then, that Sloss Vento intends to highlight
her sense of responsibility in matters concerning the education of Catholic children,
but she continues to press her point regarding Mexico's responsibility and the continued influx of "braceros" and unauthorized laborers in Texas.

Perales' invitation is related to his own participation in various Catholic organizations. For example, he authored a series of texts dated from 24 October 1947 to 5 July 1953 under the heading of "Arquitectos de Nuestros Propios Destinos." In a document entitled, "Más acerca de la Conferencia Regional de Damas Católicas," Perales points to the Southeast Regional Conference of the National Council of Catholic Women. The list of conference topics is extensive, and they clearly emphasize the participation of Catholic women within the domestic sphere. For example, some of the topics involved: "Institutos Católicos de Maternidad; Foros para discutir el asunto del Matrimonio; Programas de la Vida Familiar . . . La Enseñanza de la Religión en el Hogar; La Responsabilidad de la Mujer en lo que respecta al Bien Vivir en la Comunidad . . ." / 'Catholic Maternity Institute; Forum for the discussion of issues on Marriage; Programs on Family Life . . . Teaching Religion in the Home; The Responsiblility of Women in matters of Good Living in the Community . . . (Ms., Alonso Perales , 24 October 1947, Box 9). Perales' participation in this direction corresponds clearly to his initial project which was intended to construct a collective space of representation for people of Mexican descent. His project, then, involved work in the public sphere as well as in areas of action within organizations tied to the traditional views of the Catholic Church. For example, in an address presented during the 1947 Congress of the International Union of Catholic Women's Leagues which took place in Rome, Italy, Pope Pius XII states:

Most of you must continue to give the greater part of your time and of your loving attention to the care of your homes and families. We must not forget that the making of a home in which all feel at ease and happy, and the bringing up of children are very special contributions to the common welfare . . . woman's work in the home still goes hand in hand with her contribution to the social and national economy. (Papal Directives for the Women of Today)

Interestingly, the list of topics dealt with in the Southeast Regional Conference regarding the role women were to play in bringing about change in the destinies of people of Mexican descent closely parallels the vision set forth by Pope Pius XII. Thus, because Perales invites Sloss Vento to the conference, it becomes clear that although he is supportive of her "noble" endeavors, he does in fact attempt to involve her in those activities considered appropriate for women and which are authorized by a greater discourse, that of the Pope.

Testimony and a Legacy

After the death of her husband in 1960, Marta Pérez de Perales became involved in the project of documenting his endeavors as a means of preserving his legacy, and she turned to a number of friends who would support her effort. For example, in a letter written to Marta Perales, José Tomás (J.T.) Canales, who was a major collaborator in the Harlingen Convention of 1927,[2] explains the following: "I am writing the Hon. Mr. Alvarado who is in the office formerly occupied by your good husband 308 International Bldg San Antonio, Texas and send him data about who were the original movement that created Lulac" (J.T. Canales letter to MP, 8 September 1960,

Microfilm 2309, Reel 42). He would respond to her the following month regarding her letter "donde me avisa que va a trasladar los restos de mi estimado y fino amigo Alonso S. Perales, (su muy querido esposo) para Alice, el Sábado, día [sic] 15 de Octubre y que piensa tener una velada en su memoria en el Auditorio de la escuela superior en Alice a las 7:30 y me hace el honor de invitarme para ser uno de los oradores en dicha velada. Con gusto iré . . . " / 'where you inform me that you will transport the remains of my esteemed and fine friend Alonso S. Perales, (your most beloved husband) to Alice, on Saturday, 15 of October and that you are planning to have a memorial service in the Auditorium of Alice high school at 7:30 and you honor me by inviting me to be one of the speakers during said service. I will be pleased to go . . .' (J.T. Canales letter to MP, 7 October 1960, Microfilm 2309, Reel 42).

In a handwritten document entitled, "Al Pueblo de Alice" / 'To the People of Alice,' which was prepared for her husband's memorial service, she writes that "Fue un gran hombre y esto lo digo al mundo entero honrado y luchador. Fué [sic] el faro que sirvió de guía a los desorientados y yó [sic], que fue su compañera por 38 años, fui testiga de sus luchas, triunfos y desilusiones" / 'He was the light that served as a guide to [those who were] disoriented and I, who was his companion for 38 years, was witness to his struggles, triumphs and disillusions.' Although the words that follow are crossed out in the document, it is important to note that here she mentions that her husband's disillusions were due to the envy of others. She continues to tell the people of Alice, "Yo lo admiré . . . Defensor de su raza y del debíl [sic] igualmente defendía al ultrajado, que a la mujer burlada . . ." / 'I admired him . . . Defender of his people and of the weak [and] he equally defended [those who were] insulted as well as the woman who was taunted' (Ts. MP speech at memorial service, Alice, TX undated, Microfilm 2309, Reel 42). Here the writer clearly represents herself not only as a witness of her husband's project, but as his companion, as his collaborator. Her personal project, then, is to tell "al mundo entero" / 'the whole world' the truth about her husband's role in the founding of LULAC. The scope of her efforts also includes documentation of his work during "thirteen diplomatic missions for the United States Department of State, in Washington, Mexico, the West Indies, and Central and South America" (MP letter to United States Department of State, San Antonio, TX, 21 July 1970, Microfilm 2309, Reel 42).

In a letter to Joe Benitez, National President of LULAC from 1973-1975, Marta Perales continues to argue regarding her husband's position as "the late leader of the Americans of Mexican extraction and the true founder of the League of United Latin American Citizens." She then asserts that "I am interested that the truth be established that Alonso S. Perales was the initiator of the idea to form the Lulac [sic] and with the cooperation of his good friends the honorable J.T. Canales, Professor J. Luz Saenz and others, organized the Lulac [sic] on August 14th, 1927, for the first time in Harlingen, Texas." Marta argues futher about the importance of establishing the truth regarding this information and she explains that "[f]or future information I have a room full of manuscripts of a life time dedication and efforts for the rights and advancement of our people" (MP letter to Joe Benitez, 14 June 1974, Microfilm 2309, Reel 42). Indeed, in her interest to find informaton for her book on Alonso S. Perales, Adela Sloss Vento would offer to help her friend with the manuscripts: "Martita, si todavía [sic] no acaba de todas [sic] los archivos, puedo venir un dia [sic] o dos y ayudarle. También quiero que se lleve material y escriba todo lo que ud. quiera poner en el libro que estoy escribiendo, algo de que el Lic. fue el verdadero fundador de Lulac" / 'Martita, if you have not yet finished with all the archives, I can come a day or two to help you. I also want to take material and write everything you want to put in the book I am writing, something about the Lic. as the true founder of Lulac" (ASV letter to Marta Perales, 31 March 1975, Microfilm 2309, Reel 42).

Marta Perales would indeed respond to Sloss Vento's invitation by writing a letter for the book. Here she states: "Yo doy testimonio bajo toda responsabilidad que lo que publica en éste [sic] libro la honorable Señora Adela Sloss Vento, es verídica y tengo toda prueba concerniente a ésta ardúa lucha por los derechos humanos y constitucionales de nuestra Raza, que mi finado esposo, Alonso S. Perales Q.E.P.D. fué [sic] el iniciador y Campeón de la idea . . . fui y contiuúo siendo testiga de toda la obra de su vida, como lo fue la formación de la Liga LULAC el 14 de Agosto de 1927 en Harlingen, Texas " / 'Taking complete responsibility I give testimony that what the honorable Mrs. Adela Sloss Vento publishes in this book, is true and I have all the proof concerning this arduous struggle for human and constitutional rights, for our Race, that my deceased husband, Alonso S. Perales, May He Rest in Peace, was the initiator and Champion of the idea . . . I was and continue to be witness of his lifelong work, as was the formation of the League LULAC on August 14, 1927 in Harlingen, Texas[3] (MP letter for Adela Sloss Ventos' book, 3 May1977, Microfilm 2309, Reel 42). Interestingly, although Sloss Vento's "authorized" text, *Alonso S. Perales: His Struggles for the Rights of Mexican Americans*, would eventually be published in 1977 by Artes Gráficas, we find only a brief reference to Marta Perales in the Preface: "My sincere gratitude to Mrs. Marta Perez Perales for her sincere friendship and cooperation" (viii). The letter written by Marta would simply be placed in an Appendix to the book which included texts written by others who give information regarding Alonso S. Perales' life.

Reconstructing Historical Memory

I conclude by returning to the question of how these various documents shed light on our understanding of personal and collective spaces of representation related to a specific historical period and a multifaceted project concerned with the situation of people of Mexican descent. Through a discursive analysis of the texts that I have chosen to emphasize, it becomes clear that at the center of the life projects of Alonso S. Perales, Marta Perales, and Adela Sloss Vento is the importance of giving voice to those who could not speak for themselves. Indeed, as I have noted, in my discussion of Alonso S. Perales' letter to Nat M. Washer and dated 4 November 1919, the writer clearly uses his own experience with segregation as the starting point for his argument. In this way, his text becomes one of self-writing which discloses his own experience as an American citizen who suffers discrimination and exclusion. By writing about his personal experience, as well as that of the an American citizen of Mexican descent who had served in the military during World War I, he contests what Pierre Bourdieu (1990) defines as the *habitus* which is "a product of history, [that] produces individual and collective practices—more history—in accordance with the schemes generated by history" (p. 54). Furthermore, these schemes can be understood as a "system of dispositions—a present past that tends to perpetuate itself into the future" (Bourdieu, 1990, p. 54). It is precisely the "schemes" generated by a history of racial bigotry within the United States that have contributed and continue to contribute to the marginalization of Mexican Americans as well as people of Mexican descent in the United States.

In speaking about a *habitus* that has produced a collective practice of segregation of and discrimination toward people of color, it is relevant to recall Foucault's (1981) critique of societal control of discourse production: "we do not have the right to say everything, [. . .] we cannot speak of just anything in any circumstances whatever, and [. . .] not everyone has the right to speak of anything whatever" ("The Order of Discourse," p. 52). Foucault notes that there are certain taboos regarding the speech of those who are not in positions of power. Alonso S. Perales, however, makes it his own responsibility to contest those "systems of dispositions" intended to silence those who were unable to speak for themselves; that is, in the words of his wife Marta, he defended those who were insulted and taunted.

Crucial to the present discussion, then, is the way in which an analysis of oppositional discourse contributes to the restructuring of those "systems of dispositions" that have negatively marked historical memory in the United States. We must not dismiss the power of the written word which stands as testimony to the historical subjugation of the Mexican-American people. Thus, by bringing to the fore the life views of Alonso S. Perales, Marta Pérez de Perales and Adela Sloss Vento, it has been my intention to contribute to the recovery of an "alter-ideological" perspective that focuses on the cultural politics and values of people of Mexican descent. Indeed, as Martha Perales notes in a handwritten essay, "Americanos somos todos los nacidos en el Continente Americano . . . Americanos nos llamamos . . [y] somos muy dueños de nuestro America . . ." / 'All of those born in the American Contintent are Americans . . . We call ourselves Americans . . . [and] we are very much owners of our America.' (Ts. MP, "Devemos [sic] ser Americanos," undated, Box 10, Folder 4).

Works Cited

Arteaga, A. (1994). An other tongue. In *An other tongue: Nation and ethnicity in the linguistic borderlands*, Arteaga, A. (Ed.). Dirham and London: Duke University Press.

Ayala, A. (2005). *Negotiating race relations through activism: Women activists and women's organizations in San Antonio, Texas during the 1920s* (Doctoral dissertation). Available from ProQuest Dissertations & Theses database. (UMI No. 3215311)

Bhabha, H. K. (1990). The third space. In *Identity, community, culture, difference*, Rutherford, J. (Ed.). London: Lawrence & Wishart, 1990.

Bourdieu, P. (1990). *The logic of practice* (Trans. Nice, R.). Stanford: Stanford University Press.

Canales, J. T. (1960, September 8). [Letter to Marta Perales], M. D. Anderson Library, Special Collections, Houston, Texas.

Canales, J. T. (1960, October 7). [Letter to Marta Perales]. M. D. Anderson Library, Special Collections, Houston, Texas.

Calhoun, J. C. (2008). Senate speech against the annexation of Mexico, January 4, 1848. in *The works of John C. Calhoun:, volume IV, reports and public letters*, Crallé R. K. (Ed.). Chicago: Wilder Press.

Dilthey, W. (1962). *Pattern and meaning in history: thoughts on history and society*. New York: Harper and Row.

Divine, R. A. et. al. (1999). *America past and present*. New York: Addison Wesley Educational Publishers Inc.

Eakin, P. J. (1992). *Touching the world: Reference in autobiography*. Princeton: Princeton University Press.

Fleishman, A. (1983). *Figures of autobiography: The language of self-writing*. Berkeley, CA: University of California Press.

Foucault, M. (1981). The order of discourse. In *Untying the text: A post-structuralist reader.* Young, R. (Ed.). Boston: Routledge & Kegan Paul.

Kanellos, N. (1998). *Thirty million strong: reclaiming the Hispanic image in American culture*. Golden, CO: Fulcrum Publishing.

Lefebvre, H. (1992). *The production of space*. Trans. Donald Nicholson-Smith. Oxford: Blackwell Publishing.

Lionnet, F. (1989). *Autobiographical voices: Race, gender, self-portraiture*. Ithaca: Cornell University Press.

Merk, F. (1995). *Manifest destiny and mission in American history*. Cambridge: Harvard University Press.

Montejano, D. (1987). *Anglos and Mexicans in the making of Texas 1836-1986*. Austin: University of Texas Press.

Orozco, C. E. (1992). *The origins of the League of United Latin American Citizens (LULAC) and the Mexican American civil rights movement in Texas with an analysis of women's participation in a gendered context, 1910-1929*. (Doctoral Dissertation). Available from ProQuest Dissertations & Theses database. (UMI No. 9302444)

Perales, A. S. (1927, November 7). [Letter to Adela Sloss Vento]. M. D. Anderson Library, Special Collections, Houston, Texas.

Perales, A. S. (1934, October 17). [Letter to Adela Sloss Vento]. M. D. Anderson Library, Special Collections, Houston, Texas.

Perales, A. S. (1936). *En defensa de mi raza*. San Antonio: Artes Gráficas.

Perales, A. S. (1936). *En defensa de mi raza, segundo tomo*. San Antonio: Artes Gráficas.

Perales, A. S. (1936). Principios contraproducentes para la Americanización en Estados Unidos. In *En defensa de mi raza*. San Antonio: Artes Gráficas.

Perales, A. S. (1936). Problemas de nuestra raza en Estados Unidos. In *En defensa de mi raza*. San Antonio: Artes Gráficas.

Perales, A. S. (1936). Lo que significa para nosotros las escuelas para adultos. In *En defensa de mi raza*. San Antonio: Artes Gráficas, 1936.

Perales, A. S. (1936). El verdadero origen de la liga de ciudadanos unidos Latinoamericanos. In *En defensa de mi raza*. San Antonio: Artes Gráficas, 1936.

Perales, A. S. (1946, August 11). [Letter to ASV]. M. D. Anderson Library, Special
Collections, Houston, Texas.

Perales, A. S. (1947, October 24). *Arquitectos de nuestros propios destinos: Más
acerca de la conferencia regional de damas Católicas*. M. D. Anderson Library,
Special Collections, Houston, Texas.

Perales, A. S. (1947, September 15). [Letter to Adela Sloss Vento]. M. D. Anderson
Library, Special Collections, Houston, Texas.

Perales, M. (1970, July 21). [Letter to United States Department of State, San Antonio, TX]. M. D. Anderson Library, Special Collections, Houston, Texas.

Perales, M. (1974, June 14). [Letter to Joe Benitez]. M. D. Anderson Library, Special Collections, Houston, Texas.

Perales, M. (1977, 12 April). *Yo que fui la esposa*. M. D. Anderson Library, Special
Collections, Houston, Texas.

Perales, M. (1977, May 3). [Letter for Adela Sloss Ventos' book]. M. D. Anderson
Library, Special Collections, Houston, Texas.

Perales, M. (n.d.). [*Al pueblo de Alice* speech for memorial service, Alice, TX]. M.
D. Anderson Library, Special Collections, Houston, Texas.

Perales, M. (n.d.) *Devemos* [sic] *ser Americanos*. M. D. Anderson Library, Special
Collections, Houston, Texas.

Pope Pius XII. (1947, September 11). Allocution of Pope Pius XII to the Congress
of the International Union of Catholic Women's Leagues. *Papal directives for the
woman of today*. Retrieved from http://www.papalencyclicals.net/Pius12/
P12WOMAN.HTM.

Ricoeur, P. (2004). *Memory, history, forgetting*. Chicago: University of Chicago Press.

Padilla, G. M. (1993). *My history, not yours: The formation of Mexican American
autobiography*. Madison, Wisconsin: University of Wisconsin Press.

Saldívar, R. (1998). Narrative, ideology, and the reconstruction of American literary
history. In *Criticism in the borderlands: studies in Chicano literature, culture, and
ideology*, Calderón, H. & Saldivar, J. D. (Eds.). Durham: Duke University Press.

Sánchez, R. (1997). *Telling identities: The Californio testimonios*. Minneapolis,
MN: University of Minnesota Press.

Sloss-Vento, A. (1931, May 7). Nuestra gratitud y estimación hacia el autor de la liga
de ciudadanos unidos Latino-americanos. *Diogenes*. M. D. Anderson Library,
Special Collections, Houston, Texas.

Sloss-Vento, A. (1947, September 25). [Letter to Alonso Perales]. M. D. Anderson
Library, Special Collections, Houston, Texas.

Sloss-Vento, A. (1947, 8 September) [Letter to Alonso Perales]. M. D. Anderson
Library, Special Collections, Houston, Texas.

Sloss-Vento, A. (1975, March 31). [Letter to Marta Perales]. M. D. Anderson
Library, Special Collections, Houston, Texas.

Sloss-Vento, A. (1977). *Alonso S. Perales: His struggles for the rights of Mexican
Americans*, Vento A. C., (Ed.). Austin, Texas: Eagle Feather Research Institute.

Sloss-Vento, A.(n.d.). *Los hechos.* M. D. Anderson Library, Special Collections, Houston, Texas.

Swindells, J. (1995). *The uses of autobiography.* London: Taylor & Francis Ltd.

Therborn, G. (1980). *The ideology of power and the power of ideology.* London: Verso, 1980.

Van Eemeren, F. H. (2010). *Strategic maneuvering in argumentative discourse: Argumentationin context.* Philadelphia, PA: John Benjamins North America.

Vento, A.C. (2008). Adela Sloss-Vento 1901-1998. *Alonso S. Perales: His struggles for the rights of Mexican Americans* [DVD]. Austin, Texas: Eagle Feather Research Institute.

Vento, A.C. (2008). Introduction. *Alonso S. Perales: His struggles for the rights of Mexican Americans* [DVD]. Austin, Texas: Eagle Feather Research Institute.

Yale-Loehr, S. (2007, April 24). *Hearing on problems in the current employment verification and worksite enforcement system before the subcommittee on immigration, citizenship, refugees, border security, and international law and the committee on the judiciary U.S. House of Representatives.* Retrieved from http://judiciary.house.gov/hearings/April2007/Yale-Loehr070424.pdf.

Notes

[1]This information is taken from a handwritten document signed by Marta Perales. Some of this information appears in a manuscript entitled "Carta para el libro de Mrs. Vento" (MP letter for Adela Sloss Ventos' book, 3 May1977, Microfilm 2309, Reel 42). All subsequent references to the University of Houston Alonso S. Perales Collection materials will appear in parentheses in the text.

[2]See Evan Anders, "Canales, José Tomás," *Handbook of Texas Online* (http://www.tshaonline.org/handbook/online/articles/fcaag), accessed November 15, 2011. Published by the Texas State Historical Association

[3]Orozco (1992) has noted that the first officers of LULAC were "Ben Garza, president; M.C. Gonzales, vice-president; Andrés de Luna, secretary; and Louis Wilmont, treasurer" (p. 279). Alonso S. Perales (1936) also gives his own view of the history of the organization of what would eventually become LULAC in "El Verdadero Origen de Ciudadanos Unidos Latinoamericanos" (*En Defensa de mi Raza*, pp. 101-104).

Diplomacy, Law, and Biography

Writing a Biography of Alonso Sandoval Perales

F. Arturo Rosales

This essay outlines the challenges which I will face in producing a biography of Alonso Sandoval Perales. Although he is one of the most important figures in Mexican American civil rights history his trajectory is relatively unknown, primarily because until recently his papers were unavailable. In 2009 the University of Houston's Recovering the U.S. Hispanic Literary Heritage Project obtained the most extensive set of data regarding this crucial figure. The papers, now housed in the Special Collections at the University's library, are not only revealing of Perales' life but they are also one of the most important collections on Mexican Americans that has ever been recovered. I agreed to produce the biography before reviewing the compilation of data, imaging the content would provide thematic avenues. However after a preliminary but thorough assessment of the papers, the task became more daunting because the repository supports almost infinite pathways to understanding Perales. I have also examined other primary sources, not in the collection, but related to Perales, in Mexico City, at the National Archives in Maryland, at the Benson Collection at the University of Texas and in other repositories. I then decided that the biography should explain political and ideological trends that influenced and motivated this San Antonio attorney in the 1930s, 1940s and 1950s.

Besides appreciating and understanding the civil rights efforts Perales and his cohorts mustered, the biography should further demonstrate how important it is for academicians to transcend post-1960s points of reference which have guided much of our assessment of this generation. Activists of the Chicano Movement accused civil rights advocates of Perales generation of denying their "Mexicanness" and instead claimed whiteness. This era also influenced a foundation for more serious scholarly appraisals which to lesser degree also viewed the generation negatively. The historian Cynthia E. Orozco in her recent book *No Mexicans, Women, Dogs, or Allowed* emphatically challenges both the rather myopic popular and scholarly perceptions of LULAC formed since the 1960s-1970s Chicano Movement. Perhaps overstated, Orozco, nonetheless, provides an insightful observation.

The public, even among La Raza, knows very little about the leaders of the civil rights leaders in Texas especially those who led the effort that resulted in the founding of LULAC. Until recently, historians had little interest in them since they allegedly acquiesced to racial oppression or middle-class interests.

Activists and scholars of the 1970s called these men *vendidos* (sell-outs) and "accommodationists. . . ." (Orozco, 2009, p. 92)

As shall be seen below, Perales is generally associated with the era known as the Mexican-American Generation. Orozco insists on revising this generally accepted terminology, to the Mexican-American Civil Rights Movement. She claims the significance of that era's political meaning was misinterpreted. In the literature on the Mexican-American era, the period is not identified as a full-fledged movement to obtain civil rights. Instead of calling this period the Mexican-American Civil Rights Movement, as she does, other scholars have identified it as the Mexican-American Generation (Orozco, 2009, p. 9). I will continue to use the Mexican-American Generation in this essay in order not to confuse it with the organization in California in the 1930s and 1940s that called itself the Mexican-American Movement. I agree with Orozco, however, that the generation strenuously battled for civil rights and deserves to be defined more precisely.

Fortunately scholars in this first decade of the 21St Century transcended the previous post 60s paradigm and have provided more complex interpretations of the Mexican-American era. Orozco herself is a leading revisionist as are Emilio Zamora, Thomas A. Guglielmo and Craig A. Kaplowitz, just to name a few. I expect that my biography will also clarify many more historical imprecise questions that still remain unanswered.

My first task in this essay is to provide a contextual framework for what will be a story of Perales life and the era in which he lived and worked as civil rights activist. Historians began in earnest to study Mexican origin people in the United States in the 1960s. The history of Mexicans in the United States is truly exceptionalist in comparison to that of other ethnic groups. They have been both a conquered people and immigrants, in the classical sense of both terms. After the Mexican-American War (1846–1848), the United States acquired from Mexico what became the American Southwest and the approximately 80,000 Mexicans and unknown number of Native Americans living in the region. The Treaty of Guadalupe Hidalgo assured Mexicans, but not the Indians, "all the rights of citizens," The agreement was not upheld, however, as Mexicans lost their lands and their political rights (Weber, 1973, passim).

Just a few years later, in 1853, with the Gadsden Purchase the United States took in even more territory from Mexico; southern Arizona and southwest New Mexico. The Mexicans living in this area also acquired full constitutional rights. The new acquisitions figured crucially in the expansion of a railroad system required for economic dominance in the modern era. In areas where they outnumbered Anglos, Mexicans maintained a modicum of political and economic influence. Americans and Mexicans in the Southwest had been trading with United States interests in the East before the takeover, and Anglo-Americans and Europeans had actually lived among and intermarried with Mexicans. Following the transition to U.S. rule, the Gold Rush, military efforts to subdue and destroy the nomadic Indian tribes, and population growth created opportunities for merchants, farmers, livestock raisers, and transportation companies (Weber, 1973, passim; Delay, 2008 passim). This expanded economic activity engaged Anglo, European, and Mexican entrepreneurs, and involved Mexicans at every level; thus, migration from Mexico increased proportionally. The dominant historical debates of this era deal with size of Mexican population (Martínez, 1975; Nostrand, 1975) land tenure issues and degree to which Mexicans in the Southwest were victimized (Alonzo, 1998, passim; Montejano 1987, passim). Built mainly with American capital, after 1880 a railroad network in the U.S. Southwest and northern Mexico radically transformed the economy of both areas. It spurred the production of industrial raw materials and linked the border region to markets of the industrial basin in the Midwest and the northeast. In the process Mexican entrepreneurship and political power in the Southwest declined, as preindustrial economic activity lost its viability and the non-Mexican population vastly outnumbered Hispanics. However, in New Mexico, a few Mexican-American elites penetrated the economic and electoral system in this era of modernization. In addition, the generally Mexican population remained politically viable because of their large numbers. At the national level, many politicians resisted the bids of New Mexico and Arizona to become states mainly because they would be incorporated with a strong Mexican presence. As a consequence these territories did not achieve statehood until 1912, over sixty years after Texas and California, areas where Anglos had achieved economic and political dominance much earlier in the nineteenth century.

But this transformation stimulated a dramatic increase in immigration from Mexico. By 1900, 127,000 Mexicans had entered the United States—a number equaling more than a third of the population that had lived in the Southwest before the U.S. takeover. Numerous communities sprang up along the length of the railway lines in new agricultural sections and in the emerging mining districts that attracted Anglos and Mexicans alike. By 1915, Mexicans lived as far north as Kansas City and Chicago (Cardoso, 1980, pp. 27, 85).

The 1910 Mexican Revolution forced out numerous refugees from every class who were trying to escape turmoil and violence. Meanwhile, World War I spurred growth in every sector of the United States economy. Labor requirements had never been so great, yet disruption in transatlantic transportation, the restriction of immigration from southern and eastern Europe, and the drafting of American laborers to fight in the war created a labor vacuum. To fill this need, employers increasingly sought workers south of the border. Immigration policy also hindered the influx from Mexico, but Congress granted Mexicans a waiver to restrictions—a testimony to the importance of Mexicans in the labor market. During this era Mexicans migrated to labor sectors—in the urban Midwest cities or in rapidly growing Southwest cities—where they had never worked before (García, 1996, passiim). For the majority of the one million Mexicans who entered the United States between 1910 and 1930, finding work, setting up homes and businesses, building churches, and organizing mutual aid societies dominated their lives. To contend with a hostile reception the immigrants created organizations to defend themselves. In 1911, for example, they held El Primer Congreso Mexicanista (The First Mexican Congress) in Texas in order to implement a strategic plan to stem the tide of legal abuses and violence (Limón, 1974). One of the most painful abuses was the disproportionate subjection of Mexicans to imprisonment and capital punishment. In many parts of the United States,

Mexicans formed organizations such as La Liga Protectora Latina, founded in Phoenix in 1915, and the Asamblea Mexicana, organized in Houston in 1924. When the 1921 depression caused severe destitution among unemployed Mexicans, the consular service formed the Comisiones Honoríficas Mexicanas to help ameliorate the problems faced by unemployment and destitution. Immigration and community studies for this era dominated the very first studies of Mexican-American history (Rosales, 1999; Águila, 2000).

Immigrants from the Mexican urban middle classes, displaced as refugees during the revolution, promoted an immigrant nationalism manifested through an often-stated desire to return to Mexico. The core ingredients of this ideology were maintaining Spanish, the celebration of Mexico's patriotic holidays, Catholicism, with special reverence to Our Lady of Guadalupe, and a symbolic identification with Mexico's pre-Columbian civilizations—in essence a nostalgic *México Lindo* (Pretty Mexico) expatriate nationalism. Mexicans relied on cultural traditions such as live Mexican vaudeville, drama, and musical productions, activities that were just as important religious, political, and economic institutions. These hopefully provided a barrier to a negative stigma and also gave the newcomers cohesion (Rosales, 1999).

The evolution of the Mexican community in the United States dramatically changed during the Great Depression. In 1930, about one and a half million ethnic Mexicans lived in the United States but as they became unemployed, Mexicans were seen as a major problem and were pressured to return to Mexico. The federal government deported thousands of undocumented aliens, while local governments, charitable institutions, and employers organized massive repatriation drives. Repatriation took place on a larger scale from more populous cities such as Los Angeles, Chicago and Detroit whose industries were hardest-hit. The Mexican government attempted to help by providing expatriates free transportation back to their homes. Families with children resisted repatriation more than single men or young married couples and consequently became more rooted. (Balderrama and Rodríguez, 1995, passim; Alanís Enciso) Nonetheless, many children, most of whom were U.S. citizens, accompanied their parents.

By the end of the 1930s, New Deal agencies designed to keep young people off the streets during the Great Depression affected thousands of young Mexican Americans, and most encountered the greater Anglo society through formal education. Mexicans born in the United States founded organizations such as the League of United Latin American Citizens (LULAC), in Texas and other like groups emerged in other states. They practiced "Mexican-Americanism," an ideology that promoted embracing and adhering to what the leaders considered mainstream culture, that of Anglo Americans. At the same time they were expected to maintain a pluralistic tradition which meant they would also not forget their Mexican roots. Basically the Mexican American leadership felt that "Americanizing" would result in an atmosphere hospitable to ending segregation codes in the school system and discrimination in general, because by doing this Mexicans would become more acceptable (Gutiérrez, 1995, passim; García, 1990 passim).

During World War II, Mexican Americans enthusiastically enrolled in all branches of the armed forces and "Home Front" efforts, such as bond drives engaged

Mexican-American civilians not serving in the military. Mexican women, like their Anglo counterparts, worked in war industries as "Rositas the Riveters." But after the war, discrimination and rejection continued. In 1947 the American G.I. Forum (AGIF) was organized by Mexican-American veterans and LULAC became leading advocates for civil rights. A wartime need for labor prompted the Bracero program, which recruited thousands of Mexicans to work in agriculture and in railroad maintenance until the program ended in 1965 (García, 2002, passim).

A 1898 native of Texas, Alonso S. Perales is usually associated with this era. Still, as indicated above a lacunae exists in appreciating his contribution to civil rights history, mainly because it is only recently that his collection has been made public. Perales' father Nicolás Perales was born in 1853 in Mexico and came to Texas in the 1880s. Perales' mother, Susana Sandoval, was a native of Texas, born in 1870 of Mexican immigrant parents. His fellow civil rights advocates are also natives Texas or came as young children from northeastern Mexico. As a consequence of this generational combination, Alonso S. Perales and his generation are relevant to all of the historical periods discussed above. Even though the first half of the twentieth century is the period they affected, the legacy of the past certainly influenced ideology and strategy used to achieve the goals for which they struggled (García, 1990, passim).

For Mexican-American history in general, unanswered questions remain as do incomplete conclusions and often misleading or incorrect rendition of events. But this is especially true for studies on the era in which Perales lived. Thus, the biography will transcend the conventional compilation of his contributions and achievements as an individual, or inclusion of his human frailties. These considerations will be a major part of my book, of course, but the work will demonstrate how Perales is both a product and a causality figure of his era. My goal is to clarify and perhaps correct some of the misconceptions and often erroneous conclusions that have emerged on the history of the Mexican-American Generation. The issues which I plan to examine in the biography are shown below.

Contextual Geographic and Social History of Texas Mexican Life

Perales grew up in Nueces County and was subjected to life as a working-class Mexican. His father was a shoemaker, but died when Perales was six years old. In his growing years, the orphaned boy worked as a farm worker and railroad laborer. The transition of the Texas economy in the twentieth century and structural effect it had on attitudes towards Mexicans needs to be discussed. As such the studies that provide a general context of this experience are extremely important. Numerous works provide a geographic context for South Texas, too many to be enumerated here but some are at the top of my list (Johnson; Montejano 1987; Taylor, 1934).

Personal Life and Individual Motivation

No in-depth studies have been written about Perales' personal life, probably because the bulk of his documents had not been available. Certainly, Perales has been mentioned, if only briefly in numerous works on Mexican-American civil rights, but the full extent of his life experiences are little known. Adela Sloss Vento, a contemporary of Perales published in 1977 a book tribute to the civil rights activist which is quite useful for information but short on interpretation (Sloss Vento). All biographies should feature expressions of family life as will this one. Alonso S. Perales and his wife Marta Pérez did not have any children although they adopted three late in their marriage, after 25 years. Both he and Marta strictly embraced Catholicism and carried on a busy social life within both Mexican-American and Anglo circles, often at the elite levels.

Perhaps the most important characteristic of Perales' psychological make up is the way Catholicism affected his personal formation. In addition, he mustered boundless energy and passion for any endeavor he attempted. All of these personal aspects of his life will be featured, mainly to determine how they affected his work on civil rights. There can be no doubt that most of the data for this section of the biography will come from the personal papers which until now have never been tapped.

Relationship Perales Had With Other Mexican-American Civil Rights Leaders

Perales lived in an era in which civil rights activism grew at an accelerated rate. In the immigrant generation, an extensive inter-immigrant network made up of businessmen, leaders of mutual aid societies, editors of newspapers, and Mexican consulates helped spread Mexican exile nationalism throughout the United States. The nearest that this networking came to transcend regional lines, however, was the formation of La Alianza Hispano-Americana (Hispanic-American Alliance), which began in Tucson during 1894 as a mutual aid society and political organization It spread throughout the Southwest, and by the 1920s had accumulated a respectable record in protecting civil rights for Mexicans.

The same occurred with networking among Mexican-American era activists, except that it transcended the more parochial level that characterized the immigrant generation.[1] In 1929 in Corpus Christi, Perales and other civil rights leaders organized the League of United Latin American Citizens (LULAC) and then in 1948, a generation later the American G. I. Forum (AGIF) was founded by Dr. Hector García, a physician. Both groups attained a national following by the 1950s and they exist to this day. Interestingly, the Mexican-American Generation's growth of organizations overlapped with the waning years of expatriate influence in the 1920s. Alonso S. Perales participated deeply in the fray. He collaborated for at least three decades with intimate friends such as José de la Luz Saenz, a cofounder of LULAC, Carlos E. Castañeda, the well known Mexican-American librarian and history professor at the University of Texas at Austin; and with José T. Canales, another cofounder of LULAC and crucial figure in Texas politics.

Contrary to popular belief, however, by the 1940s Perales did not belong to LULAC. He was forced out in 1937 after Council 16 in San Antonio, to which he belonged and led informally, was eliminated at the national LULAC meeting in Houston. Members of Council 2, the other San Antonio Council who were constantly at odds with Perales and his followers maneuvered a motion which forbade the existence of more than one council in each city. Nonetheless, Perales organized another San Antonio-based organization, the League of Loyal Citizens (LLA), and a partner organization called the Committee of One Hundred. Through these he maintained a working but uneasy relationship with many LULAC councils, and a strong collaboration with Mexican-American leaders from throughout the nation, especially in the 1940s. The main figure in LULAC Council 2 and probably the leading figure orchestrating the elimination of Council 16 was Manuel C. Gonzales, a perennial rival to Perales and at times one his harshest critics. In fact, Perales had many clashes with other Mexican-American leaders such Dr. Hector García, Eduardo Idar, and at times even with allies such as José T. Canales. Very little of this has been uncovered, but the evidence of both his fraternal alliances and conflicts is scattered extensively throughout the collection.

Organizational Efforts for Civil Rights Attainment

It is crucial also to understand the working efforts that stimulated the Mexican-American civil rights organizations in Texas during the 1920s, such as the Sons of America, the Knights of America, and the League of Latin American Citizens, all precursors important to the founding of LULAC. The organization has been the subject or featured in various published articles and is the sole focus of at least three books. Its early formation has received less attention. O. Douglas Weeks in the *Southwestern Social Science Quarterly* in 1929, the same year the organization was founded, signaled the emergence of this organization. According to Weeks, LULAC was middle class, accepted only U.S. citizens for membership and tended towards assimilation. In his book *LULAC,* Benjamin Márquez (2006) also viewed the early formation of the organization although not as profoundly as Cynthia Orozco who had some access to the Perales collection when she researched for her dissertation in the 1970s. It is also important to note that early Mexican-American civil rights activity existed alongside expatriate nationalism, and at times the two ideologies clashed.

The Perales collection is extensive and revealing of the organizational activities that led to various groups but which have not been uncovered by scholars. Just one example will suffice here. To this very day, nothing has been published, which relates how and why Perales in 1937 organized the San Antonio organizations discussed above such as the LLA the Committee of One Hundred. The data in the Perales collection provide the background for this. When LULAC Council 16, which Perales helped found in San Antonio during the 1930s, was dissolved in 1937 after the internecine battle with LULAC Council 2, most of the Council 16 members joined with Perales in the new groups. Emilio Zamora (2009) in his recent groundbreaking book *Claiming Rights and Righting Wrongs in Texas,* only mentions the organization once and states that it was an affiliate of LULAC (p. 114). Similarly David Montejano in an article on a Mexican-American soldier beaten up during World War II mentions the organization in a footnote (Montejano, 2005). More comprehensive is Mario T. García's book on Catholic Mexican Americans, where he briefly mentions the organization stating that Perales organized the group in the 1930s (García, 2010, p. 75). Similarly, the Committee of One Hundred has only been mentioned in passing and only in one essay available through the internet. Unequivocally, Perales advocacy in the late 1930s and until the 1950s was accomplished through the LLA and the Committee of One Hundred (Gritter).

Ideology On Equality And Identity (Perales And His Generation)

If crystallized, both the popular and scholarly perception of the Mexican-American era would be the key term assimilation. Ernesto Chávez (2002) mirrors what countless of other historians have observed about Mexican-Americanism:

> Founded in 1929 in Corpus Christi, Texas, LULAC's central concern was to empower Mexican Americans through assimilation. It stressed the notion that Mexican Americans were U.S. citizens and therefore should have all the rights of Americans. Thus, LULAC "pledged to promote and develop among [themselves] what they called the 'best and purest' form of Americanism.Yet, in so doing, LULAC members limited who they sought to empower; they imagined a community composed of American citizens of Mexican descent. (p. 2)

Even Cynthia Orozco, who disparages the previous interpretations of LULAC, makes such an assertion. For example, in discussing the Círculo Cultural Isabel la Católica a women's Catholic organization founded in San Antonio during 1938, she describes the group by writing, "Unlike the League of United Latin American Citizens (LULAC), which emphasized Americanization and assimilation, this civic group merged Mexican nationalism with ideas of uplift" (Orozco, 2009, p. 161). In *Chicano!* I also draw the same conclusion: "Mexican Americanization was in large part dominated by middle-class reformers who advocated assimilation and working within the system as the solution to problems facing Mexicans in the United States (Rosales, 1997, p. 109)." The evidence in the Perales papers suggests that we will by degrees have to revise this notion. Communications and ideological statements scattered throughout the collection show that identity and self-image were more akin to what John Nieto Phillips describes for New Mexico. That is, that Hispanic New Mexicans could remain "Spanish American" and still be able to become a good U.S. citizen because Spanish conveyed whiteness is just as good as being Anglo (Nieto-Phillips, 2008). In this case, time and time again, Mexican Americans just used the word Mexican American or Latin American instead of Spanish American as did the *manitos* of New Mexico.

One of the most oft repeated notions of self-identity of the Mexican-American Generation is that the "Latin American" was used as a euphemism ostensibly because the activists were ashamed of being Mexican. In their well known survey of Mexican-American history, Matt Meier and Feliciano Ribera (1994) write "In Texas, Latin American is simply used for Mexican, historically a term of disparagement in that state (Meier and Ribera, p. 7)."

Cynthia Orozco gives a more nuanced view of the usage of the term. The term Mexican American was initially promoted in the turbulent initial organizational meetings that resulted in the formation of the League of United Latin American Citizens (one of the precursors of LULAC), but as has been noted above, Mexican-American leaders did not want persons born in Mexico to join their group unless they had been naturalized. She writes explaining this:

Scholars have considered "Latin" a euphemism for "Mexican," and indeed it was. But "Mexican American" was not the final choice for the organization, either. Both "Mexican" and "Mexican American" would have reminded activists of the Harlingen debacle. Yet "Latin American" referred to Mexican Americans' connections to Mexico and nations south, though still not implying an invitation for Mexican citizens, Latinos such as Puerto Ricans and Cuban Americans, or Latin Americans to join. The use of "Citizens" was a way for México Texanos to assert 100 percent U.S. citizenship and a reminder to Mexican immigrants that they were not eligible to join. (Orozco, 2009, p 153)

Racism, Race and Whiteness

An essential goal of many Mexican-American activists was to be classified as white. Seemingly this stance from our perspective today stems from a denial of Mexico's racial realities and a form of self-hate. But other reasons also accounted for this stance. It became obvious to U.S. Mexicans, even in the immigrant era, that if they were to be classified as colored it could subject them to *de jure* segregation. As Thomas A. Guglielmo (2006) puts it:

To understand Mexicans' and Mexican Americans' wartime struggle, one must grasp their complicated location in the racial orders of the U.S. South and Southwest, more particularly, Texas. On the one hand, all federal and Texas state laws either accepted people of Mexican descent as white or refrained from explicitly defining them as "Negro" or "colored." Therefore Mexicans were entitled to naturalize as free white people. Both they and Mexican Americans were entitled—sometimes in theory, sometimes in practice—to attend white schools, travel on white railroad cars, adopt white children, marry white partners, and serve time in white prisons. (p. 1215)

But there has been no greater criticism of this generation on the part of some historians than the stance on whiteness. Part of the critique is accusatory because according to the critique, Mexican-American civil right leaders failed to seek equality for all Americans. They accepted the notion that claiming whiteness would not subject them to "separate but equal" laws that legally separated African Americans and other people of color from white Americans. Basically then, the conclusion is that Mexican-Americanism approved segregation by default. The number of historians who have observed this trait among Mexican-Americans civil rights activists is numerous. These are only a few examples. Lorena Oropeza explains:

Throughout the 1950s, moreover, the American G.I. Forum joined forces with LULAC to argue successfully against the segregation of Mexican-descended people on the grounds that they were "white." Instead of mounting an attack on segregation itself, these organizations asserted that segregation should not apply to Mexican Americans. Cognizant that the United States historically had recognized but one great racial divide between black and white, these ethnic activists continued to insist that Mexican Americans, especially in view of their wartime sacrifices, belonged to the racial category that had access to full citizenship (Oropeza, 2003, p. 205).

The Texas journalist-historian, Michael Phillips (2006) also makes a similar observation.

> The American G.I. Forum, however, held a similar stance to LULAC vis-à-vis racial identity and the black civil rights movement. To both organizations, Mexican Americans were white and African Americans would have to fight their own battles. "LULAC has been the lone spokesman on Civil Rights for over a quarter of a century," the group's president, Paul Andow, sniffed in a 1963 policy statement just three days before Martin Luther King Jr. and other black civil rights leaders held their famous March on Washington. "We have not sought solutions to problems by marching to Washington, sitin's or picketing or other outward manifestations . . ." (p.162)

At least one scholar has perversely misconstrued the actual facts in order to bolster the concept of denying citizenship to Mexicans because of a socially constructed non-white status. Angela D. Dillard, a professor of African American Studies at the University of Michigan wrote the following:

> Being nonwhite not only made Mexican-Americans targets of increased discrimination; it also weakened their claims to legal protection as American citizens. *During the Repatriation Movement of the 1930s* (my emphasis), for example, the government decided that all persons born in Mexico or of Mexican-born parents "who are not definitely white, negro, Indian, Chinese or Japanese, should be returned as Mexicans." (Dillard, 2001, p. 81)

Significantly, the quotation the author uses was meant to instruct workers in the 1930 census and had nothing to do with repatriation. The term "returned" signaled enumerators to indicate on the census form persons who they thought were of the Mexican race; not those to be sent back to Mexico which seems to be what the passage is trying to convey.

The Perales collection contains a great amount of grit that will help clarify the issue of whiteness beyond what has been offered thus far. I will provide just a few examples which to my knowledge have never been acknowledged in publications. In February 1946, Perales sought to strategize with A. Phillip Randolph on how to pass the permanent FECP bill by outlawing filibustering by opponents in Congress (Alonso S. Perales to Phillip Randolph, Feb 12, 1946, Microfilm 2309 Roll 20). Then, in October of 1957, Perales wrote President Dwight D. Eisenhower to congratulate him for showing tremendous courage in sending troops into Little Rock, Arkansas to enforce integration. He tells the President that Mexican newspapers have been very supportive of his action (Alonso S. Perales to Dwight D. Eisenhower, Oct 1, 1965, Microfilm 2309, Reel 18). In 1944, Carlos E. Castañeda, now in a high post with the FECP, writes Perales where he lauds the Negro civil rights movement because they have so much more power even though they have experienced more adversity than Mexican Americans. "Hay mucho que debemos de aprender de esta minoría, (There is much that we can learn from this minority)" he states. Interestingly, he writes the letter in Spanish so that his secretary will not understand (Carlos E. Castañeda to Alonso S. Perales, n.d., Microfilm 2309, Reel 25). The collection will provide a great opportunity for more scholars to enter into the debate and my biography will also provide a more ample and complicated understanding of whiteness concerns.

Mexican Americans and Mexican Immigrants

While Alonso S. Perales lived in the immigrant era (his parents were born in Mexico), he truly embodied the Mexican-American rubric. Born in Texas in 1898, his connection to Mexico the nation was from the perspective of diplomacy although the culture that he grew up in was Texas Mexican. This important factor guided his political and identity formation. The intense allegiance to a conservative Mexico manifested by middle- and upper-class refugees provided a foil for Perales and his associates who wanted to substitute the identification Mexicans had to Mexico with that of Anglo American United States.

Much has been made of rejection of Mexican citizens as members of LULAC when the organization was formed in 1929. As Lorena Oropeza (2003) puts it:

A first order of business was differentiating U.S. citizens of Mexican descent from more recent arrivals. League membership was restricted to American citizens. Although Mexicans and Mexican Americans shared a common culture, a common language, and, most fundamentally, a common experience of oppression, LULAC members, many of whom came from centuries-old Tejano families, quickly decided that the organization's detachment from immigrant concerns was a strategic necessity.

David Gutiérrez (1995) is perhaps the most adamant about claiming a dichotomy between the Mexican Americans and immigrants, and in this practice he included Perales as one of the purveyors of the division. According to him:

This required that "intelligent and progressive" Mexican Americans focus their energies exclusively on American citizens of Mexican descent. According to Perales, the unrestricted immigration of hundreds of thousands of Mexican workers had reinforced negative stereotypes to the point that "being considered a Mexican [in Texas] signifies contempt, abuses, and injustices." (p. 84)

One of the first scholars to revise Gutiérrez conclusions is Cynthia E. Orozco:

Gutiérrez mentions the Harlingen convention of 1927, one of the first known clashes between Mexican Americans and Mexicans and a significant chapter in the history of LULAC, but he does not discuss it as a defining event, as I argue it was. LULAC's relations with immigrants are more complex than Gutiérrez suggests; LULAC's concepts of community, nation, and identity must be examined. Its strategy of Raza political empowerment was especially important. (Orozco, 2009, p. 7)

In fact, Gutiérrez misinterprets the tesimony given Alonso S. Perales, along with Ben Garza, the first president of LULAC and José T. Canales, at congressional hearings regarding a restrictionist immigration bill in 1930. Supposedly, they

> offered their organization's qualified support of restrictive immigration legis-lation pending before a House subcommittee in Washington. They were care-ful to insist that LULAC would support the immigration bill if its sponsors could prove "that Mexicans—that is Mexicans from Mexico are a menace to the American working man . . . (Gutiérrez, 1995, p. 85)

A different assessment from the record of the testimony shows that Perales was more interested in condeming the racist language used to describe Mexican immigrants. In the Perales papers and in other primary sources in the LULAC collection at the University of Texas it is clear that the trio went to Washington D.C. in order to defeat the pending restrictionist legislation.

There can be no doubt that in the organizational efforts of what became LULAC, many of the leaders wanted to restrict Mexican citizens from joining, a desire that was not universal, however. A 1927 meeting held in Harlingen to plan the unification of three groups that held Mexican-American civil rights goals resulted in a walkout when Alonso S. Perales and his cohorts pressed for an exclusive U.S. cit-izenship requirement. Interestingly, Manuel C. Gonzales, a future LULAC president walked out with other Texas-born activists and many Mexican citizens who attend-ed the meeting (*México en el Valle*, Aug 20 1927, Microfilm 2309, Reel 14). Three years later, Gonzales and Clemente Idar attempted to discredit the effort by Perales in the testimony discussed above which was interpreted as an attempt to block pas-sage of the bill. Idar in fact was an American Federation of Labor organizer and sup-ported the anti-immgrant bill. Cynthia Orozco, who covers the walkout extensively in *No Mexicans, Women, or Dogs Allowed,* does not mention the walk-out role of Gonzales. She states, "The controversy did not end when Mexicans—and possibly some México Texanos—walked out. Indeed, the press covered the controversy and fueled the dialogue (Orozco, 2009, p. 131).

Surprisingly, I found very little in the Perales collection that demonstrated that Mexican-American civil rights leaders paid attention to the event of repatriation dur-ing the 1930s depression, a topic which historians today see as one of the major vic-timization episodes regarding Mexicans in the United States. This could possibly support the allegation by some historians that Mexican-American leadership held an anti-Mexican immigrant bias. But rather, Perales often showed concern about the treatment of Mexican immigrants. In 1926, he was living in Washington D.C. and responded to an anti-Mexican editorial in the *Washington Post*. In the letter, Perales praises the editor's "aim to protect the America laborer" but condemns the "unjust attack" the editor "made upon the defenseless Mexican peon" (*Washington Post.* September 5, 1926). Then Perales wrote to his congressman, John Garner, in May of 1929, protesting the inhumane jailing of "illegal aliens" and their families in South

Texas because of the draconian measures of the restrictive immigration act in 1929 (Perales, 1936, pp. 44-45).

In one of the few references to repatriation that I found in the collection, Manuel C. Gonzales, LULAC president at the time, commented in a 1931 issue of *Lulac News* when he observed a caravan of repatriates trekking through San Antonio on their way to the border. Gonzales stated that the repatriates were returning to their homeland where they were welcomed into their own culture and at least not face the discrimination to which they were subjected in Texas. Mexican Americans on the other hand, he thought, had to remain and face the music. He concluded that this was an opportunity and a challenge in disguise to end discrimination without including the added burden of having Mexican immigrants in their midst (*Lulac News,* November 1921, Microfilm 2309, Reel 1). More compassionate was Cleofas, Calleros, a civil rights leader in El Paso. In 1936, in a newspaper advice column on the meaning of citizenship, he answered the query of a man born in Santa Fe to a woman from Chihuahua. Unequivocally he told the man, who was repatriated from California in 1931, that he was indeed a citizen and had a right to return to the United States (*Actualidades,* Nov. 18 1936, Microfilm 2309, Reel 1) That same year as director of the El Paso Catholic Welfare Conference, he sought to prevent the deportation of numerous undocumented workers who had failed to legitimize their status and would have left many of their family members behind (*El Paso Herald-Post,* February 24, 1936).

The collection provides a great deal of information on the Bracero Program as indicated below and on the attitudes held by Mexican Americans on undocumented workers in the late 1940s and 1950s. Two recent works by Kelly Lytle Hernandez and Carlos Kevin Blanton reveal uncovered information and provide new interpretations on this. Lytle Hernández, in a thorough history of the U.S. Border Patrol, discusses at length the 1954 effort to rid the country of undocumented Mexicans called "Operation Wetback" which LULAC and AGIF supported (Lytle Hernández, 2010, passim). Blanton's essay deals with the controversy over the Lyle Saunders pamphlet called *The Wetback In The Lower Rio Grande Valley Of Texas.* Support and opposition for this publication wrecked the relationship between Perales, his allies and Dr. Héctor García and George I. Sánchez. The first group felt it was an affront to Mexican origin people in Texas and the former supported the publication (Blanton, 2009). While both Lytle Hernández and Blanton have provided immeasurable contributions, their studies would have been more thorough if they had had access to the Perales papers.

Perales and International Involvement; Post World War I

As a young man, Perales was orphaned at age six and as indicated above worked as a laborer. Truly ambitious, however, he attended Draughn's Business College in San Antonio where he learned shorthand and stenography, and then obtained white-collar employment in the city. Drafted during World War I, Perales after his discharge accepted a civil service position with the Department of Commerce in Washington, D.C. and worked as an English instructor. While there, he continued his education and attended George Washington preparatory school in 1922, received a

B.A. law degree in 1927 at the National University and in 1930, a jurisprudence degree from the same institution.

While pursuing his education, Perales served with the Department of State, which dispatched him to thirteen diplomatic missions to the Dominican Republic, Cuba, Nicaragua, Mexico, Chile and the West Indies. In 1924, Perales returned to Texas and took the Texas bar exam in 1925 before he even obtained a degree and passed. He returned to Washington to obtain a college degree because he thought it necessary to have at least a B.A. to be a genuine lawyer. His posts in the Department of State ranged from translator to legal advisor, depending upon the educational level he had reached when offered the assignment. Perales' final mission was to Nicaragua in 1931, and then his Department of State career seems to have ended. He attempted to obtain various positions on diplomatic missions but was constantly rejected in the 1930s even though he knew State Department officers in high places. In the meantime, he had returned to Texas permanently and became involved in practicing law and in civil rights activism. One reason that he sought to return to a diplomatic career in the 1930s was because of the economic harshness of the Great Depression. The Perales collection will yield crucial information on this phase of his life.[3] I suspect that his zealous dedication to civil rights might have sabotaged his chances in the Foreign Service, although he found these diplomatic skills useful building an international and diplomatic platform for exposing violations of the rights of Mexican Americans.

World War II, International Issues and Alonso S. Perales

I agree in most respects with Cynthia Orozco's assertion quoted above that little scholarly attention has been paid to the Mexican-American Generation. But I believe there has been more scrutiny of this era than what she allows. Perhaps she makes this statement because the major works on the Mexican-American era were being prepared simulatneously with her book. (Guglielmo, 2006; Zamora, 2009). More accurate is that the generation before the World War II has been given scant attention, a period rich in significance for setting the tone for more publicized activity during and immediately after the War. During the time that Perales served in diplomatic missions in Nicaragua he established important connections. Anastasio Somoza appointed him in 1938 Texas Consul General for Nicaragua a position he parlayed into being able to participate in Pan American level activity. In 1944, for example, he traveled to Mexico City to attend Third Conference of the Inter-American Bar Association where he gave several interviews to Mexican newspaper and addressed the Mexican Chamber of Deputies. In April of 1945, he represented Nicaragua at the United Nations Conference at the International Organization at San Francisco, that meeting resulted in the formation of the United Nations. Perales could not attend the International Foreign Minister Conference in Mexico City which resulted in the Chapultepec Accord condemning racism in the hemisphere. He was able to keep in close contact with Mexican officials and intellectuals, however, through the Comité Contra el Racismo, a Mexican organization that kept tabs on discriminatory acts against Mexicans in the United States and published its finding in a magazine called *Fraternidad*.[4]

After reading much of the correspondence and documents pertaining to this activity, it is obvious that although Perales represented the Nicaraguan government and possibly used its funds to travel, his main goal was to apply international support to end discriminatory practices against the Mexican origin population in the United States through this forum.

Perales also exerted a strong homefront battle to end discrimination against Mexicans. In November of 1941, William H. Blocker, the U.S. Consul in Ciudad Juárez, was asked to conduct a confidential study on the degree of discrimination that existed in the United States towards Mexican Americans. [5] Blocker was chosen because he was a Texan and a veteran consulate official who supposedly understood Mexicans and Mexico. The Department of State expected the main part of investigation to take place in Texas because the region exhibited the greatest amount of racism and prejudice against Mexicans. Obviously the administration and the Department of State were bracing for war and correctly understood that mistreatment of Mexicans could undermine war efforts. Importantly, this request preceded both the Pearl Harbor attack and the Emergency Farm Labor Supply Program, popularly known as the Bracero Program.

Blocker interviewed numerous Mexicans, both nationals and Mexicans in the Southwest, but mainly in Texas. At the same time the federal government established the Fair Employment Practices Commission (FEPC) to prevent racial discrimination in the workplace. The FECP wanted to hold hearings in Texas and factions within the Department of State did not want to stir the waters, especially after the United States entered the war. The Commission eventually was at loggerheads with a powerful faction within Department of State, led by Blocker and George S. Messersmith, the ambassador to Mexico. Mexican-American activists, especially Alonso S. Perales enthusiastically cooperated with Blocker providing him with much cannon fodder. But perhaps unbeknownst to Perales, Blocker quickly identified him as a mettlesome troublemaker in more than one piece of correspondence in the files of his confidential report. This probably led to Perales not receiving a commission in the military which he strenuously sought.

It is intriguing that Perales did not comment much in his correspondence on the hearings controversy. Perhaps this was because Carlos E. Castañeda of the University of Texas obtained an important position with the FECP and did not want to jeopardize the delicate negotiations taking place between the Commission and the Department of State. More dynamic activity took place after this study was finished, and Perales led the charge in trying to obtain legislation to criminalize discrimination against Mexican-origin persons who the leadership saw were not subject to separate but equal codes, which affected so negatively African Americans and other people of color.

The Mexican-American Soldier, Perales and the American G.I. Forum

A recurring major theme in the literature describing Chicano leadership is that community leaders who emerged after World War II were responsible for the creation of a new political activity and consciousness in the Chicano population throughout the Southwest. Furthermore, that these new leaders were primarily war veterans.' Some of the first attempts to assess the Mexican-American Generation were positive. For example, in a 1971 research note in *Aztlán* Albert Camarillo indicates the following of the termed "The G.I. Generation:"

> . . . experiences shared by Chicano servicemen during the Second World War have been implied to be the most significant reasons for their increased community activities once they returned to the United States. Hundreds of thousands of Chicanos served in the armed forces, and thus had a greater opportunity to view United States society and intermingle with the non-Chicano population outside of their barrios. (Camarillo, 1971)

Camarillo anticipated studying the Mexican-American veteran mainly in California, but it is Texas where the greatest amount of civil rights activity took place (García, 2002, passim). Dr. Héctor García in 1948 took a leading role in founding the American G.I. Forum AGIF, a dynamic organization that zealously sought the protection of civil rights for Mexican-American World War II veterans. It was also organized in response to the refusal of a funeral director in Three Rivers, Texas, to bury Félix Longoria, a soldier killed in the Pacific theater (Carroll, 2003, passim; Ramos, 2000, passim). Dr. García was a veteran and younger than Alonso S. Perales, who as has been pointed out did not serve in the military during World War II. It seems that after the AGIF organized, Perales' influence began to wane as younger leaders like Dr. García and Dr. George I. Sánchez began to take on greater leadership roles. Besides, serious health problems troubled the older leaders by the 1950s: J. Luz Saenz died in 1953 at age 65; Carlos E. Castañeda lived to the age of 62 when he passed away in 1957; and Alonso S. Perales died three years later at age 62. The three in the 1950s knew that they burned the candle at both ends for too many years.

Post-Alonso S. Perales Era

In the 1960s and 1970s many Mexican Americans were educated in Anglo systems, lived in integrated suburbs and were subjected to Anglo-American mass media. Mexican Americans, now more integrated into mainstream society, made dramatic strides in breaking down obstacles, from school segregation to economic and social mobility. A crowning achievement of this generation was the formation of the "Viva Kennedy Clubs" in the 1960 presidential election; when John F. Kennedy was elected they took partial responsibility for his victory.

Perales did not live to see this era. On the surface it seems like many of the aspirations of his generation were realized, but this was not necessarily the case. Even though blatant forms of prejudice which preoccupied the civil rights struggles of his era diminished, subtler forms of discrimination remained. The late 1960s and early 1970s were a time of intellectual ferment and rebellion in the United States. Caught up in the mood, young Mexican Americans sought a new identity while struggling for the same civil rights objectives of previous generations. This atmosphere generated the "Chicano Movement," which was fueled by the conviction that a racist American society deliberately subordinated Mexican Americans; its participants rejected assimilation, which they perceived the previous Mexican-American Generation had fostered. The Movement produced provincial variations probably influenced by activity of the previous generations. Certainly the formation of La Raza Unida Party and its regional manifestations are an example of this (Rosales, 1997, passim).

In the 1980s the term "Hispanic" took on a special generic meaning referring to any person of Spanish-American ancestry living in the United States. Many critics argued that the term represented a rejection by the Mexican-American leadership of both cultural nationalism and the radical postures offered by the Chicano Movement. It would be interesting to see how Perales would have perceived the Chicano Movement if he had lived. To be sure, Chicano Movement activists in Texas like José Angel Gutiérrez admired his life-long dedication to civil rights while at the same time disparaging some of Perales cohorts like Congressmen Henry B. González, a protégé of the pioneer activist. In the early 2000s, immigration from Mexico and Latin America continued unabated, a condition that has to be taken into account as we trace the continuing development of Mexican communities throughout the United States. Since the 1960s, the massive influx of Latino immigrants reinforced Hispanic culture in the United States. The 2010 census counted about 35 million Latinos living in the United States, eighty percent of who were ethnic Mexicans. All in all, the culture and identity of Mexican Americans will continue to change, reflecting both inevitable generational fusion with Anglo society and the continuing influence of immigrants, not only from Mexico, but from throughout Latin America. By now Mexican-American Generation attitudes towards immigration have changed. Latino Civil Rights organizations such the National Council of La Raza, LULAC, the Mexican American Legal Defense and Educational Fund (MALDEF) all support providing relief for undocumented workers from Latin America, a position which has to be understood as having evolved from the Perales era.

Bibliography

Primary Sources

El Paso Herald-Post.
Washington Post.
Alonso Perales Microfilm Collection (APMC), Hispanic History of Texas Recovering the U.S. Hispanic Literary Heritage Project University of Houston.
Private archives of F. Arturo Rosales, Arizona State University.
National Archives Record Group 84 350/64/13/05

Secondary Sources

Alanís Enciso, F. S. (n.d.). *Rezumando nacionalismo: La repatriación de mexicanos de los Estados Unidos 1929-1934*. Retrieved from http://www.colef.net/ seminariosociales/documentos/DES-SP-054.pdf.
Alonzo, A. C. (1998). *Tejano legacy: Rancheros and settlers in south Texas, 1734-1900*. Albuquerque: University of New Mexico Press.
Águila, J. (2000). *Protecting 'México de afuera': Mexican emigration policy, 1876-1928*. (Doctoral dissertation). Available from ProQuest Dissertations and Theses database. (UMI No. 9990715).

Balderrama, F. E. & Rodríguez, R. (1995). *Decade of betrayal: Mexican repatriation in the 1930s*. Albuquerque: University of New Mexico Press.

Blanton, C. K. (2009). The citizenship sacrifice: Mexican Americans, the Saunders-Leonard report, and the politics of immigration, 1951–1952. *Western Historical Quarterly 40*(3), 299-320.

Chávez, E. (2002). *Mi raza primero! (My people first!): Nationalism, identity, and insurgency in the Chicano movement in Los Angeles, 1966-1978*. Berkeley: University of California Press.

Camarillo, A. (1971). A research note on Chicano community leaders: the GI generation, 1938-1950: An extended research note. *Aztlán 6*, 145-150.

Cardoso, L. (1980). *Mexican emigration to the United States, 1897-1931*. Tucson: University of Arizona Press.

Carroll, P. J. (2003). *Felix Longoria's wake: Bereavement, racism, and the rise of Mexican American activism*. Austin: University of Texas Press.

Delay, B. (2008). *War of a thousand deserts: Indian raids and the U.S.-Mexican War*. New Haven: Yale University Press.

Dillard, A. D. (2001). *Guess who's coming to dinner now? Multicultural conservatism in America*. New York: New York University Press.

García, I. M. (2002). *Hector P. García: In Relentless Pursuit of Justice*. Houston: Arte Público Press.

García, J. R. (1996). *Mexicans in the Midwest, 1900-1932*. Tucson: University of Arizona Press.

García, M. T. *Católicos: Resistance and affirmation in Chicano Catholic history*. Austin: University of Texas Press, 2010.

García, M. T. (1990). *Mexican Americans: Leadership, ideology and identity, 1930-1960*. New Haven: Yale University Press.

Gritter, M. (n.d.). *Good neighbors and good citizens: People of Mexican origin and anti-discrimination policy*. Retrieved from http://www.newschool.edu/uploaded-Files/NSSR/Departments_and_Faculty/Political_Science/Recent_Placements/GritterSample09.pdf.

Guglielmo, T. A. (2006). Fighting for Caucasian rights: Mexicans, Mexican Americans, and the transnational struggle for civil rights in World War II Texas. *Journal of American History 92*(4), 1212-1237.

Gutiérrez, D. G. (1995). *walls and mirrors: Mexican Americans, Mexican immigrants and the politics of ethnicity*. Berkeley: University of California Press.

Heber Johnson, B. (2003). *Revolution in Texas: How a forgotten rebellion and its bloody suppression turned Mexicans into Americans*. New Haven: Yale University Press.

Hoffman, A. (1974). *Unwanted Mexican Americans in the Great Depression: Repatriation pressures, 1929-1939*. Tucson: University of Arizona Press.

Limón, J. E. (1974). El primer congreso mexicanista de 1911. *Aztlán 5*, 145-150.

Lytle Hernandez, K. (2010). *Migra!: A history of the U.S. border patrol*. Berkeley: University of California Press.

Martínez, O. J. (1975). On the size of the Chicano population: New estimates, 1850-1900. *Aztlán 6*(1), 43-67.

Márquez, B. (2006). *LULAC: The evolution of a Mexican American political organization*. Austin: University of Texas Press.

Meier, M. S. & Ribera, F. (1994). *Mexican Americans, American Mexicans: From conquistadors to Chicanos*. New York: MacMillan.

Montejano, D. (1987). *Anglos and Mexicans in the making of Texas, 1836-1896*. Austin, University of Texas Press.

Montejano, D. (2005). The beating of Private Aguirre: A story about west Texas during World War II. In Rivas Rodriguez, M. (Ed.) *Mexican Americans and World War II* (pp. 41-66). Austin: University of Texas Press.

Nostrand, R.L. (1975). Mexican Americans circa 1850. *Annals of the Association of American Geographers 65*(3), 378-390.

Nieto-Phillips, J. M. (2008). *The language of blood: The making of Spanish-American identity in New Mexico*. Albuquerque: University of New Mexico Press.

Oropeza, L. (2003). Antiwar Aztlán The Chicano Movement Opposes U.S. Intervention in Vietnam. In Plummer, B. G. (Ed.) *Window on freedom: Race, civil rights, and foreign affairs, 1945-1988* (pp. 205-206). Chapel Hill: University of North Carolina Press.

Orozco, C. E. (2009). *No Mexicans, women, or dogs allowed: The rise of the Mexican American civil rights movement*. Austin: University of Texas Press.

Phillips, M. (2006). *White metropolis: Race, ethnicity, and religion in Dallas, 1841-2001*. Austin: University of Texas Press.

Ramos, H. A. J. (2000). *The American G.I. forum: In pursuit of the dream, 1948-1983*. Houston: Arte Público Press.

Rosales, A. F. (1997). *¡Chicano! The history of the Mexican American civil rights movement*. Houston: Arte Público Press.

Rosales, A. F. (1999). *Pobre raza: Violence, justice, and mobilization among México lindo immigrants, 1900-1936*. Austin: University of Texas Press.

Sánchez, G. J. (1993). *Becoming Mexican American: Culture and identity in Chicano Los Angeles, 1900-1945*. New York: Oxford University Press.

Sloss Vento, A. (1977). *Alonso S. Perales: His struggles for the rights of Mexican Americans*. San Antonio: Artes Gráficas.

Taylor, P. S. (1934). *An American-Mexican frontier: Nueces County, Texas*. Chapel Hill: University of North Carolina Press.

Weber, D. J. (1973). *Foreigners in their native land: Historical roots of the Mexican Americans*. Albuquerque: University of New Mexico Press.

Zamora, E. (2009). *Claiming rights and righting wrongs in Texas Mexican workers and job politics during World War II*. College Station: Texas A&M Press.

Notes

[1]The Perales collection is replete with data that relate this story of Mexican-American era civil rights struggle.

[2]Numerous documents exist in the Perales Collection on his education pursuits and on his Foreign Service career.

[3]See large amount of correspondence with Comité throughout 1945 and 1946 in the Perales Collection.

[4]The discussion on William C. Blocker and the confidential report is summarized from extensive correspondence and documents in National Archives Record Group 84 350/64/13; See also Zamora, passim.

Connecting Causes, Alonso S. Perales, Hemispheric Unity, and Mexican Rights in the United States

Emilio Zamora

To achieve international cooperation in solving international problems of an economic, social, cultural, or humanitarian character, and in promoting and encouraging respect for human rights and for fundamental freedoms for all without distinction as to race, sex, language, or religion.

UN Charter, 1945

Nagata, 1945

Introduction

The United Nations conference held at San Francisco's Veteran's War Memorial Building began winding down as delegations from fifty countries prepared to take part in the signing ceremony of the new organization's charter. When it came time for Nicaragua to sign, on June 23, 1945, Dr. Mariano Arguello Vargas, Minister of Foreign Affairs, walked to the austere stage of the Herbst Theatre and seated himself at a large round table. The rest of the Nicaraguan delegation, made up of government and military officials, stood between him and a raised display of national flags as the official photographers recorded yet another nation committing to international cooperation for global peace, democracy, and justice.[1]

Although the event looked like all the other forty-nine signing ceremonies, Nicaraguan officials had dispensed with tradition and assigned one of the coveted positions in their delegation to a person who had been born and raised in the United States. Alonso S. Perales, a co-founder of the League of United Latin American Citizens (LULAC) and one of the most prominent U.S. civil rights leaders of the twentieth century, held the post of lead counselor to the delegation. His selection and assignment may have seemed odd to a casual observer, but not to someone who had followed Perales' extensive and distinguished diplomatic career for Nicaragua and the United States, or knew of his close relationship with the Anastasio Zomosa regime (Perales to Sumner Welles 26 Mar 1938: 1 and attached material). By the time the first UN meeting took place, Perales had served as the Nicaraguan Consul General in San Antonio, Texas for eleven years; he also had participated in at least thirteen U.S. diplomatic missions in Latin America since the 1920s (Perales, 1948; Perales, "El Lic. A. Perales Fue Nombrado" 1).

Nicaraguan officials no doubt thought that Perales' experience in the diplomatic field and his familiarity with U.S. society and inter-American relations would give them a negotiating advantage in the culturally diverse and potentially contentious inaugural UN meeting. There was no guarantee, however, that Perales would devote his entire attention to Nicaragua's national interests. Both when departing from San Antonio and while in San Francisco, he had announced publicly that he would be representing Mexican nationals and U.S.-born Mexicans, giving voice to their fight against discrimination and inequality in the United States ("La Voz del Público" 1).[2] This did not mean that Perales intended to ignore his responsibilities to the Nicaraguan delegation. Rather, it suggests that the Central American officials had selected him knowing that they would be involved in raising the case for Mexican rights in the United States to a regional and international level of importance.

Prejudice, racial thinking and discrimination in the United States took on hemispheric importance when, during the Second World War, the State Department expanded its Good Neighbor Policy into the United States' domestic arena and the Mexican government advanced its advocacy campaign on behalf of Mexicans living in the United States.[3] Latin American leaders followed Mexico's lead and tied the global issue of racial thinking to their concern for pan-Americanism, a form of unity that was premised on mutual consultation, cooperation and reciprocity among theoretically equal nations. U.S. diplomats had consented to the broad design of mutuality during the wartime meetings of ministers held throughout Latin America. This had encouraged assertive expressions in favor of improved diplomatic relations that came to include the UN declaration for human rights and the hope that every country would adopt legal strictures against racial thinking and discrimination. Perales had taken part in this wartime discourse over the proposed diplomatic and social relations and now, as part of Nicaragua's UN delegation, was about to participate in the most important international forum on human rights with his claim on behalf of Mexicans in the United States (Thorning, 1946; Gordon Lauren, 1983).

With some exceptions, historians have overlooked the relationship between the heightened wartime attention to prejudice, racial thinking, and discrimination and the treatment of Mexicans in the United States, and they have failed to examine this community as a point where local and hemispheric issues began to correspond and connect.[4] Building on my prior work on Mexicans in the United States, here I underscore the importance of Perales as an insightful, prescient, and determined civil rights figure. Through his role in hemispheric diplomacy, Perales brought international attention to the discriminatory treatment of Mexicans in the American Southwest (Castañeda, 1958; Zamora, 2009).

The discussion that follows examines how Perales came to participate in international forums and underscores the importance of his bold and unprecedented venture into diplomatic and U.S. civil rights history. I first address how WWII set hemispheric unity in motion. The wartime unity that the United States and Mexico initiated, sustained and reflected the geopolitical concerns over security and cooperation that one would expect in the Americas during the global crisis of the 1940s. The significance that the subject of race acquired in diplomatic relations may have been less predictable before the war, but became increasingly obvious as Mexico lobbied against racial thinking in the United States, particularly among Mexican Nationals and U.S.-born Mexicans. Perales seized on the opportunity to draw attention to discrimination against Mexicans and build support for a nascent civil rights movement in Texas that he was leading at the time. I suggest that just as government and non-government representatives elevated racial thinking to prominence in the diplomatic arena, civil rights activists in Mexican communities from Texas also made the connection with a grounded civil rights cause as their principal point of departure. The story of race as a wartime issue, in other words, can be best appreciated by examining diplomatic relations, the Mexican civil rights cause in Texas, and their connection in the political biography of Perales.

Uniting the Americas

The UN delegates came to San Francisco from throughout the world, ostensibly to guarantee peace and cooperation among nation-states and between peoples. The war had revealed serious fault lines in diplomatic and social relations and demonstrated the need for a league of nations with a framework that permitted mediating differences while also protecting national sovereignty rights (Russell, 1958). The Latin American delegates shared the universal concerns for peace, cooperation, a world organization and the hope that they too could contribute to bringing about a better world. They also, however, brought experiences and ideas of their own that spoke to the larger concerns of the UN, including the future of the highly touted inter-American system of cooperation and reciprocity that was to continue beyond the war. Preserving Pan-American unity was important to these delegates; their countries' political and economic futures depended on the United States keeping its promises of non-intervention and the provision of support for economic development. Such regional interests found expression in the UN's deliberations over national sovereignty rights, future relations between small and large nations, the role of regional alliances, and the governing structure of the organization.

Perhaps the most unusual contribution of the Latin American delegation, however, was a claim that discrimination against persons of Latin American-origin in the United States represented a hemispheric version of the racial thinking and practices that had contributed to the war in Europe. Although government officials from Latin America, especially Mexico, were often tempted to use the issue as a wedge to promote national interests, the UN also provided them with an opportunity to draw on the experiences of their own nationals in the United States in the historic debates over human rights and possible remedies for racial prejudice and discrimination (Houston, 1956). Racial thinking and practices had special importance for Latin America (Vázquez García, 2001), but diplomats did not necessarily express similar concerns over racial problems in the United States, nor did they always address them with the same fervor as they did the issue of U.S. intervention.

Nicaraguan officials, for example, rarely expressed Mexico's level of concern over racial discrimination or over the United States' history of intervention. They apparently left Perales to address discrimination as he wished during the years (1934-1960) he served as their country's Consul General in San Antonio. The Mexican Consulate in San Antonio, on the other hand, by 1943 had implemented an official policy of advocacy for the rights of Mexicans living in the United States. Moreover, the consulate's lead attorney, Manuel C. Gonzales, a Mexican American who had served as the National President of LULAC in 1930-31, was given a major role in the policy's implementation. Similarly, with respect to non-intervention, Nicaraguan government officials were much less wary than their Mexican counterparts: they welcomed U.S. troops and diplomats to defend the authoritarian Somoza regime against the popular insurgency led by Augusto Sandino. Mexico's Foreign Affairs Officer, Ezequiel Padilla Peñalosa, did not necessarily mistrust the U.S. promise of non-intervention, but he often referred to it, emphasizing non-intervention as a necessary building block in the construction of inter-American unity (Crawley, 2007; Zorrilla, 1966; Torres, 1979).

The world stage may have dwarfed the problems of discrimination in the United States for delegates from some countries, but it did not minimize this issue's importance for Perales, other Latin American delegates, or even the U.S. delegation. For Perales, acknowledging the problem to illustrate an evil of global proportions strengthened the civil rights cause, discredited segregationists, encouraged change and promised to more fully integrate Mexicans and other Latin Americans into the U.S. discourse over ethnicity and equal rights in the United States. Latin Americans, on the other hand, may have been more interested in using the problem of discrimination to advocate for their nationals on foreign soil and to gain some negotiating advantage in their relations with the United States. U.S. officials had to pay closer attention to discrimination against Mexicans as Latin Americans began to address it more boldly in international venues (Gordon Lauren, 1983).

The possible new understandings and other gains that emerged from the UN meeting in San Francisco obtain additional meaning when we consider that Latin Americans had been addressing discrimination and human rights in forums over the years leading up to the conference. Beginning around 1933, when U.S. diplomats began to promote the Good Neighbor Policy in Latin America, foreign affairs officers from the Americas met frequently and raised a number of regional issues, including racial prejudice and discrimination. As will be discussed in more detail below, the well-attended Third Conference of the Inter-American Bar Association, hosted by Mexico in 1944, gave the issues a full airing and adopted a resolution condemning racial discrimination. A subsequent meeting, the 1945 Inter-American Conference on Problems of War and Peace (the "Chapultepec Conference") also hosted by Mexico, brought together an even larger number of government officials from throughout the Americas to prepare for the UN meeting. Delegates to these two international gatherings in Mexico discussed discrimination and adopted anti-discrimination and human rights resolutions. These meetings, along with the UN conference, demonstrated that the issue had achieved hemispheric and global importance. Ironically, it was changes the United States introduced in its relations with Latin America that made this new emphasis possible.

Promoting unity through Pan-Americanism. The war and consequent U.S. concerns over continental security had led the State Department to promote the Good Neighbor Policy and to seek an inter-American alliance by capitalizing on Latin Americans' anti-Axis sentiments and their longstanding tradition and imaginary of Pan-Americanism. Latin American leaders shared security concerns and ideological fears over the "hell" that German aggression had unleashed on the world, but they also welcomed the promise of improved and cooperative relations with the now friendly colossus of the north.[5] The numerous inter-American meetings that brought foreign affairs officers together beginning in the early 1930s yielded unprecedented diplomatic amicability and cooperation, including agreements to end U.S. interventions in the internal affairs of the twenty-one Latin American countries and the affirmation of human rights principles. The proclamations of inter-American unity also included agreements on commercial, financial, manpower, industrial and military cooperation that gave form to the new relations. The historic preoccupation with Pan-Americanism placed a Latin American imprint on the discourse over hemispheric unity.

Pan-Americanism had served as an idealized form of regional unity expressed by independence movement leaders like the Venezuelan Simón Bolivar, and by literary figures such as the Nicaraguan poet Rubén Darío.[6] The declaration of the Monroe Doctrine in 1823 and subsequent interventionist actions by the United States in the nineteenth and twentieth centuries strengthened a commitment to the idea of hemispheric unity among the Latin American nations, especially Mexico. Perales, astute observer that he was, reasoned that although the United States may have made the difference in the end with friendlier foreign policies, as a region, Latin America played a critically important role by agreeing with the new wartime alliance. Accord-

ing to Perales, in the process of agreeing to cooperate, Latin American leaders rene-
gotiated the terms of cooperation. They Pan-Americanized both the Monroe Doctrine and Theodore Roosevelt's "corollary" by which the United States reserved the
exclusive right to intervene on behalf of Latin American nations facing European
aggression (Liévano Aguirre, 1969; Herring, 2008; Sexton, 2011).

Pan-Americanizing relations with the United States meant agreeing with the
idea of mutual consultation in case of threats and/or acts of aggression that put the
continent as a whole at risk. The United States had consented to a non-intervention-
ist pact as early as the 1933 Seventh International Conference of American States,
held in Montevideo, Uruguay (it was during this conference that the United States
first unveiled the Good Neighbor Policy) and soon thereafter agreed to the principle
of mutual defense in the Americas. Latin Americans could now make a stronger case
for themselves as a regional federation of small, yet equal nations allied with the
United States. This provided an alternative to the big and powerful nation model that
in the end won out in San Francisco and eventually generated the all-consuming
Cold War rivalry between the United States and the Soviet Union.

Wartime agreements of cooperation also strengthened the long-standing tradition of diplomatically intervening on behalf of nationals on foreign soil. As we shall
see, Mexico extended its diplomatic reach when, beginning in 1942, its consular
corps—in collaboration with LULAC—formally implemented an advocacy policy
on behalf of Mexican-origin persons facing discrimination in the United States.
Although the State Department tacitly allowed this, in meetings held throughout the
war, American diplomats began to address the inherent contradiction between the
doctrine of non-intervention and the diplomatic protection of human rights. The tension between such fundamental concerns in the evolving system of inter-American
cooperation and reciprocity, in other words, created yet another pressing issue that
diplomats also sought to reconcile during the meetings leading up to the UN conference (Goldman, 2009).

Promoting unity through a strong Mexico-United States alliance. As the United
States' chief ally in the Americas, Mexico played a special role in wartime cooperation between Latin America and the United States. In addition to the early and consistent public pronouncements of inter-American unity made by Foreign Affairs
Officer Padilla Peñalosa, the Mexican government entered into numerous international agreements of cooperation. These accords made available hundreds of thousands of *braceros* (contract workers), primarily for American agriculture; 15,000
Mexican nationals who served in the U.S. military; security measures that allowed
the United States to set up radar installations on Mexico's coasts; and critical war
supplies like tungsten, copper and rubber for North American industrial plants.

As noted above, cooperation also involved permitting Mexico's diplomatic intervention on behalf of its nationals in the United States. Any tensions that may have
resulted from this paled next to the need for wartime unity in the Americas that Padilla
Peñalosa assiduously promoted in diplomatic meetings held throughout the Americas.
In large measure, Mexico's embrace of inter-American cooperation was rooted in
anti-Axis views and security concerns. Officials expressed these views and concerns
often and long enough to suggest a major consensus in support of the Allied cause and

of the United States as the titular head of the Americas. Practical considerations, however, also encouraged wartime unity. Mexico hoped that cooperation would result in U.S. support for the development of its postwar economy. Although the United States would fail to keep its promise, the hope was sufficiently strong to give added meaning to the idea of inter-American cooperation during the war.

The proximity of Mexico to the United States and the interdependence the two countries had achieved over time also explain the close relations that emerged during the war. The sheer amount of cooperation increased exponentially and seems to have set Mexico's postwar future apart from that of other Latin American nations. The wartime practice of racial discrimination against Mexicans in the United States, as well as Mexico's defense of its nationals on foreign soil, represented an additional distinguishing feature in the construction of unity in the Americas. Mexico, in other words, stood in for all of Latin America as a reliable barometer of material cooperation and negotiated relations. Discrimination, meanwhile, became an issue of hemispheric importance as Mexico implemented its advocacy policy in concert with the United States' decision to apply the Good Neighbor Policy at home. Mexican civil rights leaders made use of the unprecedented diplomatic opportunity to project the issue of discrimination against Mexicans onto the national and international screen.

LULAC and the Mexican Cause

LULAC emerged at the start of the Depression and began its impressive growth during the Second World War, alongside the more explicitly political Committee of One Hundred American Citizens (COHC) that Perales favored because he exercised greater influence in the organization and could speak more freely as its representative. From the beginning, both organizations distinguished themselves as ethnic or Mexican-Americanist alternatives to the more Mexicanist or transnational community organizations like the highly popular mutual aid societies, and from unions such as Local 172, a politically aggressive CIO affiliate that represented pecan-shelling workers from San Antonio (Zamora, 1993; Vargas, 2005).[7] Historians concur that LULAC and COHC gave expression to a moderate voice among members of an upwardly mobile and U.S.-born sector of the Mexican community. They also agree that the early history of LULAC was intimately tied to the political biographies of a small cadre of leaders that included Perales, one of the principal spokesmen for the organization between the 1920s and the 1950s (San Miguel, 1987; García, 1989; Marquez, 1993; Kaplowitz, 2005; Orozco, 2009).

In arguing for equal rights, Perales was joined by other leading figures in their respective professions and the civil rights movement, including New Mexico Senator Dennis Chavez, the lone voice for Mexican rights in Washington between the 1930s and 1950s, and Dr. Carlos Castañeda, who served as a professor at the University of Texas between 1936 and 1958 and expounded on the long-time presence of Mexicans in the American Southwest and the group's continued minority standing. San Antonio Archbishop Robert E. Lucey reinforced Perales' message during the wartime years, applying values from religious and social gospels to condemn racial prejudice and discrimination as moral problems of the highest order. José de la Luz Saenz, a long-time teacher and WWI veteran, also took to the court of public opinion with his extensive writings on constitutional rights, the crass violations of these rights, and the Mexican contributions of hard work, long hours and low pay in a growing wartime economy. Fellow LULAC leader and attorney Manuel C. Gonzales seconded Perales' bid for civil rights legislation and worked closely with LULAC and the Mexican government to condemn discrimination against both U.S.-born Mexicans and Mexican nationals during the war (Luján, 1987; Almaráz, 1990; Zamora, 2002, 2009; Bronder, 1982).

Chavez, Lucey, Castañeda, Saenz, Gonzales and many others in organizations like LULAC and the COHC reiterated the view that the U.S. government should address discrimination within its borders to demonstrate sincerity in the building of unity in the Americas. Even in this company, however, Perales stood out. Using the COHC as his principal base of operations (Orozco, 2011), he launched persistent critiques in books, speeches, newspaper articles, and radio interviews, building a reputation as the most active proponent of civil rights legislation for Mexicans living within the United States (Perales, 1936, 1937; Perales, 1948; Sloss-Vento, 1977). He also demonstrated impressive insight in recognizing the wartime opportunity to join with other Pan-Americanists from Latin America in reframing the problem of discrimination against Mexicans as a larger issue in Latin America-U.S. relations.

Perales brought expertise as well as a passionate energy to the fight against discrimination and the effort to link the Mexican cause to the larger wartime concern over discrimination and human rights. Armed with a still fresh record of diplomatic service in Central America, he left Washington, D.C. in the early 1920s to assume a position of leadership in the Texas-based social movement for Mexican-American rights.[8] He quickly became a leader with the Sons of America, a mutual aid society in San Antonio with an explicit Mexican-Americanist political identity. The organization gave special importance to U.S. citizenship as a precondition for membership and advanced a constitutionalist critique of racial discrimination and inequality. Perales also set out to promote broad-based unity and a claim for equality on the basis of constitutional rights and proven loyalty on the battlefields of the First World War.

This initiative involved others, but no one else matched Perales' ceaseless protests and persistent calls for unity, frequently through Spanish-language newspapers, especially the popular San Antonio-based daily, *La Prensa* (San Antonio: 1913-55). He also led important organizing efforts in South Texas, where Mexicanist mutual aid societies and other community organizations hosted his well-attended presentations. Perales often joined with other U.S.-born Mexicans, including his close political companions José de la Luz Saenz and José Tomás Canales, as well as the lone Mexican-American organizer for the American Federation of Labor Clemente Idar, to call for unity and for the establishment of a statewide organization, a goal eventually embodied as LULAC (Sloss-Vento, 1977; Zamora, 1992, 2002; *La Prensa,* "El Lic. Perales" 7+; *El Cronista del Valle,* "Va a Formarse" 4+).

Prior to the Second World War, LULAC and COHC leaders did not have close ties with Mexican nationals. Although they spoke about a common cause against segregationists (a group not known for making distinctions based on nativity or citizenship), they denied Mexican nationals membership in their organizations mainly because they thought they could make more effective claims for equal rights by presenting themselves as patriotic, U.S.-born Mexican Americans. Initially, the men who became the leaders of LULAC claimed to be speaking for both Mexican nationals and U.S.-born Mexicans. However, at an early organizing meeting, held in Harlingen, Texas in 1927, a decision was made to exclude Mexican nationals. LULAC co-founder Canales later told an interviewer that it was not until the eve of the Harlingen convention that Perales finally agreed to the proposed exclusion (Canales interview, 1929). Perales and his fellow activists likely understood and anticipated the negative reaction that occurred: untold numbers of Mexican nationals and their sympathizers bolted from the meeting, accusing Perales, Saenz, Canales and Idar of sowing divisions. Perales probably exacerbated matters when, not long after the first organizational meeting, he commented in a newspaper article that Mexican nationals might not want to join LULAC because doing so would indicate that they were rejecting their Mexican birthright ("Una Aclaración" 1).

In the 1930s, however, Perales strove to reconcile the public perception of distance and bias by reminding everyone that LULAC understood the experiences of discrimination suffered by U.S.-born Mexicans and Mexican nationals as linked and championed the rights of both groups. For Perales, the seemingly wholesale disdain for Mexicans by major segments of the larger society required a narrow ethnic strategy that claimed constitutional rights on the basis of U.S. citizenship. This did not mean, however, that LULAC overlooked obvious organic ties or its own responsibility to speak on behalf of all Mexicans. Although the organization could be faulted for breaking ranks, Perales' logic and LULAC's practice of solidarity explain the ease and confidence with which he and other LULAC leaders could make the semantic and theoretical leap to an expanded hemispheric claim for equal rights during the Second World War. Perales consistently maintained that all Mexicans, regardless of citizenship or length of residence in the United States, faced the same discriminatory fate ("La Ignorancia Como Causa de los Prejuicios Raciales," 20 Aug. 1923, Microfilm 2309, Reel 12: 1+; Perales, "El Problema de los México-Americanos," Oct. 1923, Microfilm 2309, Reel 12: 1+; Zamora, 2009, 1+).

Perales and other fellow founders of LULAC seemed willing to alienate Mexican nationals for the sake of establishing an ethnic organization in 1927. This changed by the 1930s when Mexico was championing the cause of Mexicans in U.S. soil with Gonzales basically in charge of that campaign. The overlapping leadership of Gonzales and Perales' public concern for Mexican nationals during the late 1930s no doubt undid much of the negative public perception of LULAC as an exclusively ethnic organization. A strong sense that the fledgling LULAC needed to be shored up as much as possible, even at the expense of defending Mexican nationals, thus gave way to a new view that the organization could afford to repair fences by making explicit overtures to nationals, through Gonzales and Perales and other LULAC leaders.[9]

LULAC and the Call for Hemispheric Equality

It took little effort to widen this view of the shared fate of Mexican Americans and Mexican nationals to include persons from Central and South America, especially since segregationists were not known for making fine distinctions. Expressing the claim for equality in hemispheric terms was also an inviting proposition, given the wartime language of unity and understanding that was being applied to relations between nations and groups living within national borders. Moreover, the United States' developing policy of friendly relations with Latin America placed the United States under greater scrutiny. This, in turn, encouraged civil rights leaders to offer their assessments of discriminatory practices and the degree to which U.S. officials were living up to their promise of good neighborliness. Perales also recognized that Latin American diplomats were aware of discrimination against their nationals on U.S. soil and that the related worldwide concern over race had made them especially sensitive to the strategic use of discrimination in diplomatic relations. He neither invented this diplomatic tool nor was responsible for its widespread use. His contribution was to capitalize on the opportunity to bring added attention to discrimination against Latin Americans in the United States. Perales' public statements, like the one he made before a congressional committee in 1945, suggest that he understood the historic opportunity to speak broadly and with authority in Pan-Americanist terms:

The discriminatory situation in Texas is truly a disgrace to our Nation. Mexicans—regardless of citizenship—and, for that matter, citizens of Honduras, Venezuela, Colombia, Argentina, and the other republics, have been humiliated merely because they happened to be of Spanish or Mexican descent, time and again. (Perales, 1948, p. 121)

As will be described below, by the end of the 1930s, LULAC leaders were increasingly making common cause with Latin Americans in the United States. This outreach created pressure to do more to square their organization's problematic membership policy with its leaders' expanded hemispheric view. They simply could not continue to exclude non-U.S. citizens at the same time as they were calling for an end to discrimination in the Americas. LULAC found a clever compromise in 1946, when John Herrera, an attorney, LULAC officer from Houston, and future LULAC president (1952-53), announced that during the war his local council had been interpreting the organization's constitution to mean that Mexican nationals were eligible for membership if they promised to seek U.S. citizenship. He sought and received a favorable ruling from state officers and soon thereafter announced the new interpretation at a LULAC state convention.[10]

First steps in broadening the demand for civil rights. One of the earliest indications that LULAC was starting to treat discrimination against Latin Americans in the United States as a hemispheric issue deserving the attention of officials from Washington, D.C. and Mexico City occurred in December 1939. Perales, already a well-established spokesman for LULAC, issued a blunt critique of the Pan-American Round Tables of Texas (PARTT), a predominantly Anglo women's organization, for declaring goodwill and understanding between the United States and Latin American nations while simultaneously refusing to denounce the work of segregationists at home (Perales, "El Movimiento Pan-Americanista Que se Desarrolla en Este Estado," 3 Dec. 1939 3, 6; Perales, "El Abogado Alonso S. Perales se Retira de Todo

Movimiento Panamericanista de Texas," 25 Nov. 1939, Microfilm 2309, Reel 13: 1; Perales to Florence R. Griswold, 25 Nov. 1939, Microfilm 2309, Reel 12: 1+). Since its founding in 1916, PARTT, and especially its headquarters chapter in San Antonio, had been waging a vigorous public campaign for improved relations with Latin America. This campaign was further stimulated when President Franklin Roosevelt began promoting the Good Neighbor Policy in the Americas during the early 1930s. Like the Lion's Club, the Rotary Club, and the Kiwanis Club, the Pan American Round Tables maintained relations with affiliates in Latin America and members prided themselves on serving as cultural ambassadors for the United States (Frantz, 2011).

Although by 1939 Perales was well known in many circles for his strong stance against discrimination, even by the close of the 1920s, he was becoming conspicuous among fellow civil rights leaders for his vigorous critique of racial thinking and practices as obstacles to continental solidarity (Perales, "El Resultado" 7; Perales, "La Evolución" 7). None of these early denouncements, however, appears to have been directed against an organization of the prominence of PARTT in the U.S. Pan-Americanist movement; nor had anyone of Perales' stature boldly accused well-meaning Anglos of being as guilty as nativists in undermining wartime unity. Obviously seeking dramatic effect, he announced that he would end his eight years of collaboration with the Pan American Round Tables of Texas and would disassociate himself from any other organization that professed Pan-Americanism yet failed to protest "the growing injustices and humiliations that are daily being directed against the Mexican residents in Texas" (Perales, "El Movimiento Pan-Americanista" 3, author's translation). He ended his association with the organization, although articles in *La Prensa* indicate that this changed by 1941 when he once again began to appear in public programs alongside officers of the organization.

Raising public awareness of domestic discrimination. By January 1941, Perales was raising the level of the discourse over Pan-Americanism in the United States to a higher plane. Noting that segregationists were continuing to undermine continental unity, he began calling on the federal government to initiate public education programs against racial prejudice and discrimination. According to Perales, nothing less than the outcome of the war was at stake, "Current circumstances make it imperative that the peoples of the Americas unite and cooperate." He was holding the U.S. government responsible for racial discrimination and inequality at about the same time that government officials from Latin America, especially Mexico, were beginning to intervene on behalf of their nationals living in the United States (Perales, "El Lic. Alonso S. Perales Sugiere" 3).

Perales also campaigned for government-sponsored programs to inform the Anglo public of the merits and the contributions of Mexicans and other Latin Americans to U.S. society, both historically and during the contemporary period. The purpose would be to meet the pressing wartime need to combat racial prejudice and improve understanding in ethnic and international relations. Even so, Perales became disenchanted with half-hearted or ineffective efforts at changing hearts and minds and began to place greater emphasis on civil rights legislation as the best way to prohibit discrimination and demonstrate sincerity in the construction of an inter-American alliance. For him, organizations like the PARTT and their public programs of speakers, student forums, and recognitions of fellow pan-Americanists simply did not guarantee immediate and effective results. The slow pace of change in ridding the country of racial discrimination was keeping the United States from building the unity the war required. Perales said as much during a radio-broadcast interview: "I believe we ought to put an end to it [discrimination] right now, if we really want to get the peoples of the Americas together" (KONO Radio Broadcast, "What Does it Take to get the Peoples of the Americas Together," 3 Mar. 1941, Microfilm 2309, Reel 12: 1+).

Another factor prompting Perales' appeal for federal intervention was the failure of efforts to convince the Texas legislature to pass a civil rights law that extended protections to Mexicans (based mainly on their official classification as Whites). On at least one occasion, Perales and fellow LULAC leaders like Castañeda along with Archbishop Lucey convinced a friendly legislator to introduce a bill guaranteeing equal rights to all Latin Americans. Segregationist legislators, according to Castañeda, re-wrote the ill-fated bill because they feared that civil rights guarantees would be extended to African-origin persons from Latin America, and that African Americans would subsequently claim similar legislation. The consistent opposition to civil rights legislation in Texas provides a reliable measure of segregationist thinking in the country as a whole. That, combined with the timing of President Roosevelt's issuance of Executive Order 8802, explains Perales' decision to seek a legal remedy in Washington (Zamora, 2009).

Making the most of Executive Order 8802. Responding to pressure from African American civil and labor rights leaders, in June 1941, President Roosevelt signed Executive Order 8802, which banned discrimination based on race, creed, or national origin in war industries, and established the Fair Employment Practice Committee (FEPC) to enforce the law. The FEPC became a presence in the American Southwest beginning in 1943 and quickly started applying the nation's non-discrimination policy among Mexican workers. The opening of FEPC offices in Dallas and San Antonio, the appointment of Castañeda to a major supervisory role over Mexican complaints in the American Southwest, and legal settlements favoring Mexican workers all encouraged Perales to renew his demands for civil rights legislation.[11]

Although Roosevelt's intent was to limit employment discrimination, LULAC leaders like Perales and Castañeda often pointed to Executive Order 8802 and the work of the FEPC to argue that the government could use the same justification and harness the same will to approve a more broadly defined civil rights law. To support this view, Perales often returned to the familiar contention in civil rights circles that Latin American countries were asking for anti-discrimination legislation as evidence that the United States practiced what it preached. The U.S. State Department, under pressure from the Mexican government, further amplified the discourse in 1942, when it expanded the Good Neighbor Policy into the domestic arena with a public education program that acknowledged Mexican and Puerto Rican contributions to the war effort and urged the Anglo public to be more understanding.

The State Department also encouraged Texas officials to adopt a state-level good neighbor policy in response to Mexico's 1943 decision to ban the employment of *braceros* on Texas farms. Mexican government officials hoped to make the most of their strategic advantage: the very same employers who exploited Mexican migratory labor could now be made to demand that Governor Coke Stevenson grant Mexico whatever was necessary to lift the ban on *braceros*. Governor Stevenson subsequently approved a Texas Good Neighbor Policy, established a Good Neighbor Commission (GNC) to investigate complaints of discrimination by Mexicans and encouraged legislators to consider passage of non-discrimination legislation. According to Perales and fellow LULAC leaders, these initiatives fell far short of their declared intent and underscored the need for the Mexican government to keep the *bracero* ban in place. Mexican government officials apparently agreed, because they refused to send *braceros* to Texas during the war and kept the state at center stage in the growing hemispheric debate over racial thinking. Texas had drawn the most attention from Mexican government officials, in part because of its large agricultural economy and the unfavorable reputation of its segregationists, but also possibly because of LULAC's earnest and effective efforts to draw attention to the problem in Texas (Zamora, 2009).

Challenging the commitment to equal rights in Texas. Although Texas legislators proposed several bills during the 1940s that called for prohibiting discrimination, the two legislative houses agreed on only one joint resolution, the 1943 "Caucasian Race Resolution." This resolution, like the state's Good Neighbor Policy and its Good Neighbor Commission, essentially declared Mexicans another White group as a way to avoid a more broadly based civil rights law. The Caucasian Race Resolution was issued to placate a growing insistence on civil rights legislation as a wartime expression of continental solidarity. Perales took the LULAC lead in questioning the sincerity of Texas officials by bringing before the GNC hundreds of affidavits that documented claims of discrimination that the agency had not investigated and, in some cases, had failed to mediate successfully. He also joined two other LULAC leaders in requesting admission to a bath house that had refused to accept Mexicans and in successfully filing suit on the grounds that the owner had violated the Resolution when he refused them admission. A subsequent decision by a federal appeals court, which favored the bath house owner, prompted Perales to once again question the intent of the Good Neighbor Policy in Texas and renew his attack.[12] By this time, he and other LULAC leaders, such as the Houston-based Herrera, were closely collaborating with Mexican consular officials who, in turn, would use reports and newspaper articles supplied by the civil rights leaders to level their own statements of scornful reproach against the State Department and Texas officials. The highly controversial cases of discrimination against Mexican-American veterans and Mexican diplomats underscored the seriousness of the problem.[13] The setbacks in Texas, as well as the still inviting possibility of enacting anti-discrimination legislation, no doubt encouraged Perales to seek out the new international front that eventually led him to the UN meeting of 1945 (Perales, "Por El Lic. Alonso S. Perales," 5 Feb. 1944, Microfilm 2309, Reel 12).

The International Front

Perales' association with inter-American forums as a critic of discrimination offers the most obvious examples of his comprehensive international vision of human rights and diplomatic interventions. His diplomatic and consular work, on the other hand, provides the most immediate explanation for his international activism and the attention he attracted when he expanded his claim for Mexican rights to include other Latin Americans in the United States. Perales' experience in diplomatic missions and his consular assignment prepared him for his ventures into the international arena. This background no doubt gave him the necessary confidence to move beyond the civil rights arena. He also made frequent use of his stature and sense of authority as a diplomat by publicly addressing issues of inter-American importance. He demonstrated an impressive knowledge of diplomacy, acquired in some cases through first-hand experiences meeting with Latin American diplomats and also by participating in U.S.-sponsored plebiscites, inter-American dispute settlements and complex trade agreements. It was this kind of experience-based understanding that helped Perales successfully bridge the cause of Mexican civil rights with the hemispheric challenge of building unity in the Americas.

Perales offered one of his best informed statements in a speech presented to the PARTT in San Antonio (Perales, "Resume of Address Made by Alonso S. Perales Before the Pan American Round Table of San Antonio, Texas, at the St. Anthony Hotel," 16 Nov. 1936, Microfilm 2309, Reel 12: 1+; Perales, "Conferencia Sustentada Por el Lic. A. S. Perales Ante la Mesa Redonda Pan Americana," *La Prensa,* 29 Nov. 1936: 3, 8). Although he steadfastly endorsed U.S. policy in Latin America, Perales also recognized that Latin Americans had capitalized on the need for unity as a way of shaping their relations with the United States. In his view, this had begun in 1933, when Secretary of State Cordell Hull affirmed the principle of non-intervention at the Montevideo Conference of American States. During his Round Tables speech, Perales also pointed out that the United States had endorsed resolutions on economic, commercial and tariff cooperation, all of which laid the groundwork for the reciprocal trade agreements of the late 1930s. He characterized these obvious signs of unity as a process of pan-Americanizing the Monroe Doctrine to the extent that mutual consultations were now going to take the place of unilateral decisions by the United States.

Perales' sweeping commentary on relations in the Americas also included well-founded observations on the construction of hemispheric unity. The United States had finally acquiesced to long-standing appeals for unity with a Good Neighbor Policy that promised a more democratic order and reciprocity in the area of political and economic relations. Of course, Perales did not acknowledge that the impending global crisis had prompted the call for unity or that the developing system of inter-American cooperation and reciprocity might not alter the unequal and asymmetric relations of power in the hemisphere. This restraint reflects Perales' stance as a loyal U.S. diplomat primarily interested in communicating a common American purpose and affirming the United States' commitment to playing a leading role in building unity. He did not use this opportunity to tie international relations to the cause of human rights, but he did establish the basis for presenting such a proposal later. He also strengthened his position as an authority on inter-American unity, able to employ both strategic vision and diplomatic skills.

The Inter-American Bar Association meeting. The first major venture Perales made into the international arena occurred at the Third Conference of the Inter-American Bar Association, held in Mexico City between July 31 and August 8, 1944. He represented the Texas Bar Association, along with fellow delegates and LULAC insiders J. T. Canales and M.C. Gonzales. With their help and that of other delegates, mostly from Latin America, Perales managed to convince the General Assembly to adopt a revised version of a resolution he had authored which called on the delegates to seek the adoption of civil rights legislation in their respective countries.

Perales' original resolution, written in the first person, contained the wartime language of Pan-Americanism and used the experience of Mexicans and the larger Latin American community to address racial thinking and practices in the Americas (Perales, "Resolution Introduced by Alonso S. Perales, Delegate to the Texas Bar Association," 1 Aug. 1944, Microfilm 2309, Reel 12). He opened with the basic premise that "the unity of the people of the Americas depends mainly upon their mutual respect." He followed by noting that the longstanding and widespread practice of discrimination in U.S. work sites and schools undermined both the possibility of hemispheric cooperation and the well-intentioned efforts of the Roosevelt administration (presumably a reference to the FEPC). Perales added that Mexicans, regardless of citizenship, and "all citizens of the Latin American Republics" were treated unequally, even as the war was providing better employment opportunities. He concluded with a two-part proposition to the delegates. The Inter-American Bar Association was to seek a treaty among all the American nations to ensure "that no country will permit the citizens of the other American States residing within its territory to be humiliated by any corporation, institution, society, organization or person because of race, creed or color." The second part of the recommendation called for "adequate penalties and or sanctions, through Federal legislation, for all cases in which the provisions of said treaty may be violated."

The conference delegates incorporated Perales' resolution, as well as earlier statements adopted in meetings held in Rio de Janeiro (1943) and Philadelphia (1944), into a recommendation that "racial discrimination be strongly condemned and that positive steps be taken to ameliorate and eliminate them" (Inter-American Bar Association, 1944, p. 25). Possibly taking a cue from Perales, the delegates added a justification for their recommendation that singled out conditions in the United States:

> Despite the efforts of the national governments of the American countries, there still exist, as shown in the reports which motivate this recommendation, particularly in the United States of America, acts of discrimination violative of the fundamental human rights, and which effectively contribute to the lack of confidence and the disunion of the people. (Inter-American Bar Association, 1944, p. 25)

Soon after the conference, Perales stated that he was pleased that the assembly had condemned discrimination but lamented that he had been unable to fully accomplish his goals. He did not elaborate, but unsurprisingly, he did offer a critique of the U.S. delegation that revealed a measure of independence from his country's representatives on the issue of Mexican rights in the United States. He suggested some disagreement with his countrymen when he pointed out that the assembly's practice of determining the size of a delegation on the basis of a country's population had given the United States a large number of votes and an undue influence on the deliberations. His primary interest, however, was Mexicans and discrimination, a topic that he continued to publicly address after the conference. According to a correspondent for *La Prensa*, Perales met with Mexican government officials, including members of the Congress of the Union and the Foreign Affairs Office, to report on the problem of discrimination in Texas and to request that Mexico continue to ban Braceros from areas in the United States like Texas known for their disdain of Mexicans. Perales ended the interview by pointing out that the problem of White supremacy was so serious that segregationists were blind even to the sacrifices Mexicans were making on the battlefields (Allen Hinojosa, "Antes de Salir de la Capital" 1944, p. 4).

The Chapultepec Conference. Neither Perales nor other LULAC leaders attended the next international forum, the Inter-American Conference on Problems of War and Peace (the Chapultepec Conference), held in Mexico City between February 28 and March 8, 1945. Perales, however, maintained contact with Mexican officials who were themselves to be conference delegates or were to have influence over the delegates. He also continued raising the issue of discrimination through his communications with Mexican consular officials, who regularly transmitted his complaints to the Mexican Embassy in Washington, D.C. and the Mexican Foreign Affairs Office in Mexico City for transmission through U.S. diplomatic means. Perales and Ignacio Lozano, his close friend and editor of *La Prensa*, also called on the public to send letters to the delegates, denouncing discrimination. Although we cannot gauge the effect of the letter-writing campaign, Perales' views were known as far away as Mexico City, thanks to the extensive reach of *La Prensa* (Perales, "La Próxima Conferencia de Cancilleres y el Porvenir de Nuestros Pueblos," 17 Jan. 1945, Microfilm 2309, Reel 13: 1+; Perales, "Informe Núm. 5 Acerca del Estado de las Gestiones Encaminadas a Terminar con la Discriminación," *La Prensa* 18 Feb. 1945: 5).

The Chapultepec Conference was attended mainly by government officials. They discussed resolutions, declarations and a charter inherited from previous meetings of diplomats that had addressed organizing principles and frameworks for what eventually became the United Nations. The Chapultepec Conference delegates departed from established procedure on the subject of human rights. Ordinarily, diplomats would adopt resolutions condemning discrimination and calling on governments to observe principles of human rights. This time, Bolivia, Cuba and Mexico secured the necessary assembly support for a Declaration on the International Rights and Duties of Man that was to be forwarded to the forthcoming inaugural UN meeting (Borgwardt, 2008, p. 44). In a clear attempt to establish consistency with the fundamental principle of non-intervention, the Declaration called for an end to a different kind of intervention, the "diplomatic protection of citizens abroad," yet it also asked for guarantees of a "minimum standard of civilized justice" for nationals on foreign soil (Department of State, 1947, p. 159).

The delegates also approved the Declaration of Mexico, which emphasized the rights of individuals, including women, and the obligation of governments to ensure or promote these rights. The resolution stated that world peace could not be sustained "until men [sic] are able to exercise their basic rights without distinction as to race and religion" and reaffirmed "equality of rights and opportunities for all men, regardless of race or religion." It also directed a recommendation to the governments in the Americas to "make every effort to prevent . . . acts which may provoke discrimination among individuals because of race and religion" (Murray 1950, 525).

   The UN Conference. We do not know the extent of Perales' participation in the contentious debate over human rights at the inaugural UN meeting in San Francisco. The Chapultepec meeting demonstrated that the tenet of non-intervention presented an obstacle to the implementation of human rights. The long history of U.S. intervention, which included a unilateral claim of defense (embodied in the Monroe Doctrine), had made non-intervention a key element in negotiating the system of inter-American cooperation and reciprocity the United States was proposing. Latin Americans' determined support for non-intervention coincided with similar concerns voiced at the UN meeting and undermined the possibility of maintaining even a diplomatic form of intervention on behalf of nationals on foreign soil. Discrimination and violations of human rights thus could not justify intervention, unless—as with the Nazi atrocities—the problem was of egregious proportions, in which case an international court could render appropriate judgments and remedies.

   Many delegates reportedly were enthusiastic about supporting aspirational human rights provisions and were convinced that the UN should endorse them, but few were willing to commit the world organization to a definite and effective plan of implementation. As a consequence, the language of enforcement changed from guaranteeing human rights to encouraging and promoting them (Perales, "La Conferencia de San Francisco," *La Prensa*, 15 Jun. 1945: p. 5). A well-known scholar of the history of the UN, summing up this turn of events, has concluded that, "Human rights and racial nondiscrimination foundered on the rock of national sovereignty" (Gordon Lauren, 1983, p. 18).

   Despite the obvious lack of provisions that would guarantee effective enforcement, the delegates favoring human rights could still claim a significant victory. The UN Charter declared that the organization was "determined to reaffirm faith in fundamental human rights, in the dignity and worth of the human person, in the equal rights of men and women and of nations large and small." The UN was also committed to promoting and encouraging "respect for human rights and for fundamental freedoms for all without distinction as to race, sex, language, or religion" (Russell, 1958, pp. 1035-36).

   Perales acknowledged the disappointing language attached to the human rights statements, but he was hopeful. He reported to the readers of *La Prensa* that

   despite all the efforts in favor of incorporating a list of human rights, everything suggests that we will not achieve this now, but that in the end the basic principles that will guarantee those rights will have been presented. (Perales "La Conferencia de San Francisco y el Porvenir," *La Prensa* 27 May 1945: p. 3)

In another public statement, he noted that the success of the UN Charter now depended on the good faith of the governments that had signed the document. And, since our officials are our servants, it is necessary that our people become fully familiar with the provisions of the Charter, especially the section related to the economic and social aspects of our lives so that we can insist that our respective governments commit themselves to serve our working people and our brave defenders of our nations. (Perales, "La Carta Mundial," *La Prensa* 9 July 1945: p. 2)

This mirrored his longstanding view supporting an educated citizenry, essential to holding elected and appointed officials to account.

If Perales was disappointed in the outcome of the UN deliberations on human rights, he did not show it upon his return to San Antonio. He and other LULAC and COHC members continued to campaign for a civil rights bill in Texas, and often turned to human rights provisions adopted in international forums and public statements by Mexican officials to argue that discrimination would continue to undermine relations with nations in the Americas and throughout the world. Perales, in other words, was following his own advice by appealing to his government in order to fulfill the promise of the UN Charter. The major obstacles that he and fellow LULAC leaders continuously faced may have also helped them appreciate the partial victory in San Francisco as a substantial achievement (del Moral, "El Ministro de Relaciones Exteriores," *La Prensa* 6 May 1945: p. 1).

Perales' experience in the civil rights cause, especially the setbacks that reinforced his self-determining and grateful outlook, also explain why he occasionally would declare that he had more faith in enacting civil rights laws in Austin than in Washington, D.C. In hindsight, we could question his view "that the central government cannot pass legislation that can prohibit such humiliations because of constitutional limitations" (Perales, "La Próxima Conferencia," *La Prensa*: p. 5). At the time he made this observation, however, restrictionist states' rights advocates were exercising great influence on public opinion, especially in the South. This had become all too evident when the campaign to make the FEPC a permanent agency met eventual defeat at the hands of the bloc of conservative congressmen from the South who did not want an effective monitor on U.S. civil rights matters.

Despite his doubts about federal action, Perales offered a constitutionalist argument that explained why he favored campaigns that addressed the federal government and an international strategy to influence national politics. He always pointed out that the case against discrimination could be more effective if it were linked to the logic of wartime unity. However, he also always reminded his readers that the Fourteenth Amendment remained the fundamental basis for claiming rights in the United States and that Article VI, Clause 2 of the Constitution allowed international treaties to become part of the supreme law of the land.

Conclusion

On the surface, Perales' singular undertaking in the international arena seems strikingly ironic. He and his fellow LULAC leaders appeared to be embracing what they had for so long rejected. Where they had once emphasized narrowly ethnic politics and claimed U.S. citizenship rights on constitutional grounds, they were now turning to the hemisphere as a whole for the moral and, possibly, legal wherewithal to strengthen their hand at home. The irony fades, however, when we consider that the World War had created political opportunities and a strategic climate that an astute civil rights leader like Perales could not help but recognize and use to further the cause of equal rights for Mexicans.

The United States' decision to build hemispheric unity as a war measure won over Latin Americans who shared security concerns and saw the opportunity to redefine relations between American nations on the basis of the wartime language of justice and democracy. Cooperation and reciprocity in defense, production and trade went hand in hand with the equally serious business of agreeing on international norms and understandings on a number of issues, including national sovereignty, interventions in the internal affairs of another country, juridical frameworks for world peace, organizational forms for a league of nations and human rights. The issues of discrimination and human rights were especially vexing because they had to be reconciled with the principle of non-intervention (although, as Mexico discovered, these issues could be used to justify diplomatic intervention on behalf of nationals and to leverage national interests).

LULAC was prepared for the obvious opportunity for collaboration as Mexico set out to implement its advocacy policy on behalf of nationals in the United States. The young civil rights organization had excluded Mexican nationals from its membership rolls but nevertheless had made common cause with them. Moreover, the U.S.-born and upwardly mobile Mexican members were culturally adept at agitating in both the English- and Spanish-speaking worlds. Finally, especially among liberal Anglos in large southwestern urban centers like San Antonio, they could make a special claim on constitutional rights, based on their citizenship and long-standing contributions to society.

Perales was especially well-positioned to lead in the international arena, given his legal training and vast diplomatic experience. We should not, however, overlook another important characteristic that explains much of his success. The records in his archival collection, especially his private correspondence with fellow activists like Saenz and Canales, reveal that the core cadre of LULAC leaders were serious, consistent and disciplined in their dedication to their political work, and that Perales was the most impressive of all. He often directed activities in Texas from Washington, D.C. and Nicaragua, while also shouldering his extremely demanding legal studies and diplomatic work. He also led several organizing campaigns that took him across the vast terrain of South Texas and traveled to Mexico City and San Francisco. All along, he found the time to maintain a legal practice and write an astonishing number of works including newspaper articles, books, speeches, testimonies, resolutions and affidavits that recorded the feelings and views of hundreds of aggrieved Mexicans in Texas. This output was prodigious by today's standards.

The study of Perales' work in the international arena raises an important question regarding the limited range of the discourse on human rights. In Perales' papers, we find little evidence that diplomats expressed much concern over discrimination and inequality in the lives of other afflicted groups throughout the Americas or that they included much discussion of such people in the deliberations over human rights. The declarations that emerged from international meetings in 1944 and 1945 condemned discrimination and promoted human rights in general terms and, in some cases, with explicit reference to groups such as women and Latin Americans. Indigenous and African-origin persons in Latin America often faced similar and, in some cases, more challenging experiences than Mexicans in the United States, but this did not seem to warrant a fuller account of discrimination and inequality in the Americas.

This limited view could be an accurate rendering of most diplomats' stance, but since it arises from the detailed records that Perales kept and published, it could simply be an artifact of his own highly focused concerns. He was the consummate defender of the rights of Mexicans and Latin Americans. It would not be surprising, then, to find most, if not all, of his interest—at least in his correspondence—directed towards these two groups. Moreover, wartime relations gave Mexico a singular opportunity to lobby on behalf of Mexicans in the United States, and Mexican officials followed this noble, if self-serving, strategy in collaboration with an important civil rights organization. Explanations for the attention Mexicans' rights received at international forums, however, do not negate the possibility that Latin American diplomats were not as disposed to include their own minority groups in the discussions and debates as were Mexican, or even U.S. government officials.

A related question that arises from a study of Perales' collected work concerns the apparent distance between him and the more substantial group of African-American leaders who also pursued an international strategy alongside their push for equal rights in the United States. This is especially striking in Texas where the histories of Mexican and Black populations from the Southwest and the South overlapped.[14] Neither the Perales papers nor the records of the National Negro Congress and the NAACP reveal any collaboration, despite common interests and the fact that Perales and his African-American counterparts attended the same international forums, including the UN inaugural meeting (Plummer, 1996; Borgwardt, 2005). The lack of cooperation is especially striking in Texas where the Mexican and Black populations were substantial and both communities were waging causes for equal rights.

The lack of a close connection between Mexican-American and African-American leaders may have had more to do with geography than with ideology. Mexican Americans were far removed from places like the Northeast, where African Americans were waging a vigorous civil rights campaign. This distance may have made it easier for African Americans to embrace prevailing views of Mexican Americans as primarily a regional immigrant community, outside the purview of a national civil rights agenda. The best evidence that African Americans would have, under other circumstances, made use of opportunities for a united front is their collaboration with New York City-based Puerto Ricans on civil rights issues and island politics. Also, the records of the National Negro Congress and the NAACP, and secondary literature, suggest that the African-American leadership had a longer history of participation in international forums, dating back to the Pan African Congress of the 1920s.

Geographical distance may have undermined the possibility of Brown-Black solidarity, but it did not prevent African Americans from also leveling a critique against the wartime alliance that the United States was building in Latin America. They, too, pointed to racial discrimination at home as an obstacle to hemispheric defense, Pan-Americanism and the Good Neighbor Policy. This criticism is well documented in the extensive communications between NAACP Secretary Walter White and Nelson Rockefeller, then head of the Office of the Coordinator of Inter-American Affairs. Finally, at the international level, an alliance with Mexicans might have been awkward since their leadership was mostly limited to Perales, whereas the African-American leadership had many members, longer diplomatic experience, and more significant ties with U.S. government officials. Still, Perales would have been able to contribute his own unrelenting spirit of hemispheric engagement as well as the influence of the Mexican lobby in the United States and the rest of the Americas. We can only speculate about how such an alliance might have improved both groups' chances for success.

Works Cited

Allen Hinojosa, F. (1944, August 6). Antes de salir de la capital de México, el Lic. Alonso Perales concede una entrevista a 'La Prensa.' *La Prensa*, p. 4.

Allport, G. W. (1954). *The nature of prejudice.* Reading, Mass.: Addison-Wesley Publishing Company.

Almaraz, F. (1990). *Knight without armor: Carlos Eduardo Castañeda, 1896-1958.* College Station: Texas A&M University.

Blanton, C. K. (2006). George I. Sánchez, ideology, and whiteness in the making of the Mexican American civil rights movement, 1930-1960. *The Journal of Southern History 72*(3), 569-604.

Bronder, S. E. (1982). *Social justice and church authority: The public life of archbishop Robert E. Lucey.* Philadelphia: Temple University Press.

Borgwardt, E. (2005). *A new deal for the world; America's vision for human rights.* Cambridge, Mass.: The Belknap Press of Harvard University Press.

Borgwardt, E. (2008). FDR's Four Freedoms and Wartime Transformations in America's Discourse of Rights. In Soohoo, C., Albisa C., & Martha F. Davis (Eds.) *Bringing human rights home* (pp. 31-55). Westport, CT.: Praeger Publishers.

Canales, J. T. (1929, February 17). [Interview notes by Oliver Douglas Weeks]. Oliver Douglas Weeks Papers, Box 1, Folder 4. Mexican American Library Collection, Nettie Lee Benson Collection, University of Texas at Austin.

Castañeda, J. (1958). *Mexico and the United Nations.* New York: Manhattan Publishing Company.

Chasteen, J. C. (2008). *Americanos, Latin America's struggle for independence.* New York: Oxford University Press.

Crawly, A. (2007). *Somoza and Roosevelt; Good Neighbour diplomacy in Nicaragua, 1933-1945.* Oxford: Oxford University Press.

Darío, R., & Bueno Álvarez, J. A. (Ed.). (2000). *Azul.* Madrid: Editorial EDAF.

Darío, R. *Cantos de vida y esperanza.* Derusha, W. & Acereda, Al. (Eds. & Trans.). Durham: Duke University Press, 2004.

Del Moral, A. (1945, May 6). El Ministro de Relaciones Exteriores de México define la actitud del país en relación a los problemas mundiales. *La Prensa*, p. 1.

Dudziak, M. L. (2012). *Wartime: An Idea, its history, its consequences*. New York: Oxford University Press. *El abogado Alonso S. Perales se retira de todo movimiento panamericanista de Texas*. (1939, November 25). Microfilm 2309, Reel 13: 1.

El Lic. A. Perales fue nombrado cónsul de Nicaragua. (1934, May 11). *La Prensa*, p. 1.

El Licenciado Perales objeto de gran distinción. *La Prensa* 18 Apr. 1945: 2.

El Licenciado Perales sugiere dos medidas concretas al gobierno de los Estados Unidos. (1941, January 19). *La Prensa*, p. 3.

Frantz, H. B. (n.d.). Pan American round table. *Handbook of Texas Online*. Retrieved 2011, November 2 from http://www.tshaonline.org/handbook/online/articles/vwp01.

García, M. T. (1989). *Mexican Americans: Leadership, ideology and identity, 1930-1960*. New Haven: Yale University Press.

Herring, G. C. (2008). *From colony to superpower: U.S. foreign relations since 1776*. New York: Oxford University Press.

Houston, J. A. (1956). *Latin America in the United Nations*. New York: Carnegie Endowment for International Peace.

Kaplowitz, C. A. (2005). *LULAC, Mexican Americans, and national policy*. College Station: Texas A&M University Press.

[KONO Radio Broadcast]. Microfilm 2309, Reel 12: 1-6.

Lauren, P. G. (1983). First principles of racial equality: History and the politics and diplomacy of human rights provisions in the United Nations charter. *Human Rights Quarterly* 5(1), 1-26.

Lauren, P. G. (2008). A human rights lens on U.S. history: Human rights at home and human rights abroad. In Soohoo, C., Albisa, C. & Davis, M.F. (Eds.) *Bringing human rights home* (pp. 1-29). Westport, CT.: Praeger Publishers.

La voz del público. (1945, May 3). *La Prensa*, p. 7.

Liévano Aguirre, I. (1969). *Bolivarismo y Monroismo*. Bogotá: Editorial Revista Colombiana.

Luján, R. (1987). *Dennis Chavez and the Roosevelt Era, 1933-1945* (Doctoral dissertation). Available from ProQuest Dissertations & Theses database. (UMI No. 8809278)

Lynch, J. (2007). *Simón Bolivar, a life*. New Haven: Yale University Press.

Magnífica pieza oratoria del canciller Ezequiel Padilla. (1945, May 4). *La Prensa*, p. 1.

Márquez, B. (1993). *The evolution of a Mexican American political organization*. Austin: University of Texas Press.

Murray, P. (Ed.). (1950). *States' laws on race and color and appendices; containing international documents, federal laws and regulations, local ordinances and charts*. Cincinnati: Women's Division of Christian Service, Board of Missions and Church Extension, Methodist Church.

Nagata, Y. (1945, June 23). Nicaragua Signs United Nations Charter. [Photograph]. San Francisco UN Conference. United Nations Photo Library, UN Archives and Records Management, New York, New York.

Orozco, C. E. League of United Latin American Citizens. *Handbook of Texas Online*. Retrieved 2011, November 2 from http://www.tshaonline.org/handbook/online/articles/wel01.

Orozco, C. E. (2009). *No Mexicans, women, or dogs allowed: The rise of the Mexican American civil rights movement*. Austin: University of Texas Press.

Perales, A. S. (1923, August 20). *La ignorancia como causa de los prejuicios raciales*. Microfilm 2309, Reel 12: 1-3.

Perales, A. S. "El problema de los México-Americanos." Oct. 1923, Microfilm 2309, Reel 12: 1-6.

Perales, A. S. (1936, November 16). *Resume of address made by Alonso S. Perales before the Pan American Round Table of San Antonio, Texas, at the St. Anthony Hotel*. Microfilm 2309, Reel 12: 1-6.

Perales, A. S. (1939, November 25). [Letter to Florence R. Griswold]. Microfilm 2309, Reel 13: 1-5.

Perales, A. S. (1944, February 5). *Por el Lic. Alonso S. Perales, Director de la Liga de Leales Americanos*. Microfilm 2309, Reel 12: 1-2.

Perales, A. S. (1944, Aug. 1). *Resolution introduced by Alonso S. Perales, delegate to the Texas Bar Association*. Microfilm 2309, Reel 12: 1-2.

Perales, A. S. (1945, January 17). *La próxima conferencia de cancilleres y el porvenír de nuestros pueblos*. Microfilm 2309, Reel 13: 1-5.

Perales, A. S. (1936). *En Defensa de mi Raza*. San Antonio: Artes Gráficas.

Perales, A. S. 1938, February 11. [Letter to Sumner Welles. 26 Mar 1938, and attached transcription of article from *El Centroamericano*, León, Nicaragua]. Alonso S. Perales Folder, Franklin D. Roosevelt Library, Hyde Park, New York.

Perales, A. S. [Survey notes]. Oliver Douglas Weeks Papers, Box 1, Folder 4, Mexican American Library Collection, Nettie Lee Benson Collection, University of Texas at Austin.

Perales, A. S. (1927, August 12). Va a formarse una agrupación para la unificación de la raza. *El Cronista del Valle*, p. 4.

Perales, A. S. (1927, August 23). Una aclaración al márgen de la convención de Harlingen, Texas, los ciudadanos mexicanos no podrían tomar parte en ella, las propias leyes mexicanas se los vedan, so pena de perder su nacionalidad. *El Cronista del Valle* , p. 1.

Perales, A. S. "El resultado de la junta que hubo en Harlingen, solo ciudadanos americanos de orígen mexicano." *La Prensa* 29 Aug. 1927: 7.

Perales, A. S. (1927, March 1). El lic. Perales defiende a los braceros mexicanos. *La Prensa*, p. 7.

Perales, A. S. (1927, September 7). La evolución de la raza mexicana en Texas. *La Prensa*, p. 5.

Perales, A. S. (1936, November 29). Conferencia Sustentada por el Lic. A. S. Perales ante la mesa redonda Pan Americana. *La Prensa*, pp. 3, 8.

Perales, A. S. (1939, December 3). El movimiento Pan-Americanista que se desarrolla en este estado. *La Prensa*, pp. 3, 6.

Perales, A. S. (1945, April 2). Informe núm. 10 del estado en que se hallan las gestiones encaminadas a terminar con la discriminación. *La Prensa*, p. 6.

Perales, A. S. (1945, May 27). La conferencia de San Francisco y el porvenir de nuestros pueblos. *La Prensa*, p. 3

Perales, A. S. (1945, June 15). La conferencia de San Francisco. *La Prensa*, p. 5.

Perales, A. S. (1945, July 9). La carta mundial. *La Prensa*, p. 2.

Perales, A. S. (1948). *Are we good neighbors?* San Antonio: Ártes Gráficas.

Plummer, B. G. (1996). *Rising wind; black Americans and U.S. foreign affairs, 1935-1960*. Chapel Hill: University of North Carolina Press.

Ramirez, O. V. Perales, A. S. & Public Affairs Forum. (1941, March 3). *What does it take to get the peoples of the Americas together*.

Ramos, L. Y. (2011). Not similar enough: Mexican American and African American civil rights struggles in the 1940s. In Behnken, B. (Ed.) *The struggle in black and brown: African American and Mexican American relations during the Civil Rights era* (pp. 19-48). Lincoln: University of Nebraska Press.

Russell, R. B. (1958). *A history of the United Nations charter: The role of the United States, 1940-1945*. Washington, D.C.: The Brookings Institution.

San Miguel, G. (1987). *'Let all of them take heed:' Mexican Americans and the campaign for educational equality in Texas*. Austin: University of Texas Press.

Sexton, J. (2011). *The Monroe Doctrine: Empire and nation in nineteenth-century America*. New York: Hill and Wang.

Sloss-Vento, A.& Vento, A. C. (Ed.). (1977). *Alonso S. Perales: His struggle for the rights of Mexican-Americans*. San Antonio: Artes Gráficas.

Thorning, J. F. (1946). The United Nations and the Good Neighbor Policy. *World Affairs 109*(4), 257-61.

Torres, B. (1990). *Historia de la Revolución Mexicana; periodo 1940-52, México en la Segunda Guerra Mundial*. México, D.F.: El Colegio de México.

United Nations. (1945). *Documents of the United Nations conference on international organization, San Francisco, vol. 1*. United Nations Information Organizations.

Valencia, R. (2008). *Chicano students and the courts: The Mexican American legal struggle for educational equality*. New York: New York University Press.

Vallance, W. R. (1944). *Resolutions of the third conference of the Inter-American Bar Association*. Washington, D.C.: Inter-American Association.

Vargas, Z. (2005). *Labor rights are civil rights: Mexican American workers in twentieth-century America*. Princeton: Princeton University Press.

Vázquez García, H. (2001). *De Chapultepec a la OEA: Apogeo y crisis del Panamericanismo*. La Habana: Editorial de Ciencias Sociales..

Weeks, O. D. (1928). The League of United Latin American Citizens; A Texas-Mexican Civic Organization. *Southwestern Political and Social Science Quarterly 10*, 257-78.

Zamora, E. (1993). *The world of the Mexican worker in Texas*. College Station: Texas A&M University Press.

Zamora, E. (2002). "Fighting on Two Fronts: José de la Luz Saenz and the Language of the Mexican American Civil Rights Movement." In Aranda Jr., J. F. & Torres-Saillant, S. (Eds.) *Recovering the U.S. Hispanic literary heritage, volume IV* (pp. 214-39). Houston: Arte Público Press.

Zamora, E. (2009). *Claiming rights and righting wrongs in Texas, Mexican job politics during World War II*. College Station: Texas A&M University Press.

Zorrilla, L. G. (1966). *Historia de las relaciones entre México y los Estados Unidos de América, 1800-1958, tomo II*. México, D.F.: Editorial Porrúa.

Notes

[1]The ceremonial details have been gleaned from the official photographs and caption information secured from the United Nations Photo Library. According to the editors of the San Antonio daily, *La Prensa*, the members of the Nicaraguan delegation included Doctor Mariano Arguello Vargas, Chairman of Delegation and Minister of Foreign Affairs, Doctor Guillermo Sevilla Sacasa, Ambassador to the United States, Coronel Luis Manuel DeBayle, Director General of Public Health, Alonso S. Perales, Counselor to the Delegation and Consul General in San Antonio, Texas, Marcelo Jover, Secretary and Cultural Attache to the Nicaraguan Embassy, Coronel Guillermo Rivas Cuadra, Military Attaché and Commander of the National Air Force, Lieutenant Francisco Aguirre Baca, Military Attaché, Major Carlos G. Zelaya, Private Secretary to the Chairman and Consul General in San Francisco. United Nations records also note the following delegates: Colonel Irving A. Lindberg, Advisor and Collector General of Customs, Manuel S. Canyes, Legal Advisor, and Julio C. Quintana, Assistant Secretary and Consul General in Los Angeles. United Nations, *Documents of the United Nations Conference on International Organization,* 1945: 50-51.

[2]I refer to Mexican-origin persons as Mexicans. When necessary, I will note their nativity as Mexican Nationals and Mexican Americans, or U.S.-born.

[3]The use of racial thinking derives from Gordon Allport's definition of prejudice as having both cognitive and emotional dimensions. I employ the concept to underscore the cognitive side of prejudice. Racial discrimination, on the other hand, refers to conduct and the exercise of power to create and reinforce social inequality between racially defined groups. I use racial thinking and discrimination interchangeably throughout the essay. Allport, *The Nature of Prejudice.*

[4]The internationalization of race in foreign relations had long served as a basis for leveraging civil rights in the United States. It began with WWI and continued into the Second World War as African-American and Mexican-American civil rights leaders pointed out the contradiction between the wartime language of justice and the democracy and the stark reality of discrimination and segregation at home. The claims for equal rights in foreign relations resumed after the war, although Cold War politics limited the nation's commitment to civil rights. Zamora, *Claiming Rights and Righting Wrongs in Texas;* Zamora, "Fighting on Two Fronts: José de la Luz Saenz and the Language of the Mexican American Civil Rights Movement," pp. 214-39; Dudziak, *Cold War Civil Rights.*

[5]Mexico's Foreign Affairs Secretary gave public expression to the hope often heard at the founding meeting of the United Nations that the international organization would prevent the return of the "hell" of war. "Magnífica Pieza Oratoria del Canciller Ezequiel Padilla," *La Prensa* 4 May 4 1945: p. 1.

[6]Bolívar is known for promoting unity among the newly independent countries and for establishing the first federation of independent nations, the Gran Colombia, soon after leading his country's independence movement. Dario is credited with initiating the Modernist movement in Latin American literature during the early 1900s. He gave voice to the view that Latin America had achieved a form of cul-

tural maturity and independence from Europe that it could use to seek better rela-
tions with the United States. Lynch, *Simón Bolívar;* Chasteen, *Americanos, Latin
America's Struggle for Independence*; Darío, *Cantos de Vida y Esperanza*; Darío,
Azul.

[7]A survey conducted among LULAC members indicates that the organization
sought a membership of U.S.-born professionals, businessmen, and skilled trades-
men. Questionnaire results can be found in the Oliver Douglas Weeks Papers, Box
1, Folder 4, Mexican American Library Collection, Nettie Lee Benson Collection,
University of Texas at Austin. See also Weeks, "The League of United Latin American Citizens," pp. 257-78.

[8]An ambitious young man, Perales arrived in Washington, D.C. after completing his
military service in WWI and may have worked in the Department of Commerce
while attending National University. He received a B.A. and law degree in the mid-
1920s and entered diplomatic service primarily through the State Department.
Perales participated in thirteen diplomatic missions to the Dominican Republic,
Cuba, Nicaragua, Mexico, Chile, and the West Indies in the 1920s and 1930s,
while maintaining contact with his civil rights colleagues through correspondence,
frequent visits, and extended stays in Texas. Orozco, "Alonso S. Perales."

[9]Although historians have acknowledged that LULAC leaders distanced themselves
from Mexican nationals during the organization's early years and that some of
them, especially Gonzales and Perales, later spoke on their behalf, they do not
explain this turn of events in relation to Mexico's advocacy policy. This explanation appears in my recent publication. García, *Mexican Americans; Leadership,
Ideology and Identity, 1930-1960*; Marquez, *The Evolution of a Mexican American
Political Organization*; Orozco, *No Mexicans, Women, or Dogs Allowed;* San
Miguel, *"Let all of them take heed"; San Miguel, Mexican Americans and the
Campaign for Educational Equality in Texas*; Zamora, *Claiming Rights and Right-
ing Wrongs in Texas.*

[10]Minutes of LULAC Council 60, January 10, April 18, 1946, and Manuel C. Gonzales to Herrera, April 26, 1946, Minutes of LULAC Council 60 Papers, Houston
Metropolitan Library, Houston, Texas.

[11]Clete Daniel and Emilio Zamora examine the history of the FEPC's relationship
with the Mexican community in the United States. The latter pays closer attention
to LULAC leaders like Perales who often pointed to the government's affirmative
response to employment discrimination in war industries to buttress their calls for
civil rights laws. Daniel, *Chicano Workers and the Politics of Fairness;* Zamora,
Claiming Rights and Righting Wrongs in Texas.

[12]Terrell Wells Swimming Pool et. al. Jacob Rodríguez 182 S.W.2d 824 (Texas Court
of Civil Appeals, San Antonio, 1944).

[13]Two of the most celebrated cases occurred in 1945. They included Macario García, a medal of honor winner from a small town near Houston, and Eugenio Prado,
a Mexican senator from the northern Mexican state of Chihuahua and president of
the Mexican Congress. Restaurant owners from West and East Texas refused them
service for being Mexican. Zamora, *Claiming Rights and Righting Wrongs in
Texas*, pp. 102-06.

[14]Although historians have recently begun to demonstrate cases of interracial unity between Mexican and Black workers and civil rights activists in Texas, they have not yet discovered widespread cooperation. Consult the following representative works: Blanton, "George I. Sánchez, Ideology, and Whiteness in the Making of the Mexican American Civil Rights Movement, 1930-1960," pp. 569-604; Zamora, *Claiming Rights and Righting Wrongs in Texas*; Ramos, *"Not Similar Enough: Mexican American and African American Civil Rights Struggles in the 1940s,"* pp. 19-48.

The Legal Career of Alonso S. Perales

Michael A. Olivas

Back to the Future: Latino and Latina Lawyers in the Twenty-first Century

As has been noted throughout, Alonso S. Perales, born in 1898, was one of very few Mexican-American lawyers in Texas and the country when he began his practice in 1925. In preparation for my own Chapter, I asked my high school classmate and friend, University of California-Irvine demographer Rubén G. Rumbaut, to share some lawyer data estimates he was preparing for his authoritative *Immigrant America, A Portrait* 4th edition, using merged 2008, 2009 and 2010 samples of more than 9 million cases in the ACS file. (Portes and Rumbaut, 2006) The American Community Survey (ACS) is an ongoing statistical survey by the federal government; each year it samples a small percentage of the population, allowing more regular and comparable data for demographic purposes. The figures reported in this Chapter approximate the 2010 estimates.

The merged ACS data show a 2010 national population of nearly 307 million, of whom over 32 million (10.1%) were Mexican Americans. [Of those 32+ million, over 11.6 million were born in Mexico (36.2%).] The lion's share of the 32+ million Mexican Americans were in California (also 11.6 million), followed by Texas (8.1 million)–over 60% reside in these two states.

Overall, lawyers and judges constitute approximately 1,042,000 (0.7%) of the 141 million workers, ages 25 to 64 in the 2010 civilian U.S. labor force. Of the 1,041,092 lawyers-judges in the United States ages 25-64 in the civilian labor force (between 2008 and 2010), 386,085 were women and 655,007 were men. Of these, 51,074 were Hispanic lawyers-judges: 23,233 females, and 27,841 males.

Among employed persons 25 to 64 in 2010, there were 12.5 million Mexican Americans (about 9% of all workers between those ages in the U.S.). And of those 12.5 million Mexican-American workers, 21,393 were lawyers and judges (0.2% of the Mexican-American total): 9,367 females and 12,026 males.

Finally, of the 21,393 Mexican-American lawyers and judges nationally, California and Texas have the largest share; both states have seen significant increases, but California has now surpassed Texas: the 2010 ACS estimates show that there were about 7,080 Mexican-American lawyers-judges in California (33% of the U.S. total), followed by 6,569 in Texas (31%). [Coming in well behind are New Mexico (which showed a notable increase from 2006 to 979) and Illinois (868)—both well up from 2006— while Arizona has gone well down to 711.]

Additional Latino subgroup data are also revealing: there are approximately 51,074 Latino lawyers and judges in the United States (between 25 and 64, in 2010). Cubans, with nearly 6,800, come in second to the 12,400 Mexican Americans, while Puerto Ricans follow with 5,300. These data only include the 50 states and DC, which does not count those practicing law in Puerto Rico.

    21,393 Mexican
     6,797 Cuban
     5,302 Puerto Rican
     6,034 Other Spanish-Hispanic-Latinos
     5,361 Other Central/South American
     1,912 Peruvian/Ecuadorian
     1,478 Salvadoran, Guatemalan
     1,466 Colombian
   51,074 TOTAL: Latino/a lawyers-judges (ACS, 2010)

As a final footnote to these data, the gains in the numbers of Latino and Latina lawyers have many caveats and hidden dimensions. For many years and at all levels of the law, the number of "Other Central/South American" and "Other Spanish-Hispanic-Latinos" law students and law graduates, when combined with the other larger subgroups, has surpassed Mexican Americans—who constitute 63% of the overall general Latino population. This is true even with the oddity and unevenness of the Census categories and groupings, such as some of the artificially constructed Census categories and the exclusion of Puerto Rico from the data (Rumbaut, 2011).

In addition, there are many cumulative educational and demographic features at play here: the generally poor schooling available to Hispanic schoolchildren, (Gándara and Contreras, 2010) the declining use of affirmative action in admissions, state ballot measures that restrict the use of race (to be affected by *Fisher v. UT*, scheduled to be heard by the SCOTUS in October, 2012), the increasing cost of legal education, the lack of comprehensive immigration reform, and the economic slowdown, especially evident in the legal economy. The ratio between Latina and Latino lawyers in 2010 was more balanced than the overall lawyer figures, where women constitute 37% of all lawyers between the ages of 25 and 64 in 2010. In the same period, of the 51,074 Hispanic lawyers-judges, 23,233 (45%) were females, and 27,841 (55%) were males (Molina, 2010; Chavez, 2011; Mendoza, 2012; Cruz and Molina, 2012).

This is a world the early Latino and Latina lawyers would not recognize. Certainly, the more than 50,000 such lawyers would have astounded Alonso S. Perales, the third Mexican-American lawyer in Texas, who began practice in 1925. Even when *Hernandez v. Texas* was heard in 1954, there were fewer than two dozen Mexican-American lawyers in Texas. And many of us thought we would never see the day when a Sonia Sotomayor would serve on the United States Supreme Court. Their successes as lawyers and advocates for their people surely paved the way for those who followed.

The Life of a Mexican-American Lawyer in Texas in the Early Twentieth Century

Perales and the others carried on extraordinary careers, given the enormous odds against them and the racist headwinds that blew against their efforts, especially their civil rights and community work, where hostile legislators, judges, and public officials sought to subordinate Mexican Americans, especially in Texas, long considered the equivalent of Mississippi for this community. There is a surprisingly robust scholarly literature on early Texas legal cases, particularly those having to do with education, including authoritative works by Guadalupe San Miguel, George Martinez (who has a different kind of Chapter in this project), Richard Valencia, Carlos Blanton and others. Given the widespread existence of lynchings of Mexicans and Mexican Americans up through the time of the Great Depression, community leaders organized efforts to bring racial mobs to justice; according to one authoritative and careful study, the public record reveals that through 1928, nearly 600 Mexicans were lynched in the United States, an astounding number, given the relatively small regional population and the terms of the Treaty of Guadalupe Hidalgo (Carrigan and Webb, 2009). In Houston, there were organized legislative efforts by Mexican-American lawyers in the 1930s and 1940s to secure employment benefits for Mexican-American workers, and attempts to prevent excessive force and deadly police violence against Mexicanos, including bringing police brutality case to a grand jury (Rosales, 1985, 85-87). There has begun a small fleshing-out of WWII-era cases, following the *testimonio* lead of *Are We Good Neighbors?*, the extraordinary work—extraordinary in the sense that there are very few such works in this genre, evidence of his lawyerly instincts— compiled by Perales in 1948 to record the extensive Jaime Crow practices in the state. One of the spores of this publishing project may have been the epistolary nature of a WWI diary published by Perales' friend and collaborator José de la Luz Saenz, who published his diary in 1933 with the San Antonio Spanish-language publisher Artes Gráficas. This work, which is a rare volume, archived in only a few collections, collected letters, editorials, souvenirs, and wartime letters-from-the-front that appeared in *La Prensa* and elsewhere (Zamora, 2002, 2012).

Thus, we know the anthropological and sociological details of public housing denials, public accommodation exclusionary practices, and employment discrimination, all made known in the public record by Texas lawyers such as Perales and his contemporaries: J. T. Canales, Gus Garcia, Carlos Cadena, John Herrera, Manuel C. Gonzales, Ed Idar, Jr., James DeAnda, Alex Armendariz, and others, including non-lawyers such as physician Dr. Héctor P. García and educators George I. Sánchez, Jovita González, Carlos Castañeda and José de la Luz Saenz (Wilson, 2003; Salinas, 2003; Guglielmo, 2006; Olivas, 2006, 2008; Haney Lopez and Olivas, 2008; Gross, 2003, 2007; I. Garcia, 2008; Strum, 2010).

While there are scattered files that shed light on the long legal career of Perales, regrettably, the complete files and papers of his practice have not survived (or surfaced), so observers of this interesting period of his career do not have a clear record of his thirty-plus years of practice. Letters cited in the Chapters by Cynthia Orozco, Lupe Salinas, and F. Arturo Rosales all speak to legal matters and general practice details, while Emilio Zamora spells out his international law practice and diplomatic experiences. Fortunately for observers these many years later, he appears never to have thrown away a piece of paper, and the records in various places show he attended high school and Draughn's Business College in Corpus Christi where he learned to take shorthand and became a stenographer (which later came in handy when he was taking *testimonios* for *Are We Good Neighbors?*), although he did not graduate from high school, consistent with the widespread practice of Mexican schooling in Texas, which rarely extended to high school. He worked in San Antonio as a company clerk and was drafted at the end of World War I; after completing a year of military service, he received an honorable discharge in 1920. He then held a civil service positions with the Department of Commerce and the Department of State, which dispatched Perales on over a dozen thirteen missions to the Dominican Republic, Cuba, Nicaragua, Mexico, Chile and the West Indies.

Simultaneously, he began legal studies at Georgetown in 1922-23 and then spent a year at National University, which later merged to become the school of law at George Washington University and awarded him his LLB. In those times, law school did not require a college degree or completion of studies beyond two years. Before becoming a licensed lawyer, Perales returned to Texas in 1924, worked with a law firm, continued his study of law under the supervision of a lawyer, and traveled the State to organize for the merger of the mutual aid societies that formally became consolidated into LULAC in 1929. He took the Texas bar exam, passed it, and was admitted to the Texas Bar in 1925. (He completed additional law studies after being admitted into the bar, and later petitioned GWU to receive his LL.B., even though he was not required to have the degree.) Perales then decided to move to McAllen, Texas, and took out advertisements in *La Prensa*, the important San Antonio Spanish-language newspaper—whose owner he would later represent in a complex and internecine dispute over a Mexican community hospital—and in several other Valley newspapers, announcing the July 15, 1927 opening of law offices in McAllen and Rio Grande City, in the South Rio Grande Valley of Texas. In his ad, he indicated that that he would also deliver lectures "on behalf of our Race," which he had been doing intermittently in his barnstorming efforts across Texas since 1924. In 1931, he played a supporting role in the appeal of the important *Salvatierra v. Del Rio ISD* school desegregation case, the only time he joined J.T. Canales and M.C. Gonzales in litigation. He returned to San Antonio in 1933, to open his general practice law office in affiliation with the firm of Still, Wright & Davis, and began doing legal work for the Bexar County Attorney's office in 1934. He engaged in the private practice of law in one form or another from 1925 until 1960.

Perales as Litigator

Even without his practice records, it is evident he built a substantial practice that allowed him and his family to enjoy a sold middle class life, one that was characteristically modest. (He and his wife Martha also adopted three children.) While he was not primarily a litigator, he had a general transactional practice, and tried a number of cases at the trial and appellate levels that established a record of both his general commercial practice, representing predominantly Mexican-American clients in civil and criminal matters, and his civil rights practice, trying to strike down punitive practices and discriminatory policies that harmed community members, such as racially restrictive covenants and police custody. These cases were tried in varied federal and Texas state courts in a twenty year stretch from 1939 (when he was with the firm Davis, Wright & Perales) until 1959, months before his death.

Cases tried to decision by Alonso S. Perales:

Spanish Book & Stationery Co. v. U.S., United States Customs Court July 6, 1939, Not Reported in F.Supp, 3 Cust. Ct. 512, 1939 WL 7271

Lozano v. De Martinez, Court of Civil Appeals of Texas, San Antonio. July 22, 1942 164 S.W.2d 196

Clifton v. Puente, 218 S.W.2d 272 (Tex. Civ. App.—San Antonio 1948, writ ref'd n.r.e) (co-counsel, Carlos Cadena)

Alaniz v. State, Court of Criminal Appeals of Texas. May 4, 1949 153 Tex.Crim. 374

Mendoza v. Mendoza, Court of Civil Appeals of Texas, San Antonio. February 4, 1953 255 S.W.2d 251

Powe v. Powe, Court of Civil Appeals of Texas, San Antonio. April 28, 1954 268 S.W.2d 558

Barrera v. Barrera, Court of Civil Appeals of Texas, San Antonio (October 24, 1956) 294 S.W.2d 865

Ydrogo v. Haltom, Court of Civil Appeals of Texas, Eastland. May 10, 1957, 302 S.W.2d 670

Villarreal v. U.S., 254 F. 2d 595 (5th Cir. 1958)

Valdez v. Amaya, Court of Civil Appeals of Texas, San Antonio. September 9, 1959 327 S.W.2d 708

Spanish Book & Stationery Co. v. U.S., **United States Customs Court July 6, 1939, Not Reported in F.Supp, 3 Cust. Ct. 512, 1939 WL 727 [R.D. 4616, Reappraisement 122966-A]**

In *Spanish Book & Stationery Co. v. U.S.*, Perales represented a San Antonio drug store and women's toiletries importer in a customs tax dispute against the United States, concerning the proper taxable rates for a variety of Mexican merchandise, consisting of: "certain perfumes, face powders, lotions, and other toilet articles imported into the United States at the port of San Antonio, Tex. . . . The merchandise was invoiced and entered in United States currency at certain unit values, less certain non-dutiable charges, and was appraised on the basis of the foreign-market value in Mexican currency at certain unit values, less 20 per centum, and 5 per centum, packed, tax included for the face powder and lotion, and less 20 per centum, and 10 per centum, packed, tax included for the perfume, which represented an advance over the entered values." Perales argued that the customs appraisal was too high, as the Mexican supplier had negotiated a differential rate for his client, requiring a lower tax.

As evidence, he presented an artfully drafted affidavit from the supplier, indicating that his Mexican firm billed different companies at different rates, setting out examples and showing that the rate (which would have required his buyer, Perales' client) to pay a lower customs rate:

> It will be noticed that on the invoice for La Nueva China, of Monterey, we billed the TABU powder at $2.09 (to this firm we make an extra discount of ten percent and for that reason the price is $1.88). On the one for Cabrales Hnos. we billed it at $1.46 and at this same price we billed it to Pablo Fong. On the invoice for Fourtoul Bee & Co., at $2.00 and on the one for Perfumeria "El Asia," S. A. at $1.79. To this last firm we make an extra discount of ten percent and therefore the price is practically $1.611.
>
> It will thus be seen that on five invoices the prices are $1.88, $1.46, $1.46-$2.09 and $1.611. The price at which we billed this same article to The Spanish Book and Stationery Co. is $0.47 U.S. Currency, which at the $3.60 exchange rate is equivalent to $1.692.
>
> Possibly our diversity of prices is not very much in accord with commercial usages of the United States, but we follow the standard of making prices for each customer, according to whether he buys more or less, whether he pays cash or buys on credit, and we even take into consideration the importance of the establishment where our articles are to be sold. (Italics omitted)

Indeed, this was common business practice in the United States as well, and the data proved that the price for this good was in the middle of the range of prices regularly charged customers for the powder. But U.S. Customs Judge Tilson was not persuaded that the official, higher Customs appraisal value was incorrect, notwithstanding:

> The evidence is sufficient to establish that the invoiced and entered prices are the prices actually received for this merchandise, but the evidence is not sufficient to overcome the presumption of correctness attaching to the values found by the appraiser, or to establish any other value under the statute. An appeal to reappraisement can be availed of only for the purpose of establishing a value for the merchandise, and not for establishing the honesty and good faith of the importer. The latter is a matter for consideration if and when a petition for remission of additional duties is filed. (citations omitted)

Thus, he rendered a decision for the United State Customs Appraiser, upholding the higher tax rate for the goods: "On the record before me I find the proper foreign-market values of the merchandise in this case to be the appraised values." This was a routine Reappraisement Decision (R.D. 4616), one that took more than two years between the hearing (officially entered at San Antonio, Tex., April 22, 1937) and the decision date of July 6, 1939 (Entry No. 71).

Lozano v. De Martinez, **Court of Civil Appeals of Texas, San Antonio. July 22, 1942 164 S.W.2d 196**

In the 1939 Customs Court decision, Alonso S. Perales found himself in court for a somewhat-routine commercial dispute against Assistant U.S. Attorney General Webster J. Oliver and Charles J. Miville, a special attorney chosen to assist at argument for the defendant United States. In *Lozano v. De Martinez,* the dramatis personae were more intriguing, and the mix of lawyers more complex. Perales and two colleagues represented an ousted board of directors for a Mexican-serving hospital (directed by La Beneficencia Mexicana de San Antonio) against insurgent board members who were represented by Gus Garcia, Perales' mentee and protégé. Moreover, the incumbent Board being removed was led by Ignacio E. Lozano, perhaps the most influential Spanish-language newspaper publisher in the United States, who had fled from Mexico to San Antonio; he had founded *La Prensa* in 1913 and later founded *La Opinión* in Los Angeles in 1926. He was a major social and political figure, as establishment in San Antonio as Mexican exiles could be during this period. Indeed, his influence and reach were national, as his newspapers were the largest chain of Spanish-language papers in the country. Authoritative publishing histories of the United States have characterized his influence as significant and wide-ranging (Kanellos and Martell, 2000, 39-43; Kanellos, 2007).

Lozano had assisted with the founding of the Hospital in 1930, including much of the fundraising, and it had grown to seven clinics in San Antonio. He had remained involved in Board governance, alternating with his wife, Alicia Lozano. The Hospital had operated under the governance of the original Board since its incorporation in 1930 and reincorporation in 1939, but in 1941, a new and insurgent Board sought during a complex Beneficencia meeting to reorganize the Board and to draw up and incorporate a new structure and to name new Directors. The trial that led to this appeal had found that the reorganization was proper, as the former Board members had not paid their dues in the association, and thus were ineligible to serve as Board members:

"In accordance with the notice, such meeting was held on March 12, 1941, and plaintiffs (appellees) as named above were elected directors or trustees of the Beneficencia Mexicana de San Antonio, a corporation, by the majority of the members thereof. . . . The defendants (appellants) are no longer members of the Beneficencia Mexicana de San Antonio under the by-laws passed March 28, 1941, because of their failure to pay dues as provided for therein after March 28, 1941." (p. 196)

Perales' strategy was to argue that the entire series of events leading up to the Board coup and reorganization were null and void, inasmuch as proper notice had not been given for the meeting, and that the new Board did not have the authority to take over the Hospital. However, the trial judge, sitting without a jury, had found for the insurgents, led by Sofia O. de Martinez, and the appeals court affirmed that decision: "So that, regardless of any irregularities which may have occurred prior to the events disclosed in the above findings, the subsequent events there disclosed had the effect of curing such irregularities and establishing the legal status of the corporation and of appellees as directors thereof, with the participation and approval of practically all the members of the corporation" (197). It turned out that almost the entire Beneficencia Mexicana membership, predominantly women, had shown up for the 1941 meeting, made certain that they had paid their dues, and then, in effect, called the question, catching the sitting Board off-guard.

It is hard to believe that the original Board, composed almost entirely of establishment men and male doctors involved in the provision of medical services, could have been outmaneuvered for such trivial grounds as failure to be current in their associational dues, but Garcia's clients prevailed over Perales' clients in this high stakes community governance event, one that had been simmering for several years. The "Handbook of Texas Online," in an entry written on the Hospital dispute, characterizes it as a struggle between local women community volunteers and predominantly male trustees: "The board of trustees was composed of men, probably doctors, and the board of directors was made up of women. Alicia Lozano was president until 1938, when María de los Angeles G. de Velasco replaced her. In 1938 a serious dispute over management resulted in a court settlement, and the women took over the clinic's management" (Orozco, 2012 (a), 2012 (b); R. Garcia, 1991).

***Clifton v. Puente*, 218 S.W.2d 272 (Tex. Civ. App.—San Antonio 1948, writ ref'd n.r.e)**

It may be unfair to view Perales' first two reported cases, the 1939 *Spanish Book & Stationery Co. v. U.S.* and the 1942 *Lozano v. De Martinez,* as average and common cases, although no case is trivial to its parties and lawyers. But whatever the reach of the two commercial and corporate governance cases, and his co-counsel role in *Salvatierra,* the 1948 *Clifton v. Puente* case was a significant step up in several ways. Whereas he had opposed Gus Garcia in *Lozano,* in this important civil rights case, he joined Carlos Cadena as co-counsel. Most importantly, they and their clients won, prevailing in this racial covenant matter. These several lawyers interacted with each other, leading up to the 1951 trials of *Pete Hernandez v. Texas,* the murder and jury composition trial that was resolved by the U.S. Supreme Court in May, 1954, and which included Garcia, Cadena, John Herrera, and the young James DeAnda as co-counsel (Olivas, 2006; Haney Lopez and Olivas, 2008).

Just before the *Puente* case, on June 15, 1948, Garcia, Cadena, and Herrera, as well as Anglo lawyers filed suit against the Bastrop Independent School District, leading to *Delgado v. Bastrop,* an important unpublished 1948 federal court decision that held the Mexican schools were unconstitutional, unless school districts could find legitimate reasons to isolate Mexican schoolchildren, such as the spurious assertion that the children did not speak English or that they would follow the crops and drop out, necessitating special Mexican schools. Historian Steven H. Wilson, who has written authoritatively on this period, especially on the activities of James DeAnda, has written of *Bastrop*:

> Texas was in the federal Fifth Circuit, and its Jim Crow laws were not directly affected by a ruling in the Ninth Circuit. Price Daniel, the Texas attorney

general and a future governor, nevertheless issued an advisory opinion inspired by the court's *dicta*. He forbade automatic, blind segregation of its Mexican-descended pupils, but continued to justify the maintenance of separate classes for "linguistically deficient" students. Daniels' advisory opinion became an issue in the next suit that Mexican Americans filed in Texas, *Delgado v. Bastrop ISD*. U.S. District Judge Ben C. Rice of the Western District of Texas decided that linguistic segregation in the Bastrop school district, located near Austin, violated the Fourteenth Amendment because, as it was implemented, Bastrop's segregation was "arbitrary and discriminatory." Like Price Daniel, Judge Rice did not criticize all language segregation. But he declared that the Bastrop district could segregate any individual student—Anglo or Mexican-American—only after school authorities had determined the students' English proficiency through "scientifically standardized" examinations. . . .

After describing the plan to comply with the federal court order, the state's chief school officer wrote that he trusted that superintendents, principals, and teachers "will move forward courageously and harmoniously, without prejudice, and without bitterness, as we strive to work out for ourselves a more practical democracy." Most districts either ignored the mandate, or set standards that made it extremely easy for school administrators to prevent any Mexican Americans from sharing public classrooms with Anglo Americans. (Wilson, 2003, pp. 159-160, citations omitted)

The State of Texas chose not to appeal, lest the decision take root in the Fifth Circuit, causing mischief with the many African American cases making their way forward, including school desegregation, the many other public accommodations cases, and the *Sweatt v. Painter* case that was ripening down in Austin, fewer than thirty miles down the road from Bastrop (Shabazz, 2004; Chin, 2010).

On May 3, 1948, the Supreme Court decided two decisions in four racial covenant cases, known collectively as *Shelley v. Kraemer,* holding that judicial enforcement by various courts of such covenants violated the equal protection doctrine by constituting state action. These cases were the culmination of a decades-long legal strategy by the NAACP Legal Defense Fund attorneys, involving dozens of attorneys and literally hundreds of cases. Even more notable than the Mexican Revolution-driven exodus of Mexicans to the United States, especially in such Mexican immigrant communities as San Antonio was the extraordinary exodus of African Americans from the South to the more industrial North. This great migration of blacks from Southern rural areas to sprawling and congested Northern and Midwestern industrial cities prompted various efforts to establish and maintain racial segregation in housing, especially against African Americans. In an attempt to restrict the newly arrived blacks from owning homes, many cities, towns, counties, and municipalities enacted specific racial ordinances that prohibited black families from renting, purchasing, or otherwise occupying property except in places specifically marked for such groups, such as in Louisville, Kentucky. In *Buchanan v. Warley*, the Supreme Court in 1917 had invalidated such a racially restrictive ordinance.

In the racial thermodynamics of the early twentieth century, and thwarted by the *Buchanan* decision, many invalidated ordinances were repealed or left unenforced in formal transactions. But the entire racial covenant business became, in the alternative, deeply privatized by attaching the same racial restrictions on using and conveying property through private means, or restrictive covenants that travelled with the deeds and land. These were widespread across all regions, especially those cities with informal means of governance such a homeowner pacts or neighborhood associations. In 1926, in *Corrigan v. Buckley*, the Supreme Court upheld private covenants, holding that these *de facto* segregatory and discriminatory covenants were not state action: "it is obvious that none of these constitutional Amendments prohibited private individuals from entering into contracts respecting the control and disposition of their own property." Even the authoritative American Law Institute Restatement on Property allowed such covenants as acceptable practices, allowing that "social conditions [might] render desirable the exclusion of the racial or social group in question."

As a part of the larger comprehensive NAACP strategy to build up a docket of challenges to racially restrictive covenants in both public housing and the private markets, there were many challenges, which led to stutterstep wins and losses, especially after the return of minority veterans from WW II. Legal scholar Leland B. Ware (1989) has noted, "by 1946, at least 100 civil actions were pending" (p. 742). After desegregation efforts and civil rights litigation had stalled, private racial covenants grew to effectuate and implement segregated housing. As one authoritative scholar of the NAACP litigation targeted towards housing integration noted, the racial restrictions had morphed so widely that a system of counter-covenants had grown up to weaken the actual effect of the formal language:

Despite the limitations imposed by the covenants, black home buyers invariably found ways to circumvent them. The most prevalent device was the use of a white "strawman" to purchase property. Under this system, a white buyer would purchase a home, then immediately resell the property to a black purchaser. The white homeowners in the affected area would then be required to bear the burden and expense of filing a civil action to seek enforcement of the covenant. White homeowners also circumvented the covenants by simply disregarding the covenants and selling directly to black purchasers. Because the demand for housing in black communities was far greater than the available supply, white homesellers frequently obtained substantially higher prices from black purchasers than they would have received from white buyers. As a result, despite the elaborate mechanisms that were created to perpetuate segregated communities, white homeowners and real estate agents had a significant economic incentive to sell properties to black purchasers. The influx of black families into urban centers continued throughout the 1920s and 1930s and, with the advent of the Second World War, the number of blacks migrating to urban centers increased dramatically. During the war, the defense industry created thousands of new jobs located in or near large cities. As more minorities moved to the urban centers, the demand for housing increased, causing conditions in ghettoes to deteriorate rapidly. (Ware, 1989, p. 742)

This was the state of affairs just prior to the *Puente* litigation in which Carlos Cadena and Alonso S. Perales were engaged. It was this very issue of public and private housing discrimination that Perales had undertaken to document in *Are We Good Neighbors?*; the many notarized *testimonios* he gathered and advertised were clear and compelling evidence of the racial zoning used against Mexican-origin residents, even against returning veterans and even in San Antonio, a predominantly Mexican-American city, and the home-in-exile for many *Mexicanos de afuera*, many of whom never had returned to their Mexican homeland, and who were rearing and educating their U.S. citizen children, recipients of birthright citizenship in the United States (R. García, 1991; Rivas-Rodriguez, 2005; R. Ramos, 2008).

The recent 1948 *Shelley v. Kraemer* decision had not been tested in San Antonio or applied to Mexican Americans. Carlos Cadena in particular was active in this project, spurred on in part and financed in part by private funds that University of Texas Education professor George I. Sanchez had secured to undertake litigation and advocacy for private Mexican housing access and for acceptance into the growing benefits that were formally available to citizens and returning veterans, but were not *de facto* being accorded to this group, particularly in San Antonio, a majority-Mexican city by this time (R. Garcia, 1991; Jones-Correa, 2000–2001; C. Ramos, 2001; Blanton, 2006, 2012).

The *Puente* facts as set out in the land dispute included the following:
(3) Deed dated March 28, 1947, from Clifton and wife to P. J. Humphreys.
(4) Deed dated December 4, 1947, from P. J. Humphreys to Abdon Salazar Puente.

I. N. Clifton's claim is based upon two deeds from Southwestern Acreage Company, one dated December 2, 1947, and the other dated December 16, 1947.

It is readily apparent that Puente's title, emanating from the common source at a date prior in time to that asserted by Clifton should prevail, unless there be some special provision in the conveyances mentioned which would defeat said title. Appellants claim that there is a provision of this nature. The deed from Southwestern Acreage Company to Ward, which is a part of Puente's chain of title, contains numerous restrictive covenants, one of which prohibits the sale or lease of the property to 'persons of Mexican descent.'

This deed contains the following forfeiture provision:
The conditions and restrictions are covenants written with the express understanding that in the event of any violation thereof all title to the then owner and occupant shall be forfeited to the grantor, and upon demand, such property and all improvements thereon shall be surrendered to the seller. All covenants and agreements herein contained shall extend and inure to and be obligatory upon the heirs, administrators, successors and assigns of the parties hereto.' (pp. 272-273)

That is, if the anti-Mexican covenant were to have force of law, Clifton would prevail due to Abdon Puente's inability to purchase any land with such a restriction. However, urged by Cadena's and Perales' advocacy and skill in applying *Shelley v. Kraemer*, the court struck down the covenant:

In the absence of the exhibition of a chain of title from the sovereignty of the soil or from a common source, the element of possession may be controlling. But here both Clifton and Puente claim under a common source by different chains of title. A comparison of titles is therefore involved. Puente's title is the better title and he is entitled to judgment unless by judicial action the restrictive racial covenant and the forfeiture clause dependent thereon be recognized and enforced so as to deny Puente's claim to title. It is as much an enforcement of the covenant to deny to a person a legal right to which he would be entitled except for the covenant as it would be to expressly command by judicial order that the terms of the covenant be recognized and carried out. No valid distinction can be predicated upon the position of a party (alleged to be an ineligible grantee) as a plaintiff or as a defendant. Under the decision of the Supreme Court, above referred to, judicial recognition or enforcement of the racial covenant involved here by a state court is precluded by the 'equal protection of the laws' clause of the Fourteenth Amendment. (p. 274)

The impressive decades-long restrictive covenant strategy leading to *Shelley*, and the eventual frontal assault on segregation that was *Brown*, were testament to the legal acumen and persistence so much in evidence (Tushnet, 1987). While the history of Mexican-American and other Latino racial isolation is not as well-known and their litigation was not as comprehensive as that of the NAACP, particularly with the absence of a dedicated law firm advocating for these issues, there was early litigation by Anglo lawyers on behalf of Latinos, such as the 1943 *Doss v. Bernal* in California, and there were a number of cases brought in public education and public accommodations, even with fewer Mexican-American lawyers than was the case in Texas (Jones-Correa, 2000–2001; C. Ramos, 2000-2001; Romero and Fernandez, 2012; D. García, Yosso, and Barajas, 2012).

Further examination will also reveal litigation by Latino plaintiffs concerning public benefits, access to government resources, and public accommodations in the first half of the twentieth century. Even if not always assisted by Mexican-American lawyers, who were scarce, in virtually all Western states and throughout the country, these plaintiffs litigated, advocated and made their voices heard, even if the structural features of the polity made it exceedingly difficult to change the existing order. They had learned many bitter lessons, prevailing in hard-fought litigation such as in a number of the desegregation cases, only to see victories overturned by the implementation phase or by resistance from restrictionist Anglo leaders, across sectors (Romero, 2004, 2007; Valencia, 2008; Arellano, 2010).

In his authoritative article that analyzed the role of judicial discretion in the many Texas civil rights cases, legal scholar George A. Martinez presciently noted this very point, in a turn of phrase that would be recognizable today:

This article has explored a jurisprudential point: legal indeterminacy in the context of Mexican-American civil rights litigation. The article argues that because of legal uncertainty or indeterminacy the resolution of key issues was not inevitable. Judges often had discretion to reach their conclusions. In this regard, the article concludes that the courts generally exercised their discretion by taking a position on key issues against Mexican-Americans. The article points out that exposing the exercise of judicial discretion and the lack of inevitability in civil rights cases is important for two major reasons. At one level, exposing the exercise of judicial discretion is significant because it helps reveal the extent to which the courts have helped, or failed to help establish the rights of Mexican-Americans. Thus, the article concludes that the courts could have done significantly more to help establish such rights.

The article, however, seeks to do more than establish that important conclusion. The article argues that exposing the lack of inevitability in civil rights decision-making may help break down barriers to racial reform. (Martinez, 1994, p. 618, citations omitted)

The application of *Shelley* to San Antonio covenants was also clear evidence of the longstanding vision and advocacy by Perales to eliminate the various residential racial restrictions and oppressive legal regime aimed at Latinos. Legal scholar Christopher Ramos (2001), in a careful study of San Antonio's long history of racial isolation and segregation rather cynically concludes, noting the continuing modern-day hypersegregation in the city, that the *Puente* case "may have also been too little, too late." (p. 165) Perales did not live long enough to see the uses to which his research and that of others was put in fashioning the detailed fair housing laws and regulations, but these administrative regimes for housing have become quite formal and detailed (Ware, 1993; Bender, 2010). Ironically, some vestigial racial statutes remained on the books through the early twenty first century, until enterprising researchers discovered them and moved to have them removed by state legislatures (Chin et al., 2006).

Alaniz v. State, 153 Tex.Crim. 374, 220 S.W.2d 653 (1949)

In this case, the only criminal case ever tried to a reported decision by Alonso S. Perales (who had co-counsel J. O. Faith, of Karnes City, Texas) was before District Judge H. D. Barrow, in Karnes County. His client, Severo Alaniz, was convicted of assault to murder with malice, received fifteen years, and appealed to the Court of Criminal Appeals, in Austin, and on May 4, 1949, Judge Beauchamp wrote the opinion upholding the appeal in a few terse paragraphs: "We see no ground for contention that the evidence does not support the jury's finding that he was guilty of assault to murder with malice. We are unable to consider the bills of exception and discussion of the questions raised by them would be improper. The judgment of the trial court is affirmed" (654-655).

Texas then and now has a bifurcated highest court: the Texas Supreme Court is the final authority on civil matters, while the criminal docket final authority is the Texas Court of Criminal Appeals. Ernest S. Goens was the State's Attorney of

Austin. Perales sought an appeal for another hearing, where he raised several technical, procedural questions, and three weeks later, on May 25, 1949, received his final answer—the rehearing was denied.

The facts, unremarkably, turned on a drunken brawl in a small bar in Kenedy, Texas. The brothers Severo and Ramon Alaniz and the deceased, Manuel Sosa, were involved in a knife fight, after which Sosa died some time later. Both Alaniz brothers were charged for the death, following testimony from quite a bit of bloody evidence on all three antagonists, damning wound evidence, and a number of eyewitnesses to the fight. (No one testified as to exactly who administered the *coup de grace* that killed Sosa.) However, Ramon was found to be so mentally incompetent that he was confined in a state facility for the insane, and as a result was statutorily unable to be tried or to serve as a witness, for or against his brother Severo: there was no reversible error "because of the absence of Ramon Alaniz, who seemed to have been confined in a state hospital for the insane. It was admitted that Ramon Alaniz was also charged by indictment with the same offense as appellant, and under the statute, he would not be allowed to testify for appellant. It was also not shown that there was any probability of Ramon Alaniz recovering his sanity at any time" (p. 655, citations omitted)

Under these unfortunate circumstances of not being able to point with any value to the alternative theory of the case (i.e., "the brother did it, not my client"), Perales invoked the theory that his client had been convicted of murder with malice and that there had been insufficient evidence in the trial to determine that Severo—rather than Ramon or another participant in the barroom brawl, which had spilled out into the streets and into a nearby alley—had struck the fatal blow. The Court, however, observed that the conviction had not been under the greater charge of murder, but rather the lesser offense, for assault to murder. The decision noted: Ramon Alaniz

> was involved in the difficulty and was charged, under a separate indictment, with the same offense. Appellant [Severo] sought to have the brother's testimony admitted in evidence saying that he was the one who inflicted the death wound. The complaint in this respect as well as others are embraced in four bills of exception which are found in the record. We note, however, that the motion for new trial was overruled on November 27, 1948. (p. 654)

In addition, they were convinced that, no matter the insane Ramon's involvement, Severo had been shown to have been involved:

> "That appellant was engaged in the difficulty resulting in the death of a party is not disputed; that he was a principal to the murder might well have been supported, had the jury so determined. We see no ground for contention that the evidence does not support the jury's finding that he was guilty of assault to murder with malice." (pp. 654-655)

There were several technical issues of timing, notice, and jurisdiction, but the Court appears to have considered them either cured or *de minimis*, and gave them short shrift, summarily concluding, "the matter is regulated by statute and we have no power to change it, or to make an exception thereto" (655).

Judge Graves, who dismissed the request for rehearing and who entered the final judgment, noted of one matter that had been raised about the conduct of trial Judge Barrow, in ordering the jury to continue deliberating:

> Bill No. 4 relates to the verdict of the jury in that after having deliberated, they returned into court a verdict of guilt of an assault to murder and a punishment of fifteen years. The trial court called to their attention the portion of the charge relative to an assault to murder and refused to accept this verdict, but directed them to retire and again consider of their verdict. They soon returned with a verdict of guilt of an assault to murder with malice and a penalty of fifteen years, which verdict the careful trial court received and they were discharged. There was no objection registered or made to such proceedings, and we see no error shown therein.

Finding no error in the record, the motion will be overruled (656).

Here, there is simply not enough information or collateral documentation about the trial sixty years later to know if the mistakes made by either side were, indeed, mistakes or "no error." There are no surviving lawyer notes or participants alive to amplify the record. The short opinion makes it a point to note that Perales had not objected or preserved the matter for appeal on the jury charges ("There was no objection registered or made to such proceedings") and with regard to the technical notices complained of, the Court also hints that the issue on appeal was required to have been noted at the time to preserve any record of error ("It appears that appellant's attorney could have exercised more diligence than he did exercise.") Without a fuller rendition of exactly what happened with the complex facts and complicated procedural matters that arose with the unavailable but likely guilty insane brother, and whose fault it was, that of Perales, co-counsel J. O. Faith, the State AG, or the trial court, we cannot assign blame. Rather, the mistakes seem minor, in context. Even in today's more modern courts, with enhanced protections of the record, unless a trial judge is clearly erroneous or biased, clearly not the case here, appellate reviews of trial decisions are likely to uphold convictions. Perales may have tried other criminal cases, not all of which would have reported decisions, but without further documentation, it appears the 1949 *Alaniz* case was his only foray into criminal defense.

Of course no court is infallible, and a year later, in *Aniceto Sanchez v. State*, Houston lawyers John Herrera and the newly licensed James DeAnda would also unsuccessfully appeal a jury verdict to the same court, and lose. It would be only one year later that the *Hernandez v. Texas* lawyers would claim that Pete Hernandez, tried by an all-Anglo jury in his murder trial for killing Joe Espinosa in a barroom fight in Edna, Texas, had not been judged by a jury of his peers. This team (consisting of John Herrera, James DeAnda, and with the additional support of Gustavo Garcia and Carlos Cadena) would appeal a Jackson County, Texas jury decision that he had not received a fair trial, and lost in the same Texas Court of Criminal Appeals, on the grounds that Mexicans were white by law in the State, so he had received a fair trial. In 1953, the

U.S. Supreme Court accepted the case for appeal, and after hearing Garcia and Cadena argue the matter, overturned the murder convention in 1954 (Sheridan, 2003; Wilson, 2003; Olivas, 2006; Gross, 2007; Haney Lopez and Olivas, 2008; I. Garcia, 2008).

Mendoza v. Mendoza, Court of Civil Appeals of Texas, San Antonio (February 4, 1953), 255 S.W.2d 251

Given his strong views about the sanctity of marriage, as expressed in a number of his essays and letters, Alonso S. Perales must have taken on a divorce action and property settlement case with some disdain or reluctance; in *Mendoza v. Mendoza,* he represented a divorcing husband at the original divorce action, and with co-counsel Harry B. Berry, also represented him in this 1953 appeal concerning a land dispute and whether or not the land parcel constituted community property, which under Texas family law, would have had to be split with the wife, who had sought the divorce.

The trial judge in Starr County, Sam G. Reams, had rendered a decree granting the divorce, determined the parcel to be community property, and divided the property between the Mendozas—ordering them to partition it and to split the proceeds. The husband appealed. The Court of Civil Appeals Judge A.J. Pope held that "land conveyed to husband by his parents before marriage of husband was his separate property and remained such, though a second deed conveying the same land to husband was executed by his mother after marriage of husband and death of his father" (p. 251).

In addition, Judge Pope determined that the appropriate remedy for the wife was to seek to be reimbursed for her contribution to the land, in alleviating the attached debt. He reversed this part of the original decree and ordered the matter be reconsidered by the lower court judge: "the use of the wife's separate funds after marriage to discharge the debt against the husband's separate property did not transform separate property into community property. Appellee's remedy is to obtain reimbursement" (252). In other words, the trial judge had mistaken the obligations that arose when she helped pay the debt, but the preexisting ownership interest was not reformulated into community property simply by her contribution.

In the technical sense, the more serious matter was the property issue, and although the record shows that Perales had an extensive family law practice—likely one filled with uncontested divorces or ones not requiring a full reported court decision—the *Mendoza* case appears to have been his only divorce matter in a reported case.

Powe v. Powe, Court of Civil Appeals of Texas, San Antonio (April 28, 1954) 268 S.W.2d 558

Once again collaborating with his partners Harry B. Berry and Marvin T. Deane in the San Antonio firm, Perales took this civil case to a jury, the only civil case he ever tried to a jury at the trial level rather than to a judge. They represented the appellant widow Bertha Price, whose husband had entered into a complicated parol real estate family trust in San Antonio in 1940, with joint interests by two brothers and a sister in the name of the sister and her husband, for her benefit and that of the brothers. Because the husband of their sister (their brother-in-law) received a WWII draft notice and they feared the possibility that he might die in combat, they switched plans and gave her interest to one of the brothers—who, ironically, then died in 1952. The brother's widow, represented by the Perales firm, repudiated the family trust arrangement, and sued. The children's parents who had given the original property to become the corpus of the trust, A. E. Powe and Lillian E. Powe, had moved into a residence located upon one of the lots, and continued to reside in that house until the death of Mr. Powe in March, 1943, after which the widow (their mother) continued to reside there at the time of the trial. Bertha Price argued that the entire property had reverted to her, and sought to evict her late husband's mother from the property and to exercise full dominion over the lot.

However, Bexar County 57th District Court Judge C. K. Quin construed the trust in favor of plaintiffs (that is, all the parties save the widowed Mrs. Price), and she appealed. After sorting out the complex transaction, including technical issues of proper service and the statute of limitations, and parsing the wildly conflicting stories, Court of Civil Appeals Judge Norvell held that the evidence heard by the jury was sufficient to uphold the jury's special finding that an oral agreement had been made for both purchasing the property and for placing it in the name of one for the benefit of each, notwithstanding that one of the parties had not present when the property was actually purchased.

Judge Norvell summarized, "What has been said effectively disposes of this case. In the state of the record and the instructions of the trial judge, we are of the opinion that appellant's points relating to argument of counsel do not present a reversible error. . . . All of appellant's points have been considered. None of them present a reversible error and the judgment is accordingly affirmed." Perales' client Bertha Price had to be satisfied with the prorated portion of the estate that had been held in the trust for her late husband's interest, far less than she had sought.

Barrera v. Barrera, **Court of Civil Appeals of Texas, San Antonio (October 24, 1956) 294 S.W.2d 865**

In another dispute that arose out of an earlier divorce settlement, Perales and Ronald Smallwood represented the ex-wife, Amalia Garcia Barrera, in District Court of Webb County, Laredo, Texas against her former husband, José María Barrera. In a bench trial, Judge E.D. Salinas had ruled against her in a dispute over the non-payment of taxes that were owed on the property. Mr. Barrera sued his former wife to recover $1,000 for waste of the property, arguing that she let the property deteriorate and that she had not performed the necessary repairs. In addition, he had paid the delinquent City, County, and School District taxes, totaling $317.14. The husband was the remainderman, while the wife was the life tenant, who was allowed to reside on the property and who was required to pay all the taxes for her portion of the land. After a serious flood, the real property was damaged, and there was some dispute over the extent of habitability and whether or not the ex-husband had told her not to make any repairs to the house or the garage.

They had been divorced on March 27, 1951, and the decree included a property agreement that contained the following paragraph: "Amalia García Barrera, in addition to the amount of money set out in Paragraph 1, above, shall be entitled to the use and occupancy of the property. . . it hereby being understood, however, that the garage located on said premises shall remain in the possession of and be used by José María Barrera" (866-867). The trial judge found for Mr. Barrera, and rendered a judgment of $642.50—to include the taxes and the "waste" of the unrepaired property. Amalia Barrera appealed, and was represented by Perales and his co-counsel.

Chief Justice W. O. Murray of the Court of Civil Appeals of Texas, San Antonio, reversed and found for Amalia Barrera. He held that it was well-established that it was the remainderman whose duty it is to make repairs and not let the property decline in value or become uninhabitable. In addition, he found that she had tried to make the repairs, even though it was not her duty, and he had told her not to do so: she "testified that when she undertook to repair the house, [her ex-husband] told her not to do so, not to spend any of her money on the house because it belonged to him. [He] testified to the same thing. The effect of this statement was to relieve appellant from the duty of making repairs" (867).

In addition, José María had jumped the gun and paid all the taxes himself, even though the duty to do so was hers: "The situation in which appellee finds himself was brought about by his voluntary act in paying the taxes before they were due and without asking the taxing authorities to separate such taxes" (867-868). Had he been concerned about the possible consequences of non-payment, he could have paid his portion of the taxes before they were past due, and then made a demand on her. He could also have requested that the various public taxing authorities separate the tax due on the realty (a portion of which he which he occupied), from that occupied by her, on which she had the duty to pay. The court found that he had done so gratuitously and voluntarily, and that she owed nothing either for the alleged waste or the taxes he had paid.

As a result, the appellate court held: "The judgment of the trial court is reversed and judgment here rendered that [Mr. Barrera] take nothing" (869). This was a complete victory for Perales and his client, who must have found it sweet that her ex-husband lost, inasmuch as it was his stubbornness that had let the property deteriorate and his lack of trust in her willingness to pay her portion of the taxes that led to the entire dispute.

Ydrogo v. Haltom, Court of Civil Appeals of Texas, Eastland (May 10, 1957) 302 S.W. 2d 670

Just over six months passed before Ronald Smallwood and Perales were back in an Appeals Court, and another Chief Justice, Justice Grissom. Opposing them, apparently *pro se*, was Charles T. Haltom, who had conveyed several real property lot titles to Sacarias Ydrogo, Perales' client. In the original bench trial, the suit in trespass to try title to lots was brought before Judge Eugene C. Williams of the 37th District Court, Bexar County (San Antonio). Ydrogo the grantor appealed a "trespass suit to try title" that was resolved in favor of Haltom, as he had a general warranty deed from Ydrogo conveying the disputed property in controversy to him. Ydrogo's claim was that such a title was inadequate. The appellate court resolved the matter in a single terse paragraph:

Ydrogo's points are that Haltom failed to [clear] title from the sovereignty of the soil or from a common source and that the deed was not admissible in evidence. The evidence was admissible. When Haltom proved the conveyance by a general warranty deed of the property in controversy to him by Ydrogo, he did all that was necessary to establish a prima facie case authorizing the judgment appealed from. Under the circumstances the defendant was the common source of title. Ydrogo offered no evidence. The judgment is sustained by the following authorities. . . . (670)

"The evidence was admissible." "Ydrogo offered no evidence." These are harsh words and peremptory rulings at the appellate level, a process arduous and expensive enough that most unpersuasive cases do not get through the filter. Without all the details lost forever in the record, we can only assume that Perales' client stubbornly insisted upon going to court, even without a prayer of winning, and against all odds, then took it up to the Court of Appeals. But there is a slight thread running through several of these cases, as when Ignacio Lozano and his fellow Hospital Board members are ousted for non-payment of dues, where one wonders if sufficient client counseling were occurring, to run interference (for example, before a big governance fight, making sure his client were officially dues-paid member eligible to vote and hold office in corporate matters) and to talk the clients out of losing litigation, especially when the amounts were small and the case precedents were so stacked against the clients' interests.

Villarreal v. U.S., 254 F. 2d 595 (5th Cir. 1958)

Alonso S. Perales and his law partner Ronald Smallwood argued together once more for a hapless plaintiff, this time in Perales' only recorded appearance before the Fifth Circuit, in a Federal Tort Claims Act matter. Nine-year-old Guadalupe Villarreal, Jr. received serious injuries from the explosion of a "dud" ordinance shell, which he had picked up in his own yard after it had been left there by his older brother who in turn had found it on private property located behind the family's yard. Perales' clients had sought to hold the federal government accountable for the injuries caused to the boy by the explosion of material that had been once owned by the federal government, but had simply been on the adjacent private property, partially buried under dirt for what was likely a number of years. After a full trial before the United States District Court for the Western District of Texas, Chief Judge Chief Judge Ben H. Rice, Jr. entered judgment and denied any recovery to the family.

The Court of Appeals then held that evidence fully supported the trial judgment, finding that the United States was not negligent for the ordinance or any injuries that resulted from the children playing with it, and affirmed the holding: "The district judge, on evidence fully supporting them, made findings completely negativing [sic] plaintiff's claims of negligence and gave judgment for defendant." Citing a number of similar claims, the Circuit tersely held in a one page decision: "The judgment was right. It is affirmed."

Perhaps the most notable matter was the identity of the *Villarreal* trial judge, Western District Chief Judge Rice, who, it will be recalled, had heard and decided the important *Delgado v. Bastrop* case a decade earlier, the unpublished opinion that struck down the Mexican schools in the central Texas town of Bastrop, unless the school could proffer a good faith reason for maintaining separate schools. The State chose not to appeal, so the would-be resultant Fifth Circuit case would not reach into the Deep South, which, before it was split into the Fifth and Eleventh Circuits, would have desegregated the South, albeit with "all deliberate speed." *Brown v. Board* (*Brown* II), 349 U.S. 294, 301 (1955). That case was tried before Judge Rice by a number of Mexican-American lawyers, including Carlos Cadena, John Herrera, and Gus Garcia, as well as Californian A.L. Wirin, who had tried *Mendez* and other public accommodation cases in California (Blanton, 2006). With James DeAnda, these three Tejano lawyers tried *Hernandez v. Texas* before the U.S. Supreme Court in 1954. After the case, the Bastrop Independent School District passed a policy re-implementing Mexican-schools, due to linguistic and cultural features of predominantly Spanish-speaking classes (G. Martinez, 1993; Gross, 2003, 2007; Blanton, 2006, 2012; Valencia, 2008; Wilson, 2003).

Valdez v. Amaya, Court of Civil Appeals of Texas, San Antonio (September 9, 1959) 327 S.W.2d 708

The *Valdez v. Amaya* matter was the last case ever tried to a decision by Ronald Smallwood and Alonso S. Perales, and Perales died exactly eight months later, on May 9, 1960. As he had in *Barrera*, he argued to Chief Justice Murray of the Court of Civil Appeals of Texas, San Antonio. The wrongful death suit was brought by the lawyers on behalf of Benilde Valdez and her children, for the wrongful death of her husband and their father, Sabas Valdez. Defendant Manuel Amaya, as City Marshal of San Diego, Texas had arrested Sabas Valdez and placed him in the city jail of San Diego. Valdez had just received a severe beating at the hands of a civilian third party and was in urgent need of medical attention at the time of his arrest, a fact clearly known by Marshal Amaya. Sabas Valdez was released from custody the following morning and died two days later from his injuries.

The trial court dismissed the cause of action against the City of San Diego, causing Perales and the plaintiffs to dismiss their cause of action as to Marshal Amaya, and to undertake this appeal from the judgment sustaining the dismissal of charges against the City; the City argued that City Marshal Amaya was exercising police power by arresting and detaining Sabas Valdez and, therefore, the City could not be held liable for his negligence under the doctrine of *respondeat superior*. Additionally, if the Marshal were not acting in his official capacity as a police officer, then the City could not be held liable under any other theory, as he had no authority to act for the City in any other capacity. This put Perales and his clients between a rock and a hard place.

The appellate court held:

The Valdez lawyers contended that the City should have been liable for the negligence of the Marshal in failing to furnish the seriously-injured Valdez immediate emergency medical treatment at the time he was placed in the City jail, when it was obvious that he needed such treatment. We cannot agree. The

Marshal, in arresting Sabas Valdez and placing him in jail, was exercising police power and, regardless of what his negligence was in this connection, the City is not liable for the damages caused by any such negligence, under the doctrine of *respondeat superior*. (709)

Citing a number of authoritative cases, the Court affirmed the trial court judgment in an opinion just over one page long.

Again, Perales had advocated the interests of his clients, even in a longshot case where the negligence seemed arguably evident. However, Duval County District Court Judge C. W. Laughlin, was a thorough trial judge, and his opinion had pinned down the various facts and allegations, so that Chief Justice W.O. Murray (who had earlier found for Perales' client in the *Barrera* case) was obliged to uphold the ruling, as there were no reversible errors. In more modern times, following a more fulsome tort litigation history, the Marshal would have likely had some statutory degree of liability to provide better care for a prisoner in his custody (Ross, 1998).

There is one additional legal matter of significance in which Perales was involved, early in his career, when he teamed with J.T. Canales (then practicing in Brownsville) and M.C. Gonzales (then in San Antonio practice), who had tried the first Texas desegregation case concerning Mexican Americans, *Salvatierra v. Del Rio ISD*. After the 1930 Court of Appeals decision, it appears that the appellant's petition for writ of error was dismissed for want of jurisdiction on March 18, 1931 by the Texas Supreme Court. Then, on April 15, 1931, the motion for rehearing of the petition for writ of error was overruled. Next, the appellants, who by this time included Perales as co-counsel, filed their Statement as to Jurisdiction on Appeal to the U.S Supreme Court on July 27, 1931. The U.S. Supreme Court dismissed the case for want of jurisdiction on October 26, 1931, noting that it was "treating the papers whereon the appeal was allowed as a petition for writ of certiorari . . . certiorari denied." While Canales and Gonzales were the *Salvatierra* trial lawyers, along with John L. Dodson, of Del Rio, young Perales was listed on the brief for the 1931 Statement as to Jurisdiction on Appeal, which was eventually denied. This appears, at least by document review, to be the only time he joined these two Mexican-American colleagues in a formal case, joining together the first three Texas Mexican-American lawyers.

Conclusion

It is easy sport to second-guess some of the cases that Alonso S. Perales brought for his clients, cases that are remarkable more for their breadth of subject matter and widespread venues than they are for their actual precedential value. That is, all save the *Puente* case, which has greater civil rights significance (especially its application of *Shelley v. Kraemer*), and the intersection with one of the most accomplished *Tejano* lawyers of his time, Carlos Cadena, who tried *Bastrop*, *Hernandez v. Texas* and other important cases—including another SCOTUS case, the *per curiam* decision in *Lopez v. Texas*, 378 U.S. 567 (1964)—and who went on to a distinguished career as the first Mexican-American law professor (at St. Mary's University) and a very highly regarded appellate judge, including service as the Chief Judge of his

Appellate Court, in his own right. He, James DeAnda, and other *Tejano* lawyers founded the Mexican American Legal Defense and Educational Fund (MALDEF) in San Antonio in 1968 (Wilson, 2003; San Miguel, 2007; Kohout, 2012; MacDonald and Hoffman, 2012).

While the true existential case of this period was one concerning Mexican-American jury participation, the 1954 *Hernandez*, and Perales played no direct legal role in the landmark case, he was out to capture what he considered bigger game, particularly in his choice of the venues to pursue his discursive goal, communicating with both his *raza* and the larger community. His practice, from the available litigation files, appears to have been a successful general commercial trial and appellate practice. *Puente* was the one case he actually tried where his advocacy was in the larger civil rights litigation genre, and his widespread and longstanding advocacy and scholarship for housing benefits and the general rights of Mexican Americans was evident. His peripheral role in the 1930 *Salvatierra* case was the other exception, after the case had been tried and appealed, after which he was involved in the Supreme Court *certiorari* process.

In concluding this exploratory study of Alonso S. Perales as a lawyer, one cannot help but feel that measuring out his life by his sketchy law practice files and the published court decisions does not do him justice. That is, without a better sense of his professional life as a counselor, one cannot know why he took some of these cases to trial, only to lose, and predictably. For example, he may have just had unlucky or bad clients. But more striking, at least to me, was the work that is suggested here, particularly his intersections and working relationships with other lawyers, especially the intriguing A. L. Wirin, who figures so thoroughly in the overall Mexican-American civil rights litigation, ranging from his home in California, to Texas, Arizona, and elsewhere, and the extraordinary David C. Marcus, who also figures prominently in a number of these cases, in several states. These cross-racial and cross-regional connections must be explored with various archival resources (such as the Southern California ACLU files) and with scholars who have honed in on Wirin and Marcus but do not have the full measure of these remarkable men (Mazon, 1988; Blanton, 2006, 2012; Strum, 2010; Carpio, 2012).

Finally, the most intriguing relationship hinted at is his regular and often-contentious interaction with University of Texas scholar Dr. George I. Sánchez, as suggested by Carlos K. Blanton's comprehensive work on Sánchez. New Mexico native Sánchez—also a former LULAC national president—is the only genuine competitor that Perales has for being the *Tejano* public intellectual of his time, even though he was not an academic and did not have academic resources for his writing. In turn, Sánchez interacted regularly and substantively with most of the Mexican-American lawyers who weave in and out of this Perales project, and provided funds for undertaking some of the important litigation, from a variety of private philanthropic and government funds (Salinas, 1971; Rangel and Alcala, 1972; Blanton, 2012).

Sánchez worked often with James DeAnda, who, after his work with the *Hernandez* case, moved from Houston to Corpus Christi to establish a private practice, and who wound up trying a number of important post-*Brown* school desegregation and civil rights cases with the assistance of Sánchez and physician and AGIF funder

Dr. Héctor P. García (Wilson, 2003; I. Garcia, 2003; Blanton, 2012). For example, he tried *Herminio Hernandez et al. v. Driscoll Consolidated Independent School District* (1957), *Trinidad Villareal et al. v. Mathis Independent School District of San Patricio City* (1957), *Chapa v. Odem Independent School District* (1967), *Chapa v. Odem Independent School District* (1967), and, most importantly, *Cisneros v. Corpus Christi ISD* (1970). DeAnda later became a federal judge in Brownsville and Houston, as well as a co-founder of MALDEF (Wilson, 2003, 165-171; MacDonald and Hoffman, 2012).

And as Emilio Zamora has noted in his Chapter, we do not yet know the fuller contours of Perales' international legal work, where the record is more evident in diplomatic discourse and various legal drafting exercise than in formal written litigation results. Scholarly work remains to be done in the several diplomatic files and international records (Calderón-Zaks, 2011). The work of Mary L. Dudziak in her careful exploration of African Americans in the international imagination and the extent to which elites in the United States facilitated formal desegregation, could be usefully employed in understanding the racial and political isolation of post-WWII Mexican Americans (Dudziak, 2000).

For a long time, Perales and the others had supported the Fair Employment Practices Committee (FEPC) and the Texas state Good Neighbor Commission (GNC), which took in and logged many formal complaints about discrimination, and Perales, M.C. Gonzales, and other Mexican-American leaders also used transnational channels to work with Mexican and Latin American officials to draw attention to the treatment of Mexican Americans and Mexicans in Texas (Zamora, 2005; Guglielmi, 2006). In 1945, when an anti-Mexican bill was passed by one chamber of the Texas Legislature, Perales, Carlos Castañeda, and M.C. Gonzales pulled out all the diplomatic and public stops to support better, anti-discrimination legislation in the form of the "Spears Anti-Discrimination Bill." (Gonzales and he had worked together on the 1930 school desegregation appeals.) One historian has noted of this period that Perales and the others were exploiting all avenues—foreign, state, and national—to strike down the bad bill and to pass the more progressive version:

Perales issued a press statement on behalf of the Committee of One Hundred and the League of Loyal Americans, decrying the discrimination at Pecos [in which Mexican Americans were denied restaurant entry]—which should "make every right thinking and fair-minded American blush with shame"—and calling on the legislature to pass the Spears bill. Meanwhile other Mexican Americans continued to work hard to pass [the Spears Bill]. Perales, Castañeda, and Gonzales all appeared before the senate Committee on State Affairs in early March, [1945] calling for the passage of legislation because such existing institutions as the GNC were ineffective. (Guglielmi, 2006, p. 1229)

In other words, after immersing ourselves in the Perales archives, we know more about this exceptional lawyer, but, crucially, we also know how much more is yet to be studied, documented, and told from his archives and in other hidden treasure troves.

References, Cases Cited

Arellano, G. (May 6, 2010). Mi casa es mi casa: How Fullerton resident Alex Bernal's 1943 battle against housing discrimination helped change the course of American civil rights. *Orange County Weekly*.

Bender, S. (2010). *Tierra y libertad: Land, liberty, and Latino housing*. New York, N.Y: New York University Press.

Blanton, C. K. (2006). George I. Sanchez, ideology, and whiteness in the making of the Mexican American civil rights movement, 1930-1960. *The Journal of Southern History*, *72*(3), 569-604.

Blanton, C. K. (2012). A legacy of neglect: George I. Sanchez, Mexican American education, and the ideal of integration, 1940-1970. *Teachers College Record*, *114*(6), 1-34.

Carpio, G. (2012). Unexpected allies: David C. Marcus and his impact on the advancement of civil rights in the Mexican-American legal landscape of southern California (Sanchez, G. J., Ed.). In *Beyond alliances: The Jewish role in reshaping the racial landscape of southern California* (pp. 1-32). West Lafayette: Purdue University Press.

Calderón-Zaks, M. (2011). Debate whiteness amid world events: Mexican and Mexican-American subjectivity and the U.S. Relationship with the Americas, 1924-1936. *27 Mexican Studies/Estudios Mexicanos 325-359*.

Carrigan, W. D., & Webb, C. (2003). The lynching of persons of Mexican origin or descent in the United States, 1848 to 1928. *Journal of Social History*, *37*(2), 411-438.

Chavez, M. (2011). *Everyday injustice: Latino professionals and racism*. Lanham, Md: Rowman & Littlefield Publishers.

Chin, G. J., Hartley, R. E., & University of Arizona. (2006). Still on the books: Jim Crow and segregation laws fifty years after Brown v. Board of Education, a report on laws remaining in the codes of Georgia, Lousiana, Mississippi, Missouri, South Carolina, Virginia and West Virginia. East Lansing, Mich.: *Michigan State Law Review*, 447-476.

Chin, G. J. (2010). Sweatt v. Painter and undocumented college students in Texas. *Thurgood Marshall Law Review 36*, 39-61.

Christian, C. E. (1989). Joining the American mainstream: Texas's Mexican Americans during World War I. *The Southwestern Historical Quarterly*, *92*(4), 559-595.

Cruz, J. L., & Molina, M. S. (2010). Hispanic National Bar Association national study on the status of Latinas in the legal profession; few and far between: The reality of Latina lawyers. *Pepperdine Law Review*, *37*(3), 971-1038.

De León, A. (1982). *The Tejano community, 1836-1900*. Albuquerque: University of New Mexico Press.

De León, A. (1983). *They called them greasers*. Austin: University of Texas Press.

Dobbs, R. F. (2005). *Yellow dogs and Republicans: Allan Shivers and Texas two-party politics*. College Station: Texas A&M University Press.

Dudziak, M. L. (2000). *Cold War civil rights: race and the image of American democracy*. Princeton: Princeton University Press.

Gándara, P. C., & Contreras, F. (2010). *The Latino education crisis: The conse-quences of failed social policies*. Cambridge, Mass: Harvard University Press.

García, I. M. (2000). *Viva Kennedy: Mexican Americans in search of Camelot*. College Station, Texas: Texas A & M University Press.

García, I. M. (2003). *Hector P. Garcia: In relentless pursuit of justice*. Houston, Texas: Arte Publico Press.

García, I. M. (2009). *White but not equal: Mexican Americans, jury discrimination, and the Supreme Court*. Tucson: University of Arizona Press.

García, M. T. (1989). *Mexican Americans: Leadership, ideology & identity, 1930-1960*. New Haven: Yale University Press.

García, R. A. (1991). *Rise of the Mexican American middle class: San Antonio, 1929-1941*. College Station: Texas A & M University Press.

Gomez, L. E. (2007). *Manifest destinies: The making of the Mexican American race*. New York: New York University Press.

Gonzales, P. B. (2006). Whither the Nuevomexicanos: The career of a southwestern intellectual discourse, 1907-2004. *The Social Science Journal (43)*2, 273-286.

Gonzales, P. B. & Massmann A. (2006). Loyalty questioned: Nuevomexicanos in the Great War. *Pacific Historical Review, 75*(4), 629-666.

Griswold del Castillo, R. (2008). *World War II and Mexican American civil rights*. Austin: University of Texas Press.

Gross, A. J. (2003). Texas Mexicans and the politics of whiteness. *Law and History Review, 21*, 195-206.

Gross, A. J. (2007). "The Caucasian cloak": Mexican Americans and the politics of whiteness in the twentieth-century southwest. *The Georgetown Law Journal, 95*(2), 337-392.

Guglielmo, T. (2006). Fighting for Caucasian rights: Mexicans, Mexican Americans, and the transnational struggle for Civil Rights in World War II Texas. *Journal of American History, 92*, 1212-1237.

Haney López, I. & Olivas, M. A. (2008). Hernandez v. Texas: Jim Crow, Mexican Americans, and the Anti-Subordination Constitution (Moran R. L. & Carbado, D., Eds.). In *Race Law Stories* (pp. 269-306). New York: Foundation Press.

Jones-Correa, M. (2001). The origins and diffusion of racial restrictive covenants. *Political Science Quarterly, 115*, 541-568.

Kohout, M. D. (n.d.). Cadena, Carlos Cristian. *Handbook of Texas Online*. Retrieved August 2, 2012, from http://www.tshaonline.org/handbook/online/articles/fcaas.

Kanellos, N. (2007). Recovering and reconstructing early twentieth-century Hispanic immigrant print culture in the U.S., *Hispanic Literary History 21*, 438-455.

Kanellos, N. & Martell, H. (2000). *Hispanic periodicals in the United States, origins to 1960: A brief history and comprehensive bibliography*. Houston, Texas: Arte Público Press.

MacDonald, V. M. & Polk Hoffman, B. (2012). 'Compromising la causa?' The Ford Foundation and Chicano intellectual nationalism in the creation of Chicano history, 1963–1977. *History of Education Quarterly 52*, 251-281.

Márquez, B. (1993). *LULAC: The evolution of a Mexican American political organization*. Austin: University of Texas Press.

Martinez, G. A. (1994). Legal indeterminacy, judicial discretion and the Mexican American litigation experience: 1930-1980. *U.C. Davis Law Review 27,* 555- 618.

Mazon, M. (1998). *The zoot-suit riots: the psychology of symbolic annihilation.* Austin: University of Texas Press.

Mendoza, M. G. (n.d.). Very few Latino attorneys argue before the Supreme Court. In *National Law Journal.* Retrieved February 8, 2012 from http://www.law.com/ jsp/nlj/PubArticleNLJ.jsp?id=1202541721954.

Molina, M. S. (2011). Role models: theory, practice, and effectiveness among Latina lawyers, *Journal of Civil Rights & Economic Development 25,* 125-139.

Montejano, D. (1987). *Anglos and Mexicans in the making of Texas, 1836-1986.* Austin: University of Texas Press.

Munoz, L. K. (2001) Separate but equal? A case study of Romo v. Laird and Mexican American schooling. *OAH Magazine of History* 15, 28-35.

Olivas, M. A. (Ed.). (2006). 'Colored men' and 'hombres aquí': Hernandez v. Texas and the emergence of Mexican-American lawyering. Houston: Arte Público Press.

Olivas, M. A. (2008). The 'trial of the century' that never was: Staff Sgt. Macario Garcia, the Congressional Medal of Honor, and the Oasis Café. *Indiana Law Journal 83,* 1391-1403.

Olivas, M. A. (2010). Review essay—The arc of triumph and the agony of defeat: Mexican Americans and the law, *Journal of Legal Education 60,* 354-367.

Orozco, C. E. (2009). *No Mexicans, women, or dogs allowed: The rise of the Mexican American civil rights movement.* Austin: University of Texas Press.

Orozco, C. E. (2012a). Lozano, Alicia Guadalupe Elizondo de. *Handbook of Texas Online* Retrieved July 31, 2012 from http://www.tshaonline.org/handbook/online/ articles/flo69.

Orozco, C. E. (2012b). Clínica de la beneficencia Mexicana. *Handbook of Texas Online* Retrieved July 31, 2012 from http://www.tshaonline.org/handbook/ online/articles/pqcpu).

Leininger Pycior, J. (1997). *LBJ and Mexican Americans: The paradox of power.* Austin: University of Texas Press.

Ramirez, J. A. (2009). *To the line of fire: Mexican Texans and WWI.* College Station: Texas A&M University Press.

Ramos, C. (2001). Educational legacy of racially restrictive covenants: their long term impact on Mexican Americans. *The Scholar: St. Mary's Law Review on Minority Issues 4,* 149–84.

Ramos, R. A. (2008) *Beyond the Alamo: Forging Mexican ethnicity in San Antonio, 1821-1861.* Chapel Hill: University of North Carolina Press.

Rangel, J. C. & Alcala C. M. (1972) Project report: De jure segregation of Chicanos in Texas schools. *Harvard Civil Rights-Civil Liberties Law Review 7,* 307-391.

Rivas-Rodriguez, M. (Ed.). (2005). *Mexican Americans and World War II.* Austin: University of Texas Press.

Rivera, J. M. (2006). *The emergence of Mexican America: Recovering stories of Mexican peoplehood in U.S. culture.* New York: NYU Press.

Romero II, T. I. (2004). Our Selma is here: The political and legal struggle for education equality in Denver, Colorado, and multiracial conundrums in American jurisprudence. *Seattle Journal for Social Justice 3,* 73-142.

Romero II, T. I. (2007). Bound between & beyond the borderlands: Region, race, scale and a subnational legal history. *Oregon Review of International Law 9,* 301-336.

Rosales, A. F. (1985). Shifting self-perceptions and ethnic consciousness among Mexicans in Houston 1908–1946, *Aztlán: A Journal of Chicano Studies 16,* 71-94.

Ross, D.L. (1998). Examining the liability factors of sudden wrongful deaths in police custody. *Police Quarterly 1,* 65-91.

Portes, A. & Rumbaut, R. G. (2006). *Immigrant America: A portrait.* Berkeley: University of California.

Salinas, G. (1971). Mexican-Americans and the desegregation of schools in the southwest. *Houston Law Review 8,* 939-951.

Salinas, L. S. (2003) Gus Garcia and Thurgood Marshall: Two legal giants fighting for justice. *Thurgood Marshall Law Review 28,* 145-175.

Salinas, L. S. (2005). Latinos and criminal justice in Texas: has the new millennium brought progress. *Thurgood Marshall Law Review 30,* 289-346.

Sánchez, G. J. (1993). *Becoming Mexican American: Ethnicity, culture and identity in Chicano Los Angeles, 1900-1945.* Oxford: Oxford University Press.

San Miguel Jr., G. (1987). *'Let all of them take heed': Mexican Americans and the campaign for educational equality in Texas, 1910-1981.* Austin: University of Texas Press.

San Miguel Jr., G. (2005). *Brown, not white: School integration and the Chicano movement in Houston.* College Station: Texas A&M University Press.

Saucedo, L. M. (2012). Mexicans, immigrants, cultural narratives, and national origin. *Arizona State Law Journal 44,* 305-341.

Shabazz, A. (2004). *Advancing democracy: African Americans and the struggle for access and equity in higher education in Texas.* Chapel Hill: University of North Carolina Press.

Sheridan, C. (2003). 'Another white race': Mexican Americans and the paradox of whiteness in jury selection. *Law and History Review 21,* 109-144.

Steele, R. (2008). Violence in Los Angeles: Sleepy lagoon, the zoot suit riots, and the liberal response, in *World War II and Mexican American civil rights,* del Castillo, R. G. (Ed.). Austin: University of Texas Press.

Strum, P. (2010). *Mendez v. Westminster: School desegregation and Mexican-American rights.* Lawrence: University Press of Kansas.

Tushnet, M. V. (1987). *The NAACP's legal strategy against segregated education, 1925-1950.* Chapel Hill: University of North Carolina Press.

Valencia, R. R. (2008). *Chicano students and the courts: The Mexican American legal struggle for educational equality.* New York: NYU Press.

Valenzuela, A. (1999). *Subtractive schooling: U.S.-Mexican youth and the politics of caring.* Albany: SUNY Press.

Ware, L. B. (1989). Invisible walls: An examination of the legal strategy of the restrictive covenant cases. *Washington University Law Quarterly 67,* 737-772.

Ware, L. B. (1993). New weapons for an old battle: The enforcement provisions of the 1988 Amendments to the Fair Housing Act. *Admininstrative Law Journal 7,* 59-119.

Ware, L. B. (2002). Race and urban space: Hypersegregated housing patterns and the failure of school desegregation. *Widener Law Symposium Journal 9*, 55-71.

Wilson, S. H. (2003) 'Brown' over 'other white': Mexican Americans' legal arguments and litigation strategy in school desegregation. *Law and History Review 21*, 145-194.

Zamora, E. (2002). Fighting on two fronts: José de la Luz Saenz and the language of the Mexican American civil rights movement, in *Recovering the U.S. Hispanic Literary Heritage Volume IV*, Aranda, Jr. J.F. & Torres-Saillant, S. (Eds). Houston: Arte Público Press.

Zamora, E. (2005). Mexico's wartime intervention on behalf of Mexicans in the United States, in *Mexican Americans and World War II*, Rivas-Rodriguez, M. (Ed.). Austin: University of Texas Press.

Zamora, E. (2009). *Claiming rights and righting wrongs in Texas, Mexican workers and job politics during World War II*. College Station: Texas A&M University Press.

Zamora, E. (2012). José de la Luz Saenz; experiences and autobiographical consciousness, in *Mexican American civil rights pioneers*, Quiroz, A. (Ed.). Champaign, Illinois: University of Illinois Press.

Cases tried to decision by Alonso S. Perales:

Spanish Book & Stationery Co. v. U.S., United States Customs Court July 06, 1939, Not Reported in F.Supp, 3 Cust. Ct. 512, 1939 WL 7271.

Lozano v. De Martinez, Court of Civil Appeals of Texas, San Antonio. July 22, 1942 164 S.W.2d 196.

Clifton v. Puente, 218 S.W.2d 272 (Tex. Civ. App.—San Antonio 1948, writ ref'd n.r.e).

Alaniz v. State, Court of Criminal Appeals of Texas. May 04, 1949 153 Tex.Crim. 374.

Mendoza v. Mendoza, Court of Civil Appeals of Texas, San Antonio. February 04, 1953 255 S.W.2d 251.

Powe v. Powe, Court of Civil Appeals of Texas, San Antonio. April 28, 1954 268 S.W.2d 558.

Barrera v. Barrera, Court of Civil Appeals of Texas, San Antonio (October 24, 1956) 294 S.W.2d 865

Ydrogo v. Haltom, Court of Civil Appeals of Texas, Eastland. May 10, 1957, 302 S.W.2d 670.

Villarreal v. U.S., 254 F. 2d 595 (5th Cir. 1958)

Valdez v. Amaya, Court of Civil Appeals of Texas, San Antonio. September 9, 1959 327 S.W.2d 708.

Other cases cited:

Romo v. Laird, et al., No. 21617, Maricopa County Superior Court (1925) [unpublished, reprinted in Laura K. Muñoz, Separate But Equal? A Case Study of Romo v. Laird]

Doss v. Bernal [Superior Court of the State of California, Orange County, No. 41466, 1943]

Mendez v. Westminster, 161 F.2d 774 (9th Cir. 1947)

Delgado v. Bastrop, Civ. No. 388 (W.D. Tex. June 15, 1948) (unpublished opinion)

Shelley v. Kramer, 334 U.S. 1 (1948)

Gonzales v. Sheely, 96 F. Supp. 1004 (D. Ariz. 1951)

Hernandez v. Texas, 347 U.S. 475 (1954)

Brown v. Board (Brown I), 347 U.S. 483 (1954)

Brown v. Board (Brown II), 349 U.S. 294, 301 (1955)

Herminio Hernandez et al. v. Driscoll Consolidated Independent School District; Civil Action (Civ.A.) 1384, U.S. District Court for the Southern District of Texas (S.D.Tex., 1957), Corpus Christi Division [published opinion at 2 Race Relations Law Reporter 329 (S. D. Tex., 1957)]

Trinidad Villareal et al. v. Mathis Independent School District of San Patricio City et al., Civ. A. 1385 (S. D. Tex., Corpus Christi Division, 2 May 1957)

Lopez v. Texas, 378 U.S. 567 (1964)

Chapa v. Odem Independent School District (S.D.Tex., 1967) [Corpus Christi Division, Civ. No. 66-C-72].

Cisneros v. Corpus Christi ISD, 324 F. Supp. 599 (S. D. Tex., 1970), 404 U.S. 1211 (1971) ("The stay will be reinstated pending action on the merits in the Fifth Circuit or action by the full Court") 459 F.2d 13 (5th Cir. 1972), cert den. 413 U.S. 920 (1973)

Contributors

Mario T. García is Professor of Chicano Studies and History at the University of California, Santa Barbara. A Guggenheim Fellow, he is the author of numerous books on Chicano history including *Desert Immigrants: The Mexicans of El Paso, 1880-1920*; *Mexican Americans: Leadership, Ideology & Identity, 1930-1960*; *Memories of Chicano History: The Life and Narrative of Bert Corona*; *Católicos: Resistance and Affirmation in Chicano Catholic History*; and *Blowout! Sal Castro and the Chicano Struggle for Educational Justice*.

Donna M. Kabalen de Bichara is Professor and Chair of the Department of Humanities Studies at the Tecnológico de Monterrey. She is a member of the Research Center, Memory, Literature, and Discourse, where her research centers on the self-writing of Mexican Americans as well as women's border literature. Dr. Kabalen de Bichara is a member of the advisory board of the Recovering the U.S. Hispanic Literary Heritage Project and is also a member of the Sistema Nacional de Investigadores in Mexico. She is the author of *Telling Border Life Stories: Four Mexican-American Women Writers* (Forthcoming, Texas A&M University Press).

George A. Martínez is Professor of Law at the Dedman School of Law at Southern Methodist University. He received his B.A. from Arizona State University, M.A., in philosophy, from the University of Michigan, and his J.D. from Harvard University.

Benjamin Márquez is a Professor of Political Science at the University of Wisconsin, Madison. His research interests include social movements, urban politics, and minority politics. He has published numerous articles and books on the relationship between race, political power, social identities, public and political incorporation. He is the author *of Power and Politics in A Chicano Barrio: A Study of Mobilization Efforts and Community Power in El Paso*. (Lanham: The University Press of America, 1985) and *LULAC: The Evolution of a Mexican American Political Organization* (Texas 1993). His most recent book, *Mexican-American Political Organizations: Choosing Issues, Taking Sides*. (2003: University of Texas Press) won the 2004 Best Book Award by the Race, Ethnicity, and Politics (REP) Section of the American Political Science Association. His current book project, *Democratizing Texas Politics: Race and Party Politics 1945-2002* will be published by the University of Texas Press in 2013.

Joseph Orbock Medina is a doctoral candidate in American history at the University of California, Berkeley. He researches the politics of twentieth-century Latino unity in Texas, California, and New Mexico. Mr. Orbock holds an M.A. in Latin-

American history from Texas State University-San Marcos, where in 2008 he was recognized as the Outstanding Graduate Scholar by the College of Liberal Arts.

Norma Adelfa Mouton is a researcher, writer, and independent scholar. Her research focuses on the subjectivity of U.S. Latinos/as as expressed in autobiographical conversion narratives and autobiographical fiction. She has published on the work of Teodoro Torres, on a collection of sermons by Rev. Gregorio Valenzuela and on the autobiography of Rev. Santiago Tafolla, Sr.

Cynthia E. Orozco is Professor of History at Eastern New Mexico University, Ruidoso, and author of *No Mexicans, Women or Dogs Allowed: The Rise of the Mexican American Civil Rights Movement and co-editor of Mexican Americans in Texas History*. She wrote 80 articles for the *New Handbook of Texas* encyclopedia and was associate editor of *Latinas in the United States*. She has written over 50 newspaper articles. A museum consultant and motivational speaker, she has appeared on CSPAN Book TV and NBC News. She is a fellow of the Texas State Historical Association and was named New Mexico LULAC Educator of the Year in 2012.

Retired Judge **Lupe S. Salinas** is the Eugene M. Harrington Professor of Law at Texas Southern University's Thurgood Marshall School of Law. At the University of Houston Law Center (UHLC), Salinas' interest in civil rights intensified after he discovered Alonso S. Perales' book *Are We Good Neighbors?* in the undergraduate library. His discovery of this documentation of anti-Mexican discrimination prompted him to found the Chicano Law Students Association at UHLC. In 1971, Salinas published a student article with the *Houston Law Review* about Mexican-American school segregation. Salinas cited Perales' book as supportive of the proposition that Mexican Americans constitute an identifiable ethnic minority group for equal protection purposes.

Aaron E. Sánchez is a doctoral candidate in the department of history at Southern Methodist University. He specializes in twentieth-century Chicana/o intellectual, cultural, and literary history.

Virginia Marie Raymond practices law in Austin, Texas.

F. Arturo Rosales is the author of *Testimonio: A Documentary History of the Mexican-American Struggle for Civil Rights, Chicano! The History of the Mexican-American Civil Rights Movement*, and *Pobre Raza: Violence, Justice, and Mobilization Among México Lindo Immigrants*.

Emilio Zamora is Professor in the Department of History at the University of Texas at Austin. He specializes in Mexican-American history, Texas history, oral history, and transnational (U.S./Mexico) working-class history. Zamora has authored three books, co-edited three anthologies, assisted in the production of a Texas history, text and written numerous articles. His scholarship has garnered him six best book awards, a best article prize, and a Fulbright García-Robles fellowship in 2007-08. Dr. Zamora is a member of the Texas Institute of Letters, a Fellow with the Texas State Historical Association and a Fellow of the Barbara White Stuart Centennial Professorship in Texas History at the University of Texas.